Murmured Conversations

Murmured Conversations

A TREATISE ON POETRY AND BUDDHISM BY THE POET-MONK SHINKEI

TRANSLATION, COMMENTARY, AND ANNOTATION BY

Esperanza Ramirez-Christensen

STANFORD UNIVERSITY PRESS
STANFORD, CALIFORNIA

Stanford University Press
Stanford, California

Printed in the United States of America on acid-free, archival-quality paper

Library of Congress Cataloging-in-Publication Data
Shinkei, 1406-1475.
[Sasamegoto. English]
Murmured conversations : a treatise on poetry and Buddhism / by the poet-monk Shinkei ; translation, commentary, and annotation by Esperanza Ramirez-Christensen.
p. cm.
Includes bibliographical references and indexes.
ISBN 978-0-8047-4863-6 (cloth : alk. paper)
1. Renga--History and criticism. 2. Japanese poetry--To 1600--History and criticism. 3. Buddhism--Japan--History--To 1500. 4. Shinkei, 1406-1475--Translations into English. I. Ramirez-Christensen, Esperanza U. II. Title.
PL732.R4S52813 2008
895.6'13409382943--dc22 2008002361

Typeset by Bruce Lundquist in 10.5/14 Adobe Garamond

To my sisters Alma Teresita, Fe, Caridad, and the late Norma,
for their care and solicitude through the years

Contents

Acknowledgments

It seems eminently fitting that I should be writing these Acknowledgments while on leave from the University of Michigan as Edwin O. Reischauer Visiting Professor at Harvard in 2005–6. It was at Harvard that I first conceived the project of translating the whole of the medieval Japanese poetic treatise *Sasamegoto* (Murmured Conversations) (1463–64). This translation, to which are added my own commentaries, extensive annotations, and biographical notes, was already completed in 2002, but remained unpublished due to events of a personal nature that may be described as a case of life overtaking scholarship, as a colleague has aptly put it.

In my efforts to demarcate a mental space relatively insulated from the debilitating effects of personal tragedy, I owe everything to the unflagging encouragement of friends, family, and colleagues. Among them, Edwin Cranston, teacher and dear friend in poetry always, Fumiko Cranston, tireless in her praise of the dispirited, and Howard and Aki Hibbett, sophisticated guides to the delights of the city, ensured that I would feel at home in Cambridge after all these years. They confirmed that there is a life of literature, art, and the mind that has its own timeless legitimacy above the slings and arrows of academic fashion, power politics, and racism. Andrew Gordon and Susan Pharr, past and present directors of the Reischauer Institute, facilitated my visit. Phyllis Birnbaum and Ashok Modak, dear old friends from the early 1970s in Berkeley, and Emily Dalgarno, the author of studies on Virginia Woolf and my companion on walks in the woods and around the ponds of Concord, saw to it that I took care of my health while completing the book. Marybeth Berry shared her wisdom and way of coping with life's tribulations. My sister Cari Taylor kept vigil during my stay in the hospital, and my nephew Norman Taylor Jr. taught me forbearance by his own example. Alice Cheang came from Albany to speed my recovery, and even kindly annotated a couple of my uncertain Chinese translations. My thanks also to

Lorna Porras-Johnson, tireless fellow activist back in the days of the Philippine Anti–Martial Law movement, and to Pierrepont Johnson for making me feel at home in Belmont; and to the late Daniel Boone Schirmer, leader of the Friends of the Filipino People in Boston and Cambridge, who mobilized these cities' venerable tradition of anti-imperialism to help end the Marcos dictatorship's violent suppression of democratic dissent.

For their moral support under lonely and trying circumstances, I wish also to take this opportunity to thank my loyal friends in Ann Arbor, Michigan: Romulo and Necie Aquino, Miranda Brown, Harry and Sally Joy, Frank Lum and the late, sorely missed Gemma Lum, Paz and Bernard Naylor, Hitomi Tonomura, and Adelwisa Weller. Thanks also to Sookyoung Wang for always being there, whether in Ann Arbor or elsewhere.

Similarly, this is an opportunity to acknowledge the many students in both modern and premodern periods who have participated in my seminars through the years: Alex Bates, Charles Fox, Isamu Fukuchi, Nahoko Fukushima, David Henry, Jason Herlands, Jan Leuchtenberger, Hoyt Long, Michelle Plauché, Robert Rama, James Reichert, Jeremy Robinson, Catherine Ryu, Richie Sakakibara, Lili Selden, Peter Shapinsky, Atsuko Ueda, Timothy Van Compernolle, Kristina Vassil, and Patricia Welch. These students formed an intellectual and scholarly milieu around topics that I engage in my work on classical Japanese literature and Buddhism, the poetics of waka, renga, and haikai, issues of gender and women's writing, and contemporary critical theory. Among them are many who have themselves become professors in the U.S. and Japan, their training further decisively shaped by my talented and indefatigable colleague, Ken Ito. In all cases, their dogged pursuit of humanities and culture studies research during a thoroughly market-oriented age in the academy is an inspiration to us all.

Additionally, Lili Selden, Nahoko Fukushima, and Jeremy Robinson helped to double-check the location of numerous citations and bibliographical references for this book at various times in its protracted history. Nicholas Tustin persuaded me to shift from the Wade-Giles Chinese romanization to Pinyin, and promptly proceeded to edit the manuscript accordingly. Finally, thanks also to the timely attention and work of the people at Stanford University Press, without whom this book would never have seen production: Norris Pope, Muriel Bell, and my editors Mariana Raykov and Peter Dreyer. To all, my heartfelt gratitude for coming to the rescue of a manuscript unfairly neglected by its author.

ER-C, Spring 2006   Reischauer Memorial House   Belmont, Massachusetts

List of Abbreviations

The following abbreviations are used in the Commentary and Notes. For complete citations, see under title in the Bibliography, pp. 361–70.

Butten	*Butten kaidai jiten*
BT	[Teihon] Bashō taisei
DNBZ	Dai Nihon bukkyō zensho
FGS	*Fūgashū* (seventeenth imperial waka anthology)
GR	*Gunsho ruijū*
GSIS	*Goshūishū* (fourth imperial waka anthology)
GSS	*Gosenshū* (second imperial waka anthology)
GYS	*Gyokuyōshū* (fourteenth imperial waka anthology)
HD	*Haikai daijiten*
HF	Ramirez-Christensen, *Heart's Flower*
HJAS	*Harvard Journal of Asiatic Studies*
Hyōshaku	Kubota Utsubo, *Shinkokinwakashū hyōshaku*
JCP	Brower and Miner, *Japanese Court Poetry*
Kenkyū	Kidō, *Sasamegoto no kenkyū*
KKS	*Kokinshū* (first imperial waka anthology)
KM	*Konjaku monogatari*
KT	[*Shimpen*] *Kokka taikan*
KYS	*Kinyōshū* (fifth imperial waka anthology)
Mikkan	Suzuki, "*Sasamegoto* mikkan"
MN	*Monumenta Nipponica*

MYS	*Man'yōshū* (first Japanese poetry anthology)
NKBT	*Nihon koten bungaku taikei*
NKBZ	*Nihon koten bungaku zenshū*
NKT	*Nihon kagaku taikei*
Oi	Shinkei, *Oi no kurigoto*
RH	*Rengaronshū, Haironshū*
RS	Kidō, *Renga shironkō*
SIS	*Shūishū* (third imperial waka anthology)
SKKS	*Shinkokinshū* (eighth imperial waka anthology)
SKS	Shōtetsu, *Sōkonshū*
SKT	*Shinshaku kambun taikei*
SM	*Shōtetsu monogatari*, ed. Hisamatsu Sen'ichi
SNKBT	*Shin Nihon koten bungaku taikei*
SSG	Shinkei, *Sasamegoto*, ed. Kido Saizō (the base text for this translation)
SSG rev. ed.	Shinkei, *Sasamegoto* (the revised edition line), ed. Ijichi Tetsuo
SSG Suzuki	Shinkei, *Sasamegoto*, ed. Suzuki Hisashi
SSRS	*Shinkeishū ronshū*
SSS	*Shinkei sakuhinshū*
ST	*Shikashū taisei*
STKBS	*Shinsen Tsukubashū* (second imperial renga anthology)
T	*Taishō shinshū daizōkyō*
Teikin	Kenzai, *Shinkei-sōzu teikin*
TKBS	*Tsukubashū* (first imperial renga anthology)
Tokoro	Shinkei, *Tokoro-dokoro hentō*
WBD	*Waka bungaku daijiten*
WBJ	*Waka bungaku jiten*
WRS	*Wakan rōeishū*
Zenhyōshaku	Kubota Jun, *Shinkokinwakashū zenhyōshaku*
ZGR	*Zoku gunsho ruijū*

Murmured Conversations

Introduction

Murmured Conversations is an annotated translation of *Sasamegoto* (1463–1464), one of the most important poetic treatises of the medieval period in Japan, and considered the most representative in its thoroughgoing construction of poetry as a way to attain, and signify through language, the mental liberation (*satori*) that is the goal of Buddhist practice. In one sense, this argument is a clear reflection on its author, Shinkei (1406–1475). Shinkei was a Tendai cleric with the rank of Provisional Major Bishop (*Gondaisōzu*) and headed his own temple, the Jūjūshin'in, in Kyoto's Higashiyama hills. He is best known today as one of the most brilliant poets of *renga* (linked poetry), as an equally distinctive voice in the classic *waka* form, and as the poet who, in his critical writings, formulated the principles of renga as a serious art in the Muromachi period (1392–1568).[1] *Sasamegoto* is the major work in this critical enterprise. That it is also a representative work in the larger cultural history is due to its articulation of renga, and poetry in general, as an existential praxis, a Way.

The idea that the practice of the arts, or of any skill for that matter, constitutes a Way (*michi*) is a defining characteristic of medieval Japanese cultural history. The term refers to the existence of guidelines and standards to follow, as embodied by the works and teachings of past and present masters. In this sense, the Way is akin to an academy or college without walls, a virtual institution of learning constituted by various circles of students, teachers, and an archive of circulating texts defining its history, traditions, and models. However, what is distinctive about the medieval notion of praxis is that it is everywhere—and inevitably—informed by what used to be called "the wisdom of the East," mainly Confucianism, Taoism, and Buddhism, philosophies that teach self-cultivation in harmony with a larger whole, be it the way of Heaven, of the cosmic Tao, or of immanent Suchness. This means that the skill of doing and making is also the *embodied* endeavor to overcome the small, narrow, and constricted self by means of an unflagging discipline aiming to release the large and generous self. Hence the Way is an existential praxis whose goal is not technical competence per se; beyond competence, there is a consummate praxis that is also, paradoxically, identified with the realm of freedom, of a "self-less," intuitive spontaneity equal to, because in harmony with, the universe. *Sasamegoto* lays out a renga—or, more broadly, an *uta no michi* (Way of Poetry) by inscribing a history, a set of models, and principles of authentic practice for its own time. But its distinctive character lies in its author's conviction that poetic praxis is equally the conduct of a life lived purely and a pedagogy of the mind aimed at liberating the Buddha-nature in oneself, the one being a manifestation of the other.

Most of the renga handbooks that proliferated during the Muromachi period were concerned with defining its poetic vocabulary and techniques, or with explaining the complex body of rules and procedures governing linked verse sessions. In brief, they were principally practical guides to composition. *Sasamegoto* is a distinctive exception in the comprehensiveness of its approach and its deep-probing inquiry into the mental foundations of the poetic process. The comprehensiveness also reflects the fact that the treatise is conceived within the background of the whole classical waka tradition. One of Shinkei's aims was apparently to locate renga firmly within the mainstream of Japanese poetic development, instead of being perceived merely as an anomalous genre, with no vital link to the great past. By tradition, Shinkei meant, of course, courtly literature in general—the Heian narratives and the successive imperial waka anthologies, as well as the *Man'yōshū*. More specifically, however, he had in mind the works of Fujiwara Teika and the other poets of the *Shinkokinshū* period. Not only did they represent for him the apogee of waka's history; he rightly saw that their techniques of syntactic fragmentation and elliptical ambiguity were particularly relevant for a genre like renga, because of the brevity of each successive verse unit, and the formal separation between them, which required a subtle rather than obvious connection to be poetic at all.

Poetic appeal, what Shinkei loosely calls *en*, is in a sense what *Sasamegoto* is all about. By the time the treatise appeared, the long 100-verse form of renga had been on the scene for some two centuries and a half, since the beginning of the Kamakura period (1185–1333). By late Kamakura, the formal structural requirements of the genre—that is, the integrity of the single fourteen- or seventeen-syllable verse, and the resulting firm separation between contiguous verses, had already been perfected in the work of commoner renga masters like Zen'a and his disciples Junkaku and Shinshō. In the Nambokuchō period (1336–92), Nijō Yoshimoto (1320–88) compiled the first official renga anthology, the *Tsukubashu* (1356–57), in collaboration with the most famous renga master of the time, Zen'a's successor, Gusai. And in 1372, he consolidated existing practices and rules for composing the 100-verse sequence into a definitive canon called *Renga shinshiki* (The New Renga Code). In Shinkei's view, the "ancient" period of Gusai and Yoshimoto marked renga's first flowering, a valuable precedent well worth close study and emulation. He valued the work of the old renga masters for their firm and intelligent handling of *tsukeai*, the link between verses, and Gusai in particular for the added dimension of spiritual profundity in his poetry.

Constituted of a clear and strong poetic diction, a resonant tension in the link between verses, and a degree of poetic inwardness in feeling and content, the serious renga style espoused by Gusai and Yoshimoto failed to hold the field in the forty or so years following their deaths. In the first few decades of the Muromachi period, that is to say, well into Shinkei's own time, the overall quality of renga suffered a marked decline. Various reasons have been advanced for this. One is the popularity of the style of Gusai's disciple Shua, which was characterized by verbal and technical ingenuity, arrestingly witty conceptions, and an almost total lack of poetic overtones. Such a style predictably made a strong impression on linked-verse enthusiasts then and later; it became a model for imitation by practitioners who had neither Shūa's wit nor his talent. In short, renga reverted back to its basic and primitive nature as an amusing game of words, in which the object is to surpass the preceding verse in cleverness rather than to relate to its integral meaning. Another reason that has been advanced for the decline of serious renga was the growing commercialism in linked-verse milieus throughout the country. The increasing demand to learn renga even among the lower, uneducated classes gave rise to professional *rengashi* (teachers of linked verse), itinerant "monks" who taught renga for a livelihood without necessarily possessing any particular learning or poetic training themselves. Somewhat like professional gamblers, they also pitted their skills at versification against those of amateurs at popular renga matches, in which money was at stake and victory was apparently won on the basis of the ingenuity of the link and the quantity of verses one could produce in a single session. But all this was an inevitable consequence of renga's sheer popularity. The most logical reason for the form's decline during the so-called middle period must simply be the absence of any poets of real stature who could steer it back to the course set for it by Yoshimoto and Gusai.

This was the state of the art when Sōzei, Shinkei, and the other poets later dubbed the *renga shichiken* (seven sages of renga) appeared on the scene and in the ensuing five or so decades in their various ways provided the leadership and focus that had been wanting. *Sasamegoto*, Shinkei's extensive formulation of the "True Way" (*makoto no michi*) of renga is the major contribution to this enterprise. As stated earlier, part of his procedure was to distinguish a tradition for the art in the shape of the *Shinkokinshū* period in waka and the *Tsukubashū* in renga. The fact that he invariably illustrates his points by quoting from the poetry of these two periods serves, among other things, to make this evident.

Another, and without doubt the most central, aspect of Shinkei's approach is its thoroughgoing emphasis on *kokoro*. Such an emphasis on *kokoro*, understood in its primary sense of "meaning," "feeling," or significance, manifests Shinkei's strong reaction to the current and opposite tendency to view renga as a game of words, or *kotoba*, a competition of wits that did not necessarily have to signify anything. This is nothing more than the fundamental nature of all linked poetry, be it renga or the haikai of the Edo period (1600–1868), and the basis of its overwhelming popularity. The renga or haikai verse is at base a playful and liberating exercise in verbal self-assertion. The *maeku* is in every instance a riddle, question, or problem propounded by another; success in confronting the other with a solution gives pleasure, and failure frustration. The view of renga as a verbal exercise is a natural consequence of the fact that it is in a sense an artificial speech, a "foreign" language with a lexicon adopted from the vocabulary of classical literature and a grammar of sequencing evolved from the practice of the ancient Kamakura-Nambokuchō masters. In the popular understanding, the ability to "speak" the language fluently and fast was the whole point; the object was to demonstrate one's knowledge and skill in summoning the words that correspond to or are associated with those in the preceding verse, and to derive some personal satisfaction thereby.

It is this peculiar tendency to regard verbal dexterity, articulateness per se, as the aim of renga practice that moved Shinkei to deal in *Sasamegoto* with the fundamental question of what constitutes poetry, what endows language with the charismatic appeal or attractiveness that he calls *en*, his general term for poetic beauty. Predictably, perhaps, his answer was that words should signify something beyond themselves; they must be expressive. And the something they must express is nothing more or less than the mind of the poet himself. In other words, *Sasamegoto* places man, the human being himself, in the center of the poetic nexus, not his craft or skill with words. The poet is first and foremost a person striving to know himself and the world around him, and only secondarily an artisan of language. In this second sense of "mind" or "spirit," *kokoro* does not refer, however, to the individual subjectivity as such. It is rather the inner process of contemplating the self and the universe from a distance, as it were, the discipline of meditation (*shikan*, *zen*) whose effect is the liberation of the ego from subjectivity. Although poetic (or Buddhist) training (*shugyō*) necessarily consists on the first level of learning how to wield the special language of renga with skill and intelligence, its ultimate aim is to arrive at this disinterested mental state that is the only true source of great poetry, the mind-ground (*shinji*) achieved through meditation, the Buddha mind.

In Shinkei's distinctive poetics, moreover, mental detachment is not to be confused with a state of dry or cynical indifference. On the contrary, it is through the process of disengagement from the small, ego-centered self that an individual is able to realize fully the pathos and yet the marvel of his own existence, and, by extension, that of every person, as the site of a network of temporal and hence mutable circumstances that is at once real and empty at the same time. From this perspective, a poetic sensibility is equivalent to the state of heightened receptivity, a kind of inward spaciousness, that enables an authentic poetry, including the meaningful dialogue requisite in renga as a collective genre. *Sasamegoto*'s ideal renga discourse is not an exercise in self-assertiveness but a moving conversation about universal human experience and the underlying truths of existence.

This is not to say that a renga sequence should sound like a philosophical discourse. The type of poetry that *Sasamegoto* defines in so many words is what in modern criticism would be described as symbolic, the genre that Robert Brower and Earl Miner in *Japanese Court Poetry* have identified as "descriptive symbolism" in the work of the *Shinkokinshū* poets. Shinkei calls it *yūgen*, *ushin*, *taketakaki tei*, and so on, but all these styles have in common that the poet's subjectivity is wholly absent from the poem, and that the imagery is but a device to reveal, to render palpable, the true face of the Real (*jissō*) as understood in a Mahayana Buddhist sense.

The foregoing account aims simply to provide a general literary-historical and conceptual background for reading *Sasamegoto*; a closer analytical presentation of its content will be found in the commentaries I have written for each section, which are in turn based on the annotation, without which much of the treatise is unintelligible.

Sasamegoto is in two parts. The first was written in the fifth month of Kanshō 4 (1463), when Shinkei was on religious retreat in Hachiōji Shrine in his home village in Kii Province (Wakayama Prefecture), praying for the resolution of the battles for succession to the headship of the Hatakeyama daimyō clan, who had become his temple's principal patrons. The second part, conceived as a supplement to the first, was undertaken a year later, in the fifth month of Kanshō 5 (1464), when the wished-for resolution had come to pass, the victorious Hatakeyama Masanaga was appointed Deputy Shogun, and Shinkei was back in his temple in the capital. In the Prologue, the work claims to be no more than a trivial, inconsequential conversation between two amateur poetry enthusiasts. However, it quickly proves to be a wide-ranging dialogue between a visiting master who is an authority on renga and waka, and a local renga amateur, who frequently represents the common, ignorant, and misguided view, but is desirous of learning the True Way. The colophon quoted below from one of the common-edition texts explains the origins of the work; marked by a self-deprecation that is a convention in such colophons, it is believed to have been appended by Shinkei at a later date, when someone requested a copy of the two parts or volumes.

> Around the first ten days of the fifth month in the fourth year of Kanshō [1463], while I was on a religious retreat at the collective shrine in Ta'i Village, Kishū, certain renga enthusiasts importuned me so strongly for a book of instructions that it was difficult to refuse. The task was so hurried, and the writing so deficient, that these two volumes deserve only to be cast into the fire after an initial glance. However, although they are in dire need of corrections, I am presenting the manuscript drafts as requested. (*RH*, p. 23)

Part One is Shinkei's basic, introductory teaching; here he deals with renga's history and tradition and simultaneously delivers a scathing critique of the state of the art in his day; defines the stylistic qualities of superior poetry in both renga and waka; analyzes the nature of linking or tsukeai from a structural viewpoint; and illustrates a number of bad poetic practices. In all this, his main concern, however, is to define the Way of Poetry as essentially a process of spiritual cultivation; in Shinkei's critical discourse, most literary questions have a tendency to return to the main issue of the nature of poetic sensibility, and that in turn to the Buddhist philosophy of mind.

Part Two may be said to be the innermost or esoteric section of the treatise; some of the questions raised in Part One are taken up again for re-examination, the central principles of the Way are stated and confronted directly, and their grounding in Buddhist intellectual philosophy manifestly revealed. As will be evident to the careful reader, Buddhism is present here not only as the conceptual ground but as a method of exposition. I refer to the fact that Shinkei frequently resorts to citation and anecdotal example from Buddhist scripture, in addition to Chinese secular classics such as the Confucian *Analects* (*Lunyu*, J. *Rongo*), Japanese Buddhist works, especially Mujū's *Collection of Sand and Pebbles* (*Shasekishū*), and a variety of poetic anthologies and critical works. In the Notes, these eclectic sources have been identified whenever possible and whole long passages from them translated in order to lay out the discursive context of the quotation in the original source and hence clarify the nature of Shinkei's creative appropriation of it in *Sasamegoto*. Attention to the sources reveals the breadth of Shinkei's learning, certainly, but also the nature of the treatise as a virtual mosaic of quotations, a radically intertextual piece of writing, whose bearing is not infrequently unintelligible without tracking the reference and its usage in various other discourses.

In many places, the style of exposition in *Sasamegoto* may be characterized as renga-like. One is confronted with a series of quotations and indirect references without an explicit explanation of the connections among them or between the main argument and the example. More radically, Shinkei's discourse is Zen-like in the way it occasionally concludes a section by rejecting the absolute validity of the dichotomy implicit in both the question posed by the interlocutor and his reply to it. Section 49 on the Close Link and the Distant Link, for instance, while clearly upholding the superiority of the Distant over the Close, ends by warning against an attitude of partiality for either one. This is consistent with the mutually defining concepts of mutability (or contingency) and impartiality that ground, yet also self-deconstruct, his argument. It is one with the grand finale of the treatise, its sweeping declaration, after all the discriminations so painstakingly argued, that "The true Way of Poetry is akin to the Great Void; it wants in nothing and is in nothing superfluous." It is for all these reasons that I have felt it necessary to append a commentary after each section (except for the Prologue).

For the longest time, I hesitated to include the collection of fifty verse pairs illustrating the Ten Styles at the end of Part One; it is not supported by any accompanying exposition and is believed to have been appended at a later date. However, mindful of the necessity for fidelity to my source text, and the potential that some graduate student might find it useful as a source for the complex problem of the Ten Styles concept, I eventually included it as well, and so the translation is complete.[2] The text used for the translation is edited and annotated by Kidō Saizō in *Rengaronshū Haironshū*, *NKBT* 66 (1961). It belongs to the manuscript-draft or common-edition line of *Sasamegoto* texts that were in popular circulation in the Muromachi period, and of which some seventeen copies have been preserved. For comparative purposes, I have also consulted the version edited by Ijichi Tetsuo in *Rengaronshū Haironshū Nogakuronshū*, *NKBZ* 51 (1973). It belongs to the variant or revised-edition line stemming from a revised manuscript believed to have been written by Shinkei himself while in the Kanto during the Ōnin War. Only two copies of this later version exist, evidence that it did not circulate as widely as the original edition. Its major feature is a generally better organization of material; discussions of a given topic, located in two or three places in the manuscript-draft line, are here gathered in one place. This said, however, the editing is not necessarily an unqualified improvement; the transfer and amalgamation into one of two or three sections answering to separate (though related) questions in the original has resulted in diffusing the original thrust and specific significance of certain passages. I have therefore decided to base the translation on the earlier version in the interest of clarity, and of preserving the initial, random shape of Shinkei's discourse as he responded to a request for a book of instruction from the local amateurs in his home village. This text retains a kind of immediacy; the writing has the feel of a conversation (despite—or perhaps precisely because of—the abbreviation of the interlocutor's part), which at times rises to the eloquence of a sermon and at other times reads like the outline of a lecture to be elaborated orally. The translation follows the numbering of the sections in the Kidō edition; similarly, aside from a few minor modifications, I have for convenience adopted the titles Kidō provides for each section.

Part One

ONE

Prologue

On those occasions when my good friend and I fondly converse about the fleeting affairs of this world, we find ourselves straying irresistibly even into the unfamiliar, shadowy road along Waka Bay.[1] Inconsequential though these words may be that pour from our lips, we need have no fear of unwelcome ears behind the walls, for these are no more than murmured conversations beneath a lowly thatched roof.[2] Since it is said that no fewer than eight hundred million thoughts pass through the mind in a single night, it would be a grave sin contrarily to ignore them and pretend that not one had anything to do with poetry.[3] Moreover, these words are by no means intended to guide people whose judgment is as yet immature. They are merely an account of our own perplexities as we walked uncertainly on the way of Poetry.

TWO

Renga History

About the Way of waka, nothing more need be said, for in one anthology after another since ancient days, men have selected excellent poems for preservation, polishing, as it were, all the countless stones from the beach at Ise Bay, and planing finely the various woods from the timbered mountains at Izumi.[1] Renga too belongs to the same Way, but it is but a few ages since men began to explore it, and so like the deep recesses on this side and that side of Tsukuba Mountain, there are many aspects of the art that remain obscure.[2]

Truly, the Way of waka reaches back to a time as distant as the far end of the floating bridge of heaven,[3] from whence generation after generation of gifted poets have shown the Way so clearly; how could anyone possibly go astray? As for renga, it too has remained undecayed for generations, ever since its linked leaves of words were first gathered and recorded in the *Man'yōshū*.[4] After a long history, it poured forth from the Minase River with added color and links greater in number than before.[5] Over a hundred years later, there emerged two or three wise devotees who actively brought it to heights of popularity and so ushered in a broadening of the Way.[6] Furthermore, at the end of their era, the renowned sage [Nijō Yoshimoto] appeared.[7] In his day, one of the earlier wise devotees [Gusai] was still living, who attended him night and day, helping him to determine the rules and precedents that serve as a beacon light upon the Way of renga.[8] However, it seems that the light has waned, since theirs was the work of but a single era.

COMMENTARY

Sasamegoto's account of renga history has since become standard in modern reconstructions of it. It was the *Yakumo mishō* (Eightfold Cloud Treatise [1221]) by Retired Emperor Juntoku (1197–1242; r. 1210–1221) that first cited

Man'yōshū 1635 as the oldest example of linked poetry, that is, its archaic form as "short renga" (*tanrenga*). This is essentially a waka poem divided into two parts, an upper 5-7-5–syllable verse, composed by one person, and a lower 7-7–syllable verse, composed by another in reply. It features the formal elements of the basic renga verse form as an individual link, as well as its pragmatic aspect as dialogical discourse. Nijō Yoshimoto (1320–1388) traced the beginnings of renga farther back, to the examples of *katauta mondō* (half-poems, each of 5-7-7 syllables, used in pairs for dialogues) in the ancient chronicles *Kojiki* (712) and *Nihongi* (720). This is evidence that the earliest renga poets and scholars considered the dialogical as the nexus of renga structure.

The next major development in renga history is the rise of so-called chain renga (*kusari renga*) with multiple links. The exact process by which this came about is not clear. It has been suggested that the practice of verse capping, in which someone utters the final 7-7–syllable lines of a waka and someone else then provides the initial 5-7-5–syllable lines, was involved in the process, since the latter verse, by formal necessity, would in turn have elicited another 7-7–syllable couplet to round off the sequence. Once this basic three-verse sequence, in which verse 2 combined with both verse 1 and verse 3 to form two distinct links, was established, it was possible to repeat the process all over again, starting with verse 3 as the beginning of a new round, and so on. The historical tale *Ima kagami* (1170) includes scattered accounts of linked-verse composition in the late Heian period, among them the following 3-verse sequence, which illustrates in microcosm the idea above and interestingly shows us a woman in witty discourse with the men:

nara no miyako o omoi koso yare	To the old capital at Nara my thoughts turn in longing. (Fujiwara Kinnori, d. 1160)
yaezakura aki no momiji ya ika naramu	Double-petaled cherries and the crimson leaves of autumn, how do they fare? (Minamoto Arihito, d. 1149)
shigururu tabi ni iro ya kasanaru	Perhaps the colors piling deep with each passing rain?[9] (The Echigo Nurse)

Although Shinkei makes no mention of it, the Chinese *lianju* (J. *renku*), a minor poetic form during the Six Dynasties and Tang periods, also played a part in the rise of chain renga. The *lianju* resembled renga in being a series of couplets composed by three to five poets. It is first mentioned in the *Kaifūsō*, the first collection of Chinese poems by Japanese poets (comp. 751), but was actually composed only from the mid-Heian period on. Various poetic practices and terminology associated with the *lianju* were apparently adapted to renga composition, among them the establishment of the *hyakuin* (100-verse sequence) as the standard length, strictures against similar sounds and images in consecutive verses, and the patterned arrangement of the verses in the manuscript record (*kaishi*).[10] Ultimately, however, the Japanese renga developed in a conspicuously different way from the Chinese form: in a *lianju*, the verses are integrated into a long poem with a recognizable topic, whereas in renga, where only consecutive verses are mutually related, there is no such semantic synthesis or total unified effect, and the aesthetics of thematic sequencing are more akin to music.

Shinkei's reference to the Minase River indicates the decisive influence of Fujiwara Teika (1162–1241), Ietaka (1158–1237), and other *Shinkokinshū* poets in the formation of the long form and its aesthetics during the early Kamakura period. These poets belonged to the mainstream waka tradition, and they brought their weighty heritage to bear upon renga, while taking from the new genre insights that fed their experimentation, in waka, with syntactic fragmentation and the use of the caesura at the end of line 1 or line 3 for arresting effects. Teika's diary, the *Meigetsuki* (Bright Moon Record) (1180–1235), includes several references to renga sessions held by Retired Emperor Go-Toba (1180–1239; r. 1184–1198) in his detached palace along the Minase River, and he would later dub renga his "elegant solace in old age" (*rōgo no suki*).[11]

However, the men who would, nearly a century later, from late Kamakura through the Nambokuchō period, actively cause renga to flourish, leading to a "broadening of the Way" (*michi hiroki koto ni nareru*), were leaders of the sessions held among the lower-ranking and commoner milieu, the so-called *jige renga*, as distinct from that of the court nobility (*dōjō*). These earliest renga masters were Zen'a (fl. ca. 1275–1333) and his disciples Gusai, or Kyūsei (ca. 1282–1376), Shinshō (fl. ca. 1312–1345), and Junkaku (1268–ca. 1355). From the mid-Kamakura period on, renga spread among commoners in Japan as no other poetic form had done before, not even waka. In Kyoto, the populace gathered in the precincts of temples like the Hōshōji and the Bishamondō to compose verses under the direction of professional *rengashi* (teachers of linked verse), who were usually poet-monks familiar with the rules of composition and the prescribed forms for such occasions. These gatherings, called *hana no moto renga* (renga under the flowers), because they were held in springtime under the cherry blossoms, were immensely popular and soon acquired the importance of annual events (*nenjū gyōji*). They were held as prayer offerings in connection with the Flower Pacification Festival (*Chinkasai*) held in the Third Month of each year to invoke the protection of the gods against epidemics, and in that sense had a ritual function.

Renga meetings, held not only in the shrines and temples of Kyoto but also in the mansions of the great daimyo in Kamakura and the surrounding provinces, constituted the milieu from which Zen'a and the other early renga masters sprang. Zen'a—believed to have been a priest belonging to the Jishū branch of the Jōdo Shinshū—frequently led "renga under the flowers" at temples and was instrumental in establishing one of the earliest versions of the rules, the *Kenji shinshiki* (New Code of the Kenji Era) from 1277. And it was Zen'a's disciple Gusai, now acknowledged as renga's first major poet, whose tutorship of the Regent Nijō Yoshimoto in renga subsequently had a decisive influence on the compilation of the first official renga anthology, *Tsukubashū*, in 1356–57. Their collaboration also produced a new synthesis of the rules then available, the *Renga shinshiki* (New Renga Code) (1372), which, with minor variations, defined the form for the rest of its history.

THREE

On the *Tsukubashū*

Now, then, when the renowned sage of Nijō governed the realm as Regent, he consulted that wise devotee Gusai and compiled the *Tsukubashū*, the anthology that brought together remarkable examples of all the various renga configurations in existence. Could it perhaps serve as a beacon on the Way of renga?

With the *Kokinshū* as a model, the Nijō Regent intended to make the *Tsukubashū* another peerless anthology that could become a beacon lighting the way for future poets. So it may be seen as a source of various styles that those who seek to master the Way of renga ought to reflect upon, a book they ought to investigate and learn. But from the middle period on, it is said, even the name *Tsukubashū* itself fell into obscurity. Thus the Way of renga came to lack any guideposts, and everyone composed just as he pleased.

COMMENTARY

Yoshimoto compiled the *Tsukubashū* during the years 1356 and 1357, with the invaluable assistance of Gusai and his disciples.[1] In scheme and format, the *Tsukubashū* is clearly modeled on the imperial waka anthologies. It is composed of twenty sections, variously subdivided under the topics of Spring (two sections), Summer, Autumn (two sections), and Winter; Sacred Rites (Shintō), Buddhism, Love (three sections), Miscellaneous (five sections), Travel, Celebrations, Miscellaneous Forms, and Hokku. Of the total 2,190 verses included, 119 are *hokku* and the rest are verse pairs (of *maeku* and *tsukeku*) selected from countless contemporary and earlier sources. The absence of complete texts of 100-verse sequences is notable and may be ascribed primarily to pragmatic considerations—the anthology would have dwarfed any waka anthology in scale. Nevertheless, it reveals that for most of renga's history, it was the individual links, rather than the aesthetics of sequencing across longer blocks of verses, that was the focus of attention. It was not until Shinkei's own age that the aesthetic concern for sequence began to develop as an added refinement of the form. Otherwise, Yoshimoto's choice of verses reflects a catholic taste and a definite historical perspective. Conscious that the *Tsukubashū* was in fact the first ever renga anthology, he included, in addition to the compositions of his contemporaries, examples from the *tanrenga* of the Heian period, the *haikai renga* and *hana no moto renga* of the Kamakura period, and *ushin renga* from the time of Go-Toba and the *Shinkokinshū* poets. Indeed, even the legendary poetic exchange between Yamato Takeru and the firelighter from the *Kojiki* and *Nihongi* appears in the anthology.

Of the approximately 460 poets included, those represented by twenty or more verses included Gusai, 126; Cloistered Prince Son'in, 90; Yoshimoto, 87; Sasaki Dōyo (1296–1373), 81; Ashikaga Takauji (1305–1358), 67; Tameie, 37; Zen'a, 32; Teika, 25; Tameuji, 25; Ietaka, 23; Retired Emperor Go-Saga (1220–1272), 22; Shūa, 22; Ashikaga Yoshiakira (1330–1368), 21; Shinshō, 20; and Ryōa, 20. Among the five contemporary poets with the highest number of verses in the anthology, Gusai is strictly speaking the only professional renga master; the other four were thus honored because apart from being enthusiastic practitioners, they were the social leaders of the renga milieu, providing the occasion for renga composition by regularly sponsoring sessions at their residences or in the temples around the capital, and lending their prestigious cooperation in the enterprise of producing the very first official renga anthology in Japanese history. Shōgun Ashikaga Takauji and his trusted ally Sasaki Dōyo, an official of the Mandokoro, represented the warrior-class renga circle; Yoshimoto and Cloistered Prince Son'in (d. 1354), son of Retired Emperor Go-Fushimi, and Tendai Abbot, led the sessions of the aristocratic nobility; and Gusai represented the commoner renga milieu.

The so-called middle period (*nakatsukoro*) in the treatise's historical construction generally refers to the almost half a century after the deaths of Yoshimoto and Gusai. Shinkei consistently cites it as a period of decline in the quality of renga composition, in contrast to the previous age, which was distinguished by the activities of such masters as Gusai, Junkaku, and Yoshimoto. Various reasons have been advanced for the decline of the orthodox renga style espoused by Yoshimoto and Gusai. In *Oi no kurigoto*, Shinkei, for one, ascribes it to the overwhelming popularity of the style of Gusai's disciple Shūa, which was heavily oriented toward verbal rhetoric, witty turns of phrase and wordplay, in contrast to Gusai's plainness and inwardness. (On Shūa, see "Biographical Notes.")

To construe a middle-period decline of renga, when "the Way came to lack any guideposts" (*shirube naki michi ni narite*), reveals Shinkei's ambition to provide, with this treatise, precisely that missing direction, first by restoring the work of Yoshimoto and the early masters to the field of contemporary knowledge and practice; and second, by constituting a new renga aesthetics that foregrounds thought and feeling (*kokoro*) over the mere play of language. As is well known, modern scholarship dates the Muromachi renga revival, which was also the peak of its flowering, to the work of Shinkei and the other "seven sages of renga" (*renga shichiken*), which in turn inspired the poetry of Shinkei's disciples Sōgi and Kenzai, both recipients of the *Sasamegoto* treatise.

FOUR

Post-*Shinkokinshū* Waka

I hear that the quality of waka also started deteriorating from the middle period. Can it be that the Way of waka has indeed waned?

According to the old poets, it was truly during the age of the retired sovereign at Minase Palace [Retired Emperor Go-Toba] that there appeared a great number of waka masters surpassing even those of antiquity. This was indeed the time when they conjured up a variety of new configurations, penetrated into the innermost recesses of the Way, and achieved an unparalleled success in the world. But that did not last long. From the time of Retired Emperor Go-Saga, the color faded from the dew on the leaves of words and the fragrance waned from the heart's flower.[1] Thereafter, waka followed a downhill course, growing ever more shallow, until Imagawa Ryōshun became a disciple of the Reizei Middle Counselor and after long years of study, gained knowledge of the old anthologies and revived the Way of waka.[2] Then, during Ryōshun's lifetime, the gifted Shōtetsu was born. As Ryōshun's student from youth until maturity, Shōtetsu searched deep into the forest of words and delved exhaustively into the wellsprings of the mind-heart; like ice born of water, he illumined both the shallows and the depths of poetry.[3] His light indeed shunned not the wild thickets.[4] Thus once again the mind and language of those former times became widely known in the world.

COMMENTARY

The modern valuation of the eighth imperial anthology, *Shinkokinshū* (1205), as representing the apogee of waka history, finds unequivocal documentary support here in *Sasamegoto* and Shinkei's other writings. The same goes for our appreciation of its poetry of complex technical and imagistic effects, as well as its subtle profundity. It should be noted, however, that

Shinkei's valuation included a third factor, and that is *Shinkokinshū*-style poetry's unparalleled "success in the world" (*yo ni tokimekitamaishi koto*). It is clear from this chapter that he sees Shōtetsu's waka as a revival of the superior qualities of *Shinkokinshū* poetry, but in fact the age was under the dominance of the conservative Nijō school, and the Reizei school to which he and his waka mentor belonged was distinctly out of official favor. Shōtetsu, by all accounts the major waka poet of the Muromachi period, was not included in what would turn out to be the very last of the twenty-one imperial anthologies, the *Shinzoku Kokinwakashū* (1439).[5] While future centuries would validate Shinkei's poetic judgment about the *Shinkokinshū* and Shōtetsu, waka literary history, and renga's as well, *Sasamegoto*'s literary historical construction was an unorthodox one in its own time. That Shinkei would resist the dominant view and write against the prevailing tide causes us to reflect on the historical contexts of evaluation, the relativity of center-margin distinctions, and the power given each generation to read and revise history as it comes down from the past.

FIVE

Ancient and Middle-Period Renga

When one compares the expressive diction of those first two or three renga masters with works of the middle period, they seem as different as the crow in the mountain depths and the heron by the river bank.[1] Was there really such a complete change from one period to the next?

As our predecessors have said, no matter how biased one may be, one must admit that there was a very great change.[2] When one examines the works of the early masters, one sees that they took infinite care with the maeku, attentive to even such technical points as consonantal and vocalic rhyming in order to relate to it.[3] But from the middle period on, it seems that poets were concerned only with weaving flowers and crimson leaves into their own words, while wholly discarding the mind-heart of the preceding verse. They merely strung together images of the moon, flowers, and snow even in the most unsuitable places, and so their verses, lacking the vital link to the mind-heart of the maeku, merely sat there like a row of lifeless cadavers in impeccable garb. On the contrary, it is precisely in engaging the previous verse that even the most trivial words come to life with an appeal they have never had before.

COMMENTARY

This and the following chapter constitute Shinkei's most important statement in *Sasamegoto* I on the central question of *tsukeai* (linking) in renga. Here, he is in effect saying that the link between verses has priority over the words of each verse as such. Thus the single verse might be beautiful and impressive in itself, but it is utterly lifeless (the metaphor of the cadavers is quite revealing here) if it does not relate to the meaning (*kokoro*) of the previous verse, or *maeku*. On the other hand, it might be quite plain and seemingly trivial as such but will suddenly acquire a new life when viewed from the perspective of its link with the maeku. In short, the essence and vitality of renga as a poetic genre lies in the transaction or engagement (*toriyori*) between the verse units, not in the verse units as such; and linking is as it were a *process of animating words* through the act of understanding.

SIX

The Character of the Work of the Early Masters

What does it actually mean to say that the attitude and style of the middle period are altered from the work of the early masters?

The verses of the old masters, it seems to me, are deeply linked in the conception [*kokoro*], and only incidentally in the diction [*kotoba*] or external configuration [*sugata*]. The masters had a keen faculty for discerning what to take and what to discard in the maeku, whereas poets of recent times merely divide the words arbitrarily and link up to any number of them.

yoshinoyama futatabi haru ni narinikeri	On Mount Yoshino, it's turned to springtime for the second time.
toshi no uchi yori toshi o mukaete Go-Toba-in	From within the old year, already I greet a new year.[1] Retired Emperor Go-Toba

If the second verse had been composed today, it would probably have been criticized because it does not link up to "Yoshino."[2]

sasatake no ōmiyabito no karigoromo	Midst the bamboo grass a palace courtier, splendid in hunting robes.
hitoyo wa akenu hana no shitabushi Teika-kyō	Dawn breaks upon a night asleep beneath the flowers.[3] Lord Teika

If the second verse were composed today, someone would surely complain that neither "courtier" nor "hunting robes" has a corresponding word association.

musubu fumi ni wa uwagaki mo nashi	Not even the name is written on the face of the knotted letter.
iwashiro no matsu to bakari wa otozurete Junkaku	Like Iwashiro's pine, "I wait" is all the message it brings.[4] Junkaku

Here it would doubtless be objected that there is no reference to *uwagaki* in the lower verse.

saohime no katsuragiyama mo haru kakete	Saohime, goddess of spring, has spread her tresses on Mount Katsuragi.
kasumedo imada mine no shirayuki Ietaka-kyō	Yet high above the haze, the peaks are white with snow.[5] Lord Ietaka

Again, it would be said that there is nothing in the second verse to link to Saohime and Katsuragi.

musubu no kami ni sue mo inoramu	I shall pray to the god that binds, that he may unite our destinies.
ikuyo to mo shiranu tabine no kusa makura Shinshō	I know not how many nights I shall journey, grasses for pillow.[6] Shinshō

It would be said that "god" and "pray" have been left out in the lower verse.

funa kogu ura wa kurenai no momo	A boat glides along the coast crimson with peach blossoms.

karakuni no tora madaranaru inu hoete Shūa	Land of China a tiger-streaked dog raises a howl.[7] Shūa

Here, it would be objected, there is no word correspondence to "boat."

uwagi ni shitaru mino o koso make	Now I roll up the straw raincoat that I wear on my shoulders.
karisome no makura dani naki abine shite Ryōa	I have not even a makeshift pillow, sleeping on a journey.[8] Ryōa

If this were a recent poem, critics would object that there is no connection at all to the preceding verse.

uma odorokite hito sawagu nari	The horse rears up in shock, and the people scream in alarm.
hayakawa no kishi ni atareru watashibune Gusai	The ferryboat has rammed up the bank of the swift river.[9] Gusai

Doubtless it would be argued that there is no word association for "horse."

These verses are masterpieces because of their authors' intelligence in discarding unnecessary elements in the maeku. There are countless others of the same kind, but I cannot record all of them here.

COMMENTARY

Continuing from the previous chapter on the question of tsukeai, Shinkei states that a proper link is based on the meaning, conception, or feeling (*kokoro*) of the maeku, not on its words (*kotoba*) or external configuration (*sugata*) as such. Or stated in another way, it is the integral meaning of the verse *as a whole* that determines the importance or unimportance of each word in it, and the skilled practitioner is one who possesses an acute sense of discrimination in this regard; poetic intelligence in renga is, then, the faculty of knowing "what to take and what to discard" (*torisute*). The shallow or unskilled poet, on the other hand, disregards the meaning of the maeku; he handles it as a series of discrete words, and arbitrarily links to any one of them according to external factors like conventional verbal associations (known as *yoriai*), or his desire to use such impressive images as flowers, moon, and so on. As a consequence, the verses are only loosely or slackly connected; they want the tension that is the mark of verses linked from within, from the meaning or conception. Another way of putting this is that Shinkei regarded the renga link as a dialogic exchange based on the poet's *reading* of the maeku. Sole reliance on conventional word associations indicates a refusal to read the maeku for the other poet's meaning or intention; that would be no more than a mindless automatism whose effect is to reproduce the dictionary, so to speak, of the poetic tradition. Ultimately, therefore, the central issue of tsukeai directly hinges on the question of value, that is, the ethos of language usage for interpersonal communication, on the one hand, and creativity as a desired value, on the other.

Shinkei cites the eight verse pairs that follow as examples of the intelligence with which renga masters of the early period (i.e., the time of Retired Emperor Go-Toba and Teika, and later that of Yoshimoto and Gusai) appended their *tsukeku* or following verse. Two points should be noted: one, that the verses are linked through the conception of the maeku; and, two, that the poet has skillfully selected which words are important in the maeku and accordingly linked up to them.

SEVEN

The Style of Ineffable Depth (*Yūgen*)

Now, in the Way of renga, is it the Style of Ineffable Depth [*yūgen*] that one should single out and strive to perfect?

The ancients have said that every verse should bear the stamp of that style, and certainly its mastery is the poet's most important task. Nevertheless, there appears to be a vast difference between what the old masters conceived of as the Style of Ineffable Depth and what others now understand by it. What the masters held up as example was poetry that gave primacy to the mind-heart [*kokoro*]; what most people comprehend by the Style of Ineffable Depth is an external configuration steeped in grace and charm [*sugata no yasabamitaru*]. The compelling beauty that springs from the mind [*kokoro no en*] is difficult to attain. So it is with people; putting on a fine outward appearance is the way of the many, but rare indeed is he who seeks to master his own mind. That is why the poems that the ancients considered the finest examples of this style are nowadays indiscernible as such.[1]

Poems in the Style of Ineffable Depth

aki no ta no kario no io no toma o arami waga koromode wa tsuyu ni nuretsutsu Tenchi-tennō	For the rough thatch of the rice guard's hut amid reaped fields of autumn the sleeves of my robe are ever damp with dew.[2] Emperor Tenchi
sasa no ha wa miyama mo soyo ni midaru nari	Bamboo-grass leaves— the very mountain seems astir with a wild rustling,

ware wa imo omou
wakare kinureba
Hitomaro

as a longing grips my mind
for the wife I left behind.[3]
Hitomaro

wabinureba
ima hata onaji
na ni wa naru
mi o tsukushite mo
awamu to zo omou
Motoyoshi shinnō

Such misery this;
let my name grow again common as
the channel stakes of Naniwa,
I would cast this body away
to gaze on you once again![4]
Prince Motoyoshi

wasurenamu
yo ni mo koshiji no
kaeruyama
itsu hata hito ni
awamu to suran
Ise

In a world so apt
in forgetting, once gone over
the Koshi highway, along the
Hill of Returning and Someday,
shall I ever meet you again?[5]
Ise

yamazato o
kiri no magaki no
hedatezuba
ochikatabito no
sode wa mitemashi
Sone Yoshitada

Oh, that a hedge of mists
did not a barrier raise round
the mountain hamlet—
I would see at least the sleeve
of some traveler passing yonder.[6]
Sone Yoshitada

wasurenu ya
sa wa wasurekeri
au koto o
yume ni nase to zo
iite wakareshi
Teika-kyō

Have I forgotten?
Oh yes, something I did forget—
that I said when
we last parted, "Think of our
meeting as nothing but a dream."[7]
Lord Teika

tare zo kono
me oshinogoite
tateru hito

What man is this
that wipes tears from his eyes
while standing off

hito no yo wataru michi no hotori ni Jichin-oshō	to the side of the road others must follow on life's journey?[8] Priest Jichin

Likewise, in renga, it is important to distinguish the true Style of Ineffable Depth from what merely appears to be that style.

honobono to kasumi ni hana no nioikite	Dimly comes the scent of flowers in the haze.
sokotonaku oborozukiyo ni kari nakite	Faintly, on the night of the hazy moon, the wild geese cry.
yūgure no susuki o kaze ya wataruramu	Is the wind passing over the miscanthus grasses at dusk?

Verses like these, written by untalented people and reading ever the same, although their authors change, are of the type that is highly praised day after day in every renga session.[9]

itazura ni hana no sakari mo suginuramu Ryōa	Uselessly— the flowers' splendor too shall pass.[10] Ryōa
itsu idete oboro ni tsuki no nokoruramu Gusai	When did it rise, the moon still lingering through the haze?[11] Gusai
furusato no hitomura susuki kaze fukite Gusai	In the old village, a clump of miscanthus grasses blowing in the wind.[12] Gusai

Verses like these can hardly issue from indifferent mouths. It is necessary to discriminate between gold and gilding, between gold and brass. Again, among the so-called stalwart verses [*takumashiki ku*], the same distinction exists.[13]

neriso ga wa
shiba o makuzu no
hanakazura

For a rope to tie round
the brushwood, a vine wreath
of arrowroot flowers.

kedamono wa
tsune ni kokeji o
hashirikite

A hairy beast
often comes bounding down
the mossy path.

The mind and diction of these verses are utterly lacking in quality [*shina*]; they are the work of the meanest sort of poets.[14]

midorigo no
hitai ni kakeru
moji o miyo
Ryōa

Look upon
the letter written on
the infant's brow.[15]
Ryōa

itarikeri
tani ni akatsuki
tsuki ni aki
Sōzei

The spirit soars!
Daybreak in the valley,
autumn in the moon.[16]
Sōzei

These verses, the work of skilled poets, are said to have been especially admired by their own authors. In short, it is of utmost importance to distinguish between the verse of truly compelling beauty and one that is merely full of charm; between the "stalwart" verse and the merely "rough" [*araki*] one. It is said that the masterpieces are to be found among those verses in which the mind and the words are spare [*kokoro kotoba sukunaku*], cold, and slender [*samuku yasetaru*]. The renga poet must examine those poems of the old masters that they themselves esteemed [*jisan no uta*] and then measure his own work accordingly. It is difficult to see a masterpiece in a verse with a knobby, stumbling diction and in which the total effect is corpulent and warm [*futori atatakanaru*]. Training is the most essential factor in this regard.[17]

A Few Self-Esteemed Poems of the Old Masters

miru mama ni yamakaze araku shigurumeri miyako mo ima ya yosamu naruramu Go-Toba-in	As I look on, the mountain wind turns gusty as with coming rain— feels the night colder too this very moment in Miyako?[18] Retired Emperor Go-Toba
omoiizuru oritaku shiba no yūkeburi musebu mo ureshi wasuregatami ni Onaji	At times when I remember, as smoke of kindling drifts up the evening sky, choked, I yet find solace in this memory that will not die.[19] Retired Emperor Go-Toba
kiri no ha mo fumiwakegataku narinikeri kanarazu hito o matsu to nakeredo Shikishi-naishinnō	The paulownia leaves have piled too deep to tread a way through— Though surely it cannot be that I am waiting for someone.[20] Princess Shikishi
sorenagara mukashi ni mo aranu akikaze ni itodo nagame o shizu no odamaki Onaji	The same, yet altered from the past, the autumn wind, as I ponder an old grief that turns again and yet again, an endless thread in a spool.[21] Princess Shikishi
iwazariki ima komu made no sora no kumo tsukihi hedatete mono omoe to wa Go-Kyōgoku-sesshō	You never told me this: that till your "I am coming soon," I should anxious scan the clouds in the sky, as suns and moons came between us.[22] The Go-Kyōgoku Regent

omou koto
nado tou hito no
nakaruramu
aogeba sora ni
tsuki zo sayakeki
Jichin-oshō

Of the sorrow
in my heart, why comes no one
to inquire?
I gaze up at the sky, and oh,
how keen and clear the moon![23]
Priest Jichin

miyamaji ya
itsu yori aki no
iro naramu
mizarishi kumo no
yūgure no sora
Onaji

Deep mountain trail—
since when did it start to wear
the hues of autumn?
Clouds I had not seen before
gloaming in the evening sky![24]
Priest Jichin

asajifu ya
sode ni kuchinishi
aki no shimo
wasurenu yume o
fuku arashi kana
Michiteru

Will the blowing storm
rend the unforgettable dream
that sickens in my sleeves,
rank weeds laid waste
in the chill frosts of autumn.[25]
Michiteru

shimeokite
ima wa to omou
akiyama no
yomogi ga moto ni
matsu mushi no koe
Shunzei-kyō

Having marked the site,
brooding on the impending time
in the autumn mountain—
the faint trill of pine crickets
biding in the mugwort weed.[26]
Lord Shunzei

furinikeri
shigure wa sode ni
aki kakete
iishi bakari o
matsu to seshi ma ni
Shunzei-kyō
no musume

Chill upon my sleeves
the winter rains have fallen
while I waited
"till autumn," you said,
mere words, for you had tired.[27]
Lord Shunzei's
Daughter

katae sasu
ofu no uranashi
hatsu aki ni
nari mo narazu mo
kaze zo mi ni shimu
Kunaikyō

On the pear-tree branch
slanting out toward Ofu Bay
it may or may not soon
be autumn, yet how the wind
sinks cool into one's soul![28]
Lady Kunaikyō

haru no yo no
yume no ukihashi
todaeshite
mine ni wakaruru
yokogumo no sora
Teika-kyō

The bridge of dreams
floating in the spring night
breaks off—
trailing away from the peak,
a cloud in the dawning sky.[29]
Lord Teika

toshi mo henu
inoru shirushi wa
hatsuseyama
onoe no kane no
yoso no yūgure
Onaji

Years have passed;
the only answer to my prayer
the hollow booming of
the bell on Mount Hatsuse in
the dusk that belongs to another.[30]
Lord Teika

kinō dani
towamu to omoishi
tsu no kuni no
ikuta no mori ni
aki wa kinikeri
Ietaka-kyō

Where but yesterday
I had thought to visit
in Ikuta Woods
in the land of Tsu, already
the autumn has come![31]
Lord Ietaka

omoiiru
mi wa fukakusa no
aki no tsuyu
tanomeshi sue ya
kogarashi no kaze
Onaji

I who love you am
the autumn dew clinging deep in
the grasses of Fukakusa;
the end you promised might prove
but the chill gusts of winter.[32]
Lord Ietaka

utsuriyuku
kumo ni arashi no
koe su nari
chiru ka masaki no
katsuragi no yama
Masatsune-kyō

From within the
darkening clouds, the voice
of the tempest sounds—
Is the bright ivy gusting down
Mount Katsuragi even now?[33]
Lord Masatsune

katsuragi ya
takama no sakura
sakinikeri
tatsuta no oku ni
kakaru shiragumo
Jakuren

On Katsuragi, sky-high
on Takama's slopes, the cherries
have burst into flower:
masses of white clouds trailing
beyond the peak of Tatsuta.[34]
Jakuren

kogarashi ya
ika ni machimin
miwa no yama
tsurenaki sugi no
yukiore no koe
Tomochika

In the bitter storm,
how can I bear to wait to see—
the pitiless sound
of cedar boughs cracking
under the snow on Mount Miwa.[35]
Tomochika

omoiiru
fukaki kokoro no
tayori made
mishi wa sore to mo
naki yamaji kana
Hideyoshi

To plumb the depths
of my yearning heart, I walked
to the very end
of the mountain trail, and saw
my love went deeper still.[36]
Hideyoshi

tsu no kuni no
naniwa no haru wa
yume nare ya
ashi no kareha ni
kaze wataru nari
Saigyō

It is all a dream
that springtime at Naniwa
in the land of Tsu—
the dry rustling of the wind
over withered leaves of reeds.[37]
Saigyō

toshi takete mata koyubeshi to omoiki ya inochi narikeri sayononakayama Saigyō	Now full of years, did I ever think then I would cross it once more? O mountain in midst of night, a lifetime do I bear here![38] Saigyō

Even when one understands the meaning of poems like these, to recognize them as supreme masterpieces is perhaps difficult. Because they are unadorned with fancy, rhetorical phrases and their spirit and diction are possessed of an ineffable remoteness [*yōonnaru*], it is not an easy task to single them out and realize what exactly there is in each one that makes it great. Such famous poems are numerous; one cannot possibly quote them all.

COMMENTARY

The opening passage of this chapter is a central one in *Sasamegoto*, because it expresses Shinkei's view that *yūgen*, a major aesthetic ideal of the medieval period, is primarily a state of mind and spirit (*kokoro*) and not a matter of graceful or refined poetic configuration (*yasabamitaru sugata*). He then goes on to equate *yūgen* with his own central ideal of *kokoro no en*, beauty of the mind-heart, the intense, charismatic appeal of a mind in touch with the deep truths of human existence, palpable in the poems as a wordless conviction of feeling. In this interpretation, *yūgen* is not a specific style but immanent in all poetry that reveals a spiritual depth; in this sense, it is quite close to Teika's concept of *ushin*, the mode of meditation.

As in the two previous chapters on tsukeai, Shinkei shows a tendency to oppose *kokoro* to *kotoba* and *sugata* as the poem's essential, internal core as against its external form. Such a distinction goes hand in hand with his corresponding deemphasizing of verbal ingenuity and technique as such, and both reflect his basic attitude that poetry is an expression of the person himself, the quality of his mind, and not primarily of his or her skill with words.

EIGHT

Learning and the Study of Renga

How much knowledge should one strive to accumulate in order to reach the highest realm in the Way?

It is written in the *Yakumo mishō* that knowledge does not necessarily mean mastering the classics of China and India, and that it may be confined to the *Man'yōshū*, *Kokinshū*, *Ise monogatari*, and other works of the same kind.[1] Those that exhibit a refined diction and behavior of appealing sensibility are the *Genji monogatari* and *Sagoromo*. No one is more reprehensible, said a man of former days, than the poet who makes no effort at all to inquire into these works.[2] About the *Man'yōshū*, the middling poets of our day feel that its language and spirit are awesome and impossible to understand with ease, and they will consequently have none of it. Yet ever since it was transcribed into the kana syllabary in the Pear-Garden Hall, the *Man'yōshū* has become pleasurable reading, even for women, it is said, truly unsurpassed in the wide variety of its diction and its richly moving poems.[3] It is known that Lord Teika always made it a point to say, "If you train your spirit upon the poetry of the pre-Kampyō era, how can you not achieve the Way?" He must have had the poems of the *Man'yōshū* in mind.[4]

Among Lord Teika's writings on various aspects of learning in the Way is the following: "In the first two or three years, you must study the quiet and gentle poems of the women, and thereafter the Intricate Style, the One-Figure Style, and so on. Still later, you must train in the so-called Style of Meditation, which harbors deep feeling within it, and the Lofty Style, which has a meager and cold quality. Having mastered these, then you may study the Style of Power, also called the Demon-Quelling Style."[5] Teika reportedly placed the Demon-Quelling Style at the very heart of the Way. But then he also said, "If I declare this to be the highest style, then everyone will want to study it exclusively, and for the immature poet that would be folly." And therefore he kept this matter secret.[6] Again he has written: "There are many who understand that to be an excellent verse that is graceful, quiet and innocent of striking features. They are wrong."[7]

In training for the Way, one must study both the flower and the seed. Already in the *Kokinshū*, we read: "All fallen are the seeds, the flowers alone flourish," and "Men's hearts are turned to flowers." Further, "To consider alluring beauty as its basis simply shows that one is ignorant of what poetry is."[8] All these are words of censure directed against the tendency toward insincerity. Since even in those days, such things were already being said, no doubt in our own time, not even a single seed has survived.

COMMENTARY

The question of whether Teika actually intended "pre-Kampyō" to cover not only the age of "the six poet-immortals" (*rokkasen*) but the more ancient *Man'yōshū* poetry as well must depend on an analysis of the context of the quoted passage in Teika's *Kindai shūka* (Superior Poems of Our Time). In the context of *Sasamegoto*, Shinkei's interpretation was obviously motivated by a desire to promote the study of that ancient classic as against the commonly held view of its difficulty. The point is important, since this chapter reflects his attempt to define the minimum requirements of a renga poet's classical education. As we have seen, he cites works from Heian courtly literature for their refined language and graceful attitudes, such qualities as were crucial to his grand aim of elevating renga to the social and aesthetic status of waka. The *Man'yōshū*, however, belongs to a pre-courtly sensibility; as distinct from the *Kokinshū*, which he elsewhere calls "the sole mirror of the Way," a standard model for the young poet, he cites it for exhibiting an unsurpassed breadth and diversity of poetic diction. More important, he refers to it again in Part II of *Sasamegoto* in the context of a central passage defining poetic beauty as primarily a quality of mind (*kokoro*) and only secondarily of diction (*kotoba*) and configuration (*sugata*). He writes: "The verses of those whose minds are 'adorned,' though graceful in diction and configuration, ring but falsely in the ears of those who have attained to Truth. . . . It is rare to find adorned configurations even among the famous poems and self-esteemed verses of the old poets. The poems of high antiquity (*jōdai no uta*, i.e., the *Man'yōshū*) in particular emphasized a keen directness (*surodonaru*) of expression, and therefore their excellence is indiscernible to the 'adorned' eyes of later ages" (*SSG*, p. 176). Evidently, then, Shinkei included the *Man'yōshū* in the renga poet's classical education, not only for the diversity, but more significantly, for the unadorned authenticity of its diction. And in doing so, he indicated that the refined elegance of a courtly sensibility should be accompanied by a true and honest emotion, for otherwise it falls to the level of mere artifice.

With regard to the study of poetic styles, Shinkei concurs with Teika's *Maigetsushō* (Monthly Notes) in the idea that the style of simplicity and grace should be mastered at the very beginning of one's training, and that the Demon-Quelling Style can be achieved only at the end. His progressive classification of the various styles may be outlined thus:

(1) the quiet and gentle poems;

(2) the Intricate Style; the Style of Singular Conception, and so on.

(3) the Style of Meditation; the Lofty Style;

(4) the Demon-Quelling Style.

This is merely a provisional list that Shinkei draws up for pedagogical reasons, to illustrate the principle that the various styles should be mastered gradually, each in its own time. Nevertheless, it is worth noting that level 3, *ushintei* "which harbors deep feeling within it," and *take takaki tei* "which has a meager and cold [*yase samuki*] quality," constitute his concept of high poetry, and that furthermore, he seems to have been fascinated by the stark power of *kiratsutei* in level 4. As for Teika, he set apart four styles and called them "the fundamental configurations" (*moto no sugata*) that the poet should practice constantly; these are the Style of Ineffable Depth (*yūgentei*), the Categorical style (*koto shikarubeki tei*), the Classic and Correct style (*uruwashiki tei*), and the Style of Meditation (*ushintei*). Of these the last, *ushintei*, occupies a central place in Teika's poetics, just as it does in Shinkei's.

A third aspect of Shinkei's concept of poetic study is his prescription, based on the *Kokinshū* Mana (Chinese) Preface's criticism of the popularity of beautiful and empty rhetoric, for greater attention to the substance ("seed" or "fruit") of the poem, an authenticity of feeling or thought. As is well known, classical poetics has always called for an ideal balance between form and content. All the leading poet-critics, including Teika, Nijō Yoshimoto, Kamo no Chōmei, and Shinkei himself, seem to have paid lip service to this eminently sensible principle, even while emphasizing one or the other in their actual theoretical discussions. Meaning or content as such obviously has no inherent aesthetic value in poetics apart from the words used to express it, and consequently the tendency has been to pay more attention to the formal elements of diction, imagery, and rhetorical technique as these function to produce the expressive quantity that is the poem. This was particularly true in the medieval period of Teika and the *Shinkokinshū* poets, whose concern for careful craftsmanship and subtle artistry generated numerous brilliant poems and what Shinkei acknowledges to be the glorious peak of waka's history. He himself, however, while inheriting the intricate and subtle aesthetic of the *Shinkokinshū*, made *kokoro* the basis of his own poetics, reinterpreting it, and in the process bringing the concept to its most profound development in the history of Japanese poetics. This is not the place to discuss the development of Shinkei's reading of *kokoro* not primarily as "meaning" but as "heart-mind," and its genesis in certain crucial though isolated passages in the criticism of Shunzei and Teika, which he developed into a concept of poetic imagination inspired by the Buddhist philosophy of temporality and emptiness.

The allusion to the Mana Preface in the last paragraph of this chapter is therefore significant, although here *kokoro* or the "seed" should be interpreted primarily and only in the sense of substance as distinct from a beautiful but empty form (*hana* or *en*). In the Mana Preface, the author Ki no Yoshimochi (?–919) was expressing his dissatisfaction with Japanese poetry from a moralistic Confucian perspective; he seems to have regarded the predominance of love poetry as evidence of a lack of seriousness, perhaps with its minor status in Chinese poetry at the back of his mind. Indeed, the vastness and sheer compass of the Chinese poetic achievement must early have presented a constant challenge to any serious Japanese critic, leading him to question whether the aesthetic grace and subtle emotionalism of a five-line poem could ever equal the breadth, the moral gravity and social pertinence of the Chinese example. Shinkei's emphasis on *kokoro* may be seen as evidence of a desire for poetry made of sterner stuff—a weightier content, certainly, but especially the qualities of truth and authenticity suggested by the "seed" metaphor. His inclusion of the *Man'yōshū* in this chapter and his implicit approval of the graceless and even "vulgar" Demon-Quelling Style are but manifestations of this main characteristic of his thought, which was to find its ultimate expression in his transformation of aesthetic beauty into a moral-religious value through his concept of *kokoro no en*, the compelling or charismatic beauty of the heart-mind.

NINE

The Role of Waka in Renga Training

The fellows in the countryside who delight in renga spurn waka. "The Way suffers when we compose waka," they say. What do you think of this?

This is what a former master said. It is precisely because some poets eschew the uses of waka in their training that their verses are so unappealing. This means, does it not, that one should instill the most excellent poems in one's heart and weave the shadow of their presence in every verse. And not only that, but constantly recite fine Chinese poems as well. It is the subtle presence of these poems that imbues the verses of the old masters with a certain nobility, grace, and loftiness—those intriguing qualities that are inexpressible in words. Renga arose by stringing together what were originally dialogue-poems into 50 or 100 verses, so there should not even be a hair's breadth of difference between it and waka.[1] In recent years, however, inasmuch as those who have no understanding of the waka spirit began to consider them as two disparate arts, the true essence of renga has been lost; it has become no more than a succession of mechanical verses lined up stiffly in a row.

COMMENTARY

Renga is of course quite distinct from waka; the rhythm of the single 5-7-5– or 7-7–syllable verse is necessarily quicker, more crisp and cleanly delineated than that of waka's 5-7-5-7-7–syllable form, which can be more flowing and subtle in movement. The fact that one has to convey an integral message within a briefer compass also means that renga diction made greater use of ellipses, and of nominals and verbals stripped of modal suffixes. Thus, unless a poet had thoroughly internalized both rhythms through constant practice, it was inevitable that he would produce a strange hybrid when working in the form that was not his métier. Already in the Nambokuchō period, Imagawa Ryōshun reports that renga poets scorned the renga of waka poets, calling them *uta renga*, while waka poets in turn derided the waka of renga poets, calling them *renga uta*. (See Ryōshun's *Rakusho roken*, ed. Sasaki Nobutsuna, *NKT* 5.196 [Kazama Shobō, 1957].)

Shinkei's insistence on the oneness of two forms that are obviously quite distinct may be understood as an attempt to promote in renga the aesthetic ideals of waka (and of some Chinese poetry), which he sums up as a quality of nobility (*shina*), grace (*yū*), and loftiness (*take*), that hovers about the poem like a shadow or unseen presence (*omokage*). More than a century earlier, Yoshimoto had made a similar attempt to elevate the new genre to the status of waka, but as will be recalled from chapters 2 and 3 of *Sasamegoto*, Yoshimoto's influence did not long survive him, and in popular renga circles, the irresistible notion that linked poetry is essentially a game of words and wit persisted with great vigor far into Shinkei's time.

The cornerstone of renga as a word game was the device of *yoriai*, linking through the conventional verbal correspondences that were codified in handbooks similar to rhyming dictionaries or thesauri. These handbooks represent in effect the systematization of the vocabulary inherited from the waka poetic tradition; they established the images proper to each theme, and the cluster of words associated with each image. When wielded with imagination and true wit, *yoriai* could and did produce exciting verses, but more often it caused renga to degenerate into a dull activity where the verbal correspondences stood isolated as the sole link between the verses. In other words, there was no attempt to connect to the integral meaning of the maeku (cf. chapters 5 and 6), and the result was as Shinkei says, "a succession of mechanical verses lined up stiffly in a row," a sequence of units signifying nothing. In telling the poet to read and recite waka as part of his training, Shinkei meant him to acquire a feel for the concealed but palpable connections between its upper and lower sections (as we shall see, he specifically had *Shinkokinshū*-type poems in mind), and thus to evoke in the renga link a similar "inexpressible" *omokage*, instead of the wooden and thoroughly exposed verbal joinings of *yoriai*.

TEN

On Hokku

Our rustic poets say that the fundamental style of the hokku is one that is generally lofty, calm, and moves with ease in a single measure from beginning to end. Is it indeed so?

A former master has said that, in truth, since the hokku is patterned after the head poem in waka, it should be calm, graceful, and expansive in effect. However, although this is indeed true for anthologies and such formal collections, for sequences of 100 poems, or 50 or less, the style of the head poem will vary according to the time and circumstances of composition.[1] Likewise, hokku, composed day after day on the same topics, as it were, would inevitably become dull if they all had a uniform style. The hokku of the old masters do not manifest such a deep concern for manifold effects. But then neither do they all conform to but a single one.[2] Nowadays, since it has become the fashion to esteem hokku and head poems alone, composing them has turned into an ostentatious affair, with everyone striving for all manners of effects in order not to sound like the next fellow.[3] Thus, as they say in China, "literary styles have undergone a threefold transformation."[4]

Head Poems

ika ni nete
okuru ashita ni
iu koto zo
kinō o kozo to
kyō o kotoshi to
Kodai no Kimi

How long did I sleep
that when I awoke this morning
people should say
of yesterday it was last year,
and today it's this year?[5]
Kodai no Kimi

shirazariki
yama yori takaki
yowai made
haru no kasumi no
tatsu o mimu to wa
Teika-kyō

I had not known it—
weighed by years heaped higher
than those hills,
I should see yet again upon them
rise, the bright haze of spring.[6]
Lord Teika

yahatayama
mitsu no koromo no
tamatebako
futatsu wa tachinu
kumo yo kasumi yo
Shōtetsu

In Yahata, the eightfold
hills, threefold robes
in a jeweled box,
two have been spread out,
the haze, the clouds![7]
Shōtetsu

Hokku

nake ya kyō
miyako o niwa no
hototogisu
Nijō-taikō

Sing out today,
all the capital your garden be,
O cuckoo![8]
The Nijō Regent

ima koko o
hototogisu tote
tōrekashi
Onaji

Here now, with a
"*hototogisu*!" Would you were
flitting by at last.[9]
The Nijō Regent

fuke arashi
momiji o nusa no
kamunatsuki
Gusai

Blow, winds of storm,
the red leaves as holy streamers
before the Godless Moon![10]
Gusai

ana tōto
haruhi no migaku
tamatsushima
Shūa

Awe-stilled I gaze:
the gem isle of Tamatsushima
polished by spring sun.[11]
Shūa

The effect of these head poems and hokku seems to shift restlessly from one to the next.

COMMENTARY

The final statement sums up what is in effect Shinkei's negative reply to the original question of whether the lofty, calm, and simple style constitutes the hokku's "fundamental form" (*hontai*). While conceding in the beginning that such a style is indeed proper for formal collections of waka and renga, Shinkei then goes on to illustrate his view that there is no one single essential hokku form; a variety of forms are generated by the particular circumstances obtaining in each session, the inevitable shifts in taste from one period to another, and the poet's desire to be novel and original. To illustrate his point, he quotes three head poems from the Heian, Kamakura, and contemporary Muromachi periods respectively. All deal with the same subject—the beginning of spring, but are couched in vastly different styles. The four hokku examples are all from the Kamakura-Nambokuchō periods, but they too manifest the distinct effects that similar poetic materials can produce under varying circumstances.

Shinkei's argument regarding the multiplicity of hokku styles is firmly based on its special and independent role as the sole verse in the whole sequence that is required to "record" the actual event by alluding to the place, the season, and so on; none of the subsequent verses can do so, since they are conditioned by the maeku and the sequence's formal rules of progression. Or, to put it in another way, the actual context of the session is to the hokku what the maeku is to each of the subsequent tsukeku, or the assigned topic to a waka poem, namely, an a priori set of conditions (called *en* in Buddhist philosophy) crucially determining its content and style. And since no actual context or event ever repeats itself exactly, the hokku will theoretically assume a different form with each and every session. Ultimately, Shinkei's stand on the multiplicity of styles, or the absence of an "essential form" has its basis in the Buddhist principles of temporality and emptiness.

ELEVEN

Double Meaning in Poetry

The people of these parts have various opinions about double meaning in a verse; some have a taste for it, while others shun it. How is that?

According to the old masters, double meaning is the lifeblood of poetry.[1] It should by no means be shunned. Poem masterpieces that employ double meaning are innumerable, and it is an unskillful practitioner who cannot even compose a punning verse. On the other hand, there are those who, being too clever, produce only verses with double meanings on each and every occasion. To be so deeply engrossed in this matter that it becomes an obsession also makes for a kind of impediment.

te ni musubu iwai no mizu no akade no mi haru ni okururu shiga no yamagoe Go-Toba-in	The rock-pool water drips from my cupped hands but whetting desire— spring has vanished ahead on the Shiga mountain trail.[2] Retired Emperor Go-Toba
tomoshisuru takamadoyama no shikasuga ni onore nakademo natsu wa shiruramu Juntoku-in	In the torchlights burning upon Takamado Hill, the deer may suppress their cries, but in their eyes summer is clearly manifest[3] Retired Emperor Juntoku
konu hito o matsuho no ura no yūnagi ni	Waiting for someone who comes not on Matsuho beach in becalmed twilight,

yaku ya moshio no
mi mo kogaretsutsu
Teika-kyō

as if burning like the salt seaweed,
my body is seared again and again.[4]
Lord Teika

izuku ni ka
koyoi wa yado o
karigoromo
hi mo yūgure no
mine no arashi ni
Onajiki kyō

Where shall I
lodging for tonight borrow?
Hunting cloak pulled
close as the evening gathers
on the windswept mountain crest.[5]
Lord Teika

kaze soyogu
nara no ogawa no
yūgure wa
misogi zo natsu no
shirushi narikeru
Ietaka-kyō

With the wind rustling
among the oak leaves on Nara River
in the evening dusk,
the lustration rite is the sign
the season is yet summer.[6]
Lord Ietaka

ama no kawa
aki no hitoyo no
chigiri da ni
katano ni shika no
ne o ya nakuramu
Onajiki kyō

To ford the River of Stars
even for the one promised night
in autumn, is it so hard—
that in Katano Fields a deer
rends the air with his cries.[7]
Lord Ietaka

But such masterpieces are too numerous to quote here.

Similarly, among hokku with double meaning:

shita momiji
chiri ni majiwaru
miyai kana
Gusai

Red leaves scatter,
mingling with the dust below—
the holy shrine.[8]
Gusai

suga no ne no
nagatsuki nokoru
yūbe kana.
Shūa

As the sedge root,
the Long Moon remaining in
the evening sky.[9]
Shūa

It is generally difficult to compose waka and renga without resorting to double meaning. This is why it is said to be the lifeblood of poetry. However, it necessarily includes much that is vulgar, so one must exercise the greatest discernment in its use.

COMMENTARY

Shinkei's assertion that double meaning is the lifeblood of poetry (*uta no inochi*)—which is to say the source of its vitality, will probably seem exaggerated to Western readers. To anyone with the least experience in Japanese classical poetry, however, it will be no more than a statement of fact. The overwhelming importance that double entendre assumed in this poetry was inevitable in view of the poem's brevity. A form of ellipsis, punning allusiveness was a potent device for maximizing the limited space of the poem; through it, the poet could superimpose a strand of meaning or situation distinct from, yet related to, what the words say on the primary level, and thus evoke a larger universe, a complex and resonant poetic texture mostly lost in translation, since that frequently involves rendering explicit what remains artfully half-concealed in the original. The poetic effect of the pun is perhaps best typified when it occurs at the end of a *jo*, an introductory section usually describing an external scene or situation not directly related to the poem's main statement, but forming as it were a metonymical adjunct to it. The first poem is a good example; here the punning word *akade*, by relating to the poem's upper and lower parts simultaneously, becomes the pivot upon which the whole structure hangs (thus its name, *kakekotoba*); it fuses outer and inner worlds in a word, so to speak, by transforming the one into a metaphorical equivalent of the other. If metaphor is quintessentially the language of poetry, then it may indeed be said that the pun, which is the most common Japanese metaphorical device, is "the lifeblood of poetry."

TWELVE

The Manifold Configurations of Poetry

Again, our local amateurs agree that the highest style is one that is graceful, simple, and gentle. Should we bend our efforts, then, toward cultivating such a style?

Generally speaking, it is the true Way to compose in a style of quiet simplicity; it is particularly suitable for people of insufficient skill. But if one cultivates only this style, would he not gradually lose the use of his imaginative powers? Lord Teika himself has said: "There are many who understand that to be a masterpiece that is gentle and innocent of striking features, but they miss the point."[1] The point is that in the Way of Poetry, one inevitably advances through a diversity of forms in the process of training. The ancients have illustrated the manifold configurations of poetry through analogy with various phenomena.

> "As lapis lazuli heaped in a crystal bowl" means to aim for an effect of purity and cold.
>
> "Like a five-foot stalk of blue-flag iris newly watered." The effect is one of spaciousness and a cool wetness.[2]
>
> "Not to be overpowered though one stood alone before the August Seat in the Great Hall of State of the Imperial Palace." This means the poem must be resolute and strong.[3]
>
> "In their immensity even the empty space constrains them, in their minuteness, the space in a poppy seed is yet too big for them." Like Jōzō and Jōgen, poetic inscapes room marvelous transformations.[4]
>
> Among Chinese poems, those of Jia Dao are said to be meager, Meng Haoran's cold.[5]
>
> Of the poem "As beset by yearning / [I seek] my beloved's abode" [*Omoikane/ imogari*], it is said that it strikes chill in the heart even when recited on Chaplain Kanzan's memorial day in summer.[6]

Once Lord Teika earnestly asked his father Lord Shunzei for advice concerning the style of his poetry in these words:[7] "Until I was thirty, my art had a gracefulness and refinement of expression; I was composing poems that were apparently good enough to earn the praise of the world. But when I turned forty, my poems became bony and seemed to lose their alluring beauty. Isn't this why they fail to please the ears of even the common crowd? Ah, how well do I know it! My art has strayed into a wayward path. Tell me how I should change my practice?" Thus he said, weeping disconsolately all the while. This was Lord Shunzei's reply: "A very serious question indeed! I myself have pondered long and well about your poems. They possess a configuration quite distinct from my own, but that is certainly no reason to lament. Though I would wish it otherwise, I myself can only compose on the level of the flesh, whereas you with your natural gifts have penetrated to the very bone. I have often looked with envy on your art, but for an old man of eighty to attempt to learn it would be but a futile endeavor, and I must be content to admire it." Moved to tears, he added, "In all things, to reach the bone is the highest achievement.[8] If you continue in this way to sharpen your poetic faculties, you will become the greatest poet in all the realm."

COMMENTARY

One of the most central in *Sasamegoto* I, this chapter constitutes a development and ultimately a confirmation of an attitude already suggested in chapters 8 and 11. Once again, Shinkei concedes the basic correctness of the orthodox and, it must be noted, Nijō-school style of quiet simplicity and gracefulness (expressed as *utsukushiku sunao ni yawarakanaru* or *sunao ni odashiku*), and once again, he subverts its claim to supremacy by locating it at a lowly stage of training, "particularly suitable," as he says in an uncharacteristic burst of sardonic wit, "to people of insufficient skill." He then quotes Teika to the effect that such a style cannot, contrary to common opinion, be of the finest, and proceeds to illustrate other styles or effects that must by implication represent what he himself regarded as "the highest style" (*mujō no tai* in the question).

Significantly, four out of the six metaphorical examples are mutually related and may be said to belong to the same stylistic category. In three out of these four, the effect is described as "cold" (*samushi*), and further modified as "pure" (*kiyoshi*) in one case and "thin" or "meager" (*yasetaru*) in another. The fourth instance is the metaphor of the wet iris stalk, whose cool and immaculate freshness naturally places it in this group. A second category, symbolized by Jōzō and Jōgen, is the style of ambiguity that gives a poem the "magic" power to expand to the infinity of space or then again shrink and vanish into the most elusive subtlety. In *Sasamegoto* II, Shinkei describes it as "constituted exclusively of nuance" (*omokage bakari o nomi yomu*), quotes a poem each from Teika and Shōtetsu as illustration, and declares them to be akin to the supreme Dharma Body of the Buddha. The third distinct category, illustrated by the man unintimidated by imperial majesty, is what has earlier been referred to as the Style of Power or the Demon-Quelling Style. These three distinct though not necessarily exclusive stylistic categories, then, represent the poetic qualities that Shinkei thought superior to the orthodox ideal of simplicity and gracefulness. And the anecdote that ends the chapter is in effect a reiteration of this argument, in that it views gracefulness and a refined diction (*yawaraka ni kuchi no shina mo ari*) as popular qualities belonging to a lower stage of training, as manifestations of the "skin," or even the "flesh" of poetry, but not its very "bone."

THIRTEEN

The Roots of Poetry in Temporality

Our rustic poets make a great point of including auspicious words each time they compose a verse. When someone recites a verse that is just slightly inauspicious, they frown and lower their gazes in displeasure.[1] What do you feel about this?

The mind and language of the Way of Poetry are rooted upon a sense of mutability and sorrow for the human condition. It is through poetry that people convey to one another their emotion about things that have moved them deeply; its influence should soften even the hearts of barbarous demons and stern warriors, leading them to a realization of the truth about this transient world. Yet here I come by chance upon a renga session where I find nothing but intoxication with vain appearances, mutual self-congratulation, and auspicious words like "a thousand years," "ten thousand years," "cranes," "turtles," and "the happiness of the home" being bandied about. How utterly insensitive! Words of congratulation, indeed. Where is the man that lives to a hundred, what manner of creature survives for a thousand years? Though he prospered yesterday, today will see his downfall; though we see him at morning, by evening he will have turned to smoke. Pleasure and pain, they pass more quickly than a flip of the palm. Therefore the poets of old saw the essence of poetry in temporality and the expression of sorrow for the human condition.

> Among Chinese poets, Du Fu may be said to have sung a lifetime of sorrow.[2]
>
> The *Lotus Sutra* says: "If you desire to be enlightened concerning this sutra, contemplate the illusory nature of this world."

Nevertheless one must guard against using taboo expressions during renga sessions to celebrate the New Year, or those held in the houses of nobility and feudal lords. Surely everyone understands this much and there is no need to explain it here.

COMMENTARY

This whole chapter may be read as a demonstration of Shinkei's desire to elevate the character of a renga session by converting it from a mere amusement or an ornament to a convivial social occasion, to a more meaningful activity involving the contemplation of the verities of human existence, in particular, its temporality or transience. Temporality is everywhere the governing principle and foundation of Shinkei's thought and poetry; in this, he was no different from other major intellectual and artistic figures of the medieval period. Tsurayuki in the Heian period saw poetry as, so to speak, "the spontaneous overflow of powerful feelings" at the sight of natural phenomena and as generated by man's experience of himself in the world. Shinkei goes further and states definitively that what is specifically moving about nature and man is one's awareness of their existential fragility, and that it is this awareness that constitutes the node of a poetic sensibility. In other words, like Kenkō in *Tsurezuregusa*, he sensed beauty to lie precisely in the very imperfection of things, in their constant becoming. Furthermore, he rightly saw that by showing man's fragility to himself and to others, poetry that is rooted in mutability should bind human beings in a common sympathy, leading them from the barbaric and anarchic workings of the ego into the gentle light of civilization. It is clear that he viewed the renga session, a collective activity, as a potential instrument in this civilizing process. It is an attitude that recalls the historic circumstance that the earliest renga masters, those who led the annual renga ritual under the cherry blossoms at the shrines and temples of Kyoto, were Jishū priests who saw these sessions as an opportunity to convert others to the faith.

FOURTEEN

Poetic Process as a Contemplation

Out here in the country, a renga session adjourns by a little past noon, or 2 PM at the latest. Should it drag on just a little longer, people grumble that it is against the prescribed custom. What exactly is the proper duration of a session?

It is said that the sessions held by the Nijō Regent and other poets of consequence often lasted from morning till midnight. Of course, not every session has to last that long, but, still, one that does not continue from dawn until dusk cannot hold much appeal.[1] People who compose verses frivolously, with no sense of shame before the assembled gathering, say, "What's the use of giving so much thought to a verse? It's all the same in the end anyway, whether one ponders this way or that. In fact, verses that come from too much introspection are quite incomprehensible." Since words are said to be the messengers of the soul, how trivial and agitated, then, such people's souls must be!

What is called a masterly verse depends on none other than this quality of the soul. It is such a verse as must issue from a man whose spirit is minutely permeated by beauty and made tranquil by it [*kokoro o mo hosoku en ni nodomete*], and whose mind is deeply imbued with a sense of life's moving power [*yo no aware o mo fukaku omoi'iretaru hito*]. In this way, a word or two might well spell all the difference in the total configuration of a poem. But this difference, which is variously perceived as a quality of refinement, gentleness, and tensility, as a certain meagerness and coldness, or a compelling remoteness—such a verse about which floats the wordless fragrance of the mind [*iwanu kokoro ni nioi*] can only issue from the lips of the contemplative man.

A Poem by the Go-Kyōgoku Regent [Fujiwara Yoshitsune]

hito sumanu	Along the floorboards
fuwa no sekiya no	of the impregnable fort of Fuwa
itabisashi	uninhabited by men
arenishi nochi wa	in the wake of time's ravages—
tada aki no kaze	only the chill gusts of autumn.[2]

Since former times, the word "only" in this poem has been noted for its inexplicable profundity. That astute priest Shōtetsu among others has remarked, "It is truly impossible to dismiss it lightly. To think that that noble poet had such perspicacity, how awesome!"[3] Precisely there lies the divide between the ignorant and the enlightened. It is because the gifted poet dissolves his mind [*kokoro torakete*], because the verse issues from the very depths of his being, that its composition takes time, and a session might well continue until dusk. The verse of the untalented, on the other hand, merely rolls off the tip of his tongue; it thus requires no time at all. And since it is possible to spend long years of training without acquiring the mind's ear, there are many such people who become merely dexterous and nothing more.

COMMENTARY

Starting out from the simple question about the proper duration of a renga session, this chapter launches into a long and central passage describing the "mind-ground" (what is called *shinji* in *Sasamegoto* II) upon which the process of poetic composition transpires. This process involves entering a state of introspection (*chinshi*) in which the mind becomes minutely absorbed in and is rendered coolly tranquil by beauty (*kokoro o hosoku en ni nodomete*), identical in Shinkei's poetics with a realm where things are experienced in all their fleeting, evanescent character. Also described as *kokoro o torakete*, this mental activity evidently aims, paradoxically enough, at the dissolution of the mind (the divisive egoistic mind) in the process of becoming minutely permeated by the object of its contemplation. Shinkei's understanding of poetic process is similar to Teika's concept of *ushintei* (Style of Meditation) as representing, not only one among ten styles, but no less than the *hon'i*, or essential nature, of poetry.

Considering Shinkei's arguments for a minimalist diction in the light of the poetic process described here yields the paradoxical conclusion that the more polished and worked-over a verse is, the more transparently it becomes the mirror of a realm or space from which the poet has wholly absented himself. In other words, the work of paring down a verse to its essentials involves the poet in a like process of self-abnegation whose object is complete fusion with the "mental ground" that is the ultimate source of true poetry. Introspection, the technical chiseling away at words, and the poem artifact itself apparently constitute a closed circle. The configuration of the ideal verse or poem is so organic and precise that a single word might indeed spell all the difference (as *tada* allegedly does in Yoshitsune's poem) as the keystone holding a whole arch in place, maintaining the vital link of forces ultimately supported upon the ground of the mind, or more properly, the ground of Mind, which is seen as coextensive with the universe in *Sasamegoto* II. Isolated from this ground, technical dexterity or verbal finesse as such might, as Shinkei says, "impress at first hearing, but will disenchant in the next, as the words lose their vital tensility" (*Tokoro* III, p. 226).

FIFTEEN

The Wisdom of Nondiscrimination

Can one reach the highest stage in the Way by concentrating only on one style and training in it exclusively?

A former master has said that it is precisely in not discarding any one style that a man shows unparalleled wisdom. To leave out so much by concentrating only on one style would seem quite regrettable.

> "The gentleman associates all around and does not discriminate. The small man discriminates and does not associate all around."[1]
>
> Bo Yi and Shu Qi among sages were the pure-hearted ones, Yi Yin was the lover of harmony. But of them all, it was Kongzi [Confucius] who was the timely one.[2]
>
> The Buddha was aptly called "the most-honored of two-legged beings"; in his heart, there was no discrimination among the Three Vehicles.[3]

COMMENTARY

The original question reflects the Nijō-school position that there is only one single correct style, the orthodox one, and that the highest achievement lies in mastering it. Shinkei's reply, in contrast, represents the Reizei-school position that the novice should train in all the ten styles and thereby discover the one that best suits his or her individual character. We have noted this basically liberal, pluralistic attitude in Chapter 10, where he says that the style of the hokku will vary according to the specific circumstances of each session; and again in Chapter 12, which advances the view that the poetic imagination gains in power through wide and searching experience in various stylistic configurations, and, further, that the Way is in effect a process of approaching the realm of consummate mastery by stages. Apart from the Reizei-school influence, Shinkei's liberal attitude is thoroughly grounded in the universalistic, comprehensive character of Mahayana or Tendai intellectual philosophy. The doctrine that the Three Vehicles are One is but an instance of this, as is "the perfect fusion of the Three Truths" that comprises the heart of Tendai metaphysical belief (see Chapter 27, n. 3). A pluralistic, all-embracing attitude is not the same, however, as a literally undiscriminating one. Good poetry is good regardless of its particular style, and the same holds for bad poetry, but good poems have certain qualities in common, and it is these that interest Shinkei, or any other critic for that matter.

SIXTEEN

Right Teaching and the Individual Poet

Should we study the Way by seeking out our predecessors, or are the comments of fellow poets in the various renga sessions a sufficient guide?

A foolish question. It is said, "Discover the new by inquiring into the old."[1] The learning and practice of those who have not received the proper teachings of the Way are thoroughly useless. Once someone has been set upon the wayward path, even encountering the wisest sage will not avail him. Therefore the human heart has been likened to a lacquered bucket, or then again to white thread that awaits the dye to be transformed to any color. The same truth holds when one desires to achieve enlightenment regarding the Buddhist Law, for which it is written that "Someone possessing the right knowledge is the great cause and condition."[2] In other words, "Know that things have no nature in themselves; it is through the conditions that the Buddha-seed arises."[3]

Just recently, there was reportedly someone who wished to study with a certain master of the bamboo flute. When the master inquired, "Have you played before?" he replied, "Yes, I have been practicing a little." Thereupon the master refused him, saying, "In that case, I am unable to teach you." An interesting answer, indeed, and one whose moral applies to all the other arts as well. It is important to realize that the mind that has once blundered into the evil path cannot be recalled to its original innocent state.

COMMENTARY

Shinkei's main thesis in this chapter is that like a white thread awaiting the dye, the individual talent is decisively moulded by external circumstance, and therefore it is of the utmost consequence that it be exposed to the proper teaching. The proper teaching, moreover, is available only from "those who have achieved before" (*sendatsu*)—the past poets of the tradition and the older living poets who maintain it. This is by no means a conservative stand that contradicts his liberalism in the previous sections; the Confucian adage "discover the new by inquiring into the old" speaks for itself and needs no explanation. *Sasamegoto* itself constitutes an "inquiry into the old" in that it holds up for examination the achievements of the Kamakura-Nambokuchō poets in renga and of those of the *Shinkokinshū* age in waka. These represented what Shinkei regarded as the "proper teachings" of the Way and played a crucial role in the formation of "the new"—that is to say, his own poetry and thought.

Apart from the tradition, a great teacher (*meishi*) is an equally momentous "cause and condition" (*innen*) for enlightenment in poetry, but much harder to come by. "A sage appears but once in a hundred years," Shinkei writes near the end of *Sasamegoto* II, and he for one never ceased to count it his good fortune to have been born in the same age as Shōtetsu. As he would say later in *Oi no kurigoto* (p. 417), even a keen intelligence will not survive an inadequate mentor:

> A man may be born with tremendous natural talent, but if he meets with an inadequate teacher and receives the wrong teachings, he will end up with a reputation for mediocrity despite his keen intelligence. It is the proven experience in all endeavors that one reaches the ultimate by studying under a great teacher and applying oneself to his instruction day in and day out. Renga poets rely solely on their own deluded understanding and apparently compose just as they please, without bothering to inquire into the foundations of the art. And therefore their work is said to be replete with thoughtless blunders.

SEVENTEEN

The Influence of Companions in the Way

Is it true, then, that a man may be known by the company he keeps?

As the world does not always conform to our desires, we cannot always avoid associating with all kinds of people. But when it comes to the practice of the various arts, it is of utmost importance to have suitable friends about us. No matter how earnest a renga gathering might be, when there are mingled among those present even a pair of unpeaceable souls, it will depart from the true spirit of the Way.

Ziyou rowed for quite a long distance in his boat in order to visit his friend Andao. That he should leave without meeting Andao and say, "Riding upon the moment's mood, I came; the mood spent, I return," shows a remarkably subtle and profound sensibility.[1]

Mencius's mother changed her residence three times [for her son's sake.] Truly a moving example [of the fact] that one should choose one's friends.[2]

"The good man can truly like people, and truly dislike them" means that the good man cherishes the Way.[3]

When Ziqi passed away, Boya broke the strings of his lute.[4]

"If you would know the man, look to his friends; if you would know the father, look to the child." Chastening words, indeed.

Similarly, according to Tendai teaching, "It is of utmost importance to be close to a virtuous friend."[5] In other words, "All the various phenomena arise through causes and conditions, and therefore there is nothing that possesses its own nature."[6]

COMMENTARY

This chapter continues logically from the preceding one; just as a proper teacher and familiarity with the tradition are crucial in setting the student upon the right path, so good friends are essential in ensuring that he stays on it, by means of mutual encouragement, stimulation, and kindred sympathies. In both cases, it must be noted, Shinkei bases his opinion on the Buddhist principle of dependent origination—that is, that nothing exists in its own right apart from external factors of causes and conditions (*innen*).

Shinkei's view of the crucial role of friends may also be seen as a natural consequence of renga's generic character as a collective art wholly dependent upon the quality of its participants. Egolessness and the keen awareness of temporality, which he sees as moral imperatives in the conduct of one's life, assume the character of artistic necessities in renga, since a poet who is wholly absorbed by his own verse will obviously be incapable of relating to the maeku in any significant way. As in life, so in renga, the individual unit has only a provisional existence as such; generated by the maeku, it will in turn condition the tsukeku and itself be transformed in the process. The renga verse is empty; it must each time transcend and find itself outside, within a network of invisible relations, or *innen*. It is indeed curious how Buddhist principles provide such apt metaphors for the poetics of renga. The question is whether Buddhism is merely a metaphor for Shinkei, a convenient language for illuminating the central charcteristics of the genre, or in fact the very foundation of all his thought. But the question is no doubt of merely speculative interest, since all thought and language are ultimately but a metaphor, and it was precisely Shinkei's harsh and paradoxical task to insist that poetry push itself to the utmost limit, beyond which metaphors would cease to apply.

EIGHTEEN

Poetry and the Mundane Mind

Some people say of waka and renga that it is precisely when they sound interesting even to the ear of the rude peasant and the insensitive savage that they show themselves true to the Way. What do you think?

In any art or endeavor, understanding is not possible for someone of shallow dedication and insufficient training. No doubt the ignorant and unaccomplished can grasp the simplest verses or those that employ the Close Link. But those whose mind is lofty and ineffably remote [*kedakō yōon no kokoro*] are quite beyond the understanding of the ordinary man.[1]

> The configuration of Lord Teika's poetry has been likened to the vision of an ethereal maiden appearing fleetingly in a hazy, moonlit night, leaving a trail of fragrance as it vanishes.
>
> Most people are probably content merely to recognize the poems of Hitomaro and Akahito. It is to the eyes of those who have achieved the Way that their profundity and subtlety are discernible.
>
> Rare is the man who truly knows the poetry of Du Fu, so it is said.[2]
>
> When the Buddha was about to preach the Dharma, the assembly of five thousand arrogant priests and laypeople rolled up their prayer mats and left.[3]
>
> The Metamorphosis Body and the Reward Body of the Buddha might be within the ordinary understanding, but the Dharma Body is almost totally beyond anyone's grasp.[4]

COMMENTARY

This chapter flatly rejects the notion that popular appeal is the measure of a poem's authenticity, or that a poem is "true" to the degree that it is comprehensible and interesting even to the untutored. Such a notion is on the face of it quite democratic; it at least assumes that peasants have an innate capacity for understanding poetry. The question is what kind of poetry, and it is here where one will find it difficult to argue with Shinkei. For he means specifically poems of "lofty and ineffably remote mind" (*kedakō yōon no kokoro*)—the words speak for themselves—and indeed he is not interested in the lesser kinds, except to criticize them for triviality or, on occasion, to confirm their usefulness as a means by which ordinary minds can reach their own understanding of the truth. It should always be borne in mind that Shinkei's thinking is ultimately grounded in the ethos of compassion and impartiality with which the treatise closes (see Chapter 60).

The terms "common," "vulgar," "rustic," and the like frequently recur in Shinkei's writings, where these are functions not of social class but of mind. The difference between low and high is that between a man who is taken in by appearances and allows them to govern his existence to the end, and one who is fired by a deep longing for the true and the real behind the passing show of things, and consequently pursues the Way until his mind expands to the utmost limits of the Universe. It is this boundless and numinous quality of mind that Shinkei compares to the Dharmakaya in the last illustration. The difference, then, is between ignorance and awareness, as expressed in this passage from the Epilogue to *Iwahashi*:

> A man who is ignorant of the Way is blind to the shifting of the four seasons, unaware of the deeply compelling Principle [*en fukaki kotowari*] amid the forms and colors of the ten thousand realms; he spends his whole existence before a blank wall with a jar pulled over his head (*Iwahashi batsubun*, p. 327).

NINETEEN

The Issue of Fame as Index of Poetic Value

Is someone who is popular with each and everyone alike to be regarded as a superior poet? Or should we not be guided by whether or not he is esteemed by people of discernment, though neglected by the ignorant?

This is what a predecessor said. By and large, the poet who has acquired worldly fame probably deserves it, but the praise that he receives from people of shallow understanding means nothing at all. It is the opinion of a sage, though he be alone in it, that is regarded as a matter of honor in the Way. History abounds in examples of wise persons who were forced into obscurity.

> "Do not grieve that people do not know you; grieve rather that you do not know people."[1]
>
> Not even Kongzi [Confucius] was blessed by the times, and Yan Hui was unfortunate.[2]
>
> "Best of all is when the good in the neighborhood love him and the bad hate him."[3]
>
> Even the Buddha's venerable name had not been heard by three hundred million, it is said.[4]
>
> A pine tree at the foot of the valley grows old alone.[5]

COMMENTARY

Directly consequent upon his rejection in the preceding section of popular taste as the arbiter of poetic truth, Shinkei here acknowledges that since the common people or the majority are incapable of appreciating the greatest minds, they must perforce remain in obscurity. This is not to say that he himself regarded obscurity as necessarily evidence of virtue, or that he welcomed it. As his editor Kidō Saizō observes, the allusion to Bai Juyi's poem on the lonely pine hints of Shinkei's own melancholy awareness of being remote from any worldly fame at this time (*Sasamegoto no kenkyū*, p. 38; hereafter *Kenkyū*). And, as if to prove *Sasamegoto* right even at its author's expense, despite the high regard of Sōgi and the worshipful attitude of Kenzai—certainly "sages" both, Shinkei always remained just beyond the limelight, both in his lifetime and afterward.

TWENTY

Poetry Is an Existential Discipline

How should we train the mind to reach the highest realm?

Someone has said that whether in undergoing Buddhist training to discover the ultimate source of the mind [*kokoro no minamoto*], or in studying the Way of Poetry to gain insight into the deeply moving power of things [*aware fukaki koto*], the highest realm is quite beyond the reach of those who put their trust in an enduring life, who are wholly absorbed in the objects of the senses, value worldly goods, and, being complacent, have neither worries nor fears.

> The Buddha let his horse return to the palace and went alone into the deep mountains. For six years, he underwent austerities so severe the birds would make their nests in his topknot, it is said.[1]

> Again it is said in Chinese poetry that the excellent verse springs from the tranquil spirit of a recluse.

One need not go so far as to lead a solitary life remote from the world, but still, not constantly to clarify the mind and reflect, while watching the moving clouds at evening or the flickering lamp at night, that this world of ours comes and goes in a dream, that for the high as for the low, the wise and the foolish, this thread of life that bides not till the close of day is frailer even than a filament of hair—to remain unaware of all these things while relying solely on oneself, believing that it will go on for a hundred years and a thousand years, to be wholly absorbed in the objects of the senses, cherish one's name, and be led astray by the myriad illusions of existence—that indeed is the height of foolishness! When the body turns to dust and ashes, whither goes its vital spark of life? And not only this body but all the myriad phenomena of the universe, whence do they come, whither disappear—we must pursue this question to the utmost!

COMMENTARY

This eloquent chapter is commonly cited as evidence that Shinkei identified the Way of Poetry with the Way of Buddhism. Kidō objects that this is not accurate, since the aims given for the two activities are different (*Kenkyū*, p. 39). Buddhism's object is to "discover the ultimate source of the mind" (*kokoro no minamoto o akiramemu*), while that of Poetry is to "gain insight into the deeply moving power of things" (*aware fukaki koto o satoran*). In other words, the aim of Poetry is apparently a negative ideal, to move human beings to the consciousness of the tragic character of mundane existence; while that of Buddhism is actively to discover the truth that lies *beyond* the tragedy of mundane existence; the one does not go as far as the other. Indeed, to go so far would inevitably involve the poet in a renunciation, or at least a questioning, of his passionate attachment to an art that traffics in the illusory reality of words. Nevertheless, since poetic training involves its subject in an attitude of detached renunciation common to both, it may be said to be a means toward the enlightenment that is Buddhism's object. It does not carry the poet as far as Buddhistic training would, but it ideally functions as a catalyst that sets him on the right path. Such, at any rate, seems to be the rationale for Shinkei's declaration in Chapter 13 that Poetry is rooted in the sense of temporality and sorrow for the human condition (*mujō jukkai*): a sensibility not grounded upon a tragic and ironic vision of existence has no authentic appeal, nor indeed is it poetic at all. This is palpable in the poem examples cited earlier in the discussion of *yūgen*, many of which are deeply felt meditations on the illusoriness of desire in the face of mortality and time.

The distinction that Kidō wishes to draw between Buddhism and Poetry here is largely valid for Part I of *Sasamegoto*, but not for Part II, whose central motivation is in fact the identification of the two Ways. In this connection, it should be noted that, even here, Shinkei's emphatic final statement about pursuing to the utmost the question of the origins and end of all phenomena is tantamount to saying that the object of poetic training is also to "discover the ultimate source of the mind." Ultimately, the religious justification for poetry that is to be found in the works of Shunzei, Teika, Saigyō, and Shinkei is based on nondualism, itself a Buddhist concept. And it also grounds the medieval Japanese sense of praxis (*michi*, the Way), in which there is no real dichotomy between the spiritual and the secular. The vitality of the medieval Japanese arts (of the rock garden, *ikebana*, Nō drama, the tea cult, and poetry) that survived into modern times is no doubt related to their roots in religious practice, their nature as symbolic embodiments of a purified Dharma world.

TWENTY-ONE

Poetry Is a Self-Consuming Passion

Our local amateurs are of the opinion that one should practice composing verses with dexterous ease so as not to disrupt the flow of the session. Is this so?

It must be so, indeed, since renga is an art that depends on the quality of the group and the nature of time and circumstance. But this is by no means to say that one composes in an utterly offhand manner. The man of profound dedication who has thoroughly fused his spirit with the Way, seeking the luster concealed in the jewel, the fragrance outside the flower—such a man is walking the true path.[1] I cannot speak for the likes of the great sage Mañjuśrī, were he to appear in an earthly incarnation, but for me poetry is not something that arises without effort.[2] For those who lack the ability to distinguish between the good and the bad and feel no shame before the Way's subtle profundity, it is apparently easy.

It took Ki no Tsurayuki twenty days to compose a single poem.[3]

Kunaikyō's poetic labors were so exhausting that she spat blood.[4]

Lord Kintō meditated up to three years to compose the poem "Dimly, dimly" [*Honobono*].[5]

Nagayoshi died of grief when his poem met with censure.[6]

It was I believe the Chinese poet Pan Yue who was so deeply absorbed by poetry that his hair had turned white by thirty.[7]

Buddhism likens the highest stage in the Way to the flavor of clarified butter; it must mean a spirit that has been refined to the utmost.[8]

COMMENTARY

Shinkei begins by conceding that the ability to compose verses with dexterous ease (*surusuru to shite)* under a variety of circumstances is the sine qua non of the renga poet. This apparent dexterity, however, is something that comes with constant practice, as his young disciple Kenzai reports in *Shinkei-sōzu teikin* (Bishop Shinkei's Teachings):

> Renga is something one should labor over beforehand, practicing and concentrating one's mind from morning till evening, and then do with ease during the session itself. The verse of someone who practices strenuously at ordinary times will sound good even though it seems just to issue spontaneously from his lips. The one who does not ordinarily practice makes a show of laborious effort, sweating profusely, dropping his head over his hands, bending back as he ponders, and it is all indeed a pathetic sight, but not of a true artist. (*Teikin*, p. 1121)

The *Teikin* passage clarifies the labor that enables apparent ease of performance during the session itself. This *Sasamegoto* passage reiterates the view already articulated in Chapter 14 on the proper duration of a renga session, namely, that the creation of superior poetry is a laborious, time-consuming process. Indeed, here Shinkei goes so far as to imply in his illustrations that the serious poet sets such a high value on Poetry (the Way) that he would sacrifice his youth, his health, and even finally his life for it.

Surely, the people for whom poetry is such a self-consuming, high, and rigorous passion are rare. It is clear to see from Teika's poetry that he was one of these, Shōtetsu perhaps even more so, and Shinkei too obviously. However, to require the same commitment from the numerous others for whom renga was merely an elegant, amusing game—though, like some games, endlessly fascinating and even habit-forming—seems patently quixotic. But Shinkei was a priest irrepressibly drawn to the dangerous allure of words, to the craft of the artificer conjuring worlds from nothing. Consequently, he would train into this art all the chaste and demanding passion that makes for saints in the religious sphere, mastering the words as his Buddhist mind demanded, until all specific meanings are refined out of them and they stand as pure signs pointing to the Emptiness beyond. Certainly, all his Buddhist analogies indicate that this is how he conceived of the poetic process, as a life-and-death struggle with the solidity of language, having as its object to push it to that extreme edge where it ceases to speak and merely stands as a mute witness to the stupendous silence at the heart of the ten thousand dharmas. Impracticable as it may be for a collective art like renga (though it should be recalled that group meditation was common practice in temples), there seems no doubt that this insistence on the numinous possibilities of language represents one of the most thoroughgoing expressions of the fusion of religion and art that characterizes the Japanese medieval aesthetic.

TWENTY-TWO

Worldly Glory Versus Reclusive Concentration

In the Way of Poetry, should one cultivate society in the hope of winning personal fame?

An old master has said that that too must depend on each individual soul. Some people are obsessed with their names and preoccupied with personal glory; others, having arrived on a higher plane, delight in the quiet life and keep their hearts pure of worldly desires.

Lord Teika is said to have admonished his son Lord Tameie about his poetry in these words: "One does not produce poetry this way, surrounded by the trappings of night court service, with the lamp burning brightly, and wine and delicacies scattered about. This is why your poems are so inferior. The late lord my father could compose truly superior poems precisely because his way was so different from yours. Late at night, he would sit before an oil lamp turned down so low one could hardly discern it, a simple soot-darkened robe over his shoulders and an old cap pulled low over his ears. Leaning against an armrest and hugging a paulownia wood brazier for warmth, he would intone to himself in a low voice, and deep in the night when everyone else had gone to sleep, he would be bent over weeping uncontrollably."[1] How venerable indeed is this figure bent in earnest concentration! Does it not explain why, despite his having risen to official prominence, Lord Tameie's poems were excluded from the Cloistered Prince's *Fifty-Poem Sequence*? The Retired Emperor himself noted in the Epilogue that the leading poets of the age all thought Tameie's poems utterly inferior.[2]

It is said that when he composed poetry, Lord Teika would bind up his hair, wear an everyday court robe, and not permit himself the slightest lapse from solemn decorum.[3]

COMMENTARY

Expanding on the view of poetry as an activity of high seriousness, this chapter implies through the anecdote involving Shunzei, Teika, and Tameie that the great poet does not demean his art by employing it to win social advancement or personal glory. The long description of Shunzei in the throes of poetic labor has an iconic quality that underscores Shinkei's view that poetic composition is a process of deep-going meditation best carried out in solitude, away from the distraction of public gatherings. The discrepancy between Tameie's rapid ascent of the bureaucratic ladder (as compared to his two talented immediate kin) and his inferior poetic caliber at the time speaks for itself. It must be borne in mind, however, that these anecdotes, a common feature of premodern poetic treatises, constitute paradigms of value that do not necessarily have historical veracity. They signify iconically, as an index to the critical and cultural attitudes of the writer and his or her times.

TWENTY-THREE

Criticism Is a Function of One's Own Limitations

These fellows in the countryside have all sorts of comments to make after a cursory hearing or reading of other people's waka and renga. Can they be correct under the circumstances?

In fact, a former master has said regarding this matter that it is difficult in any art to grasp something that goes beyond your own limitations. If you make light of a verse upon which the poet has broken his bones, so to speak, in strenuous reflection, you are bound to miss his point completely. The Way of Poetry has always had many skilled practitioners, but those who possess a keen discernment, thorough training, and a profound sensitivity to its ideals are exceedingly rare. Whether in Buddhism or in poetry, understanding what is of the essence is altogether a different matter, so said an old master.

COMMENTARY

Shinkei unequivocally expresses his conviction that only the poet who has himself arrived at the most profound understanding of the Way is capable of evaluating superior work. Here, as in Chapter 14, it is significant that the distinction he wishes to draw is between mere competence or skill (*jōzu*, *tassha*), on the one hand, and a keen perceptivity, on the other. This is related to his statement in *Sasamegoto* II that it is more difficult to understand and appreciate someone else's verse than to compose one's own. Such a peculiar emphasis on perceptivity over and above execution is a reflection of the central importance of *kokoro* in his poetics; presuming that the poet possesses the requisite technical competence, it is above all the quality of his mind as it relates to the external universe in the act of composition that is decisive in determining the quality of the verse or poem. The keener and more profound that mind is, the better the poem.

Shinkei's peculiar emphasis on perceptivity (which is, in premodern poetics, also the critical faculty) is intimately connected with the unique character of poetic composition in renga. Here the creative process is composed of two moments: grasping the maeku's significance, and recreating it in another form. Poetry is, of course, in every instance an act of penetration (or, in current terminology, appropriation) and interpretation before it is an act of creation, although the former is seldom clearly legible to the reader. Renga is unique, however, in making the first act always present and palpable, indeed the very stuff of its nature as *linked* poetry.

TWENTY-FOUR

Sitting with a Master

Rustic poets often abuse others by claiming that they have heard such and such while sitting in frequent sessions with some master. What do you think?

A hundred or even a thousand times may a person sit on the same mat with a master, it does not follow that he then understands the Way. If he does not inquire thoroughly into the master's mind, if they do not lay bare their hearts to each other, it will be for him like loitering among another's treasures. Lord Shunzei has said that it is essential in the Way to discuss traditional practices and precedents. But to do so with someone who is insensitive and dull-witted would be like playing the zither before a cow, as the saying goes.

COMMENTARY

Perceptivity is crucial, not only in the task of evaluating another's work, but also in the context of the master-disciple relationship. As stated in Chapter 16, an excellent teacher constitutes "the great cause and condition" in the fruitful development of individual talent. However, if the student is not perceptive, either due to insufficient wit or lack of artistic sensibility, not even the greatest master can help him. Here, it is more important to note Shinkei's emphasis on an inquiring attitude, or the desire to seek out the deepest truths in the Way, as evidence of a student's receptivity. In Part II he illustrates the importance of the questing attitude by declaring that "it is far better to criticize the Dharma and fall into hell than merely to make offerings to numberless Buddhas" (*SSG*, p. 184). Clearly, the point is not merely to gape and boast of being witness to the master's teachings as to a treasure, but to make that treasure one's very own. Discipleship, then, is a process of active penetration and "appropriation," fueled by desire. It is as well to remember, however, that in the medieval pedagogy of the Way, this process is less an appropriation, a word that denotes knowledge as a "body" to be acquired, than the mutuality of understanding suggested by the Zen slogan, "by mind transmit the mind."

TWENTY-FIVE

Constant Practice Is Decisive

Is it possible, after accumulated practice in the Way, to lay it aside for a while without impairing one's ability?

Regardless of the years spent in the dim light of fireflies and snow, if you lapse from training and concentration even for a while, your ability must surely deteriorate without a trace. The Classic says, "Three times within a day, examine yourself."[1]

Ton'a, who played the best bamboo flute [*shakuhachi*] in his day, has said: "If I stop playing for three days, the right sound would not emerge."[2] This is something to keep in mind in all the various arts.

Master Bontōan abandoned the Way of Poetry and wandered around the provinces of Azuma and Tsukushi for many years. When someone remarked, upon his return to the capital, "You must have lost your touch completely," he reportedly answered back, "And why should I have lost my touch? It is precisely outside the renga session that one practices true renga!"[3] These too are words that apply to all the various arts.

COMMENTARY

The point of Bontō's retort to the insinuating remark that he had lost his touch during his long travels in the "backward" regions is that a significant part of renga training necessarily consists of voluntary practice, outside the contingencies of a renga session. Bontō is in other words drawing a distinction between practice and performance; as in the musical arts, the one is possible only on the basis of the other, which may therefore be called "true renga." Bontō is exaggerating, of course, since participation in actual sessions is in itself a crucial part of renga training in view of its extemporaneous nature. Ultimately, Shinkei's point in citing Bontō's remark must be that the intuitive poetic faculty exhibited in a renga performance is predicated upon a constant and strenuous process of self-examination outside of it. In other words, the performance constitutes an occasion for analyzing where one has failed and how one can improve, and this process of refining one's art to perfection is a private and solitary endeavor; performance is but a manifestation of and a further stimulus for it.

TWENTY-SIX

Valorizing the Deviant or Obscure

Rustic poets dismiss those verses that differ from their own as obscure or deviant. What do you think?

That cannot be helped, since such people have set their hearts on the particular style that pleases themselves. Gifted poets, however, being intent only on rising to the skies, give free rein to their minds, with no thought for the bridge to get them there. It is doubtless wiser to admire a verse that deviates from your own taste.

Indeed, Priest Shōtetsu always used to say: "How inferior my poetry must seem to others, since I always try to avoid composing as they do." Such wisdom should chasten one.

COMMENTARY

This chapter is in effect a restatement of the pluralism enunciated in Chapter 15, and of the idea, expressed in Chapter 18, that superior poetry is beyond the grasp of a limited mind. Here, the argument is couched as a question of means and ends but is, as always, grounded on *kokoro*. The gifted poet begins from poetic inspiration, the unfettered exercise of mind or imagination that is also the end of all poetry; only after experiencing this heightened moment does he decide on the style or configuration that will best express it. The ungifted, on the other hand, fixes upon a predetermined style—needless to say the orthodox one, to begin with, and moulds his mind according to it; as a consequence, his poetry sounds like everyone else's. In Part II, Shinkei says of such people that "they see only the finger pointing at the moon," mistaking the means for the end, and in their paucity of imagination are reduced to producing bad imitations, "licking the spittle of the old poets," as it were (*SSG* 191; *Murmured Conversations*, Chapter 52).

This brief chapter is, then, an attempt to justify the unfettered exercise of mind or imagination in its boundless quest for the underlying truths of the universe, which is, as in Chapter 20, also the journey back to its own source (*kokoro no minamoto*). Like Shōtetsu, the gifted poet might be pained by his own isolation, and by uncomprehending charges of obscurity and deviancy, but he has the wisdom to be true to his own poetic vision.

TWENTY-SEVEN

The Difficulty of Comprehending Superior Poetry

How is it that the verses of those who have reached the farthest realm tend to sound ever more remote?

A former master has said that what is called training and mental application [*shugyō kufū*] means to have a profound awareness of the 100-verse sequence as a whole, paying due regard to the spirit and the words of the maeku down to the last syntactic particle; the pitfalls of clashing across one-verse or several-verse intervals; and being mindful even of how the next person may link up to one's own verse.[1] The workings of such a mind, which is sensible to what comes before and after, must of necessity be difficult to grasp for someone who can only hear the verse as it is, in isolation.

> It is said that none could understand Ono Tōfū's calligraphy after it had reached the consummate realm.[2]
>
> In Buddhism the spirit that has arrived at the Perfect Teaching, the All-Encompassing Oneness [*engyo ennyū*], discarding none of the ten thousand things, is beyond ordinary logical understanding.[3]

COMMENTARY

As Shinkei puts it, the consummate renga verse sounds remote and is difficult to comprehend, because it is a manifestation of a mind that has arrived at the state of "perfect fusion," or all-encompassing comprehensiveness, as understood in Tendai doctrine. More specifically, it is a mind that is "sensible to what comes before and after," that is to say, to the progressively widening function of the single verse in relation to the one immediately preceding and following it; to the larger block of verses of which it is a part;

and, finally, to the whole sequence. Obviously, a person who can only see the verse as such, in isolation, will fail to grasp its true significance, since that exists only in relation. Like the dharmas, the single verse is conditioned by what precedes it and is therefore empty; yet it also conditions what follows it and is therefore real. Its absence or alteration would inevitably change the composition of the whole, and therefore it is like the one that contains the all within it. This chapter is interesting less as a reply to the question of obscurity than for what it reveals of Shinkei's Buddhist-inspired conception of renga as a poetic structure.

TWENTY-EIGHT

The "Vulgar" Verse

What kind of configuration does the so-called "vulgar" [*bonzoku*] verse have?

A verse may be vulgar in its formal configuration or in its feeling and conception. One can easily detect vulgarity in the configuration, but it is somewhat more difficult to discern in the feeling or conception.

matsu ueokamu furusato no niwa	Pine trees would I plant there— the garden of the old village.
yume sasou kaze o tsuki mimu tayori nite	Luring dreams away, the wind would draw me to gaze at the moon.

In its configuration, the tsukeku above seems satisfactory enough, but is not the conception unnatural? What man would deliberately set about planting young pines in order to be awakened from dreams and gaze at the moon?

haru wa tada izure no kusa mo wakana kana	In spring the plants, every single one of them— new shoots!

The poetic appeal of spring's seven grasses lies precisely in our seeking, and finally discovering, a green shoot or two peering between the patches of snow. The thought of indiscriminately plucking all sorts of plants strikes me as utterly inferior.

COMMENTARY

Bonzoku is a Buddhist term for the ordinary layman in the state of blind ignorance, in which he is still compelled by the cravings of the senses and the narrow discriminations of the mind. In the secular sense, *bonzoku* spans a range of meanings from merely "dull, trite, and commonplace" to "common, vulgar, inferior, and mediocre." Shinkei's use of it here coincides with the latter sense of vulgar and inferior, lacking in quality. The term has occurred earlier, in Chapter 11, where he warns against the indiscriminate use of double meaning, as it "necessarily includes much that is *vulgar*."

Although he distinguishes between vulgarity in external form (*sugata*) and in conception or feeling (*kokoro*), because the former is easily detectible in the diction, syntax, or rhythm of the verse, Shinkei gives only examples of the latter here.

In the first verse pair, the tsukeku provides the reason for the intention expressed in the maeku of planting young pine trees, and may in effect be paraphrased thus: "I shall plant pine saplings in the garden so that later on, when they are grown, the sound of the wind blowing through them may wake me from my dreams and draw me to gaze at the moon." There is absolutely nothing vulgar in the imagery and diction of this verse; indeed, read symbolically as a desire for Buddhist liberation (illusory dreams vs. the moon of enlightenment), the conception is even exemplary. What Shinkei objects to is the poet's very deliberate logic, his almost calculating attitude, which is incongruous with the whole poetic imagery of pine, breeze, and moonlight. As Emerson remarked, "If you go expressly to look at the moon, it becomes tinsel." Moreover, there is also an incongruity between the gravity of the desire for spiritual enlightenment as such and the poet's lighthearted conception of it in the context of the verse, which accordingly gives an impression of affectedness and insincerity. Thus, in Shinkei's opinion, the *kokoro* of the verse—understood as the sensibility behind it, is lacking in quality.

The second example, a hokku, is an expression of delight at the abundance of young shoots in the meadow, which is burgeoning forth in the new warmth of spring. Here, Shinkei objects that the poetic appeal (*en*) of the image of "young shoots" (*wakana*) lies precisely in their rarity, in the pleasure of discovering them peering here and there in the snow after one has been searching them out on new-shoot gathering excursions. The idea of having all of them at one time, ready to be plucked, is wanting in delicacy, in a fine sense of discrimination. The question of realism is needless to say irrelevant in this judgment; the whole revolves around the issue of tact, a certain requisite decorum in the production of poetic beauty of a moving, evocative quality. From that perspective, Shinkei is no doubt right. Nevertheless, the verse does not necessarily seem vulgar; indeed, it has a certain freshness, precisely because it handles an old classical image in a new manner. Unfortunately, a verse with nothing but novelty to recommend it would not be particularly worthy in Shinkei's valuation. (This and the next four chapters, 29 to 32, are concerned with bad poetic practices, what are called *uta no yamai*, "poetic ailments," in traditional criticism.)

TWENTY-NINE

Plagiarism

In waka, what is called "plagiarism" [*dōrui*], stealing the words or conception of another's poem, is said to be highly taboo. How would it be in renga?

A former master has said that in composing poetry, one should exercise particular care in this regard. These fellows in the country apparently think nothing of passing off a verse composed by someone else in a session the day before as their own—merely changing a word or two in it. None of them can truly call a verse his own. Thus, when even the verse in which the serious poet has put so much of himself surfaces again the following day under changed ownership, in time, the single verse comes to have a multiplicity of authors. This is an impropriety that the old masters greatly deplored. When Lord Masatsune used the line *ashihiki no yamazu* [as feet dragging over the mountain ceaselessly], based on the line *sue no matsu yamazu* [as the Sue pine mountain ceaselessly] composed by Lord Ariie the year before, he reportedly earned the censure of the leading poets of his day, who thought it an utterly reprehensible thing to do.[1]

ka ni medete hana ni mo yurusu arashi kana	For its sweet scent let it tarry among the flowers, the mountain wind.
chiru o mite hana ni wasururu arashi kana	By whirling flowers enchanted, I forgot to chide the mountain wind![2]

---

hana o idete hana yori mo koki nioi kana	Exuded by the flower yet deeper than the flower, this fragrance!

ume no hana ai yori mo koki nioi kana	Plum blossoms: far deeper than indigo, this fragrance![3]

Can we tell who was the original author in each of these pairs of hokku? It is really deplorable. Let the verse be ever so subtle and profound, if it violates an earlier poet's diction and conception, it does no more than transmit the work of another.

miyako tote tsumoru wa mare no miyuki kana Sōzei	It *is* the capital! beneath piled drifts of rare shining snow.[4] Sōzei
yama tōki miyako wa mare no miyuki kana Chiun	Far from the hills, the capital lies, in rare shining snow! Chiun

These two verses were composed at about the same time, but since neither of their authors was such as would infringe on the other's conception, their similarity is really remarkable. One must make a distinction between this kind of case and the others.

COMMENTARY

Dōrui, here translated as "plagiarism," literally means the occurrence of identical or closely similar words or conception in two distinct poems, with the implication that the one was copied from the other. The practice of plagiarism was strictly prohibited in waka, renga, and later haikai, although, as will be apparent from Shinkei's remarks at the beginning of this chapter, it was widespread in popular renga circles.

Plagiarism should, of course, be distinguished from the sanctioned practice of allusive variation (*honkadori*), a favorite device with the *Shinkokinshū* poets and one of the established techniques of linking in renga. The distinction between the two apparently lies in the character of the poet's intention:

in plagiarism, the poet surreptitiously takes the words or conception of another work with the intention of passing them off as his own; in allusive variation, the poet takes from another work with the understanding that it is known to his audience, and with the intention of effecting a variation upon it. In other words, allusive variation is a creative process that depends for its effect precisely on the audience's knowledge of the earlier work, while plagiarism is a concealed parasitic act that does not acknowledge its source or infuse new life into it by a creative metamorphosis.

The distinction being drawn in this chapter of *Sasamegoto* is between outright plagiarism and coincidental similarity, as illustrated by the anonymous takeoffs on Shinkei's hokku, in the one case, and the similar verses by the two contemporary poets Sōzei and Chiun, in the other. Although the conception, and the diction of half of line 2 and all of line 3 in the last case are startlingly identical, Shinkei declares that this is purely unintentional. He is obviously speaking from his knowledge of the character of the two poets, for they were his contemporaries, and he praised them as pioneers in the renaissance of renga in his own time. Nevertheless, it seems more likely that one "borrowed" from the other without being aware of it, for they often composed renga together, along with the other seven sages.

The practice of *dōrui* was probably inevitable in renga, given the time pressure involved in a 100-verse session and the art's essentially collective nature. In the process of participating in numerous sessions with a regular or constantly shifting group, it is more than likely that a poet occasionally came up with an expression or conception invented by someone else in another session, without being conscious that he was, in effect, plagiarizing. Renga's character as a continuous sequence produced by a group militated against the consciousness of individual authorship. As commonly practiced, it was often merely a pastime or entertainment, and it was only when serious poets like Shinkei began to work for its aesthetic elevation, and anthologies were compiled as models of composition, that the question of authorship and the quality of the individual poet became matters of crucial concern. From what we know of Shinkei's philosophy, moreover, he would have viewed *dōrui* as inimical to the development of individual talent and originality.

THIRTY

Excessive Straining After Effect

In waka, what is called *irihoga*, excessive straining after an effect, is frowned upon.[1] Is it not to be found in renga also?

Such verses are indeed common; they are said to exhibit *irihoga* either in their conception or in their configuration.

ki o kiru ya shimo no tsurugi no sayamakaze	Will it fell the trees? the frost-sword gusts of the mountain wind.[2]

This verse manifests a certain boldness and dexterity, but the first line seems somewhat strained. In its place, something like *Saenikeri* [piercing keen] would perhaps make the verse more supple and expansive. The idea of cutting down trees with a sword is also unsatisfactory.[3]

natsukusa ya haru no omokage aki no hana	The summer grass: an image of springtime and fall flowers.

This verse exhibits *irihoga* in its total configuration, which is somewhat labored.[4]

COMMENTARY

In both these illustrative cases, the poets err through excess, through a want of proportion, restraint, and precision in wielding their poetic tools. It should be noted that Shinkei does not fault these verses for being unnatural in the sense of deviating from a decorous norm. In Chapter 26, we saw how he defends poets from charges of excess and deviancy by an appeal to the essential freedom of the creative imagination. In fact, he himself had a tendency to use the kind of inverted and illogical syntax cited by Retired Emperor Juntoku in *Yakumo mishō*. His judgment is based rather on whether or not the work succeeds as poetry; from this point of view, even the most exaggerated conception or unnatural diction is justified, as long as it contributes to the moving quality, charismatic appeal, or evocative power that constitutes his ideal of *en*, of the quintessentially poetic.

THIRTY-ONE

Semantic Confusion

In waka, there is a form of poetry known as *miraiki* [lit., prophetic record], which is viewed with disapproval.[1] Does it not exist in renga as well?

This type of poetry reportedly crops up in any renga session, and one is strictly admonished against it.

fukade yo ni ame ga shitagae hana no kaze	Cease to blow, and to a tranquil world submit, O flower wind![2]
hototogisu nakazuba aki no tsukiyo kana	Ah, cuckoo, but for your song, a moonlit night in autumn![3]

Such verses are among the worst of the *miraiki* type.

COMMENTARY

The term *miraiki* referred to a type of eschatological writing purporting to prophesy the future, in particular, the final phase of Buddhism, a dark and anarchic age when the Buddha's teachings have been forgotten in the world. *Miraiki* is also the title of a collection of fifty poems once believed to have been written by Teika under a pseudonym, but now generally believed to be a forgery. The poems hinge exclusively on various types of wordplay, such as *engo* and *kakekotoba*, but employed in a way that obscures the syntax and consequently the sense of the poem (see *Miraiki* in *NKT* 4: 380-83). The manuscript appears to have been transmitted in the Reizei branch of

Teika's descendants through Abutsu, Tameie's second wife, who states that "the Kyōgoku Middle Counselor Lay Monk [Teika] composed these poems to show the style favored by modern poets, such practices as an unacceptable manner of yoking words together, and the way that people's poems will become henceforth; he gave them the name 'fifty prophetic poems'"(cited in Sasaki's *Miraiki* introduction, p. 60).

The manuscript, which exists in a great many copies, was widely regarded as genuine through the Muromachi and until the Edo period. Shōtetsu, for instance, apparently viewed it as a positive model of its kind: "Double meaning [*shūku*] is of great importance in poetry. In the so-called *Miraiki*, Teika also talks about double meaning" (*SM*, p. 221). The rival Nijō school, however, strictly proscribed the work as containing negative examples of the exaggerated and undesirable use of wordplay and unusual diction, possibly motivated by the Reizei poets' known predilection for them. At the same time, its title became a generic term for affected, unnatural puns; unstable syntax; awkward allusions to older poems; unusual word combinations, and other verbal flights—the pejorative equivalent, in short, of the *shūku* (double meaning) technique discussed in Chapter 11. The following opinion on the subject by Kenzai, Shinkei's disciple, probably reflects his view on the matter:

> The prophetic poem [*miraiki no uta*] is a style that is much too high-flown. And the "rainy poems" are given to such excessive pondering, the meaning becomes obscure. [However] if you understand this to mean only that you must wholly refrain from these two styles, then your work will surely end up soporific and dull. It is essential to have a nuanced understanding of this matter. Among the poems Shōgetsu [Shōtetsu] composed in a lifetime, not even ten are free of obscurity.[4]

THIRTY-TWO

Incomprehensibility

In waka, the phenomenon called *mushin shojaku* has been noted as early as the *Man'yōshū*.[1] What is the case with renga?

One frequently encounters this type of configuration in renga. As a rule the forms that have been isolated in waka have their exact equivalents in renga.

tsuki yadoru mizu no omodaka toya mo nashi	In the water reflecting the moon, arrowhead grass [or "hawk"] though it's no bird coop.[2]
hana ya saku ame naki yama ni kage wa kumo	Flowers in bloom? Over the rainless hills, the shadows are clouds.[3]

It is this sort of verse that is known as *mushin shojaku*.

COMMENTARY

Mushin shojaku, a technical term culled from *kambun* syntax, literally means "not to be grasped by the mind," that is to say "incomprehensible." More specifically, it describes a poem or verse whose lines do not cohere into a total meaning because there is no logical connection running through them. It is not a case of syntactic fragmentation or elliptical diction for aesthetic effect, but of sheer obscurity.

As indicated by the question above, the term appears as early as the *Man'yōshū* (see n. 1 for the citation there). *Mushin shojaku* also occurs in the following passage from the *Mumyōshō*, within the context of a section dealing with mediocre poets who try to imitate the great:

> Or then again, someone attempts to compose in the manner of the poem that in some vague way seems to conceal a deep meaning, and in the process ends up becoming confused himself and producing sheer nonsense [*mushin shojaku*]. The poems of such people do not belong to the realm of ineffable depth [*yūgen*]; where they do belong is the Daruma sect." (p. 86)

The Daruma sect refers to the Zen sect, and more specifically to the Zen koan, those paradoxical intellectual puzzles propounded by master to disciple, whose answers are invariably far-fetched, logically unconnected to the question, and incomprehensible to a noninitiate.

It is not clear from the whole bearing of this chapter what Shinkei really thought of *mushin shojaku*. As distinct from the sections on *bonzoku* and *miraiki*, there is curiously no overt word of condemnation here; Shinkei contents himself with observing that the phenomenon exists in renga, just as in waka, and gives two illustrations without comment.

As shown by the pair from the *Man'yōshū*, though overtly incomprehensible, *mushin shojaku* poems sometimes concealed lewd humor (see nn. 1 and 2); in other words their obscurity was deliberate camouflage, which did not necessarily render them inaccessible to those in the know. Much early haikai in the *Inu Tsukubashū* (Doggerel *Tsukubashū*) reads like the paradoxical but suggestive verse in the first example, and, as Shinkei reports, it was of a type that was frequently encountered even in his time. All this raises the question of Shinkei's role in the polarization between "refined" (*ushin*) and "vulgar" (*mushin*) renga. As is well known, the latter would emerge as the independent genre *haikai*, and replace renga as the principal poetic medium in the Tokugawa period. The separation between "refined" and "vulgar" (*ga* and *zoku*) was already accomplished by Sōgi's time. This did not prevent him or his disciple Sōchō from composing haikai as a break from the chaste rigors of renga, but that fact is in itself evidence that the two were quite separate in their minds.

We have seen that Shinkei abhorred vulgarity as a manifestation of a want of sensibility, of a petty, narrow mind, and, indeed, morally as a sign of insincerity. He did not censure wit, wordplay, and even low-life imagery as such, so long as they functioned to bring out a genuine poetic emotion or idea. What he objected to was the unmotivated use of such devices for their own sake; in other words, ingenuity, be it verbal or conceptual, that is empty of feeling and bereft of an intellectual attitude. From this point of view, much early haikai would have been unacceptable to him. He could not have foreseen how Bashō would elevate that genre through principles amazingly like his own. Unfortunately, this does not answer the question of his role in the refined/vulgar dichotomy. All that can be said is that his pluralist inclinations, his refusal to narrow poetry to one single orthodox style, would have caused him to deplore the later stultification of renga in minute rules and predisposed him to the fresh developments in the haikai world. In the end, it seems the wisest course to read *ushin* as "serious" rather than "refined" in the context of Shinkei's works, since *kokoro* here refers to a moral and philosophical dimension in aesthetics, particularly in its identification with the Buddhist mind of meditation. We should recall, in this connection, his censure of the "configuration steeped in grace and charm," "the fine outward appearance," as mere imitations of *yūgen* (Chapter 7).

THIRTY-THREE

The Close Link and the Distant Link

In waka, there are the two modes called the Close Link [*shinku*] and the Distant Link [*soku*]. Are they not present in renga as well?

It is because most people do not discern this distinction that they are often bewildered by the precise nature of the link between verses. There are many superior poems among those employing the Distant Link, according to Lord Teika.[1] There is no doubt that the Close and Distant Link modes also exist in renga.

Verses in the Distant Link Mode

hajime mo hate mo shiranu yo no naka	Unknown its beginning, or yet its ending: this our world.
wata no hara yosete wa kaeru okitsu nami	The vast sea plain: from the offing the waves roll in but to roll back again.[2]
kore ya fuseya ni ouru hahakigi	Is this then the broom tree that grows by the lowly hut?
inazuma no hikari no uchi no matsu no iro	In a flash of lightning, the color of the pines![3]

In each of these verse pairs the poet, discarding the maeku's words and configuration, has made the link solely through the mind.[4] But such verses are too numerous to cite here.

Poems in the Distant Link Mode

sato tōki
yakoe no tori no
hatsukoe ni
hana no ka okuru
haru no yamakaze
Teika-kyō

With the first call
of the oft-calling morning fowl
in a distant village,
the breezes send from the hills
a breath of spring flowers.[5]
Lord Teika

sagi no iru
ike no migiwa ni
matsu furite
miyako no hoka no
kokochi koso sure
Onaji

A heron stands in
the pond by whose bank years
deepen on the pines:
How remote from the capital
is the feel of this scene![6]
Lord Teika

omou koto
nado tou hito no
nakaruran
aogeba sora ni
tsuki zo sayakeki
Jichin

Of the sorrow
in my heart, why comes no one
to inquire?
I gaze up at the sky, and oh,
how keen and clear the moon![7]
Jichin

makomo karu
mitsu no mimaki no
yūmagure
nenu ni mezamasu
hototogisu kana
Onaji

A shadowy dusk
over the pastures of Mitsu where
men reap the wild rice:
Half-lidded, eyes flicker wide
at the cry—*hototogisu*![8]
Jichin

shii no ha no
ura fukikaesu
kogarashi ni
yūzukuyo miru
ariake no koro
Shōtetsu

In the wind gusts
blowing back the undersides
of the oak leaves,
apparition of moonrise
in the dark pre-dawn hour.[9]
Shōtetsu

Such masterpieces are innumerable; it is impossible to cite them all.

Verses in the Close Link Mode

The manner of linking is commonplace.

kōri no ue ni nami zo tachinuru	Over the icy surface waves have risen!
sayuru yo no tsuki no kageno no hana susuki Ryōa	In the chill night across fields of moonlight, miscanthus in flower.[10] Ryōa

aruru yakata o ima tsukuru nari	They are restoring now the ruined manor.
kataoka no sato no atari o tani ni shite Ryōa	Turning the area round the village of Kataoka to rice fields.[11] Ryōa

One should refrain, however, from partiality to either the Close Link or the Distant Link. To fall into a uniform configuration is to depart from the spirit of the Way.

COMMENTARY

Shinku (the Close Link) and *soku* (the Distant Link) refer to the structural continuity or discontinuity of a waka poem. In *shinku*, the lines of the poem, being closely connected phonologically, syntactically, and semantically, constitute an immediately apprehensible unity, while in *soku*, a caesura divides the poem into two disparate parts, giving the impression of a fragmented, discontinuous surface structure. The issue of the distance between two contiguous verses is central to an understanding of renga structure—specifically the nature of the link—and of renga aesthetics.

In the course of analyzing the *shinku/soku* dichotomy here, Shinkei clearly draws a distinction between the verse as such, a formal entity constituted of words (*kotoba*) arranged into an integral shape or configuration (*sugata*), on the one hand, and some underlying deep level of meaning (*kokoro*), on the other. That is to say, "discarding the maeku's words and configuration," in the case of the Distant Link, is equivalent to going beyond its overt and specific *sense* in favor of some deep, broad meaning, that is to say, *significance*, which includes and simultaneously transcends it. The following statement on *soku* in the *SSG* rev. ed. text (p. 121) is enlightening in this regard.

> A *soku* poem is said to be one wherein it does not matter that the upper and lower parts are put together in a seemingly unnatural and arbitrary way as long as they cohere in the mind [*Kami no ku to shimo no ku to kokoro da ni tsūjihabereba aranu sama koto o mo hoshiki mama ni tsugitaru wa soku no uta naru beshi to nari*].

In *soku*, then, the connection between the two verses seems "unnatural and arbitrary" on the surface but "coherent" on a deeper level. And this apparent discontinuity or incoherence is precisely because the tsukeku does not relate directly to the words and specific sense of the maeku but to a deeper significance suggested by it.

If we look back at the broom-tree verse example for a moment with innocent eyes, the radical disjunction between maeku and tsukeku is immediately apparent. The maeku is simply asking whether "this" (the referent is indeterminate) is indeed the fabulous broom tree, while the tsukeku is a vivid picture of pine trees seen in a lightning flash. The words "growing by the lowly hut" have been wholly discarded in the tsukeku, and pine trees have really nothing to do with the broom tree as such. What the poet has done is to interpolate the broom tree's deeper significance as a symbol of the profoundly elusive quality of material reality. He has, in other words, gone straight to the invisible kernel of the maeku and animated it, setting off an undercurrent of meaning in which the two verses begin to vibrate together on the same frequency, as it were.

It cannot be reiterated frequently enough that renga's poetry lies not in the individual verses but in the relations between them. This means that its poetry is always in an absolute sense invisible in, and has to be extrapolated from, the linguistic surface of the verses themselves. But there are varying degrees of "visibility." The Close Link operates primarily on the level of verbal, semantic logic—including the poetic logic of double meaning, associative words (*engo*), and thematic similarity—and is therefore easily apprehensible. The Distant Link engages the conceptual level, seeing difference in similarity, or the other way round, outside of the predetermined meanings of words. It is therefore difficult to grasp at once, but once it has been grasped, it sets off an implosion of meaning in which the two verses, apparently so disparate, dissolve together into a deeper, larger unity.

Soku, the most extreme manifestation of renga's unique poetry, also lies at the core of Shinkei's poetics, in that it brings into concrete application his thoroughgoing emphasis on *kokoro*, the mind, and ultimately the creative imagination as he understood it, over and above the words or verbal configuration of a verse. For *soku* is based solely on the process of introspection described earlier in Chapter 14. What connects maeku and tsukeku in this instance is a universal principle that the poet intuits and interpolates from the maeku during a heightened state of awareness in which things lose their intractable particularity and are perceived in all their openness as both "empty" and "real." This tranquil, expansive, and liberated state of mind is equivalent in Shinkei's poetics to the creative imagination. In its keen perceptivity, it is wholly open to the maeku, to its words and specific messages certainly, but also to the whole world of possibilities suggested by it, its indeterminate horizon. It is in relation to this empty unverbalized horizon that the poet composes the "distantly linked" tsukeku, which has the effect of instantaneously animating it with an unexpressed—or, better yet, inexpressible, meaning.

How does one embody an intuition, a mental attitude, or a view of the world in a brief three- or two-line verse? It is manifestly impossible. Consequently, what *soku* does is not to express the idea or principle as such but to suggest it. In other words, it acts as a mere catalyst setting off a reaction in relation to the maeku. Together, the two verses are only agents of a higher discourse happening outside them (but only possible through them); they are the charged forms of a poem that has been transported beyond itself.

As for the waka poems cited above, they all have in common the fact that there is no direct continuity, either syntactically or logically, from line 1 to line 5. In all of them, the break comes at the end of line 3, marked by a caesura that also coincides with the end of one image and the beginning of another. In other words, the effect of each poem arises from the juxtaposition of two images, which set off each other. The separation creates a tension; a kind of spark ignites between the two, which suddenly illuminates or releases the unspoken feeling intended by the poet and causes the two parts to fuse into an internal unity of mood, thought, or feeling, in short, of *kokoro*. This tense relationship is obviously similar to that which obtains between maeku and tsukeku in renga, as we have seen in the cited examples. It is significant to note that the poems are by the *Shinkokinshū* poets Teika and

Jichin, and by Shinkei's waka mentor Shōtetsu, who, of course, worshipped Teika. From the literary-historical perspective, Shinkei's *soku* concept may be said to represent the most extreme development of the aesthetics of discontinuous structure subsequent to the *Shinkokinshū* poets. There seems no doubt (indeed, this chapter is evidence of it) that it was his study of their peculiar stylistic techniques that made him see the importance of *soku* and its eminently suitable application in a genre like renga, where the separation between upper and lower parts was a given condition of the form itself; that formal separation permitted a greater imaginative freedom than in waka, where the two hemistichs still had to add up to a single, integral unity on the level of configuration, or *sugata*.

Shinkei refrains here from defining *shinku*, except to note that it is a "commonplace" manner of linking, but it seems clear from the two examples cited that what distinguishes it from *soku* are a comparatively shallower conception and a corresponding emphasis on verbal correspondences as a means of connection. In the first pair, the tsukeku closely follows the syntactic shape of the maeku and is essentially a translation of its two terms into different quantities: the unlikely image of waves undulating over ice is transformed into waves of plume grass rippling over silvery, moonlit fields. The imagery is rather lovely and Ryōa displays a lot of imaginative wit, but the connection lacks the profound implications of the *soku* verses cited earlier. The same may be said of the second example, whose conception as such, having to do with the destructive effects of time, carries deeper possibilities that are not, however, realized. In *shinku*, as in *soku*, one experiences the same pleasurable surprise generated by any renga link, that of a riddle successfully solved, an obstacle safely overcome, but in *soku*, the shock of recognition is far more powerful. Ultimately, however, it is important to note that Shinkei regards the *shinku/soku* distinction as only a *provisional* dichotomy, to be subsumed under the metalinguistic principle of nondualism and impartiality.

THIRTY-FOUR

On *Hen-jo-dai-kyoku-ryū* as the Structure of the Renga Link

It is said that one composes waka according to the sequential pattern of *hen-jo-dai-kyoku-ryū*. Does the same hold for renga?

According to a former master, this pattern is of utmost importance in renga. For example, if the short verse contains *kyoku*—that is to say, intends to make a Statement, then the long verse should adopt the *hen-jo-dai* posture and leave something unsaid. Or again, if the long verse intends a Statement and is emphatically saying so, then the short verse should take the *hen-jo-dai* stance and let it flow through.

tsumi mo mukui mo sa mo araba are	As for sin and retribution, if it be so, so be it!
tsuki nokoru kariba no yuki no asaborake Gusai	The moon lingers over snowy hunting fields in a glimmering dawn.[1] Gusai
kaeshitaru ta o mata kaesu nari	The field already plowed lies plowed again.
ashihiki no yama ni fusu i no yoru wa kite Zen'a	The wild boar that lurks in the foot-dragging mountain comes in the night to call.[2] Zen'a
kōri tokete mo yuki wa te ni ari	Though the ice has melted snow alights on the palm.

chirikakaru nozawa no hana no shita warabi Junkaku	Fronds of fern under scattering flowers on the meadow marsh.[3] Junkaku

In each of the three verse pairs above, since the preceding short verse intends a Statement and is straining hard to do so, the following long verse consequently takes the *hen-jo-dai* stance, leaving something unsaid and giving it over to the maeku.

omokage no tōku naru koso kanashikere	The image of a face growing distant in the memory brings sadness.
hana mishi yama no yūgure no kumo Ryōa	Over hills where I saw flowers, the dimming clouds of twilight.[4] Ryōa

mae ushiro to wa futatsu aru shiba no io	In front, in back, two doors does it have the brushwood hut.
idete iru made tsuki o koso mire Shinshō	From its rising till its falling, he gazes at the moon![5] Shinshō

In the two pairs above, since the preceding long verse intends a Statement and is openly saying so, the lower verse falls into the *hen-jo-dai* stance, merely acknowledging the maeku and allowing it to flow through. In renga, therefore, it is the rule that the upper verse leaves something unsaid, entrusting it to the lower verse, while the lower verse expresses itself incompletely, so that it may be completed by the upper verse. This means that excellence, that quality of moving the heart and mind, is not to be found in a sequence wherein each successive verse is wholly complete in itself.

In waka, since one does not wish to express a Statement in two places in the same poem, one frequently resorts to the use of prefatory words [*jo no kotoba*][6] or pause words [*yasumetaru kotoba*] called *hampi no ku*.[7] Without a clear awareness of these things, I should think that you would inevitably end up with a shallow interpretation of even the most excellent poems. The Buddhist sutras likewise possess a certain pattern called "Introduction–Proper Teaching–Propagation" [*jo-shō-ruzū*]. To begin with, the Introduction preaches various parables and instances of karmic connection [*innen*]. Thereafter the Proper Teaching section expresses the very principle of the sutra itself; and finally the Propagation section enumerates the various merits accruing to its transmission. Everyone knows about these parts without realizing that they correspond to the *hen-jo-dai-kyoku-ryū* structure of poetry. Furthermore the "Beginning-Amplification-Turn-Summation" [*ki-shō-ten-gō*] sequence of the four-line Chinese poem comes to the same thing.[8] There are thus numerous examples of both waka and renga that employ prefatory words; the ancient poems in particular seem invariably to include them.

Some Poems with a Preface

hototogisu
naku ya satsuki no
ayamegusa
ayame mo shiranu
koi mo suru kana

Is the cuckoo singing—
midst the sweet flag, lissome
blossoms of summer,
I know not *reason* nor *flower*
why yearningly turns my heart![9]

shikishima no
yamato ni wa aranu
karagoromo
koro mo hezu shite
au yoshi mogana

Not to be had in
all of Yamato's myriad isles,
this robe of Cathay;
Ah, for a way to meet her
without *a moment's* delay.[10]

yamashiro no
yodo no wakagomo
kari ni da ni
konu hito tanomu
ware zo hakanaki

If only to reap the
young oats of Yodo in Yamashiro,
even for awhile
he comes not to whom I trust,
and pathetic indeed am I![11]

michinoku no
asaka no numa no
hanagatsumi
katsu mishi hito ni
koiwataru kana

In Michinoku
along the marshes of Asaka
water-oats bloom;
brief was the moment I saw her
yet my longing goes on and on.[12]

yoshinogawa	*Yoshino River*:
iwanami takaku	*spraying high among the rocks*
yukumizu no	*the current flows*
hayaku zo hito o	*swiftly*, a yearning for her
omoisometeshi	did suffuse my heart.[13]

There are also poems in which some lengthy pause words have been inserted in the middle lines.

ta ga misogi	For whom the Lustration?
yūtsukedori zo	Tied with sacred cord, the cock
karagoromo	*rends* the mountain air,
tatsuta no yama ni	trailing *sheer* down Tatsuta
orihaete naku	its long, bright *train* of sound.[14]

ukaibune	Cormorant fishing boats—
aware to zo omou	it is a sight to break the heart;
mononofu no	*a myriad men of arms*
yaso ujigawa no	flickering lost on the Uji River
yūyami no sora	as darkly looms the evening sky.[15]
Jichin-oshō	Priest Jichin

ikomayama	Down Mount Ikoma,
arashi mo aki no	anon the storm winds blow with
iro ni fuku	the hues of autumn,
tezome no ito no	*whirling skeins of dyed thread*
yoru zo kanashiki	in a night edged with sadness.[16]
Teika-kyō	Lord Teika

Similar to the poems quoted above are those renga verses wherein the Statement is made in the maeku and completed in the tsukeku by means of a Preface. They represent a style of linking that seems to have been a dominant one in the work of the old renga poets.

kami no igaki ni	By the holy fence of the god,
hiku muma mo ari	a horse is being pulled along.

misogi seshi
mi no hi wa suginu
mishimenawa
Shinshō

The Purification Rites
of the Day of the Snake are over:
the sacred guard-rope.[17]
Shinshō

utsutsu ka yume ka
akete koso mime

Is it reality? Dream?
When the night opens, we'll see.

tabi ni motsu
nosaki no hakone
utsu no yama
Shūa

Carried on a journey
a box with rice tribute to Hakone,
along Mount Empty.[18]
Shūa

kokoro yori
tada ukikoto ni
shiojimite

My very soul has
grown seasoned in the brine
of unchanging sorrow.

irie no hotade
karaki yo no naka
Gusai

As nettles growing by the inlet
the bitterness of this world.[19]
Gusai

Such verses are too numerous to set down here.

COMMENTARY

This chapter constitutes Shinkei's most valuable and original contribution to the analysis of the renga link, and he does it by employing a little-known concept of waka structure as well as by analogy to waka poems using a *jo* (preface or foretext). *Hen-jo-dai-kyoku-ryū* is a term describing the structural sequence of the five lines of a waka poem. The *Sangoki* explains it in the following manner:

> *Hen* [the first line] is the starting point signifying that one is about to begin, *jo* [the second line] is when one has actually begun, *dai* [the third line] is the poem's topic; one should directly manifest the topic in this line. In *kyoku* [the fourth line] one expresses something delicately elegant in an interesting manner, and with *ryū* [the fifth line], one lets the poem flow away, like a five-foot length of vine gracefully undulating on the water. (p. 350)

As described in this passage, the movement of a waka poem may be characterized as a slow buildup to its central highest point, line 4, or *kyoku*, followed by a quick (though perceived as extended) fade-out. *Hen-jo-dai-kyoku-ryū* may thus be loosely translated as "start, takeoff, topic, statement, fade-out." The same progression is suggested by Shinkei's explanation in Part II, Chapter 40, *SSG* 173-74.

Briefly put, Shinkei sees renga's basic structural unit, the verse pair, as an oscillation between what may be called a Statement (*kyoku* in *kyoku-ryū*) and its Context (my functional translation of *hen-jo-dai*). Thus if the maeku takes the one aspect, then the tsukeku should take the other. This is due to the fact that the Statement remains abstract until it is manifested in a concrete set of circumstances, and conversely, a Context remains silent, it does not speak, until the Statement gives it voice—a meaning and purpose. In other words, the relationship between Statement and Context is a functional, reciprocal one, even though the latter seems subordinate because it is said merely to let the Statement "flow through" (*iinagasu*), instead of coming up with a new one to confront it.

The riddle verse, such as the second, third, and fifth maeku in the verse pairs cited above, seems like a good representative of what Shinkei means by the Statement, or *kyoku*. What comprises a Statement as such is apparently the presence of intentionality or purpose in the verse, the sense that the poet is trying to get a point across. In the riddle, intentionality is especially marked by the proposition's paradoxical character which emphatically demands a solution, viz., "Though the ice has melted / snow alights on the palm." The Context as such, on the other hand, is unemphatic and indifferent, innocent of purpose, empty: "Fronds of fern / under scattering flowers / on the meadow marsh." In nearly all the examples in this section, the tsukeku (which happens to be the Context) consists of a purely objective image without a point as such; its significance appears only in relation to the maeku. In this case, the falling white petals come to correspond to the "snow," and the "fern fronds" are the "palm" or hand upon which they are falling.

Except for the first tsukeku by Gusai and the fourth by Ryōa, the verses quoted in this chapter are generally dry and lacking in poetic feeling. However, it must be said of them all that each links up firmly and securely with its maeku, producing an impact, as when disparate fragments suddenly fall into place. Dating from renga's first flowering in the Kamakura-Nambokuchō period, these verses have a certain archaic flavor, but it is precisely this lack of an aesthetic aura that makes them perfect illustrations for the bare-bones structure of the minimal verse-pair unit. Based primarily on the operation of wit and intelligence, they confirm renga's nature as primarily a craft of composition and design, and only secondarily a poetry of refined sensibilities.

"In renga, therefore, it is the rule that the upper verse leaves something unsaid, entrusting it to the lower verse, while the lower verse expresses itself incompletely, so that it may be completed by the upper verse." This statement summarizes Shinkei's analysis of the relationship between contiguous verses. It is perhaps best described as a reciprocal dependency, similar to the relation between space and form in the visual arts. An uninterrupted series of forms (Statements) without the silent mediation of space (Contexts) would result in a turgid texture. Indeed, as he says in the *SSG* rev. ed. text, "if each verse is wholly complete in itself, the minds [*kokoro*] will not connect, and the verses will merely be standing in a lifeless row" (p. 106). That he is so emphatic about the pitfalls of making a statement at every point in the sequence reflects a pervasive tendency in his time, and perhaps at all times, for the poet to display his talent by a verse that sounds great and impressive as such, instead of "humbling" himself with an "empty" verse that properly mirrors the previous poet's statement. As in life, so in renga, the ability to listen and respond that is the basis of all genuine communication is a difficult discipline. And that is why the Way for Shinkei is equivalent to the cultivation of an impersonal identification with Beauty or Poetry as such, and a corresponding disengagement from the personal ego; the vitality of the genre simply depended on it.

Shinkei's aim in quoting the waka poems in this chapter is to draw an implicit analogy between their structure, which consists of preface and statement, and the renga verse pair. The most obvious similarity is that in both cases, there is no direct and overt syntactic and/or semantic continuity from one part to the other. Furthermore, like the Context verse in renga, the preface is empty of intention as such; it is but an objective description of scenery, or not even that—merely an undifferentiated image mentioned without motivation. Yet through the juxtaposition, it comes to function as a concrete context, and ultimately a metaphor, for the statement in a manner similar to the operation of the one verse upon the other in renga. Further analysis reveals that the link in both cases inevitably falls into a metonymical (synecdochic) cast tending strongly toward the metaphorical. In an early article, I showed the close conjunction of metonymy and metaphor in *Genji monogatari*'s narrative progression.[20] The structure of the renga link is apparently similar. At any rate, it is obviously upon the double character of the pivot word or of partially homonymic words in these waka that the whole analogy with renga so to speak "hinges."

THIRTY-FIVE

On *Rikugi*: The Six Types of Poetry

Waka distinguishes among six types of poetry called the "six principles" [*rikugi*].[1] Would they not exist in renga as well?

I have once inquired of a former master regarding this matter. In general, you will find that verses vary one from the other according to the idea of the six principles. Let us roughly illustrate this by verse examples.

Fū

na wa takaku
koe wa ue nashi
hototogisu
Gusai

The Allegorical Mode

High is its name
and unsurpassed its song,
the *hototogisu*.[2]
Gusai

This verse extols the Regent Nijō Yoshimoto by implicitly comparing him to the *hototogisu*. Such a verse, which expresses its meaning by reference to other phenomena, must be in the Allegorical Mode.[3]

Fu

izuru hi wa
yomo no kasumi ni
narinikeri
Gusai

The Mode of Precise Delineation

The rising sun:
into haze in the four directions
transfigured!
Gusai

Here the poet's meaning has been stamped upon every word and runs through the whole. Such a verse in which the sense is finely drawn must be in the Mode of Precise Delineation.[4]

Hi	**The Metaphorical Mode**
shita momiji chiri ni majiwaru miyai kana Gusai	Red leaves scatter mingling with the dust below: the holy shrine.[5] Gusai

Here the word "dust" [*chiri*] is presented in the guise of the homophonous word "scatter," and a connection is drawn between them. This is probably what is meant by the Metaphorical Mode.[6]

Kyō	**The Symbolic Mode**
samidare wa mine no matsukaze tani no mizu Gusai	The long rains: pine winds across the peaks, the valley streams![7] Gusai

This verse, which illustrates a certain meaning or significance in phenomena by evoking it in something visible and audible, must be in the Symbolic Mode.[8]

Ga	**The Direct Mode**
natsukusa mo hana no aki ni wa narinikeri Monshin	The summer grass into flower fields of autumn has turned.[9] Monshin

This verse states its meaning directly. Such a verse, speaking plainly with no attempt at indirection in the diction or conception, is in the Direct Mode.[10]

Shō	**The Panegyrical Mode**
Hanatsubaki migakeru tama no migiri kana Jō'a	Camellia blossoms: a garden of polished white gemstones.[11] Jō'a

This is a verse of praise and celebration; it is in the Panegyrical Mode.[12] The interlinear Notes in the *Kokinshū* Preface tell us that this mode must have a religious significance. These interlinear Notes, however, are believed to have been written and added to the Preface at a later date, and the commentaries criticize them as inconsistent. There exists some oral tradition about who their author might be. At any rate, I have relied on the main text in classifying the hokku verses above.[13]

COMMENTARY

In the notes to this section, I have attempted to analyze Shinkei's concept of *rikugi* with reference to the *Shi Jing* and the *Kokinshū* Kana Preface. The process reveals that these two works had only a general influence, an indication, no doubt, that in neither one nor the other is the concept discussed or illustrated conclusively and clearly. Nevertheless, some general trends can be observed. In the *Shi Jing*, the six types are classified according to two parameters: one of content and/or social function (*feng*, *ya*, *song*) and the other of form or means of expression (*fu*, *bi*, *xing*). The *Kokinshū* Preface reflects the same division, except that *feng* is shifted from the content/function axis to that of form. The displacement increases with Shinkei, who places *ya* as well into the second category, leaving only *song* in the first.

To summarize: Shinkei's "six principles," with their external correspondences in the *Shi Jing*, the *Kokinshū* Preface, and the English translation that seemed most appropriate to his understanding of them, are the following:

1	Feng 風	*soe uta*	The Allegorical Mode
2	Ya 雅	*tadagoto uta*	The Direct Mode
3	Song 頌	*iwai uta*	The Panegyrical Mode
4	Fu 賦	*kazoe uta*	The Mode of Precise Delineation
5	Bi 比	*nazurae uta*	The Metaphorical Mode
6	Xing 興	*tatoe uta*	The Symbolic Mode

Quite apart from their imperfect correspondence to—and indeed occasional wide divergence from—both the Great Preface and the *Kokinshū* Preface, Shinkei's six principles constitute valid and illuminating categories in their own right. His explanations for each is clear and succinct, and the carefully selected hokku clarify through example what remains unelaborated in the prose.

As suggested above, Shinkei was apparently less interested in drawing demarcations based on content (these had, after all, long been established by the topical divisions of the imperial anthologies) than in explicating the primary modes of conveying meaning in poetry. From this perspective, the relevant ones are the following four among the six: the Direct Mode, on the one hand, and the Allegorical, Metaphorical, and Symbolic Modes, on the other. All together, they account for the denotative and figurative uses of language in Japanese poetry. The three figurative modes are distinguished from one another in that both terms of the analogy are present in a poem in the Metaphorical Mode, while the subject or referent is withheld in the Allegorical and Symbolic Modes. These last two are in turn distinct in the nature of their concealed referents: the Allegorical refers to a person, time, place, or situation, in other words, to the actual and particular circumstances motivating its composition; while the Symbolic evokes a concept or principle of wider, universal validity. As for the remaining two types, the Mode of Precise Delineation, while showing us Shinkei's critical perspicacity, properly belongs to an evaluation of a writer's particular style and not to a pragmatic theory of poetic modes, while the Panegyric is equally aberrant in being the only type based on content.

Shinkei's concept of the six principles is thus not wholly consistent, nor can it be said to be exhaustive. Its weaknesses are intrinsic to any attempt to apply to Japanese poetry an imperfectly understood system of classification conceived for ancient Chinese poetic production, and not the least unsatisfactory aspect of which is that the types should arbitrarily number six in all. As mentioned in the note at the beginning of this chapter, the Chinese *rikugi* concept had held an inordinately great prestige in Japan ever since its inclusion in the *Kokinshū* Preface. It became part of the *Kokin denju*, that body of arcane teachings said to have been secretly and orally transmitted from Fujiwara Teika, which was to acquire such a mysterious hold over people's imaginations in the Muromachi period, that is to say, in Shinkei's time. Thus, it may be said that in applying the *rikugi* concept to renga, Shinkei was simply following one of the main motivations for his writing *Sasamegoto* in the first place; namely, to demonstrate that renga as a poetic art had intrinsically as much validity, seriousness, and prestige as waka, since waka categories applied to it as well. In the process, he isolated at least three principles that certainly have great validity for all Japanese classical poetry.

The Allegorical Mode is particularly relevant, because classical poetry has always been a form of social communication, a kind of social event. The allusions to actual persons, places, and happenings, either explicitly announced in the prose introduction (*kotobagaki*) or left implicit in the lyrical diction and recoverable only by historical research, are, in fact, among its most fascinating aspects; it is this same practice, indeed, that is reflected in the development of lyrical fiction. This was especially significant in renga, a collective endeavor that inevitably generated hidden conversations among the members below the purely poetic transactions on its surface. As for the Metaphorical Mode, it is no exaggeration to say that it comprises the most vital and essential aspect of classical poetry. All the best-known techniques, like the *jo*, *kakekotoba*, and *engo*, are but instances of it, and, in short, the brevity of the waka form simply required it. Its relevance in renga is even more far-reaching, since the link between two verses frequently coincides with a metaphorical identification of two terms. Lastly, the Symbolic Mode may be said to represent the highest development of classical poetry. It evolved from the *Shinkokinshū* period, when poetry came to be viewed as an expression of the most ineffable principles, quite apart from social or temporal context. The best work of the *Shinkokinshū* poets, as of Shōtetsu, Shinkei, and Bashō, inevitably falls into this category.

Ultimately, Shinkei's insistence on dealing with the unwieldy concept of *rikugi* should be seen as an attempt to abstract a systematic theory of poetic modes heretofore neglected in Japanese literary criticism. Though only partially successful, it is revealing evidence of the searching cast of mind that also led him to employ the *hen-jo-dai-kyoku-ryū* concept to analyze the structure of renga, and with highly illuminating results.

THIRTY-SIX

Poetry Contests and Criticism

Through the ages, it has been the practice in waka to hold poetry contests [*uta awase*], during which the poets' names are withheld from the company while the poems are subjected to varying praise and censure until even their slightest flaws are brought to light.[1] Is there nothing like this in renga?

Indeed, is it not because renga has heretofore lacked just such a critical attitude that every amateur and ungifted practitioner has been content to compose in any way he fancies, and the Way has become so shallow? It is only recently that I have started hearing frequent reports of a similar practice in renga, whereby the poets are divided into rival groups of Left and Right, and each verse is given a verdict of win or lose after being subjected to various criticisms before the assembly.[2] Such competitions, if they included the participation of superior poets and became popular, would certainly constitute a guiding light in the Way.[3]

COMMENTARY

To date, no one has made a study of the renga contest, so it is not possible to determine to what extent its rules and procedures were established and when. There exist a number of so-called renga contests, but these are actually hokku or tsukeku arranged by an individual poet into pairs or rounds and submitted to a famous master or senior poet for judgment. One of these is the *Bontōan renga awase jūgoban* (Master Bontō's Renga Match in Fifteen Rounds) from 1415, consisting of 30 of what Bontō considered his best tsukeku, arranged into 15 rounds and submitted to Retired Emperor Gokomatsu (1377-1433; r. 1392-1412) for his marks and judgment. Again in 1521, Sōgi's disciple Sōseki (1474-1533) chose from his oeuvre 40 hokku and 200 tsukeku, arranged them into 120 rounds, and asked Sōchō to evaluate them; this manuscript is called the *Sōseki renga awase hyakunijūban* (Sōseki's Renga Match in 120 Rounds). And at the request of the poet Jun'a from Shirakawa, Shinkei himself put together the *Shibakusa-nai renga awase*, 100 hokku in 50 rounds and 200 tsukeku in 100 rounds, at Mount Ōyama in 1473.

From the late Muromachi period, there is the manuscript called *Shichinin tsukeku-han* (Evaluations of Tsukeku by Seven Poets), the record of a contest held at the Honnōji Temple in 1490, which included among its seven participants the famous trio Sōgi, Shōhaku, and Sōchō. Each poet composed a tsukeku to sixteen difficult maeku, and they all debated the merits and demerits of each verse afterward, with Sōgi giving the final marks; this would be more in the line of what Shinkei means in this chapter.

It seems possible that renga contests were rarely convened with the degree of formality and ceremony that attended waka contests, but that informally, they were held quite frequently and, as Shinkei hoped, became part of a renga poet's training. At any rate, it is evident from this chapter that he desired to foster a higher standard of poetry in renga than was being produced in his day. And one of the ways he saw of encouraging this was to hold competitions in which superior poets could display their talents and serve as models, while inferior poets could be stimulated by the rivalry and criticism to improve their work.

THIRTY-SEVEN

Marks and Grade Points in Renga

When assigning points in waka, it is the practice to scrutinize the poem and comment on it down to the tiniest detail. What ought to be the practice in renga?

According to someone whom I have asked about this matter, one who assigns marks in renga should by all means comment on any questionable points in the verses and make sure that he and the poet come to a mutual understanding regarding these. There is obviously no use in giving points or receiving them if those verses whose sense is unclear, or which include irrelevant elements, were merely to be passed over in silence. Such laxness is unheard-of in waka; particularly in this regard, renga should not deviate in the slightest from waka practice.

COMMENTARY

It was the practice in waka, renga, and later, haikai, for practitioners to submit their work to their teacher or other respected poets for evaluation. The teacher indicated the "grade" for each verse or poem through marks or points called *ten*, a system of circles and lines of varying value. The marks were originally used only for pedagogic purposes, but they acquired an extrinsic importance in the Kamakura and Nambokuchō periods, when much renga was composed during speed competitions or games where prizes were awarded to those who composed the most and the best, and even betting became part of the renga scene. As renga spread widely among the commoners, the number of self-proclaimed judges who made it their business to hand out marks increased. These were the *tenja*, professional "referees" who arbitrated on rules and points and expected to be paid for their services, many of whom were apparently only nominal priests with neither clerical office nor rank. It is against this background that Shinkei's insistence on strictness and thoroughness in handing out marks should be viewed. The marks handed out by professional *tenja* must have been useless, since they did not write out comments or care to examine the verses from a serious pedagogical motivation.

THIRTY-EIGHT

One's True Poetry Emerges in Old Age

There are some skilled poets who shy away from the idea of studying poetry in their old age and give it up before that time. Is that how it should be?

The Way is made precisely to be cultivated by the calm and liberated spirit. Therefore one can begin to practice it properly and with the keenest discernment only after one has passed middle age. Old age is indubitably the time when the verse that is truly one's own emerges.

It is said that Lord Ietaka had reached fifty before achieving fame.[1]

Ning Yue was forty when he began his studies, but he achieved the Way of Letters.[2]

Confucius was likewise forty when he ceased being deluded.[3]

Zong Shi acquired a fondness for learning at seventy and became a royal adviser.[4]

"If one listens to the Way in the morning, one can die content in the evening."[5]

COMMENTARY

Shinkei's belief that "the verse that is truly one's own" (*makoto no waga ku*) is achieved only in old age is a natural consequence of his view of Poetry as a spiritual discipline, a gradual shedding of worldly desires and illusions until the original mind or mind-ground (*shinji*) emerges in all its purity. By "the verse that is truly one's own," he does not imply a unique and special personality, for that is just a concatenation of environment and circumstance, but rather a mind that has attained to the realm of suchness and pure being. It is this unencumbered mind that is capable of producing the kind of poetry that he describes as "chill and meager" (*hie yase*): austere and without illusion, especially with regard to the artifice of language.

For obvious reasons, it is realistically impossible to attain to such a mental state before an advanced age; life involves us in too many unavoidable transactions along the way. As Shinkei says, "Confucius was forty when he ceased being deluded," that is to say, he first saw himself and the world shorn of illusion only on the threshold of middle age. And it is only then, when the Way is most difficult, precisely because unmitigated by dreams, that the true disciplining of the spirit can begin.

THIRTY-NINE

The State of Renga in Our Time

Listening to the renga being composed nowadays in the countryside, one sees no sign that the Way is being pursued with the proper application and mindfulness. Everyone seems in too much of a hurry to honor each other with a proper wand.[1]

It is true that ever since such versifiers have filled the world, the high-mindedness and deep sensibilities intrinsic to the Way have disappeared. It has become no more than senseless chatter rolling off the tip of the tongue, with no trace of spiritual cultivation whatsoever. No wonder then that these so-called 1,000- or 10,000-verse sequences assail the ears from every roadside and marketplace these days. Even the few who are initiated in the Way use it solely as a means of livelihood, employing themselves in vulgarizing it day in and day out. Verily are these the times of the Counterfeit and Degenerate Dharma for the Way.[2] Nevertheless, it is well to remember that since in all things, a moment's thought is equivalent to the ultimate, neither the gifted nor the ungifted, the peaceful nor the unruly can do other than content themselves with each day as it comes.[3] With regard to the Way of Poetry, we are all like "the poor son" whom the Buddha must entice to the right path by means of manifold devices—we cannot reach it by a direct route.[4] The Way as such would only elevate those that are already high and demean those already low.[5] Therefore, just as Buddhism recognizes the difference between the wise [who work out their own salvation] and the foolish [who must depend on the Buddha's compassion], likewise in the Way of Poetry, we can do no more than abide by each individual's inborn talent or lack of it. Such is the given condition for the Way, in which not even the Buddha, Confucius, or Hitomaro can help us. "In accord with the beings' natures [the Buddha's preaching is] differently perceived"—such is the explanation.[6] In other words: "They listen to the same thing but hear it differently."

The practice of the Way may be said to have begun flourishing from around the Ōchō era [1311–12]. At the time, its most accomplished poet was the priest

Zen'a, and among his disciples were Junkaku, Shinshō, Gusai, and Ryōa. Thereafter, during the Jōji [1362–68] and Ōan [1368–75] eras, the priest Gusai became the Way's undisputed sage; his disciples were men of exceptional talents like Shūa and Sogen.[7] After their deaths, during the Ōei era [1394–1428], Master Bontō may be regarded as the Way's beacon light. Toward the end of that era, we find men like Mashimo Mitsuhiro[8] and the priest Sōa of the Shijō [Jishū] school who were known for their refined sensibility and graceful diction.[9]

Following them in the Eikyō era [1429–41], the well-known figures were Priest Sōzei and Chiun. Having studied with Priest Shōtetsu for many years, both were also conversant with waka. It was from this period that the Way of renga, which had for some time lain in a moribund state, began to rise again.[10]

But now that Shōtetsu's influence, which shone like a light from the promontory of a great rock, has been snuffed out, the Way, alas, lies shrouded in darkness once more.[11] Henceforth, though a gifted man may appear in the world, what light can he receive, whose guidance seek, in order to illumine future generations? To behold the turbid waters of the Yellow River clear or be present at the appearance of a worthy sage happens but once in a thousand years, and who can remain to await it? I can only look back with a heart full of yearning for those bright times that now are past.[12]

All this idle talk of poetry, too, is but a passing amusement, of no more substance than the morning dew or the evening clouds before their fading. An ephemeral solace, indeed, for is it not said even of the Buddha's Dharma that to become wholly obsessed by it is to fall into the layman's confusion? Let us rather, instead of wishing enlightenment in the Way of Poetry, seek to comprehend the One Great Cause that is pressing upon us at this very moment, and liberate ourselves once and for all from the cycle of life and death![13] Frittering the time away in vain pursuits, we flounder before a path of such utter darkness that even a thousand regrets may not suffice to recall us to the light.

So it must be yet still, the more I ponder upon these things, the less it seems to me that any of the Buddhist laws and doctrines recognizes a permanent distinction between the layman and the saint. It is rather the man who, being deceived by the manifold teachings that are themselves devices, holds himself apart from the ten worlds before his very eyes and believes that he is transmigrating through the triple spheres—it is rather such a man who is a fool![14] And yet not even he can be following an errant path, since all things, when seen with enlightened eyes, share but one single nature. Inherently akin to the Great Emptiness is the human mind; no matter which Way one cultivates, no matter which teaching endeavor to follow, none will leave their traces upon it. [There are] a myriad phenomena in the triple spheres, and no master in any one of them. And the principle that good and evil are but delusions—a wonder of all wonders indeed! Yet, at the same time, all things exist immanently, just as they are—ah, how wearying to the soul is all this obstinate pondering! So be it. If it be so, so be it.

Some Verses by the Old Poets[15]

Verses in the Mode of Ineffable Depth

sode o kazasu wa
na no mi kasa nite

kasugano no
ue naru yama no
harugasumi
Junkaku

A sleeve held over the head
is a hat solely in name.

Spring haze
trailing over the mountain
above Kasuga Field.[16]
Junkaku

tomo ni sumamu
to iishi okuyama

naki ato ni
hitori zo musubu
shiba no io
Gusai

Deep mountain where you said
together we would dwell.

After your passing,
all on my own I twine together
the brushwood hut.[17]
Gusai

furusato to
naru made hito no
nao sumite

ogi fuku kaze ni
koromo utsu nari
Ton'a

Long after it fell
into an abandoned village, she
lived there still.

The echoing thud of the fulling hammer
as the wind rustles over the reeds.[18]
Ton'a

kaze no oto made
samuki yūgure

aki wa tada
hito o matsu ni mo
uki mono o
Gusai

Even the sound of the wind
is cold the gathering dusk.

In autumn when just
waiting for someone is itself
a miserable thing.[19]
Gusai

wakare omoeba
namida narikeri

Thoughts of parting
bring on the tears.

matsukaze mo
ta ga inishie o
nokosuramu
Gusai

Wind in the pines—
whose is the past it would
trace in the mind?[20]
Gusai

Verses in the Lofty Mode

kazou bakari ni
tsuyu musubu nari

Such that one can count them,
the dewdrops have formed.

harusame ni
moyuru warabi no
te o orite
Junkaku

Fingers curled,
new sprung ferns in
the spring rain.[21]
Junkaku

amari ni tōki
yama wa shirarezu

The mountain so far away
is beyond knowing's ken.

wakare uki
washi no takane ya
futachitose
Shūa

That desolate parting
on the high peak of eagles—
two thousand years ago.[22]
Shūa

michi shireru
fumi to yumi to wa
kikoekeri

For knowing the Way
of letters and the bow,
so famous.

karigane kaeru
mikazuki no mae
Ryōa

Wild geese flying home
before the three-day moon.[23]
Ryōa

hi o nagaku nasu
shiba no to no uchi

The days seem longer
within the brushwood gate.

kono yama no
nishi wa haretaru
sumai nite
Shinshō

Where I dwell,
the mountain is open clear
to the west.[24]
Shinshō

kawa no yodomi ni hana zo nokoreru	Where the river slows in a pool, they linger still, the flowers.
miyoshino no natsu miru made no osozakura Jūbutsu	In august Yoshino manifest into the summer, the late cherries.[25] Jūbutsu

Verses in the Mode of Meditation

maki tatsu yama no samuki yūgure	Cold the gathering dusk in the mountain where firs rise.
yukiyukite kono kawakami wa sato mo nashi Gusai	Trekking on and on, here upriver, there is not one single village.[26] Gusai
kore yori wa masaru kokoro ni nari ya semu	Could the heart come to feel even more exalted than this?
waga nochi no yo no aki no yūgure Ryōa	The dimming autumn evening is my world beyond.[27] Ryōa
nushi koso shirane fune no saokawa	Unknown its master, the punt with pole adrift on Sao River.
naraji yuku kizu no watari ni hi wa kurete Gusai	Over the Kizu Channel on the waterway to Nara, the day is fading.[28] Gusai
hito ni shiraruru tani no shitamichi	Known to everyone, the trail down the valley.
kaze kawaru tsumaki no yama no asayū ni Onaji	Morning and evening shifts the wind in the mountain where they gather kindling.[29] Gusai

oya ni kawaru ya
sugata naruran

tomoshibi no
akaki iro naru
oni o mite
Onaji

So changed from the father
is this visible appearance.

Gazing at a demon
red bright of hue in
the lamp flame.[30]
Gusai

Verses in the Intricate Mode

mizu ya noborite
tsuyu to naruramu

tamadare no
kogame ni saseru
hana no eda
Shinshō

The water—does it rise
to become the dew?

Drops beading
on the flowering boughs
in a small jar.[31]
Shinshō

sono na o mo
nushi ni toite zo
shirarenuru

shizu ga iori no
sono no miyamagi
Ryōa

As for the name,
you're sure to find out
by asking the owner.

Deep mountain trees in
the grounds of a rustic hut.[32]
Ryōa

kozo yori hito no
kazu zo sukunaki

konokami ni
toshi wa hitotsu no
ototo nite
Gusai

Compared to the year before,
fewer in number, the people.

To the firstborn
being a younger brother
by one year.[33]
Gusai

fune no uchi nite
oinikeru kana

ukigusa no
kakehi no mizu ni
nagarekite
Zen'a

Living on a boat,
I have grown old.

A floating weed
on the water flowing out
of the bamboo pipe.[34]
Zen'a

izuru yori iru
yamanaka no tsuki

Coming out but to go in,
the moon within the mountains.

saoshika no
iki ka to mieshi
kiri harete
Gusai

What seemed to be
the breath of the stag,
the mist is clearing.[35]
Gusai

Verses in the Classic Mode

tsuki koso muro no
kōri narikere

Upon the ice-storage cave,
the moon itself is glistening ice.

mikumano no
yama no kogarashi
fukisaete
Ryōa

Across the mountains
of sacred Kumano, a withering wind
sweeps clear and cold.[36]
Ryōa

furu ame mo
sa no mi wa moranu
matsu no kage

The falling rain
drips but scant and slow in
the pines' shadow.

koke ya iori no
noki o tozuran
Shinshō

Grows the moss in the hollow
of the cottage eaves?[37]
Shinshō

samuku kikoyuru
uranami no oto

Cold the lapping of
the waves within the inlet.

kamome naku
kono yo no ikani
fukenuran
Gusai

Seagulls cry,
how deep is the night
gone?[38]
Gusai

izumi suzushiku
matsukaze zo fuku

Cool beside the spring water
the wind stirs in the pines.

sumiyoshi no
ura no minami ni
tsuki fukete
Onaji

Far south across
Sumiyoshi Bay, the night
ages with the moon.[39]
Gusai

kieyaranu inochi ni hana o sakidatete	Before this life yet to expire, the flowers have gone on ahead.
kareno no tsuyu ni nokoru mushi no ne Ryōa	Cries of insects lingering in the dew on withered fields.[40] Ryōa

Verses in the Arresting Mode

kokoro takeku mo yo o nogarenuru	With what bold and intrepid heart did he at last renounce the world.
midorigo no shitau o dani mo furisutete Onaji	Shaking off even the clinging arms of his innocent child.[41] Ryōa
kinuta no oto zo takaku kikoyuru	How loud and clear sounds the beating on the fulling block.
aki samuki mine no iori ni hito sumite Ton'a	In the chill of autumn in the hut high on the peak, someone is dwelling.[42] Ton'a
kozue ni noboru aki no shiratsuyu	Climbing to the treetops, the white dew of autumn.
yama no ha no matsu no moto yori tsuki idete Shinshō	Beneath the pines along the mountain ridge, the moon emerges.[43] Shinshō
ima wa toshi koso tachikaerikere	Now it is that the very year turns around and comes back.
oinureba itokenakarishi kokoro nite Gusai	With a heart childlike as before, for having aged.[44] Gusai

hito no kazu koso amata miekere	So numerous in number the people to be seen.
somagi hiku masaki no tsuna ni te o kakete Onaji	Pulling the timber, the hands grasping the cord of twined ivy.[45] Gusai

Verses in the Categorical Mode

hito ni towaremu michi dani mo nashi	There are not even the paths for people to come and visit.
hana no ato konomoto fukaki haru no kusa Ryōa	After the flowers, the shade of the trees is thick with spring grasses.[46] Ryōa
mayoishi michi mo sato ni koso nare	Where I had lost my way turns out to be a village.
shiranu no no kusa karu shizu ni yukitsurete Onaji	Taken in hand by a peasant reaping grasses across fields unknown.[47] Ryōa
kakowanedo kiri ya magaki to narinuran	They are not confined, but the mists seem to have gathered thick as a wall.
shika no ne komoru yūgure no yama Onaji	Deer calls faintly secluded in the dusk-shadowed mountain.[48] Ryōa
kuyuru kokoro ni tsumi ya kiyura	From a remorseful heart the sins will dissipate.
mi o sutsuru shiba no iori no yūkeburi Shinshō	Evening smoke in the brushwood hut where one casts off the self.[49] Shinshō

harusame ni nareba urawa ni shio yakade	For the spring rain falls, no salt fires are burning along the beach.
fune ni tamareru mizu o koso kume Junkaku	They're busy bailing out water that has pooled in the boats.[50] Junkaku

Verses in the Mode of Singular Conception

namida no iro wa sode no kurenai	The hue of his tears is crimson on his sleeves.
nani yue ni kakaru ukina no tatsutagawa Shinshō	For what reason did such scandalous rumors rise, a Tatsuta River?[51] Shinshō
katae wa usuki mine no momijiba	Paler on the other branch, the crimson foliage on the peak.
hitogokoro omoi omowanu iro miete Onaji	The human heart in passion or dispassion will reveal its hue.[52] Shinshō
hirano koso kitano ni tsuzuku mori to nare	Hirano is indeed the shrine grove extending from Kitano.
naniwazu yori wa tōki tsukushiji Jūbutsu	But leagues away from Naniwa Bay is the Tsukushi highway.[53] Jūbutsu
matsu hikazu o ba hedatekinikeri	I number the days of waiting ever widening between us.
au made to iishi inochi no iki no matsu Gusai	Till we meet again, live, you said, so I breathe on, a living pine.[54] Gusai

kokoro yori
tada ukikoto ni
shiojimite

irie no hotade
karaki yo no naka
Onaji

My very soul has
grown seasoned in the brine
of unchanging sorrow.

As nettles growing by the inlet
the bitterness of this world.[55]
Gusai

Verses in the Mode of Preserving the Old

yuki o atsumete
yama to koso mire

fuji no ne wa
hito no kataru mo
yukashikute
Junkaku

I see it is indeed a mountain
that gathers to itself the snow.

The peak of Fuji—
even the tales people tell
evoke wonder.[56]
Junkaku

kami shimo o
sadamuru kimi ga
matsurigoto

taezu nagaruru
kamo no kawamizu
Zen'a

The upper and the lower
to determine is the sovereign's
way of governing.

Ceaselessly it flows,
the water of Kamo River.[57]
Zen'a

itsuwari ōki
fude no ato kana

e ni kakeba
hana mo momiji mo
tokiwa nite
Ryōa

Great are the deceptions
in the traces of the brush.

Set down in a painting,
even flowers and crimson leaves
last for all time.[58]
Ryōa

mijikayo nareba
inori-akashitsu

waga tanomu
yashiro no mina no
kamo no ashi
Ietaka-kyō

For the night was short,
I prayed until the dawn.

Legs of the duck, Kamo,
hallowed name of the shrine
I wholly trust to.[59]
Lord Ietaka

nado itazura ni tsutomezaruran	Why live thus unprofitably, not laboring and striving?
tera chikaki asuka no sato ni suminagara Jūbutsu	Though residing close to a temple in Asuka Village.[60] Jūbutsu

Verses in the Stark Mode

fushiogamu yori miyuru mizugaki	Visible the sacred barrier from where he lay prostrate in worship.
kore zo kono kamiyo hisashiki miyabashira Gusai	These be the very shrine pillars harking back to the age of the gods![61] Gusai
inochi omoeba sue zo mijikaki	When one reflects on life, the end is short, alas.
oi no ato furiwakegami no ko o mochite Jūbutsu	Past old age he has a child still wearing a pageboy haircut.[62] Jūbutsu
kanete toubeki hi o shiranu kana	One knows not beforehand the day it's likely to come.
hototogisu nakunaru tsuki wa sadamarite Shinshō	The cuckoo— the month it's said to sing is fixed, however.[63] Shinshō
yumiya zo kuni no osame to wa naru	With the bow and arrow lies the security of the country.
kakashi tatsu aki no yamada o kariagete Shūa	Gathering up the harvest in autumn over upland fields where scarecrows stand.[64] Shūa

naku tazu mo ono ga negura o isogu nari	Crying, the cranes also to their own roosts hurry back.
shimo okisoete kurenu kono hi wa Gusai	This day that ended, gathering layers of frost.[65] Gusai

The gods of Sumiyoshi and Kitano surely bear witness. I have written down these thoughts just as they floated up in my mind. Truly, they are even more uncertain than searching for the real in the darkness.[66]

COMMENTARY

Setting aside the immediately preceding verses in ten styles as a separate section added later, Chapter 39 is to all intents and purposes the conclusion of the treatise in its first circulated version. Read as such, it must be said that this ending, with its shifting and finally unresolved perspective, its negative valuation of the present state of renga, and its equally pessimistic prognosis about its future, is full of ambivalence. It is clear that Shinkei wished to take the long view and admit the truth that people are born with various degrees of talent, which is precisely why the Buddha invented various expedient devices in accord with their differing capacities. The fact remains, however, that he saw his era as one of poetic decline paralleling the alleged Counterfeit and Degenerate Age of the Buddhist Dharma. No doubt, this analogy was facilitated by the death only four years previous of Shōtetsu, the waka mentor to the leading renga poets, to whom he attributed the renaissance of the form in his own time. Moreover, Shinkei expressly declares the unimportance of poetry relative to the more exigent and transcendent claims of religious enlightenment. True, he seems subsequently to retract this construction of poetry as a vain pursuit by saying in effect that it is as such neither wrong nor irrelevant, because from an enlightened perspective, everything is interrelated, and everything counts in that all-encompassing vision. But this vision, which is incipiently that of emptiness and nondualism, precisely undoes all the painstaking distinctions that he draws in the body of the treatise. It is this contradiction between the positive value of differences, on the one hand, and their equivalence, hence emptiness, and simultaneously their absolute existence as such on a higher level, on the other, that remains unresolved in *Sasamegoto*, Part I. Thus, writing in 1463, while on a perilous mission in Wakayama, Shinkei ends on a tremendously fragile note. However, this same ambivalence became the occasion, the *innen*, so to speak, for beginning all over again two years later, when he was safely back in the capital and rethinking his concept of the nonduality of the Ways of Poetry and Buddhism, which is the distinguishing feature of Part II, containing what might be dubbed the "esoteric" or inner chapters of the treatise.

Part Two

FORTY

About *Hen-jo-dai-kyoku-ryū*

Regarding the Six Types and the principle of *hen-jo-dai-kyoku-ryū* about which I asked earlier, I remain uncertain that I have grasped these matters fully.

This is what former masters have said. The amateur who has only a vague understanding of these matters, though he may compose the most wonderful verses, is incapable of distinguishing among the styles of the anthologies of various ages, nor can he discern the good or bad in other people's waka and renga. That is why the *Kokinshū* made a point of explaining the Six Types. Likewise, in works like the *Meigetsuki*, Teika himself is said to have dealt with both matters in great detail.[1]

To discern the particular quality of another's verse is said to be far more difficult than to compose an interesting verse oneself. This is to say that the Way lies less in the making of verses than in the discipline of illuminating the intelligence of another.[2] I have previously written in general terms about the Six Types.[3] As for *hen-jo-dai-kyoku-ryū*, it refers to the five-part structure of the waka poem.

> *Hen* [Prelude] is the point when, having come to visit someone, you are still standing outside the door;
>
> *Jo* [Beginning] is the stage when you inquire whether he is home, and so on;
>
> *Dai* [Topic] is the part when you state the purpose of your visit;
>
> *Kyoku* [Statement] is when you reveal the matter of it; and
>
> *Ryū* [Dissolve] is when you bid him farewell and leave.

In renga, you should be able to sense this structure by reciting the upper and lower verses together as one. Lack of attention to this matter frequently results in absurd compositions, where the hat has somehow ended up on the feet and the shoes on the head. Those practitioners who do not grasp its significance do not care how twisted, bulky and cramped the sequence itself appears, since they are interested only in their own artificially contrived verses. They apparently have little sense for the expansive, smoothly flowing rhythm of the whole. What this means is that between any two verses, there must always be something left unsaid in the one that flows through in the other. It means to make the maeku your own and compose and recite your verse together with it.

Hen-jo-dai-kyoku-ryū may be said to be the Five Corporeal Parts of the waka poem, and the Six Types, the Six Roots that give rise to a manifold poetry.[4] If you are uncertain about these two, you will surely also lose your bearings when it comes to the Prelude-Break-Climax [*jo-ha-kyū*] structure of the myriad arts,[5] the Introduction–Proper Teaching–Propagation [*jo-shō-ruzū*] arrangement of the sutras and treatises,[6] the concept of cause and condition [*innen*], and of allegory [*hiyu*].

Now in the work of the old poets, we find lines like "long-enduring moon" [*hisakata no tsuki*], "foot-dragging mountain" [*ashihiki no yama*], "jeweled-spear road" [*tamahoko no michi*], "Nara of the good blue earth" [*aoniyoshi Nara*], and "august shining Kataoka" [*shinateru ya Kataoka*].[7] Or then again, there are lines like "mountain pheasant of the foot-dragging mountain" [*ashihiki no yama no yamadori*], and "village of the mountain pheasant's autumn's end / tail feathers" [*yamadori no aki no sue o no sato*], where an extra phrase has been inserted within the line but the meaning is in effect no more than "foot-dragging mountain pheasant" and "mountain pheasant's tail feathers." Such a phrase, called *hampi no ku*, creates a pause that draws out the line, making it supple and graceful.[8] The so-called cutting phrase [*kyakku*] is a similar device; however, it is a major flaw, because it retards the flow of sound and association in the poem. For example, in lines like "mountain pheasant's / in moonlight tail feathers upon the hill" [*yamadori no / tsuki ni onoe no*] and "autumn wind / through the pine needles drooping / sleeves blowing" [*akikaze no / matsu no ha shioru / sode fukite*], the natural flow of associations is broken by the insertion of "in moonlight" and "pine needles" in the middle, and therefore such phrases are considered an infirmity. This shows how important it is to be able to discriminate in all these matters.

COMMENTARY

This is essentially a further elaboration on Chapter 34's discussion of the structure of linking between any two contiguous verses in renga (*tsukeai*), but goes further in characterizing the movement of the whole sequence as a smoothly flowing *jo-ha-kyū* progression. As before, we are made to understand that linking in renga is an implicit (not overtly articulated) connection instituted over a gap or break, so that what seems on the surface to be *discontinuous*—as in waka with the insertion of "pillow words" or "pause words" that are not directly related to the statement—is on a deeper level continuous after all.

This continuity, clearly, is not a logical one; the tsukeku is not a discursive and rational elaboration of the maeku but rather its illumination. The analogy of the link to the Buddhist concept of causation (*innen*) as the interdependency of external cause and internal condition, or to the operation of allegory (*hiyu*) as a narrative or imagistic illustration of a concept, is an illuminating one. In all these cases, the point is not the image or the story as such but what it is pointing to. Thus, to link up to the maeku by simply adding more images or continuing a set plot or piling one idea on another without implicitly giving it a point is to end up with a "twisted, bulky, or crammed" (*kudakechijimi futomitaredo*) sequence; in sum, an incoherent and unintelligible babble.

Consequently, in renga, the ability to read, to appreciate, to discern "the good or bad" in others' works—in other words, the critical faculty—is here valorized over facility in composition per se. This is because, as an activity that fuses "reading" and "writing" in one and the same gesture of establishing a relation, renga is simply impossible without the supreme faculty of understanding.

FORTY-ONE

The Central Place of Grace [*en*] in the Poetic Process

Someone once asked a great master of former days, "Tell me exactly, how should one compose poetry?" To which the master replied, "Miscanthus reeds on a withered moor, the pale moon at dawn."[1]

This means to train your mind upon that which remains unsaid [*iwanu tokoro*] in the poem until you awaken to its chill and stilled aspect [*hiesabitaru kata*]. The verses of those who have arrived at the ultimate realm are in a mode none other than this. Thus to a verse that suggests "miscanthus reeds on the withered moor," they respond wholly with the mind of "the pale moon at dawn." Those who have no discipline in such matters will without doubt fail to grasp the import of such a link.

Again, when teaching poetry, the old masters would tell their students to keep the following poem in mind while mulling over their own.

honobono to	Dimly, dimly,
ariake no tsuki no	in the faint pool of moonlight
tsukikage ni	shadowing the dawn,
momiji fukiorosu	red leaves come fluttering down
yamaoroshi no kaze	in a gust of wind from the hills.
Minamoto Saneakira	Minamoto Saneakira[2]

This too means to compose your poem gracefully, in a measure long-drawn-out and tranquil, while setting your mind upon its aura and overtones [*omokage yojō*]. It means that those who would enter the Way must put the ideal of grace [*en*] at the core of their training. Grace, however, is by no means simply a matter of a charming refinement in the diction and configuration of a verse. Rather, it has its source in the heart of a man with but meager worldly desires, one who is keenly aware of the trackless passing of all phenomena and values human feeling so well, he would not begrudge even his own life in return for another's kindness. The verses of those whose hearts are "adorned," though refined in style and diction, would ring but falsely to the true ear. This is because the mind in such verses lacks spiritual clarity. Among the famous old poems and verses esteemed by their own authors, not even rarely do we find any that employ style as a mere adornment. The poems of antiquity, in particular, valorize direct, penetrating expression, so that their excellence is all but invisible to the adorned eyes of later ages.[3] Even Teika is said to have referred to Ietaka and himself as "makers of poems" [*utazukuri*]. "It is Jichin and Saigyo," he declared, "who are the true poet-seers [*utayomi*]."[4]

> Men choose profundity of mind; beasts choose shallow appearance, so it is said.[5]
>
> Layman Pang was content to weave twigs into baskets and sell them in the market.[6]
>
> Fu Yue was only an old man tilling the fields, yet he appeared in the king of Yin's dream.[7]
>
> Zhang Han resigned his position and went back to his village to fish for sea bream, yet he attained a name for wisdom.[8]
>
> Sima Xiangru did not own a single robe and walked around in a loincloth, but his ability could not be hidden.[9]

Still, as they say, if a ruler does not adorn himself, his ministers will not respect him, and so in the Way of Poetry, as well, the adornments of diction and configuration are essential.

COMMENTARY

This section, considered one of the most important in the treatise, includes the often cited passage on the medieval religio-aesthetic ideal of spiritual grace (*kokoro no en*), a quality of mind grounded in the existential knowledge of the emptiness and temporality of phenomena, and a consequent renunciation of mundane desire. Paradoxically, this consciousness is joined to a valorization of human feeling (*hito no nasake*), a bodhisattva-like compassion that is of higher worth than life itself. On the level of poetic style, such spiritual grace ideally manifests itself in the "chill and stilled" aspect of *sabi*, as symbolically evoked in images of phenomena (withered grass, the fleeting moonlight at dawn) at their most reduced or depleted stage, just before their disappearance. However, it is not the images themselves but the mind manifest through them that is in question. "That which remains unsaid" in the poem, its "aura and overtones" are the signs of a mind itself "depleted" in a meditation on emptiness, bereft of the discursive thinking of the rational mind, which is by definition a mind aiming to grasp its object. In other words, what manifests itself in the poem is a nondualism of mind and phenomena. The distinction drawn between "poet-seers" and "poem-makers" would seem to hinge on the absence or presence of the subject/object separation, and would be underscored again, much later, by the Bashō school's similar discourse on poetry that "becomes" (*naru*) as distinct from that which one "makes" (*suru*). The final qualification, where Shinkei seems to retreat from the unworldliness exemplified by the lives of the figures he cites, signals a characteristic turn in his mode of exposition. It marks his general position on various issues and reveals it to be one of an impartiality sufficiently absolute as to be open to what is required by a particular situation. In the mundane world of actual life, a leader needs the visible signs of superior status to be respected and therefore effective, and, similarly, poetry requires refined language in order to set it apart as a pedagogical instrument from the hurly-burly of mundane discourse.

FORTY-TWO

Verses on the Moon, Flowers, and Snow

It seems that no matter where the session one attends is held, people make a great fuss about verses on the moon, flowers, and snow and consider it highly improper for low-ranking persons to compose them.[1]

According to the accounts of our predecessors, this is something that came to be practiced only in our own time. Back in the days of the Nijō Regent [Yoshimoto], they say, the lowly young priest Shūa thought nothing of composing all of thirty-seven verses on flowers at a 1,000-verse sequence held among the high nobility and courtiers.[2] This is by no means a case of a poet overstepping his social rank; rather, in those days, it was the quality of the verse itself that was the determining factor. In assigning topics for poems, one did not give the moon, flowers, and snow to particular persons just because of their superior rank or venerable age. Moreover, such persons are not particularly desirous of composing auspicious congratulatory verses either; it is because these practitioners, being so inordinately concerned to flatter their superiors, invent such irrelevant rules, that the pure-mindedness of the Way has practically been abandoned.

> In Buddhism too, there are men who study the word [*ku*], and others who seek its intention [*i*].[3] Those practitioners who make such a fuss about particular seasonal images correspond to those who have attained only to the word.

> The unenlightened pay homage to the word, the enlightened to the intention.[4] The words are the teachings [*kyō*], and their intention is to transmit the ultimate principle [*ri*]. The teachings are provisional, the ultimate principle is what is truly real [*kyōgon rijitsu*].[5]

> To believe that phenomena exist wholly outside the mind is to keep turning round in the cycles of birth and death; to realize the One Mind [*isshin*] is to cast off birth and death for all time.[6]

> To penetrate to the source of the mind for even a single moment is to transcend life and death forever.
>
> The Reward Body that is born of action is a provisional fruit within a dream. The unconstructed Three Bodies [*musa sanjin*] are the true Buddha of the enlightened mind.[7]

Nevertheless, the poet who does not have the intention grounded in *dhyana* meditation and Buddha-wisdom, as well as the words indicating it, cannot be called a master.[8]

COMMENTARY

As in the previous section, a poetic issue, here the practice of reserving the highly prized verses on the moon, flowers, and snow to participants of high rank, turns into an occasion for defining poetic training as the cultivation of an enlightened state of mind. Where, before, the focus was on a sense of compassion founded on the realization of temporality, here it is the Tendai concept of impartiality or nondualism that is being advanced in order to criticize the common fixation on particular words and images as such, as well as the unfounded correlation between "beautiful" verses and superior social rank. Linguistic partiality and snobbery (or servility) are both seen as detracting from the "pure-mindedness of the Way" (*michi no makoto*). It is characteristic of Shinkei's dialectical mode of exposition that having argued the error of an inordinate fixation on words that are only contingent and provisional, and affirmed intention as, in contrast, the ultimate principle of the real, he ends by reinstating words, this time from the position of the middle way (*chūdō*), and with the explicit understanding that the good poet's language springs from meditation practice and the pursuit of Buddha-wisdom. From the perspective of the One Mind, no doubt, there is no separation between consciousness and language, but it takes practice to attain to that level of freedom, as well as to a disciplined indifference to the mundane social currency of linguistic usage.

FORTY-THREE

The Verse of Ineffable Remoteness (*Yōon*)

People in these rustic parts do not care that their verses are all flabby and awkwardly stumbling; being most impressed with skillfully painted surfaces, they brush aside those verses whose diction and figuration have a certain ineffable remoteness [*yōon*].[1]

A venerable old sage has said that the same holds true of all the arts, but in the Way of Poetry, in particular, one sets the highest value on sensibility, aura, and overtones [*kansei omokage yojō*]. In truth, the ineffably profound and moving resides precisely in what is left unsaid, in what is empty of overt meaning [*iinokoshi kotowari naki tokoro ni yūgen. aware wa arubeshi*]. In waka, as well, the so-called mode of ambiguity [*fumyōtei*] that is constituted solely of nuance [*omokage*] is the awesome mode of the ultimate realm.[2] Teika himself has written, "Verily it can only be the work of one man and none other."

"Are we to gaze at the moon and the flowers with the eye alone? To lie awake anxiously through the rainy night, and then stand before the petal-strewn drenched shadow of the trees, yearning after what has passed, this indeed. . . ."[3] How profoundly beautiful are these words of Kenkō's.

In the *Pipa xing*, after the sound of the lute has stilled and the moon sunk in the Xunyang River, it says, "At such moments, silence is more moving than speech"; this suggests a sensibility far from common.[4] The Chinese love poem says,

> Days of peach blossoms opening in the spring breeze,
> Season of paulownia leaves falling with the autumn dew.[5]

Waka and renga composed on Love should perhaps also be in this mode. It is the configuration of the allegorical or the metaphorical mode. Thus, a former poet has said that composing a Love poem requires a more intense concentration than three or four of the other [kinds] combined. This means that such poems on Love and Lament must issue from the very depths of the mind.

A Composition by Teika[6]

aki no hi no
usuki koromo ni
kaze tachite
yuku hito matanu
sue no shirakumo

On the thin cloak
of autumn sunlight, rippling,
a wind rises, without
a pause, the figure moves on
a cloud in the blank horizon.

A Poem by Priest Seigan [Shōtetsu][7]

aki no hi wa
ito yori yowaki
sasagani no
kumo no hatate ni
ogi no uwakaze

Frailer than the thread
the spider hangs suspended
the autumn sunlight
along a distant web of cloud,
a passing wind upon the grass.

These superior poems [*shūka*] are truly in the mode of the Dharma Body [*hosshin no tei*], manifestations of spontaneous enlightenment without instruction [*mushi jigo*]. Their meaning is difficult to grasp in the language of words. Likewise, the appearance of the heavenly maiden of Wushan[8] and the aura of the misty waters of the Five Lakes[9] are inexpressible in words.

He who would see me in the world of form,
Seek me in the realm of sound,
Is a man who walks the wrong path
And will not see the Tathāgata.[10]

Awakening to my original non-arising and non-ceasing,
I passed beyond the way of language,
Was set free from all chains of delusion,
And leaving cause and condition far behind,
Understood that my own void is equal to the great void.[11]

COMMENTARY

This chapter is deservedly considered the locus classicus for Shinkei's view of superior poetry and for a medieval hermeneutic that, paradoxically, locates the poetic sublime beyond language. But what does that mean? First, that it is neither the words themselves nor their particular arrangement, nor even the sense they are (or are not) making, but rather their evocation of the ambiguity of things that is in question. This is not, clearly, to reject the poem's diction, configuration, and meaning as such, but rather to pinpoint their combined effect as the place where value resides, since this effect, this evocation of the ineffable, requires more than a technical manipulation of language. Producing the ineffable is possible only through the mental/spiritual discipline and concentration of the seeker after Buddha-wisdom.

It is possible to mistakenly take the concept of ambiguity as a taste for a romantic nostalgia or idealized ethereality due to the invariable appeal of poets like Shinkei and Shōtetsu to the hazy form of the Wushan goddess for illustration. But the point, surely, is once again the temporality of phenomena, their relativity, and, consequently, their emptiness. A female figure turns into clouds, into rain; a love meeting might have been only a dream, but how to explain the charismatic impression indelibly stamped in the king's memory? The appeal of the strewn petals in the wake of the cherry blossoms' splendor, the impact of the charged silence after so much impassioned music in the *Pipa xing*, and the sorrow shadowing peach blossoms and paulownia leaves in Xuanzong's palace are as inevitable as the presence of death in life and possible only because of it. One is not possible without the other, and so they are immanently interdependent, and nothing is only what it seems to be.

The sublime, which is here equated with the ultimate Dharma Body (*dharmakāya*), is then the poem that is a meditation on emptiness, understood as the indeterminacy of thing and event, their porous margins, that which remains unsaid in the poem but constitutes its horizon. Without entering too deeply here into the illustrative poems by Teika and Shōtetsu, it will nevertheless be seen that, in both, the images react with each other to produce this sense of the uncanny merging of things through the agency of a mysterious wind. It is a matter of the poet's seeing beyond the fixed forms and sounds of phenomena, or the predetermined meanings of language (as the passages from the two sutras at the end suggest), and grasping the principle that undoes them.

FORTY-FOUR

Renga Rules and Buddhist Precepts: The Question of Morality and Freedom

The people of these rustic parts are very strict when it comes to the rules against similarity and clashing within specified intervals,[1] yet they seem unable to distinguish between the good and bad in the verses themselves.

It is said that the way of exercising the rules against similarity and clashing must depend upon the particular session. These rules represent discriminations made for the sake of convenience upon a base of nondiscrimination; they are in that sense like the prohibitions and precepts in Buddhism. But prohibitions and arguments about doctrine do not yet constitute the direct route [to enlightenment]. In the sutras, one encounters innumerable instances of license; the reason for this is that the right Way lies in the mind-ground [*shinji*] itself.[2] Consequently, in the work of poets who have entered the true Way, there are many things that do not adhere to formal rules.

> There are people who are lax about precepts and exacting in wisdom, others who are lax about wisdom and exacting about precepts.[3]
>
> A sharp mind, though non-Buddhist, will penetrate through the wrong views to arrive at the True Dharma; a dull mind, though Buddhist, will turn even the right views into the wrong teaching.[4]
>
> Precepts are at base like the empty space [*kokū*]; they cause the man holding them to stumble in confusion.[5]
>
> The man who has achieved insight into non-arising is he who has ultimately grasped the precepts.

Among the saintly reincarnations of the ancient past, those who placed the central emphasis on the mind-as-ground, ignoring precepts and prohibitions, are too many to be numbered. They are true worthies who were very far from taking the means for the intention.

> Bishop Gembin left his temple and was said to have become a common ferryman, and later even a caretaker of upland rice fields.[6]
>
> Priest Kyōdai kept to a strict diet of turtles, it is said.[7]
>
> Holding his child on his knees, Priest Jōzō caused the leaning stupa tower [of Yasaka Temple] to right itself through the power of his prayers.[8]
>
> The venerable Priest Zōga rode in attendance upon Archbishop Jie astride a cow, wearing at his side for a sword what looked like a dried salmon.[9]

Still, the precepts are the wisdom lifeblood of the Buddhist teaching; they represent the time-proven determinations of the various arts, the best means of ascending to the ultimate in the various religious sects.[10] Therefore one should not be lax in observing them. The five prohibitions in Buddhism are in effect merely another name for the five cardinal virtues of Confucianism.[11] Were benevolence, righteousness, propriety, wisdom, and trustworthiness to disappear even for a time, it would mean the destruction of the ways of civilization.

We are told that all the arts seem to have in common the three stages called [in Tendai] the seed, maturation, and achievement. Someone in the seed stage should not study the course meant for those in the stages of maturation and achievement. Confucius is said to have declared that even "at seventy, I do not overstep the rules."[12] This shows us that in renga, as well, one ought not to make light of the prohibitions against similarity and clashing.

Both in waka and renga, there are verses that are sullied outside yet pure within, and verses that are pure outside but sullied within.

Poems of Unadorned Configuration and Profoundly Compelling Heart-Mind

kashikomaru	Soul trembling in awe
shide ni namida no	before the god, my tears fall
kakaru kana	on the holy streamers
mata itsu ka wa to	as I take leave, not knowing
omou wakare ni	when, if ever, I can come again.[13]
Saigyō	Saigyō

ninaimotsu	Bearing on his back
zōki no ireko	a rough woven basket, feet
machi ashida	bare in cheap clogs,
yo wataru michi o	trudging his way in the world:
miru zo kanashiki	the heart wells at the sight.[14]
Jichin	Jichin

asatsuyu o	Finally to see through
hakanaki mono to	to the empty thing that is
mitsuru made	the morning dew,
hotoke no ani ni	my body has lived on to become
mi wa narinikeri	the Buddha's older brother![15]
Nakazane	Nakazane

These are poems that are, so to speak, sullied on the outside and pure inside. They are like patched cotton garments with gold concealed in the seams; wretched in appearance, they hold a treasure within. Again, there are many poems that are pleasing in configuration but wayward in mind.

oshikaranu	This useless body
miyama oroshi no	buffeted by the mountain winds
samushiro ni	on pallet of straw—
nani to inochi no	why does it drag on through
ikuyo hitorine	untold nights of sleeping alone?[16]

Such poems are innumerable; they are pure without and sullied within, like glittering brocade worn over some soiled thing. Putting on a clean appearance is the way of all men; truly uncorrupted minds are rare.

COMMENTARY

The issue raised here is a crucial one for renga, a collective activity of human interaction impossible without rules of procedure, and using a special poetic language that is unintelligible without the grammar or, more specifically, syntactical rules of progression assured by the rules. Yet Shinkei initially takes a position on a higher plane: "these rules represent discriminations made for the sake of convenience upon a base of nondiscrimination." That is, the predetermined procedures enable and facilitate the activity by specifying what is allowed or forbidden at every point of the 100-verse sequence. But they cannot cover every eventuality, since renga is precisely an art enshrining the specific temporality of its occurrence, an extemporaneous composition honoring the distinct minds of the participants and the potential for the unexpected each time someone responds to a maeku composed by someone else. Thus the rules have to be exercised with flexibility, tact, and a deep and wide understanding both of people and of poetry; their application must depend on the particular session—the specific progression reached at any point, the time and occasion, the participants, and so on, concrete temporal factors that will always exceed any previous determination. Since the aim of the activity is distinct from the rules established to enable it, to fixate on the latter is to "invert the proper order of things."

This is the same as to say that the Way of Poetry, which is in Shinkei's view identical to the Buddhist pursuit of wisdom, lies in a higher place than the decorum of social conformity or the seductions of technique. This is clear when, in the analogy of renga rules to Buddhist precepts, he cites several instances of license among sages intent on pursuing their aim of mental liberation even at the cost of violating mundane morality and social decorum. Lest the neophyte take these anecdotes as a call to sheer anarchy, however, he next takes the opposite tack to confirm the importance of the rules/precepts as a means of attaining the goal of wisdom, and deserving of respect as the time-proven discriminations collectively arrived at by past and present practitioners. This is the same as to say that the heritage of tradition has its place in renga as in any other sphere of human practice. Moreover, as Buddhist training proceeds by stages from the seed to its maturation by constant practice and the final attainment of the goal of freedom, so in renga, one must not blindly imitate the style of the masters—including their apparent license, presumably—without the wisdom they have attained through practice. The citation of Confucius's famous declaration, that "at seventy I could follow my heart's desire without overstepping the rules," confirms the concept of attainment (and the freedom that is its goal) as the culmination of a long process. It also reflects the earlier statement that "the man who has achieved insight into non-arising is the one who has ultimately grasped the precepts," in the sense, no doubt, that he understands why they are necessary yet also that they are provisional devices with no absolute existence, and so remains unfettered by them.

The final section illustrates the initial implicit distinction between adherence to the letter of the law and attention to the character of the mind applying it. The first three poems, distinguished by a directness of expression, are informed by piety and compassion. The last one, while skillfully employing the poetic technique of double meaning in three places, says nothing more than that the speaker feels cold sleeping alone. It may be "poetic" in its verbal skill, but curiously, it arouses no feeling.

FORTY-FIVE

Poetry and Zen Meditation, the Cosmic Body, and the True Word

In the sessions held here among country folk, a verse that cannot be understood by everyone alike, even if it is composed by a master, is regarded as to that degree inferior.

In all the arts, there is a vast difference between learning and mental application. You may spread out before your eyes all the teachings of the sages, the anthologies of the ages, but without experiencing for yourself the chill and the heat of it [*reidan jichi no tokoro nakuba*], you will not arrive at the ultimate. Priest Saigyō himself was reportedly always saying that "the Way of Poetry is wholly the practice of Zen meditation" [*kadō wa hitoe ni zenjō shugyō no michi*].[1] Verily, to attain the Way, there is no other teaching apart from the direct route of instantaneous enlightenment [*tongo jikiro*].

According to Tsunenobu, "Waka is the wellspring of reclusion [*inton no minamoto*], the direct route nurturing the awakening of wisdom [*bodai o susumuru jikiro nari*]. The principle of Suchness and the Real [*shinnyo jissō no ri*] is contained within its thirty-one syllables." The import of these words earned Teika's sincere praise.[2]

It is said that in old age, Lord Shunzei was beset by anxiety, thinking, "The Great Event comes to everyone without exception. I must be suffering from a blind delusion to spend all my time in poetry, forgetful of my imminent fate." While he was thus afflicted with doubts about poetry, there suddenly appeared clearly manifest before him the great god of Sumiyoshi, who smiled and said in ringing tones: "Do not belittle so the Way of Poetry. By means of it, you will without fail accomplish rebirth in the Pure Land. Poetry is a discipline in the direct route to enlightenment in this body [*sokushin jikiro no shugyō nari*]."[3]

In this way, the five-part structure of the poem [*hen-jo-dai-kyoku-ryū*] corresponds to the Five Great Constitutive Elements, the Five Buddhas of the mandala, the Five Wisdoms; to wit, the all-encompassing manifestation of the illumined cosmic universe.[4] Again, the Six Types of poetry [*rikugi*] are the Six Realms of Illusion, the Six Types of Action, the Six Constitutive Elements in unobstructed fusion; in a word, the Dharma Body in essence [*hosshin no tai*].[5] The so-called Initiation Rite to the *Kokinshū* is no different from the formal transmission of the secret teachings, which is held to be an important ritual in the Esoteric sect of Buddhism.[6]

In essence, the Way of Poetry is the True Word [*darani*] of our country. When you employ it as an instrument of vain sophistry, it means that your reading of the sutras and commentaries and your practice of Zen meditation are all equally blind delusions.[7]

COMMENTARY

This is possibly the most bewildering chapter of *Murmured Conversations*, given the greater than usual absence of explanations and links among its parts, or indeed between the question and Shinkei's response. It is also the chapter where Esoteric (Mikkyō or Shingon) concepts are most overtly foregrounded. The initial opposition set up between knowledge of the accumulated poetic anthologies and commentaries, on the one hand, and direct mental application, on the other, is not unknown in renga criticism. Nijō Yoshimoto had already sketched a similar dialectic in his treatises between learning and practice, or the ability to spontaneously compose interesting verses at the session itself, and placed the greater value on the latter. Shinkei delves deeper into the poetic process, however; his concern is to point to the nature of that process as Zen (*dhyana*) meditation, "the direct route of instantaneous enlightenment," and to the nature of the poem as an embodiment of the true aspect of Suchness (*shinnyo, jissō*), ultimate reality as understood in Mahayana teaching. Moreover, the chapter recounts Shunzei's miraculous vision, in which the Sumiyoshi deity of poetry confirms its status as a direct means of attaining enlightenment and rebirth in the Pure Land; in that sense, the anecdote functions as a defense of poetry against those who see it as mere empty words. Finally, and inevitably, an equation is posited between the poem as the Dharma Body (Dharmakaya) and poetic language as *dharani*.

As cited in the Notes, the immediate source for these mystical equations are the Esoteric Buddhist (Mikkyō) speculations in the Teika putative manuscript *Sangoki*, where the five lines (5-7-5-7-7) of the waka poem are seen as equivalent to the five constitutive elements—earth, water, fire, wind, and space—of the cosmic universe, and each in turn as equivalent to the five parts of the body—legs, belly, breast, forehead, and head. Again, the thirty-one syllables of the waka poem are seen as the thirty-two marks of the Tathagata, with the mind hidden within them counting as the thirty-second "syllable." In other words, the poem may be understood as a symbolic figuration of the cosmic body, or what the *Sangoki* calls its provisional body (*keshin*, *kari no mi*). Shinkei goes further, adding to this list of equations the Five Buddhas of the Esoteric mandalas and the five wisdoms (*gochi*) they represent. These five are Dainichi or Mahavairocana, embodiment of the Wisdom of the Nature of the Dharma Realm Body (*hokkaitaishō-chi*), surrounded by four other buddhas that manifest the other aspects of Dainichi's wisdom, namely: the Wisdom of Accomplishing Metamorphosis (*jōshosa-chi*), of Marvelous Perception (*myōkanzatsuchi*), of the Nature of Equality (*byōdōshō-chi*), and of the Great Perfect Mirror (*daienkyō-chi*). Taken together, as Shinkei states, the five-line poem is the "all-encompassing manifestation of the illumined cosmic universe," that is, the various marvelous signs of the Buddha-wisdom as it illumines anything at all in the universe. The same goes for the equation of the Six Types of Poetry (*rikugi*) with the six worlds or states of being (*rokudō*), the six types of positive action (*rokuharamitsu*), the six constitutive elements in unobstructed fusion—equal, in a word, to the Dharma Body.

This list of progressively wider equations then comes to rest, as an inevitable logical conclusion, on the construction of the poem as *dharani*. These are verbal formulations, chanted orally or contemplated silently, aiming to empower the subject to attain a state of mind equal to—or at one with—the wisdom of the Dharma Body, capable, that is to say, of conjuring up through the power of meditation the marvelous transformations everywhere manifest in the universe. This is not the place to elaborate further on the grand view of poetry and poetic process enunciated here. Suffice it to say that Shinkei's implicit reply to the question of why some masters' verses are incomprehensible is that they issue from a realm of wisdom unknown to the ordinary mundane mind, and that outside it, poetry is, indeed, no more than vain sophistry. This chapter may be taken as the locus classicus of Shinkei's equation of poetry and a Buddhist construction of the world.

FORTY-SIX

The Link Between *Maeku* and *Tsukeku*

It seems that poetasters from the middle period down to this day comprehend excellence to lie wholly in what is immediately pleasing and whose meaning [*kotowari*] is clearly perceptible in the single verse as such. They are apparently indifferent to the way in which it links up to the preceding verse [*maeku*].

A great poet has said that in waka, even the plainest poem will seem fascinating when it shifts away from and goes around its topic, while in renga even the most ordinary verse will seem absolutely inspired when seen in relation to its maeku. For instance, a statement like "The Great Buddha is in the southern capital [Nara]" is so simple even a three-year old can comprehend it. But imagine it as a quick retort to someone who remarks, on seeing an acolyte on his way to Kitano [lit., Northfield] Shrine, "The little monk is off to worship at Northfield," and it will seem quite smart. In waka, circumventing the topic constitutes a mode of composition, and one that requires great skill.

Seeing the Falling Flowers at the Imperial Apartments, by Lord Kintada

tonomori no	O gentle lads
tomo no miyatsuko	of the household royal,
kokoro araba	if you have a heart,
kono haru bakari	were it only in this springtime,
asagiyome su na	forsake the morning sweeping![1]

Composed Along the Banks of the Oi River, on "Crimson Leaves Floating on the Water," by Lord Fujiwara Sukemune

ikadashi yo	Raftsman, wait,
mate koto towamu	for I would of you inquire—
minakami wa	how strongly blows

ika bakari fuku / the windstorm, down the
mine no arashi zo / mountain slopes upriver?[2]

This mode of poetry on the natural scenery, when composed to suit the time and circumstance, can be deeply moving.

COMMENTARY

The implicit analogy that grounds this chapter is between the process of linking up to the maeku in renga and the relation between a waka poem and its assigned topic. This is to say that the topic is to the poem as the maeku is to the tsukeku. Shinkei's point is that as in waka that circumvents the topic (*dai o megurasu*), alluding to it indirectly instead of verbalizing the words themselves in the poem, in renga the link between the two verses is not visible or explicit but must be read in the taut space separating them. This is the same as to say that the single verse as such is, strictly speaking, meaningless apart from its maeku. It might be impressive or it might possess a clear significance on its own, but that fact only shows that it is not really related to the maeku. On the other hand, a verse that seems incomprehensible by itself, or not particularly significant as such, like the statement "The Great Buddha is in the southern capital," will assume its proper wit, here somewhat sardonic and *haikai-teki*, when understood as a kind of response to "The little monk is off to worship at Northfield." The taut opposition between "little monk" / "Great Buddha" and "Northfield" / "southern capital," similar to the work of the early Kamakura-Nambokuchō–period renga masters, announces that a link has been achieved.

As will be evident in the commentaries cited in the endnotes on the poems above and others like them, the orthodox practice in waka was to explicitly mention the words of the topic in the diction of the poem. However, the putative Teika treatise *Sangoki* and Imagawa Ryōshun's *Isshiden* (or *Benyōshō)* (1409) laud the subtle, evocative effect achieved by their deliberate omission and claim that this technique requires greater skill. It is interesting to note that in such cases of *rakudai* (lit., dropping [the words of] the topic), the link between topic and poem is only implicit and requires an active act of interpretation or decipherment, exactly as in renga. Equally notable is that in some cases, as in the two quoted by Shinkei here, the poems were composed right before the site of the scene being evoked, and consequently, there was no felt need to name the words of the topic. In other words, where referentiality was not an issue, it was deemed permissible to "circumvent" the topic. The conclusion to be drawn is that although the practice of composing by predetermined topics is commonly adduced as evidence of the nonreferential character of much waka poetry, it can equally be taken to evidence the opposite observation, namely, that waka was a practice of animating the referent or contextual circumstance, whether that be an actual scene and event or an imagined one as set forth by the *dai*. And that, ultimately, renga practice is not much different when the maeku is seen as the context that generates the tsukeku.

FORTY-SEVEN

The Nature and Goal of Criticism

It is the common opinion here among us country folk that the fellow who criticizes another's waka or renga even slightly is doing something foolish. If that is so, ought one to forget all about the good and bad in someone's verse after the session is ended?

People who think so cannot possibly be devoted to the Way. It is true of any activity that what makes no impression in the mind is quickly forgotten after the event.

> In Buddhism, debating about the sutras and treatises and criticizing the sayings of the ancient sages are an important means by which one arrives at the mind-ground.
>
> The purification of a Buddha realm and the conversion of sentient beings through teaching is the grand project of the Great Vehicle [Mahayana].[1]
>
> It is better to criticize the Dharma and fall to hell than merely to make offerings to numberless buddhas, so it is said.[2] For it is through the understanding of the Dharma gained thereby that salvation from arising-and-ceasing comes. For instance, one stumbles and falls to the ground, but it is also through the ground that one stands up again.[3]
>
> Good medicine is bitter to the taste but it cures the illness.[4]
>
> Falling on the inked line, the tree becomes building material. Bowing to admonitions, the ruler becomes wise.[5]
>
> Honed, even the dull sword will cut. Polished, even the stone turns into a jewel.[6]
>
> Because he listened to the admonitions of Di Huang, King Wen of Wei realized that Ren Cha was a wise minister.[7]

> The grand minister, cherishing his emoluments, does not admonish his lord. The petty minister, fearful of punishment, is silent about his faults.[8]

> Phenomena do not arise of themselves; they first come into being through circumstance [*en*].

An incalculably long time elapses before the instant of enlightenment, but from that instant even the long time before will seem no more than a moment. As the Buddha said, "I see that time in the remote and distant past as if it were this very day,"[9] and therefore when once you have turned the mind over from the errant path, there will appear to be no difference at all between the long period of training and this very moment of awakening.[10]

> The moment when your mind first awakens to the Way is already in and of itself true wisdom.[11]

> If you are skilled in overturning things, you are the same as a Tathagata.[12]

But there are people like the sutra-mouthing priests and obscurely meditating Zen monks whose long years of practice bear no fruit. Again, there are all too many in the various arts who have themselves fallen into a wholly wrong path yet persist in abusing others.

> The gentleman makes it his life's task to help others; the small man thinks it a virtue to cause others harm.[13]

> To remain unmoved through the vilest abuse and the most searing slander—this is wisdom.[14]

COMMENTARY

The unspoken concern behind the question is that in its nature as a collective activity, renga requires the exercise of tact and social decorum in order not to offend any member of the group. Criticizing someone's verse would therefore be considered "foolish" (*okogamashi*). More, if one takes literally Nijō Yoshimoto's view of renga as an activity aimed wholly at the enjoyment of the session itself (*tōza no ikkyō*), here too criticism would be irrelevant. Shinkei's response is squarely consistent with his distinct view of renga as a serious practice whose aim is the mental liberation sought by the Buddhist practitioner, here expressed as "the purification of a Buddha realm and the conversion of sentient beings through teaching."

Criticism is so vital to the Way of Poetry that Shinkei goes so far as to cite the striking slogan, "It is better to criticize the Dharma and fall to hell than merely to make offerings to numberless buddhas." As is well known, renga was held as a ritual offering (*hōraku*) to buddhas and native deities in order to gain worldly benefits such as a cure from illness or victory in an upcoming battle. Even offerings made for the salvation of one's soul apparently fell short of the buddhahood that was Mahayana Buddhism's goal. According to *Shasekishū* (see n. 2), the merit accruing from religious offerings might win one rebirth in heaven, the sixth state of being, which is one stage higher than that of the human person, but as the fruit of self-interested phenomenal outflows (*uro*), such a reward remains within the polluted realm and does not liberate one from karmic transmigration. In the same vein, in *Sasamegoto*, poetic training consists in cultivating the "mind-ground" (*shinji shugyō*) itself to attain the purified wisdom of perception that empowers one to produce a purified Buddha realm with each poem, so to speak.

Criticism, in other words, is here seen as the way to understanding; in particular, criticism is apparently encouraged because it shows a true concern for the matter at hand and can be the seed and circumstance that leads to mental awakening. Since ultimate reality, the Real (*jissō*) is just the way things are, one could sustain an injury in the course of thinking it something else, but that apparent harm also turns to benefit, in that one thereby comes to grasp the truth. For "one stumbles and falls to the ground, but it is also through the ground that one stands up again." And the Zen literature emphasizes that no one else but yourself can walk the apparently treacherous path for you.

The other citations from secular Confucian sources are meant to illustrate the rigorous effort or diligence (significantly, one of the "six perfections" in Buddhism) required to persist in the Way under the rigors of proper criticism, until the mind becomes as clarified as a stone polished into a jewel, or as acute as a honed sword. From then on, one ceases to be "overturned" by things, but rather acquires the skill of "overturning" them to produce benefits. Criticism (*hōhen*, lit., praise or blame), however, can also come from the desire for fame and profit, or even perverted pleasure in abusing others, rather than for the truth; such self-interested judgment leads only to harm and continued delusion for its subject. But the object of it must "remain unmoved through the vilest abuse and the most searing slander," for this is wisdom or courageous forbearance, which is another of the six perfections.

FORTY-EIGHT

Selecting Friends of the Way

I have asked you earlier about this, but there must be many instances when one needs to be selective in one's companions?

A wise man has said that one ought not to associate at all with people of mean human sympathies, those who behave violently, lacking tranquility in their hearts. Like mugwort among hemp plants, even the twisted mind will grow straight under the influence of friends.[1] Countless writings of antiquity have shown us the importance of this.

> The small man makes material wealth his treasure; the gentleman makes his friends a mirror [to emulate].[2]
>
> The company of gentlemen is like water, the commingling of small men like thick liquor.[3]
>
> From a wayward friend, one cannot part company too soon.[4]
>
> Encountering goodness is like savoring honey; meeting evil like grasping a flaming brand.[5]
>
> Bai Juyi collected Yuan Zhen's poems and wrote of him: "Your writings remain, your voice as pearls in each scroll; your bones might rot in the earth of the fields, but your fame will never be buried."[6]
>
> Sugawara Michizane gathered his [Chinese] poems and sent them from distant Tsukushi to the Ki Middle Counselor in the capital.[7] How profoundly moving are both these instances of friendship.

The man who has achieved understanding in any art is inevitably drawn, as to a fragrance, to a friend of deep sensibility, cherishing and yearning for him though the encounter was as fleeting as a morning beneath the flowers, or a night before the moon. Prince Shōtoku's words describing the Great Teacher Bodhidharma as "starving for nourishment on rugged-sloped Kataoka mountain" are said to allude to the Bodhidharma's languishing in sadness for want of a worthy vessel to receive his teachings in our country.[8] Priest Seigan [Shōtetsu] always used to say, "In wind and in rain, throughout the day and night, my thoughts are ever with my waka friends"—there is a depth of feeling in these words.

COMMENTARY

The issue of friends is first raised in *Sasamegoto* in Chapter 17, which concludes with a statement about the applicability of the twin concepts of dependent origination (*engi*) and absence of self-nature (*mujishō*) in the matter of choosing one's companions in the Way. Chapter 17 thus provides philosophical ground for affirming the decisive effect of the social environment in one's development. Here, the emphasis is the recognition and support that kindred spirits render each other; what friends have in common is expressed as deep feeling (*nasake fukashi*), a term whose usage in Shinkei's other writings points to a sense of the moving quality of things (*mono no aware*) in both their emptiness and interconnectedness, and equally to a feeling of compassion directed toward phenomena and persons alike. It is striking, moreover, that three out of the four relationships cited in illustration are Japanese, and three again are between poets: Bai Juyi and Yuan Zhen, paralleled by Ki no Haseo and Sugawara Michizane, and in Shinkei's own time, Shōtetsu and his disciples. The legendary case of Prince Shōtoku and Bodhidharma (see n. 8 for the narrative of their fateful encounter) makes the same implicit point that people of kindred spirit intuitively recognize one another and transmit each other's words and works, whether it be in the realm of poetry or religion. As we know, Shinkei saw no intrinsic difference between these two endeavors, seeing in them both the bodhisattva's mission to promote the wisdom and compassion that are also the roots of the deep human sympathy exemplified by these four relationships. It is instructive to note, indeed, that the fateful encounter between the foreign Zen patriarch and the Japanese prince is marked by a poem exchange, the form par excellence for expressing mutual *nasake* in traditional Japanese culture.

FORTY-NINE

The Close Link and the Distant Link

These days it seems that only waka and renga in the Close Link mode are being composed, and the Distant Link has become rare.

It is indeed all too true, as a former poet noted, that the Distant Link has been wholly neglected. Lord Teika did say that "the superior poem is to be found only in the Distant Link; it is quite rare among those in the Close Link."[1] Much has been written about the distinctions among the closely linked in conception, the closely linked in configuration, or again, the distantly linked in conception and in form. I shall dispense with them here.

The Close Link is based on form [*usō*]; the Distant Link on the formless [*musō*].

The Close Link is the teaching [transmitted in words]; the Distant Link is [the direct insight of] Zen.

The sutras of complete meaning [using words directly]; the sutras of incomplete meaning [using figuration as means].[2]

Conventional truth; the ultimate truth.

The gate of doctrine; the gate of emptiness.

If you did not set your mind upon enlightenment, how could you free yourself from the delusions [*shōji*] in the Way of Poetry? And yet even the highest enlightenment of the emptiness school [*kūmon daigo*] is considered inferior in that it is still based on a relativizing discrimination [*ushotoku*]. In the Tendai school, form *is* emptiness; the ten worlds—including the six worldly and the four saintly realms—are all ultimately one, undifferentiated and beyond form.

The *Lotus* [Sutra] says: "make the emptiness of the various dharmas your seat."[3]

It is said that of the fifty years during which the Buddha was preaching, thirty were spent in explaining the idea of Ultimate Emptiness [*hikkyō kū*].

However, in every art it is crucial to bear in mind that in the beginning you progress from the shallow into the deep, but having arrived there, you again emerge into the shallow.[4]

> Through the cause you arrive at the effect [the fruit of wisdom]; thereafter, through the effect you return to the cause.[5]

As the formless Buddha Body manifests itself in the form of the Reward Body in response to circumstance, so poetry based on form is one manifestation of poetry grounded on Emptiness. One should not, therefore, make light of its contingent efficacy as a means. The formal icons of wood and clay spring from the Great Wisdom; the sutra scrolls of paper and ink flow from the Dharma realm.[6] The single Great Cause for which the Buddha manifested himself in the world rose out of the Lesser Vehicle [Hinayana].

However, to teach and convert others by preaching a doctrine based only on conditioned discriminations [*ushotoku*] is an offense even more heinous than if you had plucked out the eyes of all the creatures of the three thousand realms.[7]

The mind of the true poet should not be fixated on either form or formlessness, the Close Link or the Distant Link; it must be like the undifferentiated mind-ground of a Buddha.

COMMENTARY

This chapter equates the Close Link / Distant Link distinction to a series of binary formulations taken from Buddhist philosophical discourse. It provides the conceptual ground for grasping a complex issue that was presented in Chapter 33 almost exclusively through concrete waka and renga examples, and may be considered the clearest indication, in that its subject is central to the essential nature of renga as *linked* poetry, of the basis of Shinkei's poetics in the Mahayana Buddhist conception of language and mind.

In brief, the Close Link (*shinku*) is defined as conventional linguistic usage requiring little or no interpretation, in that the words mean just what they say: it is the same as the use of language to teach the Buddhist doctrine using the conventional logic of discourse. In contrast, the Distant Link (*soku*) is generated by the emptiness of the dharmas, the view, exhaustively analyzed in Nagarjuna's *Chūron* (The Philosophy of the Middle Way; Skt. *Madhyamaka-kārikā*), that since all things arise wholly through causes and conditions, they are empty, void of an essential, immutable identity. And the same must go for language: the individual unit (phoneme, word, or statement) does not, theoretically, mean in itself; its semantic value is determined first by its place in the system of mutual differences that constitutes it, and second, by the specific discursive context in which it occurs. It is specifically this indeterminacy, what we might call the *musō*, or "formless," aspect of words in themselves when pried loose from the predetermined system of interconnected usages in which they are ordinarily embedded, that enables the Distant Link. The Distant Link is characterized by an apparent wide gap between maeku and tsukeku; the connection between the two verses is not immediately apprehensible using the meanings of words as set forth, for instance, in the ordinary lexicon, whether of everyday speech or in the dictionaries of renga associations. What transpires here is rather a metaphorical shift, a poetic event that uses the immanent "emptiness" of words, or their ambiguity, to effect a transference of semantic fields from one verse to the next. Because the metaphor is unprecedented, the link is not recognizable except by an interpretive reading, such as those required by "the sutras of incomplete [or indeterminate] meaning" (*furyōgi-kyō*, Skt. *neyartha*).

Does Shinkei then mean to valorize *soku* over *shinku*? If *soku* is taken as the mark of a searching mind, then the answer must be yes. For, "if you did not set your mind upon enlightenment [*satori*], how could you free yourself from the delusions in the Way of Poetry [*kadō no shōji*, lit., birth and death of poetry]," that is, the delusion that words mean as such, that linguistic categories are real, and relative discriminations absolute? Then poetic language would eventually stultify into orthodoxy and convention. The *satori* or Zen of language is most visible in the Distant Link, where words are set free to float and align themselves into new and unprecedented configurations.

Nevertheless, in a characteristic final note affirming an impartial attitude, Shinkei admonishes the renga poet to keep an open mind, limber enough to respond to every circumstance, and not become attached to either Distant or Close Link. The conventional language and logic of the Close Link also have their uses in a session; they could be what is required, depending on time, place, and occasion. What is important, to put it pragmatically, is that convention be recognized as neither more nor less than what it is. And such is possible only because one has made the required journey from the shallows to the deep and returned again to the shallow, but from a different, mind-transforming place. Returning from the journey, the "shallow," that is, the mundane, is also transformed; it becomes a purified Buddha realm, which, seen from the mind's eye, is what Shinkei characterizes as *aware*, "moving" in the sense of "marvelous," "numinous."

FIFTY

On the Issue of the Ultimate Style

Among the ten styles of poetry, which one should be considered as the ultimate?

In the past, when the Retired Sovereign [Go-Toba] issued an imperial decree to decide this same question with the great poets of his time, Priest Jakuren, the lords Ariie, Ietaka, Masatsune, and others declared the Style of Ineffable Depth [*yūgentei*] to be the most exalted one. His Majesty, however, along with the Regent Yoshitsune, the lords Shunzei, Michitomo, Teika, and others held that it is the Style of Meditation [*ushintei*] that is the most noble and consummate.[1] It is poetry in which the mind has dissolved and is profoundly at one with the numinosity [*aware*] of things; poetry that issues from the very depths of the poet's being and may truly be said to be his own waka, his own authentic renga.

A Poem by Lord Teika

harusame yo
konoha midareshi
murashigure
sore mo magiruru
kata wa arikeri

Ah, the spring rain:
in a whirl of withered leaves,
the winter shower
even after it had vanished,
could yet confound the senses![2]

A Poem by Priest Seigan [Shōtetsu]

mi zo aranu
aki no hikage no
hi ni soete
yowareba tsuyoki
asagao no hana

Void is the self!
As the autumn sunlight with
each passing day
dwindles starker in life
the morning glory flower.[3]

The initial line in each of these poems is truly beyond the imagination of the kind of author who must borrow another's voice. Without looking at Shōtetsu's poem closely, you might think that something like "the dew is so cold" [*tsuyu samumi*] would still have placed it in the consummate Style of Ineffable Depth, but it is precisely that first line as such that makes the crucial and marvelous difference. It shows the poem to be wholly the product of a practice located in the elemental ground of the mind.

The ancients recognized that there are people who have a penetrating eye for poetry, and others who don't. Certainly, those who have arrived at the mind's source have it. The voice hearers and condition perceivers of the Way, on the other hand, do not harbor the Great Doubt; consequently, for them, the Great Enlightenment is not possible.[4] In Teika's classification of the Ten Styles, we find the following examples.

kokyō ni haha ari shūfū no rui
ryōkan ni hito nashi bo'u no kon

In the old village a mother weeping in the autumn wind;
At dusk in the empty travel inn, the rain seeps into the soul.[5]

omoiideyo
ta ga kanegoto no
sue naramu
kinō no kumo no
ato no yamakaze

Recall, if you can,
whose was the promise that
ended in this trace:
the lingering mountain wind
in wake of yesterday's clouds.[6]

Teika classified these under the Demon-Crushing Style, a rather amazing thing to do, and baffling to the ordinary eye.[7] Again, Tsurayuki marked these two poems from the *Man'yōshū* as superior.[8]

hi kuretari
ima kaerinamu
ko nakuran
sono ko no haha mo
ware o matsuran

It has gotten dark;
I shall be going home now;
the children must
be crying, and their mother
will be waiting for me.[9]

sakagame ni
waga mi o irete
hitasaba ya

How I would love
to crawl into a wine jar
and be soaked through—

hijiki iro ni wa	not caring if my bones turned
hone wa naru tomo	the color of pickled seaweed![10]

These too do not strike one as superior poems, do they? Even Teika remarked that it is much too improbable.[11] Nevertheless, no doubt, Tsurayuki had his reasons for praising them as he did.

COMMENTARY

Shinkei's esteem for the poetry and criticism of Shunzei and Teika is such that it is tempting to conclude that he is in agreement with them in affirming *ushintei*, the Mode of Meditation, rather than *yūgentei*, the Mode of Ineffable Depth, as "the ultimate style." That would not be wrong, but it should be recalled that previously, in Part I, Chapter 7, he also confirms the overwhelming importance of *yūgentei*, and declares that "its mastery is the poet's most important task." This apparent inconsistency is resolved by noting that in the earlier instance, he defined *yūgentei* as poetry in which the heart-mind (*kokoro*) is paramount, and named it "the compelling beauty of the heart-mind" (*kokoro no en*). In other words, he understands great poetry primarily as a manifestation of spiritual grace and conviction, and so there is no substantive difference between *ushintei* and *yūgentei* in this regard. In this chapter as well, the focus in *ushintei* is the non-egoistic mind, one that has "dissolved" its own narrow concerns and relates to things in the profound spirit of *aware*, which here refers to a recognition of the numinosity of phenomena, the utter uniqueness of each and every thing in its very temporality and ontological dependency, a self-overcoming nondualism of "subject" and "object" that paradoxically enough gives rise to the poet's "own waka, his own authentic renga" (*waga uta waga renga*). From this point of view, "the ultimate" refers to the attainment of the illumined mind in meditation and is in this sense synonymous with *ushintei*.

The correlation of *ushin* with the mode of meditation is apparent in the poem examples from Teika and Shōtetsu: the first evokes the utter serenity of a state of samadhi in which the perceiving mind becomes indistinguishable from the object of its perception: the finely falling, soundless spring rain; and the second illumines the marvelous interdependency between the frail autumn sunlight and the increasing vitality of the morning glory, and discovers therein the emptiness of phenomena as such, namely, the first line, *mi zo aranu.*

That Shinkei is nevertheless open to other modes of "the ultimate" is clear from his citation of examples of poetry in the Demon-Crushing Style, which here are unadorned statements of truth, plain fact, or simply unmitigated desire. Again, they indicate that "the ultimate" names varieties of authenticity and conviction, whether in the expression of the Buddhist knowledge of being and nonbeing, Confucian filial piety, the emptiness of love, the ineluctable moral and emotional claims of the family, or the equally irrefutable wish for an intoxication beyond recall.

FIFTY-ONE

Discipline in the Mind-Ground

It is said of the Way that no matter how talented and keen-witted[1] a practitioner may be, he will not attain the ultimate if he neglects the discipline in the mind-ground [*shinji shugyō*].

There is no doubt that the man of utter dedication who has a lofty attitude to his art and aims for the realm of ineffable depth is of the greatest value in the Way. Lord Teika has written about this in great detail, saying: "Since ancient times, not a single one among those with only a superficial attitude to their art has ever won the world's praise. Practitioners who take the Way for granted will surely receive the punishment of both gods of poetry upon their heads."

His heart fixed on composing the superior poem, the Lay Monk Dōin went barefoot on monthly pilgrimages to the Sumiyoshi deity until he was eighty.[2]

Priest Tōren, wishing to consult someone about the question of *masoho no susuki*, borrowed a straw raincoat and set off for Watanabe in the rainy night, not waiting for the break of dawn. When a participant in the session remarked, "You're certainly in a great hurry!" he reportedly answered, "Does a man's life wait for tomorrow?"[3]

For many years, Minamoto Yorizane prayed to the deity of Sumiyoshi: "I offer my very life to be able to compose a superior poem!"[4]

Even Śāriputra, first in wisdom [among the Buddha's Ten Great Disciples], entered enlightenment through the power of faith.

When Prince Shitta [Skt. Siddhārtha] cast off his princely rank and went off alone into the deep mountains, it was an act motivated by awakened faith and the conviction of temporality. Consequently, he became the Great Teacher, leading us out of the three realms of illusion and illumining the Dharma World.[5]

When the venerable Kashō [Skt. Kāśyapa] went into seclusion on Mount Keisoku [Skt. Kukkutapada], it was because of his profound desire for the Great Event [of enlightenment].[6]

COMMENTARY

Talk of the ultimate style, whether in the mode of *ushin* or *yūgen*, inevitably leads to the issue of how one achieves it. Here, as in the preceding section, Shinkei underscores the decisive importance of discipline in the mind-ground (*shinji shugyō*) as the foundation for reaching the highest level of poetry. Such a discipline, which is the same as the pursuit of mental liberation (*satori*), requires dedication and great faith, since neither the outcome nor the span of a poet's life is certain, as Tōren well knew when he rushed off in the rain to pursue the question of a species of miscanthus grass, or Yorizane, when he offered his very life to achieve the ultimate. The desperation of these men who seek the heights of attainment, it is worth noting, could easily be construed as the kind of attachment that Buddhism admonishes against. But significantly, such deep-seated desire is legitimized in this treatise by the identification of its object with the single great event (*ichidaiji*) of religious enlightenment. This is the sole justification for the poet's engagement with language, which is otherwise no more than vain sophistry. The meaning of the deliberate juxtaposition of the anecdotal allusions to poets and to the buddha and bodhisattvas (Śāriputra, Kāśyapa) speaks for itself.

FIFTY-TWO

Orthodoxy and Plurality

Here in the country, the village old men and untutored youths tell each other that anything other than the orthodox verse style is not in accord with the Way.

This is what the old poets say. That may be true, indeed, with regard to the language of renga, but its mind and configuration ought to be of various kinds. The distinctions among the ten styles are based precisely on such differences.[1] It is said of authors who invariably say the same thing that they see only the finger pointing at the moon.[2] Again, in imitating the conception and words of others, they are said to be licking the spittle of the ancients, something our predecessors regarded as shameful.[3] Ryōshun declared that the author who limits himself to the orthodox configuration [*seichoku no sugata*] will never attain to the name of poet immortal [*kasen*]. However, he wrote, this is not to say that one lets the mind go in all directions at once. It must mean that to dress always in light yellow or unfigured white robes is regrettably to ignore the rest of the five colors.

> In Buddhism as well, the mind and its external manifestation differ greatly among the several sects. A single exclusive sect would not constitute a world. This is also the reason for the existence of the three teachings of Confucianism, Buddhism, and Taoism.

In this way the several sects are mutually different but their wellspring is one.[4]

COMMENTARY

Possibly one of the most attractive features of Shinkei's thinking, to this contemporary reader at least, is his advocacy of plurality and difference. This apparent valorization of originality is not, of course, as in the West, an outgrowth of an ideology of freedom and individual liberty. Rather, it is the logical consequence of the Buddhist philosophy of emptiness and temporality. Phenomena have no intrinsic and permanent nature; they are constituted by a dynamically changing network of circumstance. Since, for a theory that fully takes the factor of time and mutability into consideration, nothing is ever exactly the same as another thing, the kind of repetitiveness fostered by conformity to the orthodox style contradicts the Buddhist understanding of the truth about the world.

Difference, nevertheless, requires to be grounded in an implicit theoretical oneness, otherwise it could not be perceptible at all; it would be beyond cognition and understanding. Thus, the ten styles (and we should understand "ten" as merely a provisional number emerging from the historicity of Japanese practice) are theoretically the various manifestations of a cosmic impersonal Mind, just as the teachings of Confucianism, Buddhism, and Taoism are different philosophies generated by particular circumstances of time and place and ever subject to the vicissitudes of historicity. Linked poetry, which is precisely a genre enshrining the mutual correlation of things—another way of saying that nothing is ever absolutely different or the same as something else—is itself a concrete demonstration of the truth of the unspeakable One that "grounds" plurality through the endless play of language.

If we take the One as the moon of enlightenment, and in turn the "wellspring" (*minamoto*) or source of the various forms, then to invariably adhere to any particular form (style in this context) is, as Shinkei says, "to see only the finger pointing at the moon" or, more shamefully, to lick the spittle of the ancients. In this way, the pursuit of enlightenment in poetry means to achieve access to the source, the ultimate software, if you will, that drives the mind.

FIFTY-THREE

Reclusion

Among the poet immortals who feel deeply about the Way are those who, cherishing a life of tranquil reclusion, do not appear at the usual poetry sessions and are thus unknown to others. One hears that many more of their kind have arrived at the wellsprings of poetry than among those who have garnered a public celebrity. I find this baffling.

The old sages say that it is indeed among such persons that the true poet is to be found.

> It was to the householder Yuima's humble hut under the trees that the great saint Monju [Skt. Mañjuuśrī] came to bow in reverence.[1]
>
> At Kizan peak beneath a meager pine, Kyoyū heard the empty sound of the wind and awakened to the dream of human existence.[2]
>
> Content with only a bowl of rice and a gourdful of water, Gan Kai lived in obscurity amid the grass.[3]
>
> Sonshin was so poor he slept on a so-called straw bed—a mere bundle of straw laid out as a mat, yet he was a sage man.[4]
>
> To the very end, Kai Shisui refused to come out of the mountain and so perished there, but on the Cold Meal Day [of his memorial], cooking fires are dark all across the land.[5]
>
> Priest Saigyō cast himself as a beggar, yet a wise world illumined his name.[6]
>
> To the stone seat marking Kamo no Chōmei's hut, Retired Sovereign Go-Toba twice made an imperial visitation, so it is said.

For the true poet immortal, there is neither profit nor merit. He must be as the Buddha preached through the householder Yuima.[7]

> Without taking the scroll in one's hands, one is always reading this sutra; no words issue from one's mouth, yet one is everywhere chanting the scripture.[8]

> The gentleman will grieve for the Way, the small man will lament his poverty.[9]

Keeping their minds pure as the waters that reflect the moon, such persons truly find joy in the flower of the groves of poetry. Yet are there many who mock such graceful poets and hold them in contempt.

> Even the sweet dew may turn to poison; it all depends on the tongue within.[10]

> Not even divine power can overcome the force of karma, so it is said.[11]

> Clever is the hawk, yet is it mocked by the crow.

> Even the Buddha was derided by the five thousand arrogant priests.[12]

Again, there are in the world many poets of a wild and reckless disposition who take their own lives but lightly; one can mistake them for people who have cast off mundane desires. But in fact they are even worse than those who openly pamper their bodies and are wallowing in the senses. It is quite certain that they harbor numerous flaws in their hearts.

Similarly, we find among the diverse fields of the Way people of shallow motivation who profess a love for it and make a show of their efforts, while remaining uncommitted in their hearts. They are particularly numerous in the field of Buddhist practice.

> A man of old used to say that the true natures of such people are revealed by their words and works.

> Uncoiling but an inch of its body, the snake reveals its size; by a single utterance a man shows himself foolish or wise.[13]

> The humane are sure to be courageous; the courageous are not necessarily humane.[14]

COMMENTARY

This section foregrounds the contradiction between genuine attainment of the mind, such as that of the poet immortals (*kasen*), and public celebrity. Quite apart from the fact, abundantly demonstrated in our own time, that celebrity is a function of the limits of common understanding, and that high achievement is precisely located beyond those limits, Shinkei's explanation for this contradiction is apparently that true poets do not actively seek celebrity. "For the true poet immortal, there is neither profit nor merit. He must be as the Buddha preached through the householder Yuima." To practice poetry for fame and profit would be, in the language of the *Vimalakirti Sutra*, to remain within the realm of things that are conditioned in nature, whereas the realm of reclusion, the goal of leaving the householder's life, is precisely to abide in the unconditioned, that which does not depend on the dualistic partiality that generates all mundane desire.

It might be remarked that in this chapter, Shinkei is in danger of going beyond even the activity of poem-making, and that is in a sense accurate. However, his pronouncements here conform to his view of the highest among three stages of a poet's training (the so-called *keikandō*), when having reached technical as well as artistic maturity, the poet's concern turns to observing the Way, in particular, the attitude of impartiality that enables a responsiveness to all phenomena without bias (see *HF*, 198–200). "Keeping their minds pure as the waters that reflect the moon," persons who "truly find joy in the flower of the groves of poetry" can do so only on the basis of a serene disinterest, since any partiality immediately obscures the emptiness—an inward spaciousness—necessary for phenomena to register themselves on the mind with a new freshness and immediacy. The final allusion to Confucius on the inevitability of courage among the humane indicates that the pure-minded person does not set him- or herself above the mundane, but rather that true courage is possible only when one's conviction of what is right overrides all fear for the mundane security of the self, a fact that again underscores the need for impartiality.

FIFTY-FOUR

The Impartiality of Divine Response

To gather a band of wild fellows to string senseless words together—can such be a happy offering [*hōraku*] to the gods and buddhas? One should think that in such cases, it is rather the work of those who have achieved the Way that is certain to elicit the divine response.

According to the old sages, no matter how ill-trained and wild such practitioners might be, the divine response would not be any less. One receives an infinitely greater blessing in welcoming even one terribly sinful priest than in summoning the Buddha and his five hundred worthy arhants. Again, the teachings say: though he be a blind sinner who has broken the precepts and has a wife and children, accord him the respect due even to a Sharihotsu [Skt. Śāriputra] and a Mokuren [Skt. Maudgalyāyana].[1]

> The Buddha-mind is the mind of Great Compassion.[2]

> In the practice of the six perfections, the perfection of giving [*dambaramitsu*] comes first.[3]

However, it is also said that one must not worship at a temple built as offering by an impure priest.[4]

COMMENTARY

As is well known, it was a common practice throughout the medieval period to make offerings of poetry (waka, renga, *kanshi*) as well as Nō plays and other performing arts at temples and shrines as a celebration of the benefits of the Dharma (*hōraku*). In chapter 4 of the *Vimalakīrti Sutra*, Vimalakirti gives a rather eloquent reply to the question of what *hōraku* (the joy of the Dharma) means, and it is clear there that the term refers to the delight one takes in the pursuit, attainment, and practice of wisdom. As records of *hōraku renga* indicate, however, the practice of giving delight to the gods, buddhas, and bodhisattvas through artistic performance aimed to solicit their blessing of a specific request by the celebrant or the sponsor, whether this be success in an upcoming battle, the repose of a relative's soul, safe childbirth, recovery from illness, or some other such mundane request. Indeed, "linked poetry under the flowers" (*hana no moto renga*), held among the cherry blossoms in shrines and temples as a ritual to ward off pestilence, early contributed to the form's popularity.

This is the only section in the treatise where reference is made to a phenomenon that was taken for granted in its time but seems to us now to be an indication of the ritual aspect of the arts throughout the medieval period, their inscription in popular religious life. Shinkei's answer to the question of whether the poor quality of a performance would have an adverse effect on divine response is firmly in line with the opinion expressed in his major source, the *Shasekishū*, on the basis of a passage in the *Sutra of the Ten Wheels*, namely, that imperfect observance (of the precepts) is not to be condemned outright, but rather turned into the seed of future benefits, and that such an attitude is in conformity with the Buddha's compassion and with the fact that among the six perfections, that of giving and generosity comes first (see also n. 1). In sum, in this view, it is a mistake simply to condemn undisciplined practitioners of renga; one should rather build on their enthusiasm as an opportunity to teach them the higher reaches of the Way of Poetry, which is, after all, trained on the same aim of mental liberation, though for the many, it is achieved by stages. That this attitude does not signal approval of rule-breaking is evident in the final qualification, which forbids the worship of images and in Buddhist halls constructed from ill-gotten wealth. The difference would seem to be one of intention: there is less evil in having the right views but failing to uphold them due to human weakness than in a deliberate act of deception aimed at misleading others.

FIFTY-FIVE

Heredity, Social Status, and the Way

A man might have achieved the ultimate in the Way but the world will not esteem him if he is obscure and lacks social status. On the other hand, even the most incompetent fellow, when he suits the times and succeeds, moreover, to a famous house, is respected by all. It is disturbing.

> Yao was wise, but his son foolish, and Shun was wise, though his father was obstinate.[1]
>
> A house is not the house as such; it is that which is transmitted through it that makes the house. It is not the man as such that makes the man, but what he knows.[2] A person can enlarge the Way; the Way by itself cannot enlarge the person.[3]
>
> The gentleman is not ashamed of inquiring of those beneath him, and in doing so arrives at the Way.[4]
>
> A person's face is venerable because it manifests his/her mind.
>
> The Yellow Emperor believed in the words of a mere herd boy. Tokushū bent to the admonitions of a peasant.[5]
>
> It is said that even the scholar must listen to the teachings of the lowly.[6]
>
> Fishing along the shores of the Wei, Taigong Wang rode home on the right-hand side of King Wen's carriage.[7]
>
> The Minister Kibi was the son of a Lieutenant of the Left Gate Guards, but his reputation reached even China.[8]
>
> Ōe Tokimune was a mere grass-reaper walking behind a packhorse.[9]

A lowly beggar priest, Matsumuro Chūzan was appointed leader of the eight Hossō sects in the great debate.[10]

The conditions of body, mind, and environment plunging one into the deepest hell are wholly within the mind of the Most Venerable One; the Vairocana body-and-ground is not beyond a single thought of the deluded.[11]

COMMENTARY

Shinkei clearly does not dispute the accuracy of the observation in the question, namely, that worldly esteem is based primarily on an inherited name and social status, not genuine individual achievement. Therefore, his two initial citations are directed at refuting the ignorant belief in the prestige of inheritance, pointing instead to the fact that it is the individual rather than his father or his famous house that matters. In both instances, there is a recognition that the Way—the store of knowledge, practice, and insight into the principles of an activity, moral or artistic—is a formless abstraction unless embodied by specific persons and continuously renewed by their thinking and practice through time. The Nō artist Zeami's recognition of this principle is strikingly evident in his stricture that his teachings "must not be passed on to someone—though he be an only son—who is lacking in ability" (see n. 2).

In the same vein, Shinkei's reference to stories from China and Japan of obscure, lowly persons whose talents were nevertheless recognized by others just as keen-witted is meant to refute the common, unthinking worship of an inherited celebrity. The final citation from the Tendai treatise, *Kombeiron*, serves to wrap up the reply, which in this context must, I believe, be taken as a refutation of inheritance (that is, karma) as signifying any permanent identity. While karma might doom one to a lowly, obscure status in this life, because the whole cosmic universe is informed by the Dharma Body, the light of its wisdom penetrates even those lower regions and dissolves the ignorance that plunged one there. Consequently, fame and obscurity (believed to be signs of a good and bad karma) are mere worldly and provisional distinctions without permanent substance. The ascription of wisdom to beggar and peasant, herd boy and grass-reaper and the unexpected rise to high office of persons of lowly birth are no doubt meant to advance the view of an immanent equality among people, irrespective of their social circumstances.

FIFTY-SIX

The Mark of Temporality in Talent, Training, and Fame or Obscurity

Are there not many cases in which men who are approximately equal in studiousness and poetic ability much later prove themselves manifestly superior or inferior to one another?

Indeed, one sees in all the arts that a man who is in no way inferior from youth through middle age may suddenly find himself left behind by the others. When one neglects the Way, even an interval of two or three years can become as vast as the distance between earth and sky.

A long time ago, there lived the poets [Fujiwara] Takanobu and Sadanaga; they were equally famous, the one being the other's match in studiousness and ability.[1] However, Takanobu was appointed to court office, while Sadanaga donned the black robe, changing his name to Priest Jakuren.[2] Freed from court attendance, he applied himself to the discipline of poetry night and day, until the time came when, both now being full of years, people ceased to speak of them in the same breath. Takanobu was always lamenting, "If I had died early, my fame would have endured in the world; instead, I have lived on to see it dwindle away."[3] There is a depth of feeling in these words. As the saying goes, there are young shoots that early burst into flower, but having flowered bear no fruit.[4] This means that vigilance is the essential in any endeavor.

Truly, there are only too many who show unmistakable talent right from the start and are destined for a brilliant future, but are subsequently cut off before their time. Nothing is more dismal and frustrating than this.

Even the likes of Yan Hui and Li were unfortunate.[5]

Sweet springs quickly run dry; the straight tree is the first to break.[6]

The twice-fruiting tree withers; the heavily loaded ship capsizes.[7]

It is the way of the world that in living too long, even the good man turns complacent, exposing more and more disagreeable traits as time passes.

> Confucius also said, "Who has reached old age and does not die—he is as a thief."[8]

> Priest Kenkō writes, "At the longest, a man should live only until forty"—these are embarrassing words.[9]

Around the middle period, there lived the poets Ton'a and Kyōun.[10] Kyōun's station in life was apparently an unhappy one; he was said to be continually lamenting his lot. Told that four of his poems were to be included in the *Shinsenzaishū*, he bowed nine times before the editor and wept copious tears of joy. Then he learned that ten or so poems by Ton'a had also been selected, and the following day, he went and tore out his own poems from the anthology.[11] Perhaps Ton'a was a poet who suited the times. As the saying goes, "the times make the tiger or the mouse." When the time is right, even the mouse will be as a tiger, but when the time is wrong, even a tiger will be as a mouse. Thus do unfortunate men fall into obscurity like a distant gleam behind the clouds.

It is said that when the end was near, Priest Kyōun discarded all the poems and manuscripts he had written until then, burying them behind his old hut at Fujimoto in the Higashiyama hills. It is deeply affecting to reflect that he died with a lingering grudge against poetry in his heart. Again, of Priest Nōin, we hear that he too buried all his poem collections when he died at the place called Kosobe.[12] No doubt these men did not cherish any hope that future poets would understand their work. Their stories are truly pitiful.

> Men's praise or blame is not for the good or bad;
> fortune or poverty decides who is celebrated, who rejected.[13]

COMMENTARY

The interlocutor's question about the disparity that in time opens up between two people about even in ability and effort at the beginning of their poetic careers is clear, and the first part of Shinkei's response is also clear: the disparity results from Jakuren's withdrawal from mundane affairs in order to devote himself to his art; this is truly to make full use of one's time and to be fortunate enough to be able to do so. The remainder of the response then develops the leading idea—namely, the weight of time and circumstance—in a negative direction, in that neither of these factors is fully under our control. There is young talent cut down before its prime, on the one hand, and a lingering old age blighted by ugliness and shame, on the other. And, finally, not even the utmost dedication can conquer the force of circumstance: the condition of one's birth, one's distance from or proximity to power, the taste and fashion of the times. Hence those who by all rights should be celebrated may remain obscure and vice versa. For persons who suffer such misfortune, the man of sensibility can only respond with a deep sense of *aware* as compassion and sympathy, precisely because there is no outliving time. Here in these anecdotes of poets who perished with dissatisfaction (*urami*) in their hearts, who buried their poems in despair over gaining even future readers' responsive understanding of their work, we can measure the medieval sense of temporality and the aesthetics of the privative that arose from it.

In the *Sōkonshū*, there is a poem composed by Shōtetsu on 3.24.1452, occasioned by a visit to the site of Nōin's resting place in Kosobe, Osaka:

> Adjoining that village is a place called Kosobe. It was where Priest Nōin lived long ago; beside the rice fields was a grave where it is said that as he was dying, he had buried in great numbers the poems he had composed until then, including the waka manuscripts he owned. I looked for it last year when I visited the hot springs, but this time, after closer inquiries, I discovered that it was farther out, in a tiny spot surrounded by a bamboo fence, which was probably the garden of Nōin's house; someone had built a hermitage on its traces and was living there even now.

mukashi hito
tazura ni uzumu
utazuka ni
matsu no koto no ha
kuchi ya nokoreru

On the rice field
where he buried them long ago
in a poem grave mound,
do the waiting leaves of words
moulder as they linger behind?
(*Sōkonshū* 7455, pp. 752-53)

This piece seems a fitting epigraph to Shinkei's observation about the permanent disappointment of poets who died in obscurity, lamenting their world's indifference or inability to understand their poetry. In particular, the double valence of *matsu no koto no ha*, "pine tree" and also "waiting" in conjunction with *kuchi*, "decay, waste away," brings out the irony of poetic words that should be everlasting as the pine, and their mouldering entombment in the earth. This moving anecdote has a particular resonance when read in our own time of empty, inflated celebrity and the dire rarity of readers with sufficient judgment to appreciate the words of the past.

FIFTY-SEVEN

The Difficulty of Achieving the Way: The Transmission of Mind Is Beyond Language

The world is filled with practitioners of all sorts, but only a few, it would seem, have plumbed the depths of the Way.

According to our predecessors, those who excel in this Way number just one or two. If they wrote thus even in the old days, then such persons must indeed be rare. Rising higher even as one gazes, hardening even as one chips away—such is the Way.[1] Thus is it said to be a realm impossible to reach without the accumulated discipline of unflagging concentration.

> A thousand miles starts right underfoot;
> the tall mountain rises from a speck of earth.[2]

Similarly, in Buddhism, the voice hearers and condition perceivers have an understanding of what is called "temporality in [contemplation of] decay" [*hai'e no mujō*], the decomposition and rotting away of this body, but "temporality with each thought" [*nennen no mujō*], which permeates the mind before each and every phenomenon, belongs to the stage of the bodhisattva's Great Enlightenment. The poet of such an unflagging discipline must be practically nonexistent.

> The deluded are as the hairs on a cow; the enlightened as the fabulous horn of the kilin [Chinese unicorn].[3]
>
> Qu Yuan of the state of Chu declared that alone among all, he was sober.[4]
>
> Even the sages Yao and Shun had their worries, so it is said.[5]
>
> When the Buddha signified the hidden eye of the True Dharma [*shōbō genzō*], the ineffable mind of nirvana [*nehan myōshin*], Kasyapa's face alone broke out in a smile.[6] Truly is it a Way transmitted only from one mind to another, through subtle signs, of what cannot be established by language [*tanden. mitsuin. furyū monji*].[7]

COMMENTARY

Continuing from the initial assertion in the previous chapter that one attains excellence in poetry only by unworldly dedication, this chapter defines poetic training per se as an unflagging mental application (*nennen no shugyō*) equivalent to the enlightened state of the bodhisattva. This is apparently a realm that need not observe the material putrefaction of the body as evidence of impermanence, but holds to it rather as a principle or conviction in each and every moment of thought (*nennen no mujō*). It is, we might add, this consciousness of temporality, coupled with emptiness, that is understood in Shinkei's Buddhist-inspired aesthetics as the highest poetic realm, where each and every phenomenon without bias is endowed with *aware*, a moving quality, and also with *yūgen*, ineffable depth. In other words, the poetic way of seeing does not grasp the conventional materiality of objects—their arising, abiding, and ceasing—as the basis of a positivist or, at the other extreme, nihilistic perspective, but understands the temporality of phenomena in a "higher" sense as a manifestation of the mysterious principle (*ri*) that connects everything in the Dharma realm (*dharmadhatu*) such that every arising is at once also a ceasing, so that in truth there is neither arising nor ceasing, and there is only the inconceivable Middle Way.

The final reference to the iconic story of the Buddha's holding up a flower and Mahakasyapa, alone among the multitude gathered there, smiling in silent comprehension (the *nenge mishō* parable), functions in the context of this section to underscore the point that understanding the subtle Dharma, the true eye of the teachings (*shōbō genzō*), and, implicitly, the highest poetic realm of being and seeing, is only achieved through unflagging discipline of the mind, what Shinkei elsewhere calls *shinji shugyō*, training in the mind-ground, that is, Zen meditation.

The Zen school asserts that what has been transmitted and understood in the *nenge mishō* parable is beyond language and doctrine. The Tendai school to which Shinkei belonged, where Zhiyi's *The Great Stillness and Insight* (*Makashikan;* Ch. *Mohe zhiguan*) was the primary text for meditation, makes the same assertion. But it nevertheless recognizes the power of language as a skillful means (*hōben*) of bringing the practitioner closer to the brink of enlightenment, so to speak, like a finger that points at the moon without claiming that the two are the same. Mujū's *Shasekishū* includes the following passage clarifying the Tendai position, which may be defined as a nondualism of ends and means, the oneness of language and truth, such as is embodied in *shingon* ("the true word," or *dharani*), which a poem can also be. It is most likely one of Shinkei's sources in this chapter:

> The distinction between meditation [*zen*] and teaching [*kyō*] is on the level of method [*hōben*]. There should not be any difference between them at the time of enlightenment. Therefore an ancient sage has said, "The teaching is the Buddha's words, meditation is the Buddha's mind; for the several buddhas, mind and mouth correspond with one another." Again, it is said, "You know through practice, I practice what I know." The various teachings set up language to banish language; borrow thought to reject thought. Adhering to the potentiality generated by teaching, they distinguish between the raw and the ripe, advance from the shallow to the deep, enter the formless through form—these are the skillful means for reaching those of average or inferior nature. *On the other hand, ever since Kasyapa transmitted the Eye of the True Dharma* [shōbō genzō], *the meditation school* [zenmon] *has upheld single transmission, subtle signs, and noncstablishment of language* [tanden mitsuin furyu monji]*; from the start, it did not set up language or have any concepts or truths.* This mode goes beyond the skillful means [*hōben*] of the several doctrines. The various sects indeed speak of the ultimate place that lays waste all verbalization, that arrests the way of language, but they nevertheless set up a secondary level and recognize stages. Accordingly, they are likened to the turtle dragging its tail [leaving a trail back to the nest it would hide]. This is because language is hard to forget and consciousness easily roused. For this reason, Bodhidharma came to the West, spreading the direct pointing school, transmitting only the mind's sign. *By mind, one transmits the mind*; without setting up a gate, recognizing no path or rules, in touch only with the highest in one's nature. As an ancient sage says, "The gate-less is the gate of liberation, the thought-less is the thought of a person of the Way." Therefore, with regard to the methods of meditation and [verbal] teaching, superficially speaking, they are not the same, but from the standpoint of the True Word, one should not separate and distinguish between them. (Mujū Ichien, *Shasekishū*, VB.10, "The Avatars Delight in Poetry," p. 255; emphasis added)

FIFTY-EIGHT

Mutually Supportive and Antagonistic Arts

Among people who practice poetry, one finds many who study a mixture of other arts [*nōgei*] as well. Is this advisable?

This is what the old sages said. One does not expect the person who has achieved true greatness in one art to pursue others beside it. Nevertheless, the various arts are said to be either mutually supportive or antagonistic, so combining them is alright in the first case but bad in the other. For example, scholarship, Buddhist discipline, and calligraphy are all in a mutually supportive relation to poetry. *Go*, *shōgi*, *sugoroku*, and other forms of gambling constitute a mutually reinforcing series. The various wind and stringed instruments support the arts of dancing and chanting. The same relation exists among kickball, sumo, and the martial arts. On the other hand, *shōgi*, *sugoroku*, sumo, and such are in a mutually antagonistic relation to poetry, Buddhist teaching, and scholarship; combining them is very bad practice. The ancients here and on the continent only spoke in praise of "the man who walks alone"; therefore it is the man who brings his practice and study of one art alone to consummate mastery who becomes the mirror of the Way and earns the adulation of the world. Thus did our predecessors say.

COMMENTARY

The treatise is unequivocal in its opinion that greatness in an art (*nōgei*, *michi*) is achieved only by specialization. However, if one must cultivate other arts besides poetry, then they must be confined to those that support it, namely, scholarship (*gakumon*), Buddhist discipline (*butsudō shugyō*), and calligraphy (*shuseki*); together, these constitute in effect the art of letters. As we have seen, the idea of the oneness of poetry and Buddhism was widespread in the medieval period, when many of the poets were also monks.

Furthermore, to be a poet was also to be a scholar of poetry as a field of knowledge, with its own history, archives (anthologies and treatises), and traditions of practice. Thus, as distinct from specialization in the modern sense, the teachers and critics of poetry in premodern Japan were invariably practicing poets themselves; there was not yet the divorce between knowledge and practice that we see today.

It is noteworthy that gaming and the martial arts are here deemed to be in an adversarial relation to letters. It suggests that *bunbu ryōdō*, "the twin Ways of letters and arms," which is believed to have constituted an ideal in the Muromachi period, probably had its source among samurai who wished to identify themselves with the civilized arts of peace, and among the monks and poets who tutored them. Shinkei himself was one of the latter, but his censure of "the way of the warrior" (*mononofu no michi*) is unmistakable in some poems he wrote during the Ōnin War (1467–77).

FIFTY-NINE

The Practice of Poetry in Our Time

The State of Confusion in Modern Renga

These days there is virtually no one who does not practice the Way of Poetry. It is a remarkably thriving period, is it not?

This is how our forerunners tell it. A state of wild disorder, with persons of disparate levels shouting each other down. The confusion while the session is in progress, the superficiality, with people walking out early in disorderly fashion, as if it were the most natural thing to do. A host of Cao Zhis firing off verses in the space of seven paces, whipping up Mu Wang's eight swift horses—verily is it a sorry spectacle crying out for a sage of the Way.[1]

> When the fierce beasts are in the mountains, poisonous insects dare not rise. When a sage is present in the world, there are no men of crooked plots.
>
> When the hawk is asleep on his perch, the sparrows make boisterous noise.[2]
>
> The difficulty lies, not in doing, but in putting into practice. Again, the difficulty is, not in putting into practice, but in a consummate doing.[3]
>
> It is in the ages of counterfeit and degenerate Dharma teaching, long after the Buddha's death, that temples and icons multiply by the wayside. This is verily the age of the Dharma's destruction.[4]

So be it, and yet in a world of decline, when human nature itself is diminished from the past, those who cherish the Way in our time, though only in its external forms, must be deemed men of deep compassion.

> In a world bereft of the Buddha, treat the arhant as a Buddha; in times bereft of arhants, pay homage even to rule-breaking ignorant men in priestly garb—thus is it said.[5]
>
> A land lacking gold and silver deems even lead and copper to be treasures.

COMMENTARY

The first part of Shinkei's reply to the interlocutor's positive valuation of renga's overwhelming popularity in their time is characteristically critical, given the high ideals that he cherished for the Way. Fortunately for the modern reader, we are also treated to (no doubt an exaggerated version of) the conduct and atmosphere of renga sessions on the street, so to speak, which was apparently a rather informal, rough-and-tumble affair. Despite Shinkei's initial disdain, it is refreshing to catch a glimpse of the dynamic disorder that reigned there, the boisterous argumentation (about the rules, whether someone's verse conforms to them or not), the intense competition to be the first to fire off a response to the preceding verse, or even to keep taking a turn so as eventually to monopolize the floor. It all evokes an aggressive verbal exhibitionism or one-upmanship such as is not uncommon in our own day, whether in the academy or the talk shows of the mass media. If there were, and why not, among these Muromachi enthusiasts forerunners of the redoubtable Edo haikai poet Saikaku (1642-1693), famous for composing verses so fast that the calligrapher could barely keep up with him, we can imagine them straining against the leash of the rules, including that of decorum, and indeed producing verses that were more like comic haikai (haikai renga) than the sober (*ushin*) poetry Shinkei is advocating in this treatise. Since there are virtually no extant records of the sequences produced in these popular sessions, it is tempting to speculate that there was less interest in preserving them for posterity than in enjoying the one-time performance for its own sake and, further, that one did not need to be literate to participate in such sessions, as long as one could deliver verses in the 5-7-5– and 7-7–syllable meter. The liberating influence of wielding a poetic language that need not observe the social hierarchy inscribed in everyday linguistic usage is incalculable, both for commoners and for the serious poets of Shinkei's milieu.

That the treatise aims, not at criticism pure and simple, but rather at the reform of the popular version of renga by skillful means is clear from the next part of this section. In effect, the analogy of the state of the art with the lapse into "the counterfeit and degenerate Dharma teaching" (*zōbō. mappō*) after the Buddha Sakyamuni's passing renders it all the more imperative to cherish and esteem even such "rule-breaking ignorant men in priestly garb" (*hakai muchi no sōgyō*), that is, licentious poets, for their spirit of compassion (*nasake fukaki*) in abiding in the Way of Poetry, despite the lack of a "sage" to guide them. The qualified retreat from an initial extremist or positivistic position is characteristic of *Sasamegoto*'s nondualistic mode of thought and argument, as well as its essentially pedagogic orientation.

The Pedagogic Method Should Suit the Student's Capacity

In the Way of Poetry, as in Buddhism, the man of shallow dedication will not succeed, despite the clarity of the teachings of past sages. It is wholly a matter of whether or not the latent capacity (*kikon*) ripens into maturity. The light of the various anthologies through the ages is like Heaven's radiance impartial, but it will not fire the raw kindling of an immature mind. Likewise, it is said in Buddhism that the one whose mind is awakened for all time is he who has truly imbibed the teachings.[6]

> To see with the eye and be unable to grasp it with the mind—this is like carving on ice, like drawing pictures on water.[7]
>
> Even the good medicine of Giba or Henjaku will not cure the illness of one who, having no will to recover, does not follow the healer's instructions.[8]

In both Buddhism and Poetry, it is also said that in teaching practitioners of yet immature mind, one should adjust the method according to their level of understanding. For the father may be wise but the son foolish, and the master may have penetrated to the bone of the art but his disciple be unable to carry it on. It is like the old wheelwright who criticized Duke Huan of Qi's book-reading.[9] Thus did the Buddha also modify his preaching in various ways according to the disparate levels of people's understanding, as indicated in the terms "in accord with the [being's] capacity" [*zuiki*] or "the meeting of minds" [*tōki*].[10]

> The Buddha said, "Stop, stop, it may not be preached! My Dharma is ineffable and difficult to conceive."[11]
>
> The duck's legs are short, but to stretch them would be distressing; the crane's legs are long, but it would be painful to cut them.[12]
>
> The foolishness of expedient means [*hōben*] is right, the wisdom that is lacking in means is wrong, so it is said.[13]

Again, the Reizei Middle Counselor, Lord Tamehide, is reported to have taught the following.[14] Have the dull and soporific poet study those poems of stark, startling effect, while training the overly active mind on poetry that is calm and expansive. This is indeed a sage teaching.

> The sage has no mind; he makes the mind of others his own. The sage has no language; he makes the language of others his own.[15]

> By wholly contingent names and words, he draws and guides the sentient beings.[16]

COMMENTARY

The argument for a skillful—because compassionate—pedagogy here rests on the concept of the "latent capacity" (*kikon*) for enlightenment that beings possess, and of the operation of internal cause and external condition (*innen*) in stimulating that capacity to mature, on the one hand, and in responding to that stimulus, on the other. In other words, "the light of the various anthologies through the ages is like Heaven's radiance impartial, but it will not fire the raw kindling of an immature mind," where the poetic models are the external condition and the poet's mental maturity or immaturity (responsiveness or lack of same) the internal condition.

According to Kidō's gloss, the wood and fire metaphor here is culled from Mujū's *Shasekishū*, which explicates how the compassion of the buddhas and bodhisattvas operates in conjunction with people's latent good "roots" or capacity and their deep faith to save them from the bad effects of karma. The exposition begins by emphasizing the force of karma, which not even divine power can overcome, a fact that accounts for universal suffering. Salvation is thus essentially a collaboration between the sufferer and the savior; what the bodhisattva does is to reinforce the power of good roots and faith by shouldering the being's suffering as his/her substitute, thus allowing him/her to be more receptive to the Dharma that leads to salvation. In other words, the bodhisattva's compassion is merely the external or "supplemental condition" (*zōjōen*) that activates the internal cause, the latent capacity within the being's nature. While the benefit to be derived from it is certain, this compassionate divine response may be present or absent, or may be swift or slow, depending upon the being. Here Mujū resorts to the same analogy that Shinkei further extends into the realm of poetic pedagogy, defining that in effect as the dynamics of *innen*, or stimulus and response, in the teacher-student relation, which he also clearly views as a reader's relation to the text:

> Speaking in terms of analogy, the natural capacity of sentient beings is like wood, and the bodhisattva's compassion is akin to fire. By means of fire, brushwood burns; this external fire is like the supplemental condition. It has the power to awaken the fire within the wood. If only the external condition mattered, and it did not have to await the fire within the wood, the fact of burning would be the same, whether the wood be dry or raw. But in fact, because the process awaits the fire within, the time it takes to burn the wood varies. In this way, *the power of the buddhas' and bodhisattvas' compassionate vow is given in equal measure to all sentient beings, but when their natural capacity is in a raw [i.e., underdeveloped] state, there is no response. "Raw" means that there being an impediment, the "water" of sinfulness, the wood is not enflamed by the responsive fire of compassion. A heart of meager faith that does not quicken in wisdom and understanding—such is the veritable figure of rawness; it is like raw wood that does not catch fire.* Where faith and understanding are true, the divine response is not in vain; it is like dry wood that easily catches fire. The buddha-nature within the mind of the sentient beings is akin to the fire-nature in the wood. When the wood finally dries up, the good roots spring to life. The power of the buddhas' and bodhisattvas' vow is as the fire coming from without; while the fire-nature might be present within the wood, it does not appear without their skillful means. Again, the external condition of fire might be present, but it will not become manifest without the fire-nature within. In this way, though the buddha-nature is present, without the compassion and skillful means of the buddhas and bodhisattvas, it will not be realized in fact. This mutual working of internal cause and external condition is the universal principle of nature. (Mujū Ichien, *Shasekishū* 2.9, "The Bodhisattvas' Taking On of Suffering as Substitutes," pp. 126-27; emphasis added)

It is illuminating to discover, in Daniel Stevenson's essay on the *Mohe zhiguan* (J. *Makashikan*) and Tiantai history, that the concept of stimulus and response dynamics (J. *kan'ō*, Ch. *ganying*) is to be found in some fifth- and sixth-century Buddhist exegetical texts in China, and that it gave rise to a narrative genre, "tales of miraculous response" (*yingyan ji*) during the North-South and early T'ang dynasties, in which salvation centers around the "responsive interaction between devotee and sacred object," be it a sutra, bodhisattva, pilgrimage site, or relics and images.[17]

The discourse of responsive interaction is employed in *Sasamegoto* and Shinkei's other critical writings, not only in a pedagogical context, as here, but as the underpinnings of an ethics/aesthetics of the act of dialogical linking in renga, whereby the tsukeku is conceived as a response to the stimulus provided by the maeku, and the heart-mind (*kokoro*) is the active agency that holds the two verses in the tension of a mutual animation, such that each is meaningful only through the other. Ultimately, it may be said indeed that the whole ethics/aesthetics of *aware* as responsive compassion, as articulated in Shinkei's writings, would have been greatly influenced by Zhiyi's application of the *ganying* concept in the *Makashikan* and elsewhere, an issue, however, that calls for a whole separate essay.

It remains to notice that the teacher's (or bodhisattva's) responsiveness is manifest in the recognition of the student's specific level of understanding, and the skillful invention of a method that conforms to it, in order to release the "fire-nature in wood," so to speak. In other words, a skillful pedagogy is precisely the mark of compassion, and "the wisdom that is lacking in means is wrong," for it would only obstruct understanding. Thus do the deities and bodhisattvas "dim their light and join the dust" (*wakō dojin*) in order to succor beings. Finally, Taoist principle and the Buddhist discourse of compassionate pedagogy (which is, in effect, what *hōben* is) come together in the two highly "fragrant" quotations—because resounding with the unspoken logic of all that precedes them—in *Sasamegoto*'s renga-like method of explication. That the sage has neither mind nor language of his/her own is precisely the open-mindedness or impartiality necessary to enable the process of self-overcoming in a truly dialogical relation with the other.

The Three Buddha-Bodies, the Three Truths, and Poetic Levels

In waka and renga, there are poetic configurations akin to the Three Bodies of the Buddha—the Dharma Body, the Reward Body, and the Response Body, and to the Three Truths of the Empty, the Contingent, and the Middle.[18] The verse that is wholly open, whose meaning is directly visible as such, would correspond to the Response Body. Since this is like the Buddha manifesting himself in the five parts of the body and the six roots of perception, even the most dull-witted practitioners can apprehend it. The verse that exercises the imagination and is crafted with skill would correspond to the Reward Body. Awaiting the catalyst [*ki*] of a person's capacity, it may on occasion become apparent, but at other times remains concealed, so it cannot be distinguished except by persons of intelligence and understanding. The verse that is conceptually simple [*kotowari sukunaku*] yet feels ineffably remote and lofty [*yōon ni kedakaki*] corresponds to the Dharma

Body. It is not easily accessible, whether by sheer intelligence or diligent study. Yet it is clearly manifest to the eye of someone who has undergone the longest training, the utmost mental discipline. It is the measure of a mind abiding in the Middle Way of the Real [*chūdō jissō no kokoro*].

COMMENTARY

This chapter is for once comprehensible as such without too much explication; it simply equates three poetic styles of ascending levels of difficulty with the Buddhist three-bodies (*sanjin*) concept on the one hand and the Tendai three-truths nexus on the other. The first level, the Response Body (*ōjin*) in which the Buddha appears in a sensible phenomenal form according to the particular need of beings, would be the verse whose meaning is explicit, whether it is a descriptive evocation of a scenery or a statement of openly discursive logic; this would correspond to the provisional reality (*ke, kari no*) of mundane perception. The second level, corresponding to the Reward Body (*hōjin*), would be a verse that holds an unspoken symbolic significance that is discernible or not depending on one's level of understanding, which is also a measure of the merit accruing to the poet of advanced training; such a verse would correspond to the truth of the "empty" (*kū*) in that it cuts through the mundane meanings of words and causes the verse to assume a significance greater than the sum of its parts. And, finally, poetry corresponding to the Dharma Body (*hosshin*) and the Middle (*chū*) Way combines the simplicity of the first level with the complexity of the second. Outwardly serene and unexceptional, with no particular thought to transmit or feeling to express, like the poems in the mode of ambiguity (*fumyōtei*) by Teika and Shōtetsu cited earlier, closer analysis reveals it to be a subtle, dynamic, and multilayered figuration of a contemplative state of mind. The ineffable remoteness of such poetry is owing to the impression that the bounded, personal self is absent, or that the mind has wholly become one with the object of its contemplation.

SIXTY

The Question of the True Buddha and the Ultimate Poem

Practicing Buddhism in pursuit of the true Buddha, or undergoing the mental discipline of Poetry in order to realize its numinous ground, one wants to determine exactly the form of the true Buddha, the configuration of the ultimate waka or renga. Is this a foolish attitude?

What is called the true Buddha or the true poem cannot possibly have a predetermined configuration. It is merely a feeling [*kansei*] or an inner power [*toku*] that manifests itself according to the time and in response to circumstance. The heart of Poetry is like heaven-and-earth giving rise to teeming phenomena and a myriad mutations. Such is what is known as the Buddha's Metamorphosis Body [*tōrushin*].[1] And neither the Dharma Body nor the Tathagata in his Metamorphosis Body can possibly have one true form. Therefore it is said that only the poet who does not remain fixed in one place can have the right understanding. And thus it is that when someone asked an ancient master, "What is it that can be called a Buddha?" he replied, "The oak tree in the garden."[2] When this person asked the master's disciple what this could mean, the latter declared, "These words are not my teacher's. Stop slandering him!"[3]

> All the teeming phenomena and the myriad forms are the Dharma Body.
> Therefore I bow in reverence before each grain of dust.[4]

In Buddhism, the Wisdom School aspires to the lofty, while the Compassion School trusts in the miraculous grace of the lowly;[5] so too in the Way of Poetry, the School of Compassion apparently has its followers. They answer to those who chant the Buddha's name [*nembutsu*], a practice meant wholly for the simple and dull-witted, those most weighed down by the burden of ignorance. Putting learning and discipline aside, they set their tongues to chanting the holy name night and day in the belief that this is the ultimate practice. The Wisdom School, on the other hand, corresponds to Tendai teaching and its Zen meditation practice. However, where the goal of true reality is concerned, the lowly way of the Compassion

School is by no means different from the other. For example, on a cold night, one might wear silken brocade and another cover himself with patched hemp, but the two are the same in being enabled to ward off the chill wind. There is absolutely no difference once they have fallen asleep.

> The joy of nonaction in the Western Pure Land
> Is finally to float free of what is and what is not.[6]

Discriminating between this and not-this, raising delusory thoughts like waves before the wind, such a mind still remains in the eighth stage of consciousness. But once arrived at the tenth stage, the mind is no longer swayed by distinctions of good and bad.[7] When the wisdom that illumines the conjurer's tricks has awakened, and all blind delusions have been eradicated, then and only then do the sense fields and the intelligence, object and subject, cease to be delusions.[8] It is all entirely a matter of awakening to a compassion without conditions, of using circumstance to generate the space of an openness beyond form.[9]

COMMENTARY

This is to all intents and purposes the conceptual finale of *Sasamegoto*'s construction of a poetics based on a Mahayana Buddhist understanding of reality. The formulation of the initial question itself reveals Shinkei's thought to be a double articulation—Buddhism, poetry—of the same entity; each illumines what the other is about in a mutual exchange of languages.

In the preceding chapter, we have already glimpsed what seemed to be his final position in the definition of the highest level of poetic style, what we might call the sublime ("ineffably remote and lofty") as equivalent to the Dharmakaya, the "measure of a mind abiding in the Middle Way of the Real." For is not the middle way precisely the destination of the poet who has set his mind on enlightenment? That turns out, however, to be only a provisional determination, true if one is intent on establishing a hierarchy of styles, or mapping out the poet's progress from the shallow to the deep. But as is well known, in Buddhism, the deep is no place to tarry. Having reached there, one returns to the mundane with a more open mind in order to teach others the way out of suffering. In other words, just like a bodhisattva, who is a composite of wisdom *and* compassion, the true poet does not become attached to a particular style or poem configuration but must be sufficiently generous to respond in kind to a variety of occasions and circumstance.

Hence "only the poet who does not remain fixed in one place can have the right understanding" (*shōken*, the right view); this is to recognize the utter reality of time and change, and that each context requires its own response, and that compassion, or responsive understanding, is precisely this admission of the uniqueness of each context. And the Zen koan of the oak tree in the garden, which goes beyond the original formulation in the *Mumonkan*, indicates how the same words when uttered in another time and context no longer obtain, and it is a mistake to be fixated on the words themselves rather than their intended meaning. Without saying so, Shinkei implicitly presents the two-line verse that follows, an ecstatic affirmation of everything as the purified and all-embracing Dharma world (*dharmadhatu*), as the intended meaning of the koan. This is the same as to say that in the numinous light of an achieved liberation from mental bondage, later articulated as the dualistic formulations of positivist assertions of is/is not, good/bad, anything at all can be material for poetry, is "poetic" in the sense of the subject's ecstatic or holistic awareness of the interdependency of all phenomena, including that of the mind (here, *chi*, knowledge and wisdom) and its objects (*kyō*), which could not possibly be constituted as one without the other, and hence are one.

It is the paradoxical truth about the wisdom of nondiscrimination that it is not attained without an initial cognition of (conceptual, linguistic) distinctions as the means to go beyond them; hence the school of Tendai meditation, as set forth in *Makashikan*, trains the mind to see objects of thought from a dizzying array of different standpoints and levels, precisely to illumine their constructed nature and so transcend them. And it is only from this "transcendent" position that one can practice the "unconditioned compassion" (*muen no jihi*) that is clearly *Sasamegoto*'s central concern, because this compassion is precisely the ability to see beyond form or distinguishing feature (beyond race, class, gender, ability, history, etc.) in order to affirm the reality of local form and feature in a responsive understanding. Such is the lesson of the oak tree in the garden, which is the same as to see each hue and fragrance as the Middle Way. The other two-line verse in this chapter is from a hymn to the Western Pure Land and goes like this:

The joy of quietude and nonaction in the West
is finally to float free of what is and what is not;
With great compassion burning as incense the mind,
to wander in the Dharma realm,
A Buddha incarnate blessing all things equally,
with no partiality to any one.

SIXTY-ONE

The Ten Virtues

In the writings of the ancients, it is said that the man who does not possess all the ten virtues cannot truly become a sage of the Way.

INTELLIGENCE SKILL LEARNING MENTAL DISCIPLINE DEDICATION TO THE WAY CALLIGRAPHY A SAGE TEACHER DWELLING IN TRANQUILITY OLD AGE SOCIAL POSITION

In fact the perfect man who does not lack any single one of these is extremely rare. Therefore it is said that the sage appears but once in a hundred years, and the saint encountered but once in a thousand years. Whether in the great continent or in our country, to be born in the age of a sage of the Way is almost beyond the realm of possibility.

The Seven Treasures of a Dharma Vessel[1]

FAITH PRECEPTS SHAME REPENTANCE LEARNING WISDOM RENUNCIATION

The Seven Thieves in the Way of Poetry[2]

DRUNKENNESS DOZING IDLE TALK WEALTH LACK OF ARTISTIC SENSIBILITY FAST TALKING INTELLECTUAL ARROGANCE

COMMENTARY

The ten virtues (*jittoku*) enumerated here as the factors constituting a sage (*meisei* or *myōshō*) of the Way of Poetry or renga are a composite of various aspects: mental (intelligence), spiritual (mental discipline, dedication to the

Way), technical or professional (skill, learning, calligraphy, a sage teacher), and personal situation (dwelling in tranquility, old age, social position). They represent Shinkei's ideal of the poet who has achieved the highest state. Not surprisingly, intelligence and artistic skill here are dedicated to high religious principles. In his last critical essay, *Oi no kurigoto*, he reduces these ten qualities to only three: *suki*, artistic spirit; *dōshin*, dedication to poetry as a Way, an existential pursuit of authentic being; and *kanjin*, dwelling in tranquility. In this way, he distills the artistic, religious, and social aspects that constitute the Way of the ideal human being as poet. Needless to say, no one aspect can be isolated from the rest, since they are all mutually related; art divorced from the spiritual dimension is of limited value, as is artistic activity motivated primarily by desire for worldly fame and profit, which is the tendency precluded by the requirement of *kanjin*. As explained earlier in *Sasamegoto* (Chapter 20 above), *kanjin* does not have to mean actual physical reclusion, dwelling apart from others, but is rather a state of mind characterized by tranquil detachment from mundane concerns, such as desire for fame and fortune, that inevitably drive the person living in society.

It should be noted that these ten qualities are different from what is ordinarily understood by the term *renga jittoku* ("the ten virtues of renga"), where "virtue" is understood in the sense of "merit, benefit, or effect." This concept also arose from the Buddhist dimension of renga practice but within the popular milieu, perhaps the Compassion School mentioned earlier in contrast to the Wisdom School. Specifically, it is the belief in the miraculous efficacy of renga as a prayer offering (*hōraku*) and refers to renga's early connection with the worship of Tenmanjin (the apotheosis of the Heian minister and poet Sugawara Michizane), the deity enshrined in the Kitano Shrine, to whom the populace addressed requests of a secular nature, like prayers for a safe childbirth, recovery from an illness, higher social status, victory in battle, success in a commercial venture, and so on. The *Renga hidenshō* (Secret Teachings of Renga), attributed to Sōzei; *Bajōshū* (On Horseback), attributed to Shinkei; and Sōgi's *Tsukuba mondō* contain passages on the *jittoku* concept, with *Bajōshū* even mentioning "twenty-five merits" that were reportedly revealed to the superintendent (*bettō*) of Anrakuji in Kyūshū in an oracular dream.

The bearing of the *jittoku* concept in the popular milieu may be gleaned from the following text of the *Kitano tenjin renga jittoku* (The Ten Virtues of Renga [as revealed] by Kitano Tenjin), a calligraphic scroll attributed to Shinkei's disciple Kenzai, who held the shogunal appointment of Master of the Kitano Shrine Renga Meeting Hall; the scroll is still in the Kitano Shrine archives. Each virtue is illustrated with a 5-7-5–syllable verse, rendered in paraphrase below, by Nijō Yoshimoto (identified in the text as "Regent and Great Minister"), Gusai, and Shūa—the three major renga poets of the Kamakura-Nambokuchō periods.

One, attaining buddhahood without undergoing religious training. "That one has in truth no father and mother is because one is a buddha."
—Nijō Yoshimoto

Two, winning the favor of the deity without going on pilgimage. "Whose is the sword that splits the rock? The deity of Furu."
—Priest Gusai

Three, wandering through the four seasons without moving. "Parting the boughs, plum trees that I saw in bloom, to autumn leaves are turning."
—Priest Gusai

Four, enjoying blossoms and the moon unhampered by time or rule. "Lying at my leisure, the moon and the flowers for pillow."
—Nijō Yoshimoto

Five, viewing famous places without traveling. "Come from afar, which cloud would that be, on the crest of Fuji."
—Priest Gusai

Six, cherishing the past in the present without being old. "I sit facing it and marvel, is it indeed the moon on which he gazed long ago?"
—Priest Shūa

Seven, imagining parting from one's lover without being in love. "The moon must know—how it goes with the person I used to see."
—Nijō Yoshimoto

Eight, escaping the mundane world without renouncing it. "How admirable is the flowing water—unable to abide in this world."
—Priest Gusai

Nine, divining the mind of someone with whom one is not familiar. "Up to three times has he seen rebirth—on the hard rock."
—Nijō Yoshimoto

Ten, associating with high rank though one is not of noble birth. "It nourishes anybody's child, the lord's parental love."

—Priest Shūa

(Text in Ijichi Tetsuo, *Renga no sekai* [Yoshikawa Kōbunkan, 1967], p. 52)

As may be deduced from this scroll, the advertised merits of renga practice are based on its nature as a collective activity involving persons from different social classes and as a poetry grounded on a concept of existence as continuing change and variation. Put positively, the renga experience was seen as a means of mental liberation from the mundane circumstances of birth, status, and the fixed and specific constraints of time and space. As such, it is related to the principal teachings of both Zen and the Amidist sects. Ultimately, the gist of Shinkei's treatise and of the popularizing slogans of the *renga jittoku* is the same: mental liberation through poetic practice. The difference is that the treatise addresses the essential question of what is actually required to get there.

SIXTY-TWO

Epilogue

The rough generalities contained in these two volumes are truly of no consequence. The true Way of Poetry is wholly akin to the Great Void; it lacks in nothing and is in nothing superfluous.[1] Each and every human being finds his own way to perfection; ultimately, enlightenment does not depend on others.[2] When the Great Way is abandoned, there is benevolence and righteousness; when great knowledge appears, there are only great lies.[3]

> In the state of delusion, both right and wrong are wrong;
>
> Before the great awakening, both what-is and what-is-not are not.[4]
>
> Outside the truth that all the various phenomena [in their Suchness] are the Real [*shohō jissō*], there is only delusion.[5]
>
> The causes of a multitude of suffering are rooted in insatiable desire; in a word, destroy the roots.[6]

Jūjūshin'in Shinkei

COMMENTARY

How are we to characterize the bearing of this epilogue? Clearly, all the distinctions, categories, and admonitions expounded in the body of the treatise are here rejected from the perspective of an achieved state of enlightenment or wisdom where they do not apply anymore. In other words, such distinctions of right and wrong, of is and is not, are crucial as instruments (*hōben*) of teaching and conversion, but invalid outside of the pedagogical context that necessitates them. Generated by the mind, by language, and by circumstance, they are at base empty. The buddhas and bodhisattvas practice two things, according to the *Makashikan*: preaching and silence. The prose of logos is for teaching, and so is the figuration of poetry. The archives and precepts of the Great Way (Taoist or Buddhist) exist because the Great Way does not. The great knowledge systems are constructions, useful for those who can read, but instruments of deception for the ignorant who cannot discriminate. Everything can either be a path to wisdom or a means of self-aggrandizement. Knowledge is self-perpetuating, and so is desire; at some point, one has to step out of language and begin the path of self-transcendence by the uprooting of desire. Outside of language that is dedicated to wisdom, there is only the silence of understanding, and of the suchness of all the dharmas. In this way, the Epilogue is a summary of the essential principles of the treatise, and simultaneously a pointed admonition to begin the existential journey that is the Way.

Reference Matter

Notes

Introduction

1. For a literary biography, critical analyses, and translations of Shinkei's poetry, see Esperanza Ramirez-Christensen, *Heart's Flower: The Life and Poetry of Shinkei* (Stanford: Stanford University Press, 1994); hereafter *HF*.

2. A partial translation, comprising about half of the treatise's sixty-two chapters, has long been available in Dennis Hirota, "In Practice of the Way: *Sasamegoto*, an Introduction Book in Linked Verse," *Chanoyu Quarterly* 19 (1977): 23–46. The same appears in Hirota's later compilation, *Wind in the Pines: Classic Writings of the Way of Tea as a Buddhist Path* (Fremont, Calif.: Asian Humanities Press, 1995), pp. 133–69, striking evidence of the continuing effect of Shinkei's eloquent thought in the modern discourse of the Way.

Chapter One

Here and below, *SSG* refers to Kidō Saizō's edition of *Sasamegoto* in *NKBT* 66, the basis of the translation, and *SSG* rev. ed. to Ijichi Tetsuo's edition in *NKBZ* 51. Translations of passages from various primary sources cited below are mine unless identified otherwise.

1. "Waka Bay" (Wakanoura), on the coast of what is now Wakayama City, Wakayama Prefecture, has been famous in poetry since the eighth century because of its apt name. Shinkei was visiting his home village in Wakayama when he wrote the treatise.

2. An allusion to the proverb *kabe ni mimi ari*, "the walls have ears." It is used here, not in any literal sense, but merely as a figure of speech in keeping with the self-depreciating tone of the Introduction.

The reader should note also that this line is the source of the title *Sasamegoto* (lit., murmured words) rendered here as "murmured conversations," that is, words not suitable to be spoken out loud before the knowledgeable or the expert on the one hand, and the wholly ignorant on the other.

3. An allusion to the following lines from the *Anle ji* (J. *Anrakushū*), a doctrinal text of the Jōdo Shinshū sect of Buddhism written by Daochuo (562–645), one of the Seven Venerable Priests of the sect: "For each day and each night that passes by, every human being born into this world is afflicted with eight hundred and forty million thoughts—so says the *Jōdo Bosatsu Sutra*" (cited in *SSG*, p. 121, n. 6). This seems to have been a widespread belief in the Kamakura period; there are references to it in the *Hōgen monogatari* (Tale of the Hōgen War) (ca. 1219–22) and *Taiheiki* (Account of the Great Peace) (ca. 1346–72). See *NKBT* 31: 159 and 35: 281.

Chapter Two

1. An allusion to a passage in the Kana Preface to the *Shinkokinshū*, saying in effect that the human heart is an inexhaustible source of poetry: "No matter how numerous the stones one picks from the clean shores of Ise Sea, they never run out. Neither do the dense trees cease to grow in the timbered mountains of Izumi, though one may cut them [down]. This is the way of all things, and the way of poetry is the same." *Shinkokinwakashū zenhyōshaku*, ed. Kubota Jun (Kōdansha, 1977), 1: 82; cited hereafter as *Zenhyōshaku*.

2. In this chapter, Shinkei is referring to the Kamakura (1185–1333) and Nambokuchō (1336–92) periods, the initial stage of renga development, which culminated in the compilation of the first official anthology *Tsukubashū* (1356–57) and the consolidation of the rules of composition in the *Renga shinshiki* (New Renga Code) of 1372. "Deep recesses on this side and that side of Tsukuba Mountain" (*Tsukubayama no konomo kanomo oku nokorite*) is an allusive variation on *KKS* 1095, "A Song of Hitachi."

tsukubane no	Though there be shade
kono mo kano mo ni	*on this side and that side*
kage wa aredo	*of Tsukuba Mountain,*
kimi ga mikage ni	no shade is there to surpass
masu kage wa nashi	the gracious shelter of my lord.

Shinkei alters "shade" (*kage*), read also as "shelter" or protection in the poem, to the deep recesses (*oku*) of the mountain, which still remain unexplored. The relevance of this allusion also stems from the fact that renga was known as "the Way of Tsukuba" (*Tsukuba no michi*); Tsukuba Mountain was in Hitachi Province (now Ibaragi Prefecture). The renga poet and patron Nijō Yoshimoto (1320–1388) traced the beginning of linked verse to the *katauta mondō* (half-poems, each of 5-7-7 syllables, used in pairs for dialogues), which were among the songs included in the ancient chronicles. He wrote a renga handbook, the *Tsukuba mondō* (Tsukuba Dialogues), whose title derived from a pair of *katauta* from the *Kojiki* (712) and *Nihon shoki* (720), which he saw as the most ancient evidence of renga activity. This was a poetic exchange between Yamatodake no mikoto (the August Brave of Yamato), the legendary prince who subdued the eastern tribes for the ruling Yamato kingdom in Nara, and an attendant called *hitomoshibito* (man who lights the fires).

Niibari	Since I passed
tsukuba o sugite	Tsukuba and Niibari,
ikuyo ka netsuru	how many nights have I slept?
	(Yamatodake no mikoto)
Kaga nabete	Counting the days—
yo ni wa kokonoyo	of nights there are nine nights,
hi ni wa tōka o	of days there are ten days.
	(*hitomoshibito*)

NS 25, 26 in *Nihon shoki*, pp. 140–41; trans. W. G. Aston, *Nihongi* (Tokyo: Charles E. Tuttle, 1972), p. 207. See also *Tsukuba mondō*, pp. 34, 74, 76–77.

3. An allusion to the creation myth of Japan. The *Nihon shoki* (pp. 80–81) recounts how the primal couple, the male and female deities Izanagi and Izanami, stood on "the floating bridge of heaven" and thrust down a jeweled spear into the ocean, whereupon an island formed at the spear's point. They then descended and dwelt there, giving birth to the other islands of Japan. The Kana Preface to the *Kokinshū* says of the origins of waka: "This poetry first appeared at the dawn of the creation of heaven and earth," referring to the poetic exchange between

Izanagi and Izanami as they circled their new abode and pronounced themselves man and wife. *Kokinshū*, ed. Ozawa Masao, *Kokinwakashū*, *NKBZ* 7 (Shōgakkan, 1971), p. 49.

4. The *Man'yōshū* includes the following poem, of which a nun composed the first part and Ōtomo no Yakamochi the second part, also commonly cited as the first example of linked verse. The precedent for doing so was set by Rtd. Emperor Juntoku (1197–1242; r. 1210–1221) in his treatise *Yakumo mishō* (The August Eightfold Cloud Treatise) (1221), which includes a discussion of renga until the mid-thirteenth century, when the long form was already in existence. *Yakumo mishō* in Sasaki Nobutsuna, ed., *NKT* 3: 9–94 (Kazama Shobō, 1956), pp. 21–25.

MYS 1635. "A poem in which the nun composed the first part, and Ōtomo no Sukune Yakamochi, at her request, continued with the last part as a reply."

saokawa no	Damming the waters of
mizu o sekiagete	Sao River to flow into the land,
ueshi ta o	I planted this field.
[Ama tsukuru]	(composed by the Nun)
karu wasaii wa	The rice from the first harvest
hitori narubeshi	should then be yours alone.
[Yakamochi tsugu]	(continued by Yakamochi)

The exact significance of the poem is not clear, but most critics agree that it is couched in double meaning. Shimazu Tadao summarizes the various interpretations in the *Man'yōshū* commentaries and concludes that the metaphorical significance may be paraphrased thus: Nun, "How I have toiled and suffered to bring up my daughter!" To which Yakamochi, taking the role of a prospective suitor to the girl, replies with irony, "Certainly, the fruits of your labor [your daughter] should then belong to yourself alone" (Shimazu, *Rengashi no kenkyū* [Kadokawa Shoten, 1969], pp. 1–11).

In the *Man'yōshū*, this poem is preceded by "Two poems sent to a nun by a certain person," *MYS* 1633–34, which are evidently related to it, since they employ the same imagery of the toil of planting and its expected reward. However, it is not clear whether the "certain person" is a prospective suitor of the nun's daughter or in fact the father claiming his rights over the girl. At any rate only the previously quoted *MYS* 1635 need concern us here, and the fact that it was considered the earliest renga because it was composed by two people in dialogic exchange.

5. This refers to the rise of longer renga sequences, as distinct from the short, two-verse renga, during poetry sessions held by Rtd. Emperor Go-Toba (1180–1239; r. 1184–1198) in his villa on the Minase River. Here, famous poets of the age, like Teika and Ietaka, would compose linked verse as an amusing pastime after the formal rigors of waka composition. The participants were divided into a "serious" (*ushin*) group of courtier poets and a "comic" (*mushin*) group of lower-ranking nobility. The idea was for both groups to compose tsukeku to the same maeku, but the criteria for determining which was the better is not clear. It should be noted that linked verses from this period, although longer than before, were not continuous "sequences" as we know them from the Muromachi period. Known as *fushimono renga*, they were rather a series of fifty verse pairs incorporating antithetical topics like "Black and White," "Fish and Fowl," "*Genji* Chapter Names and Place-names," and the like.

6. This is the century with its midpoint some time during the reign of Emperor Hanazono (1297–1348; r. 1308–1318). The "two or three wise devotees" (*kashikoki irogonomi*) referred to are the best known among the renga masters of the late Kamakura and Nambokuchō periods, namely, Zen'a, Gusai, Junkaku, Shinshō, and Shūa. As their names frequently recur in

Sasamegoto and indeed Shinkei's other works, I have supplied whatever biographical data is available on them in "Biographical Notes."

7. Nijō Yoshimoto (1320–1388) was the greatest patron of renga in the Nambokuchō period (1336–92), a man whose literary and scholarly tastes, combined with his political stature, helped to raise the still *nouveau* poetic form to a position of social prestige almost equal to that of traditional waka. For more on him, see "Biographical Notes."

8. Gusai, or Kyūsei (ca. 1282–1376), the most famous renga master of the Nambokuchō period, was renga's first major poet. As the leader of the commoner renga milieu, he helped Yoshimoto compile the first official renga anthology, *Tsukubashū*, and to consolidate existing practice into the set of formal rules called *Renga shinshiki* (New Renga Code), which would govern renga composition until the Edo period. See "Biographical Notes" for a fuller account of him.

9. *Ima kagami*, ed. Itabashi Tomoyuki, vol. 53 of *Nihon koten zensho* (Asahi Shinbunsha, 1957), p. 325.

10. For an early standard source on Japanese *renku* (C. *lianju*) and renga, see Nose Asaji, *Renku to renga* (Yōshōbō, 1950), chap. 2, on *renku* from the Heian period, which includes extant pertinent documents.

11. For the pertinent citations from Teika's *Meigetsuki* diary, see Shimazu, *Rengashi no kenkyū*, pp. 42–45.

Chapter Three

1. The comprehensive source for modern *Tsukubashū* scholarship remains Kaneko Kinjirō's magisterial *Tsukubashū no kenkyū* (Kazama Shobō, 1965). This is not only a work of textual research; it encompasses historical studies of renga structure and aesthetics from the Heian period on, including *renku*; the social class composition of the various renga milieu; the link between renga practice and religious belief; and the organization of the anthology and sociopolitical circumstances of its production.

The earliest modern annotated edition of the *Tsukubashū*, which is based on a collation of several manuscripts, was edited and annotated during World War II by Fukui Kyūzō, with the aid of the then young scholars Kaneko Kinjirō and Ijichi Tetsuo, who traveled across the country to examine and copy old manuscript versions. This is [*Kōhon*] *Tsukubashū shinshaku*, published by Waseda Daigaku Shuppanbu in two volumes, the first in 1936 and the second in 1942. Ijichi would later publish annotated selections from *Tsukubashū* in *Rengashū* (*NKBT* 39) from 1960.

Chapter Four

1. Go-Toba (1180–1239), Teika (1162–1241), Ietaka (1158–1237), Hideyoshi (1184–1240), and other major *Shinkokinshū* poets had all died before the accession of Go-Saga (1220–1272; r. 1242–1246). During Go-Saga's rule as Cloistered Emperor, the *Shokugosenshū* (1251), an anthology of inferior merit, was compiled, showing how much contemporary waka as practiced by the conservative Nijō school of poetry had degenerated since Teika's time. See Robert Brower and Earl Miner's discussion of this school in *Japanese Court Poetry* (Stanford: Stanford University Press, 1961) (hereafter *JCP*), pp. 345–56.

The twin metaphor that Shinkei uses here to refer to the decline of the mind-heart (*kokoro)* and diction (*kotoba)* of poetry has been the cornerstone of Japanese literary criticism since it was first articulated by Ki no Tsurayuki in the opening lines of the Kana Preface to the *Kokinshū* (p. 49): "Japanese poetry has its seed in the human heart, which springs into numerous leaves of words."

2. Imagawa Ryōshun (1326–1420) is the great representative and vociferous defender of the Reizei school of poetry, which, along with the rival Nijō school, comprised one of the two mainstreams of poetic activity after Teika's death. The Reizei Middle Counselor was Reizei Tamehide (d. 1372), with whom Ryōshun studied waka for a period of around twenty-five years. On the Reizei school, see *JCP*, pp. 338–413; and see "Biographical Notes" s.v. "Ryōshun" for a fuller account.

3. In 1394, when he was thirteen, Shōtetsu (1381–1459), who would become the major waka poet of the Muromachi period, had occasion to meet Ryōshun and Reizei Tametada (1361–1417) at a poetry meeting sponsored by one of the shogunal administrators. Ryōshun accordingly became his teacher for the next seventeen or eighteen years.

An allusion is made here to the proverb "Kōri wa mizu yori idete, mizu yori tsumetashi" ("Ice is born of water but is colder than water"), which is to say that the pupil is taught by his teacher but later rises above him. In short, Shinkei means that Shōtetsu surpassed his master Ryōshun in the range and quality of his poetry.

4. "His light indeed shunned not the thicket" (*kano hikari ya yabu shi wakazarikemu*). This line means that the influence of Shōtetsu's teachings was not confined to the society at the capital but also reached poetic circles in the provinces. Shōtetsu was the first great waka poet sprung from the *jige*, or commoner, class, and his works and teachings thus had a wider circulation than would be possible for other waka poets, who traditionally came from the old aristocracy and would not have been comfortable teaching commoners. The line is an allusive variation on the poem below.

KKS 870, Miscellaneous. "Composed and sent to express his happiness to Isonokami Nammatsu, who was unexpectedly granted court rank, though he was not in service at the palace but was in seclusion in the place called Isonokami." Furu no Imamichi.

hi no hikari	*For the light of the sun*
yabu shi wakaneba	*shuns not the wild thickets,*
isonokami	even in Isonokami—
furinishi sato ni	this village grown ancient,
hana mo sakikeri	the flowers are in bloom!
	Furu Imamichi

Isonokami, now in Tenri-shi, Nara Prefecture, is associated here with the phrase *sono kami* (anciently, formerly), alluding to a period when it was supposed to have been the capital during the reigns of Emperors Ankō (r. 453–456?) and Ninken (r. 488–498?). By Nammatsu's time, however, it had become a rustic retreat, overgrown by weeds and tall grass. The *Nihon sandai jitsuroku* (p. 603) entry for 1.7.886 mentions the elevation of Nammatsu from the seventh to the fifth rank, thus placing him in the coveted courtier class. The poem is, of course, a grateful allusion to the Emperor's impartiality in rewarding a subject absent from his sight in rustic Isonokami.

5. For the circumstances around the compilation of the *Shinzoku Kokinshū* and Shōtetsu's exclusion from it, see *HF*, pp. 38–39; the chapter "Shōtetsu and Shinkei" is an account of the master-disciple relation between the two poets.

Chapter Five

1. The heron-crow metaphor derives from the saying *sagi to karasu* ([as different as] the heron and the crow) or *sagi o karasu* ([like making] a crow of a heron), which is to paint vice

as virtue, or pass off wrong as right. Not only is the quality of the poetry written by Gusai, Junkaku, and Shinshō as distinct from the compositions of the middle period as black is from white, but the implication is that the latter works are counterfeits of the genuine article. The crow is also a symbol for a professional, as opposed to the amateur.

2. That is to say, no matter how much one would like to believe that the poetry of the middle period is as good as that of the old masters, it isn't.

3. Japanese consonantal and vocalic rhyming are similar to alliteration and rhyme in Western poetry, and like them seem to have been adopted to reinforce the aural quality of the verse, as well as to effect a smooth transition from one line to the next. Consonantal rhyming (*goin sōtsū*) is the use of the same consonant, and vocalic rhyming (*goin renjō*), of the same vowel, in the last syllable of one line and the first syllable of the next. The first is alliterative in effect, and the second resembles rhyme. They are first mentioned in connection with linked verse in the *Chirenshō*, a handbook Yoshimoto wrote for his son Moronaga in 1374, containing his explanations of the different renga styles, as well as critical appraisals of the poetry of Gusai, Shūa, and more recent poets. The poet Bontō (see Chapter 25, n. 3) gives the following examples in his *Chōtanshō* (1390), a renga handbook in which he recorded the teachings of Yoshimoto.

Consonantal Rhyming:

yama tō**ki**	Far mountains
kasumi ni uka**bu**	set afloat in the haze,
hi no sashite	touched by sunlight.

Vocalic Rhyming:

sora ni na**ki**	Not from the sky—
h**i**kage no yama **ya**	sunlight striking the mountain
ame no uchi	in the falling rain.

Bontō discusses rhyming (*hibiki*, echoing) as devices to effect a smooth transition (*utsuri*) from one line to the next in what is called the "closely linked verse" (*shinku*) in both renga and waka (*Chōtanshō*, pp. 153–55). Note, however, that whereas Bontō sees rhyming only within the single verse, Shinkei observes its application across two verses, that is, within the context of the issue of linking maeku and tsukeku in renga.

Chapter Six

1. *Tsukubashū* (hereafter *TKBS*) 1024, Miscellaneous: Rtd. Emperor Go-Toba; 23, 24. "Renga of the fifth year of Kempō [1217], Fourth Month, Metal-Senior/Swine day." (Numbered citations from the *Tsukubashū* are from the abridged text edited and annotated by Ijichi Tetsuo in *Rengashū*; otherwise they refer to the complete but unannotated text appended at the back of Kaneko Kinjirō's *Tsukubashū no kenkyū*. Critical or evaluative commentary about the nature of the link between verses is based on my own reading, which expands or augments the primarily philological headnotes in the *Tsukubashū* text edited by Ijichi and the *Sasamegoto* text edited by Kidō.

Readers should remember that when renga verse pairs are quoted, only the name of the author of the *tsukeku*—the lower verse that links up to the preceding verse, or *maeku*—is given.

In this verse pair, the integral meaning of the maeku clearly hinges upon *futatabi*, and that is what Go-Toba has selected for expansion in his tsukeku. *Futatabi* (the second time; once again) in the maeku doubtless refers to the cherry trees in the mountain, which bloom later than those in the city or the lowlands. In other words, the poet fancies that their flowering heralds a second spring in the same year. Go-Toba picks up *futatabi* in the tsukeku and reinterprets it by means of an allusive variation to the following poem from the *Kokinshū*.

KKS 1, Spring. "On the day of the coming of spring in the old year." Ariwara Motokata [885–953].

toshi no uchi ni	*Within the old year*
haru wa kinikeri	*springtime has come!*
hitotose o	what now the year—
kozo to ya iwamu	shall we call it last year,
kotoshi to ya iwamu	or the new year call it?

Motokata's playful confusion, meant to suggest irrepressible spirits at spring's arrival, is occasioned by the fact that sometimes the Japanese civil calendar months did not correspond to the natural seasons, as is the case here, when spring has already come in the Twelfth Month, whereas it should coincide with the First Month of the new year. In Go-Toba's rereading then, the maeku's second spring is not due to the cherries' second flowering but to spring's early arrival in the old year.

2. That is to say, from an arbitrary viewpoint that ignores the meaning of the maeku, "Yoshino" would have been singled out because it is a "marked" word in the Japanese poetic lexicon, carries a weight as such, and the modern poet would no doubt have automatically linked up to it by the image of "flowers" (i.e., cherry blossoms) for which it is famous. Shinkei's remarks after each pair are all in this vein; his point is that a word that seems important as such is not necessarily so in the integral context of the verse. It is the total meaning that determines the relative weights of the words in the maeku, not an external scale of value judgments.

3. *TKBS*, Spring: Former Middle Counselor Teika; 1, 2. In the maeku, "bamboo grass" (*sasatake*) functions as a pillow word for "courtier" (*ōmiyabito*), based on its association with "bamboo grove" (*chikuen*), a word that in Chinese usage refers also to imperial princes.

According to Ijichi's commentary, Teika makes the connection through a somewhat well-concealed play on words. From "bamboo" in the maeku, he derives the word *yo* (each length of the bamboo trunk from one joint to the next), which then by further association yields the homophone *yo* (night) in the tsukeku (*Rengashu*, p. 44). However, in the context of *Sasamegoto*, it would be more relevant to observe the skill with which Teika has expanded upon the maeku's conception. He imagines the courtier in the bamboo grove as someone who went out hunting and was so enamored of the flowering cherry trees that he spent the night beneath them. Apart from this, there is also a tonal amplification from one verse to the next, in that the courtier's hunting costume is enhanced by the cherry blossoms. In this way, the expected criticism that neither "courtier" nor "hunting robe" has a word association in Teika's verse is blunted by consideration of its total conception, as opposed to searching for mere isolated verbal correlations.

4. *TKBS* 825, Love. Priest Shinshō; 17, 18. (Note the disparity in authorship here.) A *musubu fumi* (knotted letter) is a letter folded from the sides to make a long and narrow band, which is then loosely knotted in the middle or at one end. The name of the receiver, written in heavy ink strokes across the knot, was called the *uwagaki*. When knotted in the middle the *musubu fumi* was frequently used for love missives, as here.

As in the previous pair, the link is primarily conceptual or situational. Apart from that, the tsukeku picks up *musubu* (tie or knot) and makes an allusion to the knotted branches of Iwashiro's pine (*iwashiro no musubi matsu*), the focal motif in a sequence of four poems in the *Man'yōshū* (MYS 141–44), of which the following is the first.

MYS 141. "[One of] two poems composed by Prince Arima, then grieving over his lot, when he tied together the pine branches."

iwashiro no	At Iwashiro,
hamamatsu ga eda o	the boughs of the shore pine
hikimusubi	together I twine—
masakiku araba	if good fortune attends me,
mata kaerimin	I shall return and see them again.

The custom of tying together the tiny branches on the pine tree in order to signify a vow, or to ensure luck on a journey, is an ancient one. The belief was that if the branches stayed knotted, one would have success and good fortune; if they came untied, one would meet with ill luck. According to the *Nihon shoki* (2: 334–35), Prince Arima, an ill-starred son of Emperor Kōtoku (r. 645–654), was incited by Soga Akae to plot treason against the government of Empress Saimei (r. 635–661). Betrayed by Akae, he was put to death at Fujishiro-nosaka by the shores of Iwashiro, in Hitaka District, Kii Province.

The word *matsu* thus has two meanings in the tsukeku: "to wait" and "pine tree." The allusion to the *Man'yōshū* poem injects some pathos into the total poetic situation here, as one imagines the sender of the letter waiting in vain like the pine tree for Prince Arima's return. The link is in the nature of a narrative progression, or elaboration on the letter with no addressee in the maeku.

5. *TKBS* 11, Spring: Junior Second Rank Ietaka; 1, 2. "Composed for a 'Black and White' renga session during the time of Rtd. Emperor Go-Toba."

These two verses display the early renga practice called *fushimono*, whereby the poets adopt twin topics and incorporate each of these in alternate verses. Thus for the topics "Fish and Fowl," for example, the first verse would make an indirect allusion to the name of a fish, the second to some type of fowl, the third to a fish, and so on through the sequence. This is similar to the playful device in waka known as *mono no na*, examples of which make up the tenth volume of the *Kokinshū*. In this case, "tresses" suggests black, while the snows on the peak of Katsuragiyama are, of course, white.

In the maeku, *saohime no katsura* (Saohime's tresses) functions, through the duosemic pun, as a kind of pillow word and preface for Katsuragiyama, located on the boundary between Osaka-fu and Nara Prefecture, and famous as one of the sacred mountains of the wandering band of ascetics belonging to the Shugendō sect of Buddhism founded by En no Gyōja. Quite apart from the alternating allusions to black and white, connection is made here through the logical and syntactic continuation from *haru kakete* (to put on spring) in the last line of the maeku to *kasumedo* (albeit hazy, a reference to spring) in the first line of the tsukeku. The waka-like continuity is typical of the renga of the court poets.

6. The connection here pivots on the phrase *musubu no kami* (god that binds), referring to the god Dōsojin of the Izumo Road north of Ichijō Avenue in the capital, then popularly believed to bring men and women together—which is the point of the preceding verse. The same god, however, was also regarded as a patron and protector of travelers, thus the associated reference in the tsukeku. As in the last but one example, the tsukeku's conceptual interpretation of the maeku lends pathos to the situation, as the poet imagines the lover departing for a journey from which he may not return.

7. *TKBS* 1414, Miscellaneous, where this is attributed to Priest Seijun. Seijun (d. 1371), regarded as one of the pioneers of renga in Kamakura, is known to have composed the hokku for a 10,000-verse sequence held there in 1320. His poetry is included also in the *Shinsenzaishū*, the imperial anthology compiled at the request of the Shōgun Ashikaga Takauji in 1356.

Karakuni (China) in the tsukeku springs from *kurenai* (crimson) in the maeku through the mediation of the phrase *karakurenai* (China red, a deep crimson color). The link does not end there, however. The tsukeku also refers to the Chinese "peach-blossom spring" (*tōgenkyō*), Suzuki Hisashi notes in his modern Japanese rendering of *Sasamegoto* in Haga Koshirō, ed., *Geidō shisō shū*: 89–227, *Nihon no shisō* 7 (Chikuma Shobō, 1971) (hereafter "*SSG* Suzuki"), p. 97. It does seem more fruitful to assume that the poet is interpreting the scene being described in the maeku within the context of the famous *Taohuayuan ji* (Account of the Peach Blossom Spring) by Tao Qian (365–427), an enthralling anecdote of how a fisherman of the Taiyuan period (376–396) came upon a stream on whose banks peach trees were blooming in profusion, and rowing further discovered an ideal realm where people lived forever in harmony. See James Robert Hightower, *The Poetry of T'ao Ch'ien* (Oxford: Clarendon Press, 1970), p. 254; also Ikkai Tomoyoshi, ed. and trans., *Tō Emmei* [Ch. *Tao Yuan-ming*], *Chūgoku shijin senshū* 4 (Iwanami Shoten, 1958), p. 141.

Both *SSG* Suzuki (p. 97) and Fukui Kyūzō (*Tsukubashū shinshaku*, 2: 183) have observed that the visual quality of the poem is reminiscent of certain Chinese scroll paintings. I think it is certainly true that the natural setting of the first verse is framed into a picture in the tsukeku, with the addition of the tiny detail of a barking dog, which also figures in Tao Qian's account. The tsukeku excels in evocation, summoning up the Chinese poet's vision of utopia in a few simple words.

8. Source unknown. The maeku is presented as a kind of puzzle, in which the reader is provoked to wonder why the speaker is thus emphatically (the force of *koso*) rolling up his raincoat. The answer is, of course, provided by the tsukeku. It is perhaps because the link does not employ any conventional associations that Shinkei states that modern practitioners would see no connection at all.

Ryōa (fl. ca. 1333–1383) was Zen'a's youngest disciple and took his place as master of the *hana no moto renga* of the commoners. Like Gusai and Shūa, he was a frequent participant in the sessions at the residences of Nijō Yoshimoto and Cloistered Prince Son'in. He is known to have received the secret traditions of the *Kokinshū* from Yoshimoto in 1373. His style is characterized by ingenuity and a haikai-like flavor of everyday life and humor. There are twenty verses by him in the *Tsukubashū*. Kidō, *RS* 1: 266–73.

9. In the *Renga entokushō*, a renga treatise dealing with the various techniques of linking, Kenzai (1452–1510) writes of this very same tsukeku: "One must realize that in the ferry that experiences shock as it rams against the riverbank, there is also a horse. It is thoroughly foolish to say that there is no association here for the word 'horse'" (p. 124). Since Kenzai was a disciple of Shinkei's, it is almost certain that he is transmitting his teacher's interpretation here. See "Biographical Notes" on Kenzai.

Chapter Seven

1. Of the seven poems referenced here, the first five are among those cited as examples of the *yūgen* style in a manuscript attributed to Teika called *Teika jittei*, an anthology in which the poet gives poem examples for the ten styles of waka enumerated in his *Maigetsushō* (1219), compiled sometime between 1202 and 1213. See *Teika jittei* in *NKT* 4: 362–63.

It should be noted briefly here that the authenticity of the *Teika jittei* has been questioned by some Japanese scholars, notably, Taniyama Shigeru in *Yūgen no kenkyū* (Kyoto, 1943), pp. 168, 170–72, and Higuchi Yoshimaro in *Teika Hachidaishō to kenkyū* (Mikan Kokubun Shiryō Kankōkai, 1957), 2: 118–30. Most authorities nevertheless favor attribution to Teika, particularly in the light of a passage in the *Maigetsushō* in which he seems to imply that he had previously undertaken a work on the *jittei*, or ten styles (see *Maigetsushō*, p. 514). This argument is weakened, however, by the fact that the authenticity of the *Maigetsushō* itself has been the subject of controversy; see, e.g., Tanaka Yutaka, *Chūsei bungakuron kenkyū* (1969), pp. 225–50. The question of the forged Teika manuscripts is a complex one that need not detain us here; suffice it to say that Shinkei, Shōtetsu, and other Reizei-school poets accepted them as genuine, and that their influence on medieval Japanese poetics was quite decisive.

2. *GSS* 302, Emperor Tenchi (d. 671; r. 688–671). The sociopolitical reading of this poem holds that Emperor Tenchi was moved to tears of compassion when he saw the poor hut of the watchman guarding the rice harvest in the autumn fields. Yamagishi Tokuhei, ed., *Hachidaishūshō* (Yūseidō, 1960), 1: 241. The dew that seeps through the rough shelter of crudely woven grasses is the same that wets the emperor's sleeves and symbolically becomes the thread of sympathy binding lord and subject. *Kario* signifies both "harvested rice ears" and "temporary hut"; each meaning reinforces the other, since "autumn fields" immediately conjures up images of ripe grains, while the season itself suggests loneliness and melancholy. A fine delineation of the autumnal atmosphere, coupled with the suggestion of pathos in the human situation, results in a moving, elegiac quality here.

3. *SKKS* 900, Travel, Kakinomoto Hitomaro (fl. ca. 680–710); also in *MYS* 133, where it appears as a *hanka* to the *chōka MYS* 131, which has the following headnote: "Composed when Kakinomoto Hitomaro, having parted from his wife, was on his way to the capital from Iwami Province."

Kubota Utsubo comments that the tone of immediacy and the strong flood of emotion that characterized the preceding *chōka* have subsided to a quieter mode here. He observes, furthermore, that the excellence of the poem (i.e., the quality of *yūgen*) lies in the tonal harmony between the early winter landscape of softly rustling bamboo leaves and the delicate yearning it awakens in the poet's heart as he listens on the mountain trail (*Shinkokinwashū hyōshaku* [Tōkyōdō, 1964–65], 2: 130–31; hereafter *Hyōshaku*). The third line, *midaru nari* (seems/sounds stirred, disturbed), is especially crucial in effecting this resonance between natural scene and emotion; the simplicity of the lower section as set off by the natural description is especially fine.

4. *GSS* 961. "Sent to the Kyōgoku Consort after their affair had become known."

Prince Motoyoshi (ca. 890–942), a son of Emperor Yōzei, was famed for his amorous adventures. He wrote this poem after it was discovered that he had been having an affair with Uda's consort even while that Emperor was alive (*Hachidaishūshō*, 1: 335). The resulting scandal forced the lady to cut off relations, but as we see the prince's persona is prepared to risk his reputation again, and even his life, for another meeting. The poem is characterized by an intensity of feeling coupled with technical dexterity. The third and fourth lines function on two levels of meaning involving a wordplay in which *na ni wa* suggests both *na ni tatsu* (to become the subject of rumor or scandal) and Naniwa, the old place-name for Osaka Bay and its surrounding areas. *Mi o tsukushi* means "to risk or sacrifice one's life" as well as "channel markers" (*mio tsukushi*), poles driven into water routes to guide passing ships. It is an associative phrase (*engo*) for Naniwa, since the channel markers in Osaka Bay were especially famous.

5. *SKKS* 858, Partings. Kubota Utsubo remarks that this poem has the appearance of having been written by a lady and sent to her lover when she was about to embark on a journey to the Hokuriku provinces. It is an expression of her insecurity about the man's fidelity during her absence, as well as an attempt to hold on to something that she felt was about to vanish. *Hyōshaku*, 2: 105.

The poem shows a conspicuous use of the *kakekotoba* (pivot word, pun) device. *Koshiji* (lit., the road [that one] crosses) refers both to the path that the lady is about to follow on her journey and to Koshi, another name for the provinces in the Hokuriku region, located along the northeastern shores of the Japan Sea. Kaeruyama (lit., mountain of returning) and Itsuhata (homophonous with *itsu hata*, lit., when again, someday) are both ancient place-names in Hokuriku, Echizen Province, respectively located in Nanjō District and Tsuruga District. The poem leans somewhat heavily on wordplay, but there is irony in the juxtaposition of Koshiji and Kaeruyama (she wittily images the road leading to Koshi as the road coming back) and a delicate tinge of pathos in the opening phrase, *wasurenamu yo ni mo* (in a world apt to forget).

6. *SKKS* 495, Autumn. The poem is the undisguised complaint of a person from the capital who is temporarily in seclusion in the mountains. The subjunctive mood of the verb *hedatezuba* (if [the mist] did not cut off [this mountain dwelling]), the futile yearning in the suffix *mashi* (then *would* I see . . .), and the contrastive force of *wa* (I might not have company, but I would see *at least* the sleeves) all serve to emphasize the desire for company engendered by autumn days when the thick mist hovers over the mountain forever, it seems, and there is no relief from the tedious isolation.

7. *Shūi gusō* 268. One of ten poems grouped under the topic "Ill-Fated Love After the First Meeting" in Teika's personal anthology, the *Shūi gusō*, compiled around 1216 and including 3,653 of his poems. In the anthology, the second line ends in the *rentaikei* inflection (*keru*) and the third line reads *waga kokoro* (my heart, my love).

The poem has historically been cited as an instance of Teika's penchant for obscurity. Teika's self-proclaimed admirer Shōtetsu admits as much and proceeds to explicate it thus:

> This is not an easy poem to understand. When Shōjōin [the Shōgun Ashikaga Yoshimochi, 1386–1428; r. 1394–1423] was in office, he asked both Kōun [1345?–1429] and myself about it, but the bearing of our responses was different. In the judgment of those in the capital at the time, mine was the more appropriate one. This is what I said: "Having vowed a love that afterward seemed unreal, I said to forget it and think of it wholly as a dream; but I cannot forget because I have forgotten how it was supposed to be. I told myself when we parted to turn it into a dream and forget it, but I cannot because I have forgotten what I said." Teika's poems are in this way highly concentrated and involved, composed by becoming wholly that [persona's] self. No one can match him when it comes to love poetry. . . . Kōun's response was that *wasurenu ya* is intended as a question directed to the other, saying, "Have you forgotten?" and so on. (*Shōtetsu monogatari* [ca. 1433], ed. Hisamatsu Sen'ichi in *Karonshū Nōgakuronshū*, *NKBT* 65 [Iwanami Shoten, 1961], p. 192, translation mine; poem text has *keri* in line 2 and *waga kokoro* as line 3; see also Robert Brower, trans., *Conversations with Shōtetsu* [Ann Arbor: Center for Japanese Studies, University of Michigan, 1992], pp. 101–2)

As anthologized in the *Rokkashō* (Selections from Six Poets), an anonymous commentary to this poem, possibly stemming from the renga poet Shōhaku (1443–1527), seems mainly to agree with Shōtetsu's reading and clarifies the troublesome syntax of the first two lines thus:

> I said, when we parted, "Think it but a dream," but have I forgotten? [No!] Therefore I have indeed forgotten [what I said]—is what it means. It is an instance of the feeling one has afterward, having met and then parted with someone. They met once only and for the last time, and then he said, think what went before as a dream, don't think of me, we must not long for each other, let's forget that we even met; but afterward he is unable to forget and finds himself again longing for her. When he said to forget it and treat it as a dream, did he forget? No, what he forgot was what he had avowed. This is in the spirit of love longing. (From the *Rokkashō naichū* as cited in *Rokkashō*, p. 218, headnote to poem 1652; poem text same as in *Shūi gusō*; bracketed insertions mine)

Kubota Jun's headnote to this poem (*Fujiwara Teika zenkashū* [Kawade Shobō, 1985, 1986], 1: 47) apparently agrees in the main with Kōun's variant reading of the first line as directed to the other: "Are you saying that you have forgotten me? Well, then, I too have forgotten my own intention. For the reason that although we two parted saying we would think of this love meeting as a dream, even so I am unable to forget by thinking it was a dream." In a supplementary note (no. 268, 1: 480), however, Kubota takes issue with both Shōtetsu's and Kōun's readings, observing that "neither can be said to be the correct interpretation." My rendering is based on Shōtetsu, because it is most likely closer to Shinkei's reading. It is not clear, as Kubota claims, that Shōtetsu takes *wasurenu ya* as the negation suffix *zu* rather than the perfective *nu*; rather, he was most probably rendering the implicit negative response to the rhetorical question (*hango*), "Have I forgotten?" as "No, indeed not, I have not forgotten." That ties in better with the second line in the Shinkei and Shōtetsu version, *sa wa wasurekeri* (What I did forget was *this*!).

Still problematic, however, is the rentaikei *keru* ending in the *Shūi gusō* version: *wasurenu ya/sa wa wasurekeru*, which would read, "Is the reason I do not forget because I have forgotten this?" in a case of *kakari musubi*, whereby the medial particle *ya* generates the *rentaikei* ending, *keru*. Otherwise, the rentaikei *nu* of the negation *zu* is ungrammatical before *ya*, which usually takes a *shūshikei* inflection. It is perhaps for this reason that later versions changed to *keri*, thus introducing a caesura after line 1 by reading *wasurenu ya* as the *shūshikei* of the perfective *nu* plus the emphatic rhetorical question particle *ya* in sentence-final, rather than medial, position.

The poem is perhaps somewhat mannered, in the style of Ariwara Narihira's famous and equally involved *Tsuki ya aranu* (Is there no moon?). Both take the love experience as a delirium of the senses, a delusion immune to reason, by use of a diction, however, that ironically depends for its effect on cool logic.

8. *Shūgyokushū*, II: *Kamo hyakushu* 2608; *Rokkashō* 2031. The poem carries a tone of censure for those passive observers who weep empty tears of pity while holding themselves aloof from the toil of humanity. It is conceived in a simple, perhaps conventional, allegorical frame, in which life is seen as a road and people as travelers. However, it has a forceful directness that sets it apart from the elaborately wrought style characteristic of that age. For Jichin, see under Jien in "Biographical Notes."

9. The three verses quoted above are examples of what amateurs regarded as the *yūgen* style in linked verse. As Shinkei has previously remarked, however, poetry that is merely "steeped in grace and charm" fails to exhibit the true meaning of *yūgen*—that is, the charismatic appeal of the mind-heart. Thus, although written by different authors, the three are virtually interchangeable in general effect as in diction. *Honobono* (dimly) in the first verse becomes *sokotonaku* (dimly, faintly) in the second verse. The atmospheric effect of *kasumi* (haze) in the first verse is not much different from that of *oborozukiyo* (night of the vague moon) in the second, or of *yūgure* (dusk) in the third. The image of flowers diffusing their fragrance in the first verse turns to wild geese crying in the second verse, and to the wind blowing in the third. In other words, the verses are nothing more than a series of poetic images strung together in a facile manner in order to give an external appearance of "ineffable depth." Nowhere is there a sincere expression of deeply felt personal experience; the poet's mind or heart does not register in any of these vaguely romantic pictures. Without knowing the maeku for them, it is impossible, of course, to judge exactly their quality as *linked* verses. Still, the point must be that if their authors were dealing seriously with the maeku, they would not produce such startlingly similar work, sounding as if they were all patterned after a predetermined model. In this sense, the *yūgen* poem is inimitable.

10. In contrast to the three verses immediately preceding, this and the two that follow, although using generally the same imagery, manifest the true *yūgen* style, because one can sense a mind behind them. Here Ryōa goes beyond a charming description of the scent of

flowers; his verse is an elegy to beauty that fades too soon, and by extension, it poses the eternal question: of what use is it all?

11. Like the parallel verse in the first group, Gusai employs the image of the hazy moon, but he is not so much interested in painting a fine picture as in again evoking his hushed wonder at the instant of suddenly noticing the moon in the paling sky. The verse evokes the growing brevity of nights in spring (as compared with the winter just past) in "When did it rise, the moon . . . [?]"

According to the *Renga hidenshō* (The Secret Traditions of Renga), a collection of instructions on the techniques of linking, based on teachings handed down from Sōzei, the maeku to the verse is the following (p. 94; quoted in *SSG*, p. 128, n. 2):

yama kasukanaru haru no akebono	Mountains faintly outlined in the early spring dawn.

12. Here again the visual elements—miscanthus grass and the wind—are the same as in the third example in the first group, but there is a subtle distinction hinging on the addition of *furusato* (lit., old village, referring to one's old home), a term that immediately calls up intimations of the passing of time and suggests longing for a once familiar place. It is this human element that imparts a moving quality to Gusai's poem that is lacking in the other. In one of Shinkei's letters (*Tokoro* I, p. 200), one finds the following maeku to the verse.

tsuyu mo namida mo tada oi no sode	Only dew and tears— the sleeves of old age.

Gusai's tsukeku picks up "old age" and parallels this with the related image of the "old village." Furthermore, he evokes a gray, autumnal atmosphere that is appropriate—in the sense, for instance, that old age and austereness come together in the quality of *sabi*. In the letter, Shinkei cites this tsukeku among those where the link is made through suggestion (*omokage*), rather than visible verbal correspondences.

13. I.e., the distinction between a genuinely "stalwart verse" (*takumashiki ku*) and its poor imitation, the mere "rough verse" (*araki ku*). Judging from the four examples that follow, the *takumashiki ku* is characterized by a plain, seemingly unpoetical subject matter, which is handled in a forthright and elevated manner. This may be seen in the choice of images like beast or dog, the character written on an infant's forehead, or a rope to bind firewood—none of which has the suggestiveness and charm of the conventional images of the courtly poetic tradition.

14. The preceding two verses employ topics that are essentially unadorned, but their treatment lacks the requisite directness and purpose. What sense is there, for instance, in imagining that delicate tendrils of flowering arrowroot vines can form a rope to tie around a bundle of rough kindling, aside from displaying an arty cleverness? *Neriso* is a rope made from branches twisted together; it is often used to tie together kindling (*shiba*). *Makuzu* refers to both "arrowroot" and the act of "twisting" or "twining" (*maku*). Similarly, in the second verse, there seems to be an attempt at wit in the incongruous juxtaposition of beast and moss (both have hairy textures), but lacking a point, the association is inconsequential. In short, these two verses nullify the inherently plain imagery by an empty indirectness or conceit. Instead of genuine strength, we have a kind of playful roughness.

15. *TKBS*: Priest Ryōa, 38. The maeku is the following:

inu koso hito no mamori narikere	It is surely the dog that is man's guardian.

In keeping with the plainness of the maeku, the tsukeku is an equally forthright statement given strength through its elevated tone and significant implications. The message of the maeku is on the physical level: the dog is an alert and faithful "guard" *(mamori)* for man and his dwellings. The tsukeku extends the significance into the spiritual realm, pointing to the religious practice of writing the character for dog on an infant's brow as a symbol or "charm" (also *mamori*) to protect the child from evil spirits. This is a good example of linking not only through diction (connection is made through an alternative interpretation of *mamori*) but through an amplification of the meaning of the maeku.

16. Here again there is a forceful directness in the sweeping first line: *Itarikeri* (It has come to this!) with the implication that a spiritual climax has been reached. The rest of the verse is a simple enumeration of the visual aspects of the experience, but in the context of the first line, each element stands pure and unadorned in a moment of pure perception. In the *Sōzeiku*, the maeku appears as follows:

neburi wa samenu	From sleep wholly awakened—
mono fukaki yama	quiet depths of the mountain.

(*Sōzei kushū* 1155–56, in *Shichiken*, p. 91) There is no need to explain how the tsukeku takes the primary stage of experience (awakening) embodied in the maeku and pushes it to its farthest reaches, as the spirit takes in the concomitant aspects of the landscape: dawn streaking the edge of the valley, the pale moon lingering in the west, and the autumnal spareness of the whole atmosphere.

17. This paragraph is important, because it contains the first occurrence of another major set of terms in Shinkei's poetics, namely, "cold and slender" (*samuku yasetaru*), which is clearly being set in opposition to "corpulent and warm" (*futori atatakanaru*). Since I discuss the quality of coolness and slenderness in another context in my concluding commentary on Chapter 14, there is no need to dwell on it here. I would only point out that this passage reveals that these terms describe the external configuration or total effect (*sugata*) of poetry of "true compelling beauty" (*makoto ni ennaru ku*), or "the stalwart verse," which are in turn what could be called "masterpieces" (*shūitsu*).

With the exception of Jichin's *Omou koto* (*SKKS* 1780) and Hideyoshi's *Omoiiru* (*SKKS* 87), the twenty-one poems that follow are from the *Jisanka* (Self-esteemed Poems), an anthology that reportedly originated in a request by Rtd. Emperor Go-Toba that sixteen *Shinkokinshū* poets each submit ten of what they regarded as their best poems. These sixteen poets are: Princess Shikishi, Fujiwara Yoshitsune, Shunzei, Teika, Ariie, Ietaka, Masatsune, and Hideyoshi; Minamoto Michiteru, Michitomo, and Tomochika; Jien, Jakuren, Saigyō, Shunzei's Daughter, and Lady Kunaikyō. However, because the event is not recorded in a contemporary source, and from the fact that all 170 poems (including ten by Go-Toba) are in the same general style, it is now assumed that the selection was in fact carried out by a single editor, himself an accomplished poet, some hundred years after Go-Toba's reign (*WBD*, p. 458). It is worth noting, however, that Teika's diary mentions in the entry for Genkyū 2 (1205).3.9 being asked by Go-Toba to submit twenty of his *jisan no uta*; the request is repeated in the entry for Jōgen 1 (1207).4.7, this time for ten (see *Meigetsukishō*, pp. 171, 205). Consequently, some scholars believe that the work is authentic and was compiled by Go-Toba himself around 1211. At any rate, it was quite popular in the Muromachi period and subsequently; Shinkei's disciples Kenzai and Sōgi wrote commentary on the *Jisanka* poems, some of which probably transmits Shinkei's opinions. Here in *Sasamegoto*, Shinkei quotes these "self-esteemed poems" as a model for the kind of sensibility and diction that the renga poet should aspire to.

18. *SKKS* 989, Travel. "On the sentiment of Travel, when he worshipped at Kumano."

Kumano, in the southeastern part of Kii Province, was famous for the three great Shintō shrines collectively known as the Kumano Sanzan; it became the object of imperial pilgrimage from 1090, when Rtd. Emperor Shirakawa (1053–1129; r. 1073–1086) made his first visit. Go-

Toba himself is known to have made the trip at least twenty-seven times between 1198 and 1221. Teika's *Meigetsuki* diary records in detail one such pilgrimage in Kennin 1 (1201).10.5–26, when he was a participant; for various reasons, Kubota Jun believes this poem was most probably composed then.

The poem is outstanding for its evocative delineation of atmosphere. We imagine the persona gazing from his window upon the dark night in the mountains, where he cannot see, but can feel the chill wind getting stronger and the early winter rains approaching; the inflexion of *shigurumeri* is particularly effective. The suggestion of loneliness and the longing for home (here the capital) that overtake the traveler are very simply suggested in the last two lines. A conventional topic of Japanese poetry is handled in a fresh, unaffected manner.

19. *SKKS* 801, Laments. "Around the Tenth Month, when the Rtd. Emperor was staying at the Minase Palace, he sent a poem to the former Archbishop Jien that said, '*Nurete shigure no*' [Drenched by the early winter showers]. In the Tenth Month of the following year, he sent Jien a number of poems on the ephemerality of existence, of which this was one."

The Rtd. Emperor wrote the poem *Nurete shigure no* after the death of a favorite lady-in-waiting known as Owari on the nineteenth day of the Tenth Month, 1204, using *shigure* (early winter showers) as a metaphor for his tears. Owari, daughter of a high priest at Saishōji, had given birth to a son by Go-Toba in the Seventh Month and did not regain her health, despite the numerous prayers he offered for her; this infant would be known as Lay Monk Prince Dokaku and become Tendai Abbot.

The theme of mutability is concretely realized in this poem, written on the first anniversary of Owari's death. *Ori* (break) refers to wood broken up for kindling; it also means "time, occasion," in which sense, it connects to the first line *omoiizuru* (recollect). *Yūkeburi* (evening smoke, here from burning firewood) also suggests smoke from a funeral pyre. *Musebu* is "to choke," in this context both from the smoke and from tears. *Wasuregatami*, finally, is a nominal meaning "memento," but it is also an adjectival phrase in the sense of "difficult to forget." The *kaketoba* device is used repeatedly, but in an unobtrusive, skillful manner; the images retain their vividness even while amplifying the poem through their overtones and polysemic value. Frail wisps of smoke rising and disappearing in the sky remain the central image, a symbol of evanescence that simultaneously recalls the poet's dead love. However, it is also a wholly everyday image, for it is the smoke that rises from people's hearths at evening. Thus private grief is given a public dimension by setting it within the common people's pattern of life. The poet's sorrow is not only for an isolated individual but for the ephemerality that is an inescapable condition of human existence. *Ureshi* (lit., glad) in the fourth line suggests that the very mark of mortality becomes, paradoxically, an enduring memento through which the poet finds his love again. Ultimately, the poem may be read as a comment on the necessity and healing power of mourning and remembrance.

20. *SKKS* 534, Autumn. "An autumn poem, one of those presented for the 100-Poem Sequences."

"100-Poem Sequences" here refers to *Shōji ninen in'onhyakushu* (The Rtd. Emperor's 100-poem Sequences in Shōji 2), also known as *Go-Toba-in shodo hyakushu* (Rtd. Emperor Go-Toba's First 100-poem sequences)—commissioned from twenty-three leading poets (including himself) by the retired sovereign in 1200. Of these poems, formally recited on 11.22.1200, seventy-nine were later included in the *Shinkokinshū*.

(For convenience, from here on I shall use the term "poet" instead of "persona" to refer to the mind or sensibility expressed in the poem; although a useful theoretical distinction for pedagogical purposes, the professed opposition in contemporary criticism between the author and his/her masks is not ultimately a real one, since it presumes that there is a recognizably determinate "real face" behind the "masks." Masks constitute a formal means of expression, a language; in the mind that dons them, there is no intrinsic duality. When the mind is stilled in emptiness, it is neither real nor unreal, and it is not subject to a determination. When, however, it expresses itself through the force of *en* or circumstance, it is wholly real in its functioning.)

The poem figures the poet's mixed feelings regarding her continued isolation. Although grown rather fond of the pensive melancholy of autumn, she is startled to realize, on looking out into the garden one day, that all the leaves of the paulownia tree now lie thick before her door. *Kanarazu* (necessarily, inevitably) in the fourth line suggests the ambivalence: it is not necessarily true that she is anxious for company, but in the face of a bleak winter, she would be almost glad of a visitor (based on Kubota Utsubo's reading, *Hyōshaku*, 1: 444). Still, ambivalence remains the primary impression here; is she just being playful or is she serious? It is impossible to tell, and the poem's subtlety lies precisely there. It is interesting to compare the novel quality of this feeling with that of Yoshitada's more determinate *SKKS* 495 (*Yamazato o*), quoted earlier by Shinkei in this chapter, and also with its *honka* (foundation poem), *KKS* 770, by Bishop Henjō.

waga yado wa	About my house
michi mo naki made	the grass is grown so rank
arenikeri	the path has vanished,
tsurenaki hito o	while I waited for someone
matsu to seshi ma ni	whose heart was cold.

21. *SKKS* 368. "Composed as an Autumn poem."

The poem would seem to echo an old theme: human aging in the midst of unchanging nature. Here, it is something as formless as the autumn wind—the same, yet sounding altered by subjective experience—that strikes pangs into the heart of the poet, possibly lamenting the passage of time and the ruin it has wrought in her life. *Nagame* (gaze vacantly, ponder) implies that she keeps recalling the past, and each recollection is cause for more brooding. *Shizu* was an ancient woven cloth of irregular pattern, in which the weft was woven from threads of hemp and similar fibers. The spinning spool of *shizu* thread figures the futility of the poet's reveries. An allusive variation is made on the following poem from *Ise monogatari* 32 (p. 163).

inishie no	As in ancient looms
shizu no odamaki	the spool of *shizu* thread
kurikaeshi	turned round and round,
mukashi o ima ni	Oh, were there some way
nasu yoshi mogana	to turn time past into now.

In *Ise*, this poem was sent by the man to a former lover. Apparently, it had no effect, because there was no reply. As in the previous piece, the complex ambiguity and interiority of Shikishi's meditation emerges by comparison with the artless simplicity of the *honka*. The past is indeed present again but only in a recollection that underscores the gap between then and now, which in turn generates another round of brooding. Her poem is essentially about obsession and difference, or the desire for—and impossibility of—repetition.

22. *SKKS* 1293, Love. "Presented for the 100-Poem Sequences."

The author, assuming a female persona, administers a highly ironic rebuke to a tardy lover in a stunningly effective language, the bare gist of which is: "Indeed, you never told me, 'Thus grieve,' but what a long period has elapsed since that night when you said, 'I am coming soon!'" The complaint is subtly conveyed through the double meaning of the phrase *tsuki hi hedatete*, which literally means "[the clouds] covered the sun and moon," but is also a figurative expression of the woman's unhappiness. Again, since *tsukihi* refers as well to "days and months"—i.e., "time," and *hedatete* may mean "divided," then the phrase becomes an allusion to the lover's protracted absence, and may be rendered as "the days and the months that divided us." The witty indirection in the inverted syntax, which withholds the object of the verb in line 1 until the last line, and the lightly elegant tone are more effective than pathetic tears. It has an equally elegant *honka* in *KKS* 691, Love, by Priest Sosei:

ima komu to	*Just because*
iishi bakari ni	*you said, "I am coming soon,"*
nagatsuki no	till the laggard moon
ariake no tsuki o	emerged in the predawn sky,
machiidetsuru kana	I found myself waiting.

The Go-Kyōgoku Regent was Fujiwara Yoshitsune (1169–1206), one of the great literary patrons of the mid-classical period, the second son of the regent Kanezane and a member of the hereditary regental branch of the Fujiwara. See under Yoshitsune in "Biographical Notes."

23. *SKKS* 1780, Miscellaneous. "Among a sequence of fifty poems."

This is from the *Rōnyaku gojisshu uta awase*, the contest sponsored by Go-Toba in 1201, in which ten poets competed, each composing ten poems on each of five topics (the four seasons and miscellaneous). The poem is marked by an utter simplicity of tone and diction. A contrast is clearly being drawn between *tou hito* (a person who comes to inquire) in the first part and *tsuki* (moon) in the second: dejected, the poet wishes that someone would come and commiserate with him; instead, it is the moon that looks upon him with solicitude. *Aogeba* in the fourth line clarifies this situation, for it not only means "When I looked up," but also "when I sought." In his solitude, the poet finds solace, as well as a model for impersonal detachment, in the moon's keen yet empty light. In the contest, this was matched with and won against a poem (quoted below) by Yoshitsune, Jien's own nephew.

yo no naka o	Trusting to things
aru ni makasete	as they are, I carry on
suguru kana	in this world,
kotaenu sora o	the while gazing on and on
uchinagametsutsu	at the vast unresponding sky.

While the conception of the two poems is quite similar, perhaps Jien's more dramatic, even loftier diction—and therefore emotion—gained it the winning mark in this instance. An even closer resemblance may be found in this poem by Saigyō (*SKKS* 1307, Love), showing how the leading *Shinkokinshū* poet influenced the others' production:

aware tote	*Why comes no one*
tou hito no nado	*to inquire* and say,
nakaruramu	it's all very sad—
mono *omou* yado no	the wind ruffling the grass
ogi no uwakaze	about my brooding abode.

24. *SKKS* 360. "On the topic 'Going Along the Mountain Path in Autumn,' when people composed Chinese poems and compared them to Japanese poems."

The occasion was the *Genkyū shiika awase* of 1205, held at the palace of Rtd. Emperor Go-Toba, though it began as a wholly private session planned by Yoshitsune in his residence. A *shiika awase* was a contest in which Chinese *shi* and Japanese waka were composed on the same topic and then compared. In this one, the *shi* was in the *shichigon niku* form, i.e., two seven-character lines. Two topics, each to be treated in thirty-eight rounds, were assigned (the other was "Spring-Viewing in the Village by the River"), and there were nineteen participants on each side (*WBD*, pp. 309–10). The manuscript is valuable for the use of the more complex topics, and as a precedent for the eclectic Japanese-Chinese poem match.

The autumn scenery is being viewed from a distance, perhaps at the entrance to the mountain road. The main interest of the poem lies in the sweeping spatial treatment and in the startling effect of the last two lines, where one is suddenly confronted with the seemingly unrelated image of crimson clouds in the setting sky. However, the phrase *mizarishi kumo* (clouds not seen before), viewed in the context of the earlier *itsu yori aki* . . . (from when [did it become] autumn), suggests that the poet is not concerned about the clouds as such, but is in fact using them as a metaphor to evoke the richly tinted beauty of the autumn foliage as seen from afar against the sky.

25. *SKKS* 1562, Miscellaneous. "On the topic 'Old Memories in the Image of the Wind.'"

Minamoto Michiteru (1187–1248), of the Murakami Genji clan, was the son of Palace Minister Michichika and the younger stepbrother of Michitomo, one of the *Shinkokinshū*'s compilers. He reached the summit of an official career as a prime minister (*daijōdaijin*).

This complicated poem is rife with visual images of devastation that convey symbolically the wrack of old age. *Asajifu* is low *chigaya* grass growing sparsely in isolated clumps; by metonymic convention, it signifies a long-neglected, ruined field, garden, and habitation. As such it anticipates the second and third lines, *sode ni kuchinishi / aki no shimo* (the autumn frost that rotted in my sleeves.) *Shimo*, logically associated with *asajifu*, also suggests "tears"; the speaker has been weeping so long that his sleeves are all "rotted" (*kuchinishi*). Thus we have the parallel images of a frost-ruined garden and sleeves wasted by tears. *Wasurenu yume* (unforgotten dream) in the fourth line justifies the use of a verb as strong as *kutsu*; this melancholy dream has held the poet in thrall for an infinitely long time. At this point, *aki* (both "autumn" and "weary of") comes into play, suggesting that the memory is of an unrequited or unfulfilled love, or perhaps that the speaker has wearied of the memory's persistence. The poem builds to a climax with the final *fuku arashi kana*, a vision of the gusty storm wreaking further devastation in the garden, while it awakens the poet and tears him away from his futile memories. In this manner, a series of disparate images are tightly compressed and manipulated in order to convey an unmistakable conviction of feeling. An absurdly literal translation shows the extreme compression and fragmentation of diction here: "Ruined garden, O / in sleeves rotted / autumn frosts / / unforgotten dream / blowing storm . . . ?"

Shinkei's disciple Kenzai observes in his *Jisankachū* (Commentary on the Self-esteemed Poems): "This is definitely a poem with a deep mind, requiring a careful analysis. Saigyō's 'It is all a dream! That springtime at Naniwa' [*naniwa no haru wa / yume nare ya*] and what is conveyed in this one are the same mind." Similarly, in *Hachidaishū shō* (Selections from the Eight [Imperial] Anthologies [1682]), Kitamura Kigin notes: "it has limitless suggestion [*yojō kagirinaku*]; the diction wholly depends on the mind, and the configuration is difficult to match" (both cited in *Zenhyōshaku*, 7: 267).

26. *SKKS* 1558, Miscellaneous. "Composed and submitted for the 100-Poem Sequences when he was well over eighty."

This is from the third of three groups of 100-poem sequences commissioned by Rtd. Emperor Go-Toba in 1200 and 1201. The poems in this group, composed by thirty leading contemporary poets and submitted in the Sixth Month of 1201, were judged in the famous *Sengohyakuban uta awase* (Poetry Contest in 1,500 Rounds) of 1202, the most extensive single source for the *Shinkokinshū*, which includes ninety poems from it.

Shunzei (or Toshinari, 1114–1204) was, with his son Teika, one of the two great poet-critics of the mid-classical period (see "Biographical Notes"). In contrast to the immediately preceding poem, this one is characterized by simplicity of tone and treatment. Nowhere is there a hint of emotionalism in the diction, which does not overtly mention any single word pertaining to death. That subject is only to be inferred from the circumstance mentioned in the prose preface, that Shunzei was then over eighty years old. Thus the first line *shimeokite* (marked out, laid aside) implies "Having disposed of the matter of where I would like to be buried," and the matter-of-fact *Ima wa* (lit., "Is it now?") would have to refer to his impending death. The only suggestion of *aware* stems from the tiny trills of the dying insects on the autumn mountain that the poet had picked for the site of his grave. *Matsumushi* (lit., pine insects) are said to correspond to the modern Japanese *suzumushi* ("bell-ring insect"; *Homoeogryllus japonicus*). As usual, *matsumushi* may also be read as "waiting insects." The poem appears under "the intricate style" (*komayakanaru tai*) in *Teika jittei* and is cited as a model of the "mode of pathos" (*mono no aware tai*) in *Shōtetsu monogatari* (*SM*, p. 207; *Conversations with Shōtetsu*, p. 125).

27. SKKS 1334, Love. "From the Minase Fifteen Love Poems Match."

For this poetry contest, the *Minase-dono koi jūgoshu uta awase* held by Rtd. Emperor Go-Toba at the Minase villa on the night of 9.13.1202, ten poets submitted fifteen poems each on fifteen varied topics of love, making 150 poems in 75 rounds. The judge was Shunzei, then already eighty-nine. As with the *Sengohyakuban uta awase*, the poems were composed against the background of excitement stemming from the compilation of the *Shinkokinshū* and included some that were considered the most ambitious demonstrations of the *Shinkokin* mode. The topic for this round was "Love in the Image of Rain."

The inverted syntactical arrangement, which opens with the verb phrase *furinikeri* (How it has fallen . . .) and shifts the noun phrase and adverbial modifier to the second line, *shigure wa sode ni* (the winter drizzle on my sleeves), is an emphatic way of conveying the force of the woman's emotion. *Shigure* is, of course, an unmistakable symbol for "tears." The poem was matched against the following by Kintsugu:

ame fureba	As rain falls
noki no shizuku no	and drips along my eaves
kazukazu ni	endlessly turns
omoimidarete	my disordered mind, with nary
haruru ma zo naki	a glimpse of clear sky.

It won too against a poem by Jien on the same topic. Shunzei's evaluation observes: "The poem of the Left alludes to the rain from 'As rain falls' to the very last line. From the Right, the sequence of words 'the winter rains upon my sleeves / by autumn [tiring]' [*shigure wa sode ni / aki kakete*] has great appeal. Therefore it deserves the winning mark" (cited in *Zenhyōshaku*, 6: 212). While Shunzei praised the rival poem's success in bringing out the topic of "love in the image of rain" in every line, he was even more attracted to the richly ironic effect of lines 2–3 in his granddaughter's piece, whereby *aki kakete* doubles as the lover's words, "By autumn [I shall come]," and as an adverbial clause in *aki kakete / iishi bakari* (no more than words you said in tiredness).

The poem is actually an allusive variation on the following anonymous *honka* from *Ise monogatari* 96 (pp. 216–17); this translation is from Helen Craig McCullough, trans., *Tales of Ise (*Stanford: Stanford University Press, 1968), p. 136.

aki *kakete*	*"In autumn," I said,*
iishinagara mo	but it was not to be—our
aranaku ni	relationship has proved no deeper
konoha furishiku	than a shallow creek
e ni koso arikere	strewn with fallen leaves.

In *Ise*, this poem was supposed to have been written by a woman unable to keep a tryst with her lover in autumn. The *SKKS* poem repeats, with slight variations, the first two lines above, but reverses the poetic situation, for it is the man who fails to come to the promised meeting.

28. *SKKS* 281, Summer. "For the Poetry Contest in 1,500 Rounds."

For Lady Kunaikyō, a member of Go-Toba's court and along with Shunzei's Daughter one of the most accomplished woman poets of her time see "Biographical Notes." In the *Shinkokinshū*, this poem appears close to the end of the Summer section (the last poem is *SKKS* 284), probably because it evokes the coming of autumn. It is an allusive variation on *KKS* 1099, "A Song of Ise."

ofu no ura ni	As the fruit on
katae sashioi	*the pear branch slanting out*
naru nashi no	*toward Ofu Bay,*
nari mo narazu mo	our love *may or may not ripen,*
nete katarawamu	but let us lie together anyway.

In Kunaikyō's poem, the pear-tree imagery, which functions as a *jo* (preface) in *KKS* 1099, becomes an actual description of scenery, and *nari mo narazu mo* means "whether or not it becomes," rather than "whether or not it may ripen." A different handling of poetic materials transforms the *Kokinshū* love poem into a seasonal poem.

29. *SKKS* 38, Spring. "Composed at the request of the Cloistered Prince Shukaku for a sequence of fifty poems."

In late 1197, Cloistered Prince Shukaku (1150–1204), a son of Emperor Go-Shirakawa, ordered seventeen representative poets to compose sequences of fifty poems, which were submitted in 1198–99; they later formed the basis of the *Omuro senka awase* (Contest of Poems Selected by the Omuro Cloistered Prince [another name for Shukaku]). Of the original nine hundred poems, including fifty by the prince, twenty-five were selected for the *Shinkokinshū*.

This poem is considered the example par excellence of *yōen* (ethereal beauty), the aesthetic principle espoused by Teika, which, along with Shunzei's ideal of *yūgen*, was predominant in the mid-classical period. There is richness not only in the visual images themselves but also in their proliferating allusions. The opening line, *Haru no yo* (spring night), is filled with light, airy charm, and, in the conventional vocabulary of Japanese poetry, inevitably suggests a night too brief and too soon gone. The next nominal, *yume* (dream), has limitless poetic and philosophical-religious connotations that need no elaboration here. The phrase *yume no ukihashi* (floating bridge of dreams), the uncertain path of ephemeral dreams, ineluctably carries allusions to the final chapter of the *Tale of Genji* that bears that title and refers to the unrealized ties between Kaoru and Ukifune, and, more generally, to his relations with the three Uji princesses, all of which came to naught. More broadly, worldly existence may be viewed as a dreamlike passage from one state of being to another. The third line, *todaeshite* (lit., broken off, interrupted, like flowing music that is abruptly stilled, leaving the notes still hanging in the air), fulfills the symbolism implicit in the lines: the poet awakens from the dreams of an all too short spring night.

The unspoken transition or, so to speak, the spacing between upper and lower sections whereby the dream turns into a cloud is, in my opinion, really the best part of this poem. The verb employed is *wakaruru* (lit., separates, parts), suggesting that a personification of lovers parting at dawn is at work. Furthermore, there is doubtless a suggestion of the dreamlike encounter between the goddess of Mount Wu and the King of Chu at Gaotang; on parting from him at dawn, she tells him to seek her in the morning cloud at dawn and the falling rain at dusk. (See *HF*, pp. 333–34, for the currency of this *Wen xuan* anecdote in medieval literature.) The poem is everywhere permeated with the nostalgia and shimmering beauty of dreams of love on a spring night. With consummate artistry, Teika has handled the topic and the various images so as to distil the essential elusiveness, the beguiling translucency as it were, of romantic love: a cloud momentarily caught in or holding captive the mind, and ultimately no more than a function of sheer temporality, apt to appear and disappear with time's passage. Shinkei's admiration for Teika is without doubt motivated by this poet's concentrated stalking of the emptiness that lies in the heart of desire. When he speaks of the quality of "ineffable remoteness" (*yōon*) at the end of this chapter, as well as an austerity both of diction and of feeling, we may well assume that he had such poems as this one especially in mind.

30. SKKS 1142, Love. "On the topic 'Praying for Love,' submitted for the 100-poem contest held in the residence of Fujiwara Yoshitsune."

Twelve poets composed a hundred poems each on the topics of Spring (15), Summer (10), Fall (15), Winter (10), and Love (50), totaling 1,200 poems, which were presented in the *Roppyakuban uta awase* (Poetry Contest in 600 Rounds) held in the residence of then Captain of the Left Bodyguards [*sataishō*] Fujiwara Yoshitsune (later Go-Kyōgoku Regent) in the autumn of 1193. The contest was enlivened by fierce disputations between the two rival schools of poetry then, notably between Kenshō (ca. 1130–1209) of the Rokujō school and Jakuren (1139?–1202) of the Mikohidari school, who seem to have engaged in lengthy verbal battles for days. This contest is a landmark in various ways: the presence of Yoshitsune, Teika, Ietaka, and others who were then experimenting with an innovative new style as opposed to the conservative Rokujō school; the literary criticism handed down by Shunzei, who was the sole judge and had to justify his opinions under fire; and as a record of the development of *daiei* (composing on given topics), particularly the increasing systematization as well as minute distinctions among the total of 100 topics under each of the larger topics of the four seasons and love.

Hatsuse is an old name for Hase Township (in Sakurai City, Nara), site of the Hasedera Temple, which has been famous since antiquity for its image of the Eleven-Faced Kannon (Skt. Avalokitesvara), the bodhisattva of great mercy, popularly believed to grant every petition. In particular, Kannon was believed to manifest herself as the man or woman whom the petitioner wishes for as spouse. The poem is mystifying at first reading but the last line, *yoso no yugure* (lit., another's dusk; *yoso*, other, stranger), suggests that the bell tolling the end of the day also signifies the time of lovers' meetings, but not for the speaker, whose prayers have not been granted. (Note that the SKKS text has *chigiri* [love vow or meeting] rather than *shirushi* [sign or mark; effect] in the second line.) An atmosphere of stillness, somehow paradoxically heightened by the booming of the bell, pervades the poem. Loneliness is immediately felt in the first line, *toshi mo henu* (How the years have passed), which forms an independent syntactic unit, and whose true significance is only fully explained in that final, highly ironic *yoso no yūgure*. What emerges is the depth of the speaker's despair, his sense of alienation from grace, as the bell tolls another loveless day in an eternity of waiting. The poetic diction is marked by a syntactic fragmentation and extreme austerity that only serve to heighten the total effect. A more literal rendering will perhaps bear this out: "Years have passed; / the answer to my prayers: / Hatsuse Mountain / the bell on high / another's dusk." Even Shunzei remarks of this poem that "held hidden within the heart, it is perhaps unclear in the words" (*kokoro ni komete kotoba ni tashika naranu ni ya*) although he did give it the winning mark (see *Roppyakuban*, p. 245).

31. SKKS 289, Autumn. "Among those composed for a 100-poem sequence."

This sequence was patterned after the 100 subtopics used for the famous *Horikawa-in ontoki hyakushu waka* (100-Poem Sequences Composed During the Reign of Rtd. Emperor Horikawa) dating from around 1105–6. The topic here is *risshū* (the coming of autumn).

Ikuta no mori (Ikuta Woods) is the name of an area near Ikuta Shrine in the present city of Kōbe, Hyōgo Pref. (formerly Settsu Province; Tsu is an ancient name for Settsu). *Kinō* (yesterday) in the first line is set in opposition to *aki wa kinikeri* (autumn has come) in the last line, with the implication that "yesterday" was still summer. The prevailing feeling here may be grasped by comparing the poem to its honka:

Shikashū 83, Autumn. "While living in Tsu province, he sent this to Ōe Tamemoto, who had gone back to the capital after completing his term of duty there." Bishop Shōin. (*Shikashū* is the sixth imperial anthology, compiled between 1151 and 1154 by Fujiwara Akisuke)

kimi sumaba	Did you live here still,
towamashi mono o	*I would have liked to visit*;
tsu no kuni no	but *in Ikuta Woods*
ikuta no mori no	*in the land of Tsu*, already
aki no hatsukaze	the first *fall* winds are blowing.

Although Ietaka for the most part adopts the language of the earlier poem, the total effect is noticeably different. Shōin's poem centers around the human situation; it is an expression of his disappointment at not meeting with the provincial governor, and his attitude to the coming of autumn is tinged with regret. Ietaka's version, on the other hand, makes the season itself the central theme; the human situation is employed only to convey his appreciation of the moving quality of the first signs of autumn in Ikuta Woods.

32. *SKKS* 1337, Love. "From the Minase Fifteen Love Poems Match."

The topic for this round was "Love in Autumn." Fukakusa (lit., deep grass) is a place-name in the northern section of Fushimi, Kyoto (formerly Kii District, Yamashiro Province). The poem develops by means of an extended metaphor, in which the woman who suffers from her lover's coldness compares herself to the autumn dew that must presently scatter before the first winter gusts. The impression of helplessness conveyed through the comparison with the frail dew is intensified in the compressed irony in the last two lines. *Tanomeshi sue* is "the promised end," the future one had been led to trust, with *sue*, "end" in a temporal sense, also meaning "tips," and thus rounding off the metaphor of dew on the grass before the wind.

33. *SKKS* 561, Winter. "Composed on the topic 'Falling Leaves,' and presented for the Kasuga Shrine Poetry Match."

Thirty prominent poets of the period participated in this contest held in the Wakadokoro (Poetry Bureau) on the 11.10.1204; the poems composed there were dedicated to the Kasuga Shrine in Nara three days later. There were fifteen rounds each on the following three topics: "Falling Leaves," "The Moon at Dawn," and "Wind in the Pines."

Masaki no kazura is an old name for *teika kazura*, a species of vine with thick, glossy leaves that turn red in the autumn; it bears clusters of white flowers in the early summer. In the ancient period, it was worn as a headdress during religious ceremonies. (For Katsuragi [or Kazuragi] Mountain, here used as a *kakekotoba* with *masaki no kazura*, see Chapter 6, n. 5.) The poem displays an excellent combination of images of sight, sound, and color, all employed to evoke a changing scene before the eye. *Utsuriyuku kumo* (lit., shifting clouds) combines with the image of cascading leaves to create an impression of motion, to which the rumbling of the storm provides a kind of sound accompaniment. It also has that indefinable quality of suggestiveness (*yojō*) stemming from the tiny detail that the colorful *masaki* leaves are not in fact present before the speaker's eyes. They are only suggested in his mind, evoked by the moving clouds that transport the imagination to another place—that is, to Katsuragi Mountain, where they must indeed be swirling before the same storm. The judgment on this poem observes the supple diction, the aural fluidity of phrasing commonly associated with the *take takaki yō* (the lofty mode), in the sequence *chiru ka masaki no / katsuragi no yama.*

34. *SKKS* 87, Spring. "Composed as a spring poem among the six presented at the Poetry Bureau."

The occasion was the so-called *Santai waka* (Poetry in Three Styles) meeting held at the Wakadokoro on 3.22.1202 at the command of Rtd. Emperor Go-Toba. Seven major poets—Go-Toba, Yoshitsune, Jien, Jakuren, Teika, Ietaka, and Kamo no Chōmei (1155–1216)—composed a poem on each of the following topics: Spring, Summer, Fall, Winter, Love, and Travel. The idea was to demonstrate the "three styles," the definitions for which vary according to the source, but according to Chōmei's record of Go-Toba's directive in *Mumyōshō* (Nameless Notes [ca. 1210–12]), in Hisamatsu Sen'ichi and Minoru Yoshio, eds., *Karonshū, Nōgakuronshū*, *NKBT* 65: 35–98 (Iwanami Shoten, 1961), these were: (1) Spring and Summer Poems—they are to be composed in a style "broad and expansive" (*futoku ōki ni yomu beshi)*; (2) Autumn and Winter Poems—their style must have a "slender, withered" effect (*hosoku karabitaru*); (3) Poems of Love and Travel—they must possess "allure and a gentle refinement" (*en ni yasashiku*) (*Mumyōshō*, p. 77; see also Roselee Bundy, "*Santai Waka*: Six Poems in Three Modes," *MN* 49, 2 and 3 (1994): 197–227 and 261–86). These embody three concepts of poetic beauty, apparently originating from Go-Toba, in the *Shinkokinshū* period and were significant in the formation of Teika's concept of the ten styles of waka (*WBD*, p. 440).

Takamayama (another name for Kongōsan) forms the highest peak in the Kongō mountain range (earlier known as Katsuragi mountain range) extending north-south for eighteen kilometers west of Nara Prefecture, on the boundary to Osaka-fu. Tatsutayama, a lower peak west of Sangō Town, Ikoma District, Nara Prefecture, belongs to the Ikoma mountain range, which starts from the northern boundary of the Kongō chain. The fact that Takama is much higher than Tatsuta is important in visualizing the effect intended by the poet; Takama rises behind Tatsuta, so that the cherry blossoms on its slope would seem like white clouds hovering behind Tatsuta's peak. The cherry blossom–white cloud metaphor is a conventional one in Japanese poetry. Cf., e.g., the following poem from the *Kokinshū*.

KKS 59, Spring. "Composed and presented by imperial command." Tsurayuki.

sakurabana	The cherry blossoms
sakinikerashi na	seem indeed to have flowered!
ashihiki no	white clouds glimpsed
yama no kai yori	in the valley between the
miyuru shirakumo	foot-wearying mountains.

Aside from reversing the poetic situation by seeing the flowers as clouds and not vice versa (shifting the exact location of the flowers on the mountain also results in a somewhat different picture), Jakuren's poem impresses one as pure, simple description, compared to the slightly more emotionally tinged poem by Tsurayuki, where the heavily inflected second line, *sakinikerashi na*, suggests that the speaker has been waiting impatiently for the mountain cherries to bloom. The verb *miyuru* (is seen) in the last line also makes the presence of the observer felt in a way Jakuren's poem does not. A more literal translation of Jakuren's version: "Katsuragi— / the cherries of Takama / have flowered; / behind Tatsuta, / trailing white clouds." As required by Go-Toba for spring and summer poems, this one is "broad and expansive" in the vast scale of the scenery depicted, the simplicity or absence of intricacy in the diction, and the calm generosity of mind implicit in both.

35. *Sengohyakuban uta awase* (Poetry Contest in 1,500 Rounds), Round 944, Winter. Matched against a poem by Prince Koreakira (1179–1221, Go-Toba's elder brother) and lost. The judge for this round, Fujiwara Suetsune (1131–1221), claimed that the poem's meaning is

difficult to understand (*kokoro egatashi*), particularly the first two lines in connection with its honka, Lady Ise's poem translated below. (*Sengohyakuban uta awase*, ed. Ariyoshi Tamotsu, 3: 511–12).

KKS 780, Love. "Composed and sent to Lord Nakahira when they knew one another but noting signs of growing coolness, she informed him that she would depart for Yamato Province where her father was Governor." Ise.

miwa no yama	*On Mount Miwa*
ika ni machimin	*how shall I forbear and wait,*
toshi fu tomo	when the thought occurs
tazunuru hito mo	that though years may pass,
araji to omoeba	no one will come to visit.

Miwa Mountain in Yamato Province (present Sakurai City, Nara Prefecture) was anciently believed to be the sacred body of the deity of Ōmiwa Shrine. The association between cedar trees and Mount Miwa stems from an anonymous poem, *KKS* 982, Miscellaneous, to which Ise's poem in turn alludes.

waga io wa	My dwelling
miwa no yamamoto	lies at the foot of Mount Miwa;
koishiku wa	if you miss me
toburaikimase	come and visit where
sugi tateru kado	the cedar stands at the gate.

From these two antecedent poems, we may imagine that the speaker in Tomochika's piece is alone in her house in the country, waiting hopelessly for the visitor, presumably a lover, who never comes. Although Tomochika repeats the first two lines of *KKS* 780 in lines 2 and 3 (*ika ni machimin/miwa no yama*), in the lower section, he shifts directly into the *Shinkokin* style of descriptive symbolism, which at once intensifies the emotion of the honka by several degrees. The scenery and winter season are used to convey a desperate melancholy not yet present in the two earlier poems.

36. SKKS 1317. "On the topic 'Deep Mountain Love,' from a poetry match at the Wakadokoro."

The reference is to an impromptu session held at the Wakadokoro on 7.25.1206 and subsequently arranged as a match. Though the complete manuscript is not extant, it is known that there were three topics given; the other two are "Hearing the Wild Geese at Dawn" and "Deer by a Farmhouse." Go-Toba called this session right after the results of another match known as the *Keishō jishin uta awase* (Poem Match of Senior Nobles and Courtiers) were announced. "Impromptu" (*tōza*) means that the topics were given on the same day as the match, as distinct from the usual *kendai*, where some days were allowed between the announcement of the topics and the submission of the poems. For the match preceding this one, for instance, Teika received the topics on 7.10 and at Go-Toba's urging submitted his poems early, on 7.20; the match itself, involving ten poets on each side, was formally held on 7.25 (*Zenhyōshaku*, 2: 330–31).

The poet handles the somewhat unwieldy topic in an interesting, witty manner. The concept itself, that the speaker's love is deeper than the mountain, is not unexpected, but its translation into a situation is imaginative. He had thought the far reaches of the mountain path to be a measure (the word used is *tayori*, "affinity, relation") of the depths of his feelings, but after actually following the road to the end, he realizes that his heart is far more profound. The poem is classified under the *yūgen* style in *Teika jittei*.

37. *SKKS* 625, Winter.

The effect of this poem, one of those Saigyō included in the Mimosusogawa solo match judged by Shunzei, is generated chiefly by the inspired juxtaposition between the upper and lower sections, as underscored by the syntax, as well as the contrast between past and present, a bygone spring and the scene of winter-withered reeds now. How that springtime must have been is left to the imagination, though it helps to know that Saigyō is alluding to the following poem by Priest Nōin:

Goshūishū 43, Spring. "Sent to someone around the New Year, when he was in Tsu Province."

kokoro aramu hito ni miseba ya *tsu no kuni no* *naniwa* atari no *haru* no keshiki o	Would I could show it to someone with heart to feel, the aura of *springtime* along the shores of *Naniwa* *in the land of Tsu*!

Here as well, the spring scene is evoked, not described; the ecstatic response of Nōin's speaker only suggests the breathtaking loveliness of that Naniwa spring to which Saigyō alludes in his poem. The shriveled leaves evoke by contrast what Nōin's spring must have been like—the reeds newly sprung and a tender green, the air suffused with a soft warmth, the haze over the bay waters. Another effect of comparing Saigyō's poem to its honka is to underscore his point, which is simply to evoke that sense of wonder at phenomenal change when viewed outside the frame of, say, causation and logical sequence, and with full regard for the riddling question of memory and time, and of reality. That would be how a person of sensibility (*kokoro aramu hito* in Nōin's poem) would view it. It is probably for this unspoken level of significance that Shunzei judged it as having the quality of *yūgen*.

38. *SKKS* 987. "Composed when he came to the vicinity of Azuma."

Azuma was a general name for the Eastern Provinces, particularly the area east of Ashigara Barrier in Sagami Province (Kanagawa). The mountain Sayononaka (there is an implicit pun on *yo no naka*, "midst of night") in Ogasa District, Shizuoka Prefecture, lies between Nissaka and Kanaya, old stations on the Tōkaidō highway. Saigyō was on his way to the Ōshū region from Ise. Centuries later, the figure of Saigyō in his mind, Bashō would write about a similar trip from Edo in *Oku no hosomichi* (The Narrow Road to the Deep North).

The poem does not employ any of the formal allusive devices, like *engo* and *honkadori*, that are responsible for the textural richness of most of the poetry in the *Shinkokinshū*. Saigyō is primarily concerned with expressing an emotion so deeply felt that it does not need the traditional trappings of the poetic idiom. In this sense, the poem best exemplifies Shinkei's understanding of *yūgen*, especially in its conviction of feeling and its manifestly spare, "unadorned" quality. Like the preceding poem, *tsu no kuni no*, it conveys the feelings of an old man, but whereas the former projects a sharp contrast between two distinct points in time, symbolically represented by spring and winter in Naniwa, this one explores the long span of years between two such points. This is perhaps an overly fine point to make, but it is prompted by a consideration of the rhetorical question, *toshi takete / mata koyubeshi to / omoiki ya*, which, with all its implications, may be paraphrased thus: "Here I am again on the road to the North. Looking back to that time when I first crossed Sayononaka Mountain, did I even imagine then that I should come this way once more, as I do now—the years heavy upon my brow?" This is immediately followed by the exclamation *inochi narikeri* (lit., "Ah, . . . life!"), which is the high point of the poem, a pithy statement open to all sorts of interpretations beyond the first reading, "that I should live to see it!" and a second reading, "Such is life. . . ." In effect, it sums up the poet's deep emotion as he contemplates the years of his life, the fact that he has lived to see this moment.

Saigyō was sixty-nine at the time (1186), traveling once more to the Northern Provinces, which he had visited on a long journey around 1144, when he would have been only twenty-seven, just four years after taking the momentous decision to renounce the world, and still uncertain perhaps of the wisdom of that move. The years between had been marked by the hardships of constant travel and religious austerities, undertaken against a background of political turmoil caused by the incessant quarrels among the monasteries, the struggle for ascendancy between the Heike and Minamoto clans that culminated in the Gempei Wars of 1180–85 and brought about the effective eclipse of the court aristocracy. Viewed in this light, that single exclamation acquires deeper meaning and the whole poem a breadth and humanity quite rare among the narrowly circumscribed personal effusions of court poetry. The element of tone is handled in an impressive manner; it is here majestically moving, with something of the quality of a slow, submerged theme in music. Kubota Jun's final comment on it is wholly sound: "A simple, honest confession nearly bare of ornament. The kind of poem that transcends commentary and will nevertheless draw much comment, but none will shake the certitude of the author's immediate emotion" (*Zenhyōshaku* 4: 659).

Chapter Eight

1. *Yakumo mishō* VI: "Knowledge does not mean reading the literature of India and China. It simply means to study thoroughly the meaning of the old [Japanese] poems. What is called learning has its source in none other than the *Man'yōshū* and the *Kokinshū*" (Sasaki Nobutsuna, ed., *NKT* 3: 9–94 [Kazama Shobō, 1956], p. 92). The *Yakumo mishō* (The August Eightfold Cloud Treatise), a compendium of waka learning since the Heian period, was written by Go-Toba's son, Emperor Juntoku (1197–1242; r. 1210–1221), sometime before his exile to Sado in 1221 in connection with the Jōkyū Disturbance, though he made emendations and additions subsequently. It is arranged into six sections dealing with poetic genres and modes; the formal procedures for poem contests at court; a classified list of the waka lexicon; commentary on types of language usage; explanations and citations of places famous in poetry; the requisite mental attitude for poetic composition and evaluations of various poets. Its broad and systematic, textbook-like coverage of the various areas of poetic learning makes it a good source for waka poetics and practice from the Heian to the early medieval period.

2. Shinkei must be referring here to the judgment made by Shunzei (1114–1204) in Round 13, "Withered Fields," of the first Winter section of the *Roppyakuban uta awase* (Poetry Contest in 600 Rounds), where he chooses the Left poem by Yoshitsune for the evocative quality of its diction, particularly its use of the words *kusa no hara* (field of grass) from a poem by Oborozukiyo, *ukimi yo ni*, in the "Hana no en" (Festival of Cherry Blossoms) chapter of the *Genji* (see *Genji monogatari*, ed. Abe Akio et al., *NKBZ* 12–17 [Shōgakkan, 1970–76], 1: 427). He chides the opposite side for criticizing precisely those words as unfamiliar: "That the representative of the Right should criticize 'field of grass' is much too extreme. Murasaki Shikibu's skill as a writer [of prose] is not only superior to that of poets, the 'Hana no en' chapter is especially fine. For a poet not to have read the *Genji* is a deplorable thing" (*Roppyakuban uta awase*, ed. Taniyama Shigeru, in *Uta awase shū*, *NKBT* 74 [Iwanami Shoten, 1965], p. 442). The usual reading for the second sentence about Murasaki Shikibu's skill in prose, *Murasaki Shikibu, utayomi no hodo yori mo mono kaku fude wa shushō no ue, Hana no en no maki wa koto ni yū aru mono nari*, takes it to mean that her own ability in poetry is not equal to her excellent prose. I take *utayomi* to be "poets," which seems more logical in the context of the preceding and following sentences. This is too complex an issue to explore here (see Taniyama's supplementary n. 46, esp. p. 539b); suffice it to say that both Shunzei and Teika were enthusiastic advocates of allusions to *Genji* in waka composition.

3. The work of transcribing the original Chinese-character text of the *Man'yōshū* into the Japanese *kana* syllabary was carried out in the Pear-Garden Hall (Nashitsubo, more com-

monly known as Shōyōsha), one of the imperial-consort apartments located northeast of the emperor's quarters. Five poets were appointed by Emperor Murakami in 951 to this task, in addition to compiling the second imperial anthology, *Gosenshū*. Thereafter known as "The Five Poets of the Pear Garden," they were Minamoto Shitagō (911–983), Sakanoue Mochiki (fl. ca. 950), Ki Tokifumi (fl. ca. 950), Ōnakatomi Yoshinobu (922–991), and Kiyohara Motosuke (908–990).

4. *Kindai shūka* (Superior Poems of Our Time): "If in diction you admire the old, in conception seek out the new; if you strive for unparalleled heights of configuration and learn from the poems of the pre-Kampyō era, how can you fail to produce good poetry?" (Ed. Fujihira Haruo in *Karonshū*, *NKBZ* 50 [Shōgakkan, 1975], p. 471.)

The Kampyō era (889–98) was the name of Emperor Uda's reign. Modern textual editors of the *Kindai shūka* generally agree that by "pre-Kampyō," Teika was referring to the work of Narihira, Komachi, and the other so-called Six Poetic Geniuses (Rokkasen) active around the years 830–80, who are credited with stimulating the revival of native waka, which had been eclipsed by the vogue for Chinese poetry subsequent to the age of the *Man'yōshū* (comp. ca. 759).

5. These various styles may be briefly described thus: (1) the Intricate Style (*komayakanaru tei*) creates a densely intricate aesthetic effect through complex rhetorical technique; (2) the Style of Singular Conception (*hitofushi no aru tei*) is characterized by a startling or arresting conception; (3) the Style of Meditation (*ushintei*) gives a sense of being immersed in contemplation upon a deep poetic realm; (4) the Lofty Style (*take takaki tei*) has a sense of transcendent fluidity produced by a tightly controlled diction; (5) the Demon-Quelling Style (*kiratsutei*) possesses a terrifying power in its meaning and diction. (Definitions based on headnotes 11, 13, 16–18 to Teika's *Maigetsushō*, p. 514.)

The quotation from Teika reflects the following *Maigetsushō* passage: "Having first of all acquired a fluent mastery of the simple and graceful configuration, you will find that the others—like the Lofty Style, the Style of Visual Description [*miru tei*], the Style of Wit [*omoshiroki tei*], the One-Figure Style, and the Intricate Style, will easily come of themselves. It is true that the Demon-Quelling Style is difficult to learn. But having undergone the utmost training, why should you not be able to compose even in such a style?" (Ed. Fujihira Haruo in *Karonshū*, *NKBZ* 50 [Shōgakkan, 1975], pp. 514–15.)

It is evident that Shinkei's citation deviates from the original passage above. Such is generally true of all his citations from other sources, with the exception of poetry. He does not quote verbatim, because he is obviously citing from memory. Isolated from their original contexts, moreover, such passages have undergone a change of emphasis in the process of being used within Shinkei's own system of thought. Strictly speaking, they are not quotations as we know them but rather interpretations, or in a sense, "translations." Thus by referring to the original "quoted" passages, one should be able to trace the external building blocks as well as their unique and specific evolution in Shinkei's poetics.

6. Cf. the following passage from *Sangoki*:

> This style [*gōrikitei*, the Stark Style] is probably the highest. It is among all the most difficult to master. It is strongly forbidden to attempt it at an early stage, for your poetry will then gradually lose its charm and come to resemble the vulgar poems in appearance. You should merely keep it in mind and desist from composing in it until you are thoroughly proficient. And then, when your mind has been rendered powerful by constant practice, and your words follow one another with invincible force, the poem of power will emerge of itself. It is a style that manifests the "bone" and is unconcerned with overtones [*yojō*]. It seems that even Kingo held it to be the Absolute Truth of Poetry. However, if I declare it to be the highest style, everyone—even amateurs and the untalented, will be so fired with the idea that they will not rest until they have tried it, and distorted it in the process by

> producing nonsensical poems. . . . In my opinion, strength of execution may be considered the mark of excellence in all endeavors, and therefore it must be said that the Demon-Quelling Style is indeed the very heart of Poetry. (Ed. Sasaki Nobutsuna, *NKT* 4 [Kazama Shobō, 1956], pp. 328–29)

The *Sangoki*, it must be noted, belongs to the group of forged manuscripts attributed to Teika, the others being *Guhishō*, *Gukenshō*, and *Kirihioke*. Dating from sometime between the late Kamakura and early Muromachi periods, they are believed to have been forged from two genuine Teika manuscripts originally preserved in the Reizei branch of Teika's descendants, but subsequently lost (see *JCP*, pp. 348–52, for a fuller account). Considered authentic all throughout the medieval period, these treatises wielded a great influence in the contemporary poetic milieu, notably on two of its central figures, Shōtetsu and Shinkei. Thus, although it is impossible to determine in what way they reflect or distort Teika's thought, there can be no doubt about their literary-historical significance.

As we have seen in the previously quoted *Maigetsushō* passage, Teika does say that the Demon-Quelling Style (also called the Stark Style in *Sangoki*) is difficult and can only be wielded after the most rigorous training. Whether he also privately considered it the highest style, constituting Poetry's ultimate principle, as the *Sangoki* maintains, is an interesting question, but the point is that Shinkei considered this opinion significant enough to include it in *Sasamegoto*. It will be remembered that he himself composed a poem in this style, which earned Shōtetsu's censure for its unrefined image, "swollen with stormy winds / it spits the moon" (*arashi o fukumi / tsuki o haku*) (see *HF*, pp. 44–45).

7. "What people generally understand by an excellent poem is one that is simple and innocent of striking features [*mumon*], uncomplicated in conception, and calmly flowing in diction. This is a superficial view. If such a poem were to be considered a masterpiece, then no doubt we would be producing masterpieces with every poem" (*Maigetsushō*, pp. 520–21).

8. Shinkei is quoting from the Mana [Chinese] Preface of the *Kokinshū*. Looking back to an ancient time when the Japanese emperors encouraged the presentation of poems on public occasions and allegedly employed them as an instrument of government, the Mana Preface deplores the subsequent decline of Japanese poetry due to the popularity of Chinese poetic composition at court, and to a shift in the temper of the times, which it describes thus:

> From then on, the age became frivolous, and people came to value wantonness and extravagance. Weightless words rose, teeming like clouds, and the current of sensual pleasure [*enryū*] gushed forth like a spring. The seeds of Poetry fell; its flowers alone flourished. The amorous used it as a messenger of "the birds and flowers," and beggars employed it as a means of livelihood. And thus it halfway became the companion of women, not fit to be presented before stalwart men.

The Mana preface then proceeds to illustrate the poetry of recent times with a critical evaluation of the Six Poetic Geniuses, and continues: "Apart from them there were numerous others, and one cannot name them all. However, most of them took alluring beauty [*en*] as the basis, and had no understanding of the meaning of Poetry" (*NKBT* ed., pp. 336–39). The "seed" (*mi*, also rendered as "fruit") is a metaphor for a poem's *kokoro*—its meaning, content, conception or intention—and "flower" (*hana*) for a poem's *kotoba*—its words, diction, and form.

Chapter Nine

1. This is a reference to the *tanrenga* (short renga) of the Heian period (794–1185), which was regarded as renga's germinal form. It was simply a waka poem divided into two parts: the upper 5-7-5–syllable hemistich composed by one person and the lower 7-7–syllable hemistich by another as a reply. It was a vehicle for witty repartee, examples of which may be found in the tenth-century *Yamato monogatari* and other poem tales, as well as in imperial waka an-

thologies from the *Gosenshū* (951) to the *Kin'yōshu* (1126). The longer sequences, called *kusari renga* (chain renga), gradually appeared from the period of the cloistered emperors (1086–1156) on, and by the Kamakura period, the 100-verse sequence, or *hyakuin*, had become the standard length.

Shinkei's reference to *tanrenga* as evidence of the essential oneness of renga and waka makes sense only as a polemical argument. If any historical connection can be drawn at all from the viewpoint of aesthetic identity, it would be to *Shinkokinshū* poetry, in which the discontinuity between the upper and lower hemistich, with its resulting subtle effect, most resembles the mechanics of renga structure.

Chapter Ten

1. The distinction being drawn here is between formal poem collections and informal poem sequences. The model for the former is the imperial anthology, which represents the poetic legacy of a whole age, wherein poems by various authors are arranged according to external principles of thematic progression and social decorum. Sequences of 50 or 100 poems, on the other hand, are normally composed by a single author or by a small group during a specific time or for a specific occasion. Thus, whereas the opening poem of any volume in an imperial anthology is meant to be typical and should conform to the orthodox formal style, that of a 100-poem sequence inevitably reflects the particular circumstances, whether material or personal, in which it was composed, and may deviate from the standard style. It is pertinent to note here in passing that it is precisely the temporal and individual character of the poem sequence that made it possible to utilize Shinkei's works in this genre as material for his biography in my book *Heart's Flower*.

2. Here as in the earlier chapters, "old masters" is a reference to Gusai, Junkaku, Shinshō, Zen'a, and other leading poets of the Kamakura and Nambokuchō periods, who for Shinkei represented renga's earliest flowering. He frequently cites these "old masters" to give his argument the authority of precedent.

3. Evidently, in Shinkei's time, it was almost invariably the hokku that remained in people's minds after a particular session. Those that had caught their fancy were much talked about and immediately circulated by word of mouth, as was true, for instance, of Shinkei's hokku from 1466 that found their way into the *Inryōken* journal (see *HF*, pp. 78–80). Thus, since hokku could make a poet's reputation overnight, everyone naturally wished to sound different and original to attract attention. It was also around this time that poets started making separate collections of their hokku, as distinct from their tsukeku.

4. This is probably quoted from "The Biography of Xie Lingyun [385–433]" in the *Song Annals*: "In the more than four hundred years from [the start of] the Han [206 B.C.E.–220 C.E.] to the Wei [220–65 C.E.], literary styles have undergone a threefold transformation in the hands of writers and scholars" (*SSG*, p. 134, n. 10). Shinkei intends by the quotation no more than a summary comment on the ever-changing variety of poetic styles generated by shifts in taste and the pursuit of novelty. As indicated in his other works, however, he did not believe that novelty was in itself a mark of great poetry.

5. *GSIS* I: 1, Spring. "Composed on the first day of the First Month." This piece by Kodai no Kimi, one of the leading woman poets of her time, is the head-poem in the Spring volume, and consequently also the very first in the *Goshūishū*, the fourth imperial anthology. Very much in the Heian orthodox style of elegant confusion, it is obviously an allusive variation on *KKS* 1, *toshi no uchi ni* (see Chapter 6, n. 1).

6. *Shūi gusō* 1401. "100-poem sequence at the residence of the Regent and Minister of the Left [Kujō Norizane], Jōei 1 [1232], Fourth Month."

On the topic "Haze," this is the head-poem of the sequence, composed when Teika was already seventy. It appears as well in the imperial anthology *Shokukokinshū* (comp. 1265), but not as a head-poem, and in the Miscellaneous rather than the Spring section. The difference in placement is most probably due to the poem's strongly personal character, and illustrates Shinkei's point regarding the distinction between the head-poem of a formal anthology and of a *hyakushu* very well.

7. *Sōkonshū* XI:8342 [Year 1453], Eleventh Month. "On 'spring's robe of haze,' from the 100-Poem Sequence Prayer Offering to Hachiman held at the residence of the Master of the Left Division of the Capital [Hosokawa Katsumoto] on the nineteenth day."

Koromo (robe) in line 2 and *kasumi* (haze) in line 5 together make up *kasumi no koromo* (robe of haze), a metaphorical image for the harbinger of spring in the classical poetic vocabulary. The verb *tatsu* in line 4 means "to arise" and refers to the formation of the clouds and haze of line 5. The same verb, *tatsu*, occurs in the common expression *haru tatsu* (spring arises or appears), and therefore the third of the "three robes" left unnamed must be "spring robe." In other words, the poem is a kind of acrostic puzzle on its topic, "The Robe of Haze of Spring." The expression "three robes" also means the three kinds of surplices (*san'e*) worn by Buddhist monks, and might furthermore be an allusion to the three branches of the Hachiman (read Yahata in line 1) Shrine to which the poem sequence is dedicated. One senses that there is another hidden meaning in the poem, probably hinging on the connection between Hachiman, the god of warriors, and the *tamatebako* (jeweled box) of line 3, but it is not clear what this might be. At any rate, like Teika's poem, this one has a strong local and particularistic character due to the allusion to Hachiman and the possible correlation with the sequence's sponsorship by the daimyō Hosokawa Katsumoto; it would therefore not have been proper as a head-poem in an imperial anthology.

8. According to Yoshimoto's disciple Bontō, this hokku was composed at the Chion'in Temple in the Higashiyama hills east of the capital. Shinkei quotes it again in his letter to Sōgi and remarks that it is "inexpressibly marvelous in its evocation of the wide, distant prospect from the hilltop" (*Tokoro* III, p. 221). The poet is in effect commanding the bird to wing off from the hilltop of Chion'in, letting its cry resound as it flies clear across the outspread city below. As Shinkei says, there is indeed something marvelous about the way the hokku instantaneously summons up such a wide vista. It gives one pause, however, to consider that the whole effect would have been utterly lost to posterity had Bontō not happened to record its place of composition, a fact that indicates how closely the hokku is bound to the actual and specific circumstances of its composition.

9. Also by Yoshimoto and using the same image of the *hototogisu*, this hokku has a dimmer, more delicate tone texture in contrast to the bright wit and visual vividness of the first. The feeling evoked is one of strong anticipation, followed by a lonely regret. No doubt Shinkei set the two beside each other to illustrate how the same poetic materials can be handled in such a way as to create a totally different effect. The same unspoken intention is evident in his juxtaposition of the two hokku that follow below.

10. Gusai images the autumn leaves whirling down the mountainside in the wintry moonlight as *nusa*, branches or wands hung with long strips of cloth or paper, used to summon the gods in Shintō ritual. The last line, *kamunatsuki* (lit., "godless moon"), is the Tenth Month of the lunar calendar, and coincides with the beginning of winter. The hokku alludes to *KKS* 313: Autumn, "Composed on the same last day (of the Ninth Month)." Mitsune (fl. ca. 900).

michi shiraba	If I but knew the way,
tazune mo yukamu	I would go and visit it—
momijiba o	autumn that went,

nusa to tamukete	waving as sacred streamers
aki wa inikeri	the red leaves before the god.

11. According to Sōzei's report, this hokku was composed "at the Gojō Tamatsushima," a branch of the Tamatsushima Shrine erected at the former residence of the revered poet Shunzei (1114-1204) on Gojō Avenue. Dedicated to the god of poetry, Tamatsushima was an object of devout worship among medieval poets, including Shōtetsu and his disciples.

Shūa's hokku is similar to Gusai's in evoking a godly presence and in the use of wit in the poetic image, which here centers on the association between *migaku* (to polish) and *tama* (a round bead or gem) in the name Tamatsushima (lit., "isle of gems"). *Tama* is cognate with its homonym, which means inner life force, spirit, and it is possible that Shūa intends the hokku also to suggest the idea of poetic inspiration as a divine effulgence in the soul. His tone of reverent awe is distinct from the wild exhilaration of Gusai in the preceding hokku.

Chapter Eleven

1. "Most people consider double meaning to be the wellspring of poetry [*uta no minamoto*] and give it the highest importance. But to go too far and use a whole string of them at one time is positively distasteful" (*Yakumo misho* VI, p. 80). What I render as "double meaning" here is *shūku* (lit., a choice or superior line of verse), referring in waka critical usage to puns (*kakekotoba*) and associative words (*engo*).

2. The poem appears in Round 287 of the "Poetry Contest in 1,500 Rounds" sponsored by Rtd. Emperor Go-Toba in Kennin 1 (1201); it was composed by Go-Kyōgoku Regent Fujiwara Yoshitsune, not by Go-Toba, as Shinkei has it.

Akade, "unsatisfied, unsated," refers to the two situations juxtaposed in the poem: the pool water dripping from the persona's cupped hands before he has slaked his thirst, and the ending of spring before he has enjoyed it to the full. One is to understand that the persona has traveled all the way from the capital to the mountains, where spring comes later, in order to catch the late-blooming cherry blossoms, only to find them gone.

3. *Fuboku wakashū* VIII, "Flares." The piece is originally from a 100-poem sequence composed by Go-Toba's son, Rtd. Emperor Juntoku, author of the *Yakumo mishō* treatise. Takamado Hill is the southeastern extension of the Kasuga Hills in the old capital of Nara. The flares or torches in the poem were used by hunters to lure out the deer on summer nights. The double meaning is in line 3, *shikasuga ni*, a conjunctival phrase meaning "although it is so"; the embedded homonymic morpheme *shika* is also the word for "deer."

The *Fuboku wakashū* text has line 4 as *onore nakite ya*; accordingly, the poem's last three lines should read "in peril / do the deer yet cry out / knowing the summer is here?"

4. *Shinchokusenshū* XIII: Love, 851; *Shūi gusō* 2447, Love. Matsuho no ura was the ancient name of Iwaya no ura, the bay along the northern tip of Awaji Island in the Inland Sea overlooking Suma and Akashi. Composed during a poetry contest at court in Kempo 4 (1216), the poem activates the various meanings of *matsu* (to wait, pine tree) and *ho* (flame, sail) in the place-name Matsuho no ura. Simultaneously, there is an implied comparison of the frustrated lover to the sailboat becalmed in the windless evening, as well as to the seaweed fishermen burn for salt along the shore. Indeed, the proliferating metaphors and *engo* quite overwhelm the first level of meaning, which is given only at the beginning and end: *konu hito o / matsu . . . / mi mo kogaretsutsu* (lit., my body is seared again and again, waiting for someone who does not come), indicating that Teika was more interested in ambience than meaning. In particular, the interminable waiting and the subject's inability to let go are brought

out by the repetitive inflexion of the final verb. The translation is patently inadequate to the several levels of symbolism here and illustrates the difficulties of rendering *shūku* in English while retaining the suggestive economy of the original. I have chosen aesthetic tact over elaborating what is only implied.

5. *SKKS* 952, Travel. "Composed during a poetry contest at the residence of the Regent and Prime Minister [Fujiwara Yoshitsune], on the topic 'Evening Storm on a Journey.'"

There are these embedded polysemic moves: *karigoromo* (hunting robe) and *kari* (borrow) in line 3; *hi mo yūgure* (day dimming toward evening) and *himo yū* (knot the cord) in line 4. Thus a bifurcation of sense occurs from line 2 to 3 and again from line 3 to 4, but the transitions remain smooth, as of a curve skillfully negotiated.

6. *Shinchokusenshū* III: Summer; 192. Nara no ogawa in line 2 is a variant name for Mitarashigawa, the river flowing by the Upper Kamo Shrine in Kyōto, along whose banks the Mitarashi (lit., hand-laving) lustration rite was held in the last ten days of the Sixth Month, i.e., of summer. *Nara* as a common noun means "oak." The point of the poem is perhaps clearer when it is read against the other below, *GSIS* 271, Summer, on which it is an allusive variation.

natsuyama no	With the *oak leaves*
nara no ha *soyogu*	*rustling* upon the *summer* hills,
yūgure wa	the *evening dusk*
kotoshi mo aki no	recalls once again this year,
kokochi koso sure	the feel of the coming autumn.
Minamoto Yoritsuna	Minamoto Yoritsuna

7. *Shokukokinshū* V: Autumn; 448. Katano Field in Kawachi Province (Osaka) was an ancient imperial hunting ground; the pun hinges on *kata* (difficult) in the place-name. *Ama no kawa* (lit., River of Heaven) is an allusion to the romantic Chinese legend about the Weaving Maiden and the Herd Boy, the celestial lovers who were allowed to meet only once a year on the Seventh Night of the Seventh Moon. The lovers, representing the stars Altair and Vega, kept their annual tryst across the Heavenly River, the Milky Way. The legend has been a favorite theme in classical poetry from the *Man'yōshū* on and is still celebrated today during the Tanabata Festival.

8. This hokku was reportedly composed at the Kitano Shrine, which worships the spirit of Sugawara Michizane and was the official center of renga activities in the capital. *Chiri* means "scatter" in reference to the scarlet autumn leaves of line 1, but "dust, earth" in relation to the rest of the verse. In the latter sense, it is an allusion to the compassionate virtue of the bodhisattvas, enlightened beings who return to "mingle with the dust" of the earth, assuming ordinary mortal guise in order to lead humans to salvation. In other words, the verse embodies the concept of *honji suijaku* (lit., dripped traces from the fundamental ground) by which Japanese deities were seen as incarnations of buddhas and bodhisattvas, a belief ultimately founded on the numinosity of the phenomenal.

9. *Nagatsuki* (lit., long moon) is the name of the Ninth Month of the lunar calendar; it refers in this context particularly to the full moon of the fifteenth night, considered the most beautiful in the year. The poet describes it as "remaining" in the sky in relation to the sun, which sank in the west just as it appeared in the east. Unlike the subtle resonance of the pun on *chiri* in Gusai's hokku, the double function of *naga* here has no apparent poetic effect and seems merely mechanical. Did Shinkei intend it as a negative example of the unmotivated and indiscriminate use of punning?

Chapter Twelve

1. This passage from the *Maigetsushō* has been quoted once before (see Chapter 8, n. 7), with a slight variation.

2. *Go-Toba-in onkuden*: "Priest Shun'e composed in a smooth, quiet manner. He is said to have declared that a poem should be composed so that it seems to glide as smoothly as a drop of water rolling down the length of a five-foot iris leaf [*goshaku no ayamegusa ni mizu o ikaketaru yō ni*]" (ed. Hisamatsu Sen'ichi, *NKBT* 65: 145; see also Robert Brower, trans., "Ex-Emperor Go-Toba's Secret Teachings," p. 36). Shinkei's quotation varies slightly from the original; it says, *goshaku no ayame ni mizu o kaketaru gotoku ni*. In the *Onkuden*, *ikaketaru* expresses the sense of water gliding down the long iris stalk or leaf, while in *Sasamegoto*, *kaketaru* simply conveys the moist dewiness of the iris stalk after being watered. Consequently, Shinkei describes the poetic effect illustrated by this image as *nurenure to sashinobitaru* (translated "a spaciousness and cool wetness"), an immaculate yet vital quality ultimately related to his concept of "coolness and slenderness" (*yase samuku*).

3. The Great Hall of State (Daigokuden) was the most august building in the compound housing the various government offices in the Greater Imperial Palace (Daidairi). Inside was the Imperial Seat, from where the Emperor held court and presided over the most important state ceremonies. The qualities of resoluteness and immovable courage illustrated by this metaphor recall the Demon-Quelling Style mentioned in Chapter 8.

4. The twenty-seventh chapter of the *Lotus Sutra* recounts how the princes Jōzō and Jōgen converted their nonbeliever father to the right views by performing supernatural feats such as emitting fire from various parts of their bodies, or making themselves so large as to fill empty space. *Hokkekyō* [a bilingual Chinese-Japanese edition of the Lotus Sutra], ed. and trans. Sakamoto Yukio and Iwamoto Yutaka (Iwanami Shoten, 1976), 3: 292–96; *Scripture of the Lotus Blossom of the Fine Dharma*, trans. Leon Hurvitz (New York: Columbia University Press, 1976), pp. 326–27.

Shinkei's source for the quotation, however, is evidently the *Mumyōshō* chapter called "Poetry Resembles the Preaching of Chūin," where Chōmei quotes the following anecdote told by Priest Yūsei:

> In commenting on the marvelous transformations of King Myoshōgonnō's two sons, it is the usual thing to say, "In their immensity, they fill the empty space; in their minuteness, they can slip into a poppy seed." When Chūin preaches, however, he says, "In their immensity, even the empty space constrains them; in their minuteness, the space in a poppy seed is yet too big for them." Now that is a wonderfully waka-like conception. One should understand poetry in this way, as a matter of lending color to old materials and turning them into something rare. As for poems that are merely novel, I should think they are easy to compose, if one were really bent on it. (pp. 47–48)

If the *Mumyōshō* is indeed Shinkei's source, it is clear that he has discarded the whole context of the quotation there, and has merely adopted Chūin's brilliant exegesis to make one of his own on a poem's marvelous power to simultaneously evoke boundlessness and the most minutely elusive feeling. He is, of course, illustrating the style of rich ambiguity commonly associated with Teika and Shōtetsu.

5. A possible source is the following line from "A Memorial to Liu Ziyu" by Su Dongpo (Su Shi) (1036–1101), giving a curt evaluation of four major Tang poets: "Meng Haoran was cold, Jia Dao meager, Yuan Zhen superficial, and Bai Juyi common" (quoted in *SSG*, p. 258, suppl. n. 7).

6. *SIS* 224, Winter, Tsurayuki.

omoikane	As beset by yearning
imogari yukeba	I seek my beloved's abode,
fuyu no yo no	in the wintry night

kawakaze samumi — the river wind gusts so cold
chidori naku nari — the plovers are crying.

In the *Mumyōshō*, Chōmei reports the following remark by his teacher Shun'e regarding this poem: "Nothing can match this poem for sheer atmosphere [*omokage*]. Someone has rightly said, 'It strikes chill in the heart even when recited on Kanzan's memorial day on the twenty-sixth of the Sixth Month'" (p. 90).

A Hieizan monk in the reign of Emperor Daigo (885–930; r. 897–930), Chaplain Kanzan is said to have attacked several emperors after his death out of resentment of the court's inadequate reward of his services. The *Ōkagami* for one attributes the blindness of Emperor Sanjō (976–1017; r. 1011–1016) to his vengeful spirit. See Helen Craig McCullough, trans., *Ōkagami, The Great Mirror: Fujiwara Michinaga (966–1027) and His Times* (Ann Arbor: Center for Japanese Studies, University of Michigan, 1991), pp. 83, 138, 257. His name appears in other medieval sources, including the *Heike monogatari* and the *Jikkinshō*.

On the Chaplain's memorial day on 6.26, the heat was reportedly more torrid than usual due to his angry spirit. The point of Shinkei's reference is to illustrate the powerful efficacy of a poem's chill *omokage* to counteract the heat of a passionate hatred.

7. This appears to be a condensed version of a longer account in the *Kirihioke*, one of the forged Teika treatises. Shinkei preserves the main outline of the story and faithfully transmits its original point. See *Kirihioke* (Paulownia-Tub Brazier), attr. to Teika, ed. Sasaki Nobutsuna, in *NKT* 4: 264–90 (Kazama Shobō, 1956), pp. 273–74.

8. "To reach the bone" (*kotsu o etaru*) clearly means to take hold of what is most essential in the art of poetry, to penetrate to its very root and foundation. It is not possible to determine solely from this anecdote what the term *kotsu* signifies in concrete terms. In a brief article on the usage of this and other "bone"-related terminology in Yoshimoto's renga treatises, Kaneko Kinjirō points out that it refers specifically to the instinctive creative power that results from long, rigorous training. Its operation is manifest in the poet's artistic control of the materials of his craft, in his infallible choice of words, for instance, or thorough handling of *tsukeai* (linking). *Kotsu* then signifies virtuosity and consummate execution; as we have seen, the *Sangoki* associates it with the Demon-Quelling Style (see Chapter 8, n. 6). Kaneko, "Yoshimoto rengaron no kotsu," pp. 27, 30.

Chapter Thirteen

1. This statement reflects upon the nature of renga as a social activity, as part of or even the main feature of a gathering to celebrate a particular occasion such as an important birthday, a victory in battle, an excursion to view cherry blossoms, and so on. As such, it would have been the natural tendency to promote a convivial atmosphere through the use of auspicious words like those scornfully quoted by Shinkei in his reply, or conversely, to censor unpropitious language that might be offensive to the members of the party.

2. The life of the Tang poet Du Fu (712–770) was marked by constant hardship and deprivation and particularly exacerbated by the sociopolitical dislocations of the An Lushan Rebellion, and he seems to have lapsed into near despair in his last years. Shinkei, whom the civil disorders of the times had driven into exile in 1463 when he wrote these lines, and who would again become a refugee with the outbreak of the Ōnin War in 1467, must have felt a special kinship with this Chinese poet. In his use of poetry as an instrument of social and moral protest, something almost unknown in Japanese poetry since Okura in the *Man'yōshū*, he would doubtless have been inspired by the example of Du Fu, who was held in very high esteem by the Song poets, as well as by the monks of the Gozan Zen temples who wrote

Chinese poetry (see Haga, *Chūsei Zenrin*, pp. 314–15). Shinkei's own nephew trained for the priesthood at Kenninji, one of the Gozan temples, and he was friendly with the poet-monk Banri Shūkyū (b. 1428). See also *HF*, pp. 80, 151, 171.

Chapter Fourteen

1. It is reasonable to infer from this statement and the information in the question that an ordinary 100-verse sequence at this time took around six hours, from dawn till noon. In Shinkei's opinion, however, a session should last for a whole day, from dawn till dusk. Twelve hours for 100 verses gives 7.2 minutes per verse, but in practice the poets surely took less than that, since some time would have been allotted for at least one intermission. No doubt, it was possible to cut the time in half, as in the sessions of the commoners, but as Shinkei says, the product would not have been of much interest. Quite apart from the obvious fact that superior poetry takes time, a renga verse is by its very nature difficult to compose because of the formal restrictions put on the individual poet. That is to say, he had at one and the same time to fulfill two requirements: one, that he relate to the maeku, a verse composed by someone else and wholly unpredictable in character; and, two, that he observe the rules of progression stipulating the numerical occurrences of themes and images in terms of the whole sequence. Such conditions make renga more difficult to compose than, say, waka. As Sōchō would later observe, waka is like mounting an assault on a castle; one can bide one's time, and the attempt need not be decisive. Renga, on the other hand, is like hand-to-hand combat on the battlefield; the moment comes, with its fixed and unpredictable circumstance (i.e., the maeku), and one can only try once and for all. See Sōchō, *Renga hikyōshū* [A Collection of Analogies to Renga], ed. Ijichi Tetsuo, *Rengaronshū*, 2: 161–85 (Iwanami Shoten, 1956), p. 181.

2. *SKKS* 1599, Miscellaneous. "Composed for the Wakadokoro Poetry Contest on the subject 'Autumn Wind Along the Barrier Road.'" This poetry contest was held on 8.3.1201, just six days after Rtd. Emperor Go-Toba established the Wakadokoro (Poetry Bureau) in his Nijō Palace for the compilation of the *Shinkokinshū*. Yoshitsune's poem was matched against one by Asukai Masatsune and won.

Fuwa Barrier in Mino Province (Gifu Prefecture) was one of the three ancient barrier forts established to guard the Heijōkyō capital at Nara; the other two were Suzuka Barrier in Ise and Arachi Barrier in Echizen. Said to date from Emperor Temmu's reign (673–86), Fuwa Barrier had already fallen into disrepair by the early Heian period.

3. The significance of *tada* in this poem whose profundity has amazed so many is explained in the following passage from Tō no Tsuneyori's *Shinkokinwakashū kikigaki*: "The word *tada* is truly rare and marvelous. The poet is saying that the wind blowing over the Barrier after it has been ruined is *only the autumn wind throughout the four seasons*. He does so because the essential nature [*hon'i*] of the autumn wind is its profoundly melancholy and moving quality. In its ineffability of feeling, this is truly an awe-inspiring poem" (quoted in *Zenhyōshaku*, 7: 336; emphasis added). For Tsuneyori's association with Shinkei and Sōgi, see *HF*, pp. 44, 135–36, 169–70.

The content and phrasing of Tsuneyori's commentary echo the corresponding *Sasamegoto* passage here. As we know, he too was a former disciple of Shōtetsu's; thus, in all likelihood, he is actually transmitting that poet's interpretation here. In fact, it came to be the standard reading of this poem in subsequent medieval-period commentaries, including Kenzai's *Shinkokin nukigakishō*, said to transmit Shinkei's teachings (*Zenhyōshaku*, 9:142), and Sōgi's *Jisankachū*, which may also be partly traced to Shōtetsu through the mediation of both

Shinkei and Tsuneyori. Given the specific reading of *tada* in this commentary, perhaps the last line of the poem should be rendered "ever only the chill gusts of autumn."

Chapter Fifteen

1. *Rongo* (Ch. *Lunyu*; *The Analects* of Confucius) II.30, p. 51, in the *Shinshaku kambun taikei* (hereafter *SKT*) series, ed. Yoshida Kengō, *SKT* 1 (Meiji Shoin, 1980). In this bilingual Chinese-Japanese text, the passages are numbered consecutively from §I to §X, not separately for each section. Unless otherwise identified, translations from the *Rongo* and other primary source-texts are mine.

2. "But of them all it was Kongzi [Confucius] who was the timely one," viz., who in the fullness of time gathered in himself all the attributes of a sage. The quotation is in *The Chinese Classics*, trans. James Legge (1861; reprint, Taipei: SMC Publishing, 1994), vol. 2, *Mencius,* bk. V, pt. II, chap. I.5. Shinkei is apparently misquoting *Mencius* here; Shu Qi does not appear in the corresponding passage in *Mencius*, and it was Liu Xiahui who represented harmony, not Yi Yin. However, his point about Kongzi's being the complete sage is clear enough. Like his brother Bo Yi, Shu Qi chose to starve to death rather than bowing to the aggression of King Wu of Zhou (r. 1122–1115 B.C.E.) against the Shang dynasty, which he overthrew, and therefore he may also be said to be one of the "pure-hearted" sages. The names of the two brothers appear together in the *Zhuangzi,* chap. VI ("The Great and Venerable Teacher"), as models of the pure man; perhaps Shinkei had this in mind when he inadvertently emended *Mencius.* See Wing-Tsit Chan, *A Sourcebook in Chinese Philosophy* (Princeton, N.J.: Princeton University Press, 1963), p. 192; and Burton Watson, trans., *The Complete Works of Chuang Tzu* (New York: Columbia University Press, 1968), pp. 78–79.

3. "The most honored of two-legged beings" is the translation of *ryōsokuson* (Skt. *dvipadottama*), one of the Buddha's epithets. Shinkei means that he was called so because of his tolerance and all-encompassing understanding.

"The Three Vehicles" (*sanjō*) are the three paths to enlightenment as practiced by (1) the *shōmon* (auditor; Skt. *śrāvaka*), who aims to be an *arhant* and achieves salvation for himself alone by listening to the sermons of a Buddha; (2) the *engaku* (condition perceiver; Skt. *pratyekabuddha*), who attains salvation through his own efforts by perceiving the principle of dependent arising that operates in the universe; and (3) the *bosatsu* (Skt. *bodhisattva*), who aims to become a Buddha and in the process saves countless other beings as well. Seen from the Mahayana (Great Vehicle) point of view, the ways of the *shōmon* and *engaku* are yet deficient and narrow, representing the Hinayana (Lesser Vehicle), because they aim only for their own salvation without helping others to achieve the same. The bodhisattva is therefore strictly speaking the only authentic Mahayana saint.

As embodied in the *Lotus Sutra*, one of the central Mahayana teachings is that the Three Vehicles are only devices (*hōben*; Skt. *upāya*) to lure the various ignorant beings to salvation, in spite of themselves, as it were. There is actually only One Vehicle (*ichijō*), encompassing the other three and aimed solely at bringing all the sentient creatures without discrimination to the enlightenment of Buddhahood. Such is the message illustrated by the famous Parable of the Burning House.

Thus Shinkei means that just as the Buddha does not discriminate among those who practice the three different paths to salvation, making the One Supreme Vehicle available to all of them regardless, so in the realm of poetry, one should not be partial to only one style to the exclusion of the others. The implication, if one is to be drawn, is that the various styles all equally lead to the one supreme and undifferentiated goal of poetic enlightenment.

Chapter Sixteen

1. *Rongo* II.27, p. 49. "The Master said, 'If a man keeps cherishing his old knowledge, so as continually to be acquiring new, he may be a teacher of others'" (*Chinese Classics*, trans. Legge, 1: 149).

2. *Hokkekyō* 3: 306 (chap. 27); see also *Scripture of the Lotus Blossom*, trans. Hurvitz, p. 329. The quotation appears in the speech of a Buddha to King Myōshōgonnō, confirming that his sons Jōzō and Jōgen were indeed "friends of right knowledge" who caused him to abandon his wrong views and thus achieve enlightenment. (See also Chapter 12, n. 4.)

3. *Hokkekyō* 1: 118 (chap. 2); also *Scripture of the Lotus Blossom*, trans. Hurvitz, p. 41.

Chapter Seventeen

1. Ziyou (or Wang Huizhi), son of the famous Jin dynasty calligrapher Wang Xizhi (321–79), is the free spirit and lover of bamboos who figures in Shinkei's *Oi no kurigoto* (see *HF*, pp. 161, 163). His friend Andao (the *tzu* of Dai Kui) is the pure-minded artist and scholar who adamantly refused to serve as minstrel to the king of Wuliang (*Mōgyū* 1.470).

Shinkei is alluding here to an anecdote found in *Mōgyū* (Ch. *Meng qiu*), ed. Hayakawa Mitsusaburo, *SKT* 58–59 (Meiji Shoin, 1973), among other places, where the following version appears under the title "You Visits Dai." One night when Ziyou was staying in Shanyin (Shaoxing, Zhejiang Province), thick snow fell, and when it cleared, the earth lay utterly bright and gleaming in the moonlight all around. Drinking alone and reciting a poem before this marvelous scenery, Ziyou suddenly felt a deep yearning to see his friend Andao, who was then in Yan (south of Shanyin). Quickly, he got into a small boat and sailed throughout the night, arriving in Yan toward dawn. When he reached Andao's gate, however, he stopped, and without going in turned around and went home again. When someone asked him the reason, he replied, "Riding upon the moment's mood, I went; the mood spent, I returned. What need was there to see Andao?" (*Mōgyū* 1: 432–33).

The anecdote is also cited in a Kamakura-period collection of instructive tales, *Jikkinshō* (comp. 1252), §V: "One Should Choose One's Friends." The author, a lay monk at Rokuhara, draws from it the moral that "Even the most convivial party will seem no more than indifferent if it does not include a friend who truly answers to one's heart" (quoted in *SSG*, suppl. n. 11; see also *Jikkinshō*, ed. Nagazumi Yasuaki [Iwanami Shoten, 1942], p. 126).

The point of the anecdote in *Mōgyū*, however, lies in Ziyou's profoundly paradoxical behavior, and that is also what impressed Shinkei, who sees in it evidence of a "remarkably subtle and profound sensibility" (*nasake fukaku*; *en fukaki* in the *SSG* rev. ed. text). In other words, Ziyou shows a mind wholly at one with the Dao, or Nature, moving when its spirit moved him in the form of moonlight and snow and stopping when the brilliant moon had faded at dawn. In particular, Shinkei saw deep feeling in his refusal to mar a pure-minded friendship based on the Dao by forcing the moment beyond its natural span, and this despite his longing to see Andao and the far distance he had come. To have gone in to his friend and talked of moonlight when the sun was up would have been utterly pointless and trivial, unworthy of a pure and lofty sensibility. (No doubt, if the story had a sequel, Ziyou would have composed a poem on that night and sent it to Andao.) In *Sasamegoto* II, Chapter 48, Shinkei cites the *Kunshishū* to the effect that the association of sages and poets is like water, thin and purifying to the mind, but durable, and that of small men like sweet wine, thick and close, but only for a while.

2. An allusion to the following famous anecdote in vol. 1 of the *Lienü zhuan*, a collection of tales about exemplary women put together by Liu Xiang (77–6 B.C.E.). When Mencius was small, he lived with his mother near a graveyard. He used to play there, jumping into

the grave pits and burying himself in earth, pretending to be dead. Thinking such games unfit for a child, his mother decided to move to another neighborhood, which happened to be near a marketplace. However, seeing how the child was exposed to the insincere and self-serving flattery of the sellers, she decided to move again, this time to a place near a school. There she saw how observing the proper performance of rites had a salutary effect on her son, and so she decided to stay. The boy grew up to master the Six Classics and became the great Confucian philosopher Mencius (cited in *SSG*, p. 258, suppl. n. 12; see also the brief citation in *Jikkinshō*, p. 131). Shinkei alludes to this anecdote to illustrate the great influence of social environment in moulding a man's mind and character.

3. *Rongo* IV.69: "The Master said, 'Only the good man can truly like people and truly dislike them'" (p. 89). This is so because the mind of a good man is clear and tranquil, like a mirror; it accurately reflects the good and bad in people without subjective distortion. Shinkei's interpretation, that this means "the good man cherishes the Way," goes a step further but does not violate the text, since it would be the presence or absence of the Way in people that is the good or bad in them.

4. This is an allusion to the anecdote in *Mōgyū* called "Boya Breaks the Strings [of his Lute]." Boya, who lived sometime during the Chunqiu period (770–450 B.C.E.), was a brilliant lute musician, and his friend Zhong Ziqi was one who infallibly divined the exact feeling that he was expressing through his playing, be it the loftiness of a great mountain or the roaring of a wide river. When Ziqi died, Boya smashed his lute, breaking its strings, and never played another note till the end of his life. This was because no one but Ziqi possessed an understanding equal to his music (*Mōgyū* 1: 341; see also *Jikkinshō*, p. 130). The original sources for the *Meng qiu* version are the *Liezi*, a Taoist text of undetermined date; and the *Lushi chunqiu*, a 26-vol. collection of legends and anecdotes thought to have been compiled by Lü Buwei (d. 235 B.C.E.), now believed to constitute a synthesis of earlier political and cosmological thought into a new, eclectic system.

5. *Kanjin ryakuyōshū*: "The *Shinjikangyō Sutra* says, 'Consider it of utmost importance to be close to a virtuous friend, and of secondary importance to listen to the preaching of the doctrine'" (*SSG* p. 143, n. 15). The *Kanjin ryakuyōshū* is a major Tendai text compiled by Bishop Eshin (or Genshin, 942–1017), founder of the Tendai Eshin school and sixth patriarch of the Jōdo Shin sect. His view that waka may be an instrument of meditation may have a bearing on Shinkei's belief in the religious uses of poetry.

6. *Daichidoron* (Skt. *Mahāprajñāpāramitā-śāstra*), XIX: "All the various phenomena arise through causes and conditions, and therefore there is nothing that possesses its own nature: this is True Emptiness" (*SSG*, p. 143, n. 6). The *Daichidoron* is a 100-vol. work by the great Buddhist philosopher Nagarjuna (ca. 150–250), which consists in its first 34 volumes of a commentary on the *Daihonhannya Sutra* but is otherwise an encyclopedic source on Buddhist thought, literature, and practice in India at the time it was written. Based like Nagarjuna's other works on the central concept of emptiness (J. *kū*; Skt. *śūnyatā*), it is distinguished by a positive emphasis on the teaching that all phenomena or dharmas as such are identical with ultimate reality. The work had a permanent influence on all subsequent developments in Mahayana intellectual philosophy, including the most important tenets of the Tendai sect. *Butten kaidai jiten*, ed. Mizuno Kōgen et al. (Shunjūsha, 1966; 2nd ed., 1977), pp. 128–29.

Chapter Eighteen

1. The Close Link (*shinku*) refers to an easily comprehensible verbal or semantic relationship between the maeku and tsukeku. The issue of the Close Link and the Distant Link is

directly taken up in Chapters 33 and 49. Here it is sufficient to note that Shinkei implicitly identifies the Distant Link with verses "whose mind is lofty and ineffably remote."

2. This is the second reference to Du Fu in *Sasamegoto* I; see Chapter 13 and n. 2. there. Du Fu's poetry is generally acknowledged to be very difficult by reason of his very originality: his complex handling of new, unfamiliar forms, and a tendency to ambiguity and densely compressed language. Shinkei might be saying, however, that the sheer breadth of its subject matter and the poet's insistent search for meaning or truth beyond the conventional verities are difficult for an ordinary mind to encompass.

3. *Hokkekyō* 1: 86 (chap. 2):

> While he [the Buddha] was speaking these words, in the assembly bhiksus, bhiksunis, upasakas to the number of five thousand straightway rose from their seats and, doing obeisance to the Buddha, withdrew. For what reason? This group had deep and grave roots of sin and overwhelming pride, imagining themselves to have attained and to have borne witness to what in fact they had not. Having such faults as these, therefore they did not stay. The World-Honored One, silent, did not restrain them. (*Scripture of the Lotus Blossom*, trans. Hurvitz, p. 29)

4. This statement is an allusion to the Mahayana concept of *sanshin* (Skt. *trikāya*), the three bodies or aspects of the Buddha, each one distinct from—yet also present in—the others, and ultimately forming a unity. (1) *Ōjin* (Skt. *nirmāṇakāya*) is the "metamorphosis body" by which he freely assumes various guises in response to the needs of each situation in the task of teaching and saving others. The historical Buddha Sakyamuni was one such guise. (2) *Hōjin* (Skt. *sambhogakāya)* is the "reward body," which the Buddha received due to the merits he accumulated as a bodhisattva; also described as the "body of bliss and enjoyment," it is the glorious form in which he appears in Paradise, or to bodhisattvas, or as an object of worship. The Buddha Amitabha in the Pure Land is one such manifestation. (3) *Hosshin* (Skt. *dharmakāya*), the "Dharma Body," is the Buddha body as such in its essential nature; it is the True Face (*shinnyō*; Skt. *tathatā*), the wholly real that cannot be represented through ordinary rational and linguistic description. Shinkei was of the opinion, however, that it can be evoked through poetry. See Chapter 43 for examples of poems by Teika and Shōtetsu corresponding to the Dharma Body, and Chapter 59 for Shinkei's analogy of poetic styles to the three Buddha bodies.

Chapter Nineteen

1. *Rongo* I.16: "The Master said, 'Do not grieve that people do not know you; rather grieve that you do not know people'" (p. 35). In the context of this chapter, Shinkei interprets the quotation to mean that the superior poet is less concerned that others recognize his greatness than that he himself discern the greatness of others.

2. This line appears to echo Kenkō's statement in *Tsuzuregusa* 211 (Nagazumi Yasuaki, ed., *NKBZ* 27), p. 257: "Nor should you trust in your learning if you have any; even Confucius was not favored by his times. You may have virtue, but you must not rely on it; even Yen Hui was unlucky" (Yoshida Kenkō, *Essays in Idleness: The Tsurezuregusa of Kenkō*, trans. Donald Keene [New York: Columbia University Press, 1967], p. 174).

The image of Confucius in the *Analects* is that of an itinerant teacher who tried to propagate the Way in various states but frequently met with a hostile reception; he was, in other words, far from being a worldly success. Yan Hui, his best-loved and most virtuous disciple, remained poor and died young.

3. *Rongo* XIII.327, pp. 299–300: "Tzu-kung asked, saying, What would you feel about a man who was loved by all his fellow villagers? The Master said, That is not enough. / What

would you feel about a man who was hated by all his fellow villagers? The Master said, That is not enough. Best of all would be that the good people loved him and the bad hated him" (*The Analects of Confucius*, trans. Arthur Waley [New York: Knopf, 1938], pp. 178–79).

If the last sentence above were rephrased as "Best of all would be that the discerning praised him and the ignorant neglected him," it would express Shinkei's view of the unreliability of popular opinion regarding excellence in poetry. In short, greatness and worldly success seldom go together.

4. The *Daichidoron*, IX, tells that after the Buddha had been preaching in the kingdom of Sravasti for twenty-five years, of its 900 million inhabitants, only 300 million had actually seen him, and 300 million heard of him, while the remaining 300 million were utterly ignorant of his existence. Cited in *SSG* rev. ed., p. 135, n. 13.

5. This line was almost certainly inspired by Bai Juyi's *Jiandi song* (The Pine at the Foot of the Valley), a poem that employs the image of a magnificent pine growing and aging deep in a remote valley to lament the fate of wise and gifted men whose talents remain unappreciated by the world, and who never gain worldly success. "The high are not always wise, / The humble are not always foolish," Bai says (*Haku Kyo-i* [Ch. *Bai Juyi*], ed. Takagi Masakazu [Iwanami Shoten, 1958–59], 1: 132–33).

Chapter Twenty

1. His mind having opened to the meaninglessness of his princely existence, Sakyamuni rode away from his father's palace one night on a white horse, accompanied only by his groom Chandaka. Later he gave his horse to Chandaka and dismissed him, bidding him return to the palace and tell the king his father of his resolve to search for a higher reality beyond the appalling human condition of birth, old age and death. Thereafter he went to live in the Uruvilva-grana forest on the eastern banks of the Nairanjana river, undergoing strict fasting and other physically emaciating austerities for six years. (*Buddhist Scriptures*, trans. Edward Conze [Harmondsworth, Eng.: Penguin Books, 1959], pp. 34–66.)

Chapter Twenty-One

1. "Seeking the luster concealed in the jewel, the fragrance outside the flower" (*tama no naka ni hikari o tazune, hana no hoka ni nioi o motomuru*) is Shinkei's imaginative variation on the metaphorical expression "look for the flower among flowers, search for the jewel among jewels" (*hana no naka ni hana o motome, tama no naka ni tama o saguru*). The latter occurs, for instance, in *Yakumo mishō*, VI: "The *Code of Abe Kiyoyuki* says, 'In general, in waka the flower is of primary consideration and the seed secondary. One must not use words that are archaic, vulgar, obscure, or outlandish. *Simply look for the flower among flowers, search for the jewel among jewels*'" (p. 75; emphasis added). The gist of this is that in composing poetry, one should not attempt to employ realistic but unorthodox language, but merely select the suitable words from within the poetic vocabulary that has been refined and purified by tradition. In the *Renri hishō* (1345–49), Nijō Yoshimoto uses the same expression in a similar sense to refer to the fine "poetic" diction of the waka anthologies, as distinct from the forceful but graceless language of noncourtly renga practitioners (*Renri hishō*, ed. Kidō Saizō, in *Rengaronshū, Haironshū, NKBT* 66: 33–67 [Iwanami Shoten, 1961], pp. 40–41).

Shinkei's creative rephrasing of the flower-jewel metaphor yields a wholly different meaning; namely, that the serious poet is not satisfied with surfaces, but seeks to penetrate the hidden depths of things. Another interpretation, related to the first, would be that the serious poet is concerned, not only with graceful, refined diction, but with creating an atmosphere (*omokage*) that evokes the invisible but profound principle in things.

2. Mañjuśrī (J. Monju) is the bodhisattva who personifies wisdom (Skt. *prajñā*), a profound and penetrating mind. In Buddhist iconography, he is depicted as sitting at the Buddha's left hand, opposite the bodhisattva Samantabhadra (J. Fugen) on his right. Shinkei's point is that for such a superhuman intelligence as Mañjuśrī's, poetry would, of course, require no effort, but it is a different matter for ordinary humans.

3. This is perhaps culled from *Toshiyori zuinō* [Toshiyori's Essentials of Waka] (1111–14): "It is a good thing not to compose poetry in a hurry. Now as in the past, nothing wise has ever emerged from rapid composition. Therefore poets like Tsurayuki took all of ten or twenty days on a single poem. However, one must be guided by the time and circumstance" (*Toshiyori zuinō*, ed. Hashimoto Fumio, in *Karonshū, NKBZ* 50: 39–270 [Shōgakkan, 1975], p. 259). The *Zuinō* is a long, rambling treatise written by Minamoto Toshiyori (or Shunrai) (1055–1129) at the request of Regent Fujiwara Tadazane for the poetic instruction of his daughter Taishi, later Empress to Rtd. Emperor Toba (1103–1156; r. 1107–1122).

4. Kunaikyō (see also Chapter 7, n. 28) is said to have been less than twenty when she died, but as many as fifteen of her poems were included in the *Shinkokinshū*. See also "Biographical Notes."

An anecdote in Chōmei's *Mumyōshō* (ed. Hisamatsu, pp. 76–77) recounts that she applied herself so strenuously to composing poetry, sleeplessly keeping at it day and night, that she fell ill and died. The account does not mention her spitting blood; possibly Shinkei's version is based on others surmising that she perished of consumption aggravated by her exhausting poetic labors.

5. It is not clear which of Kintō's poems is meant here. The famous *Honobono* poem, *KKS* 409, is anonymous and not by him.

6. Nagayoshi (or Nagatō) was a mid-Heian period poet, son of the Governor of Ise, Fujiwara Tomoyasu, and younger brother of Michitsuna's Mother, the author of *Kagerō nikki* (Gossamer Diary). He rose only to the Minor Fifth Rank, with the sinecure of Governor of Iga. However, he had the distinction of being the teacher of the famous poet-priest Nōin and was numbered among the Thirty-Six Poetic Geniuses.

Shinkei is alluding here to an anecdote in *Toshiyori zuinō* (pp. 253–54) recounting how Nagayoshi fell ill and died from brooding about Fujiwara Kintō's criticism of his poem, quoted below:

kokoro uki	It is a year that
toshi ni mo aru kana	brings sorrow to the heart;
hatsuka amari	only nine days
kokonuka to iu ni	past the twentieth, already
haru no kurenuru	spring has drawn to an end.

On hearing the poem, Kintō reportedly remarked without thinking, "Does spring then last only thirty days?" Informed of his comment, Nagayoshi immediately left the place in anger and humiliation. Composed on the last evening of the Third Month during a poetry party given by Kintō to mark the passing of spring, the poem utilizes the fact that the Third Month that year was a "small" month (i.e., lasting only twenty-nine instead of the full thirty days) to bring out the conventional sentiment that spring is all too brief. Such a conception, though far from remarkable, is valid enough, and Kintō's remark was rather careless. On his deathbed the following year, Nagayoshi would reveal that Kintō's criticism had plunged him into a state of mental depression that eventually led to his illness.

In the *Zuinō*, Toshiyori uses this anecdote as a warning that one should exercise caution in criticizing the work of poets who regard their poems with earnest devotion, even though they may occasionally include questionable points. Shinkei, however, uses it merely as a positive illustration of the life-and-death seriousness of a proper poetic attitude.

7. Pan Yue (248–300), a Jin dynasty poet who held various minor offices in the government for thirty years before retiring to his estate in the outskirts of Luoyang at fifty, was executed, along with his family, on charges of treason brought against him by a disgruntled rival. In the Preface to his *Qiu xing fu*, he says, "When I had seen thirty-two springs and autumns, my hair began to turn white" (cited in *SSG*, pp. 146–47, n. 9). It is not clear, however, whether this was due to his poetic exertions.

8. "The flavor of clarified butter" (*daigomi*) is the highest among the "five flavors" (*gomi*), or stages in the process of refining fresh milk to ghee. In Tendai doctrine, the five flavors are used as a metaphor for the five periods of the Buddha's teaching, from the Hinayana scriptures to the progressively more refined sutras of the Mahayana school, specifically the *Mahāprajñāpāramitā*, or "great wisdom," sutras in stage four, and the *Lotus* and *Nirvana* sutras in stage five, which are said to constitute Buddhism's innermost mysteries.

The five flavors are also a metaphor for the five stages of Zen concentration (*gomi Zen*), corresponding to the practice of heretics, ordinary people, Hinayana believers, Mahayana believers, and believers in the fundamental Buddha-nature of all things. This last is called *saijōjō*, "the Supreme Vehicle," the *samādhi* of the true and absolute face of reality, the utmost stage of concentration reached by Sakyamuni when he entered Nirvana.

Chapter Twenty-Two

1. The source of this anecdote may have been the following passage from *Kirihioke*:

> In the cold nights when the chill was most penetrating, the late lord my father would move the flickering lamp aside, put on just the outer cloak of his soot-darkened white purification robe, tie the cords, and pulling a quilt over him, hug the paulownia-wood brazier under the quilt, supporting his elbows against it as he sat up in bed and intoned words of poetry all to himself, utterly at one with the remote and desolate silence. ([Teika?], *Kirihioke*, ed. Sasaki, p. 274)

The preceding passage in which Teika admonishes Tameie does not, however, appear in the *Kirihioke*; also the fact that Shunzei wears the outer layer of the white robe used for religious ritual (*jōe*) in this version suggests the sacred dimension of the act of poetic composition. This quintessential image of the venerable poet was apparently an inspiration for Shōtetsu and his circle. In *Shōtetsu monogatari*, we read: "Shunzei habitually meditated on his poems with a soot-darkened cloak of purification over his shoulders, leaning against a paulownia-wood brazier. At no time, not even in his most private moments, did he ever relax and lie down when engaged in poetry" (*SM*, pp. 198–99).

2. Tameie (1198–1275) attained to the senior second rank with the office of Provisional Major Counselor at the age of forty-three. His father Teika did not reach the same rank until he was sixty-five and was first appointed to the Council of State, with the lower office of Provisional Middle Counselor, at the advanced age of seventy. Tameie's grandfather, Shunzei, did not rise beyond the senior third rank as Head Chamberlain of the Empress-Dowager's household. See also "Biographical Notes."

"The Cloistered Prince's *Fifty-Poem Sequence*" refers to the *Dōjo-hōshinnō-ke gojisshu waka*, a poetry meeting announced in 1218 and sponsored by the Cloistered Prince Dōjo, second son of Rtd. Emperor Go-Toba and head priest of the Ninnaji Temple. Including the major *Shinkokinshū* poets like Teika, who gave out the topics, Go-Toba himself, Ietaka, and Masatsune, the participants numbered twenty-two in all. Regarding the reasons for Tameie's exclusion, Kidō cites the colophon to the Naikaku Bunkō Text of this meeting, which includes Go-Toba's statement of the process of selecting the participants and his judgment of the poems. According to Go-Toba, among the poets being considered as participants, "Lord Tameie comes from a long [poetic] lineage, but he is known to be utterly inferior and unaccomplished. He is unsuitable" (*SSG*, p. 147, n. 18). Here it should be pointed out that in 1218, Tameie was still a young man of twenty, although much would have been expected of him even then as heir to the Mikohidari poetic house of Shunzei and Teika.

3. *Shōtetsu monogatari*: "Teika would open up the view in the south-facing room, sit in the exact center of it, and gazing southward far away, meditate on his poems, his robes properly arranged. This is a good way, being no different from composing during public meetings at the court of the Emperor or the Retired Emperor" (*SM*, p. 198).

Chapter Twenty-Five

1. This line is probably an allusion to *Rongo* I.4 (p. 20): "Master Tseng said, Every day I examine myself on these three points: in acting on behalf of others, have I always been loyal to their interests? In intercourse with my friends, have I always been true to my word? Have I failed to repeat the precepts that have been handed down to me?" (Waley, trans., *Analects of Confucius*, p. 84).

The *Rongo* (Ch. *Lunyu*) passage is about the importance of daily self-examination in the maintenance of personal virtue. In the context of this chapter in *Sasamegoto*, Shinkei uses it to mean the necessity for constant application and mindfulness in maintaining a high level of artistic excellence.

2. In the critical essay *Hitorigoto*, Shinkei lauds Ton'a (d. ca. 1457–60) as the foremost *shakuhachi* artist in the whole country in the years before the Ōnin War. The reasons for his high regard may be gleaned from an anecdote about Ton'a that he recounted to Kenzai: see *Kenzai zōdan* (A Miscellany of Kenzai's Lectures), in Sasaki Nobutsuna, ed., *NKT* 5 (Kazama Shobō, [1957] 1977), 413. Viewed from the standpoint of the issues raised in *Sasamegoto*, the anecdote reiterates the distinction between competence or dexterity, on the one hand, and the charismatic appeal of an art based on religious contemplation, on the other.

3. On Bontō, who received renga instruction from Nijō Yoshimoto but subsequently spent some twenty years traveling in the provinces, see "Biographical Notes."

Chapter Twenty-Seven

1. "Clashing across one-verse or several-verse intervals" translates *uchikoshi* and *tōrinne*, both of which violate the rules of renga composition. *Uchikoshi* is the recurrence of similar or traditionally associated images and expressions at one-verse intervals, a kind of *aba'* rhythm that is forbidden because it results in monotony and tediousness, and retards the forward movement of the sequence as a whole. From this rule, we may conclude that the basic unit of continuity in renga is three verses, in which the second may closely relate to the first, and the third to the second, but never the third to the first. In other words, any third verse of a three-verse unit in the sequence must break away in a new direction instead of echoing the first and reverting to the same point.

Rinne, the Buddhist term for karmic rebirth, is used in renga in the same sense as *uchikoshi*, except that it is less specific and refers generally to the idea of returning to the same point. *Tōrinne* therefore means returning from a distance, that is, the recurrence of a similar element after an interval of not one but several verses; this reveals, incidentally, that certain word pairs are so closely associated that the magnetic attraction between them operates even across longer intervals.

2. Ono Tōfū (894–964) was one of the three greatest calligraphers of the Heian period (the so-called *sanseki*), along with Fujiwara Sukemasa (944–948) and Fujiwara Yukinari (972–1027). Tōfū was the acknowledged pioneer of a native style of calligraphy as distinct from imitations of the Chinese; his is said to have been a broad, supple, and gentle brushstroke that concealed great inner strength.

3. "The Perfect Teaching" translates *engyō*, and "the All-Encompassing Oneness" *ennyū* (lit., Perfect Fusion), both of which belong to the central terminology of Tendai doctrine. *Engyō* is the highest of the so-called *kehō shikyō* (the four principles or stages of Buddhist teaching), i.e., (1) *zōkyō*, "the Tripitaka teaching," contained in the Hinayana scriptures and intended for *sravakas* and *pratyekabuddhas*; (2) *tsūgyō*, "the common teaching," which applies to Hinayana and Mahayana believers alike; (3) *bekkyō*, "the special teaching," meant only for bodhisattvas—that is, particular to the Mahayana school alone; and (4) *engyō*, "the perfect teaching," intended for bodhisattvas of the highest capacity, also described as pure Mahayana. This last corresponds to the truths expounded in the *Lotus* and *Nirvana* sutras, and specifically the esoteric principle of nondualism, *shohō jissō*, meaning that all the various dharmas (phenomena) as such, individually, severally, and in totality, are identical with the Real, that is, ultimate reality.

Ennyū refers to the perfect fusion of the so-called Three Truths (*santai*) in Tendai philosophy. They are (1) *kū*, "emptiness," the belief that since all the dharmas arise only through causes and conditions, they do not possess an intrinsic identity and are therefore empty; (2) *ke*, the "provisional" or contingent existence of all the dharmas as a consequence of causation, which may be described as temporal and mutable, but nevertheless real for a time; and (3) *chū*, the "middle" truth that grounds and encompasses the previous two and sees the dharmas as both empty and real; both logically contradictory aspects are rendered indissoluble in a third undifferentiated realm accessible only in meditation, beyond logic and linguistic description. Buddhist-inspired poets like Teika and Shinkei believed that poetry generated from within this state of meditation will evoke this third realm.

Santai ennyū, "the perfect fusion of the three truths" belongs to the realm of "the perfect teaching." The four principles of teaching and the three truths are in effect progressively widening perspectives on the dharmas. When the mind has expanded to its utmost, then the distinctions perceived during the earlier unperfected and incomplete stages instantaneously disappear; the mind sees all as present in the one, and all as One.

Chapter Twenty-Nine

1. Fujiwara Ariie (1155–1216) was, like Asukai Masatsune, a poet and compiler of the *Shinkokinshū*. The incident cited by Shinkei is recorded in Rtd. Emperor Juntoku's *Yakumo mishō*, VI, where "Stealing [*nusumitoru*] Words from the Poems of Recent Poets" appears as the first of six prohibited practices in poetry. Ariie's poem with the lines *sue no matsu / yamazu koto toe* (as the Sue pine / mountain ceaselessly, ask) was composed during a match between Japanese and Chinese poems in the Kenryaku era (1211–13); it contains a pun on *matsuyama* (pine mountain) and *yamazu* (ceaselessly, constantly), as well as the poetic place-name Sue no Matsuyama, famously immortalized in *KKS* 1093, an anonymous poem declaring a lover's constancy. Juntoku does not quote the complete poem by Ariie, but it elicited the admiration of many, including Teika and Masatsune. And then in the Seventh Month of the same year, Masatsune composed a poem with the lines *ashihiki no / yamazu kokoro ni / kakarite mo* (as feet dragging over / the mountain ceaselessly, in my heart / I think), containing the same pun

on *yama* and *yamazu*. Juntoku expresses his disapproval thus: "What is this? Masatsune is surely too good a poet to envy someone like Ariie, so how could he do such a thing? Not to mention the lesser poets who follow suit, loathe to be bested in the rush to steal from others. This is most reprehensible" (*Yakumo mishō*, pp. 76–77).

It appears from this illustration in *Yakumo mishō* that the use of similar puns was considered plagiarism; once invented, a pun acquired its author's patent and could not be used by others. The prohibition applied in the case of contemporaries borrowing from each other, since the question of credit and attribution then becomes obscure. This is distinct from the case of borrowing from the established poetic repertory of the imperial anthologies, where the original is known and the question of attribution would not arise.

2. This hokku is by Shinkei himself; it appears in *Shibakusa kunai hokku*, 45; *Shingyokushū*: Spring, 696; and *Shinkei kushū kokemushiro: Omoshiroki tei* (Style of Wit), 2130 (in *SSS*, pp. 12, 36, and 87).

3. Also by Shinkei; *Shibakusa kunai hokku* 19 (*SSS*, p. 11). It appears as well with his own commentary in *Guku Shibakusa* 5: "The saying goes, 'Ice comes from water but is colder than water; blue comes from the indigo plant but is bluer than the indigo plant.' Likewise the fragrance of plum blossoms has a deeper evocative power [*en fukashi*] than their color" (*SSRS*, p. 5).

The common saying to which the hokku alludes in a manner both intellectually clear and imagistically vivid is originally from the *Xunzi* (a fourth-century B.C.E. Confucian work), where it is meant to illustrate the truth that the disciple may surpass his master, the child his father, and so on. The hokku is conceived not only in praise of the flowers' fragrance; it is an allegorical statement to the effect that the invisible world exercises a more powerful pull on the human mind than the world of appearances. Furthermore, in Shinkei's own poetic vocabulary, this formless fragrance connotes the seductive profundity of the noumenon, suggested by and manifested in the phenomenal world but reaching beyond it.

Although Shinkei tactfully refrains from mentioning that two of the four hokku above are his, we fortunately have the evidence of his renga collections to prove his authorship. Consequently, the corresponding similar hokku, if by a different author (and not composed by Shinkei himself for illustrative purposes here), are plagiarized from his own work.

4. This hokku by Sōzei and the one that follows by Chiun both praise the beauty of the capital city under a rare covering of snow. Sōzei and Chiun were, with Shinkei, Gyōjo, Nōa, and Senjun, the leading renga poets of the mid-Muromachi period. Dubbed "the seven sages of renga" (*renga shichiken*) in modern scholarship, they established the aesthetics of the serious renga form espoused by Shinkei's students, Sōgi and Kenzai. See *HF*, especially chap. 3, for Sōzei's and Chiun's activities with Shinkei, and "Biographical Notes" for Sōzei.

Chapter Thirty

1. In the *Yakumo mishō*, for instance, *kotoba no irihoga* and *fuzei no irihoga* comprise the third and fourth of the "six unacceptable practices in [waka] poetry." Judging from Juntoku's account, *kotoba no irihoga* involves semantically illogical constructions, inverted syntax, and other cases of what were considered precious, affected diction. Some of the examples seem fairly innocuous; viz., *kiri no ariake*, "a dawn of mists" (meaning a misty dawn), instead of the more usual *ariake no kiri*, "the mists of dawn," and *kaze no yūgure*, "a dusk of winds," which is a similar case of inverted syntax. Others, like *tsuyu fukete*, "the dew grows late" (meaning the dew is thicker as the night grows late) and *kumo takete*, "the clouds grow old," are more abnormal cases of illogical syntax, evidently resorted to in the interest of compressing more than a single meaning in one line. Juntoku proscribes them not principally

because they deviate from the norm; his point is that though such expressions might sound fresh and arresting when new, their effect wears out with constant and indiscriminate use, leaving only an impression of insipidity and affectation.

Fuzei no irihoga refers to an unnatural conception or image, something like a conceit. Juntoku writes:

> This is the case when a poet, in an excessive desire to be arresting, comes up with things that sound ludicrous. . . . Someone once recounted the story of a poet who, on the topic "Dew on the *Ominaeshi* [Flower]," composed the lines "On the flower, yellow beads, / On the leaves, green beads." This conception truly struck everyone as vulgar. . . . Again, on the idea of a fisher girl diving into the sea bottom and seeing the moon there, a fellow recited, "Though she dives in [pun on "though it has set], does the fisher girl yet see the moon?" This might not be a true instance of *irihoga*, but it is certainly the conjuring trick of someone whose ability is utterly beneath what is required for poetry. . . . In general one who pursues an idea to excess in composing poems is bound to receive the censure of people of clear judgment. One must exercise prudence in this regard. (p. 79)

2. *Shimo no tsurugi* (frost sword, frost blade) is a figurative term for a freshly honed sword blade that glints pale and cold like frost. In this hokku, it is employed as a metaphor for the white and piercingly cold gusts of the frosty wind. Perhaps there is also an intended pun on *saya*, understood as the "sheath" of a sword, in the last line, *sayamakaze*.

3. While recognizing and praising the hokku's masterful diction, Shinkei finds the first line, "Will it fell the trees," unnatural and strained, in that it pursues the frost blade metaphor to an excessive degree. As a consequence, the verse takes on a certain wooden, ratiocinative character, to the detriment of poetic feeling. His suggested substitute, *saenikeri*, would convey a more immediate sensation, while simultaneously preserving the cutting edge, so to speak, of the original image. Moreover, from the viewpoint of the total configuration, it would round out the angularity of the original, lending it a more supple shape and texture by effecting a smoother continuity from line 1 to lines 2–3.

4. The second hokku is far inferior to the first; it has nothing to recommend it either in the conception or the diction. The author does not stop at saying that the green summer grasses are all that remain of the spring flowers; he goes on to imagine the summer grasses giving way to autumn flowers, an addition that dissolves the pathos evoked by the first two lines because of its repetitiveness. What he needed was a third line to bring home the feeling suggested by the first two, not a new image that crowds it out and results in a flat, unmoving, and "labored" effect.

Chapter Thirty-One

1. See "Commentary" for *miraiki*.

2. The verse incorporates a pun on *ame ga shita* (the world, the times) and *shitagae* (obey, submit, follow) and might mean, in paraphrase, "O wind among the flowers, submit to the time's tranquility and cease to blow!" Kidō (p. 153, n. 16) evidently sees no pun here, however, and tentatively reads line 2 as *ame ga shita kae*, where *kae* means "nurture, sustain," yielding the variant meaning "O flower wind, cease to blow, and nurture rather the things beneath the skies"—which sounds somewhat illogical and awkward. That the expression *yo ni / ame ga shitagae* (or *ame ga shita kae*) can be thus interpreted in two inconclusive ways in itself manifests the imprecise and confusing character of the verse's diction. This is an instance, not of poetic ambiguity, but simply of semantic confusion, which in turn diffuses the total effect of the verse, making it deteriorate into ultimately meaningless gibberish. It is not clear whether or not it was Teika himself who gave the title *Miraiki* to the collection mentioned in the preceding note, but from the example of this verse it may be surmised that the term

connotes the confusion and obscurity attending the final phase of Buddhism, when although the Buddha's teachings remain, they are only imperfectly understood.

3. In this second example, *miraiki* would apply not only to the verse's diction but to its conception, an artificial conceit wholly lacking in poetic appeal. In paraphrase, the idea behind it is this: "So lovely is the moon tonight that we might almost think it autumn, were it not for the cuckoo's call," which is, needless to say, heard only in the summer. Like the second example of *irihoga* in Chapter 30, the verse is at best indifferent and at worst utterly pointless. The poet has sacrificed the fabled beauty of the *hototogisu*'s rare song, on the one hand, and of a moonlit autumn night, on the other, to exhibit a less than sparkling wit.

4. *Kenzai zōdan*, in *NKT* 5, pp. 392–93. The term "rainy poems" translates *Uchūgin*, the title of a manuscript of seventeen poems, also falsely attributed to Teika, generally of a sunken, melancholy mood and excessive subtlety of feeling, seven of which include the rain image.

Chapter Thirty-Two

1. The *Man'yōshū* examples alluded to in the question are *MYS* XVI: 3838 and 3839, introduced by the heading "Two *Mushin Shojaku* Poems," and, according to a following note, composed in answer to a challenge that someone produce a deliberately incomprehensible poem in exchange for a prize. The sense (or non-sense) of the two may be translated thus: *MYS* 3838, "The scabs on the saddle of the great bull, *sugoroku* board growing on my wife's forehead," and *MYS* 3839 "On Mount Yoshino, round pebbles that my husband wears for loincloth, the ice fish are clinging." Conceived as a mocking exchange between husband and wife, this pair of poems have been kept deliberately obscure, but they would seem to conceal some obscenely humorous references. *NKBZ* 4.134–35.

2. *Omodaka* in line 2 refers to a species of arrowhead grass when read with line 1, and to "hawk" (*taka*) when read with line 3. *Omodaka* thus divides the verse into two parts, viz., "There are arrowheads in the water that reflects the moon," and "There is a hawk but no bird coop," which do not, however, connect to convey a coherent meaning. Even if the first two lines were read as a *jo*, or preface, to "hawk" and the third line as the main statement, the whole still remains pointless, unpoetic, and at best playfully paradoxical.

Perhaps, indeed, the paradox is the point, for the whole may be read as a comic verse with scatological implications, like the pair of poems in the *Man'yōshū*. The word *toya*, meaning a small hut for raising birds and fowl, also refers to the hawk's molting season, since it was then confined to the coop; by analogy, *toya* is also a variant term for *baidoku* (syphilis), whose victims suffered from hair loss, like molting birds. Furthermore, there is an expression, *toya ni tsuku*, that refers both to birds' being kept in the coop while molting and to prostitutes' confinement during attacks of syphilis, and therefore line 1 can be read as *tsukiyadoru*. The grass *omodaka* is also written with the characters 面高 (lit.,"a high, raised surface") either because the arrowhead leaves have a raised pattern of veins or because they shoot up from the surface of the water. From a scatological context, *omodaka* would then suggest syphilitic boils and tumors. In short, the verse indeed makes no coherent point, because the point is the riddle, a device to force the reader to scrutinize the words and discover the low-life humor underneath.

3. The second verse also makes no overt sense. Nor can it be interpreted scatologically. Perhaps the author was attempting a variation on the common conceit of mistaking clouds for blossoms and vice versa, and the reasoning might go like this: "Are the flowers already in bloom? Over those distant hills it is not raining, so those shadows cannot be rain clouds but flower clouds." This is, however, stretching the original fragmented syntax a bit too far. Or if the author was trying to be witty, his was indeed a convoluted wit.

Chapter Thirty-Three

1. This statement is based on the emphasis and marked preference for *soku* over *shinku* in the putative Teika treatises *Guhishō* and *Sangoki* in contrast to the *Chikuenshō*, which articulates the position of the conservative Nijō school. The *Guhishō* extols the marvelous effects of the Distant Link (*NKT* 4.298), and a similar opinion appears in abbreviated form in the *Sangoki* (*NKT* 4.351).

2. As if to illustrate the maeku's philosophical statement about the unfathomable origins and final end of the universe, the tsukeku juxtaposes the concrete image of distant waves rolling in upon the shore and pulling back again in a never-ending round. At the same time, however, it subtly shifts its focus to the related idea of ceaseless flux and ultimately, timelessness. The unknown temporal "beginning and ending" of the world is translated into the circularity of the waves' motion.

3. "The broom tree that grows by the lowly hut" was a legendary tree in Sonohara, Shinano Province (Nagano Pref.) that was said to appear from a distance but mysteriously vanish and change into plain evergreens when approached. "The lowly hut" (*fuseya*) was actually one of the primitive cottages maintained by the authorities in isolated areas along the principal travel routes during the Nara and Heian periods. Because the one in Nagano was so famous for the broom tree, in time, it acquired the status of a proper noun, Fuseya. Whereas the broom tree is supposed to disappear or turn into a prosaic evergreen, here the distant link is in the sudden, startling apparition of that same common evergreen pine in the lightning flash.

4. "Mind" here translates *kokoro*.

5. *Shūi gusō* 3314: Miscellaneous, "Dawn." The poem has a mellifluous quality arising from the smooth repetition of *h*, *k*, and *o* sounds. The clear structural division between upper and lower sections coincides with the shift from an aural to an olfactory emphasis, a juxtaposition that has the effect of making it seem as if the delicate fragrance in the air was summoned by the cock's calls, an unusual but marvelous effect of the *soku* technique.

6. *Fūgashū* 1784, Miscellaneous. In the *Shūi gusō*, Teika's personal anthology, we learn that this is from a "100-Poem Sequence on Living in Solitude" composed in Bunji 3 (1187). The objective image in the upper section is juxtaposed against the statement of subjective feeling in the lower section, highlighting the country/city (and solitude/society, time/timelessness) dichotomy contained in the poetic message.

7. *SKKS* 1780, Miscellaneous. The structural division coincides with the question-and-answer format of the poem, and brings out the startlingly paradoxical message that although no one comes to visit with whom he can share his thoughts, the poet finds consolation in the moon, in whose pure, transfulgent light, all thought and sorrow must vanish into emptiness. In its deepest layer, this is a religious poem; the moon may be read as a metaphor for the all-penetrating mind of the Buddha.

8. This was one of the poems composed for the *Santai waka* (Waka in Three Styles) held in Kennin 2 (1202), the twenty-first day of the Third Month. The upper part sketches a wide, brooding, and nebulous landscape, which coincides with the speaker's vague and abstracted mood—between waking and sleeping. It thus provides an effective foil for the instantaneous, piercing clarity of the *hototogisu*'s call that startles him wide awake in the poem's lower half.

Shōtetsu quotes this poem in *Shōtetsu monogatari*, giving it the highest praise and particularly noting the inspired quality of the upper half, which "confounds ordinary understanding, and whose ineffable profundity goes beyond rational sense and wholly resists description" (*SM*, p. 209).

9. The objective image in the poem's upper half is suddenly animated through the juxtaposition with the lower half, which specifies the precise shade of feeling that the blowing oak

leaves (with their pale undersides) awaken in the speaker: the ghostly, shadowy light cast by a thin crescent moon in early evening. *Yūzukuyo* refers to the evening of the crescent moon in the first seven days of the month in the lunar calendar; it sets early, leaving the small hours of the night in darkness.

10. The maeku in this pair is a paradoxical statement, a riddle to which the lovely image of the tsukeku is a witty reply. The pale moonlit fields are the "ice" and the plumed miscanthus grasses undulating in the wind are the "waves" of the maeku. Such a direct verbal and imagistic correspondence renders this a Close Link.

11. The link turns on the reinterpretation of the word *tsukuru*, which means "build, repair" in the context of the maeku as such, but "cultivate, plow" (homonym *tsukuru*) from the perspective of the tsukeku. In other words, as modified by the latter sense, the pair comes to mean "They are now cultivating the land in the village by the hill, and the place where a ruined mansion used to be has been turned into rice fields." The sense of the link is easier to grasp when one reads the tsukeku first and the maeku last; it will then be seen that they describe a continuity like that of a waka poem with a Close Link. Here, as in the previous pair, there is an associative correspondence between isolated words in the maeku and tsukeku, viz., *yakata* (mansion) and *sato* (village), *tsukuru* (build, cultivate) and *ta* (rice fields).

Chapter Thirty-Four

1. *TKBS* 561, Winter. A famous verse by Gusai that is frequently cited in renga handbooks from Yoshimoto to Shinkei and Sōgi. In his commentary on verses by the seven sages and Gusai, *Oi no susami*, Sōgi interprets the link in this manner: "This manifests the feel of morning in the mountain where the speaker is lodging. The scenery is so tremendously absorbing that he has forgotten all about the retribution of sins. The poet linked up to the maeku by adopting the persona of a hunter" (p. 143). Buddhism forbids the taking of animal life, and therefore hunting is a sinful activity. In *Renga jūyō*, a brief instruction book that he wrote for the Shōgun Ashikaga Yoshimitsu (1358–1408; r. 1368–1394) in 1379, Yoshimoto cites the verse for its attentiveness to the central point of the maeku: "[The verse] sounds generalized, but 'if it be so, so be it!' is of central importance [in the link]. It was surely conceived with particular attention to the matter of syntactic inflexion" (p. 103).

The great tension in the space between maeku and tsukeku here perfectly illustrates Shinkei's point regarding the reciprocal relationship of Statement to Context. Gusai's verse is in effect the concrete set of circumstances that anchors and justifies the maeku's sweeping declaration, and this is also Yoshimoto's point.

2. *TKBS* 1320, Miscellaneous. In the anthology the verse is attributed to Priest Saien, not Zen'a. The maeku's Statement is in the form of a riddle, to which the tsukeku is the answer: ravaged by a bear foraging for food in the night, the rice field the farmer plowed during the day has been plowed again.

3. As in the previous pair, the maeku is a riddle, a Statement of the emphatic, insistent kind (*momikudokitaru*) that calls attention to itself by an apparent contradiction requiring a solution. Here, in Junkaku's tsukeku, the falling white petals come to correspond to the "snow" of the maeku and the "fern fronds" are the "palm" or hand upon which they are falling.

4. This pair and the next represent the same kind of Statement / Context alternation in the first group of examples, except that the Statement occurs this time in the long 5-7-5–syllable verse. Here *omokage* (memory, image, traces) in the maeku most probably refers to someone from whom the speaker has been estranged by death or separation, and I have translated it explicitly as such. In the tsukeku, it becomes the remembered image of hills

alight with flowering cherry trees, where now only the darkening evening clouds remain as traces of a former splendor.

5. As in the latter two examples in the first group, the maeku is a paradoxical statement or riddle to which the tsukeku is a solution. The close verbal correspondence between *mae ushiro* (front and back) in the maeku and *idete iru* (rising and setting) in the tsukeku seems typical of links of this kind—i.e., the kind consisting of a riddle and its solution.

6. The "preface" (*jo*) is the initial two or three lines preceding and introducing the main statement of a waka poem. It is related to the statement in an indirect, metaphorical way and usually ends in a "pivot word" (*kakekotoba*) or pun upon which its connection with the rest of the poem hinges. Below, Shinkei cites six poems employing this technique; his aim is to show that the Context / Statement alternation in renga is similar to waka's preface / statement structure.

7. *Hampi no ku* is a line inserted in the middle of a waka poem (usually the third line) that creates a pause or break in its syntactic and imagistic continuity; it is essentially a preface placed in medial instead of initial position. Again, Shinkei gives three examples below. *Hampi* as such was a short robe with sleeves reaching only halfway down the arms; it was worn between inner and outer robes and thus gave its name to the waka technique.

8. The "four-line Chinese poem" referred to here is the *zekku* (*jueju*), a form consisting of four lines with five or seven words to each line, which most closely approximates Japanese poetry in its brevity and concision. It was written by all the major poets of the Tang and Song dynasties, including Li Bai (699–762), Wang Wei (699–750), and Su Dongpo (1036–1101). The first line, *kiku*, was supposed to introduce the theme; the second line, *shōku*, to continue and amplify upon it; the third line, *tenku*, to effect a turn or contrast; and the final line, *gōku*, (more commonly called *kekku*), pulls everything into a unified whole. Like the *hen-jo-dai-kyoku-ryū* concept of waka, the formal principle described above was not always reflected in actual practice but is nonetheless useful as a general guide to the poem's structure. The third line of the *jueju* would seem to correspond to the fourth line of waka—that is, the "turn" is the crux of the Chinese poem, just as the "statement," or *kyoku*, is the centerpiece of the Japanese; both represent the point toward which the preceding lines build up and from which they fall. Thus, like waka, the *jueju* may be reduced or flattened to an essentially binary structure (viz., the "turn" and the "non-turn," the marked/unmarked, positive/negative) similar to the Statement/Context alternation in renga, and this is the point of Shinkei's analogy.

9. *KKS* 469, Love, Anonymous. The first three lines comprise the preface and the last two the statement. The connection between the two lies primarily in the homophonous repetition of *ayame*, written 菖蒲 (sweet flag) in line 3 and 文目 (pattern, thus also sense, reason) in line 4. The preface, which describes the bird singing among the sweet flag in the Fifth Month, functions simultaneously as a time and place context for and a metaphorical image of the statement about the persona in love. In this connection, it is pertinent to point out that *ayame*, the flower, is etymologically cognate with *ayame* 漢女, "Chinese maiden," or 文女, "female weaver or seamstress," referring to women from the mainland who immigrated to ancient Japan, bringing those advanced skills, and their descendants (see, e.g., Shōgakkan's *Nihon kokugo daijiten*, 1: 597 [rev. ed., 1972]). Their desirability as wives is attested to by the Heian custom of having the woman's family provide clothing for her husband. Thus the statement "I love without reason" [*ayame mo shiranu / koi mo suru kana*] would imply loving without an object, or irrationally loving someone not yet fully known. This ties in with the fact that this waka is the head-poem of the first Love volume in the *Kokinshū*.

10. *KKS* 697, Love, Tsurayuki. As in the previous example, the three-line preface ends with a word, *karagoromo* (Chinese robe), partially homophonous with the initial words in

the statement, *koro* (time) and the emphatic-emotive *mo*. A metaphorical comparison is obviously being drawn between the rare Chinese robe and the lady whom the persona finds impossible to meet.

11. *KKS* 759, Love, Anonymous. The connection between preface and statement hinges on the pivot word *kari ni* in line 3, meaning "to reap or harvest" in the context of the former and "temporarily, for a while" in relation to the latter.

12. *KKS* 677, Love, Anonymous. *Hanagatsumi* in line 3 is a grass of undetermined identity that grows in marshes and puts out plume flowers in the autumn; it is believed to be a species of oat grass. The word is partially homophonous with *katsu mishi* (seen by chance, barely seen) in line 4. The juxtaposition has the effect of suggesting that the persona met a humble country lass by chance while traveling in Michinoku and is unable to forget her. In all these poems, similarity in sound has the mysterious effect of implying a similarity in sense, that is to say, of enforcing a metaphorical connection between preface and statement.

13. *KKS* 471, Love, Ki no Tsurayuki. *Hayaku* (swiftly) in line 4 provides a smooth juncture between preface and statement. It means specifically "at once, instantaneously" in the statement, but the metaphorical image in the preface also suggests the hidden force and violence of love at first sight.

14. *KKS* 995, Miscellaneous, Anonymous. The "pause" occurs in line 3, *Karagoromo* or "Chinese robe." *Tatsu* in Tatsuta Mountain also means "to cut, to tear" in association with "Chinese robe" and is therefore a pivot word. The pause line enriches the poem as a whole by suggesting an implicit metaphorical comparison between the sound of a silken fabric being ripped along its length and the long cries of the bird tearing through the silence in the mountain.

Yūtsukedori is a cock tied with a cord made from the mulberry; it was used in religious purification rites that were held especially during times of disorder.

15. *SKKS* 251, Summer, "Composed on the topic 'Cormorant River' during the 100-poem contest sponsored by the Regent and Great Minister." The pause occurs in line 3 and part of line 4, *mononofu no / yaso uji* (warriors of the eighty clans), an epithet for Uji River, with *uji* (clans) serving as a pivot word. The insertion of these pause words functions to amplify the total effect of the poem, both by suggesting the great number of cormorant fishing boats out on the river, and by implicating all men (viz., the eighty clans) in the tragic sin of killing for survival. In short, this river is here a symbol of human existence, just as in the Uji chapters of the *Genji*. The primary allusion, however, is most probably to the Gempei battles fought here, events fresh in the memory of the *Shinkokinshū* poets and later recorded in the epic *Tales of the Heike*.

The poem's honka is *MYS* 264, "A poem composed by Kakinomoto no Asomi Hitomaro by the Uji River, when he was on his way to the capital from Ōmi Province."

mononofu no	Along the weir stakes
yaso ujikawa no	on Uji River, eighty-armed as
ajiroki ni	the kingdom's clans,
isayou nami no	impeded the waves hesitate,
yukue mo shirazu mo	not knowing which way to go.

(Here I take the epithet to hinge on the numerous lateral branches of the Uji River, as of the clans.) The poem appears in the *Shinkokinshū* (*SKKS* 1648, Miscellaneous) as well; Kubota Jun speculates that since the Uji flows from the sea of Ōmi (mod. Lake Biwa), from where Hitomaro began his journey, he could be lamenting Emperor Tenchi's ruined capital and followers at Ōmi, destroyed during the Jinshin War (*Zenhyōshaku* 7: 426). This is certainly plausible, given the existence of *MYS* 29–31, Hitomaro's elegy "On Passing the Ruined

Capital of Ōmi." Jien's allusive variation on *MYS* 264 would be the distinctly Buddhist belief in the sin of killing any sentient creature, whether fish or human underlying the lament; the medial position of the epithet, as distinct from initial in Hitomaro, also makes for a more subtle, inwoven texture.

16. *Gyokuyōshū* 783, Autumn. *Tezome no ito no / yoru* (twisting hand-dyed threads) in lines 4 and 5 comprise the pause words, ending like the previous two in a pivot, *yoru*, which also means "night." They constitute a metaphorical image superimposed upon the actual scenery of autumn leaves whirling down the mountainside on a night of winds and moonlight.

As shown by the three examples above, "pause words" are similar to the preface, except that they occur in the middle instead of the beginning of a poem and are shorter in length, being more like "pillow words" (*makura kotoba*). If one may judge from these alone, the medial position seems to have a more complex effect than the initial in enriching the poem's imagistic texture and deepening its overtones.

17. *TKBS* 616, Shintō Gods. In the anthology the verse is attributed to Priest Seison, not Shinshō. The Day of the Snake in the tsukeku refers to the purification ceremony held on the first Day of the Snake in the Third Month. It involved the ritual transference of one's bodily defilements to a doll, which was then cast into a stream or river to be carried away into the sea. The practice originated in Enryaku 11 (792) during the reign of Emperor Kammu. The tsukeku functions as a preface in relation to the maeku's Statement, in the sense of giving it a context. The purification rites over, someone is going home, pulling his horse along the shrine fence. "Shrine fence" (*igaki*) in the maeku and "sacred guard-rope" (*mishimenawa*) in the tsukeku are in associative juxtaposition.

18. Again, the tsukeku is conceived as a preface to the maeku's Statement, and the two may be seen as an inverted waka. The third line, *utsu no yama* (Mount Utsu), is partially homophonous with *utsutsu* (reality) in the beginning of the maeku, in a manner that recalls the homophonous juncture in a waka with a preface, thus:

tabi ni motsu	*Carried on the journey,*
nosaki no hakone	*a box with rice tribute to Hakone,*
utsu no yama	*along Mount Empty—*
utsutsu ka yume ka	Was it reality? Dream?
akete koso mime	when the night opens, we'll see.

Apart from this, the link between the two verses turns on the verbal correspondence between *aku* (to dawn / to open) and Hakone (the place-name, which includes the word *hako*, "box"); and between *utsutsu* (reality) and *utsu no yama* (Mount Empty, a homonymous pun on the place-name). The unexpressed subject of the question in the maeku as such is probably a love meeting, which would make it an allusion to the famous poem exchange between the poet Narihira and the Ise Vestal Priestess in the *Tales of Ise*, chap. 69. Although this allusion is deflected in Shūa's tsukeku, the impression remains strong that the pair is meant as a spoof or comic caricature of the *Ise* poems (see also *Ise monogatari,* chap. 9). Shūa, it will be recalled, was famous for his smart and witty wordplays.

19. In the tsukeku, *irie no hotade / karaki* (the nettles by the inlet / bitter) functions as a preface to *yo no naka* (this world), and the whole verse may in turn be seen as constituting a preface to the maeku. The link probably alludes to the following poem in the "Akashi" chapter of the *Genji*, addressed by the Akashi Lay Monk to Genji just before the latter leaves Akashi to return to the capital (*Genji monogatari*, ed. Abe et al., 2: 258):

yo o umi ni	Become a self
kokora shiojimu	steeped in the briny sea of
mi to narite	the world's sorrows,

nao kono kishi o	yet am I from this shore
e koso hanarenu	still unable to depart.

Shiojimu (soaked in brine, salty) in the maeku corresponds to *karaki* (stinging, bitter) in the tsukeku.

There is an actual historical (diachronic) basis for Shinkei's analogy between the renga verse pair and the waka with a preface. Each pair is in effect an inverted waka, with the statement coming first and the preface last. It is significant to note that all the verses cited in this chapter are somewhat archaic in comparison with the contemporary style manifested in Shinkei's own work and those of the other seven sages. The fact is evidence of his implicit intention in this chapter, which is to engage in a structural analysis of tsukeai based on the historical practice of the Kamakura-Nambokuchō poets, on the one hand, and what he implies are its roots in the waka genre on the other.

20. Esperanza Ramirez-Christensen, "The Operation of the Lyrical Mode in the *Genji monogatari*," in *Ukifune: Love in the Tale of Genji*, ed. Andrew Pekarik (New York: Columbia University Press, 1982), pp. 21–61.

Chapter Thirty-Five

1. The source of the *rikugi*, or "six principles" concept in Japanese poetics may be traced to the *Kokinshū* prefaces, which drew in turn from the Great Preface of the *Shi Jing*. Inexplicable as it may seem, the Japanese adopted without modification the six-type classification meant to describe the poems in the Chinese *Classic of Poetry*. The Chinese Preface (Manajo) to the *Kokinshū* baldly states that "there are six types of Japanese poetry: the first is called *fū* (Ch. *feng*), the second *fu* (Ch. *fu*), the third *hi* (Ch. *bi*), the fourth *kyō* (Ch. *xing*), the fifth *ga* (Ch. *ya*), and the sixth *shō* (Ch. *song*)," without offering any explanation. Neither does the Japanese Preface, but it pursues the matter a bit further by assigning Japanese names to the six—the same that Shinkei uses here—and a corresponding waka example for each. Not long afterward, some poet-scholar, believed to have been Fujiwara Kintō (966–1041), inserted notes briefly explaining each type, apparently on the basis of the *Maoshi zhengyi*, and criticizing the poem examples for inappropriateness. These interlinear Notes have since become a permanent feature of the *Kokinshū* texts, as may be seen by Shinkei's reference to them at the end of this chapter. Although the unidentified commentator observes at the end that "in general, the idea of classifying Japanese poetry into six types is implausible," that did not dissuade subsequent poets from an exercise that had all the prestige of the ancient Chinese precedent and the *Kokinshū* behind it, and Shinkei was no exception. In the *Sasamegoto* translation, I have rendered the names of the six types according to Shinkei's explanation. (The texts used for the *Kokinshū* prefaces are the Saeki *NKBT* and Ozawa *NKBZ* editions.)

2. This is the hokku to the opening sequence of the 1,000-verse renga held at Yoshimoto's residence in the Fourth and Fifth Months of 1355, just a year before he and Gusai completed the compilation of the *Tsukubashu*. In view of Yoshimoto's role as a prominent poet, scholar, and greatest renga patron of his time, Gusai's high praise seems quite appropriate.

3. In the Great Preface (text and translation from *Chinese Classics*, trans. Legge, 4: 34–36) of the *Shi Jing*, *feng* 風 is described as a type of poetry by which rulers admonish their subjects, or subjects satirize their rulers, in an overtly innocuous yet insinuating language; it is therefore a species of didactic allegory. In Japan, since political and moral criticism was virtually unknown in the native poetry, it was found more convenient to interpret *feng* simply as a type that concealed its meaning in the guise of something else, that is to say, an allegory without didactic content. Thus for the corresponding Japanese mode, *soe uta*, the *Kokinshū*

Preface quotes an innocent-sounding waka about flowers emerging to bloom from winter hibernation and states that it is a reference to Emperor Nintoku (r. 313–399). In turn, the interlinear notes (hereafter simply "Notes") explain that the said poem was composed by Wani (an immigrant Korean scholar at the Japanese court) to urge that the time was ripe for Nintoku, then still a prince, to assume the emperorship. Such an "allegorical" reading follows the procedure of the early national histories, the *Kojiki* and *Nihongi*, which take the anonymous poems and folk songs of the oral tradition and set them within the context of their own mytho-political narrative. Anomalous as it may seem, the procedure nevertheless coincides with the fact that in waka it is the context, whether real or invented, that determines the presence or absence of "allegorical" intent. The same is true in renga particularly of the hokku, which is generated by the circumstances of the particular session; for instance, our knowledge of its context tells us that Gusai's verse is not simply a paean to the bird of summer but a eulogy cum greeting to the session's host, Nijō Yoshimoto.

4. In the Great Preface, *fu* 賦 is a narrative that employs a direct, straightforward style. The *Kokinshū* Preface calls it *kazoe uta* and gives as an example a poem containing a number of double meanings. The Notes declare that this type "expresses its meaning directly without resorting to analogies with things," and consequently fault the poem example as inappropriate due to its indirection and, indeed, incomprehensibility.

A signal departure from the original Chinese meaning occurs in the Kamakura-period treatise *Chikuenshō* (1278?), which says: "The *fu* is a composite poem; it is constituted of several meanings. The character for *fu* is also read *kubaru* [to distribute] or *tsukusu* [to exhaust]. Thus it means a poem that exhausts the greatest possible number of substantial words in a single poetic unit" (p. 416; the *Chikuenshō* is a waka treatise attributed to Fujiwara Tameaki, and is said to transmit the teachings of his father Tameie). This definition is obviously influenced by the specific Chinese genre called *fu*, written with the same character but not identical with *fu* in the *Shi Jing*. It was, however, adopted by Bontō in his renga handbook *Chōtanshō* and he illustrates it with the following verse pair containing images of the three seasons all at once.

haru natsu aki ni kaze zo kawareru	How shifts the wind with spring, summer, and autumn!
hana no ato aoba narishi ga momiji shite	After the flowers, the leaves that sprouted green turning to scarlet.

(p. 155). In the *Chōtanshō*'s unorthodox interpretation then, *fu* or *kazoe uta* seems to mean a poem that employs a profuse imagery or a multiplicity of poetic materials. It is clear that Shinkei's own understanding of *fu* has been influenced by the two treatises above, particularly in their reading of the character *fu* as *kubaru* or *tsukusu*. The momentous difference, however, is that Shinkei modified the sense of "exhaustiveness" to refer to the treatment and not the number of images involved. For him *kazoe uta* signified thoroughness and exactitude in the poet's handling of the poetic materials in order to convey his meaning; it had a qualitative not a quantitative value. Such is evident not only in his explanation of it here but even more so in the quoted example. Far from being prodigal in meaning or imagery, Gusai's hokku has only one single subject, the rising sun, and the last two lines express his meaning precisely.

Why Shinkei should have chosen to understand *fu* in this way may be accounted for by the fact that the *Chikuenshō* explanation ran counter to his own aesthetic ideal of *hie yase* (chill and meager), or brevity and concentration. Furthermore his artistic intelligence would automatically have rejected a profusion of imagery and materials as inappropriate for a short poetic form like the waka, and even more so for the renga verse. In doing so, he isolated a stylistic quality that has nothing to do with the Chinese *rikugi*, nor can it properly speaking be included in a theory of poetic modes, but it is nevertheless relevant and noteworthy in its own right.

5. Composed during a session at Kyoto's Kitano Shrine, this hokku by Gusai has been quoted once before as an example of the usages of double meaning in renga (see Chapter 11). The autumn scenery, with scarlet-tinted maple leaves falling and mingling with the dust of the earth, acquires a numinous significance as a metaphor for the illuminating presence of the bodhisattva's compassion in the dark, suffering world. As a subtle evocation of the holiness of the Kitano Shrine grounds, it is a highly appropriate poetic rendering of the circumstances of its composition.

6. In Chinese poetry, *bi* 比 is a metaphorical piece in which meaning is conveyed through analogy with things; it is therefore a technical category based on the method of expression, as distinct from *feng*, which may also be analogical but has a moral or political didactic content. The metaphorical character of *bi* has been accurately understood in Japanese poetics, as witness the corresponding name for it in the *Kokinshū* Preface, *nazurae uta* (analogical poems). The problem, however, has been how to distinguish it from the first category, *feng* or *soe uta*. The Notes suggest how this may be done. They fault the poem example given, even though it is clearly metaphorical, because it does not render explicit that a comparison is in fact being made between the two terms of the analogy. This seems a useless objection, since waka has never overtly employed the "A is like B" formulation of the English simile; the terms of a metaphor have invariably taken a paratactic or metonymical configuration. Nevertheless the Notes' objection is helpful in suggesting that it is perhaps the factor of explicitness that distinguishes *nazurae uta* from *soe uta*. Whereas in the former, both terms of the metaphor are present in the poem, in the latter the one term is absent, remains implicit, and may be determined only from the poem's actual (or invented) context. This, at any rate, seems to be what distinguishes the one from the other of Shinkei's' examples for each: there is no word in the *Na wa takaku* hokku that explicitly points to a person, Yoshimoto, as its real subject, but in the present example, both terms of the metaphor, one superimposed upon the other, are contained in the duosemic word *chiri*, and *miyai* (shrine precincts) in the last line confirms the intended double meaning.

7. According to Sōzei's renga handbook, the *Mitsudenshō*, this hokku was composed "in a valley at Nishiyama," the mountain range on the western boundary of the capital, running from Mount Atago in the north to Tennōzan in the south. Kidō suggests that the hokku might have been inspired by the following Buddhist hymn composed by Dengyō Daishi, Tendai's founder(*SSG*, p. 160, n. 4):

tani ni wa nagaruru	The sound of the stream
mizu no koe	flowing deep in the valley
shinnyo busshō	clarifies in my soul
mune ni sumi	the true likeness of Buddha-nature;
mine ni wa sasou	In the voice of the wind
kaze no oto	passing high on the peak
shohō jissō	I always hear that
tsune ni kiku	the myriad phenomena are truly real.

Doubtless the heightened quality and sense of spiritual exhilaration in Gusai's hokku has a basis in the Mahayana Buddhist perception of the nonduality of phenomenon and noumenon (*shohō jissō* above). However, it is impossible to judge whether the hokku itself was directly influenced by Saichō's hymn. There is frequently a numinous quality to Gusai's rendering of natural landscape, which is beyond doubt Buddhist in origin and must have particularly appealed to Shinkei, who frequently cites from his work and had the highest regard for him among all the Kamakura-Nambokuchō poets.

8. In the Great Preface, *xing* 興 are "allusive" pieces that start out with a description of something in the animal or vegetable world that the poet later elucidates in terms of what he wishes to convey. The corresponding type in the *Kokinshū* Preface is *tatoe uta* (illustrative poems), and the waka example is one wherein the poet illustrates the boundlessness of his love by stating that not even the vast number of minuscule sands on the beach can equal its measure. *Tatoe uta* therefore resembles the analogical character of the preceding *nazurae uta* in drawing upon external elements from the vegetable or animal world for purposes of comparison. It is distinct, however, in not effecting that sense of momentary identification between two things that is the mark of a true metaphor, the instantaneous illumination that suddenly reveals a similarity in two things otherwise so unlike. *Tatoe uta* is more akin to the extended simile in which the two terms being compared yet remain distinct and apart, the one expressly being employed simply as a means of elaborating or elucidating the other.

The *Chikuenshō* concludes rightly that *fū*, *hi*, and *kyō* are all analogical modes, and then attempts to draw the differences among them thus: "The fourth, the so-called *kyō* poem, takes two things and says they are similar, but their forms are different. It is true that *fū*, *hi*, and *kyō* all employ analogy, but *fū* compares a situation or content [*kokoro*] with another, *hi* compares a form [*katachi*] with another, while *kyō* compares one thing with another, yet distinguishes them from each other" (p. 416). This passage is useful mainly in drawing out the same distinguishing characteristic for *kyō* or *tatoe uta* that we have observed above on the basis of the waka examples from the *Kokinshū* Preface.

As may be gleaned from an analysis of his explanation and hokku example, for Shinkei *tatoe uta* referred to a mode of evoking a certain significance in something by means of material images (*sono mono ni yuetsukitaru o minashi kikinashi tatoetaru*) which, we might add, function in its place. The real subject of Gusai's hokku, the sensation or idea of the interpenetrability of all phenomena, is nowhere explicit in its linguistic surface. There we have only a statement about the protracted Fifth-Month rains (*samidare*) manifesting itself in the winds whistling through the pines on the peak and the rushing torrents of the swollen streams. However the deliberate syntax—blandly put, it yields the equation "rain = winds, streams"—alerts us to the fact that this whole imagistic complex is in fact intended as an analogue of a Buddhist principle, and that what Shinkei is illustrating here is the operation of the symbolic mode of poetry. His concept of *tatoe uta* is similar to the *Kokinshū* Preface and the *Chikuenshō* in its analogical character, and its separation of the two terms of the analogy. However, it is widely divergent from both in withholding the one term (the subject) from the poem's linguistic surface and, further, in letting the analogue stand in place of the subject, as its symbol. Perhaps Shinkei was influenced by the Chinese character for *kyō*, which may mean "to raise, activate, or set in motion," in his apparent conception of *tatoe uta* as a symbolic mode of conjuring a formless principle or meaning.

9. *TKBS* 2102, Hokku. "From the 1,000-verse sequence at the Regent's residence." Attributed to Priest Mokuchin.

The event mentioned in the preface must be the one held during the Fourth and Fifth Months of 1355 under Yoshimoto's auspices. The hokku for the opening sequence, by Gusai, was quoted earlier as an example of the Allegorical Mode.

Monshin, to whom Shinkei attributes this hokku, has twenty-five verses in the *Tsukubashū*. A member of the Askikaga bakufu's corps of Adjudicators (*hikitsukeshū*), he was one of Gusai's leading disciples and according to Sōzei's report "could produce an interesting verse even from an unpromising maeku" (*SSG*, p. 260, suppl. n. 25).

10. Comprising the second and third major divisions in the *Shi Jing*, the *ga* 雅 (translated by Legge in *Chinese Classics* as "Odes of the Kingdom") were pieces sung to musical accompaniment during festive occasions at the royal and feudal courts. They celebrated the triumphant return of troops from military expeditions, the arrival or departure of envoys, praised the virtues of guests and host at banquets, and so on. The Great Preface holds them up as representations of the customs of the kingdom, describes them as "correct," and says further that they indicate "the causes why the royal government decays and flourishes."

The *Kokinshū* Preface equivalent for *ga* is *tadagoto uta*, and the poem example given may be paraphrased thus: "Happy would be men's words, if in this world there were no deceit." The Notes explain that this type of poetry "speaks of the well-ordered administration of things, of their correctness." They fault the poem example for not conforming to this definition, and suggest the following alternative example, having to do with the peaceful state of the kingdom: "On the mountain cherries' hue have I gazed to my heart's content, in these times when no wind arises to scatter the blossoms."

A modified interpretation of *tadagoto uta*, with no bearing at all on the idea of correct government implied by the Chinese type, appears in the *Chikuenshō*, viz., "This is a poem that expresses itself plainly, in a straightforward manner, without drawing an analogy with things" (p. 416). This interpretation coincides with Shinkei's and is almost certainly based on a misreading of *tada* (correct) as its cognate root *tada* (straight, direct as opposed to crooked and indirect). Thus, a category based on function and content in the *Shi Jing* turns to one based on mode and technique in later Japanese poetics.

11. This spare, imagistically acute hokku evokes the sensation of the camellia blossoms' stark whiteness against the thick, deep green foliage by comparing them to round polished gems. It also indirectly compliments the host whose garden provided the setting for the session.

One of the leading renga poets of the late Nambokuchō period, Jō'a had the distinction of being appointed administrator (*bugyō*) of the Kitano Shrine Renga Meetings and earned Yoshimoto's praise for the elegance and vividness of his style.

12. Comprising the fourth and final section of the *Shih Ching*, the *shō* 頌 (Ch. *song*, "Odes of the Temple and the Altar" in Legge's translation) were hymns of praise sung during sacrificial rites at the ancestral temples; they celebrated the virtues of kings (and occasionally admonished them), recounted their illustrious history, prayed for abundant harvests or rendered thanksgiving. According to the Great Preface, "the Sung are so-called because they praise the embodied forms of complete virtue, and announce to Spiritual Beings its grand achievements" (*Chinese Classics*, trans. Legge, 4: 36).

The *Kokinshū* Preface correctly understood this type as songs of praise; such may be gathered from the corresponding Japanese name, *iwai uta* (celebratory poems), and the waka example assigned to it. The Notes explain, however, apparently echoing the Great Preface, that this is a type "that sings the world's praises and announces them to the gods," and consequently finds the poem example inadequate, presumably for failing to include the religious character of the Chinese type.

Shinkei at any rate follows the *Kokinshū* interpretation, as indicated by Jō'a's hokku, which celebrates the beauty of the camellias in the garden; he also wonders briefly about the type's supposed religious significance but arrives at no conclusion. It might be noted that hokku composed on formal occasions were required to include a compliment to the host or the place, so most of them would invariably fall into the Panegyrical Mode.

13. The last lines in this chapter are Shinkei's only direct reference to the interlinear Notes in the *Kokinshū* Preface that have provided some material for the preceding discussion. From this it appears that he did not rely on them exclusively for his own interpretation. The oral

tradition ascribes them to the Heian poet and scholar Fujiwara Kintō, who is known to have written an annotation of the *Kokinshū* Chinese Preface, the so-called *Kintō-kyō chū*, which is no longer extant. This was one of the sources for the Kamakura-period commentary by Kenshō (ca. 1130–1209) called *Kokinshūjo chū*. It is not possible at this time to determine which commentaries Shinkei used; the *Chikuenshō* may very well have been one of them. In any case, it is clear from the whole tone of this chapter that Shinkei regarded his own interpretation as tentative and inconclusive from the point of view of the correct and orthodox understanding of *rikugi*. (This tentative attitude is evident in the variant ending of this chapter in *SSG* rev. ed., pp. 110–11). However, a correct interpretation of *rikugi* probably does not exist, since the concept has never been clearly expounded even in Chinese poetics. Shinkei's presentation will therefore have to be evaluated on its own merits.

Chapter Thirty-Six

1. The waka contest under consideration here is of a particular kind called *hōhen no uta awase*, a form of poetry debate where the members of the two opposing teams are allowed to argue the merits of their own poems and criticize those of the opposite team, as distinct from the other practice of appointing a judge.

2. There are actually two records of renga contests (*renga awase*) dating from before Shinkei's time. Both are called *Hyakuban renga awase* (Renga Contest in 100 Rounds). In the first, the famous rival poets Gusai and Shūa vied with each other in composing tsukeku to the same 100 maeku, and in the second, Nijō Yoshimoto and the same Shūa likewise matched their tsukeku, though not to exactly the same maeku. It will be recalled that in Shinagawa in 1468, five years after writing *Sasamegoto*, Shinkei discovered a manuscript of the Gusai-Shūa contest that included Yoshimoto's commentaries and was so excited that he added his own tsukeku to theirs. See *HF*, chap. 4, pp. 106–7.

Since there are no other records of similar renga contests after the two above have come to light to date, perhaps Shinkei was right in saying that they had only just recently been practiced in his own time. As we know from one of his letters (*Tokoro* II, p. 213), he himself started judging at renga contests held at the residence of the Deputy Shōgun Hosokawa Katsumoto from 1463, after his return to the capital from Wakayama.

3. In the *SSG* rev. ed. text, Shinkei adds: "It is the established practice in any field to study by seeking out a teacher; only in the Way of renga since recent times has it become common to think that one knows everything, with the result that it has since then strayed into the wrong path and degenerated into a frivolous activity" (p. 142).

Chapter Thirty-Eight

1. The *Go-Toba-in onkuden* says: "Lord Ietaka was not well known when he was young, but from around the Kenkyū era [1190–99] his fame notably increased" (p. 147). Ietaka was between thirty-two and forty-one years old in the Kenkyū era. *Shōtetsu monogatari* echoes Go-Toba when it says, "Ietaka was more than forty when he first acquired fame as a poet. He composed any number of poems before that, but he was honored only after turning forty" (*SM*, p. 233; for the context of this remark, see *Conversations with Shōtetsu*, p. 163).

2. Ning Yue lived in the Warring States period. According to the *Lüshi chunqiu*, he could not endure farming and, having resolved to become a scholar, would study throughout the night while everyone else was asleep. Thus he completed in fifteen years what took others thirty and was later rewarded for his efforts by being appointed teacher to King Wei (r. 425–401 B.C.E.) of the Zhou dynasty. Cited in *SSG* rev. ed., p. 142, n. 1.

3. From the famous passage in *Rongo* II.20 (p. 40): "The Master said, At fifteen I set my heart upon learning. At thirty I had planted my feet firmly on the ground. At forty I no longer suffered from perplexities. At fifty I knew what were the biddings of Heaven. At sixty I heard them with docile ear. At seventy, I could follow the dictates of my own heart, for what I desired no longer overstepped the boundaries of right" (*Analects of Confucius*, trans. Waley, p. 88).

4. "Zong Shi first became fond of learning at seventy and rose to become a royal adviser" (*Tongzi jiao*, cited in *SSG*, p. 162, n. 7).

5. *Rongo* IV.74 (p. 93). In other words, if one has consistently observed the Way until old age, then one has indeed fulfilled one's destiny as a human being and can accept death with equanimity. This concluding observation belongs on a different plane from those preceding it.

Chapter Thirty-Nine

1. This locution stems from poems using the expression *nusa mo toriaezu* (unprepared with a wand), the most famous being *KKS* 420, Travel, "Composed at the site for honoring the mountain deity, when the Suzaku Rtd. Emperor [Uda, 867–931; r. 887–897] was traveling in Nara." Sugawara no Ason [Michizane].

kono tabi wa	On this journey, I come
nusa mo toriaezu	unprepared with a holy wand—
tamukeyama	but behold the mountain,
momiji no nishiki	a brocade of scarlet leaves
kami no manimani	spread for the god's pleasure.

Nusa was a wand from which hung strips of cloth or paper; it was used in religious worship to honor the deity. As the speaker has come without one, he instead offers the splendid autumn foliage to pacify the god. The point of the locution in *Sasamegoto* is simply the thoughtless haste with which modern renga practitioners cap each other's verses without due regard to quality.

2. "Counterfeit and Degenerate Dharma for the Way" translates *kono michi no zōbō mappō*, an allusion to the second and third of the three stages of the Buddhist faith after the death of Sakyamuni. These are (1) *shōbō* (Correct Dharma), the first 500 years, when the teachings still remain and self-enlightenment is still possible through correct practice; (2) *zōbō* (Counterfeit Dharma), the next 1,000 years, when the teaching and the practice remain but enlightenment is no longer possible through one's own efforts alone; (3) *mappō* (Degenerate Dharma), the subsequent 10,000 years, when only the teachings remain, no one puts them into practice, and enlightenment is wholly impossible. In Japan, the third stage was believed to have begun in the year 1052.

3. The logic of the thought here is not clear, chiefly due to uncertainty in the interpretation of *ichinen soku goku* (lit., one thought is equal/identical to the ultimate). Kidō simply notes that the source of the phrase is unknown (*SSG*, p. 163, n. 14); Suzuki (p. 151) gives an elaborate paraphrase to the effect that the ten worlds are of themselves the manifestation of true reality and Buddha-nature. Human beings live various lives and think various thoughts each according to his/her apportioned lot, and "each of these lives or thoughts is in itself an absolute thing" (*zettai no mono*). This fatality, however, is redeemed by the following statement about the Buddha's manifold devices for saving souls.

4. The parable of the "poor son" (*gūji*) takes up nearly all of chapter 4 in the *Lotus Sutra*. The son ran away from his father's house and became a common laborer, while his father gained in wealth and fame. After many years, the father discovered his son's whereabouts and wished to will all his worldly treasures to him. However, knowing that circumstances

had made his son's mind narrow and mean, and that he would neither believe such a miracle nor be able to manage such a fortune, he tactfully invented numerous devices in order to train his mind gradually to receive his inheritance. Similarly, all the sentient creatures are children of the Buddha, but because they are ignorant and unprepared to receive the great treasure of his teachings directly, he invents manifold devices (*hōben*; Skt. *upaya*) to gradually make them aware of their intrinsic Buddhahood, in spite of themselves as it were. See *Hokkekyō* 1: 222–63; *Scripture of the Lotus Blossom*, trans. Hurvitz, pp. 84–100.

5. This reflects the following passage in the *Makashikan*, vol. 5, chap. 7, "The Correct Training in *Shikan* [stillness and insight]": "The blind leader and the lame follower, though there be two of them, will stumble and fall. A blind man and a lame man walking in the dark of night is an extremely pitiful sight. To such people, one should not teach the practice of *shikan*. For *shikan* elevates those who are already high, and demeans those who are already low" (*Makashikan* [The Great Stillness and Insight], ed. and trans. Sekiguchi Shindai [Iwanami Shoten, 1966], 1: 263).

The *Makashikan* is a ten-volume work recording the teachings of Zhiyi (538–597), the third patriarch of the Chinese Tendai sect and regarded as its true founder. A systematic exposition of the principles and practice of *shikan* or meditation, the *Makashikan* comprises one of the so-called three major Tendai texts (*Tendai sandaibu*) all conceived by Zhiyi as commentaries on the sect's central scripture, the *Lotus Sutra*. The other two are the *Hokke mongu*, a twenty-volume treatise systematically explaining the content of the *Lotus Sutra* according to four principles or perspectives; and the *Hokke gengi*, a searching analysis of the most profound concepts embodied in the sutra, in particular the principle of nonduality or the identity of all phenomena with true reality (*shohō jissō*).

6. *Hokkekyō* 1: 282; chap. 5, "The Parable of the Medicinal Herbs": "The Buddha's undifferentiated preaching / Is, like the rain, of a single flavor, / In accord with the beings' natures / Differently perceived" (*Scripture of the Lotus Blossom*, trans. Hurvitz, p. 108). The Buddha compares the Dharma to the rain that falls equally upon the plants, grasses, and trees but is received differently by each according to its distinct nature.

7. Sogen (?–ca. 1380) was a priest of the Konrenji, head temple of the Jishū sect's Shijō school in Kita-ku, Takagasaki, north of the capital. A well-known calligrapher, Sogen was the author of *Shinsatsu ōrai* (1367), a kind of lexicon cum encyclopedia in fifteen sections, each dealing with the vocabulary of New Year's greetings, tea ceremony, incense burning, scrolls, horse-riding, poem anthologies, calligraphy, and other topics common to the sociocultural life of the times. A disciple of Gusai in renga, he appears under the name Soa in the *Tsukubashū*, where his twenty-four verses give him a slight edge over Gusai's other famous but renegade pupil Shūa, who has only twenty-two included there. There are today extant texts of volumes 14 and 20 of the *Tsukubashū* stemming from a copy made by Sogen immediately after the completion of the anthology's final draft. For particulars, see Kaneko, *Tsukubashū no kenkyū*, pp. 157, 302–4, and 569–72.

8. Mashimo Mitsuhiro was a vassal of the Shōgun Yoshinori (1394–1441) and held the title of Governor of Kaga (Ishikawa). In his youth, he had the good fortune to study renga with Nijō Yoshimoto's disciple Bontō before that poet departed for his long journey to the provinces. Mitsuhiro's talent was recognized by Yoshinori, among others, who once summoned him, along with four or five other leading renga poets, for a grueling session of two 100-verse sequences in one day. This event occurred at the Tendai *monzeki* temple Shōren'in, Yoshinori's residence for several years before becoming Shōgun in 1429.

It is not known when and for what reasons Mitsuhiro was forced to leave society and retire to Mount Kōya, the great Shingon monastery in Wakayama Province. Bontō visited him there twice, and both times they composed a *hyakuin* together. The second time, around 1413 or so, Bontō remarked to Sōzei that he considered Mitsuhiro his most promising disciple even in his youth, but that the enforced seclusion of Mount Kōya had turned him into a truly accomplished poet. Sōzei, who had begun studying with Bontō subsequent to the latter's return to the capital in 1408, had lived for a while on Mount Kōya and knew Mitsuhiro well; together they would compose two *hyakuin* in memory of Bontō's death in 1427. Many years later when Shinkei, who had long considered Mitsuhiro the best poet of his generation, solicited Sōzei's opinion about him, the latter agreed saying, "But of course. There was no one who could match him in his time. I too tried to be as close to him as possible when I was young." Indeed, even the redoubtable Shōtetsu would remark upon hearing of his demise that "the renga of the whole country has died" with him.

Unfortunately, his secluded life on Mount Kōya, though it might have polished his art, did nothing for Mitsuhiro's fame. Except for the few verses cited in the writings of Shinkei (and perhaps others), his work has not survived. Contrary to the usual practice, he apparently did not compile a personal anthology and he does not appear in the *Shinsen Tsukubashū*. Nevertheless, Shinkei prized the "chill and meager" quality of his poetry, and one cannot help feeling that it was this neglected poet who inspired him most among those of the immediately preceding generation. Among the hokku that Shinkei quotes from Mitsuhiro are the following:

usuku koki midori no nobe no yukima kana	Pale or deep the green of the meadow under patches of snow.
nagatsuki ya shimo ni utsurou konoha kana	October moon— fallen leaves blanching under frost.
fuke arashi ogi ni honomeku yūzukuyo	Blow, winds! glimmering on the reeds, the moonrise.

(*Tokoro* I, pp. 195–97;
RS 1: 322–25)

9. Sōa was, like the previously mentioned Sogen (n. 5) in the preceding century, a priest of the Jishū Konrenji Temple north of the capital. Virtually nothing more is known about him, however, except that he was sufficiently famous to be asked to judge the verses at a session sponsored by the Fushimi Prince Sadanari in the Twelfth Month of 1425. As here in *Sasamegoto*, in the *Tokoro-dokoro* letter cited above, Shinkei mentions him alongside Mitsuhiro as one of the finest poets of the late Ōei era (1394–1428). In particular, he cites Sōa's evocative diction and the quality of *yūgen* in the hokku verses below:

matsu no ha wa nururu bakari no shigure kana	Pine needles just barely wet: a passing shower.
kogarashi no aki fukinokosu momiji kana	Remains of the storm that blew away autumn: red leaves.

(*Tokoro* I, p. 197)

10. For Sōzei and Chiun, see *HF*, chap. 3, pp. 54–56, and other places there. See also the entry for Sōzei in "Biographical Notes." Sōzei and Chiun were the most senior of the so-called seven sages (including Shinkei) responsible for renga's renaissance in the Muromachi period.

11. Shōtetsu died in 1459, just four years before Shinkei wrote these lines. See *HF*, chap. 2, on his role as Shinkei's waka mentor and his place in the contemporary poetic milieu.

12. Shinkei means the Eikyō era (1429–41), "when the illustrious masters and predecessors of waka and renga still remained in the world and brilliant poetry gatherings were held at various places" (*Hitorigoto*, p. 468). He always remembered this era from his early twenties to mid-thirties with nostalgia; his teacher Shōtetsu (the "worthy sage" of this passage) was at his peak, the other seven sages, including Sōzei and Chiun, were still living, and the specter of the political strife that would have such a disastrous effect on his life and career had yet to rear its head.

13. "The One Great Cause" is a compressed translation of *ichidaiji no innen*, that is to say, the great event of the Buddha's appearance in this world constitutes the cause and condition for the attainment of enlightenment by sentient beings. Shinkei therefore means that it is incumbent upon everyone to inquire into the significance of this great event by studying the Buddha's teachings and pursuing the course he prescribed for release from human suffering.

14. "The triple spheres" (*sanze*) are those of time, viz., past, present, and future. "The ten worlds" (*jikkai*) are the six lower worlds of the confused and ignorant; namely, hell, hungry ghosts, beasts, demons, men, and heavenly beings, plus the four higher worlds of the enlightened; namely, sravakas, pratyekabuddhas, bodhisattvas, and buddhas (see also Chapter 15, n. 3). The ten worlds are thus the totality of the universe of sentient beings.

This puzzling statement means that the triple spheres are but a function of the ten worlds, time is but a function of space and vice versa; the one is not possible without the other. If there are no progressive stages or worlds through which one transmigrates, then neither is there a past, present, and future, and in fact there is no such thing as transmigration from the enlightened point of view. It is only a concept devised by the Buddha to lure the sentient beings to ascend the ladder to his world. It is real as far as one does ascend it, but having reached the top, one realizes that there has never been any ladder and one is where one has been all the time. In fact, the world that is before one's very eyes, in which one finds oneself, is in and of itself True Reality.

15. "Some Verses by the Old Poets." This is a selection of fifty tsukeku from the *Tsukubashū* period, classified generally according to the ten modes (*jittei*) of waka appearing in Teika's *Maigetsushō* and works attributed to him, the *Teika jittei* and *Sangoki*. The placement of this small collection of renga in ten styles in this concluding chapter of *Sasamegoto* I is obviously anomalous. The treatise—that is, Part I, which was written earlier as a complete work—effectively ends with the preceding paragraph; consequently, this portion seems like a later addition. That Shinkei nevertheless meant it to be included in *Sasamegoto* is evident in the revised edition, where the following question has been inserted to begin a separate section: "In waka, one sees various configurations of poetry divided into ten styles. Are there no such determinations in renga?" (*SSG* rev. ed., p. 111). It remains true, however, that just as in the classified waka collection called *Teika jittei*, in neither edition of Shinkei's treatise are prose explanations given for each mode. The ten modes or styles, illustrated below with five verses each, are the following:

(1) *yūgentei* 幽玄體, The Mode of Ineffable Depth

(2) *chōkōtei* 長高體, The Lofty Mode

(3) *ushintei* 有心體, The Mode of Meditation

(4) *komayakanaru ku no tei* 濃句體, The Intricate Mode

(5) *uruwashiki ku no tei* 麗句體, The Classic Mode

(6) *omoshiroki tei* 面白體, The Arresting Mode

(7) *koto shikarubeki tei* 事可然體, The Categorical Mode

(8) *hitofushi no tei* 一節體, The Mode of Singular Conception

(9) *shakotei* 寫古體, The Mode of Preserving the Old

(10) *gōrikitei* 強力體, The Stark Mode

The ninth, the Mode of Preserving the Old, is not found in *Maigetsushō* and *Teika jittei*, which have *miru tei*, the Visual Mode, instead; but the *Sangoki* does include it under the Categorical Mode. The tenth, the Stark Mode, is called *kiratsutei*, the Demon-Quelling Mode, in *Maigetsushō* and *Teika jittei*; it is included under the same category in *Sangoki*, indicating that both names refer to the same mode.

In the following notes on each verse, I have tentatively indicated, where possible, the qualities that seem to characterize each mode, based on my analysis of Shinkei's verse examples and on available scholarship on the matter. As with the issue of the six types of poetry (*rikugi*), there is, to put it mildly, little clarity on the subject of the ten modes, and I shall desist from undertaking here the kind of comparative analysis I did for the six types in Chapter 35. This is because the question of the ten modes is a major one that requires treatment as a separate project. The *yūgen* mode, which is the best known of the ten in Western scholarship, has been analyzed by Edwin A. Cranston in "'Mystery and Depth' in Japanese Court Poetry," in *The Distant Isle: Studies and Translations of Japanese Literature in Honor of Robert H. Brower*, ed. Thomas Hare et al. (Ann Arbor, Mich.: Center for Japanese Studies, University of Michigan, 1996), pp. 65–104, which includes, moreover, a complete translation of the fifty-eight poems from the *Teika jittei* illustrating the *yūgen* mode on pp. 86–100.

16. *TKBS* 1030, Miscellaneous. Junkaku picks up "hat in name only" (*no no mi kasa nite*) in the maeku and alludes to Mikasayama (lit., three-hat mountain), which rises beyond Kasuga Field in Nara, while superimposing another reading, "as in the name Mikasa" (*na no mikasa nite*). More poetically, Kaneko Kinjirō, "Shinkei no renga jittei ni tsuite," *Shōnan bungaku*, no. 13 (March 1979): 3, observes in Junkaku's link a subliminal evocation of the image of *kasumi no sode* (sleeve of haze), the diaphanous waving sleeves of a dancing girl, in the hazy landscape (hereafter cited as "Jittei").

17. The life of mountain reclusion to which the speaker had looked forward, in anticipation of sharing its tranquil pleasures with a good friend, undergoes an ironic reversal when the latter passes away before that event, and reclusion becomes utter solitude in fact. Gusai's link underscores the cutting off of all worldly ties signified by this act, while gaining pathos from the opposite, human desire for companionship.

18. The maeku strongly suggests *Ise monogatari* 123, the woman in Fukakusa Village who vows to continue waiting there after the man abandons her, even if the village turns into an overgrown moor. However, Ton'a apparently made the link through *SKKS* 483, Autumn, "On the topic of Beating Clothes [on the Fulling Block]," by Fujiwara Masatsune.

miyoshino no	In the Yoshino hills
yama no aki*kaze*	the autumn *wind* deepens with
sayo fukete	the night as chill
furusato samuku	*in the abandoned village echoes*
koromo utsu nari	*the thud of the fulling hammer.*

The poem is certainly permeated with a chill and desolate atmosphere; by this allusion Ton'a in effect shifts the old village from Fukakusa to Yoshino, where the sovereigns maintained a detached palace when the capital was still in Nara. Sōgi has the following commentary on this very verse by Ton'a in *Oi no susami*: "A terribly wasted old village where it does not seem likely that anyone remains, but there is indeed, just barely discernible, an inhabitant.

Through the melancholy rustling of the miscanthus grasses in the wind, the sound of the mallet beating cloth—the feeling is truly incomparable" (p. 145).

Ton'a (1289–1372), a representative waka poet of the Nijō school, also composed excellent renga, as witness Sōgi's inclusion of him in *Oi no susami*, a critical treatise that otherwise deals with the work of the seven sages and Gusai as models for emulation. He also has nineteen verses included in the *Shinsen Tsukubashū*. See *HF* for further information on Ton'a and Shōtetsu's consciousness of being a rival of his posthumous reputation.

19. The link is easily comprehensible when the tsukeku is read first and the maeku last; the configuration then falls into that of a waka poem. Gusai's use of adverbials and particles neatly responds to the force of *made* (rendered as "even") in the maeku to effect a clear syntactic link while deepening the feeling.

20. Gusai links up to the maeku by setting the scene of parting in the past, as evoked in the persona's mind by the wind in the pines. Kidō detects here the shadow (*omokage*) of an allusion to the "Wind in the Pines" ("Matsukaze") chapter of the *Genji*, specifically to two poems there. The first is a farewell poem composed by the Akashi Lay Monk as his wife and daughter prepare to leave Akashi for Ōi near the capital (*Genji monogatari*, ed. Abe et al., 2: 393):

yukusaki o	At the *parting* of the ways,
haruka ni inoru	as he prays for your boundless
*wakare*ji ni	fortune in the road ahead,
taenu wa oi no	what turns out not to have an end
namida narikeri	*are the tears* of an old man.

The second poem is one composed in Ōi by the Lay Monk's wife, the Nun, as she listens to the wind in the pines through the notes of her daughter's *koto*, longing for Akashi and her husband, wondering at the destiny that has brought her back to the edge of the capital. The Ōi residence, it must be noted, was inherited by the Nun from her grandfather, a former Minister of Central Affairs, and she associates it with her youth, while it was in Akashi where she became a lay nun (*Genji monogatari*, ed. Abe et al., 2: 398).

mi o kaete	In the mountain village
hitori kaereru	where I have come back alone,
yamazato ni	self all altered,
kikishi ni nitaru	it seems I've heard it before,
matsukaze zo fuku	*the wind* blowing *in the pines*.

The fourth line, ***kikishi ni nitaru***, would refer to the pine winds in Akashi, now part of the Nun's past, since she will never return there or see her husband again. We cannot know, of course, that Gusai intended an allusion to the *Genji*—the identical line, *namida narikeri*, in the maeku and the Lay Monk's poem notwithstanding. Still, such a vaguely evocative reference to the "Matsukaze" chapter poems and story—the Nun's past life with her husband in Akashi as suggested by the single term *matsukaze*—would endow the link with a narrative density and depth of feeling that possibly led to its classification under the *yūgen* mode. Here, it is instructive to note, with regard to the practice of *honzetsu* (allusion to prose works) as a method of linking in renga, that according to Sōgi, the mode of allusion must be general enough that the situation and feeling could apply to anyone and not just to the specific fictional character in the tale (*Asaji*, pp. 320–21). Thus, while the allusion grounds the link in a specific and concrete situation, the feeling arising therefrom is of universal validity and so paves the way for the poet-reader's mediated identification with the character.

21. The wordplay (count = bend or curl the fingers) here is quite transparent, as is the correspondence between *musubu* (to form) and *moyu* (to sprout), and among the images of dewdrops, new sprung ferns, and spring rain. It is undeniable, however, that the resulting

scene, dewdrops gleaming on the delicate, furled green tracery of new ferns, clearly visible ("such that one can count them") in the otherwise bare earth, is quite vivid and fresh. The smooth continuity from maeku to tsukeku gives the link a fluidity characteristic of the lofty mode. Possibly the lofty mode classification is also based on an allusion, pointed out by Yuasa Kiyoshi (*Shinkei no kenkyū*, p. 240), to *Wakan rōeishū* 12, "Early Spring," a Chinese couplet by Ono Takamura (803–852):

> shijin no *wakaki warabi* wa hito *te o nigiru*
> hekigyoku no samuki ashi wa kiri fukuro o datsusu
>
> Purple-skinned, the *new fern* is
>   *a man's hand curled*;
> Green as a gem, the cold reed is
>   an awl poking out of a bag.
>
> (*WRS*, pp. 49–50)

The loftiness would then lie in the evocation of the fresh clarity of spring's appearance (in the fiddleheads bursting their brownish purple cocoon in the spring rain) through the mediation of a Chinese poem by an ancient Japanese official. The awl poking out of a bag, incidentally, is taken from the biography of Lord Ping Yüan in the *Shi ji*, where it is said that the man of sagely eminence is like an awl concealed inside a bag; hide it as one may, its pointed end will bore a hole through and reveal itself. Takamura's variation in the changed context of a seasonal theme is startling, to say the least, but it does make the point about the unmistakable early signs of spring.

22. "The high peak of eagles" refers to Jubusen (Eagle Peak Mountain) or Ryōjusen (Skt. Gṛdhrakūṭa) in the city of Rajagrha, former Magadha kingdom, where the Buddha is said to have preached the *Lotus Sutra*. It is so long ago since the multitudes heard the sutra and parted from him on Gṛdhrakūṭa mountain that the mind cannot grasp it. Apart from actualizing the distant mountain of the maeku as Jubusen in India, Shūa rereads "distant" in the temporal sense (viz., "two thousand years ago"). The sacred subject matter, the sense of spatiotemporal remoteness, and the longing for the Buddha's presence all contribute to the aspect of the sublime here.

23. Word association: wild geese = letters; bow = three-day moon. Wild geese are associated with "letters" via an anecdote in the *Hanshu* biography of Su Wu (139–60 B.C.E.), who was held captive by the Xiong Nu but managed to send word back to Emperor Zhao by attaching a letter to the leg of a wild goose. The anecdote is recounted in the "Sobu" chapter of Book 2 of the *Heike monogatari* as the origin of the expression *gansho* or *gansatsu* (lit., goose-letter or -inscription) for "letter." (See *Heike* 1: 190–93.)

The "three-day moon" (what we call a crescent moon) is shaped like a "bow," and the geese migrating back north in spring unerringly know the "way" there. An unexpected turn, given that the referent in the maeku is surely a man famous for both writing and the martial arts (the *bunbu ryōdō* concept). Might the lofty quality be due to the implied wonder at the geese's homing instinct, their accuracy in finding their destination over a long distance? This possibility is lent credence by what Yuasa suggests is an allusive variation on *WRS* 320, Autumn, "Wild Geese" by Ōe Tomotsuna (886–957), composed on the specific topic "The Visiting Geese Know the Autumn Sky."

> *kyokyū* sarigatashi, imada utagai o *shōgen no tsuki* no kakareru ni nageutazu
> honsen madoiyasushi, nao ayamari o karyū no mizu no sumiyakanaru ni nasu
>
> For the *empty bow* is hard to elude, they leave not doubting the *bow-stringed moon*;
> And easy to miss seeing the swift arrow, they mistake still the hurling stream.
>
> (*WRS*, pp. 128–29)

Within the context of the link, "know" in the maeku would then suggest the wild geese's knowledge of the perils of being shot down by an arrow during their flight back north in the spring.

24. Shinshō effects a startling transformation in the maeku as such, which speaks only of the tranquil (or tedious) daily life of a recluse with its simple and set pattern. In his tsukeku, the days seem longer because the hut faces west and is illuminated by the setting sun. Again, "west" to a recluse is also the signifier of the Pure Land; since he has an unobstructed view (*nishi wa haretaru*) of it, his spirit can rest tranquil, take the long view, so to speak, from a spiritual affinity with that realm of grace. Kidō (in *Kenkyū*, p. 78, n. 8) is surely right in detecting here an allusion to Chōmei's lines in the *Hōjōki*: "The valley is dense with growth but *the view is open to the west* [*nishi wa haretari*]. And so I certainly do not lack for a path to contemplation" (*Hōjōki*, p. 42).

25. *TKBS* 204, Summer. The design of the link is influenced by *MYS* 375, "Composed by Prince Yuhara in Yoshino."

yoshino naru	*In Yoshino*, along the
natsumi no kawa no	*still pools of the river Natsumi*
kawayodo ni	*of the summer fruit*,
kamo zo naku naru	a quail seems to be calling
yamakage ni shite	in the shadow of the hills.

The cherry trees of Yoshino hills bloom later than those in the lowlands; the scattered petals can still be seen, collecting in the stilled pools of the river, well into the summer. An imagistically vivid link, endowed with an aspect of the sublime by the allusion to the storied past of the Nara period, when the river valleys and hills of Yoshino were a favorite retreat of the court.

26. Gusai sets up or enhances the effect of the maeku by providing a narrative context. The hiker has been following the river in hopes of lodging in a village, but the evening finds him alone beneath the looming fir trees in the mountain. The sense of loneliness, unspoken but implied, is reinforced by the maeku's allusive citation from the final two lines of *SKKS* 361 by Jakuren: *maki tatsu yama no / aki no yūgure* (the gathering autumn dusk / in the mountain where firs rise).

27. *TKBS* 1471, Miscellaneous, author listed as Anonymous; line 1 of the maeku is *kore yori mo*, and I have translated accordingly, although the verse as such is extremely vague as to the speaker's precise state of mind. Kidō seems to discard the rhetorical question in line 3 and reads the maeku within the topos of Love as "I shall probably become even more deeply absorbed in longing" [*ima yori sara ni mono-omoi ni fukeru koto darō*]; he then reads the tsukeku as involving a shift of referent to the speaker's next life (*Kenkyū*, p. 78, n. 10). Yuasa (pp. 222–23) apparently agrees with Kidō's reading, since he detects an allusive variation on the following poem: *SKKS* 1811, Miscellaneous. "When she decided to become a nun and someone stopped her." Izumi Shikibu

kaku bakari	Were I to live on
uki o shinobite	mutely enduring such misery,
nagaraeba	I should sink
kore yori masaru	into a state of brooding
mono o koso omoe	*deeper even than this.*

But although the maeku seems to be citing line 4 of Izumi's poem, the state of brooding or frustrated longing signified by *mono o omou* is not necessarily what is meant by *kokoro* in the maeku. And it is this ambiguity in *kore yori mo / masaru kokoro* that Ryōa (or whoever the tsukeku author actually was) sets out to define in the wholly changed context of the state of being of *aware* and *sabi* adumbrated by the famous autumn evening (*aki no yūgure*) poems in the *Shinkokinshū*. Kaneko, for one, reads the link as: "The autumn evening in that world beyond is probably even more profoundly lonely than the one before my eyes now" (p. 6). In particular, I believe Saigyō's *SKKS* 362, the famous *Kokoro naki / mi ni mo aware wa / shirarekeri* poem, is behind this link. Without going into a lengthy discussion of syntax and poetic rhetoric, I would paraphrase the link thus: "Could I experience a state of being even more exalted than this? So moving is the autumn evening that it is as if the heart-mind had already died to this mundane world and dwelt in the world beyond."

28. The ostensive link is through Sao River, which is located in Nara. Gusai relocates the masterless boat to Kizu Channel, like Saokawa a place-name in Yamato Province, and animates the emphatic *koso* in the maeku by adding the detail of fading daylight. As evening nears, the boat cast adrift on the waves is bound to lose its way during the crossing to Nara.

29. There is an association between *hito ni shiraruru / tani* (the valley / known to everyone) in the maeku and *kaze kawaru / . . . / asayū ni* (morning and evening / shifts the wind), based on a line in *WRS* 680 by Sugawara Fumitoki (899–981) praising the virtue of Minamoto Masanobu in rejecting thrice an appointment as Minister of the Right in 977:

> *ashita ni* wa minami *yūbe ni* wa kita
> tei tai'i ga *tani no kaze hito ni shiraretari*
>
> Southerly *at morning*, northerly *at evening*,
> Cheng T'aiwei's *valley wind is known to everyone.*

The Chinese verse is based in turn on an anecdote in a commentary on the biography of Zheng Hong in the *Houhan shu*. When Zheng Hong was young, he would go pick the fallen twigs for kindling in the Ruoxie valley. One day he came upon an arrow belonging to a Taoist immortal in the Bohao mountain; the latter, to reward him for returning the arrow, asked Zheng Hong what he wished. Zheng Hong replied: "It is always hard to carry the kindling up the Ruoxie valley. I would wish that the wind blew south in the morning and north in the evening." And so ever since that encounter, the wind has blown south at morning and north at evening, making wood gathering easier in the valley, and for that reason, it became known to everyone as "Zheng Hong's wind" (cited in *SSG*, p. 261, suppl. n. 31, and *WRS*, n. 680).

As Yuasa points out (p. 223), Shinkei himself uses this anecdotal allusion in his poetry, and the reason is his empathy for the difficulties of eking out a livelihood and the grace in the Taoist's recognition of Zheng Hong's diligence and honesty.

30. *TKBS* 1894, Miscellaneous Forms, Haikai. The link turns on a rather macabre anecdote recounted in, among others, "The Lampstand Demon" chapter of the Nagato Text *Heike monogatari*. During the reign of Empress Suiko (d. 628; r. 592–628), the Great Minister Karu was sent on the embassy to China, where he learned the way of yin-yang divination. The Chinese, however, had no desire to see this esoteric knowledge transmitted to Japan. Consequently, they forcibly detained the Minister, tore the skin off his face and stuck a lampstand on his head, thus disguising him as a veritable lampstand demon, the image evoked by the tsukeku. Later, Karu's son traveled to China to search for him and came across the demon lampstand but did not at first recognize it as his father. Whereat the creature composed a Chinese verse revealing his identity, and the son finally recognized his father (cited in *SSG*, p. 167, n. 10). The link turns on this moment of recognition; whereas the *Tsukubashū* classifies the link under "haikai" for its eccentric imagery, Shinkei reads in it a demonstration of the depth of the filial piety; the father's outward appearance (*sugata*) might be horribly changed, but the filial piety binding parent and child remains unaltered.

31. "Dew" is classified under the lexical category "Falling Phenomena" in renga; this probably occasioned the riddle-like question posed by the maeku. In response, Shinshō summons

a small, close-up image of dew forming on branches of flowers arranged in a vase; water evaporating ("rising") from the vase condenses as dew on the branch.

32. Without the verse to which the maeku is linked, it is not possible to determine the antecedent of *sono na*, since Japanese pronouns lack gender and number; I have rendered it as the neutral "the name," although it might well mean "his name"—that is, the name of the owner himself. At any rate, Ryōa rereads *sono na* to mean "their names," referring to the trees in a mountain peasant's yard. He might well be only a humble rustic but he will know the names of those great trees growing in his own yard. Kaneko (p. 7) detects a buried, subtextual evocation of a passage in the "Otome" chapter of the *Genji*, describing the northwest or winter garden in Genji's new Rokujō Palace: "The chrysanthemum hedge would bloom in the morning frosts of early winter. . . . And in among the deep groves were mountain trees which one would have been hard put to identify" [*osaosa na mo shiranu miyamagi-domo no, kobukaki nado o utsushi-uetari*] (Murasaki Shikibu, *Genji monogatari*, ed. Abe et al., 3: 74; *The Tale of Genji*, trans. Edward Seidensticker (New York: Knopf, 1977), 1: 384). The skill of the detailed turn Shinshō effects on the maeku, and the subliminal *Genji* evocation, possibly account for the Intricate Mode classification of this link.

33. Gusai's linking turn is somewhat startling, but sure-footed. He focuses on the emphatic "fewer in number" (*kazu zo sukunaki*) in the maeku's rhetoric and reinterprets it to mean "fewer in years"; consequently, "the year before" (*kozo*, meaning "last year" in the maeku) comes to refer to the earlier birth of the older brother. There is also a playful phonological echoing of initial syllable *ko* in *kozo* and *kono*, and of *hito* ("people," but also "one") and *hitotsu* (also "one") between the two verses. A rather numerically studded, intricate turn, possibly occasioned by the necessity for leaving behind, at this point in the sequence, the theme of mutability in the maeku as such.

34. A startlingly humorous turn from the pathos of old age overtaking a seafarer or fisherman. "A floating weed" as well as "flowing" in the tsukeku may be read also as signifiers of a wandering, rootless existence. The water grass that had been "growing" (homophonous with *oi*, "aging," in the maeku) in the pipe is nudged out, by the force of the swollen rains, perhaps, to end one knows not where. This pair is cited also in *Shasekishū* VB.7, "About Renga" (p. 245). Kidō observes that the maeku is alluding to the line "Young boys and fresh girls grew old in boats" [*dōnan kanjo shūchū ni oyu*] from one of Bai Juyi's "New *Yuefu*" entitled "Vast and Wide the Sea," about people exhausting their lives in search of the fabulous, illusory Penglai mountain out at sea (see *Haku Kyo-i* 1: 31). If so, however, Zen'a ignores the allusion, possibly because the previous link already turned on it.

35. Gusai achieves the link by closely following the concept of phenomena appearing and disappearing. In the maeku as such, the referent is the moon occasionally seen from within the range upon range of mountains; in the tsukeku, what "comes out but to go in" is the stag's breath, imaged as the mist that in lifting reveals the moon and then conceals it again. The intermittent calls of the stag seeking its mate through the autumn night are, however, the subliminal link.

36. The maeku images the white moonlight upon the *himuro*, an underground hollow carved out in the mountainside for storing winter ice until the summer. By mentioning Kumano, Ryōa transforms the caves into meditation cells for the priests of Kumano, thus introducing a stark spiritual dimension to the windswept landscape beneath icy moonlight.

37. Shinshō links to the maeku by repeating the concept of the rain's diminished volume in a different metonymical detail. There is also a subtle difference in emphasis: whereas the maeku focuses on the intermittent sound of raindrops beneath the pines, the tsukeku muffles

that sound through the image of moss absorbing the raindrops. The effect of the link is to bring out the fresh, moist greenness of the overcast scene.

38. The impingement of but two sounds on the consciousness of the speaker points up the silence all around and measures the lateness of the hour. A subtle link, similar in spirit to Shinkei's own cold and slender aesthetics.

39. *TKBS* 371, Autumn. The verse is cited as an example of superior renga poetry in Yoshimoto's *Gekimōshō* (1358, p. 62). Gusai locates the declining moon in Izumi Province (Osaka) by aural affinity to the word *izumi* (spring, pool) in the maeku, and has the speaker gazing south from along the bay of Sumiyoshi (Settsu Prov., mod. Hyōgō). What he does is essentially to widen the landscape from a small area of pines and spring to take in the whole vista of the night sky over Osaka Bay. There is also a more subtle link between the coolness of the pine breeze where the observer stands and the pure rays of the declining moon across the bay.

40. The late spring scene in the maeku ("flowers" as such signify the spring season) turns to late autumn in the tsukeku. The dying person ("yet to expire") is replaced by lingering insects, and the vanished spring flowers are understood as the autumn wildflowers, now withered across the fields. An extremely firm, economic, and well-designed link; the thematic shift is achieved in an elegantly seamless manner, while fully retaining the pathos of the maeku.

41. *TKBS* 1554, Miscellaneous; the verse is attributed to Junkaku in the anthology. The link, which illustrates the resolute courage required to renounce mundane existence (including the family), is wholly clear. What is arresting, as Kaneko speculates (p. 9), is the unexpected contrast between the subject's rough boldness and the child's soft vulnerability. Seen with a cold eye, there is but a tiny step from this exalted drama to comic haikai with its taste for incongruity. Incidentally, commentators observe here an allusion to the legendary life of the poet recluse Saigyō. The following passage from the *Illustrated Tales of Saigyō* (*Saigyō monogatari e-kotoba*) is particularly striking in relation to the link:

> "Grant that I may escape by autumn and unhindered carry out my plan of renouncing the world at year's end," he [Saigyō] prayed at the Sambō Temple. When he went home, his little girl of four, whom he had cherished all these years, came out to meet him at the veranda and clung to his sleeve, saying, "I'm so happy that Father has come home." He loved her above everything, so much so that his eyes grew dark with the emotion, but was this not precisely the way to cut off the fetters of delusive attachment, he thought, and kicked her down the veranda. She was crying desolately, but he refused to listen and went inside. (Quoted in *SSG*, p. 261, suppl. n. 32)

The tension between Saigyō's requisite hardness and the child's innocent vulnerability is what emerges, with a sharply ironic effect, in the renga link.

42. The link is similar to the third example, also by Ton'a, under the *yūgen* section above, and there is also an allusion to *SKKS* 483, but the syntax of this link lacks the poetic ambiguity of that mode. The arresting quality would be in Ton'a's move of placing the sound of the fulling block in a hut on the peak, a location somewhat unusual because such huts are associated with hermits, whereas beating clothes on the fulling block is woman's work, connoting especially the loneliness of a village wife waiting for a husband who does not come home. At any rate, Ton'a's move involves the clever turn of reading *takaku* ("loud" when referring to a sound) in the maeku in its other sense of "high"—thus the hut on the peak; from such an elevated position, the sound would be louder than coming from the lowlands.

43. *TKBS* 1128, Miscellaneous, Anonymous. The link is based on an unspoken analogy between the whiteness of dew and of the moonlight shining on it. Emerging from beneath the ridge, the moon as it climbs up the sky gradually illuminates the dew-laden pine trees

from the lower branches up, so that one may say that the glistening dew is indeed "climbing to the treetops." An impressive, and even aesthetically pleasing solution to the paradox presented by the riddle-like maeku.

44. *TKBS* 1575, Miscellaneous. "At a 1,000-verse sequence in the residence of the Regent [Nijō Yoshimoto], then Palace Minister." In *Fude no susabi,* Ichijō Kanera explains the link thus: "The maeku is about the beginning of the year in spring; the tsukeku links to it the idea that with old age, the heart of the child returns. It is as the saying goes—old age is a second childhood." (*Fude no susabi* in Ijichi Tetsuo, ed., *Rengaronshū*, 1 [Iwanami Shoten, 1953], p. 286)

"Now is it" (*ima wa*), referring to the New Year in the maeku, takes another referent, old age, and what returns is the childlike heart. Or again, one can say that the years turn around, returning the subject to his childhood. As with the other examples for the Arresting Mode, the link is at once startlingly unexpected and utterly right.

45. *TKBS* 1270, Miscellaneous; attributed there to Taira Takashige. Where the usual link would read in the maeku a common occasion for crowds, as say, an official ceremony, a religious festival, and such, this one introduces a quite novel and rustic image of rows of laborers dragging a pile of timber through the forest for transport elsewhere.

46. Where crowds came to view the cherry trees earlier, now that their flowering is past, "even the paths" (*michi dani mo*) leading to them have disappeared beneath the new lush growth of grasses. In this way, the categorical mode refers to a link that accounts for the maeku with a firm, sound, and inarguable conception.

47. Ryōa effects a link by extending the narrative to explain how the lost persona in the maeku found his way to a village, thus accounting for the sense of uncertainty and then relief in the maeku's inflection.

48. Ryōa's tsukeku includes the unusual expression *ne komoru* (lit., secluded cries) generated in response to "confined" and "wall" in the maeku, whose syntax and conception as such strikes one as a difficult riddle. (I render *kiri no magaki*, lit., "hedge of mist," as "wall of mist" here, because it sounds more effective in English.) The link is produced by way of an allusion to the following poem: *Senzaishū* 310, Autumn. "Composed when she presented a 100-poem sequence." Taikenmon'in no Horikawa.

saranu dani	Even without it,
yūbe sabishiki	the *evening* is desolate enough
*yamaz*ato no	in the *mountain* village—
kiri no magaki ni	*from within walls of mist*
ojika nakunari	*the sound of a stag crying.*

The sense of confinement within layers and layers of mist, in which the deer cannot make out its mate, and the listener can only hear its faint cries, is what emerges in the link through the mediation of the poem.

49. Verbally, the link turns on the double entendre in *kuyuru*, the *rentaikei* inflexion of *kuyu*, meaning "to regret, feel remorse about" in reference to "sins" in the maeku but "to burn, to smoke" in the context of the tsukeku. Semantically, Shinshō contextualizes the maeku's statement in the scene of a recluse carrying out evening prayers as part of the discipline of liberating himself from egoistic desire. A metaphorical operation occurs whereby the dissolution of sin becomes figured as smoke vanishing in the evening sky.

50. Again a narrative approach to linking; though the fisherfolk have a temporary respite during the rain from making salt, they cannot relax but have to empty the rainwater that has collected in their boats. The action of scooping briny seawater over the fires to collect salt is echoed in the tsukeku to a different purpose and with the rainwater as referent.

51. *TKBS* 974, Love. Crimson tears allude to "tears of blood" (*chi no namida*) in waka diction, a figure for extreme and desperate grief. This exaggerated image, ascribed to scandalous rumors in the tsukeku, is matched by the hyperbolic comparison there between the rise of scandal and the force of Tatsuta River, "river" simultaneously suggesting the fixed phrase "river of tears" (*namidagawa*) in the poetic vocabulary of love. There is, furthermore, a conventional association between "crimson" and "Tatsuta River" based on a poem by Narihira, *KKS* 294, Autumn.

chihayaburu	Unheard of even in
kamiyo mo kikazu	the age of the raging gods—
tatsutagawa	On Tatsuta River
karakurenai ni	swirl the waters in tie-dyed
mizu kukuru to wa	splotches of flaming crimson.

The singular conception in the link would then be the arresting correlation between the crimson of the subject's tears and the "visible" impact of the scandal that caused them, as figured in the flaming autumn leaves swirling on the Tatsuta River. One imagines that this scandal, "unheard of even in / the age of the raging gods," would be on the order of Narihira's affair with the Ise Vestal Priestess.

52. *TKBS*, Love, maeku to No. 970 by Fujiwara Tameie, and part of a three-verse sequence there; ascribed to Gofukakusa-in no Shōshō no Naishi (d. 1265?), a waka poet and one of the leading women renga practitioners included in the *Tsukubashū* (15 verses), along with her sister Ben no Naishi (fl. ca. 1243–1265; 13 verses); they were daughters of the waka and renga poet Fujiwara Nobuzane (1177–1265).

"Paler on the other branch" (*katae* is homonymous with "the other side") suggests that the one side must be deeper in color, thus the rather amazing leap to the tsukeku's philosophical statement, where the crimson of the autumn foliage, deep on one side, pale on the other, comes to figure the heart's "passion or dispassion." It is interesting to note in turn the tsukeku to this one, composed by Teika's son Tameie:

namida o shiraba	If he knew of my tears, I would
tsuki mo hazukashi	feel shame even before the moon.

Tameie in effect takes up "passion or dispassion" in a situation where a woman weeps for an unrequited love and dreads its exposure ("reveal its hue").

53. To understand Jūbutsu's smart rejoinder to the maeku, which is based on the contrastive juxtaposition of proximity and distance, it is necessary to know that Hirano Shrine is dedicated to the fourth-century Emperor Nintoku, who had his seat in Naniwa (by Osaka Bay), and that Kitano then as now enshrined the spirit of Sugawara Michizane, the Heian statesman famously exiled to Tsukushi (in Kyushu). So while the shrines of the two men are in adjacent locations in Kyoto, the places associated with them in life are quite distant from each other.

54. The ironic impact of the link is best appreciated when the verses are considered in reverse. Then it will be seen that, given the ever-widening separation, the subject who lives only for that meeting cannot hang on much longer. Syntactically, *iki no matsu* (a living pine) functions as a kind of lead-in phrase to *matsu hikazu* (number of days of waiting) in line 1 of the maeku, generating a homophonous doubling of *matsu* in its two senses of "pine tree" and "wait." The pine, being a signifier of constancy and longevity, acquires a paradoxical effect when *iki no matsu* is read as "waiting to breathe/live," that is, leading a diminished existence until the meeting, which is however less and less likely to happen. So as the days stretch on, the subject's life becomes effectively shorter. Such would be the singular conception animating this link.

55. This pair has appeared previously in Chapter 34; see n. 19 there. The arresting concept pertains to the juxtaposition of "briny" with "bitter" to reinforce the sober, admonitory construction of mundane life as a vale of sorrow and hardship.

56. *TKBS* 1319, Miscellaneous; line 1 of the maeku is *yuki o atsumuru*, a clearer inflexion. Mount Fuji has of course been famous since ancient times for its snow-covered peak all year, particularly as evoked in *MYS* 317, Akahito's *chōka*; the tenth-century *Ise monogatari*, chap. 9, also speaks of it as "the mountain that knows no seasons" (*toki shiranu yama*) for that reason. The link here thus hinges on the association between snow, mountain, and Mount Fuji; and more precisely, the subject's confirmation by sight (viz., "I see it is indeed") of the tales that have been transmitted about it since ancient times, evoking wonder and drawing the subject to see it for himself. The allusion to Akahito's *chōka* is to the final section below:

tokijiku so	and no matter the season
yuki wa furikeru	it is white with fallen snow;
kataritsugi	I shall transmit the tale,
iitsugiyukamu	speak of it for ages to come,
fuji no takane wa	the lofty peak of Fuji.

The classification of this verse under "the mode of preserving the past" clearly has to do with its ancient theme.

57. The "upper and the lower" in the maeku refers to social classes; the emperor governs by appointing an official hierarchy of ranks with corresponding duties and privileges, and by this maintains civil order. In the tsukeku, this is reinterpreted to refer to the *Upper* and *Lower* Kamo Shrines in the capital, site of important annual, official festivals, and *matsurigoto* read in its other meaning of religious worship. The sum effect of the link is a statement such as this: Just as the waters of the Kamo River flow ceaselessly from upstream to downstream, so the sovereign's rule is forever assured through civil government and worship of the nation's Shintō deities. It is a classical and conservative concept, to be sure, but it was probably still the orthodox belief, despite the political ascendancy of the warrior class by Zen'a's time.

58. The maeku as such doubtless refers to a letter full of lies, more specifically to a missive from a lover who turns out to be faithless. In an amazing and elegant turn, Zen'a bears down on "great deception" (*ōki* can mean both "numerous" and "great"), rereading it to mean a version of *ars longa, vita brevis*, flowers and autumn leaves being the classic symbols of mutability in the traditional thematics of nature and human affairs, particularly love. The construction of the sign, that is, of language and painting, as baseless lies (*soragoto*) would be Buddhist in origin. However, it is equally possible that by "great deception," Zen'a meant to celebrate art's power of rendering the ephemeral timeless. *Tokiwa* (everlasting, lit., "changeless rock") in line 3, it is relevant to note, is used in congratulatory contexts to refer to the sovereign's long reign or the pine tree's constancy. As such sentiments have a more ancient and orthodox provenance, the latter reading is probably the more sound.

59. *TKBS* 611, Shintō; attributed to Fujiwara Iemi, a Senior North-Facing Warrior, with junior fifth rank, to Rtd. Emperor Go-Uda (1267–1324; r. 1274–1287).

The verses are linked almost wholly through the verbal correlations "pray" = "Kamo Shrine" and "short" = "legs of the duck." Apart from identifying the name of the shrine where the subject prayed until the dawn, there is here no attempt to achieve a meaningful statement. Its interest lies in the comically incongruous, *haikai*-like effect of the juxtaposition of the name of the sacred shrine, Kamo, with its homonym *kamo*, meaning "duck," and the insertion of *ashi*, "legs" in line 3, so that *kamo no ashi* comes to function as a kind of lead-in phrase (*joshi*) to *mijika* (short) in the maeku's initial line. The resulting phrase, "duck's legs / short" (*kamo no ashi / mijika*) is, of course, totally inappropriate to the solemn context and is indeed probably intended to yield the mocking subtext, "Having put my trust in a duck's short legs, I prayed until the dawn," or some such. Be that as it may, the reference to ancient Kamo Shrine and Shintō worship mark the link as belonging to the *shakotei*.

60. *TKBS* 659, Buddhism. *Tsutomu* in the maeku, which means to labor and strive at some task, is given a specific religious inflexion in the tsukeku by the simple move of referring to a temple, so that it comes to mean working at the salvation of one's soul by such religious practices (*tsutome* or, in Sino-Japanese, *gongyō*) as daily prayer, sutra reading and copying, meditation, and pilgrimage. There are numerous ancient temples near Asuka Village in Nara, the oldest indeed being Asukadera.

61. Staying within the Shintō topos of the maeku, the tsukeku reinforces the subject's sense of the awe-inspiring mystery of divine power by placing the origins of the shrine in mythic times. The stark quality lies in the focus on the almost oppressive, hieratic and taboo character of the divine, set up far above and beyond the human.

62. *TKBS* 1596, Miscellaneous. *Sue*, referring to the final years of a life in the maeku, acquires the altered semantic inflexion of "end," as in the hair ends of a pageboy haircut, which are indeed cut "short," thus *sue zo mijikaki*. The tsukeku provides a reason for the maeku speaker's lament on the brevity of his final years; in its bald statement of an incongruity, its withholding of sympathy, the link is stark indeed.

63. By simply inserting the contrastive *wa* particle, and introducing the famous bird of summer, said to sing in the Fifth Month, Shinshō resolves the otherwise difficult maeku. Poems on the cuckoo commonly speak of the rarity of its calls, how long and eagerly one waits to hear it, and the inevitable disappointment when it does not sing. The cut-and-dried tone of this link therefore belies the pathos with which this bird is handled in the courtly tradition.

64. The link is made by reading *osamu* (pacify, secure, govern) in the maeku to refer to the straw scarecrows that *secure* the harvest from pests and animals; again, in its second sense—"to store, secure in a safe place"—*osamu* refers to storing the autumn harvest. Whereas the maeku states that it is military force that secures the peace in the country, Shūa feels that it is a safe harvest, that is, the orderly functioning of the rice economy, that is essential. Since rice was the currency of official taxation and rents, salaries and properties, it was obviously crucial for civil order. This is an unusually hard and sober topic for poetry.

65. The "stark" designation here would seem to be due to the atmosphere of intense, frosty cold at evening. There is perhaps an allusion to the evocation of winter frost in *WRS* 372 by Ki no Nagon, in which the crane is said to "swallow" its own voice (suppress its cries) due to the fallen frost.

> ashita ni gakō ni tsumotte oshi iro o henzu
> yoru kahyō ni ochite tsuru koe o nomu
>
> At morning piled in the tiled gutters,
> the duck alters in hue;
> At night fallen on the village gates,
> the crane swallows its voice.

If there is indeed an allusion, then Gusai's tsukeku should be understood as evoking a later moment, when the cranes' cries have been stilled by the frost.

66. The locution "the real in the darkness" (*yami no utsutsu*) is from *KKS* 647, Love. Anonymous.

mubatama no	*In* waking *darkness*
yami no utsutsu wa	black as leopard lily seed,
sadakanaru	*the real* proved

yume ni ikura mo	not much more substantial
masarazarikeri	than a vivid dream in sleep.

This final disclaimer at the end of Part I echoes the prose occurring before the Ten Styles section, as well as the modest rhetoric at the beginning of the whole treatise, which characterizes it as "an account of our own perplexities as we walked uncertainly on the way of Poetry."

Chapter Forty

1. The extant *Meigetsuki*, Teika's *kanbun* diary covering the years 1180–1235, contains no references to either *hen-jo-dai-kyoku-ryū* or the Six Types (*rikugi*). Kidō notes that Teika is reported to have authored a poetic treatise with the same title, so it is possible that Shinkei is referring to that work.

2. In the *Yakumo mishō*, Rtd. Emperor Juntoku makes the same observation, using as illustration the *Zhuangzi* anecdote of the cartwright who criticized the Duke's book reading as useless, since words do not transmit the mental attitudes and expertise gained from practice. Juntoku writes: "It is the same with poems. Even the practitioner who knows in his mind which is good and which bad does not have the power to teach it [that discrimination]. Therefore it is more important to understand poetry than to compose it [*uta o kokorouru koto wa, yomu yori wa daiji nari*]" (*Yakumo mishō*, p. 74).

3. Shinkei refers here to Chapter 35 of *Sasamegoto*.

4. The Five Corporeal Parts (*gotai*) correspond to the following parts of the body: head, neck, breast, arms, and legs. The Six Roots (*rokkon*) are the six sources of delusion—but also of illumination, when employed as the instruments of a higher understanding—in Buddhist thought: the five organs of sensation—eyes, ears, nose, tongue, body—and the mind, seat of the discursive intellect.

5. "Prelude-Break-Climax" (*jo-ha-kyū*) names the concept of dynamic structure in the performing arts of music and dance, particularly Nō; it was used by Nijō Yoshimoto and the Muromachi renga poets as well to describe the progression of a renga sequence.

6. The "Introduction–Proper Teaching–Propagation" (*jo-shō-ruzū*) concept of sutra structure is culled from ancient Chinese studies of the *Lotus Sutra*. The Tiantai patriarch Zhiyi is said to have divided the twenty-eight chapters of the scripture into two main parts: "the secondary gate" (chaps. 1–14) and "the primary gate" (chaps. 15–28), and each part into the three sections mentioned here. Thus in Part I, chapter 1 is the "Introduction," chapters 2–9 are the "Correct Tenets," and chapters 10–14, the "Propagation" section. The corresponding sections in Part II are chapters 15, 16–17, and 18–28. See Shioiri Ryōdō, "The Meaning of the Formation and Structure of the *Lotus Sutra*," in *The Lotus Sutra in Japanese Culture*, ed. George J. Tanabe Jr. and Willa Jane Tanabe (Honolulu: University of Hawaii Press, 1989), pp. 32, 34–35.

7. These are instances of "pillow words" (*makura kotoba*), stock epithets conventionally inserted before certain nominals (here "moon," "mountain," "road," and the place-names "Nara" and "Kataoka") to elevate or ornament them.

8. On *hampi no ku*, see Chapter 34 above and n. 7 there.

Chapter Forty-One

1. This question also appears in the *Bontōanshu hentōsho* (Replies of Master Bontōan), a renga manual written by Bontō for Hamana Mochimasa in 1417, based on what he learned as a student of Nijō Yoshimoto and from contemporary opinion, as well as his own practice. The work includes this passage: "When a poet asked Mototoshi how one should compose

poetry, he replied, 'Miscanthus reeds on a withered moor, the pale moon at dawn.' How is one to understand this?" (*SSG*, suppl. n. 33.)

2. *SKKS* 591. Winter. "Topic unknown." Lord Minamoto Saneakira (910–70). The poem also appears in *WRS* 402. That the extra three syllables in lines two, four, and five do not mar the excellence of the whole has been remarked in critical works like Fujiwara Tameie's *Eiga ittei* (ca. 1275), which cites it as an instance where surplus syllables (*ji amari*) dictated by poetic necessity do not sound jarring and are therefore permissible (*Eiga ittei*, p. 361).

3. "The poems of antiquity" (*jōdai no utadomo*) refers to the *Man'yōshū* (comp. ca. 759), an anthology already praised by Shinkei in Part I (see Chapter 8 above).

4. The anecdote about Teika making this distinction between "makers of poems" and "poet-seers" is recorded in Ton'a's treatise *Seiashō* (ca. late Kamakura—1360):

> According to the Minister of Popular Affairs [Nijō Tamefuji, 1275–1324], the Kyōgoku Zen follower [Teika] was always saying, "My late father [Shunzei] was indeed a great poet-seer [*uruwashiki utayomi*], while I am a maker of poems [*utazukuri*]. I tried so hard to compose as he did but it didn't work and I gave up." . . . Again, the Lay Monk, Retired Minister of Popular Affairs, is reported to have said, "There were indeed poet-seers in the past, but now everyone is a maker of poems. As for making, how is that to be done? Each one has his own idea about it, and none are the same." Again, it is said: in a letter that the Lay Monk, Retired Kyōgoku Middle Counselor [Teika], sent to Priest Jichin, he wrote, "Your compositions as well as those of my late father are indeed the poetry of great poet-seers [*uruwashiki utayomi no uta*]. As for myself and others, we are poem-makers who work by the force of intelligence [*chie no chikara o mote tsukuru utazukuri nari*]. And so in all the realm, those who make poems in this way are our disciples." (Ton'a, *Seiashō*, in Sasaki Nobutsuna, ed., *NKT* 5 [Kazama Shobō, 1957; 4th ed., 1977], pp. 113–14)

5. This saying appears in the *Kunshishū* (The Gentleman's Collection), a single-volume anthology of sayings and memorable passages from Confucian texts used for the moral upbringing of the young. From the style of the *kanbun* used in the text, it is believed to date from the late Heian period. *ZGR* 32b: 946.10.

6. "Layman Pang" (J. Hō Koji) of the Tang period studied with Shitou and was later certified by Mazu in Jiangxi for having achieved knowledge of the innermost teachings of Zen. Formerly a civil official, he renounced his wealth and position, and is said to have lived with his daughter, making bamboo baskets to sell in the market. Case 42 of the *Hekiganroku* (Blue Cliff Record) features his perspicuity as a Zen master. For a translation, see *The Blue Cliff Record*, trans. Thomas Cleary and J. C. Cleary (Boston: Shambhala, 1992), pp. 253–57; also pp. 610–11 for a biographical note. The *Hekiganroku* is a composite text with a complex history. Its oldest core is a collection of one hundred koans compiled by the Unmon-sect Zen master and poet Setchō (Ch. Xuedou, 980–1052), who also wrote a verse for each case. About a century later, another master, Engo (Ch. Yuanwu, 1063–1135) of the Rinzai sect, added introductions and annotations on phrases in the main case and in Setchō's verse, plus a longer commentary on each. Subsequently, Dai'e (Ch. Dahui, 1089–1163), one of Engo's disciples, grew alarmed at the book's popularity and fearing that the commentaries would distort Zen by their conceptual and formal approach, he collected the printed copies and had them burned. Fortunately, some escaped Dai'e's fires and became the basis for the book's reconstitution. The *Hekiganroku* has since been countlessly reprinted in both China and Japan; it is revered as one of the principal texts of Zen, particularly in the Rinzai sect, where it is considered the best guide to verbal interviews in Zen meditation practice (*Butten kaidai jiten*, ed. Mizuno et al., p. 212).

7. Wu Ding of the Yin saw Fu Yue clearly in a dream, and had him sought out; he was discovered laboring in construction, and the king elevated him to be his wise and trusted adviser. The anecdote may be found in the *Shu Jing* (J. *Shokyō*, *The Book of Documents*). See *Chinese Classics*, trans. Legge, 3: 248–53.

8. The story of Zhang Han may be read in *Mōgyū*, under "Zhang Han [J. Chōkan] Follows His Inclination." A native of Wu, Zhang was a man of talent who went to Luoyang and was appointed Grand Marshal by King Jiong of Qi. But he did not care for the bureaucratic formalities and was, moreover, put off by Jiong's excesses. Sensing perhaps the approach of disaster with the autumn winds, he was stricken with yearning for the fragrant greens and pickled sea bream of his native Wu and declared: "It is human nature to set a high value on being able to follow one's inclination. Whatever drove me to travel several thousand miles in search of fame and position?" And straightaway he abandoned his office and set off for his mountain home. The tyrannical Jiong was subsequently killed, and people praised Zhang for his perspicuity. One of them wanted to know why he was not worried about leaving a name for posterity. He replied: "To be granted fame after death is not like having a draught of wine right now." People thought this large-mindedness truly splendid. *Mōgyū* 2: 914.

9. On Sima Xiangru (J. Shiba Shōjo), see "*Shi Ji* 117: The Biography of Sima Xiangru," in *Records of the Grand Historian: Han Dynasty II*, trans. Burton Watson (rev. ed., New York: Columbia University Press, 1993), pp. 259–306, esp. p. 261. In the *Mōgyū*, under "Wenjun Minds the Hearth" (pp. 599–600), we have the following story:

> Chuo Wenjun [J. Taku Bunkun] of the Former Han dynasty was the daughter of the rich man Chuo Wangsun of Linjiong in Shu province. She was recently widowed and loved music. Sima Xiangru [J. Shiba Shōjo] attended a banquet at their house with another guest. When the wine was flowing freely, he played the zither and attracted Wenjun with his music. He had brought with him a carriage and outriders and behaved with an elegant serenity, cutting quite a sophisticated figure. Secretly observing him from behind her door, Wenjun was delighted in her heart and conceived a love for him. Fearing that Xiangru would not be chosen for her husband, she eloped with him that night, and they fled to Chengdu, his hometown. His home turned out to be no more than a bare structure of four walls. Her father Wangsun was greatly angered, and after some time Wenjun herself became unhappy. Then she told Xiangru, "Let us go back to Linjiong, borrow money from my uncles, and with it make a living at least." And so they went to Linjiong, where they sold their carriage and all their equipage and bought a tavern. Wenjun herself minded the tavern hearth while Xiangru pulled on a loincloth and worked alongside the hired help at all sorts of odd jobs, washing dirty dishes in the marketplace. Wangsun was so ashamed he locked his gate and stopped going out. His male kin came one after another to reason with him thus: "You only have one son and two daughters. What you do not lack is wealth. Wenjun has already cast her lot with Xiangru. He used to be well traveled and, though poor, has enough talent to be counted on." And so Wangsun settled on Wenjun one hundred slaves and a million in coins. The couple then returned to Chengdu, bought fields and house, and became quite wealthy. Some time thereafter, Yang Deyi of Shu became a breeder of dogs for the imperial hunts, serving under Emperor Wu. It so happened that the Emperor had read Xiangru's prose-poem, "Master Emptiness," and found it excellent, saying, "How is it that I was not born in the same age as this man?" At which Deyi observed, "Sima Xiangru from my hometown says that he wrote it himself." Amazed, the Emperor summoned Xiangru for an interview and subsequently appointed him one of his attendants. (*Mōgyū* 2: 599–600)

Chapter Forty-Two

1. Moon, flowers, and snow are major "marked" images in the seasonal vocabulary of the poetic tradition. Since they carry in themselves a great deal of charge and are highly prized, their occurrence in the 100-verse sequence (*hyakuin*) is stringently restricted according to the rules of frequency and intermission. "Moon" may occur only thrice, and each occurrence must be separated from the next by a minimum interval of seven verses; "flowers" may appear four times in total but only once on each sheet; "snow" too may appear four times, at minimum seven-verse intervals, with the added stipulation that it may not occur with

"spring snow" on the same page of the manuscript. (The renga manuscript, called *kaishi,* consisted of four sheets of paper, each folded horizontally along the middle to yield eight pages. The hundred verses were recorded on the *kaishi* by the calligrapher in a set number of verses per page: 8–14, 14–14, 14–14, 14–8. The rules of occurrence of the images were defined, therefore, by their location in this arrangement.) The rarity of these images in the structural economy of the hyakuin means it was a high privilege to compose on them; Shinkei's reply would revolve around whether the privilege should be based on merit or social status.

2. Since "flowers" had a frequency of four for each hyakuin, it would occur a total of forty times in a 1,000-verse sequence (*senku*). If Shūa composed thirty-seven flower verses at such an event, that is an amazingly high number indeed.

3. "In Buddhism too there are those who study the word [*ku*] and others who seek its intention [*i*]." Suzuki Hisashi, who annotated the *Sasamegoto* text in the *Geidō shisō shū*, glosses this statement (p. 172) by citing the *Yuimagyō* (Skt. *Vimalakīrti Sutra*): "Of those who undergo training in search of correct enlightenment, there are two kinds: those who pursue the lines of scripture, and those who seek the deep meaning of the Buddha's intention."

4. "The unenlightened pay homage to the word, the enlightened to the intention." Again, Suzuki (ibid.) cites the following passage from *Yuimagyō*: "The new student-aspirants who have not yet arrived at the Way like to study the words of the scriptures; the old aspirants who have arrived at the Way labor to understand the Buddha's intention."

5. "The words are the teachings, and their intention is to transmit the ultimate principle [*ku wa kyō, i wa ri nari*]. The teachings are provisional, the ultimate principle is what is truly real [*kyōgon rijitsu*]." The dialectics of word and teaching vs. intention and principle, and of the provisional vs. the real, are fundamental in Tendai philosophy. Some instances of the usage of these terms and the operation of the dialectic in canonical as well as popular religious texts are the following:

> *Daichidoron* IX: To rely on the principle means that in it, there is no opposition between the good and the bad, misery and fortune, or false and true. One obtains the principle through the words; the principle is not in the words themselves. It is like the situation where someone points with his finger to indicate the moon. A confused man will see only the finger and not the moon. So the one says to the other, "I am pointing to the moon with my finger in order to show it to you. Why do you look at my finger and not see the moon?" Just so, words aim to point out the principle; the words themselves are not the principle. Therefore one must not rely on the words. (Quoted in Suzuki Hisashi's additional annotations focusing specifically on the esoteric passages in *Sasamegoto*, "*Sasamegoto* mikkan [hereafter cited as "Mikkan"] II, p. 30; Suzuki's annotations in his modern Japanese translation/rendering of *Sasamegoto* in the *Geidō shisō shū* volume is identified as "*SSG* Suzuki" to avoid confusion.)

> *Hokke mongu* III.B: The ultimate principle is the true Suchness [*ri wa kore shinnyo*]. The true Suchness, being fundamentally pure, never alters regardless of the presence or absence of buddhas. *This is why the principle is called real* [*yue ni ri o nazukete jitsu to nasu*]. Phenomena [*koto*] are of the mind, of the consciousness, and so on. Generating pure and impure actions [*gō*], they shift and move without becoming fixed. That is why phenomena are called provisional [*gon*]. Outside the principle, phenomena would not be established, and outside of phenomena, the principle could not manifest itself. Phenomena have the effect of manifesting the principle; it is for this reason that skillful means [*hōben*] are highly praised [in the *Lotus Sutra*]. Principled teaching names the totality of the aforementioned principle and phenomena as the ultimate principle [*rikyō to wa mae no ri, koto o sōjite mina nazukete ri to nasu*]. For instance, it is like considering as truth both the ultimate reality and the mundane [*reiseba, shinzoku tomo ni shōshite tai to nasu ga gotoshi*]. By embodying this, the several buddhas achieve sainthood. What is called sainthood is the correct truth [*shō to wa shōjitsu nari*]. In order that the lower beings may receive it by means of the dharmas, the buddhas design teachings based on the principle. In effect, *the teachings are provisional* [*kyō wa sunawachi gon nari*]. Without

> the teachings, the principle does not manifest itself; its manifestation depends upon the teaching. This is why the Tathagata had such high praise for skillful means. (Quoted in Suzuki, "Mikkan," II, pp. 30–31; emphasis added)

The same issues, however, are taken up in *Shasekishū* XB.2, in a passage in the section called "Understanding the Essential in the Various Sects," which in fact contains the phrase appearing in *Sasamegoto* as "The teachings are provisional, the ultimate principle is what is truly real" (*kyōgon rijitsu*). It begins with an illustrative story about a woman who went mad, thinking she had lost her head since she couldn't see it in the mirror, when in fact it was only because she was holding the mirror the wrong way. When people pointed that out to her, she did see her head again, but persisted in believing that she had in truth regained what the demon had actually snatched away. Then the text continues:

> What this event illustrates is that the unenlightened mind [*mumyō no kokoro*] is like someone who has inexplicably lost his head and is looking for it. But the clear mind of original enlightenment [*hongaku no myōshin*] has never been lost. It is lost only in the sense that one thinks one has lost one's head. Thinking that one obtains it in seeing it for the first time is like achieving buddha wisdom for the first time [*shigaku no bodai*]. But how can there be a first time? Since *that* was a dream, *this* too is a dream. As the *Engakukyō* [Sutra of Perfect Enlightenment] says, "When one first realizes that the sentient beings have always been buddhas, then both life-and-death and nirvana will seem like yesterday's dream" [*T* 17: 915a]. Since the life-and-death without beginning, the sleep of total darkness, and the supreme state of buddha wisdom are all [contingent] inscriptions of initial enlightenment [*shigaku no mon nareba*], none of them leave a trace. Only of the original wisdom-insight [*honrai no chiken*]—that which is untouched by the myriad phenomena—may it be said that it is neither worldly nor saintly, and is the treasure storehouse of the self. And thus it is that the Buddha's teachings of a lifetime are all admirable expedients [*hōben*]. In effect, they are saying to those who have lost their heads that they have not in fact done so. But these are but useless words to those who are not mad. This is why, as Kashō says, "the two truths [of the worldly and unworldly] are only doctrines; they have no connection with the realm of principle [*nitai wa tada kore kyōmon nari, kyōri ni azukarazu*]." And in Tendai, "*The teachings are provisional, the ultimate principle real* [*kyōgon rijitsu*]; that is, doctrines are all expedient means." In the Hossō [sect] too, we find this: "What is called relying on words refers wholly to truth established provisionally as expedient means [*hōben anryūtai*]; it is not located in the real [*shinjitsu no tokoro ni arazu*]. It is precisely the destruction of words, referring to truth that is not established [*hianryūtai*], that—without mind and thought and without establishing words and explanations—is the true Buddha Dharma." And so it is that in any sect, until words and explanations [*gonzetsu*] are set up, meanings and principles [*giri*] understood, and is and is-not [*zehi*] distinguished, the sect's essential teaching will remain obscure. (*Shasekishū*, ed. Watanabe Tsunaya, *NKBT* 85 [Iwanami Shoten, 1966], pp. 444–45; emphasis added)

One of the most popular texts of the medieval period, the *Shasekishū* is a book of tales and sermons compiled by the monk Mujū Ichien (1226–1312) between 1279 and 1283 with the aim of illuminating Buddhist doctrine through stories as well as anecdotes from contemporary life. As evident in the numerous extant manuscript variants, the work was widely disseminated even long after Mujū's lifetime. It seems to have become a well-loved source of stories and inspiration for preaching, to judge from Shinkei's own obvious acquaintance with it. An adept of both Zen and Esoteric practice, Mujū was possessed of an encyclopedic knowledge, as witness *Shasekishū* and his other works, whose enduring relevance may be measured by the fact that Emperor Go-Nara (r. 1526–57) awarded him the posthumous title of National Teacher Daien sometime in the Tenmon Era (1532–1555). Clearly Mujū and his works may be said to embody the influence of Kamakura Zen Buddhism on Muromachi poets like Shinkei.

6. "To believe that phenomena exist wholly outside the mind is to keep turning round in the cycles of birth and death; to realize that phenomena and mind are one is to cast off

birth and death for all time." The following passage from *Shasekishū* I.9, "Stopping Delusive Thoughts Through the Skillful Devices of the Gods Who Soften Their Light," is a useful gloss on these lines from *Sasamegoto*, and may in fact have been their source. The section is introduced by the story of a monk who leaves the Kumano monastery in despair over his deep-seated attachment to a beautiful woman. While traveling, he dozes off and sees his future in a dream: he is married to the woman, but their son drowns in his thirteenth year. Awakening, he realizes the futility of his longings and returns with fresh resolve to Kumano. The dream is ascribed to the skillful devices of the gods who soften their light of wisdom (*wakō no hōben*) in order to save beings. The text continues:

> The *Yuishikiron* says: "When one has not yet attained true enlightenment, one is always within a dream. Therefore the Buddha preached that birth-and-death is a long night." [*T* 31: 39b] The Great Teacher Jion [Ci En, or Kui Ji, 632–682, founder of the Faxiang or Hossō sect] comments thus: "*To believe that there are dharmas outside the mind is to keep turning round in the cycles of birth and death; to realize the One Mind is to cast off birth and death for all time.*" When no light dawns upon the long night of birth and death, it is because one sees dharmas outside the mind and is kept turning round in the realm of delusion. Not to see dharmas outside the mind means to understand that the dharmas are the mind, the mind is the dharmas, and thus to emerge from birth and death. The person of discerning mind [*kokoro aru hito*] becomes enlightened about the One Mind that is the Source [*isshin no minamoto o satorite*] and awakens from the sleep of the three phenomenal realms [of desire, form, and formlessness]. (pp. 82–83; emphasis added)

In headnote 19 (pp. 82–83) of *Shasekishū*, the textual editor Watanabe Tsunaya observes that he still has to find the source of the said lines in Jion's (Ci En's) commentary, and cites instead its occurrence in the *Gumei hosshinshū* (Awakening to Faith Amid Delusion), written by the Japanese Hossō scholar monk and recluse Jōkei (1155–1213) after 1193. Kidō believes that Shinkei was citing from *Shasekishū* above, and not from the *Yuishikiron jukki* (suppl. n. 38, p. 262), as Suzuki has it in his modern Japanese gloss in the *SSG* Suzuki, p. 173.

7. The original text has: *ui hōbutsu muchū gonka, musa sanjin gakuzen jitsubutsu.* This line appears in *Shugo kokkai shō* (A Treatise for Guarding the Country, 818; *T* 74: 135–45), Saichō's defense of the Tendai concepts of the nondualism of the One Vehicle as against the Three Vehicles; of the real over the provisional; and the possibility of buddhahood for all beings as against any immanent discrimination among them, where the latter positions are those held by the Hossō school, specifically as represented by its contemporary spokesman then, the scholar monk Toku'ichi with whom Saichō was engaged in debate. Suzuki in *Geidō SSG*, p. 174, nn. 2 and 3, explains that in the Hossō sect, one establishes the self as the fundamental cause (*kompon'in*), and the phenomena outside oneself as the condition (*en*). According to this line of thinking, enlightenment is attained by seeking the unchanging true principle outside oneself. This kind of enlightenment, however, is merely provisional; it is just the truth of temporality (*mujō*), from which one has to be also ultimately liberated. It is, so to speak, a temporary buddha-fruit or enlightenment obtained within a dream. In the Tendai perfect teaching (*engyō*), on the other hand, the Three Bodies (that is, the Dharma Body of the ultimate principle, the Reward Body of wisdom, and the Response Body of compassion) are in themselves, immanently, One Body. And this fusion is not due to the subject's training or mental construction but to the fact that they are immanently one. Such is the Tendai concept of *musa sanjin*, the "unconstructed Three Bodies." (Nakamura Hajime et al.'s edition of *Bukkyō jiten* [Iwanami Shoten, 1989] cites precisely this passage in *Sasamegoto* under the entry for *usa. musa.*) The realm where principle and wisdom (*ri* and *chi*) become one is the realm where the myriad phenomena are One Mind. When we attain insight into this marvelous fact by which we ourselves are this One Mind, then we attain buddhahood without necessarily undergoing special training or study.

Kidō also cites the appearance of the line *ui hōbutsu muchū gonka* in the following poem from the *Shin Senzaishu* (1359): Buddhism, by the Former Abbot Kanshu, "About the line 'the Reward Body that is born of action is a provisional fruit within a dream.'"

masu kagami	The very image
migakite utsuru	reflected in the clarity of
kage mo nao	the polished mirror
omoeba kari no	is, when I think on it,
iro ni zo arikeru	nothing but a fugitive form.

It is a marvelous poem, using the mirror image to illustrate in a trice the meaning of the doctrinal words.

8. "Dhyana meditation and Buddha-wisdom" (*jōe*). These are the second and third stages of the Mahayana Buddhist course of training; the first is following the "precepts" (*kai*) or moral prohibitions. In effect, after initially rejecting words as contingent and provisional, then affirming intention as, by contrast, the principle of the real, Shinkei ends by reinstating words, this time from the enlightened position of the middle way. This dialectical progression of his thought is representative of the method typically followed in *Sasamegoto*'s method of exposition.

Chapter Forty-Three

1. *Yōon*, "ineffable remoteness," inscribed in *hiragana* in the *NKBT* base text, is written with the ideographs for "dim, hidden" plus "distant" in the Kokemushiro *SSG* text. It is more commonly read as *yūen*, as in *Waka bungaku jiten* (ed. Ariyoshi Tamotsu [Ōfūsha, 1991], pp. 661–62), which defines it as a quality of ineffable depth in the poetic realm, close in meaning to *yūgen* and *yūshin*. In *Shōtetsu monogatari*, Shōtetsu declares that to conform to what people favor as a good poem is to limit one's own capacity; he laments that people are unable to comprehend those poems that he composes with *yōon* in mind (*mata yōon naru hon'i no uta o yomeba, hito kokoroezushite urami nite aru nari*; *SM* II.65, p. 221; see complete translation in *Conversations with Shōtetsu*, p. 147). Ariyoshi glosses this passage as referring to "a poem generated from a philosophical or conceptual base, with a deep and remote poetic realm that others find hard to grasp" (*WBJ*, p. 660).

2. In the *Guhishō*, *fumyōtei* is one of the eighteen modes, and further also one of the four modes classified under *ushintei*, the others being *mono no aware tai*, *riseitei* (the mode of governing the realm) and *bumintei* (the mode of cherishing the people). Among the four, the last two are the essential manifestations of *ushin* (see *Guhishō*, ed. Sasaki Nobutsuna, *NKT* 4 [1958], p. 293). As for *fumyōtei* itself, there is not much explanation in the *Guhishō*, except for the remark that "it cannot be composed except by that person [*futto sono hito narade wa, yomiurubeki koto ni arazu*]. It must be the style of Lord Ariwara [Narihira's *Tsuki ya aranu* poem cited]. This indeed fulfills the *fumyōtei* mode" (cited in Akahane, "*Sasamegoto* ni okeru fumyōtei to yūgen," p. 31). The citation of the Narihira poem indicates that *fumyōtei* referred to an ambiguous, enigmatic quality, such that the poem's meaning is not immediately apparent. In the *Tsuki ya aranu*, it would refer to the absence of an overt connection—that is, an ellipsis between the upper and lower statements.

In his article on *fumyōtei* in *Sasamegoto*, Akahane Manabu suggests that the direct canonical source for the term is a popular poem by Bai Juyi, "Karyō no yoru, omou koto ari" (Thoughts on a Night in Karyō):

A nebulous moon, neither bedimmed nor bright,
A soft and gentle breeze, neither warm nor cold;

Lying alone on the empty bed, enjoying the air,
Dawn creeps quietly in the heart.

This "nebulous moon, neither bedimmed nor bright" (*fumyō fuan mōrōtaru tsuki*) is probably the inspiration for Genji's poem to Oborozukiyo, as well as the source of her name, which means "nebulous moon," in the "Hana no en" chapter (Tamagami Takuya, ed. *Genji monogatari hyōshaku* [Kadokawa Shoten, 1967], 2: 337; see also "The Festival of the Cherry Blossoms" chapter of the *Genji* in the Seidensticker translation, 1: 152, where the nebulous moon is rendered as "misty moon"). It is also cited in the following *Shinkokinshū* poem: *SKKS* 55. Spring. "Composed on the line 'A nebulous moon, neither bedimmed nor bright' from the poem 'Thoughts of a Night in Karyō' in the [*Hakushi*] *Monjū*." Ōe no Chisato.

teri mo sezu	Not shining radiant,
kumori mo hatenu	nor wholly clouded over—
haru no yo no	the nebulous moonlight
oborozukiyo ni	of a night in springtime
shiku mono zo naki	is truly without parallel.

The same Bai Juyi poem forms the background of a piece composed by a certain lady-in-waiting and judged by Shunzei to be the winner in round 256 of the *Sengohyakuban uta awase*:

yoshinoyama	On Yoshino hills
teri mo senu yo no	on a night when the moon
tsukikage ni	mutes its radiance,
kozue no hana wa	treetops shed flowers
yuki to chiritsutsu	fluttering like snow.

In his commentary, Shunzei praises this piece for raising the aura (*omokage*) of Bai Juyi's poem, and adds that the image of "the spring snow beneath the moon feels especially alluring [*en ni miehaberi*]" (*Sengohyakuban*, 3:159). This indicates that *en* is a quality raised by a vague, nebulous—that is, *fumyō*, scene; it is the aura of something half-hidden or held back, and therefore mysterious and alluring. This ties in with the later quotation from *Tsurezuregusa*, as Akahane points out (p. 32). But as this chapter of *Sasamegoto* develops, it becomes apparent that *fumyō* or ambiguity as related to the Dharma Body refers to *kokoro no en* (spiritual allure) and ultimately to the "ineffable remoteness" of the Buddhist noumenal realm as evoked in a poem.

3. *Tsurezuregusa*, § 137: "Are we only to look at flowers in full bloom, only at the unshadowed moon? To watch the rain while longing for the moon, be secluded behind drawn blinds, all unaware of spring's passing—in this there is more pathos, a deeper feeling [*nao aware ni nasake fukashi*]. In truth, there is more to see in the days when the treetops' blossoming is nearly over, in a garden of flowers all wilted and scattered" (p. 200). And further on, "In everything—the moon, the flowers, are we to gaze with the eye alone?" (p. 201)

4. The *Pipa xing* (Ballad of the Lute) is from the period of Bai Juyi's banishment to a minor post in Jiujiang, Jiangxi Province, in 815–19. According to its preface, he composed it on an autumn evening in 816. He was sending off a friend at Yipu Bay (the Yijiang flows from Xunyang River and empties into the Yangzi River) when they heard the notes of a lute from one of the boats over the water. It was a sophisticated style of playing too fine for the countryside, and sure enough, it turned out that the musician was formerly a famous artiste from the capital, Chang'an. With age and a fading beauty, she had come down in the world and ended up a merchant's wife, plying the waters in these rustic parts. The poet invites her to perform for them, and her playing, imbued with the sorrow and anguish of her life story, is so superbly moving that the poet composes the *Pipa xing*, a long ballad of 626 characters,

for her. Since he too was enduring an exile from the capital, he had a kindred feeling for her. Shinkei's citation is from the following passage:

Thick strings loud and violent as a sudden downpour,
Thin strings halting and faint as a close murmur,
When violent and loud, and halting and faint came together,
It was like big pearls and small pearls cascading down a silver platter.
Now smooth as a warbler's trill among the flowers,
Then tense as the stream's current choking beneath the ice,
As an icy stream beginning to freeze, the notes reach their height,
And having reached their height, come to a halt, in the next moment the sound is stilled.
Something else, a hidden sorrow, a dimly sensed anguish, rises—
At such moments silence is deeper than sound.
Then, as if a silver jar had split apart and water suddenly gushed forth,
Or armored warriors collided, with a clashing of lance and sword,
The music ended, the plectrum laid aside, leaving imaged in the heart
The chorus of four strings like a silken fabric tearing apart.
From the boats to the east and west, the voices are stilled,
All I see is the white autumn moon in the river's heart.

(*Haku Kyo-i* 2: 116–24)

5. A couplet from the *Chōgonka* (*Changhen ge*, Song of Unending Sorrow, 806), Bai Juyi's famous poem of 120 lines on the Tang Emperor Xuanzong's deep intoxication with the exquisitely beautiful Yang Guifei, its tragic outcome, and his inconsolable grief. During the An Lushan Rebellion (755–57), when the court was fleeing Chang'an before the victorious rebel army, the six divisions of the imperial guards mutinied and refused to proceed unless Xuanzong bowed to their demand for the execution of Yang Guifei and her cousin the minister. Accordingly, she was hanged from a pear tree not far from the roadside, "the curving moth-wing eyebrows expiring before his horse," as the poet puts it. The cited couplet is from a later passage, when the tides of war having turned, Xuanzong is brought back, along the same route, to Chang'an from his exile:

Heaven turns, sun shifts, the dragon horse courses back,
Reaching the spot he hesitates, loath to come away,
Below Mawei hill, beneath the muddy earth,
Her gemlike face is gone from sight, empty the death site.
Lord, ministers, all look back, till cloaks are soaked through
As eastward to the capital gate their trusty steeds take them back.
There, the ponds and parks are just as of yore,
The lotuses on Taiye Pond, the willows of Weiyang Palace,
Lotus blossoms like a face, willows like eyebrows,
Before these, how could the tears not brim over?
In days of peach blossoms opening in the spring breeze,
Season of paulownia leaves falling in the autumn rain.
In the south park of the western palace, the autumn grasses are thick,
Fallen leaves fill the steps, a crimson too deep to sweep away . . .

(*Haku Kyo-i*, 2: 100–105)

In the *Wakan rōeishū* 781 under Love, the same couplet is cited, with "autumn rain" appearing as "autumn dew"; the *Sasamegoto* text has the "autumn dew" version as well. Two other couplets in *WRS* (780 and 783) are taken from this poem. See also *Hakushi monjū* 12: 4.

6. *Gyokuyōshū*, Travel. "On 'a distant prospect on a journey,' during a Chinese and Japanese poem contest at the residence of the Kyōgoku Regent [Yoshitsune]." In Teika's personal

poem collection, *Shūi gusō*, no. 2551, with a similar headnote; in both collections, the last line is *ochi no shirakumo* (white cloud over yonder).

7. *Sōkonshū* 3.1995. "From the seventeenth [of the Seventh Month, 1433], when the mountain faction [of Tendai] came brandishing the sacred palanquins to press their case, there was such confusion that all monthly poetry meetings were cancelled. Among those I composed when people came instead to my hermitage, on 'Evening Reeds.'"

8. "The goddess of Wushan" alludes to a story in the *Gaotang fu* by Song Yu (290–223 B.C.E.) in the *Wen xuan*. The King of Chu made love to her in a dream; upon leaving him at dawn, she says, "You may find me in the high slopes on the southern face of Mount Wu, changed into a morning cloud at dawn and become the falling rain at dusk" (*Wen xuan* X, pp. 1–2; for a complete translation of the *Gaotang fu*, see *Wen xuan or Selections of Refined Literature*, trans. David R. Knechtges (Princeton, N.J.: Princeton University Press, 1996), 3: 325–49). Shinkei's reference to the goddess's appearance as "inexpressible in words" (*kotoba ni wa arawasu bekarazu*) most probably refers to her mysterious transformation into cloud and rain in Song Yu's poem. Shinkei also alludes to the goddess of Wushan in a link from the 1468 renga sequence, "Broken Beneath Snow"; for a translation and commentary, see *HF*, pp. 333–34.

The so-called "dream of Wushan" motif is in fact an important one in medieval aesthetics. Shōtetsu gives a lengthy recounting of the tale within the context of an explanation of *yūgen* in the *Shōtetsu monogatari*, thus:

> What kind of thing could the *yūgen* mode be referring to? It is certainly not a case where you could simply and clearly articulate in words and concept what you think, and claim that *this* is what *yūgen* is. Since it is said that the moving clouds and whirling snow are the *yūgen* mode, does it then refer to the atmosphere [*fuzei*] of clouds hanging in the sky or snow floating in the wind? In the work by Teika called, I believe, *Guhi* [*Guhishō*], it is written: If we were to concretely illustrate the *yūgen* mode—there was in China a king called Xiang [of Chu]. One day, saying that he would take a nap, he retired to his chambers, and a goddess descended from the sky and made love to him while he was in a state that was not quite a dream nor yet real [*yume tomo utsutsu tomo naku*]. King Xiang could not bear that it should end and sought to detain her, whereat the goddess said, "I am a goddess of the upper realms. Due to a bond in a former life, I have come here and made love to you. But I am not such as can remain on this earth." And saying this, she was about to fly away, but so great was the king's longing, he pleaded, "If that is so, at least leave me a memento of yourself." She replied, "As my memento, there is a mountain near the palace called Wushan; gaze at the clouds hanging there in the morning, at the rain falling there at evening." And she vanished. Thereafter, in his longing for the goddess, King Hsiang would gaze at the clouds hanging over Wushan in the morning, at the rain falling there at evening, as her memento. It is the mode of contemplating [*nagametaru*, written with the graph for *yomu*, "to compose, chant"] this morning cloud and evening rain that may be called the *yūgen* mode. So it is written. As for the question of wherein the *yūgen* lies here, that must depend on the inner mind [*kokoro no uchi*] of each one. It is not something that can be expressed in words or clearly discriminated in the mind, is it? Shall we say that it is this mode of drifting, suspended ambiguity [*tada hyōhaku to shitaru tai*] that is *yūgen*? Or shall we say that it is the atmosphere of four or five court ladies dressed in silken robes, gazing at the riot of flowers at the height of their splendor in the Southern Palace? You might still ask where in all this the *yūgen* lies, but it is not something of which one can say, it is this, exactly. (*SM* II: 100, pp. 232–34, translation mine; see also *Conversations with Shōtetsu*, pp. 161–62)

Kidō assumes a passage in the *Guhishō*, Ruijūbon text, as Shōtetsu's source for the anecdote illustrating *yūgen*. In the *Sangoki*, we find the following:

> In general what is called "ineffable depth" [*yūgen*] among these styles refers to the poems' unusually subtle feeling and diction [*kokoro kotoba kasuka ni tada naranu sama nari*]. What are called the two modes of "passing cloud" [*kōun*] and "whirling snow" [*kaisetsu*] are the overtones inhering within

ineffable depth [*yūgen no naka no yojō nari*]. Of course, they have to evoke feeling. "Ineffable depth" is the general term, and "passing clouds" and "whirling snow" are special designations. Among poems that are said to be ineffably deep, there are those that are yet more superior, which give the sensation of a tissue of thin clouds veiling the moon, an aura of flying snow floating in the wind; these poems, over which a shadow floats and hovers apart from the conception and the words, are what is called the mode of passing clouds and whirling snow, according to my late father. It is the mode my father pointed to, when I was a beginner, as the one that is among the various modes the essential nature of waka [*waka no hon'i*]. This means that in poetry, one must evoke this aspect of gracefulness, a gentleness in things [*yasashiku mono yawaraka naru suji*]. (*NKT* 4: 315–16)

In the *Gukenshō*, we find the following passage:

What is called the mode of passing clouds and whirling snow is a configuration of the yūgen poem. Among yūgen poems, there are special configurations called passing clouds and whirling snow. There are two types: yūgen of the mind-heart and yūgen of words. The present mode is probably yūgen of words. The *Wen xuan Gaotang fu* says: "Long ago the former king went on an excursion to Gaotang. Tiring, he took a nap and saw a lady in a dream. The lady said, 'I am the maiden of Wushan, a guest at Gaotang. At dawn I become a passing cloud, at evening, turn into moving rain. Each morning and evening, I am below the southern terrace.' The following morning, he saw that it was just as she said. And so he erected a mausoleum there and called it Morning Clouds." Again, the *Luoshen fu* says: "The deity of the river Luo is called Fufei. [She is] faint and ethereal as the veiled moon behind wisps of cloud, floats in the air like whirling snow in the drifting wind. Her shoulders are moulded slender, her waist is like fine-spun silk." It must be poems that contain this atmosphere in their mind-heart that are meant. (*NKT* 4: 355–56; for a complete translation of the *Luoshen fu*, see *Wen xuan*, trans. Knechtges, 3: 355–65)

The following passage in the *Guhishō* Ruijūbon text is cited by Hisamatsu Sen'ichi in a supplementary note (p. 284, n. 35) to *Shōtetsu monogatari* (similarly cited by Kidō for this *SSG* passage):

The *yūgen* mode is not just one; among collections of yūgen poems are those that have the configuration of passing clouds or whirling snow. Yūgen is the comprehensive name, and moving clouds and whirling snow are particular modes of it. Moving clouds and whirling snow are illustrative terms for an alluring woman [*enjo*]. In this regard, the poem that gives the sense of being gentle and refined [*yasashiku kedakaku shite*], as of wisps of clouds veiling the moon, is what is designated as "passing clouds." Again, the poem that gives the sense of being gentle, suggestive, and unusual [*yasashiku keshiki-bamite tada naranu*], as of tiny flecks of flying snow scattering in confusion before a wind that is not overly strong, is probably what is called "whirling snow." The *Wen hsüan Kaot'ang fu* says: [same text as in *Gukenshō* above]. (*SM*, suppl. n. 35, p. 284)

9. Kidō (*SSG*, n. 19) cites the following passage from *Bontō-anshu hentōsho* (The Book of Master Bontō's Replies, 1417): "The Five Lakes manifest the water against a distant prospect of mountains, and the mountains divide the waters. Distant and close, the perspectives are various, quite beyond the ordinary imagination. They would be equal to the poetry of evocation [*yojō no ku*]."

10. From the *Kongō hannyaharamitsu-kyō* (Skt. *Vajracchedikā prajñāpāramitā sūtra*; The Large Sutra on Perfect Wisdom; more commonly known as *Kongōkyō* or *Kongōhannya-kyō*), *T* 8: 748–52; the quoted passage is on p. 752a.

11. From the *Dainichikyō* (Skt. *Mahāvairocana sūtra*), formerly called *Daibirushana jōbutsu shimpenkaji-kyō*, one of the principal canons of Esoteric Buddhism. *T* 18: 1–55; the quoted passage is on p. 9b. The verse is explained thus in the *Daibirushana-kyō shiun*, a commentary on this sutra by the Tendai monk Chishō Daishi (Enchin, 814–891):

"Awakening to my original non-arising" means that realizing that you are from the start unborn is as such to become a buddha. What is more, there is in truth no awakening and no becoming; you have passed beyond the way of language. The rest is an interpretation of the *A*-graph [unborn origin] concept. Awakening to one's original non-arising is, to wit, to be a buddha; the way of the buddha's self-enlightenment is located in the exhaustion of all language and cessation of action. If you stay in this moment of [realizing] your original non-arising, you will be released from all delusion, your removal from the causal chain of birth and extinction will be like the immutable clarity of empty space. Your self-nature being thus clarified and empty of distinctions, it is the same as the true face of the Great Emptiness [*daikū no jissō*]. In sum, this is the all-inclusive, omnipresent space of the Vairocana Buddha. This prajña intuition is equivalent to the Great Emptiness; once removed from all ignorance, you awaken to your original non-arising and of all the dharmas, there is nothing that you do not know and hear. (Cited by Kidō in *SSG*, suppl. n. 45; also cited by Akahane, *Yūgenbi no tankyū*, p. 468.)

Chapter Forty-Four

1. *Sashi-ai. kiraimono* (also known as *sarikirai*) refer to the renga rules of prohibition against the perceived "clashing" of identical, similar, or conventionally associated pairs of words, or of the same lexical categories and themes, across specified intervals during the 100-verse sequence. They are rules of Intermission aimed at preventing a monotonous uniformity or, to put it another way, fostering variety in the movement of the verse continuum. The closest permissible interval for similar or closely associated word pairs, according to the rule called *uchikoshi o kirau* (clashing across one-verse intervals) is two verses. For instance, "wet sleeves" and "tears," "parting" and "returning," "cold" and "penetrates the body," "dream" and "reality": all these constitute conventional pairs of images in the poetic lexicon. While they may occur in immediate succession from one verse to the next, as is only natural, they may not do so at one-verse intervals but must be separated by at least two. This suggests that while an *aa'b* imagistic rhythm is fine, *aba'* is anathema, since the link between *a* and *a'* (say, "wet sleeves" and "tears") across a one-verse interval gives the sense of a regression, a going back to the same point (the technical term for it, culled from Buddhism, is *rinne*, karma). The frequency of the occurrence of important images like "moon," "flowers," and "snow" was also restricted (see Chapter 42 and n. 1 there), as was the recurrence of the same themes. The Spring and Autumn themes had to be separated by at least seven verses on a different theme or themes; Summer, Winter, and Love by at least five, and so on. The object was to maintain both continuity and variation in the progression of the whole sequence, but as this is a function of the integral meanings of the verses themselves rather than of isolated images, and the same word can have a totally different impact depending on context, it is easy to see why the issue of rules and their proper application can be a complex one, and how a literal interpretation of them can inhibit the imagination. See Steven D. Carter, *The Road to Komatsubara: A Classical Reading of the Renga Hyakuin* (Cambridge, Mass.: Harvard University Press, 1987), for a complete translation of the renga code established in 1372.

2. The matter of the sutras including instances of "license" (*yurusu koto*), as distinct from the precepts, in which they are not tolerated, appears also in *Shasekishū* II.10, "It is Not in Vain to Establish Karmic Affinity with the Buddha's Dharma." It explains the different attitudes to human failings or vice from the perspective of the precepts, where they are unconditionally censured, and of the sutras, where they are viewed relatively as a context or opportunity for future salvation. The following passages summarizing its content are illuminating: "The great aim of admonitions in the Precept Treasure is to control even the smallest vice, allowing it no merit at all. This is in order that the Buddha's teachings may flourish and thrive, and so that people may achieve the Way and its fruits. In the sutras, on the other hand, there might be failures but depending on circumstances, they are encouraged in anticipation of a benefit in the distant future" (p. 129). Again, "Therefore the sutras see virtue

even in vice; where just one or two parts of virtue exist out of twelve, they are not discarded. This is because though one falls into bad ways, it is seen as a cause for achieving Buddhahood in the distant future" (p. 130). Shinkei's point, however, is that poetry is a function of the "mind-ground," or the boundless imagination that gives rise to a myriad phenomena, which may not be circumscribed by rules.

3. *Nehangyō* (*Nirvāna Sūtra*) VI.4.8: "Good men, *those who are lax about the wisdom teachings are called lax, but those who are lax about the precepts are not considered lax. The bodhisattvas and mahasattvas, who are neither lax nor arrogant about the Great Vehicle, are the ones who truly uphold the precepts.* In order to guard the right teachings, they purify themselves in the waters of the Great Wisdom. For this reason, a bodhisattva may violate the precepts, but he is not therefore considered lax" (cited in "Mikkan," II, p. 31; emphasis added). This would seem to reflect Shinkei's point about training in the mind-ground (*shinji*) being of greater moment in poetry than all the fuss about rules.

4. *Makashikan* X. B: "If you do not get caught up in sectarianism, there will be no contention, whether in the matter of cause or effect. An impartial mind does not attach itself to impartial dharmas and so does not generate wrong views. Again, a partial mind that attaches itself to the 'direct' [enlightenment] gate gives rise to wrong views. If for the sake of his name or for the people's sake, in order to win victory or profit, he discriminates in favor of a school's views, he thereby generates anger, love, pride, and karmic bondage. For instance, it is like putting poison in good medicine—how can this not lead to death? Taking the poison of partial views and putting it in the True Dharma increases the suffering and aggregates. For this, the Tathagata is not to blame. *A sharp mind, though non-Buddhist, will penetrate through the wrong views to arrive at the correct view; he renders the partial impartial and becomes the Buddha's disciple. A dull mind, though Buddhist, will turn even the right teaching into the wrong; he renders the impartial partial and becomes an errant disciple.* How can one not pity him?" (*Makashikan*, ed. and trans. Sekiguchi 2: 336–37). Shinkei's point, in the field of renga, would be that although the rules are in themselves right, one who does not understand their import will apply them in a partial manner—for instance, literally, without regard for circumstance—and so defeat their purpose.

Note that *Shasekishū* I.10, "How a Pure Land Follower Made Light of the Divine Light and Brought Punishment Upon Himself," cites the same *Makashikan* passage quoted in *Sasamegoto*: "The Tendai patriarch [Zhiyi] has commented thus: 'The sharp mind of a non-Buddhist puts wrong views into right views; he takes the wrong teachings [*jahō*] and makes them right teachings [*shōbō*]; the dull mind of a Buddhist puts right views into wrong views; he takes the right teachings and turns them into wrong teachings'" (p. 88; the headnote cites *T* 46. 137a–b).

5. *Shasekishū* IV.1, "The Silent Priests." This chapter begins with an anecdote about four priests secluded in a hall to practice silence. When one of them broke the silence, another spoke out to chide him, a third spoke to scold the other two, and the fourth declared that he alone had said nothing. The moral of the story is that one should not censure others nor become attached to one's own practice, since everything has its merits and demerits. The *Sasamegoto* passage occurs in the following context:

> In general, the three fields of study—precepts, meditation, and wisdom—differ in their methods, but they are wholly one in essence. To distinguish the three entities of prohibition, offense, and agent, and then determine what is violation and nonviolation, is the way of mundane morality. You may uphold it and still be subject to retribution from [earlier] karmic outflows. Precepts are only a means of inducing meditation. Their substance is in the underlying actions in the realm of desire. Therefore the Nanzan Master of Discipline explains, "Fixating on them obstructs the Way in that they belong to mundane virtue. Violating them obstructs the Way in that you cannot then escape

the three evil worlds." Upholding them obstructs the Way because of your fixation on the precepts themselves. Violating them further estranges you from the Way since you then enter the three evil worlds. In sum, this is to remain within mundane morality. Therefore the *Hokkugyō* [Dharma verse Sutra;] says: "*Precepts are like the empty space; they cause the man holding them to stumble in confusion.*" And in the *Daibongyō* [*Mahaprajnaparamita sutra*] we find: "In nonvigilance one roundly fulfills the perfection of pure self-discipline. For there is then neither violation nor nonviolation." (p. 175; *Shasekishū* headnote 25 observes that the italicized passage above does not appear in the *Hokkugyō* but in the *Kegon daishoshō*, V)

6. Bishop Gembin was a famous early Heian cleric; he appears in "Bishop Gembin Flees the World and Vanishes," the first story in Kamo no Chōmei's collection of exemplary tales, *Hosshinshū* (Awakening of Faith Collection), which begins:

> Long ago there was a man called Bishop Gembin. He was a man of considerable intellect at Yamashina Temple, but he had a profound aversion to the mundane and had no taste for associating with colleagues at the temple. So he built a meager grass hut on the banks of Miwa River and lived there in meditation. Emperor Kammu [r. 781–806] heard about him and pressed him into service, and given no possible recourse, he forced himself to mix in society again. Nevertheless, perhaps because his heart was not in it, during the reign of the Nara emperor, when he was offered promotion to Archbishop, he refused and sent up these words:
>
> | | |
> |---|---|
> | miwakawa no | Washed clean |
> | kiyoki nagare ni | in the pure flowing streams |
> | susugiteshi | of Miwa River, |
> | koromo no sode o | I shall not sully yet again |
> | mata wa kegasaji | the sleeves of this robe. |
>
> Shortly thereafter, without even informing the people who served as his disciples, he disappeared, one knew not where.

Several years later, a former disciple on his way to Koshi finds the former Bishop in bedraggled hemp clothes laboring as a ferryman, but he flees before he can accost him. From the villagers thereabouts, he hears that this ferryman is no ordinary laborer but a cherished priest, who is constantly at prayer and takes no fees for his services, except the little he needs to eat. The story goes on to quote a poem by Gembin in the *Zoku Kokinshū* about the loneliness of watching over the deserted upland rice fields at autumn's end, and speculates that since he was always drifting like the clouds and wind, he must at one time also have worked as a caretaker of rice fields (*Hosshinshū* 1: 7–8 in *Shiseki shūran* 23). The anecdote also appears in *Kojidan* 3: 53, in [*Kaite zōho*] *Kokushi taikei*, and *Kankyo no tomo*, in *ZGR* 32b: 486.

7. *Kokon chomonjū* 2, the section beginning "According to the testament of Master Chishō," narrates how Priest Kyōdai disappeared after handing over the headship of the Onjōji [Miidera] Temple to Chishō, for whom he had been waiting for more than a hundred years. The passage continues:

> Returning to the temple, I asked Totomumaro how things were with Kyōdai. He could tell me nothing at all about the whereabouts of the old mendicant priest. For years, Kyōdai would eat nothing but fish and drink nothing but rice wine. It was his practice to go out to the cove by the beach belonging to the temple to catch fish and turtles for his priestly diet. When Totomumaro spoke to the priest, he suddenly hid himself. It was so sad. Not caring that I was heard, I cried out in pity. Now as I gazed with the faithful upon his hermit cell, I saw that the fish that had dried up through the years were the stems, roots, and leaves of the lotus flower. By this we understood that he was a paragon without equal. (*NKBT* 84, 2:78; cited by Kidō, suppl. n. 51)

Kyōdai is said to be an incarnation of the bodhisattva Miroku, as evident in the version of this story in the *Konjaku monogatari* 2, called "How Chishō Was Welcomed by Kyōdai, Metamorphosis Body of Miroku, and Entering Miidera Established a Separate School" (see

NKBT 22–26, 2: 78). Chishō Daishi (Enchin, 814–891), fifth Tendai Abbot, was also the founder of the Jimon branch of Tendai. He studied both the orthodox and esoteric branches of Tendai doctrine in China from 853 to 858, and is the author of numerous treatises. Kyōdai, according to the *Honchō shinsenden*, was from Shiga in Ōmi Province; although several hundred years old, his face remained as fresh as that of a child (*Konjaku monogatari shū* 1 [*NKBZ* 21], p. 179, n. 24).

8. The *Shūi ōjōden* includes the following account of Jōzō:

> The great priest Jōzō had the lay surname Miyoshi and was from the right division of the capital. He was the eighth child of the Consultant, Minister of the Imperial Household and Provisional Governor of Harima, Lord Kiyotsura. His mother was a granddaughter of Emperor Saga [r. 809–823]. . . . During the Tenryaku years [947–57], he lived in Yasaka Temple. At that time lords and other high-ranking nobles gathered there in scores, and, seeing the Yasaka stupa tower, said that the direction in which the tower was leaning was inauspicious; that since the tower was turned toward the castle, it too would start slanting, and so on. At which the great priest declared that he had been intending to straighten the tower for some years. The several members of the assembly all assumed it would be necessary to contribute materials for the project. But the great priest assured them that such expenses would not be necessary and he would try to straighten the tower that very night. That night, attired in court cap and robe, he went and sat on the bare path facing the tower, performed ritual prayers, then immediately went back to his quarters. Then his disciple Priest Ninpō . . . who was then wandering in the garden, happened to gaze out at the stupa tower and saw how a gentle wind came blowing from the northwest, shaking the tower and its jeweled bells and making them resound. When dawn came, he looked again and saw that the tower was perfectly straight. Several people came rushing on horseback and their gladness knew no bounds. (*Shūi ōjōden* II: 55–57, in *Dai Nihon bukkyō zensho* [*DNBZ*] 107; cited by Kidō, suppl. n. 52)

The story of Priest Jōzō straightening the leaning tower of Yasaka Temple by prayer is also to be found in the *Konjaku monogatari* 20: 1012 (*Nihon koten zensho* ed.) and *Senjūshō* 7: 431 (*ZGR* 32b). Suzuki ("Mikkan," II, p. 32) also cites a related passage from the *Yasuyori hōmotsushū* II (in *DNBZ* 147).

9. *Hosshinshū* I, "The Reclusion and Death of Priest Zōga at Tōnomine," is a highly interesting narrative underscoring the eccentric behavior and deep devotion of Zōga (pp. 14–16).

> Priest Zōga was the son of the Consultant Tsunehira and disciple of Archbishop Jie. Even as a child, his writing was so superior to others' that he was praised everywhere as someone who would have a great future. But in his heart there was a deep aversion to the world; he was not blinded by fame or profit and his most cherished wish, unknown to others, was to be reborn in Amida's paradise. Lamenting that his dedication to the Way was not as perfect as he would wish, he went to worship at the Central Hall [of Enryakuji on Mount Hiei] for a thousand nights and offered a thousand prayers to attain to perfect piety. In the beginning, he prayed silently, without so much as a sigh, but by the six- or seven-hundredth night, he was whispering, "I pray you, possess me, possess me!" Those who heard him wondered what the priest was up to, for he was apparently asking to be possessed by the goblin, and they were torn between suspicion and derisive laughter. In the end, however, they clearly heard the words "Let piety possess me!" and were much moved.
>
> In this way, the thousand nights came to their conclusion. As might be expected, his aversion to the world was now even deeper than before, and he was only waiting for an opportunity to renounce his body. Then, one day, an intramural debate was held at the temple. As was the custom, after the debates were over, they threw away food for a feast in the garden, and as expected, crowds of beggars gathered from all directions, fighting to get their hands on the food and feed themselves. Suddenly, this Consultant Zen priest [Zōga] ran out from among the assembled priests, grabbed some food, and ate it. The onlookers were scandalized; they taunted him, "You Zen priest there, have you gone mad?" "No," he declared, "I am not mad; it is this whole priestly assembly that seems to me mad!" They found these words even more amazing. "This is terrible, terrible," they agreed, and in the meanwhile, Zōga left and locked himself in his room.

Later, he went to live in the place called Tōnomine in Yamato Province [Nara], spending years in pious practice and meditation. In time, having acquired a reputation for holiness, he was summoned to be the Preceptor of the then Empress. Perversely, he went and, approaching the balustrade of the Imperial Palace, shouted out all manner of embarrassing things, then left again without a word. Another time, he was on his way to see someone who wished to make an offering to the Buddha, and was reflecting on some suitable material for his sermon, when it occurred to him that in this preoccupation with fame and profit, he was in fact courting an evil karma. Arriving late, he quarreled with the patron, blaming him for some vague matter or other, then left again without going through the planned offering. This kind of behavior was doubtless meant to estrange himself from people, so that they would cease to call on him on such occasions. *Again, during the felicitation ceremonies for his teacher the Archbishop [Jie], he broke into the ranks of the advance guard, wearing on his side a dried salmon [karazake to iu mono] for a sword, and riding a truly miserable-looking, bony old cow.* He declared that he would attend the Archbishop, but his appearance was so arresting, the onlookers could only gape in amazement. So he pulled away, singing, "So much pain for a famous name! The beggar alone is carefree!" Now, the Archbishop was not a mundane person, and said, "It is I whom he seeks to hit in my palanquin." Hearing that voice, Zōga was saddened and said, "My teacher is about to enter an evil path." At which the Archbishop was reported to have replied from within the palanquin, "This too is for the sake of the sentient beings."

When this venerable priest was nearing the end of his life, first he drew up the *go* board and played all by himself, and next he asked for the mudguard flaps [from a horse saddle], slung it across his shoulders, and went through the motions of the dance called "The Butterfly." In wonder, his disciples asked him what it all meant. He explained, "When I was only an innocent child, I was admonished against [doing] these two things, and so I stopped doing them. But the desire to do so remained in my heart, and might otherwise have bound me to the cycle of life and death." Soon he saw the saintly hosts come to welcome him, and, joyfully, he chanted this poem,

mizuha sasu	As a wisdom tooth sprouts
yasoji amari no	after eighty years and more
oi no nami	in the aging waves,
kurage no hone ni	I am met by the unthinkable—
ainikeru kana	the bones of a jellyfish!

and so breathed his last. This man's behavior would probably be called insane by later generations, but since he desired nothing less than to break through the realm of the mind and its objects, I have told his story as a cherished exemplar. Where it is the rule in associating with people to obey the high and take pity on the humble, the body becomes another's possession, and the heart-mind employed in the getting and giving of love. All this not only makes for suffering in this world but is also a great impediment to liberation from it. Outside of detaching yourself from the realm of the mind and its objects, what other means is there for the easily distressed mind to attain tranquility?

Priest Zōga's story has a wide distribution, among the other sources being *Honchō hokke genki* (Miraculous Tales of the *Lotus Sutra*, *ZGR* 8b: 168 on), *Zoku honchō ōjōden* (Biographies of Priests, Continued, *DNBZ* 107: 25), and *Shiju hyakuinnenshū* (Personal Collection of Various Karmic Stories, 8: 144, in *DNBZ* 148). He figures also in the *Konjaku monogatari* (*NKBT KM* 3: 181 and 4: 99); *Senjūshō*, and *Uji shūi monogatari*.

10. "The precepts are the wisdom lifeblood of Buddhist teaching" [*kai wa buppō no emyō*]. This statement means, more specifically, that the precepts are crucial to Buddhist teaching, since they lead to the wisdom that is its ultimate aim. For example, Suzuki ("Mikkan," II, p. 26) cites the following passages from *Daichidoron* XIII:

> Again, the mind of one who observes the precepts has no regrets; having no regrets, it is happy and carefree; being happy and carefree, it achieves concentration; having achieved concentration, it attains true wisdom, and thereby nirvana. The observance of the precepts is considered the foundation of the several good dharmas.

> Again, the person who observes the precepts is naturally able, through abstinence, to restrain the five emotions and is not subject to the five cravings. If the mind strays, he can capture it and make it turn back. This means that observing the precepts enables one to guard the several roots. Keeping the roots under guard enables Zen meditation. Zen meditation leads to wisdom, and with wisdom one achieves the Buddhist Way.

Note that the progress of Shinkei's argument here indicates his reading of the Way (*michi*) as ultimately not bound by predetermined forms and rules; yet it is these same rules and determinations that, having come down from the practice of earlier poets, initially set one on the path leading to the ultimate realm of freedom (corresponding to wisdom in Buddhism), and for that reason, they possess an essential value. This view seems to conform to the Tendai literature on precepts, which reflects two main attitudes: (1) the precepts are essential in the gradual method of training that leads to wisdom; and (2) once wisdom is achieved, the precepts become secondary; the bodhisattva may ostensibly violate them, but he cannot then be said to be *not* upholding the precepts.

11. *Makashikan* VI.B contains the following passage, making a correlation between the five Buddhist prohibitions and the five Confucian cardinal virtues, in the section on "Destroying Dharmas Everywhere," which explains how to contemplate contingent reality from the standpoint of emptiness. One should know the disease, know the appropriate medicine, and then take or apply it.

> About entering the contingent and knowing the medicine: since the marks of disease are countless, so are the cures. They can be condensed into three: mundane, nonmundane, and the highest nonmundane. . . . A sutra commentary says: "What is the intention behind mundane preaching? Say that a child-prince was falling from a high place; the king his father, in his love and pity, piles up layers of silk and cotton upon the ground in order to spare the boy pain. It is just so with the sentient beings. Just when they are falling into the three lower worlds, the Venerable One in his compassion takes mundane good models and provisionally spreads them underneath so that they may escape evil tendencies. Though the ordinary dull minds might not know it, the Venerable One walks behind them and appears in the same buddha-less world, guiding the ignorant." The *Great Sutra* says, "The secular classics and mundane writings are all Buddhist sermons; they are not outside the Way." Again, the *Konkōmyō* says, "All the good treatises of the world issue from this sutra. If one knows the mundane teachings profoundly, one will see that they are in fact Buddhist teachings."
>
> How can this be? If you put together the ten good practices, they correspond to the five prohibitions. *If you know the five cardinal virtues and the five elements profoundly, their meaning is similar to the five prohibitions.* Nurturing benevolence and compassion, not doing others harm: this is the prohibition against killing. Righteous and accommodating, he controls himself for the sake of others: this is the prohibition against stealing. A model of propriety, he binds up his hair and pays homage to his parents: this is the prohibition against adultery. Wise and intelligent, his actions are sober and conform to the principles of the Way: this is the prohibition against drinking liquor. Trustworthiness is to make a vow upon the true record and not betray the rules of honesty: this is the prohibition against idle speech. *Confucius of the Zhou set up these five cardinal virtues and made them the Dharma medicine of the mundane world in order to heal the diseases of humanity.* (*Makashikan* 2: 41–42)

The *Shasekishū* III.7, "A Story About Confucius," includes a similar analogy or conversion between the five Confucian virtues and the Buddhist five prohibitions.

> When one thinks about it, the person who does not neglect his own humanity is truly rare. Such a man, first of all, is he who practices the five cardinal virtues of benevolence, righteousness, propriety, wisdom, and trustworthiness; maintains his family; and fosters the peace of the country. What is called benevolence means to do the people good and love them widely. It is to respect the aged like one's own parents and cherish the young as if they were one's own children. A man devoid of such benevolence is akin to demons and beasts. The heart of deep sympathy and generous goodwill may be described as benevolent when its sphere is narrow, and compassionate when its sphere is

broad. The substance is the same, but there is a difference in the quality of its functioning. For instance, the substance of fire is one, but depending on the amount of fuel, it will emit a brighter or a dimmer light. Righteousness means to be straight and honest, capable of discerning the truth and judging right from wrong without prejudice or malice. From the perspective of the five precepts, benevolence corresponds to the prohibition against killing, and righteousness to that against stealing. Propriety means to respect and give way to others and maintain the order of precedence; to be restrained and humble, and not arrogant. It corresponds to the prohibition against adulterous lust. Adultery is the most extreme contempt for another. Wisdom is a lucid mind, one that discerns right from wrong, and good from bad; it spurns folly and yearns to follow the sagely way. It corresponds to the prohibition against drinking liquor. Liquor deranges the mind, in that it causes stupidity. What is called trustworthiness means to be true in heart and words, without deception, and vigilant against the tiger lurking in the mouth, the cutting blade of the tongue; not given to reckless words, thinking thrice before speaking. It corresponds to the prohibition against deceitful speech. He who perfects the five cardinal virtues will naturally escape harm and misfortune and live out his allotted lot of life. Sustaining the body he received from his father and mother, making a name for himself, dispensing merits: he is the model of filial piety. (p. 159)

12. *Rongo* II.20: "The Master said: 'At fifteen, I set my heart on learning, and at thirty I was established. At forty, I ceased to be confused. At fifty I understood the will of heaven. At sixty my ears inclined to what it heard, and *at seventy I could follow my heart's desire without overstepping the rules*" (p. 40). Shinkei's point is that the highest achievement is a freedom that does not, however, violate the established rules. At this point, one has thoroughly understood the rightness and necessity of the rules, in such a way that there is no more conflict between rule and inclination. This Confucian stand is meant to correspond to the Mahayana view that a bodhisattva may seemingly violate the rules, yet due to his deeper understanding of them, that is, his wisdom, he is ultimately upholding them.

13. *GYS* XX.2786 Shintō Rites [fifth line is *omou aware ni*]. Saigyō was paying his last respects to the deity of the Kamo Shrine in the capital before departing on a foot pilgrimage to Shikoku, a journey from which, due to old age, he was not certain of returning.

14. *Shūgyokushū* IV.2396. The fourth and fifth lines are *yo o yuku michi no / mono to koso mire*. The *Shūgyokushū* is the individual poem anthology of Jichin (also known as Jien), as collected by the Cloistered Prince Son'en, Abbot of Shōren'in, in the years 1326–28 and 1346. One edition has a total of 4,613 poems, another 5,917.

15. *Fuboku wakashō* XXXV.16543. "Old Man." The text there is different: *Asatsuyu o / hisashiki mono to / omou yo ni / hotoke no ani ni / ikade nariken* (In a world where / the morning dew is seen / as a long-lived thing, / how did I live so long as to become / the Buddha's older brother?)

16. In the *Yakumo mishō*, VI, this poem is cited as a bad example of uselessly clever word-play: "The linking of the words is endlessly strange and the configuration is truly bad" (p. 80). The double entendre in question are: *mi* (body, self) in *miyama* (deep mountain); *samu* (cold) in *samushiro* (straw mat pallet); and *iku* (live, exist) in *ikuyo* (many nights). Juntoku's main objection is most likely the awkward fit between the surface sense and the second meaning enabled by the word-play. The surface meaning generated by the syntax as such is jarring, somewhat absurd, as evident in *oshikaranu miyamaoroshi* (uncherished mountain storm) and *inochi no ikuyo hitorine* (life's several nights sleeping alone). The sense becomes comprehensible only through the double entendre, whereas the decorum of polysemy in waka apparently dictates that the surface diction make sense as such, and the second semantic level should function to deepen the feeling through the ambiguity and complexity generated by multiple meanings. Consequently, this poem sounds awkward and funny in Japanese; it has, in fact, the air of an unsuccessful *haikai* poem; its wit is somewhat dim.

Shinkei's point, however, is less technical than moral, given the context of the citation within a reference to the Confucian virtues and Buddhist prohibitions. His objection would be to the incongruity between the apparent seriousness or sincerity of the diction and the deflation of expectation when one realizes that the speaker is saying nothing more than that he feels cold sleeping alone, that his life is useless without a warm body beside him. In this view, life (and its poetic expression) is too serious for this kind of disingenuous verbal trickery. This is not even a love poem, since there is no yearning for the beloved.

Chapter Forty-Five

1. The most likely source for this statement by Saigyō, as well as the next by Minamoto Tsunenobu, and possibly the anecdote about Shunzei's doubts in paragraph three is the *Sangoki*. See n. 3 for the complete passage.

2. For Minamoto Tsunenobu, see "Biographical Notes."

3. Shinkei's source for the concept of identifying poetic composition with Zen meditation practice, and consequently with the way of instantaneous enlightenment, is apparently culled from the following passage in *Sangoki* II, which includes the *Sasamegoto* citations from Saigyō, Shunzei, and Minamoto Tsunenobu. It should be kept in mind that the author of the *Sangoki* was believed by the Muromachi poets, including Shinkei and Shōtetsu, to be Teika.

> According to [Minamoto] Tsunenobu, "Waka is the wellspring of reclusion, and as such it is the essential route nurturing the awakening of wisdom" [*waka wa inton no minamoto to shite, bodai o susumuru yōro nari*]. It is true indeed. It can be said that to reach understanding in any art is to realize that it can as such be subsumed within the principle of Suchness and the Real [*kore shinnyo jissō no kotowari ni osamerubeshi*]. What is meant by poetry here is that the determination of thirty-one syllables is modeled upon the thirty-two marks/aspects of the Tathagata [*nyorai*]. It is said that the Tathagata has thirty-two aspects, but what appears is [only] thirty-one aspects. The invisible, highest aspect does not become manifest. That is why, basing the analogy only on the manifest aspects, poetry came to have thirty-one syllables. Considered together, the five separate lines are subsumed under the five cardinal elements of earth, water, fire, wind, and space. A flaw in the earth-element line is called a flaw in the legs; a flaw in the water-element line is called a flaw in the belly; a flaw in the fire-element line is a flaw in the breast; a flaw in the wind-element line a flaw in the forehead; and a flaw in the space-element line a flaw in the head. In sum, the thirty-one syllable configuration of the poem constitutes a provisional body [*keshin, kari no mi*] of the five great elements. As for the heart-mind hidden within the thirty-one syllables, it could be called the innermost heart of the real [*naishō shinjitsu no shinri to mōsubeshi*]. Therefore to chant/compose a poem is the same as to establish a buddha [*uta isshu o yomeba, ichibutsu o kenryūsuru ni onaji*]. Further, as an ancient sage once said, composing ten or a hundred poems is to acquire merit for making ten or a hundred buddhas. Priest Saigyō has said, "Poetry is the practice of Zen meditation." It is true indeed that it is not possible to compose it without focusing the mind on a single point. In order to arrest the mind's dispersal, there is nothing better than meditation. After my late father [Shunzei] had dedicated many long years to this Way [of poetry], there came a time when he reflected that no one is exempt from the cycle of birth and death, and poetry seemed no more than mad words and clever phrases [*kyōgen kigyo*]. Realizing that it was in truth the essential way to liberation that he wished to pursue, he went on pilgrimage to Sumiyoshi Shrine to pray for guidance in the matter. While he was praying earnestly one night, in a dream he saw an old man well past ninety-nine years of age . . . seated in front of the sacred altar of the god and he seemed to be whispering in a reedy voice. Seeing him thus, my father was moved to speak to him about his problem [with poetry], and without hesitation asked him how to achieve the momentous event of liberation [*shutsuri ichidaiji no koto*]. At this, the hoary old man broke out in a smile and apparently said, "Do not even think of doing anything else. Through poetry you will be reborn in paradise," then bestowed upon him the "dimly, dimly" poem [*honobono no uta*]. This was a truly marvelous turn of events. "Then poetry does not only nurture the

mind for a while but could become a way to the future— what a noble revelation!" he said, the tears streaming down his face. It was indeed moving. From then on, as may be expected, he more and more looked up to poetry as a weighty practice [*omoki michi*]. (pp. 341–42)

4. The Five Great Constitutive Elements [*godai shosei*] are earth, water, fire, wind, and space; they constitute and give rise to all phenomena. In esoteric Buddhism, each further corresponds to a shape and color (earth = square = yellow; water = circle = white; fire = triangle = red; wind = crescent = black; and space = jewel sphere = blue. In sum they constitute the five stupas of Dainichi Nyorai's [Mahavairocana's] *sammaya* mandala.

The Five Buddhas (*gobutsu*) of the mandala refer to the five dyani buddhas of the Diamond Sphere (Kongōkai, Skt.; Vajradhatu) or the Womb Sphere (Taizōkai; Skt. Garbhadhatu), with Dainichi Nyorai at the center, surrounded in the four directions by four buddhas (Dainichi in phenomenal manifestation, as, for example Sakyamuni). For the Diamond Sphere, the four buddhas are (1) Ashuku (Aksobhya), signifying perfect and immutable wisdom, direction east, color yellow; (2) Hōshō (Ratnasambhava), representing Dainichi's wisdom of impartiality, direction south; (3) Mida (Amitabha), wisdom in action, west; and (4) Fukūjōju (Amoghasiddhi), the wisdom of accomplishing welfare of self and others, direction north. For the Womb Sphere, they are (1) Hodō (Ratnaketu), representing the virtue of buddha wisdom, direction east; (2) Kaifuke (Samkusumitaraja), representing the wisdom of impartiality, direction south; (3) Muryōju (Amitayus), buddha of boundless life, direction west); and (4) Tenkurai'on (Divyadundubhimeghanirghosa), manifestation of the buddha's nirvana wisdom, figured as a dharma drum that sounds of itself, exhorting against evil, encouraging the good; direction north.

The mandala is a visual representation or diagram of the world and/or the mind; it is used as a ritual device for meditation, in conjunction with rituals such as hand gestures called mudras, with the object of uniting oneself with the buddha and experiencing a nondual reality. For a detailed study of Japanese examples, see Elizabeth ten Grotenhuis, *Japanese Mandalas: Representations of Sacred Geography* (Honolulu: University of Hawaii Press, 1999).

The Five Wisdoms (*gochi*) are those belonging to the sixth element, consciousness or mind (*shiki*, *vijnana*), as it works on the five phenomenal elements (earth, water, fire, air, space) in the wisdom sphere, or Vajradhatu. They are: (1) *hokkaitaishō-chi* (*dharma-dhatu-svabhava-jnana)*, wisdom in the substance/essence of the dharma world, arising from the pure consciousness; corresponds to the samadhi of Vairocana at the center; the space element (Ui Hakuju, ed. *Bukkyō jiten* [Daitō Shuppansha, 1938; reprint, 1965], 972); (2) *daienkyō-chi* (*adarsa-jnana)*, "the wisdom of the great round mirror," in Yuishiki thought, the wisdom without outflows, achieved from transforming the eighth consciousness; all the dharmas of the three realms appear as a myriad merits and in a fullness of perfection that lacks for nothing; likened to the reflection of colors and forms in a great round mirror, corresponds to Aksobhya, direction east (ibid., 690); (3) *byōdōshō-chi* (*samata-jnana*), "wisdom of nondifferentiation or impartiality," achieved by transforming the seventh consciousness to contemplate, by means of the dharmas and of oneself and other sentient creatures, the truth of oneness or nondifference (*byōdō ichinyo*), thus generating the spirit of great compassion (*daijihi*) and aiding the bodhisattvas in their work of saving others; corresponds to Kaifuke in Esoteric doctrine, direction south; color yellow (ibid., 897); (4) *myōkanzatsu-chi* (*pratyaveksana-jnana*) "the wisdom of marvelous observation," transforming the sixth consciousness so that one is able to analyze and explain the various dharmas and banish doubts; corresponds to Muryōju or Amitabha, direction west (ibid., 1019, 281); and (5) *jōshosa-chi* (*krtyanusthana-jnana*), in Yuishiki thought, the wisdom attained from transforming the five senses so that all phenomenal existence is seen as one with the mind, and one is able to engage in marvelous transformations, for oneself and for others; in Esoteric thought, the northern space presided over by Fukūjōju (ibid., 570).

5. The Six Realms of Illusion (*rokudō*) are those of hell, hungry ghosts, beasts, demons, humans, and gods; a being transmigrates through them in accordance with his merits or demerits.

The Six Types of Action (*rokuharamitsu*) are the so-called "six perfections" in the path to bodhisattvahood: perfection of giving, morality, patience, effort, meditative concentration, and wisdom.

The Six Constitutive Elements in Fusion (*rokudai muge*) means that in essence the five phenomenal elements and the sixth element of consciousness are not separate but mutually interpenetrable, without obstruction, as light is to light; since the being's self is composed of the six elements, there is no permanent difference between it and the six elements of the buddha; one set is interchangeable or capable of fusing with the other, as in the slogan *nyūga ganyū*, "it enters me; I enter it," that is, the mystic body, voice, and mind of the Tathagata (*sanmitsu*), being immanent and universal, may enter and dwell in the individual's body, voice, and mind; similarly, the individual's body, voice, and mind, or actions (*sangō*), may transform into those of the Tathagata; another way of saying that all things, animate and inanimate, may achieve enlightenment in this body (*shujō sokubutsu*); also refers to the fusion or nondifferentiation of animate and inanimate entities, and gives rise to the belief in attainment of buddhahood by grasses, trees, and lands. See Ui, ed. *Bukkyō jiten*, 839, 1139–40.

The syntax of this statement follows a climactic movement, bringing us to the inescapable conclusion that a poem may be identified, on the basis of the principle of the immanent oneness of all things (*rokudai muge*), with the highest state of being, the Dharma Body.

6. "The so-called Initiation Rite to the *Kokinshū*" (*Kokinshū kanjō nado to ieri*), a reference to the cultural phenomenon of *Kokin denju*, the secret transmission of the meanings of obscure words in the *Kokinshū*. It is said to have started in the late Heian period, when Fujiwara Mototoshi transmitted them to Shunzei, but the phenomenon first assumed overriding importance in the Muromachi period, when Tō no Tsuneyori transmitted them to Sōgi (in the text called *Kokin wakashū ryōdo kikigaki*). From then on, the transmission divided into several branches. It continued to wield authoritative influence until the Edo period. The *Kikigaki* contains blanks or places marked simply "secret" (*hiji*), the burden of which are written in separate slips of paper and available only in a separate transmission to the elected heir to them. These are known variously as the "the secret of the three trees and three birds" (*samboku sanchō no hiji*), "three important items" (*sanka daiji*), or the "paper-slips transmission" (*kirigami denju*) and became an object of ridicule from the early modern period on due to their attitude of mystification. However, the *Kikigaki* itself is a fine example of Muromachi commentary in its approach of reading the poem as an integral whole rather than a string of isolated words. See Ozawa Masao, "Kaisetsu" to *KKS*, p. 35.

The "three trees" in the secret transmission refer to *ogatama no ki* (*KKS* 431), *medo ni kezuribana* (*KKS* 445), and *kawa nagusa* (*KKS* 449); the "three birds" to *momochidori* (*KKS* 28), *yobu kodori* (*KKS* 29), and *ina ōse dori* (*KKS* 248). The closing section of *Kirihioke* records esoteric information about the "three trees," purportedly as transmitted from Minamoto Kingo to Shunzei, and cites the "epilogue to the *Kokinshū* initiation rite" as source. See [Teika?], *Kirihioke*, ed. Sasaki, pp. 288–90.

7. The belief that "the Way of Poetry is the True Word of our country" (*kadō wa waga kuni no darani nari*) and that a frivolous employment of it will nullify one's Buddhist practice reflects the following chapter in *Shasekishū* V.A.12, "On the Profound Significance of the Way of Poetry." *Sōji* ("totally upholding [words]") below is the same as *darani*, whose etymology

is "upholding" or "maintaining," and refers to the power of darani or mantra words to fix the mind upon good dharma, to keep it from straying into bad dharma Buddhism. The practice of intoning darani incantations or spells is especially important in the Esoteric sect, where it refers to the True Word, a mystic syllable indicating the vow of the buddha and bodhisattvas. In each syllable of the incantation, an inexhaustible meaning is contained, and performing it dispels all impediments and summons great benefits (*Shasekishū*, suppl. n. 42, p. 513).

Reflecting on the Way of Poetry reveals its power to halt the mind's distracted wandering and to induce a still tranquility. It contains the mind in just a few words [*kotoba sukunakushite, kokoro o fukumeri*]. Without doubt it bears the import of *sōji*. What are called *sōji* are, to wit, *darani*. The deities of our land are the trace-emanations of buddhas and bodhisattvas, the advance manifestations of the [Buddha's] Response Body. The venerable Susano'o had early initiated, in his "eightfold fence of Izumo" poem, the practice of chanting in thirty-one syllables. This is surely no different from the words of the Buddha. The darani of India are even so; it is just that they are in the speech of that country; the Buddha spoke darani using that language. Thus in Zen Master Ichigyō's *Dainichigyō-sho*, it is said: "The words [in the languages] of the various directions are all darani." If the Buddha appeared in our country, he would doubtless use the language of Japan in speaking darani. *Sōji* do not, at base, have letters [*sōji moto moji nashi*]; it is the letters that manifest them. Where is the country whose writing would be powerless to manifest them? Indeed, the Master of Kōya [Kūkai] has said, "All the Five Great Elements resonate, and the Six Pollutions are wholly signs." There is no sound outside the five vocalics, no word apart from the letter A. The letter A is the root and base of the True Word in Esoteric teaching. And therefore, the scripture [*Daichidoron*] says, "All tongues and languages are the True Word." Even the thirty-one chapters of the *Dainichi-kyō* correspond of themselves to the thirty-one syllables [of waka]. Enfolding all worldly and otherworldly truths within thirty-one syllables, waka elicits the response of the buddhas and bodhisattvas, moves divinities and human beings. Though darani are in the common speech of India, employing and upholding them has the virtue of banishing sin, the effect of enabling escape from ignorant suffering. The waka of Japan as well is but the language of the common world, but when employed in poetry to express one's thoughts, it does not fail to evoke feeling. What is more, when it contains the spirit of the Buddha's teaching, it is indubitably a darani.

Different as are the languages of India, China, and Japan, since the intention [*i*] comes through, and its benefit is the same in all of them, the Buddha's teaching spreads, its import gaining adherents, its benefits of no little consequence. There is no teaching that is fixed by language [*kotoba ni sadamareru nori nashi*]. But if you grasp the spirit and express your thought, it will without fail elicit a moved response [*kokoro o ete, omoi o nobeba, kanarazu kannō arubeshi*]. When the great saint appeared in our country, he was already chanting waka. Such is the chant of the Kiyomizu Kannon [*SKKS* 1917]:

tada tanome	Only trust in me—
shimejigahara no	mugwort grasses everywhere
sasemogusa	in Shimeji plains—
ware yo no naka ni	as long as in this world
aran kagiri wa	I dwell and ever abide.

This is certainly a darani, no doubt about it. Many [Shintō] deities too are moved by poetry to grant people's wishes. In sum, the virtue of waka and the import of sōji must be understood as one with darani. Where one blames them for being frivolous words, the failing lies in the person's polluted mind. Even the scriptures, secular and sacred, all turn to samsaric delusions when employed for fame and profit. The fault is with the person. One should not for that reason lose sight of the virtue of sōji. Even sutra-reading turns to frivolous words when the circumstances are bad, according to the *Jōron*. I have written this down from my own understanding of the principle. How can there be no meaning in it? What is more, it can be seen in the sutras and commentaries as well. You must not think that it is a private opinion.

All the various dharmas are the Real [*shohō jissō nari*]. There is no color or fragrance that does not abide in the Middle Way. Rough words and fine speech all return to the essential truth [*dai'ichigi*].

One need not be so discriminating in waka and such. The actions of survival and earning a livelihood in no way betray the Real. What could fail to be in accord with the principle of the Dharma [*hō no kotowari*]? A long time ago, when I was in tranquil reclusion in the mountains, I heard the cries of a deer and composed this thought:

kiku ya ikani	How now, do you hear?
tsuma kou shika no	The very cries of the deer,
koe made mo	seeking its mate, tell it:
kaiyojissō	All things are the Real,
fusōihai to	not mutually other or different.

Again, as it is said in Shingon thought, "All the dharmas that arise are the mandala; according to circumstance, they rise and fall, shifting between delusion and insight," so all the myriad dharmas are the mandala. One may, depending on circumstance, become fixated on them and end up deluded, or pass through them and achieve insight. Their essential nature is the immanent cosmic mandala. I reflect continuously on this thought.

onozukara	"Of themselves
yakeno ni tateru	the very reeds sprouting in
susuki made	the burnt-out fields
mandara to koso	are mandala," even so
hito mo iu nare	do the people say.

(It is said that in Sakatō, the miscanthus reeds on burnt-out fields are called "matara.")

Using exoteric and esoteric Mahayana thought, I have reflected on waka, applying to it the principles of Buddhist teaching. I may be guilty of arbitrary, unorthodox suppositions and deluded views, and be subject to people's ridicule—these are all cause for circumspection. But I nevertheless write these down as an attempt [to think about waka]. If there be flaws here, excise them; let none that come after be guided by them. But if there be any reason in them, you must add your words and come to their aid.

The sage has no mind; he makes the mind of the myriad things his mind. The sage has no body; he makes the bodies of the myriad things his body. And therefore the sage has no words; he makes the words of the myriad things his words. How then can the sage's words be anything but Dharma words? If they are Dharma words, there must be reason in them. If there is reason in them, they must be *sōji*, and so darani. When one thinks of waka in this spirit, the fact that the divinities and buddhas employ waka renders it indubitably the True Word. (*Shasekishū*, pp. 223–25)

Chapter Forty-Six

1. *SIS* 1055. Miscellaneous Spring. "Seeing the piles of scattered petals by the Imperial Palace, during the reign of the Engi Emperor [Daigo, r. 897–930]." For Minamoto Kintada, see "Biographical Notes." The poem, which also appears in *WRS* 132 without attribution, is cited in the *Shunrai zuinō* (*NKBZ* 50: 113) and Shunzei's *Korai fūteishō* (*NKBZ* 50: 415), and is the subject of a tale in *KM* 24: 32, where it is attributed to the Middle Counselor Fujiwara Atsutada. In the *Zuinō*, Toshiyori includes it among a group of old poems where "the name of the object that should be mentioned on the [textual] surface of the poem is omitted and evoked instead in the mind." He objects that in this case, it is not necessarily only [cherry] flowers that scatter and pile up in the Palace. In fact, there are all sorts of dirt and refuse that the morning cleaning staff have to sweep up and deposit daily in the so-called dirt mountain (*chiriyama*) located by the headquarters of the Military Guards of the Right. Given the possibility of misunderstanding, the poem is far too reckless in omitting the word "flowers" in the poem's diction (p. 114). It is an amazingly literal-minded objection from a reader-critic who apparently prefers explicit clarity to artful indirection. One wonders if it was written tongue-in-cheek and imagines how a haikai poet would have given the poem a comic twist.

2. *SKKS* 554. Winter. "Composed on the spirit of 'Crimson Leaves Floating on the Water,' when the courtiers went to Ōi River during the time of Rtd. Emperor Go-Reizei [r. 1045–1068]."

The poem is cited, along with *SKKS* 1528 (see translation from *Sangoki* below), as an instance of "dropping the letter of the topic" (*dai no ji o otosu koto*) in Fujiwara Tameie's treatise, *Eiga ittei* (ca. 1275). As a general rule, Tameie is against leaving out explicit mention of the words of the topic in the poem itself, but adds the qualification: "However, there are also instances where it [the topic] is evoked" instead of being verbalized. His commentary continues: "Since these two poems were composed on the site itself, the topic does emerge, though entrusted to the scene that is right before the eyes, and 'crimson leaves' and 'water' are not mentioned" (*Eiga ittei*, pp. 349–50; also cited in Kubota's *SKKS Zenhyōshaku* 3: 239–40). Shinkei's most likely source for the question of circumventing the topic, however, is the *Sangoki*:

> One Must Fully Grasp the Topic. In general, when it is a matter of celestial and earthly phenomena, plants, animals, and all such things possessing material form, one should name the topic in the poem. However, there are also topics on which one composes in an evocative, subtle manner [*omowasete kasukani yomeru*]. In Chinese poetry, this is apparently considered the mark of a superior poem by a skilled poet. In fact, my father stated that in Japanese poetry as well, it is beyond the capacity of the untalented poet of inferior powers. On "Not at Home in the Flowers' Season": [Chinese couplet quoted] How ingeniously apt is the poet's interpretation of the spirit of the topic here. Again, composing on "Fallen Leaves Flowing Away on the Water": [*SKKS* 554 quoted]. And again, on "Moon Shining on the Water" [*SKKS* 1528, Minamoto Tsunenobu]:

sumu hito mo	The house feels
aru ka naki ka no	as though it might be
yado narashi	uninhabited—
ashima no tsuki no	stilled in the moonlight
moru ni makasete	gleaming through the reeds.
(Tsunezane)	(Tsunezane)

> These two poems are of a type composed right before the scene itself. While the topic does emerge in the poem, the poet relied on what he was seeing at the very moment and did not explicitly name crimson leaves on the water and so on. On "Cuckoo" during a poetry contest on the fourth day of the Fifth Month:

samidare ni	Through the pouring
furi'idete nake	rains of June, sing out!
to 'moedomo	I wish it so, but
asu no tame to ya	does it keep its voice
ne o nokosuran	in reserve for tomorrow?

> This poem is said to have been subjected to various criticisms for dropping the topic [*rakudai nari tote*]. One would have to wonder why. I have heard that in handling the words of the topic, one must be resourceful and let the imagination roam [*kokoro o megurashite yomubeki*]. (pp. 329–30)

The same poem is cited, along with two others, in the *Ryōshun isshiden* (also known as *Benyōshō*, 1409) under the section "On Poems That Express their Meaning Indirectly" (*kokoro o mawashite yomu uta no koto*). About these, Ryōshun states that they are beyond the capacity of beginners; he comments that "though these two poems were composed while viewing the scenery of the place, that does not emerge explicitly in the words, but indirectly." Significantly, this section is preceded by one on "the style of vulgar poetry" (*iyashiki uta no sama*), where he states that "there is little that is evocative and lofty [*yosei to take takaki*] in the configuration of poems that express their meaning in a manner excessively clear and complete [*amari ni mo kotowari o tashika ni iitsumetaru*]" (pp. 180–81). Again, Tō no Tsuneyori's *SKKS* commentary, the *Shinkokinwakashū kikigaki*, also mentions this poem, with the following remark: "This is a poem that circumvents the topic [*dai o mawashite*]; it is not easy to understand all at once. Such instances are numerous among the works of the adepts" (cited in *Zenhyōshaku* 3: 239). Since then, modern commentaries have remarked on the significance of this poem for the question of composing by predetermined topic and its relation to the actual scenery.

Chapter Forty-Seven

1. "The purification of a Buddha realm and the conversion of the sentient beings through teaching" (*jōbutsu kokudo, kyōge shujō*) appears in the gathas spoken by Mahakasyapa in Chapter 4, "Belief and Understanding" (*shinge-hon*) of the *Lotus*. *Hokkekyō* 1: 256.

2. *Shasekishū* II.10, "Establishing an Affinity with the Buddhist Teaching Is Not in Vain," recounts the story of a brahmin in India who made it a practice to buy the skulls of those who had in life listened to the Buddhist teaching. He erected stupas and made offerings to them and thereby achieved rebirth in heaven. The text continues, "And how much better would it be to listen oneself to the teaching, to believe and understand, and then practice it. Therefore, the *Zenjūtenshi-kyō* says, '*To listen to the teaching, criticize it, and fall to hell is better than making offerings to numberless buddhas*'" (p. 129).

In a variant *Shasekishū* text (ed. Tsukudo Reikan [Iwanami Shoten, 1943]), the line quoted by Shinkei occurs in §3.1, "The Epileptic's Clever Remark," and continues with this explanation: "*Criticizing it [the teaching] and falling into hell ultimately becomes the seed, for it is the cause of liberation. On the other hand, you may make offerings to the countless buddhas,* but receiving only the fruit of phenomenal outflows, you will not be freed from transmigration" (1: 121).

3. A line from *Hokke mongu*; also cited in Mujū Ichien's *Zōtanshū* (Random-Talk Collection), 10 vols., 1304–5, 1. In Dōgen's thirteenth-century *Shōbōgenzō* (Treasury of the Eye of the True Dharma), the line appears within a discussion of "suchness":

> There is a statement that has been made from antiquity, that has been made from India, that has been made from heaven: *if one falls on the ground, one rises from the ground; there is no way to rise apart from the ground.* What this is saying is that one who falls on the ground must get up from the ground, and cannot hope to rise except by way of the ground. It has been considered excellent to become greatly enlightened when this is brought up, and considered a path to liberate body and mind as well. Therefore, if one asks what the principle of enlightenment of the Buddha is, it is said to be like someone fallen on the ground rising from the ground. (*Shōbōgenzō: Zen Essays by Dōgen*, trans. Thomas Cleary [Honolulu: University of Hawaii Press, 1986], p. 50)

Shinkei's point here is that enlightenment entails a thoroughgoing understanding arrived at through criticism, which here must be read as a sign of honest doubt. It is only by risking "hell" that one attains to "heaven." In conjunction with Dōgen's discussion, in the nondualism of "suchness," both the falling into confusion and the emergence from it are based on the same "ground"; one is not possible without the other. Or, in the context of this chapter in *Sasamegoto*, indifference and self-satisfaction lead nowhere; criticism, in revealing ignorance and confusion, is also paradoxically the way to touch ground, so to speak, and thus stand up again, this time on firmer ground. In sum, enlightenment entails an experiential process.

4. From the *Kōshikego* (Ch. *Kongzi jiayu*, Sayings of the Confucian school), a collection of anecdotes about and dialogues between Confucius and his disciples; said to be a forgery by

Wang Su of the Wei dynasty (220–65), who compiled it from the *Zuo Zhuan*, *Guo Yu*, *Xunzi*, *Mengzi*, and other pre-Han texts.

5. From the *Shokyō* (Ch. *Shu jing*, Book of Documents).

6. Kidō (*SSG*, p. 184, n. 14) cites the *Kunshishū* for this saying. The following passage includes other images used by Shinkei in the treatise: "The crooked tree, receiving the inked line, subsequently turns straight. The dull, obeying the whetstone, becomes sharp. Things await the [proper] circumstance. Receptivity is just so. How can the blindly ignorant follow the teacher and not learn the Way? To see with the eye, yet be unable to grasp it in the mind— this is like writing on water, carving on ice; the labor is expended without result" (p. 9).

The *Kunshishū* is a late Heian-period (eleventh-century) collection of worthy and wise quotations from Confucian sources, intended for the education of young people. It clearly aims to encourage virtue and learning, as inculcated by a filial upbringing and a strict teacher. The gentleman, as distinct from the small man, is possessed of an education and the virtues of tolerance and self-reflection.

One of the *Kunshishū*'s possible sources is this *Junshi* (Ch. *Xunzi*) passage: "Falling on the inked line, the tree becomes straight; honed on the whetstone, the metal becomes sharp. A gentleman studies widely and engages in daily reflection; hence his intelligence is clarified, his actions [are] free of fault" (p. 15).

7. An allusion to one of the stories recounted in *Shasekishū* III.2, "The Man Who Admitted Defeat at a Hearing." King Wen of Wei thought himself a wise ruler and turned to his ministers for confirmation. One of them, Ren Zuo, disagreed, saying that a wise king received his mandate from Heaven, whereas King Wen had acquired the kingdom by force, having dispossessed his uncle of the throne and taken his empress. The king was greatly angered and dismissed Ren Zuo. Next, he turned to another minister, Di Huang, who confirmed that Wen might indeed be called a wise king; the proof was that a minister as wise as Ren Zuo had been born in the same age to serve him. Moved by these words, Wen recalled Ren Zuo, reformed his government, and achieved the name of a wise king (p. 147; see also *Sand and Pebbles: The Tales of Mujū Ichien,* trans. Robert E. Morrell [Albany: State University of New York Press, 1985], pp. 125–27).

In the Tsukudo edition of *Shasekishū*, the story of King Wen is followed by these lines: "The Book says, 'The tree, following the inked line, becomes building material. The ruler, bowing to admonitions, becomes wise'" (1: 128). The co-occurrence of the King Wen anecdote with this line (cited just above in *Sasamegoto*) in *Shasekishū* is one of the evidences Kidō presents to conclude that this work, rather than individual Chinese texts, is Shinkei's main source for many of the Chinese classical allusions and sayings in *Sasamegoto.* It is also evidence that the *Shasekishū* text Shinkei used is closer to the Tsukudo edition. *Kenkyū*, pp. 347–49; 364, n. 1.

8. *Honchō monzui* 2; also in *Taiheiki* 14.

9. From the *Lotus Sutra*, chap. 7, "Parable of the Conjured City" (*Hokkekyō* 2:12; *Scripture of the Lotus Blossom*, trans. Hurvitz, p. 130).

10. This idea is expressed in the *Shasekishū* thus: "In the Hossō school, where they set up a hundred dharmas, it is said that the time elapsed is only a thought on the plane of consciousness. They are only provisional dharmas and do not at base have a determinate time. A hundred is only a hundred in the mind, a year a year only in thought. They are tentatively set up on the plane of consciousness. Thus, although one speaks of incalculable kalpas on the way to buddhahood, one thinks of incalculable kalpas as a dream. In reality, they are but a moment" (*Shūi* section, item 9:5, pp. 467–68).

11. From the *Kegonkyō*, *T.* 9: 449c. The same line, however, occurs also in *Shasekishū* III.1,

"The Epileptic's Clever Remark": "The Zen Master Ichigyō's commentary says, what is called the self-realization of the mind means that from the beginning until now, non-arising is of itself buddhahood; in truth, nothing is realized, nothing attained. Again, it is said, for one who abides in this Vehicle, *the moment when the mind first awakens is in and of itself [already] true wisdom.* When arising-and-ceasing are not set in motion, one arrives at nirvana" (ed. Tsukudo, 1: 117).

12. A line from the *Shuryōgonkyō*, occurring in this context: "The Buddha spoke to Ananda: . . . 'From that non-beginning until now, all the sentient beings in their ignorance have been losing their right mind over things, have been overturned by them. Therefore, from this perspective, they see the large, see the small. [But] *if you are skilled in overturning things, you are the same as the Tathagata,* your body and mind perfectly illumined" (*T* 19: 945.111c; cited in *SSG*, suppl. n. 59, p. 264).

In *Shasekishū* V.3, "The Scholar Who Was Reborn as a Beast," the line is cited in the context of a discussion of the use of Buddhist study either for fame and profit or for spiritual salvation.

> Thinking about the question of worldliness and unworldliness, I have since perused the sacred texts and found numerous passages on it. The *Jinnōkyō* says, "When the bodhisattva is not yet a buddha, he takes the buddha-wisdom and turns it into delusion. When the bodhisattva has become a buddha, he takes delusion and makes it wisdom." The *Shugokyō* says, "There are those for whom delusion gives liberation, since it becomes the cause and condition for contemplating the true substance. And there are those for whom liberation leads to delusion, since it becomes the cause and condition for attachment." This is an important statement. When the intention is good, there is no attachment in aiming for the Way; thus, though it might look like delusion, it is really the cause and condition for liberation. But if there is fame and profit and self-interest in the heart, it might resemble virtue, but is actually the cause and condition for karmic transmigration. The good and bad is not to be determined by the outward action alone. It is by the intention that one distinguishes who rises and falls. This too is a question of one's own orientation. As the *Shuryōgonkyō* says, "*If you are skilled in overturning things, you are the same as a Tathagata.*" The three categories [i.e., the five skandhas, *goun*; the twelve locations or entrances; and the twelve worlds] and the seven great elements [earth, water, fire, wind, and space, plus sight and consciousness] are at base the Tathagatagarbha. As the *Ryōgakyō* [*Lankavatara sutra, T* 16. 480–640] says, "The Tathagatagarbha is the source of both the good and the not-good. Therefore, things have neither merit nor fault in themselves. When employed by the mind, they are grounded there, provisionally called delusion when the mind is overturned by them, and buddha wisdom when the mind is able to turn them to produce benefits. In truth, there is neither delusion nor wisdom. There is only the teaching, of which there is neither head nor tail, of the one spirit of nondifferentiation [*ichiryō musōkyō*]. How is it to be spoken? Therefore even the naming of it is but an expedient means. Within true enlightenment, there are no names, there are no minds." ("Supplements" 40.485–86; ed. Tsukudo, 1: 206–7)

13. This line appears in the *Kunshishū*, p. 11.

14. Rongo (Ch. *Lunyu*) 12. 285: "Zizhang asked about wisdom. The Master said, 'To remain unmoved through insidious abuse or searing slander—this may be called wisdom. Yes, indeed, to remain unmoved through insidious abuse or searing slander—this may be called the farthest reaches of wisdom.'"

Chapter Forty-Eight

1. *Junshi* (*Xunzi*) I.1: "Sprouting among the hemp plants, the mugwort grows straight without staking. . . . Thus, with regard to his residence, a gentleman carefully chooses the village; in associating with others, he necessarily attaches himself to worthy persons; in this way, guarding himself from error and perversity, he approaches the core of the right" (1: 21).

2. *Kunshishū*: "A proverb says, the small man makes material wealth his treasure; the gentleman makes his friends a mirror" (p. 10).

3. *Kunshishū*: "Again it is said, the company of gentlemen is like water, the commingling of small men like thick liquor" (p. 10).

4. *Kunshishū*: "According to the ancients, when a gentleman loses something, three times he searches in his own breast; the small man, having no such scruples, suspects the pure-minded. For this reason, to realize, after association, that someone lacks goodness does not compare with living apart from him; to discover that someone's heart is dishonest is not as good as to have sooner parted from him" (p. 11).

5. *Kunshishū*: "Kongzi said, never forget a person's kindness; never dwell on a person's anger. Again he said, encountering goodness is like savoring honey; meeting evil like grasping a flaming brand" (p. 10).

6. Bai Juyi collected the writings of his close friend, Yuan Zhen (779–831), under the title, *Yuan Shaoyin ji* (Vice-Mayor Yuan's Anthology), and composed the following verse in his memory:

> Your literary remains are thirty scrolls in all,
> The pearl and gold of your voice in each scroll;
> In the earth of Dragon-Gate Field
> Your bones are buried, but never your fame.

7. Perhaps an allusion to the following passage in the postscript to the *Kanke kōshū* (The Later Sugawara Collection), the last Chinese poetry anthology of the exiled minister Sugawara Michizane (845–903): "This volume of new Chinese poems from the western headquarters [Kyūshū] is now called 'The Later Collection.' When he was near death, he affixed his seal on it and sent the volume to the Middle Counselor Ki no Haseo. Upon seeing it, Haseo raised his gaze to heaven and sighed in grief" (p. 524). Ki no Haseo (d. 912), an early Heian scholar of Chinese, was Michizane's student.

8. *Shasekishū* V.10, "About Bodhisattva Incarnations Enjoying Waka," recounts the encounter between Shōtoku Taishi and the Bodhidharma thus:

> Once, when he [Shōtoku Taishi] was passing along Mount Kataoka, his horse stopped and would go no farther. Puzzled, he looked around him and saw a foreign priest who had collapsed from starvation on the road. Dismounting, he talked with the priest, then took off his purple cloak to cover him, composing this poem:
>
> | | |
> |---|---|
> | shinateru ya | On rugged-sloped |
> | kataokayama ni | Kataoka, a traveler lies, |
> | ii ni uete | starving for nourishment; |
> | fuseru tabibito | Ah, the pity of it— |
> | aware oya nashi | his mother is not here. |
>
> . . . The reply,
>
> | | |
> |---|---|
> | ikaruga ya | Were the bountiful river |
> | tomino'okawa no | Tomino'o of the flying hawfish |
> | taeba koso | ever to cease flowing, |
> | waga ōkimi no | then and then only might I |
> | mina wa wasureme | forget your gracious name. |
>
> This starving man was the Great Teacher Bodhidharma. He appears thus in Heishi's biography of Prince Shōtoku. When the prince lived in Daitōkōzan in his previous incarnation, Bodhidharma encouraged him with these words: "The people of the eastern sea yonder do not know of the workings of cause and condition and have never heard of the Buddha's teaching; they take existence to be mere food and clothing. There is a task for you there. Go and be born in that land, spreading the Buddha's teaching and helping the sentient beings." And so the prince was born in our country. (pp. 253–54)

This story of the fateful encounter between the Zen patriarch and the Japanese prince had a wide circulation, appearing not only in biographies of Shōtoku Taishi but in literary critical texts like the *Shunrai zuinō*, *Korai fūteishō*, and *Nomori no kagami*, as well as *setsuwa* collections like the *Konjaku monogatari*. The *Nomori no kagami* reads Shōtoku's poem to mean that "the weak capacity of a small, backward country is no different from a starving man's powerlessness. . . . Like a motherless child difficult to bring up, there are no people who would take it [Zen] in, or gods who would protect it." Again, Bodhidharma's reply is interpreted there to mean "were the innate capacity indeed to run dry and Zen be unable to spread, then only might I feel disappointed in you." The author of this treatise from 1295, thought to be Rokujō Arifusa, was critical of Zen and concludes his reading by declaring that "if even a reincarnated sage found it hard to teach and spread it, how can a mere worldling teach and transmit it?" (p. 92). Shinkei's point is the intimate fellowship of kindred spirits as exemplified by the poetic exchange above, and the factor that, in all three cases cited, the survivor in the partnership showed a sympathetic understanding of the other's deepest desires by transmitting his mission, whether it be in poetry or religion.

Chapter Forty-Nine

1. Lord Teika's remark here perhaps reflects a similar opinion in the *Sangoki*: "Next, on the matter of the Close Link; this refers to a poem wherein everything coheres as you go from the initial five-syllable line to each of the following 7-5-7-7–syllable lines. In other words, it is like the 'Dimly, dimly' [*honobono*] poem. Next, on the matter of the Distant Link; this refers to the case where in relation to the first five-syllable line, [only] one or two of the following 7-5-7-7–syllable lines cohere of themselves. *Someone has said: outstanding poems are rare with the Close Link; good poems frequently occur with the Distant Link.* This is probably true" (p. 351).

The following passage from *Guhishō*, however, is more apropos. It comes after the statement "There is always a caesura [*kiruru tokoro*] in a poem" and five poem examples illustrating the occurrence of a caesura after each of the waka's five lines respectively.

> The structure of poems is all like this. Their quality can be measured according to it. No doubt those that end in the fifth line may be considered good poems to begin with. Poems in the Close Link should definitely have the closure in the fifth line. The others would mostly be in the Distant Link mode. *It is true, nonetheless, that there are no outstanding poems among those using the Close Link. Even if there were, they would be quite rare.* No matter how you look at it, in the Close Link the words succeed one another in a manner too predictable, moving as it were from roots to branches to leaves, and thus invariably producing the merely ordinary and rarely the unusual. In the Distant Link, you interrupt the poem at any line, and generate thereby something marvelous. Is this not the reason that Lord Tsunenobu declared that the outstanding poems are in the Distant Link? (ed. Sasaki, p. 298)

2. "The sutras of complete meaning" (*ryōgikyō*) are those that directly express the meaning of the dharma; in the Yuishiki (Mind Only) school, they refer to the sutras having their source in the third stage of the Buddha's preaching, which expounds the middle truth. As distinct from these, "the sutras of incomplete meaning" (*furyōgikyō*) are those that speak of the dharma only indirectly, by means of parables or expedient devices (*hōben*); these are from the first and second stages of the Buddha's teaching, which preached the dharma from the standpoint of the provisional and of the empty, respectively.

Étienne Lamotte renders *ryōgi* (Skt. *nitartha*) as "precise meaning" and its negation, *furyōgi* (Skt. *neyartha*), as "indeterminate meaning." Similarly, Donald S. Lopez Jr. has "sutras of definitive meaning" as distinct from "sutras whose meaning requires interpretation" (p. 61). Lamotte says, further, that "the *Treatise* by Nagarjuna (I.539–540) considers sutras to be of precise meaning when the allegations are obvious and easily understood, and sutras the meaning of which needs to be determined are those which through skillful means (*upaya*) say things which at first sight seem to be incorrect and which demand an explanation" (pp. 17–18). Again, "the Mahayana attached the greatest importance to sutras of indeterminate and provisional meaning and which constitute the intentional teaching of the Buddha" (p. 20). (See Lamotte, "The Assessment of Textual Interpretation in Buddhism," and Lopez, "On the Interpretation of the Mahayana Sutras," both in *Buddhist Hermeneutics*, ed. Lopez [Honolulu: University of Hawaii Press, 1988]). All this is illuminating in relation to the correspondence Shinkei sees between *furyōgikyō* and the Distant Link, as well as his probable understanding and valuation of it.

3. From the *Lotus Sutra*, chap. 10, "Preachers of the Dharma":

> If a man is to preach this sutra,
> he should enter the room of the Tathagata,
> don the robe of the Tathagata,
> and sit on the Tathagata's seat,
> taking his place without fear among the multitude
> and preaching widely, with a fine understanding.
> Make great compassion your room,
> tender harmony and endurance of insult your robe,
> *the emptiness of the various dharmas your seat,*
> and so abide there, preaching the dharma.
> (*Hokkekyō* 2: 162)

4. Perhaps an allusion to *Guhishō*: "Again, there is a crucial matter with regard to composing poetry. *In the beginning stage, you must reflect from the shallow and enter the deep. But in the accomplished stage, you reflect from the deep and emerge into the shallow.* It is this that I have slowly come to understand as a product of many years of practice. That you must not reflect upon lofty and profound conceptions in the beginning stage is because you have not yet acquired the verbal facility in expressing even the ordinary. When you then attempt to study the lofty, since the grounding of your mind and character is weak, your thinking veers in the wrong direction and you fail in composing the poem. Therefore you must learn to compose from the shallow and gradually ascend the ladder into the profound" (p. 299). Note, however, that Shinkei's emphasis is not on the beginning stage, but on the accomplished one. This is how the *Guhishō* explains the accomplished stage:

> It is the nature of things that the mind must reach its level as a consequence of exhaustive training. What is meant by the adept composing from the deep to the shallow is that because he has quickly mastered and discarded the ordinary conceptions, his mind tends to first of all seek out the rare. And because he carries within him the mastery of the ordinary as a foundation, no matter how high his mind might soar, it never loses sight of the right way. Success is a matter of course. Again, when the lofty conception nevertheless escapes him, there is no pain in bringing the poem down gradually to the familiar level that he had earlier discarded. This kind of judgment is crucially important. (ed. Sasaki, pp. 299–300)

5. Kidō is of the opinion that the progression of Shinkei's thought from the preceding sentence to this one and the following is influenced more by *Shasekishū*, suppl. 9.3:

> The practice of the self-enlightened is called "examining the cause to reach the effect." Proceeding from the shallow to the deep [*asaki yori fukaki ni itarite*], it discards action and joys in nonaction, ignores form and affirms the formless. This is the formal course of training in the wisdom school. [In contrast, and this is the reverse course from deep to shallow] [t]he skillful means [*hōben*] of the buddhas who benefit others is called "the trace emanation from the original ground" [*honji suijaku*]; since it conveys the original ground's external workings, it exhibits form out of formlessness and

causes bodies to become manifest out of bodilessness. Such is the form that compassion takes in guiding the lowly [to salvation] by means of a variety of forms. (p. 467)

This *Shasekishū* passage continues with reference to the parable in the *Lotus Sutra* about the skillful means a wealthy old man used to lure his impoverished, ignorant son to assume his rightful heritage; and how the Buddha assumes even the form of evil demons and wayward gods to save beings.

6. *Shasekishū* V.A.1, "The Scholar of Perfect and Instantaneous Enlightenment Escapes the Demon-Disease": "Again, a former saint said, *'The formal icons of wood and clay spring from the Great Wisdom; the sutra scrolls of paper and ink flow from the Dharma realm.'* Truly the Buddha wisdom is temporally manifest in the carvings of icons, and the perfection of the Dharma realm manifests itself in the written sign. Therefore is it said that paying homage to Buddhist images of itself yields benefits, and chanting before the sutra scrolls unfailingly wards off pollution" (p. 201). This chapter starts with an anecdote about how a monk intones a long passage on perfect and instantaneous enlightenment from the *Makashikan* and becomes impervious to the pestilential demons sent to harass him. It is mainly about the virtue of chanting the scriptures, even without wholly comprehending them, to protect one from calamity and nurture the latent capacity for goodness in the mind.

7. *Shasekishū* VI.17, "On Preaching Based on Conditioned Discrimination": "The term 'wrongful preaching for a livelihood' [*jamyō seppō*] appears in the *Buddha Treasury Sutra* [*Butsuzōgyō*]; what is called 'conditioned discrimination' [*ushotoku*] refers to the same thing. People commonly think that conditioned discrimination means preaching with a view to receiving donations. In the sutra, however, wrongful preaching is to preach in ignorance of the true reality of all the dharmas [*shohō jissō*], on the plane of phenomenal and conditioned form, without also teaching the principle of ultimate formlessness [*musō no ri*]. It is because the truth of the noumenal and unconditioned [*mushotoku*] is not taught that it is called conditioned discrimination. *This method of preaching is a sin even worse than gouging out the eyes of all the beings in the three thousand Great Thousand realms.* It is a sin graver than that of someone who perpetuates the ten evils night and day, since people do not take him for a preacher. He may drive himself to perdition but he does not lead others there. Preaching on the plane of conditioned discriminations increases people's karmic burden of life and death and deprives them of the principle of true reality. Worse, looking to donations arises from the caring for fame and gain; it is not even worth speaking about" (p. 286).

Chapter Fifty

1. A probable source for this anecdote is *Guhishō* (ed. Sasaki, p. 292):

It seems that our predecessors as well did not find it easy to determine the ultimate style. In the Bunji era [1185–90], when the Retired Sovereign summoned several practitioners of the Way to the Sentō Palace to inquire about the requisite qualities of this style, my late father said: "The ultimate style must be poetry in the *ushin* mode. However, even within this mode, the configuration may be deep or shallow, tending to the source or [simply] its currents. What is called a poem in the ultimate style would be one that puts priority on a sound heart-mind [*tadashiki kokoro*] and does not use a clouded diction [*kotoba obomekazu*]; it is made to progress smoothly, yet this continuity is not predictable and gives it an arresting quality." Jakuren declared that the *yūgen* mode must be the ultimate in waka, and Kenshō that it must be the *reitei*. Ariie, Masatsune, Lords Ietaka and Michitomo had the same opinion as Jakuren, speaking for the *yūgen* mode. The Kyōgoku Regent [Yoshitsune], who often held fast to the gist of the words spoken by my father, declared that it must certainly be just as he had said, and the Retired Sovereign seems to have thought so as well, for he nodded in agreement. As for myself, I am not necessarily partial to my father's words, feeling that I must speak out my own opinion based on what I have acquired of understanding so far. Nevertheless, since it was my deep conviction that indeed the *ushin* mode in particular is without doubt the ultimate style in this Way, I held fast to it in giving my opinion on the matter.

2. In Teika's personal collection, *Shūi gusō*, the poem appears under the heading "A 100-poem sequence on Dwelling in Tranquility, composed in Bunji 3 [1187], winter, with Etchū-jijū [Fujiwara Yoshitsune]" (*Fujiwara Teika Zenkashū* 1:52, no. 308). The poem also appears as *FGS* 106 under Spring.

3. In Shōtetsu's individual collection, *Sōkonshū*, the poem (no. 3844) has the topic "Morning Glory [Flower]." (See p. 924, "Kaidai" in *ST* V, for the complete text of the poem; only the first two lines are included in the *SKS* base text.)

4. See Chapter 15 n. 3 above on the Three Vehicles, for the "voice hearers" and "condition perceivers" (*shōmon* and *engaku*) of the Way.

5. Part of a Chinese poem by Minamoto Tamenori that appears in the *Honchō reisō*, Part II, with the preamble, "A poem composed in the place of a man from Uryōtō, about his being moved by the imperial favor." In the *Shōtetsu monogatari*, Shōtetsu mistakenly ascribes Tamenori's poem to Po Chü-i, and cites Teika on its virtues:

> According to Teika, when pondering on a poem, you should always recite from the *Hakushi monjū* [the lines] "In the old village a mother weeping in the autumn wind; / At dusk in the empty travel inn, the rain seeps into the soul." When you do so, your spirit will become lofty and a good poem will emerge. Again, he said to recite "[You] in the Orchid Court in the flower season, beneath curtains of brocade, / [I] in Lu-shan in the rainy night, within the grass hut" [See *WRS* 555]. "At dusk in the empty travel inn, the rain seeps into the soul"—as one lies all alone in the travel inn, quietly rain starts to fall—this is truly a lonely feeling. [Teika's] poem "the autumn wind in the house that longs for her who is gone" [*naki hito kouru yado no akikaze*] is one with the spirit of such a time. (*SM*, 38, p. 213)

6. *SKKS* 1294. Love, "From the Poetry Contest in 1,500 Rounds." Lord [Fujiwara] Ietaka.

7. In the *Sangoki* (pp. 327–28), Ietaka's *omoi'ideyo* poem is indeed classified under the Demon-Crushing Style [*kiratsutei*], and the lines from Tamenori under its variant, the Stark Style [*gōrikitei*]. For the *Sangoki*'s explanation of this style, which it considers the highest, see Chapter 8 n. 6 above.

8. *Kirihioke* cites the two poems with the prefatory remark, "Among the *Man'yō* poems cited by Tsurayuki as truly possessing sincerity [*makoto*]" ([Teika?], *Kirihioke*, ed. Sasaki, p. 265).

9. *MYS* III.337. "A poem composed by Yamanoue no Okura on leaving a banquet." There is some textual variation from the original *Man'yōshū* version, but the thought is the same.

10. *MYS* III.343. "Thirteen poems in praise of sake, by the Commander of the Dazai Headquarters, Lord Ōtomo [Tabito]." Again, there is some variation from the *Man'yōshū* version.

11. After citing these two poems as those in the *Man'yōshū* that Tsurayuki praised for sincerity, *Kirihioke* continues:

> What could he have meant by that? Surely Tsurayuki said this as a mere illustration. It is hard to believe. Regarding the first, sake jar poem, when one thinks about it, of what earthly use would it be to actually put one's body in a sake jar until it rotted? It is quite an improbable poem. As for the other, while it does not suit our own time, it rings true nevertheless. No matter how frightfully raw the diction and effect might be, it is alright as long as its intention is earnest, such that we recognize some truth therein. Still, the rawness in the diction and configuration [*kotoba sugata no osoroshiki*] is unfortunate. About the sake jar poem, Kingo (Mototoshi) is reported to have said that it is deficient

> in both, being an ancient poem. When it comes to the *Man'yōshū*, one should be very careful in selecting and discarding words from it. ([Teika?], *Kirihioke*, ed. Sasaki, p. 265)

It is possible that Teika, or whoever the author of *Kirihioke* was, did not know the prose preface to Tabito's sake jar poem, contextual information that would have rendered the poem more "truthful" or "sincere." Shinkei's statement that Tsurayuki must have had his reasons for praising these poems apparently recognizes the contingent nature of critical evaluation. That is, either Tsurayuki knew more about the contexts of the poems than later ages or his criteria were different.

Chapter Fifty-One

1. "Keen-witted" (*rikon*): the base text has *yūgen* here. Since it is clearly an error, I have adopted the revised edition version. *SSG* rev. ed., p. 137.

2. Most likely an allusion to the following anecdote, "Dōin's Deep Devotion to Poetry," recounted in Kamo no Chōmei's *Mumyōshō*:

> In the depth of his devotion to this Way [of poetry], no one can match Lay Monk Dōin. Until he was seventy or eighty, he went on foot on monthly pilgrimages to the Sumiyoshi [Shrine] in order to pray that he might compose a superior poem—a truly admirable thing to do. Once at a poetry contest, when Kiyosuke as judge gave his poem the losing mark, Dōin made a point of going before him and, weeping earnest tears, expressed his disappointment. The host himself could find nothing to say and was moved to observe, "Never before have I encountered such earnestness." After Dōin turned ninety, perhaps because his hearing was failing, he would make it a point during poetry meetings to make his way up to the reciter's seat and stay very close. The appearance of this wizened old man bending his ears to listen as if there were nothing else in the world was truly extraordinary. It was after this lay monk had passed away that the *Senzaishū* was compiled. Even after his death, his reputation for deep devotion to this Way was such that Shunzei gave him priority and included eighteen of his poems. And when he appeared in a dream to tearfully express his happiness, Shunzei, it is said, was so moved that he added two more of his poems, bringing the number up to twenty. That was indeed the appropriate thing to do. (pp. 74–75)

3. Also an allusion to the *masuho no susuki* story from the *Mumyōshō*, translated below.

> On a rainy day, some men who shared kindred interests were gathered at someone's house, reminiscing about affairs of the past, when the question of what kind of reed the so-called *masuho no susuki* might be arose. "I do believe I've heard that there's a priest in the village called Watanabe who knows about it," an old man said rather vaguely. Priest Tōren was then present; after hearing this, his conversation became subdued and then without further ado, he said to the host, "Please loan me a straw raincoat for a while." The host was mystified but brought it out anyway. Having interrupted the conversation, Tōren put on the raincoat and straw sandals and was rushing out when the company, overcome by curiosity as they were, asked what he was about. "I'm going to Watanabe," he replied, "For many years now, I've been perplexed by this thing, and when I hear that there's someone who knows about it, how can I not go and ask him about it?" "Even so, wait until the rain has stopped," they admonished him, amazed as they were. But Tōren shot back, "How now, what nonsense you speak. Is life—his or mine—a thing that will wait for the rain's clearing? The rest you'll hear presently, in good time." And with those parting words, he was gone. That was the kind of splendid devotee he was. (pp. 48–49)

An explanation of the differences among three species of the reed grass *susuki* (*miscanthus sinensis*), of which the object of Priest Tōren's inquiry, *masuho no susuki*, is one, follows. The anecdote ends with the observation that the use of such items of old knowledge is common in waka practice, but one should not indiscriminately disseminate them. The anecdote appears also in *Tsurezuregusa* 188.

4. The base text has "Daini Takatō" here; I take "Minamoto Yorizane" from *SSG* rev. ed., p. 138. That version conforms to Shinkei's most likely source, the *Mumyōshō*:

> [Minamoto] Yorizane, Chamberlain and Lieutenant of the Left Gate Guards, was a great devotee of the art. So deep was his dedication to waka that he prayed at Sumiyoshi, "I shall offer up five years of my life; grant that I may compose a superior poem." Some years later, when Yorizane was suffering from a grave illness and prayers were held that he might live, the Sumiyoshi deity possessed the spirit of a woman in his household and spoke thus: "Have you forgotten what you said when you prayed to me that time?
>
> | | |
> |---|---|
> | konoha chiru | As dead leaves swirl |
> | yado wa kikiwaku | about my house, my anxious ears |
> | koto zo naki | cannot tell them apart; |
> | shiguresuru yo mo | nights when the chill rain falls |
> | shiguresenu yo mo | and nights when no rain falls. |
>
> That I granted you this poem was because you kept the faith and spoke of your devotion to me. This being so, I cannot save you this time." (pp. 95–96)

Minamoto Yorizane (1015–1044) was a member of the Seiwa Genji clan, son of the Governor of Mino Province, Yorikuni. The poem above appears in *Goshūishū* 382: Winter, "Falling Leaves Like Rain." He has a personal poetry collection called *Yorizane shū* or *Kojichū sakingo shū* containing some 103 poems. In a variant version in the *Fukuro sōshi*, Yorizane offers not only five years but all of his life (as in Shinkei's summary) to the Sumiyoshi deity. When shortly thereafter, he is inspired to compose the *konoha chiru* poem above, he does not recognize it as *the* superior poem and the deity has to appear in a dream to tell him so. See *Mumyōshō*, suppl. n. 125.

5. Perhaps a summary of the following passage from *Shasekishū* III.1:

> When the Great Teacher Shaka renounced his kingly rank, entered Dandoku Mountain [Skt. Dandaka], and bade Shanoku [Skt. Chandaka] return to the royal palace, Shanoku wept, saying, "You were born in the hallowed sanctum of the palace and sat above the upraised gazes of ten thousand men. How can you live alone in this mountain interior? I shall stay and serve you." But the Teacher made him go back to the palace, saying, "We emerge alone at birth, depart alone at death; why should we necessarily have company in the meantime? After I have achieved the supreme Way, all the sentient creatures will be my companions," and made him go back to the palace. And so indeed he became the Sole Honored One in the three realms, looked up to as savior by the four forms of life. (p. 136)

This passage goes on to extol the reasons for forsaking the worldly life.

6. The base text has "Dandokusen" here; the Sasaki text version, "Keisokusen," is the correct one. Keisokusen [Kukkutapada] is the mountain in Magadha Province where Kasyapa is said to have entered meditation, and where he waited to transmit the Buddha's robe and teachings to Maitreya, the buddha of the future.

Chapter Fifty-Two

1. The classification of waka into ten styles is an old convention in waka practice; it seems to have gained added momentum during the *Shinkokinshū* period, when poets like Teika and Rtd. Emperor Go-Toba evinced a deep interest in the distinct effects of various poems. Teika's principle of using old words for new conceptions seems to be what is reflected in Shinkei's understanding of the ten styles as marking distinctions not primarily in the poetic lexicon itself but in the gestalt (*sugata*, configuration, aesthetic shape, discursive effect) and quality of feeling (*kokoro*) generated by the poet's handling of the diction. In essence, the ten styles are manifold embodiments (*tei* is an ideograph indicating "body") of the mind.

2. A reference to a common metaphor originating from Buddhist discourse. To see only the finger pointing at the moon is to mistake the means for the end and thus merely repeat or reproduce the language without generating new effects and conceptions. It should be understood in relation to Shinkei's advocacy of mental cultivation (*shinji shugyō*) as the ground of poetic practice and inspiration, and also in relation to his concept of the three stages of poetic training, wherein the middle stage involves liberating the mind to produce "marvelous transformations" (*shimpen*) and manifold effects.

3. This is also a common saying. Bashō would later declare, affirming the liberating effects of the Danrin school for his own further development, "If Sōin had not come before us, our haikai would still be licking Teitoku's spittle" (as reported in *Kyoraishō*, p. 495). And again, "Do not even for a moment lick the spittle of the ancients; things transforming according to the shifting pulsion of the four seasons: everything is like this" (*Sanzōshi*, p. 546).

4. A clear indication of the contemporary Muromachi way of recognizing the differences among the three principal philosophies based on the belief that their source (*minamoto*, rendered as "wellspring" here) is one. In other words, this plurality is acceptable because of their supposed common origin. What could this mean? Is it merely a general comment that whatever is generated from the human mind is ultimately one, which means that differences are reducible or soluble? Both Buddhism, which espouses the proposition that forms are only provisional manifestations without an unchanging core, and Taoism with its idea of a primordial latent energy (the Tao) coursing through the cosmos, are susceptible to this kind of pluralist or eclectic attitude to distinct philosophies.

Chapter Fifty-Three

1. The story of Monju's visit to the ailing householder Yuima (Skt. Vimalakīrti) and the latter's superior wisdom in comparison to the Buddha's own disciples is told in the *Yuimagyō* (Skt. Vimalakīrti-nirdeśa sūtra), one of the oldest Mahayana texts, and considered the locus classicus of the belief that one can attain the virtues of reclusion without leaving one's own home, but merely dwelling in a simple hut there. Kamo no Chōmei's ten-foot-square hut in the Hōjōki is an allusion to Yuima's in this sutra. The famous dialogue between Yuima and Monju takes up, among other issues, the nonduality of purity and pollution that grounds the bodhisattva's enlightenment and practice of remaining in the dust of the world in order to succor others. Yuima is taken as an example of the principle that if the mind is pure, so is its earthly abode, wherever that might be. *T* 14:537–57; see also Burton Watson's translation, *The Vimalakirti Sutra* (New York: Columbia University Press, 1997).

2. Kyoyū (Ch. Xu You) is the subject of the following anecdote in *Mōgyū* 146, "Kyoyū's Gourd": "According to the *Biographies of Recluses*, Kyoyū was living in seclusion in Kizan. Lacking a proper vessel, he used his hands to scoop up water to drink. Someone sent him a gourd, and so he drank from it instead. Finished, he hung the gourd on a tree. When the wind blew, it made a creaking noise, and so he threw it away." *Mōgyū* 1: 388; see *Tsurezuregusa* 18, pp. 106–7 (Kenkō, *Essays in Idleness*, trans. Keene, p. 18), for Kenkō's version of this story. It was apparently current until the Edo and Meiji periods, since Buson and Sōseki alluded to it in their haiku.

3. Gan Kai (Ch. Yan Hui, 513–482 B.C.E.) was Confucius's best-loved and most virtuous disciple; the teacher's grief at his early death was inconsolable. The allusion is to *Rongo* (the *Analects*): "Confucius said, 'What wisdom is there in Yan Hui! A bowl of rice, a gourdful of broth, and living in some narrow lane. Others could not endure such deprivation. But Hui—his joy in the Way does not falter. He is wise indeed, is Yan Hui'" (*Rongo* VI.129).

The *Rongo* passage is repeated verbatim in *Mōgyū* 435 (2: 829) under the title "Gan Kai's

Wicker Tray and Gourd." The mention of "grass" in *Sasamegoto* might be an allusion to this Chinese verse, *WRS* 437 (p. 161) by Tachibana Naomoto: "The gourd is often empty, and the grass rank at Gan En's lane; / Barred by dense growth of goosefoot and soaked in the rain is Gen Ken's door." It is interesting to note that the *Wakan rōeishū* base text used in the *NKBT* series, now in the Imperial Household, was a gift from Shinkei's disciple, Kenzai, in 1495, according to its colophon.

4. *Mōgyū* 403 (2: 781), "Sonshin's (Ch. Sun Ch'en) Straw Pallet": "The *Sampo getsuroku* says: Sonshin's common name was Genkō. He was of a poor family and made his living weaving mats. He was learned in the *Odes* and *Documents*, and became the head official of civil affairs. All he had to protect him from the cold winter nights was a bundle of straw. At day's end he went to bed on it, and put it away in the morning." *Mōgyū* [Ch. *Meng qiu*], ed. Hayakawa Mitsusaburō, 2 vols. [*SKT* 58–59] (Meiji Shoin, 1973). This anecdote is also cited in *Tsurezuregusa* 18.

5. Kai Shisui (Ch. Jie Zhitui), a native of Jin in the Spring and Autumn period, was in the service of Duke Wen. Being inadvertently passed over in the distribution of rewards, he went off and secluded himself in Mianshan. Wanting to summon him back, Duke Wen set fire to the mountain, but unfortunately Zhitui perished in it.

In the *Keiso saijiki* (Ch. *Jinchu suishi ji*), a one-volume work by Zong Lin of the kingdom of Liang (552–57) describing Chu rituals and customs from beginning to end of the year, there is the following reference to Zhitui: "In search of Jie Zhitui, Duke Wen of Jin burned the forest where he was hiding, but Jie Zhitui held on to his pure-minded reserve and, refusing to come out of the mountain, died clinging to a tree. Moved to pity, Duke Wen forbade the making of fires on that day, and this became known as the custom of the Cold Meal" (cited in *SSG*, p. 192, headnote 5). This ritual of abstinence is held on the 105th day from the winter solstice, including the two days before and after; since no cooking fires may be lit, only cold food is eaten.

6. That is, accorded him fame. As Ijichi observes (*SSG*, rev. ed., p. 144, nn. 6 and 7), the description of Saigyō as a beggar refers to the fact that wandering priests like him had to depend on alms from others. Again, the "wise world" is most likely a comment on *Shinkokinshū* poets like Teika, Shunzei, and Go-Toba, who recognized Saigyō's greatness and gave him the highest number of poems in that anthology.

7. Suzuki, "Mikkan," III, p. 30, cites an allusion to a passage in the *Yuimakyō* where Rāhula (the Buddha's natural son, later one of the ten great disciples) explains to the Buddha why he refuses his request to visit the ailing—but apparently very keen-witted—Vimalakīrti (Mañjuśrī, the wisest of the disciples, goes instead; see n. 1 above). Apparently Rāhula had been bested in a previous encounter with Vimalakīrti. Asked by the wealthy sons of Vaisali what profit there could be in reclusion that he had renounced his kingly rank for it, Rāhula had attempted to explain that it had the advantage of accruing merits, but Vimalakīrti came by and admonished him thus: "Rāhula, you must not respond by preaching the advantage of accruing merit through reclusion. Why? Because reclusion is that in which there is neither profit nor merit. In the realm of conditioned action [*ui no nori*], it may be said that there is profit, there is accruing of merit. But you undergo reclusion for the sake of unconditioned action [*mu'i no nori*]. Within the realm of unconditioned action there is neither profit nor merit." And Vimalakīrti goes on to characterize reclusion as, among other things, abiding in nirvana, a disinterested state where there is no "I" and nothing is received, since conventional distinctions and partial views have been overcome through meditation practice (*zenjō*). See *T* 14: 475. 541c. For a fuller context, see Watson, trans., *The Vimalakirti Sutra*, pp. 48–49, or Robert A. F. Thurman, trans., *The Holy Teaching of Vimalakīrti: A Mahāyāna Scripture*, pp. 31–32.

8. Suzuki, "Mikkan," III, p. 30, cites the following passage from the *Hokke gengi* (The Subtle Meaning of the *Lotus*), scroll 8.*jō*, as Shinkei's source here: "If one interprets the letter in this way, then without taking the scroll in one's hands, one is reading the sutra; no words issue from one's mouth, yet one is everywhere chanting the scripture. Though the Buddha is not preaching, he always hears the Indian sounds; with no conscious thought in his mind, he illumines the dharma world everywhere." The passage is part of Chih-i's long and complex explanation of the word *kyō* (sutra) as immanent in phenomenal form or the six pollutions. Thus if one meditates on the color of black ink (that is, writing, the letter) for instance, one realizes that it is a concrete manifestation of the so-called ten wonders of the secondary gate (one of the two major divisions of the Lotus Sutra, the other being the primary gate). The logic here is ultimately based on the Tendai principle of the nonduality of ultimate reality and phenomena, as evident in the common slogan, "There is not one color, not one fragrance, that is not within the middle way."

9. *Rongo* XV:410: "Confucius said, The gentleman works for the Way, he does not work to eat. Till the soil, and there may be famine therein. Cultivate learning, and there may be remuneration therein. But the gentleman will grieve for the Way, he will not lament his poverty."

10. *Kanro kaerite baidoku may be kanro oyobi baidoku* (there is a one-stroke difference between the graphs for *kaerite* and *oyobi*), in which case, the source might be *Daichidoron*: "The language of ultimate truth is sweet dew that nourishes the person; empty and false words are poison that kills the person. One should know that both the sweet dew and the poison depend on the tongue within" (cited in *SSG* Suzuki, p. 204). In "Mikkan," II, pp. 34–35, Suzuki notes that the same Daichidoron passage is cited in *Yasuyori Hōbutsushū* II. 4.

11. There is a similar line in *Shasekishū* I.7, "The Gods Honor Devotion to the Way" (for complete English text of this section, see Morrell, trans., *Sand and Pebbles*). This chapter consists of anecdotes showing that the Shintō deities do not always grant the prayers of monks if they lack a true desire for enlightenment, if they carry bad karma from previous lives, or if granting the prayer would obstruct their progress toward enlightenment. The quotation occurs in the context of a story about a poor monk in the north valley of the Eastern Pagoda (Enryakuji) on Mount Hiei. For a hundred days he goes on pilgrimage to Hiyoshi Shrine in order to improve his lot. He receives a sign that the deity will fulfill his request; however, he is instead evicted from his quarters and forced to share quarters with others in the south valley of the Western Pagoda. Again he turns to the deity for help, and this time the latter reveals the following:

> "Due to a miserable karma from a previous existence, you are not destined for fortune in this one. I arranged to move you from your cold quarters in the north valley of the Eastern Pagoda to warmer quarters in the south valley of the Western Pagoda, intending to grant at least that one small favor. Anything more is beyond my powers." And so the monk resigned himself and ceased thereafter to lament his lot. Thus is it said, "Not even divine power can overcome the force of karma." (p. 74)

12. This is culled from a passage in *Hokkekyō* 1.86 (chap. 2, "Expedient Devices"); see Chapter 18 n. 3 above for the version in *Scripture of the Lotus Blossom*, trans. Hurvitz.

13. *Kunshishū*, p. 11: "Again it is said, a snake reveals an inch of its body, and one knows its size; a man utters a single word, and one knows him to be foolish or wise." The saying is also to be found in the *Huainanzi*, acc. to Ijichi, *SSG* rev. ed., p. 146, n. 1.

14. *Rongo* XIV:338 (p. 306): "The Master said, The virtuous will be sure to speak, but all who speak do not necessarily possess virtue. The humane are sure to be courageous but the courageous are not necessarily humane."

Chapter Fifty-Four

1. Mokuren, or Mokkenren (Skt. Maudgalyāyana), one of the Buddha's ten great disciples, said to have been foremost in miraculous powers, reportedly made offerings to a priest to save his mother who was then suffering in the hell of hungry ghosts. This was the foundation of the practice of *Urabon-e* (or *Obon*), the festival for appeasing the souls of the dead, still observed today in Japan in the summer.

Shasekishū II.10, "The Value of Karmic Affinity to the Buddhist Dharma," includes the following passage, which clarifies the thought here; it is part of an argument drawing a distinction between the precepts' emphasis on strict observance of rules and prohibitions, and the sutras' more liberal approach of turning violations into an occasion for doing good works and thus acquiring merit for the future.

> In the sutras, though flaws may be present, one is encouraged to look upon them as an opportunity for future benefits. In the *Jūringyō* [Sutra of the Ten Wheels], we find this teaching: "*Though he be a sinning priest and blind, wandering from tavern to tavern led by his wife on the one arm and carrying his child in the other arm, if you show him the reverence due to a Sharihotsu and a Mokuren, you will surely acquire merit.*" (p. 129; emphasis added)

This chapter continues with other quotations from the sutras to the effect that, as long as he has the correct views or belief, even a flawed priest who breaks the precepts might benefit one in the future. The apparent triviality of motivation in entering the priesthood or nunhood nevertheless becomes the occasion, the "karmic affinity" (*kechien*), for later enlightenment.

2. *Kanmuryōjukyō* (Sutra of Contemplating the Buddha of Immeasurable Life): "The Buddha-mind is that of great compassion; by this unconditioned compassion, he nurtures the various sentient beings" (*SSG*, p. 194, n. 5).

3. The "six perfections" (*rokuharamitsu*) are the following: *danna*, giving (of goods or services to others); *shira*, observing the precepts; *sendai*, patience and endurance; *biriya*, energy and assiduousness; *zenna*, meditation or concentration; and *hannya*, wisdom (Skt. *dāna, śīla, kṣānti, vīrya, dhyāna, and prajñā*, respectively).

4. This statement perhaps reflects a passage in the *Shasekishū* II.10, the same chapter cited in n. 1 above. It is an explanation of the rationale behind the precepts.

> The precepts are grounded on strict observance, emphasize present benefits, banish the roots of social evils, and prevent violations. Consequently, although virtue may be present, if it is mixed with error, it is placed under restraint. Admonition is given if even one or two faults out of ten are present. *It is said that pure-minded priests must not worship a buddha made from treasures acquired through the wrong means.* The *Nehangyō* [*Nirvāna Sūtra*] says: "Due to the strict restraints necessitated by the precepts, the person who makes offerings, though unknowingly, to the errant priest who hoards impure treasures will even so fall to hell. The pure-minded priest must not drink from that [sullied] river." In sum, the smallest fault is subject to restraint and no benefit is allowed from it. This is in order that the Buddhist teaching may flourish, and so that enlightenment and the fruit may be achieved. (p. 129; emphasis added)

Chapter Fifty-Five

1. Yao and Shun were the legendary sage emperors in the *Shokyō* (Ch. *Shu jing; Book of Documents)* and *Shiki* (Ch. *Shi ji*; *Records of the Grand Historian*) of the Confucian canon. Because Yao's own son was untalented, he chose the lowly but virtuous Shun to be his successor. The *Shokyō* describes Shun's circumstances thus: "His father is obstinate, his mother a loudmouth, and his younger brother arrogant; but he pacifies them all by filial piety and does not oppose them by force" (1.28). *Shiki* has a similar passage in the "Annals of the Five Emperors" chapter.

2. The same saying appears in the epilogue of Zeami's Nō treatise *Fūshikaden* (Style and the Flower [1418]): "This separately recorded oral transmission represents the important teachings on the art as handed down in our house to only one person in each generation. It must not be passed on to someone—though he be an only son—who is lacking in ability. For it is said, '*A house is not the house as such; it is that which is transmitted through it that makes the house. It is not the man as such, but what he knows, that makes the man.*' This surely represents the utmost attainment of the marvelous flower of a myriad fortunes" (p. 297; emphasis added).

3. Quoted verbatim from *Rongo* (XV.407, p. 355); it is another way of stating the immediately preceding citation on the relation between the received tradition in the art and the person who carries it on by revitalizing and extending it.

4. Also from *Rongo*, V.107 (p. 115): "Zigong asked: How did Kong Wenzi come to be called Wen? Confucius replied: He had a keen intelligence and loved to study; *he was not ashamed to inquire of those beneath him*. It is for this that he was called Wen." Wen, signifying "a man of letters," was the posthumous title given to Kung Yu, an official of the state of Wei. It was an ancient practice in China to award posthumous names appropriate to people's character and achievements.

5. The progression of Shinkei's thought here seems to follow *Jikkinshō* III ("One Should Not Be Contemptuous of Others") 12:

> One should never be contemptuous of other people. Even the wise person will have one flawed thought in a myriad. Even the dullard will have one right thought in a thousand. It is this one in a thousand that one should learn, this one in a myriad that one should banish. Therefore is it said that the sage breaks out of the gate of emptiness, and the saint finds his measure in a lowly peasant. This means that the good person does not hold others in contempt and is not ashamed of inquiring and learning from the lowly. Thus *the Yellow Emperor believed the words of a herd boy, and Tokushū bent to the admonitions of a peasant.* In this way, there is always something to learn from the talk in the alleys, the tales in the wayside. (*Jikkinshō*, ed. Nagazumi Yasuaki [Iwanami Shoten, 1942], p. 96; emphasis added)

The reference to the Yellow Emperor's trust in the words of a mere herd boy is an allusion to an anecdote in *Zhuangzi* 24, *Xu Wugui*. The Yellow Emperor and his attendants set out to visit the Great Cloud and lose their way. They come upon a herd boy tending his horses and ask him for directions, amazed that he should know the way. The Yellow Emperor then proceeds to ask the herd boy how to govern the realm, at which he replies: "Governing the empire I suppose is not much different from herding horses. Get rid of whatever is harmful to the horses—that's all." The Emperor is so impressed that he addresses the boy as "Heavenly Master" and twice bows his head in obeisance (*The Complete Works of Chuang Tzu*, trans. Watson, pp. 265–66).

6. This line would seem to be related to the quotation from *Rongo* V.107 appearing earlier in this chapter; see n. 4 above.

7. The story of Taigong Wang is told in chapter 32 of the *Shi ji*; he was an obscure recluse whom King Wen personally brought to court; it was by his sage advice that the Zhou defeated the Shang. This was a popular anecdote among Muromachi literati. For an allusion to it in Shinkei's renga, see *HF*, pp. 218–19.

8. *Jikkinshō* III.16: "Wise Ministers and Sage Priests of Japan and China Who Rose from a Lowly Birth": "Gyōgi Bosatsu was born in Ōtori Village, Izumi Province; Kōbō Daishi came out of Tado District, Sanuki Province. It may be said that both were no different from the common people of the countryside, but each earned a name for being an avatar [of the Dharma]. *The Minister Kibi was the son of the Lieutenant of the Right Gate Guards Kunikatsu*; the Awata Minister of the Left was the son of Tamba Provincial Governor Ariyori. Both their

fathers were of lowly rank, but so esteemed were their own talent and capabilities that they attained to the exalted office of Minister" (*Jikkinshō shinshaku*, ed. Okada Minoru [Daidōkan Shoten, 1939], p. 164).

9. *Jikkinshō* III.14 "The Origins of Ōe Tokimune": "When the Midō Regent [Fujiwara Michinaga] was on his way to some place, he became curious about a boy who was leading the packhorse while holding a book with the other hand, reading. He had the boy brought before him and noted the double pupil in his eye and the extraordinary intelligence of his face. Shortly thereafter, he summoned him and had him educated as the ward of Masahira. In time, this boy became known as Ōe Tokimune, a scholar of wide talents and vast learning who served His Majesty, transmitted the way of a Doctor of Letters, and lived to a wise old age, disseminating knowledge of the care of the body" (*Jikkinshō shinshaku*, ed. Okada, pp. 158–59).

10. Chūzan was a priest of the Kōfukuji; according to the *Honchō kōsō den* (Biographies of Eminent Monks), he was very reclusive and had no taste for office. But Emperor Murakami (r. 947–968) appointed him to represent the six Hossō sects in the great debate between Hossō and Tendai (*SSG*, p. 195, n. 21.

11. This is a quotation from the *Kombeiron* (see *T* 46: 781a), a treatise by the ninth Tiantai patriarch Zhanran (J. Tannen) (711–782). Among Japanese sources, the same passage is cited in the *Kanjin ryakuyōshū* by the Tendai prelate Genshin (942–1017) and Mujū's *Shasekishū* I.3 (p. 65), among other sources. Genshin explains it thus: "There is a vast difference between the karmas of the most saintly and the lowest of the worldly, but these are at base the same. One should realize that the mutual proximity of the affect and divine response within the several intermediate realms is based on this fact" (*SSG*, p. 266, suppl. n.74). In *Shasekishū* I.3, the *Kombeiron* passage is cited within an exposition of the doctrine of nonduality or nondiscrimination culled from the *Makashikan* and Esoteric teaching:

> In the deep mind of Esoteric teaching, since all the ten worlds are manifestations of the formless Dharma Body, in truth the body of Emma [King of Hell] and the form of the Vairocana are contained within the four kinds of Dharma Body, are endowed with the five wisdoms, the boundless wisdom. Once having entered into this inner realization, without altering their bodies, Emma and the demons and beasts will without fail open up their mind-ground to the latent Dharma Body in their nature. *Therefore an ancient worthy has said: "The conditions of body, mind, and environment plunging one into the deepest hell are wholly within the mind of the Most Venerable One; the Vairocana body-and-ground is not beyond a single thought of the deluded."* (p. 65; emphasis added)

Chapter Fifty-Six

1. For Fujiwara Takanobu (1142–1205), see "Biographical Notes." Takanobu was successively appointed Provincial Governor of Kazusa, Echizen, and Wakasa, and ended his official career as Provisional Master of the Right Capital, with the Senior Fourth Rank, before taking the tonsure in 1202 at age sixty.

2. For Priest Jakuren (secular name Fujiwara Sadanaga), see "Biographical Notes." Jakuren held Junior Fifth Rank and was an official in the Central Affairs Ministry when he took the tonsure around 1172, abandoning a secular career while still in his early thirties, in contrast to Takanobu.

3. There is a longer version of this anecdote in "The Pair Takanobu and Sadanaga" in Chōmei's *Mumyōshō* (ed. Hisamatsu, pp. 75–76); for a translation, see *The Mumyōshō of Kamo no Chōmei and Its Significance in Japanese Literature*, trans. Hilda Katō, *Monumenta nipponica* 23, 3–4 (October 1968), pp. 396–97.

4. *Rongo* IX.227: "The Master said, there are young shoots that spring forth but do not come into flower; there are those that flower but bear no fruit" (pp. 210–11).

5. *Rongo* VI.122: "The duke Ai asked, 'Who among your disciples best loves learning?' Confucius replied, saying, 'There was Yan Hui; he loved learning. His anger was not misdirected, and he never committed a fault twice. Unfortunately, he was short-lived and died. Now he is no more. And I have yet to hear of anyone who loves learning as he did'" (p. 128). According to "The Biographies of Zhongni's [Confucius's] Disciples" (§7) in the *Shi ji*, which quotes the passage above from *Lunyu*, "When Yan Hui was twenty-nine years old his hair was extraordinarily white, and he died young." In §17, we find regarding Li, Confucius's son: "Kongzi [Confucius] begot Li. His other name was Bo Yu. Bo Yu died before Kongzi, at age fifty" (*SSG*, suppl. n. 75).

6. *Kunshishū*, pp. 10–11; there is a similar line in *Zhuangzi* 20: "The Mountain Tree," in Taigong Ren's advice to Confucius on how to escape death and disaster: "*The straight-trunked tree is the first to be felled; the well of sweet water is the first to run dry.* And you, now—you show off your wisdom in order to astound the ignorant. . . . That's why you can't escape!" *The Complete Works of Chuang Tzu*, trans. Watson, pp. 213–14.

7. Kidō (*SSG*, n. 5) cites a line from the *Huainanzi*: "The roots of the tree that bears fruit a second time necessarily become worn out."

8. *Rongo* XIV.378: "Yuan Rang crouched, waiting [for Kongzi]. The Master said, 'When a child, without respect for his elders; a grown man, he distinguished himself in nothing; *having reached old age, he does not die—this is to be a thief.*' And he tapped him on the shins with his staff" (p. 335).

9. *Tsurezuregusa* 7: "We cannot live forever in this world; why should we wait for ugliness to overtake us? The longer man lives, the more shame he endures. To die, at the latest, before one reaches forty, is the least unattractive" (Kenkō, *Essays in Idleness*, trans. Keene, p. 8).

10. Kyōun (or Keiun, ca. 1293–1369) and Ton'a (1289–1372) were, along with Kyōun's father Jōben (ca. 1265–1344) and Kenkō (ca. 1283–1352), the author of *Essays in Idleness*, two of the so-called "four deva kings of waka" (*waka shitennō*) in the late Kamakura period who were leading disciples of the Nijō-school master, Tameyo (1250–1338). Ton'a, however, surpassed Kyōun in worldly fame, enjoying the patronage of Shōgun Ashikaga Takauji and Regent Nijō Yoshimoto. For more information on these two rivals, see "Biographical Notes."

11. As if to confirm the veracity of this anecdote, there is not a single poem by Kyōun in the extant text of the *Shinsenzaishū*, but four by Ton'a are included. This imperial anthology, the eighteenth, was compiled by Nijō Tamesada and presented to Emperor Gokōgon (of the Northern Court) in 1359. Originally conceived under a 1356 directive by the Shōgun Takauji, it established a precedent for the bakufu's direct involvement in the most hallowed poetic tradition of the imperial court. It also marked the ascendancy of the Nijō school just ten years after the preceding *Fūgashū* anthology compiled by the rival Kyōgoku school. The Nijō dominance and political alliance with the bakufu would subsequently continue through the final three imperial anthologies until the *Shinzoku Kokinshū*.

12. For the early eleventh-century poet Nōin, see "Biographical Notes." Kosobe, where he died, is in Takatsuki-shi, Osaka.

13. Kidō observes (n. 18) that this saying also appears in *Taiheiki* 39; see *NKBT* 36: 431, where it is clearly meant as a criticism of Ōuchi Hiroyo (d. 1379), a strong ally, then traitor to the Southern Court when he joined the bakufu forces in 1363. Awarded the provinces of Suō and Nagato, he indulged in extravagant displays of wealth in the capital and was praised by all for it.

Chapter Fifty-Seven

1. This is from Yan Yuan's (or Yan Hui's) famous admiring lament on the surpassing virtue of his master's teachings and skill in means in *Rongo* IX.216:

> Yan Yuan heaved a sigh and lamented, saying: "*Ever higher as I gaze up at it, ever harder as I chisel away at it;* I see it before me, and yet in a trice it is behind me. By orderly method, the Master skillfully leads me on. He broadens me through knowledge of letters, restrains me through practice of propriety. When I would quit, I cannot, for though already I have exhausted my talents, it seems to yet stand tall and distant there. And though I would follow, there is no way at all to do so."

The line quoted in *Sasamegoto* also appears in other treatises and in the Preface to the seventh imperial anthology, *Senzaishū* (1187–88), compiled by Shunzei: "In truth that which is harder as one chisels away at it, and higher as one gazes up at it, is none other than the Way of Japanese poetry" (*Senzaiwakashū*, p. 63).

2. Possibly from Laozi, *Daode jing* 64:

> Work at things before they come to be;
> Regulate things before they become disordered.
> A tree whose girth fills one's embrace
> sprang from a downy sprout;
> *A terrace nine stories high*
> *arose from a layer of dirt;*
> *A journey of a thousand leagues*
> *Began with a single step.*
> (*The Daodejing of Laozi*, trans. and ed. Philip J.Ivanhoe
> [New York: Seven Bridges Press, 2002], p. 67; emphasis added)

However, there is a similar couplet in Bai Juyi's *Zoku zayū mei* (Sequel to Motto Kept Close By), which is closer in wording: "A thousand miles starts right underfoot, / the tall mountain rises from a speck of earth" (cited in Ijichi, *SSG* rev. ed., p. 150, n. 12). Kidō (*SSG*, p. 198, n. 1) notes that the *Kokinshūjo chū* cites the same lines from Bai Juyi.

3. Possibly from the *Baopuzi* (J. *Hōbokushi*), a Jin Taoist text, which says, "Those who seek it are as the hairs on an ox; those who capture it are as the kilin's [Chinese unicorn's] horn" (*SSG*, p. 198, n. 7).

4. *Chuci* (J. *Soji*) VII: "Qu Yuan said, 'The whole world is muddled, I alone am clear; all the people are intoxicated, *I alone am sober*. That is why I was exiled.'" Qu Yuan was a loyal minister of Chu during the Warring States period. He attempted to resist the depredations of the oppressive Qin and restore the fortunes of Chu but fell into disfavor due to slanders by the political opposition. Exiled to Hunan, he subsequently committed suicide. The *Chuci* is a Han dynasty compilation of the works of Qu Yuan, his disciples, and later Chu poets who modeled themselves on him.

5. *Rongo* VI.148: "Zigong said, 'Say that someone contributed widely to the benefit of the people and was able to succor them, what about him? Could we call him virtuous?' The Master said, 'Why make a case of virtue? He is surely a sage, is he not? *Even Yao and Shun had their worries on this score.* Now, then, in wishing to establish himself, the man of virtue establishes others; in wishing to accomplish things himself, he lets others accomplish theirs. The ability to take one's exemplars from what is near—this may be called the way of virtue.'" (p. 148) The same line occurs in *Rongo* XIV.377 in reply to Zilu's question about the superior man. Confucius replies that such a man "cultivates himself, that the hundred clans may be at ease. He cultivates himself, that the hundred clans may be tranquil. *Even Yao and Shun worried about this*" (p. 334).

6. (Ch. Wumen Huikai, 1183–1260), *Mumonkan* (Ch. *Wumen guan*, The Gateless Barrier, 1228), Case 6, "The Buddha Holds Out a Flower": "When Shakyamuni Buddha was at Mount Grdhrakuta, he held out a flower to his listeners. Everyone was silent. Only Mahakasyapa broke into a broad smile. The Buddha said, 'I have the True Dharma Eye [*shōbō genzō*], the Marvelous Mind of Nirvana [*nehan myōshin*], the True Form of the Formless [*jissō musō*], and the Subtle Dharma Gate [*bimyō no hōmon*], independent of words [*furyū monji*] and transmitted beyond doctrine [*kyōgai betsuden*]. This I have entrusted to Mahakasyapa" (*Two Zen Classics: Mumonkan and Hekiganroku*, trans. Katsuki Sekida, p. 41; Japanese inserted).

Kidō (*Kenkyū*, p. 128, n. 12) notes that this famous *nenge mishō* (a flower held out and a smile) anecdote occurs in *Shakushi keikoryaku* (Ch. *Shishi jigulüe*) (1354), a historical account of Buddhism in China from ancient times to Sung. The *Shakushi* itself, however, cites the anecdote (*T.* 49.753b) from a sutra called *Daibontennō monbutsu ketsugi-kyō*. Suzuki ("Mikkan," III, p. 31), whose annotation I have followed here, gives the *Mumonkan* source first, and then cites Yamagishi Tokuhei to the effect that the said sutra, though presumed to originate in India, was clearly a later product, most likely of the Zen sect in China. Yamagishi speculates that the anecdote was inserted into Buddhist history in order to concretely illustrate the central Zen concept of wordless transmission (*ishin denshin*) and to give canonical legitimation to Mahakasyapa as the Buddha's chosen heir to the subtle teachings of Zen.

7. "Only from one mind to another" (*tanden*), that is, since the teaching cannot be transmitted through language; "subtle signs" (*mitsuin*), forms and configurations described by the ten fingers, by which buddhas and bodhisattvas variously signify their vows. Kidō also cites a passage from *Shasekishū* III.1 (ed. Tsukudo, v. 1, p. 118) that is similar to the passage cited by Suzuki from VB.10, "The Avatars Delight in Poetry," in the *NKBT* edition. See the commentary for a translation of the said passage.

Chapter Fifty-Nine

1. "A host of Cao Zhis firing off verses in the space of seven paces" (*shichiho no sai*, lit., "talent in seven paces" in the text) refers to exceptional ability in rapid poetic composition. It is an allusive reference to the following tale of sibling rivalry in *Shishuo xinyu* (A New Account of Tales of the World), by Liu Yiqing:

> Emperor Wen of Wei [Cao Pi] once ordered the Prince of Dong'a [his brother Cao Zhi, whose poetic talent he envied and hated] to compose a poem in the space of seven paces, saying that if the poem was not completed by then, the maximum penalty would be carried out. Straightaway, the prince responded by reciting a poem, saying, "Boiled beans are taken to make a soup / Strained lentils utilized for stock / While stalks beneath the pot are blazing up / The beans within the pot are shedding tears; / Originally from the same root grown / For one to cook the other, why such haste?" The emperor looked profoundly ashamed. (Cited in *SSG*, suppl. n. 79, p. 267)

Shinkei's point is that the rapidity of composition in popular renga sessions raises the specter of a man composing as if his very life depended on it.

"Mu Wang's eight swift horses" renders *happiki no koma*, an allusion to the eight prize horses used by Mu Wang of Zhou to ride the length and breadth of his realm. Whipping up such horses would spur them to even greater speed, and in the context of this passage in *Sasamegoto*, would be both unwise and unnecessary.

2. Probably recollected from *Wakan rōeishū* 755: "When the fleet horse in front of the carriage falls ill, the drudge horse pulls confidently ahead, / *When the hawk is quiet on his perch, the sparrows soar*" (emphasis added). This is a couplet from a poem by Xu Hun (791–854?), "Sent to the talented Li Yuan of Tangtu," saying in effect that when a man of superior intelligence like Li Yuan lives in obscurity, others of middling ability get ahead for lack of competition.

3. A similar passage occurs in *Shasekishū* III.3, "The Dialogue Between Gonyūbō and His Younger Sister, the Lady-in-Waiting": "Knowledge and practice are distinct from each other. Therefore, the *Sho* [*Shokyō*, Book of Documents] says, 'The difficulty lies not in knowing, but in doing it well'" (p. 149). The *Sasamegoto* passage is possibly an expansion of the concept in the canonical Chinese source.

4. *Shasekishū* VIII.23, "On Having One's Teeth Pulled Out," cites a relevant passage from the *Zōbō ketsugi kyō*, a sutra believed to have originated in China before the Sui period, which gives an account of the degeneration of Buddhist teaching a thousand years after the Buddha Sakyamuni's demise and advocates compassion and almsgiving (p. 176, n. 10). The passage (as quoted in *Shasekishū*) says: "*Subsequent to my death, at the end of the age of counterfeit Dharma [zōbō], Buddhist halls, pagodas, and icons will fill the waysides,* while people will lack in the spirit of reverence. *It is the sign of the demise of my Dharma*" (p. 365; emphasis added).

5. A canonical source might be this *Daijikkyō* (Skt. *Mahasamnipata-sutra*) passage cited in *Shasekishū* II.10: "The *Daijikkyō*, using an analogy to various treasures, says: 'When gold, silver, and such are lacking, even tin is considered a treasure. When there is no one who has achieved the Way, and no one who observes the precepts or even breaks them, then one must give offerings even to someone who, his head shaved and wearing a bit of surplice, bears the form of a priest'" (p. 130).

6. "The one whose mind is truly awakened for all time is he who has truly imbibed the teachings." *Shasekishū* III.1:

> Again when the Great Teacher Tendai Chisha preached the great stillness and insight [*makashikan*], in teaching practitioners of the perfect and sudden [enlightenment] the attitude of seeing into the mind, he explained that one brings about the true form [*jissō*] from the start, concentrating on seeing the one thought in three thousand [*ichinen sansen no kan*], and attaining to the principle of the middle way of color and fragrance; in this way, by means of unconditioned wisdom, one brings about the realm of the formless [*muen no chi o mote, musō no kyō o enzu*]. The ever-abiding marvelous realm is formless and utterly still. The insightful wisdom that corresponds to this marvelous realm must of necessity be mindless and unconditioned [*mushin muen*]. Thus an ancient has said: The Way, being mindless, suits the man; the man, being mindless, suits the Way. Now, what is called marvelous also has the name "that which cannot be thought." If it can be thought and measured, then it is undoubtedly an illusion, and not marvelous. Therefore the *Daichidoron* says: A marvel of all marvels—who will have faith and receive it? *The one whose mind is awakened for all time [hisashiku hosshinsuru], it is he who will have faith and receive it.* And what does "for all time" signify? When no distinctions arise with regard to all phenomena—that is called "for all time." (ed. Tsukudo, 1: 116; emphasis added)

7. *Kunshishū*: "To see with the eye, and be unable to grasp it with the mind—this is like drawing pictures on water, like carving on ice; labor is expended without effect" (p. 9; emphasis added).

8. Giba (Skt. Jivaka) was a famous healer in Rajagrha in ancient India during the time of Sakyamuni; so was Henjaku (Ch. Bian Que) in China during the Warring States period. (See Shiki, Henjaku Sōkō retsuden 45, for his biography.)

9. The reference is to the story of Duke Huan (685–643 B.C.E.) and the wheelwright in *Zhuangzi* XIII, "The Way of Heaven" (*The Complete Works of Chuang Tzu*, trans. Watson, pp. 152–53), to the effect that books are merely the chaff and dregs of men of old; they cannot transmit what is essential, which cannot be put into words. The thread of Shinkei's thought here, however, indicates that he also had *Yakumo mishō* VI in mind, particularly this passage:

> Composing poetry is something that arises from the heart-mind; it does not depend upon another's teaching. Therefore, the father may be an adept, but the child will not necessarily inherit his mind. The master may have bone-deep mastery, but the disciple will not reflect his style. Long ago a wheelwright, hearing Duke Huan of Qi reading from a book, asked him, "What is it?" Duke Huan replied, "This is called a book; it was made and handed down by men of old."

The wheelwright then said, "Well, what a useless thing that is! It might contain their words, but cannot possibly manifest their minds. It is no more than the chaff and dregs of those men of old. There is much old lore also about the making of wheels. I know in my mind everything about how it is done, but there are no words to teach it to someone else. I am now seventy, but I have not yet transmitted it to my son. Surely, this rule holds in book-reading also." And it is the same for poetry. (pp. 73–74)

10. Kidō's gloss on *tōki* (*SSG*, p. 200, n. 17) is basically the same as for *zuiki* (in accord with the [being's] capacity); I render it as "the meeting of minds," following the Buddhist usage, understanding, of course, that the Buddha or teacher is able to turn his mind to suit the student's capacity, while the student opens his to meet the teacher's.

11. From the *Lotus Sutra* II, "Expedient Devices" (*Hokkekyō* 2.82–3), where the Buddha, having proclaimed and praised his profound and subtle dharma, stops short of revealing what it is. For the second time, Sariputra entreats him to do so, and again the Buddha refuses, saying,

Cease, cease! No need to speak.
My Dharma is subtle and hard to imagine.
Those of overweening pride,
If they hear it, shall surely neither revere it nor believe in it.
(*Scripture of the Lotus Blossom*, trans. Hurvitz, p. 28)

12. From *Zhuangzi* VIII, "Webbed Toes": "The long is never too much, the short is never too little. *The duck's legs are short, but to stretch them would worry him; the crane's legs are long, but to cut them down would make him sad.* What is long by nature needs no cutting off; what is short by nature needs no stretching" (trans. Watson, pp. 99–100). The same *Zhuangzi* passage is also cited in *Shasekishū* V.A.8, "The Dialogue Between the Scholars: An Ant and a Tick": "Therefore it is said that one should not cut the crane's legs, or stretch the duck's legs. This means that each should abide in his own level, observing the Way of heaven and practicing transformation through nonaction, with a heart unafflicted by joy and sorrow" (p. 218).

13. Kidō has no gloss here, and neither does Suzuki. A similar idea is found in the *Yuimagyō*: "Wisdom without expedient means is bondage; wisdom with expedient means is liberation. Expedient means without wisdom is bondage; expedient means with wisdom is liberation" (*The Vimalakirti Sutra*, trans. Watson, p. 70).

14. For Reizei Tamehide (d. 1372), see "Biographical Notes."

15. The canonical source for this famous line is *Daode jing* (J. *Dōtoku-kyō*) 49: "The sage has no mind of his own. He takes as his own the mind of the people" (*Lao Tzu: Tao Te Ching*, trans. D. C. Lau [Harmondsworth, Eng.: Penguin Books, 1963], p. 110). It is also cited at the conclusion of *Shasekishū* V.A.12, "The Profound Principle in the Way of Poetry":

The sage has no mind; he makes the mind of the myriad things his mind. The sage has no body; he makes the body of the myriad things his body. Thus the sage has no words; he makes the [words of the] myriad things his words. How can the words of the sage not be dharma words [*hōgo*]? If they are dharma words, then they must contain truth; if they contain truth, then they must be totally upholding [sōji], and being so, then they are darani. Considered with this attitude, the fact that deities and buddhas use waka undoubtedly means that they are indeed true words [*shingon*]. (p. 225)

Here the *Daode jing* passage is used to ground the argument, ultimately based on the principle of nonduality, that waka can function as bearers of Buddhist truth, since the buddha or sage uses the beings' own mind and language to teach effectively. In another *Shasekishū* chapter, VI.5, "On Long Sermons," the same passage occurs again, but in the context of a criticism of a priest who preached an excessively long sermon during the dedication ceremonies for a new temple hall, despite the fact that music and dance performances were also scheduled, and so the audience tired of it and wished he would leave. The story continues,

> "The sage has no mind; he makes the mind of the myriad things his mind." In all things one should pay attention to the feelings of others and act in accord with the time and circumstance. With regard to the Buddhist principle as well, one can expound it at length when the audience has a desire to listen and the place is a hall where the mind can be quiet. But at a dedication with music and dance, one should have shown more sensitivity. (p. 265)

16. From the *Lotus Sutra* II, "Expedient Devices" (*Hokkekyō* 1: 106), *Scripture of the Lotus Blossom*, trans. Hurvitz, p. 34; emphasis added:

> Within the Buddha-lands of the ten directions
> There is the Dharma of only one Vehicle.
> There are not two, nor are there yet three,
> *Save where the Buddha, preaching by resort to expedients*
> *And by merely borrowing provisional names and words,*
> *Draws the beings to him.*
> In order to preach Buddha wisdom
> The Buddhas come into the world.

17. Neal Donner and Daniel B. Stevenson, trans., *The Great Calming and Contemplation: A Study and Annotated Translation of the First Chapter of Chih'i's Mo-ho chih-kuan* (Honolulu: University of Hawaii Press, 1993), pp. 74–78.

18. For "the Three Bodies of the Buddha" (*hotoke no sanjin*), see Chapter 18 n. 4 above. The "Three Truths of the Empty, the Contingent, and the Middle" (*kū, ke, chū no santai*) refer to the three characterizations of the nature of phenomena or reality in Tendai thought. They are "empty" in lacking an unchanging essence and identity; "contingent" or provisionally real in that they come into existence through circumstance; and are said to have a "middle" existence from a nondualistic perspective that does not reify either their emptiness or contingency. In the "perfect fusion of the three truths" (*ennyū santai*), the three levels of existence are viewed as present in each one, undifferentiated and beyond characterization.

Chapter Sixty

1. In Esoteric teaching, the Metamorphosis Body (*tōrushin*) refers to the changing forms—human, animal, demonic, divine—that the Dharma Body assumes according to the necessities of circumstance, in his task of guiding the beings to salvation; in general, the Metamorphosis Body constitutes the fourth Buddha Body, in addition to the Three Bodies.

2. THE OAK TREE IN THE GARDEN KŌAN. Kidō and Ijichi both cite the Jōshū (Zhaozhou, 778–897) chapter of *Gotō egen* (Ch. *Wudeng huiyuan*, Compendium of the Five Flame Histories) (comp. 1253) as the source for this Zen koan, but it also appears as Case 37 in the *Mumonkan*:

> A monk asked Jōshū, "What is the meaning of Bodhidharma's coming to China?" Jōshū said, "*The oak tree in the garden.*"
>
> Mumon's Comment: If you understand Jōshū's answer intimately, there is no Shakya before you, no Maitreya to come.
>
> Mumon's Verse
>
> Words cannot express things;
> Speech does not convey the spirit.
> Blocked by words, one is lost;
> Blocked by phrases, one is bewildered.
>
> (*Two Zen Classics*, trans. Sekida, p. 110; emphasis added)

In both sources, the question is phrased, "What does it mean to say that the founding teacher [Bodhidharma] came west [to China]?" and it also appears thus in at least two other *Sasamegoto* texts. This is a famous koan, known as *teizen no hakujushi* (The Oak Tree in the Garden). In their edition of *Bukkyō jiten* (p. 585), Nakamura et al. explain the case thus:

> This is not simply a matter of the oak tree in the objective realm. It is precisely the mental state of great enlightenment of Shakuson [the Buddha Sakyamuni] becoming one with the bright morning star; that is, when one empties the self and becomes selfless within the personal experience of yoga, then everything becomes the self. From the plane of the so-called "identity of thing and self" [*motsuga ichi'nyo*] or "nonduality of person and world" [*ninkyō funi*] (the disappearance of the subject-object distinction), one becomes the Bodhidharma himself. This is a concretely embodied demonstration, in words involving the total personality, of the [Bodhidharma's] intention in coming west.

This entry in the dictionary ends with a citation of precisely this passage from *Sasamegoto*.

Mumon Ekai's *Mumonkan* is a collection of forty-eight Zen koans, to which Ekai added his own commentary and verses. It was first introduced to Japan in 1254, when Ekai's Japanese disciple Shinji Kakushin (1207–1298) came home after six years' study in China and made it the basis of his own teaching. Due to its manageable size and simple format, the *Mumonkan* was very popular as a Zen beginner's text; reprints and commentaries on it were more numerous even than for the *Hekiganroku*, the other popular Zen source in Japan.

3. The provenance of this sequel to the koan above is not clear; it suggests the possibility that as a pedagogical text, these brief verbal conundrums were open to variation and expansion according to the inspiration of the particular circumstance. Here, Shinkei surely means to indicate that it is unsound to become attached to the letter of Jōshū's words (what "the oak tree in the garden" *means*); that is, to hold him to his earlier words is to miss the temporality of speech as well as the spirit of the reply, which is precisely as interpreted in Ekai's verse in n. 2 above. This is pointedly borne out by the verse couplet that immediately follows the anecdote in the *Sasamegoto* text.

4. Suzuki ("Mikkan," II, p. 36) cites two passages from Mujū's *Zōtanshū* and remarks at the end that the idea in them is the same expounded in a passage in the *Makashikan* Introduction by Shōan Kanjō (Ch. Zhang'an Guanding) on perfect and sudden enlightenment (*endon*). The two passages Suzuki cites from *Zōtanshū* are the following, with emphasis added to highlight the same or similar passage in *Sasamegoto*:

> I.12: Between the worldling and the saint, there is no high and low. That is certainly to attain the principle. The treatise says: In the dharma world, there is no distinction between body and essence. *All the teeming phenomena and the myriad forms are the Buddha Body.*"
>
> IX.1: "When *sanmaya* is taken in a broad sense, it will be seen that the myriad things of this world must be the *sanmaya* of the buddhas, bodhisattvas, and sage heavenly kings. One would not know it from looking, but there is nothing that is outside the meditation [*sanmai*] of the Buddha. Everything, all the dharma world, is the Buddha Body, that is, the Dharma Body. Again, it is the radiance of serenity [*jakkō*]. If you go astray about this point, then all the myriad realms turn to realms of delusion, but if you attain it, each color and fragrance becomes the Middle Way [*chūdō*]. The treatise says, In the dharma world, there is no difference between body and essence. *All the teeming phenomena and the myriad forms are the Dharma Body. I do not see any dharmas outside the Buddha wisdom* [bodai], *therefore I bow in reverence before each grain of dust.*

The *Zōtanshū* was written by Mujū Ichien, the author of *Shasekishū*, when he was nearing eighty years. Conceived as a memento for his disciples, it is believed to be his final work. More difficult and containing fewer stories than the other book, *Zōtanshū* is a compendium of Mujū's encyclopedic knowledge of the various Buddhist doctrines, while maintaining its ground in the philosophy of the Middle Way and everywhere informed by his characteristic rationality and pragmatic attitude about the efficacy of religious belief in alleviating human suffering.

5. Perhaps an echo of *Shasekishū* I.3, "Praying to the [Shintō] Deities for Release from Birth-and-Death," which includes a long speech by Abbot Kōken of Miidera explaining his somewhat unorthodox practice of Shintō worship by an appeal to the native deities as provisional manifestations of the Dharma Body and to the Buddha's infinite compassion, which adopts any guise in order to succor the beings. As this chapter in the *Shasekishū* probably, in my opinion, influenced Shinkei's thinking in this chapter, it is worth reading the following passages, the last of which reveals the reasoning behind the adaptation of Shintō deities into the Buddhist pantheon, as well as an incipient nativism:

> It is my lot that in studying the sacred teachings of the exoteric and esoteric schools in order to grasp the essential way to [obtain] release from birth-and-death, my own power [*jiriki*] is too weak, my understanding shallow. Without the power of superior karmic affinity, it would be difficult to accomplish my desire for release. Consequently, I have gone so far as to inquire about the major and minor deities even in remote areas and provinces, not to mention those in the capital. I write down the names of the various deities, great and small, in all of Japan, and petition them here in this one-mat space, all the while reciting the *Heart Sutra* thirty times and chanting Shintō spells as offerings for their pleasure [*hōraku ni sonaete*]. My practice is none other than to trust in the skillful means of the deities who soften their light [*wakō no hōben*] to lead me to liberation. The reason is that the skillful means of the Great Sage [the Buddha] depends upon the country, upon the occasion, and has no fixed pattern. "The sage has no unchanging mind; he takes the minds of the myriad people as his own"; likewise, the Dharma Body is no fixed body; it takes the bodies of the myriad phenomena as its own. This being so, the ten worlds constituting the formless Dharma Body are at once the totality of the Vairocana. In terms of Tendai thinking, the karmic causation constituting beings and their environment—that is, the three thousand dharmas of the ten worlds—are all the manifold virtues of the Dharma Body. For this reason, the latent virtue in the ten worlds manifests itself in merit-producing action, and by means of the Buddha's vow to assume an infinite variety of forms and bodies, the salvation of the nine worlds from delusive passions is effected. (p. 64)

Kōken here continues by referring to the Esoteric teaching that the fourfold mandala corresponds to the ten worlds of the Dharma Body. In the process of realizing its inner self-nature, it generates the benefits of great compassion as its external operation. Such are the marvelous workings of a marvelous body; like the waves that are inseparable from the water, there is no dependent origination apart from the wholly Real [*shinnyo*]. Kōken then goes on to identify the Shintō deities as manifestations of the same Dharma Body:

> This being so, in the ancient west [India], it became manifest in the form of buddhas and bodhisattvas and saved it. Our own country, however, is but grains of millet dispersed in a remote land. For such obstinate, strong people who are ignorant of causation and without faith in the Buddha's teaching, the empathetic, unconditional compassion [of the buddhas and bodhisattvas] provides the responsive workings of the metamorphosing Dharma Body, appearing in the form of evil demons and heretic gods, manifesting itself in the bodies of poisonous snakes and fierce beasts in order to pacify the violent, evil tribes and convert them to the Buddha's Way. Therefore, one must not valorize the Buddha bodies that arose in the other countries while belittling the corresponding forms they took in our own land. Ours is a divine land marked by the traces of great manifestations. What is more, we are all their descendants; the karmic fate that made us one with them in spirit is by no means shallow. If we look to the foreign worthies, their response will, on the contrary, be distant. Therefore nothing is better than to trust in the skillful means by which the deities soften their light in response to the capacity for good in us, praying to them to lead us to the essential path of liberation from birth-and-death. (p. 64)

Here follows an analogy between the Dharma Body and its manifestations to statues of men and beasts made of gold; one might see qualitative differences if one concentrated on their external forms, but their substance is one and the same—it is gold.

> By means of formless gold, the Dharma Body crafts the various forms of the ten worlds and the fourfold mandala in accord with beings' natures. If one ignores the form and keeps faith with the

substance, is there any that does not share in the Dharma Body's benefits? *The Wisdom School holds the lofty as most excellent, but the Compassion School holds the lowly as most marvelous.* It is like midgets comparing heights; the shortest one wins. The blessing of the Great Compassion is such that the Metamorphosis Body draws especially close to those of inferior capacity, benefiting obstinate beings in a compassion exceedingly excellent. Therefore, believing that the deities who soften their light to become as mere dust [*wakō dōjin*] are verily the utmost expression of the several buddhas' compassion, I have carried out my practices, unusual as they are, for many years now. (pp. 64–65)

6. From a hymn to the Pure Land in *Kangyō jōzengi*; it occurs in the following passage: "*The joy of quietude and nonaction in the West / is finally to float free of what is and what is not,* / With great compassion burning as incense the mind, to wander in the Dharma realm, / A Buddha incarnate blessing all things equally, with no partiality to any one" (cited in *SSG* rev. ed., p. 157, n. 17).

7. THE TEN STAGES OF CONSCIOUSNESS. In Consciousness Only (*yuishiki*) teaching, every being is held to have eight kinds of consciousness (*hasshiki*). The first six are based on the five sense organs—eye, ear, nose, tongue, and body—and the mind that processes these sensations and their objects through language. The seventh and eighth, *manashiki* (Skt. *mano-vijnana*) and *arayashiki* (Skt. *alaya-vijnana*), are deeper levels of consciousness discovered in yoga or meditation practice. The seventh, *manashiki* (lit., thinking), is self-consciousness, the self's attachment to its objects of thought, its identification of itself with the mental processes of the *arayashiki* as explained below; it is an awareness whose operation is incessant, whether one is sleeping (i.e., in dreams) or awake, and condemns one to the karmic cycles of life-and-death. The eighth is the root-consciousness of individual existence; *alaya*, etymologically, "dwelling place," is the storehouse of the seeds that germinate into the various phenomena or dharmas of the "external" world; these dharmas, in turn impressing themselves on or perfuming the storehouse consciousness, generate other seeds there, which persist even as they germinate and die from moment to moment. *Alaya* consciousness, therefore, being the seat of an endless process of cause and effect, of determinations of karmic past, present, and future, is the consciousness that grounds and maintains the mind and body as an integral existence, and according to the Consciousness Only school, all phenomena are a product of its operation. (Based on the entries on *hasshiki*, *manashiki*, and *arayashiki* in *Bukkyō jiten*, ed. Nakamura et al.)

In addition to the eight stages of the Yuishiki school noted above, the Hossō sects of the Tendai and Kegon schools added a ninth stage, the *anmarashiki* (Skt. *amala-vijnana*, the "unpolluted consciousness"), also called *shinnyo*, which was held to be the root source of all phenomena, as in the phrase *shinnyo engi* ("dependent origination from the Tathagata"). The Hossō sect, however, holding to the idea of *arayashiki engi* ("dependent origination from the storehouse consciousness," i.e., that all phenomena arise from the *araya*) claimed that the mind is already free of pollution from the eighth, or *araya*, stage itself, so that this ninth stage is unnecessary. (*Bukkyō jiten, ed.* Nakamura et al., p. 205, under *kushiki*; also Ui, p. 196.)

The tenth stage (*jisshiki*) exists in the Esoteric (Mikkyō) doctrine, as the last of the ten expounded in the *Shakumakaen-ron*, a treatise attributed to Nagarjuna (ca. 150–250 C.E.) but now considered to be of Chinese Kegon-school origin from the eighth century. It builds on the attempt of the *Daijōkishin-ron* to synthesize the *arayashiki* with the *nyoraizō*. The *Shakumakaen-ron* was particularly important to Kūkai, who utilized the esoteric elements in it to elevate the Shingon school as the highest within the Mahayana tradition. In the process of using this treatise as his source for systematizing Shingon doctrine, Kūkai influenced the simultaneous development of the Esoteric school and *hongaku* belief (*Bukkyō jiten*, ed. Nakamura et al., pp. 382–83).

Also called *kenritsudaya*, the tenth stage is when all phenomena—sentient and nonsentient—are seen as being of one and the same mind (*issai isshin*) (*Bukkyō jiten*, ed. Ui, pp. 460–61). This stage also refers to *nyoraizō* (Skt. *tathagata-garbha*), the presence of buddha-nature, or immanent potentiality for enlightenment, in all beings. By the addition of the ninth and tenth stages, Esoteric doctrine implicitly points out the inadequacy of the *arayashiki* as the ultimate source of enlightenment, since it is also the source of delusions and consequently has to be transcended by progress to the highest stage, in which dualisms and such conditioned distinctions no longer obtain. This is of course Shinkei's point in this chapter of *Sasamegoto*.

8. *Genke no chi o okoshite, genmō o nozoite nochi, kyōchi tomo ni maboroshi ni mo arazu.* In *Bukkyō jiten*, ed. Ui, p. 250, and ed. Nakamura, p. 233, *genke* is the magician's trick of transforming objects or conjuring visions; it is the second of the ten analogical illustrations of the principle of emptiness. *Kyō* in *kyōchi* is sphere, environment, the realm of the activity of the six organs of sensation and consciousness; *chi* is intelligence, mental functioning. I have rendered *kyōchi* twice as "sense-fields and intelligence, object and subject" for the sake of clarity, since the point is to erase the distinction between the two: the subject/object or mind/world dichotomy renders both illusory; it is only by cognizing their interdependency, and thus their emptiness as autonomous entities, that each attains to the Real.

9. UNCONDITIONAL COMPASSION. *Tada muen no jihi o okoshite, musō no kyō o enzuru nomi narubeshi.* "A compassion without conditions" or "unconditioned compassion" renders *muen no jihi*, which refers specifically to the Buddha's compassion, characterized as nondiscriminatory as regards its object, identical or equal as regards its measure and quality, and thus absolute. This level of compassion, being unconditional and unconditioned, is necessarily grounded in the truth of emptiness. I found the following passage from *Makashikan* on unconditioned compassion useful:

> The process [lit., cause and condition] of achieving the contemplation of the Middle involves, summarily put, five points: (1) [it is for the sake of] unconditioned compassion; (2) fulfillment of the [bodhisattva's] generous vow; (3) pursuit of the Buddha's wisdom; (4) study of the great expedient means; and (5) assiduous devotion to religious practice. First, unconditioned compassion is in effect the Tathagata's compassion. It is of the same substance as the Real [*jissō to dōtai*] and does not bear the mark of sentient beings; consequently, it is not an emotional attachment. It does not bear the mark of nirvana; consequently it is not stilled in emptiness [*kūjaku ni arazu*]. Since it is not stilled in emptiness, it is not a compassion conditioned by the dharmas. Since it is not compassion as emotional attachment, it is not induced by sentient beings. It does not bear the mark of two sides; consequently, it is called unconditioned. The *Nirvana Sutra* says, "Generating the Tathagata is called nongenerating" [*nyorai o enzuru wa nazukete muen to iu*]. It covers the dharma world everywhere, removing the basis of suffering, giving the ultimate joy. (2: 61–62)

In a supplementary note, Kidō cites the passage from *Shasekishū* III.1 (ed. Tsukudo, p. 116) below to gloss the *Sasamegoto* statement under consideration here; it includes a reference to the *Makashikan*'s explication of sudden enlightenment (*endon*):

> Again, in expounding the great stillness and insight, when the Tendai Daishi Chisha taught the method of contemplating the mind [*kanjin*] to the practitioners of sudden enlightenment, he would explain that one induces the Real [*jissō o enji*] from the very start and, focusing on seeing the three thousand in a single thought [*ichinen sanzen*], attains to the principle of the Middle Way in each hue and fragrance. Consequently, one is inducing the space of the formless [*musō no kyō*] by means of an unconditioned wisdom [*muen no chi*]. The marvelous space of the eternal abode [*jōjū no myōkyō*] is formless and stilled in suchness [*jakunen*]. And the contemplating wisdom that corresponds to this marvelous space is necessarily mindless [*mushin*] and unconditioned.

The source for the direction of Shinkei's thought here, and of the *Shasekishū*, may be the following passage from *Makashikan*, I.B:

> Again, "the right" is not three, it is not one, nor is it either three or one; yet is it nevertheless three and one. For this reason, it is called the "inconceivable right" [*fukashigi no ze*]. Again, "the right" is neither a constituted dharma [*sa no hō*] nor a buddha, not something made by heavenly being or asura. The space of the ever-abiding is formless, the wisdom of the ever-abiding is unconditioned. By means of unconditioned wisdom, one generates the space of the formless, and the space of the formless corresponds to unconditioned wisdom. Space and wisdom are an undifferentiated oneness, though one says "space and wisdom" [*kyōchi*]. For this reason it is called unconstituted [*musa*]. (*Makashikan* 1.62; for other translations of this passage, see Donner and Stevenson, trans., *The Great Calming and Contemplation*, p. 201; and Thomas Cleary, trans., *Stopping and Seeing: A Comprehensive Course in Buddhist Meditation by Chih'i* [Boston: Shambhala, 1997], p. 38)

Chapter Sixty-One

1. THE SEVEN TREASURES. The names for these seven moral and spiritual qualities are apparently analogies to the "seven treasures," or precious stones (gold, silver, lapis lazuli, crystal, agate, ruby, and cornelian), mentioned in Buddhist literature descriptions of the forests of jewels in the Pure Land. Or again, an analogy to the treasured possessions of the kings (*tenrin jōō*, lit., "wheel-turning sacred king"; Skt. *cakra-vartin rajan*) who rule the world by righteous government: the golden *cakra* wheel, white elephants, blue horses, sacred jewels, cherished women, ministers of the treasury, and great generals. Promoting the spread of Buddhist doctrine by preaching is called turning the wheel.

These seven moral qualities appear in the *Nirvana Sutra*, VII, as the seven sacred treasures (*shichi shōzai*) of someone capable of achieving the fruit of Buddhist sainthood. Mujū's *Shōzaishū* (1299) explains the significance of each of these seven qualities.

LEARNING, MORALITY, AND WISDOM. The passage below from *Shasekishū* X.B.1, "About the Possessing Spirit Who Understood Buddhist Teaching," explains the distinction, among the seven, between learning and wisdom, and underscores the crucial importance of observing the moral precepts in the attainment of wisdom:

> When you listen to what this spirit says, it seems to be in accord with the sacred teaching. It is true that learning and wisdom are two separate things. *There are seven sacred treasures: faith, precepts, shame, repentance, learning, wisdom, and renunciation.* What is called learning is knowledge of the sacred scriptures and secular classics and the ability to distinguish between Mahayana and Hinayana interpretations. Nevertheless, there are those [among the learned] who are motivated by fame and profit, are self-opinionated and arrogant, and, lacking both in true wisdom and actual practice of the precepts, become attached to things; they may be called learned, but not wise. They will surely fall into the path of delusion. A scripture says, "A person may have beauty, family, and learning, but without morality and wisdom, he is akin to the birds and beasts. Another may be placed in a lowly, scorned position barely noticed by anyone, but in possessing wisdom and morality, he may be called a superior person." It is also said, "Success or failure in the various endeavors depends upon upholding the precepts; whether or not one recognizes the buddha in oneself is a matter of whether the vehicle one takes is laggard or swift." Liberation from evil habits depends on the power of observing the precepts; enlightenment in the Buddhist Way responds to the discipline of meditation and insight [*jōe*]. This has all been determined in the sacred teaching. Thus the *Ryōgon* [*Daibutchō shuryōgonkyō T.* 945], in speaking about grasping the Buddhist teaching, says regarding the significance of the three immovable determinations: "The precepts signify mastering the heart-mind; the precepts are a means of generating meditation, and it is through meditation that wisdom arises." (p. 433)

2. This list of the seven "thieves"—that is, injurious and harmful—factors in the Way of Poetry seems to be mainly instances of improper behavior that would disrupt the requisite

mental concentration and continuous flow of verses during the renga session; they are also demonstrations of a lack of seriousness in attitude toward poetry. Their presence here would seem to indicate that dozing, inebriation, and gossiping were not uncommon occurrences at the popular and informal renga events.

What I have rendered as "intellectual arrogance" is *shōtoku*, properly, a Buddhist term synonymous with *satori*, enlightenment, or the direct and self-evident experience of the ultimate Buddhist truth. In poetics, however, it is used to refer to intellectual pridefulness and self-affectation. In the *Mumyōshō*, Chōmei quotes his teacher Shun'e: "Never, never, though you may have arrived at the point where people will permit you much, be so carried away by intellectual arrogance that you compose poems with an air of self-affectation. This is something you must never do" (p. 68). The reason is that such self-satisfaction leads in time to a degeneration of one's poetic powers; therefore, it is best to compose always with the heart of a beginner. It is poetry of subtle simplicity that best stands up to the test of time.

As for "rich people" (*tokunin*, rendered as "wealth" in the translation), unless they were serious poets, their ample resources could turn the session into a mere excuse for a lavish and ostentatious party. There was much status and prestige involved in hosting a renga session; it was an opportunity for the wealthy to show off their rare and expensive furnishings and art objects. And there are *kyōgen* plays poking fun at men of moderate means who would go so far as to beggar themselves for the prestige of sponsoring a session. No doubt Shinkei would also have seen the harm in the giving of prizes at these sessions. Kenkō, for instance, tells a satirical story about a Jishū priest walking home after spending all night at a renga session; suddenly, a beast leaps at his throat in the dark, and scared out of his wits, he falls into a stream. But when they drag him out, it is noticed that he is still clutching to his bosom the fan and boxes that he had won in the renga party. And the beast turns out to be his own dog come to meet him (*Tsurezuregusa* 89, p. 163–64; *Essays in Idleness*, trans. Keene, pp. 75–76). In sum, Shinkei apparently thought that material considerations had a disruptive effect on the quality and seriousness of the poetic pursuit.

Chapter Sixty-Two

1. Perhaps inspired by this line from the *Shinjinmei* (Ch. *Xinxin ming*, Inscription on Conviction in the Mind): "[The Great Way is] perfect like the Great Emptiness; it lacks in nothing and is in nothing superfluous" (*T.* 48.376b). The *Shinjinmei* is a 584–character poem attributed to the third Zen patriarch Seng Can (J. Sōsan, d. 606); it is a paean to the Great Way, an ultimate state of mind liberated from all partiality and dualistic thinking, and abiding in the realm of suchness. Strongly marked by native Taoist thought, the work wielded a great influence on the formation of early Zen Buddhism in China and has since been a popular text for recitation also in Japan. This passage resonates with the verse from the *Dainichi-kyō* cited in Chapter 43; see also n. 12 there.

2. Suzuki ("Mikkan," II, p. 37) cites this passage from *Makashikan* VIIB as possible source: "Next, you enter the first abode, tear apart the darkness of ignorance and gaze on the buddha-nature. According to the ten abodes chapter of the *Kegonkyō*,' . . . One who contemplates in this way swiftly achieves the merits of all the several buddhas; from the very first time that the mind awakens, it senses the true enlightenment, comes to know the nature of the ultimate reality of all phenomena and, concentrating on the wisdom body, *does not depend on others for enlightenment*'" (*Makashikan* 2: 147). The passage occurs at the end of the section explaining the eighth of the "ten vehicles for contemplating the dharmas" (*jūjō kampō*), which is the necessity of being vigilantly aware of one's level of meditational attainment in order to ensure further progress.

SELF-ENLIGHTENMENT WITHOUT A TEACHER. BY MIND TRANSMIT THE MIND. Suzuki also cites *Shasekishū* X.1 (X.B.2 in the *NKBT* ed.), "The Man Who Understood the Essential Message of Buddhist Teaching":

> In Zen priest Yixing's [683–727] *Commentary on the Dainichi-kyō*, which records the oral transmission from Subhakarasimha [637–735; J. Zenmui Sanzō], it says: "Passing on the wisdom of enlightenment [*bodai*] to someone is not a matter of giving him the nuts in one's hand. To receive it, he must necessarily have the wisdom of self-enlightenment without a teacher [*mushi jigo no chie*]. The miracle of attaining to the mind is not something that can be handed down." Among the sayings of the Great Teacher of Kōya [Kūkai, 774–835] is this: "The true purpose of esoteric teaching is to transmit the mind by means of the mind [*kokoro o motte kokoro o tsutau*]. Words [*monji*] are but rubble; words are only the dregs." Such may be read in the *Shōryōshū* [Kūkai's Literary Anthology]. As the Tendai Great Teacher Chisha [Zhiyi] said when he transmitted the three kinds of meditation [*shikan*] from Nangaku [Ch. Nanyue], "As for words, one may transmit them, but *enlightenment does not depend on others* [*shō wa hoka ni yorazu*]." Thus the truly autonomous enlightenment is attained by oneself alone. In Yixing's *Commentary*, as well, it says, "When a person sustains an injury, that he is in pain is unquestionable. But to actually know that pain, one would have to suffer the injury oneself." The founding teacher said, "This mind may be said to be like drinking water and finding out oneself the cold or the heat of it. You may learn from others that water is cold or warm, but how can you know it without actually drinking it yourself? Access to the meaning of true reality is precisely like this." (ed. Tsukudo, 2: 147–48; the *NKBT* ed., p. 442, does not include the rest of this passage after the first citation from Yixing)

3. WHEN THE GREAT WAY IS ABANDONED. Laozi, *Daode jing* XVIII: "Great Tao rejected: Benevolence and righteousness appear. / Learning and knowledge professed: Great hypocrites spring up. / Family relations forgotten: Filial piety and affection arise. / The nation disordered: Patriots come forth" (Laozi, *Tao Te Ching*, trans. Stephen Addiss and Stanley Lombardo [Indianapolis: Hackett, 1993], p. 18). Shinkei's quotation varies from the original in the second line: *Daichi idete daigi nomi nari* instead of *chie idete daigi ari*; the general sense is the same.

Continuing from the *Shasekishū* X.1 passage translated in n. 2 above, we find the passage from *Daode jing* interpreted by Mujū thus:

> Again, Laozi says, "When the Great Way is abandoned, there is benevolence and righteousness; when knowledge and intelligence appear, there are great lies." In the age of the Great Way, everyone observes the way of filial piety, so behavior is spontaneously filial in action and intention. For this reason, no one teaches it, there are no words for it. Just as there is no medicine where there is no illness, so there are no words called benevolence, righteousness, propriety, wisdom, and conviction. It is when there are unfilial children and erring men in the world that the teaching of benevolence and righteousness appears. Heshang'gong [a Taoist and important commentator on Laozi in the reign of Han Emperor Wen] says: "'When the Great Way is abandoned, benevolence and righteousness appear' means that in the age of the Great Way, with filial children in every family and loyal retainers in every house, benevolence and righteousness do not appear. But when the Great Way is abandoned and in disuse, evil and errancy arise; in a word, there is the necessity for a way to transmit benevolence and righteousness. 'When knowledge and intelligence appear, there are great lies' means that because learned and intelligent men put down virtue and elevate words, put down the substance and elevate the language [*bun*, here, rhetoric], people are led to study the language and so engage in falsehoods. And so the Five Emperors dispensed laws, and Cangxie invented writing, which is not like the Three Emperors' tying knots on rope or cutting notches on wood." When people's hearts were simple and pure, the marks they cut on wood or tied with rope were not wayward. But in the age of columns of written signs, the marks became lies. In the same way, were it not for the presence of worldly delusion, Buddhist teaching would not arise; everything would be wholly still, tranquil, and pure; there would be no traces of profane or holy. Because the wayward beings generate all kinds of deluded views, giving rise to various fixations, unavoidably, writing

> appeared and verbal explanations arose in order to guide them. Therefore the Lotus says: "Only in order to draw and guide the beings does he [the Buddha] resort to provisional names and words." (ed. Tsukudo, 2: 148)

4. MAKE OF YOUR MIND A MIRROR: THE NONDUALITY OF SUBJECT AND OBJECT. Perhaps influenced by the following passage from *Shasekishū* III.2, "About Sincere Words Evoking a Response." It is preceded by a brief anecdote about the stewards of two households, both famous but equally ugly, so that people nicknamed them "the monkey stewards" of Yoshimizu and Mimuro. One day, the Mimuro steward was sent on an errand to Yoshimizu. There, some naughty people decided the two should meet each other and waited around to see their reaction. Then the Yoshimizu steward appeared, and seeing his counterpart, stepped forward and smiled. "Well, what do you think," the people asked. "Why, it's just like seeing myself in a mirror!" he replied. At this, everyone laughed in high spirits and thought of him with affectionate regard. Under the circumstances, his words sounded quite splendid.

> As an ancient said, "You make a mirror of bronze to adjust your cap and robe; make a mirror of someone to discover your own virtues and faults; make a mirror of the past to know prosperity and decline; and make of your mind a mirror to illumine the ten thousand things." The common tendency to see only another's faults while ignoring your own, making someone a mirror without illumining your own self, is truly a foolish one. When you criticize someone, you must also reflect upon your own faults. This is what it means to make someone a mirror. . . . The Prince's [Shōtoku Taishi] *Seventeen-Article Constitution* says: "Wipe the anger from your face, resentment from your heart, and do not abuse others for being different. Everyone has a mind, and each clings to his own. Your right could be another's wrong, his right, your wrong. You are certainly not a sage, nor is he necessarily a fool. In fact, you are both deluded worldlings. Who, then, is there to decide the principle of right and wrong?" Indeed, the mundane mind's susceptibility to attachment is such that since right and wrong is based on blind emotion, both must be wrong. If you illumine your right in the mirror of another's wrong, then your right cannot be right. And the other's wrong cannot be wrong. Therefore, an ancient has said, "*In the state of dreaming, what is and is-not are both not. In the throes of delusion, right and wrong are both similarly wrong.* This being so, cast off all virtue and fault, right and wrong, and you will arrive at the Great Way, subject and object one, self and other equal." (ed. Tsukudo, 1: 129–30; *NKBT* ed. suppl.§ 21.2, p. 474)

5. SHOHŌ JISSŌ: ALL THE VARIOUS PHENOMENA ARE THE REAL. Ijichi cites *Chidoron* V: "Outside [the truth that] all the various phenomena are the Real [*shohō jissō*], all that remains is wholly, in a word, delusion" (*SSG* rev. ed., p. 159, n. 15). Suzuki in "Mikkan," II, p. 37, refers to another passage in *Daichidoron*, but it does not seem to me as relevant in this context. He also cites two passages from the *Nehangyō*, XV.20.2 and XXIV.22.6, both of which admonish the listeners that they will be followers of Mara, that is, deluded and not the Buddha's disciples, if they conceive of ultimate reality as something that can actually be grasped by the mind.

The foundational Mahayana concept of *shohō jissō* refers to the "suchness" [*nyoze*] of all phenomena, their essential being or true reality, not as described, conceptualized, or theorized by reason and language, but what they are "just as they are." It is, of course, an axiom of Mahayana teaching that how things are "as such" cannot be pinned down by language, not because there is something mysterious about them, but more because of the limitations of language—for instance, its built-in, constructed syntax, which preconditions our understanding of nonlinguistic phenomena. It is important to point out, however, that while orthodox Mahayana teaching recognizes that words cannot master or capture this suchness, they can nevertheless point to it by means of parables, analogies, and logical analysis. This is the reason for the centrality of means or skillful devices (*hōben*; Skt. *upaya*) in the teaching.

As for *shohō jissō*, the following passage from the *Lotus Sutra*, chap. 2, "Expedient Devices," is commonly cited as the locus classicus of the term:

> Sariputra, the Thus Come One's knowledge and insight are broad and great, profound and recondite, without measure and without obstruction. His might, his fearlessness, his dhyana-concentration, his release-samadhi have deeply penetrated the limitless. He has perfected all the dharmas that have never been before. Sariputra, *by making a variety of distinctions*, the Thus Come One can skillfully preach the dharmas. His words are gentle, gladdening many hearts. Sariputra, to speak of the essential: as for the immeasurable, unlimited dharmas that have never been before, the Buddha has perfected them all. Cease, Sariputra, we need speak no more. Why is this? Concerning the prime, rare, hard-to-understand dharmas, which the Buddha has perfected, *only a Buddha and a Buddha can exhaust their reality, namely, the suchness of the dharmas* [*shohō jissō*], the suchness of their marks, the suchness of their nature, the suchness of their substance, the suchness of their powers, the suchness of their functions, the suchness of their causes, the suchness of their conditions, the suchness of their effects, the suchness of their retributions, *and the absolute identity of their beginning and end.* (*Scripture of the Lotus Blossom*, trans. Hurvitz, pp. 22–23; emphasis added)

SUCHNESS. THE TEN SUCHNESSES. These so-called "ten suchnesses" (*jūnyoze*) are in effect an analysis of the various aspects of the reality of the dharmas (*shohō jissō*); it breaks down into manageable parts—i. e., appearance; nature; integral substance; latent force; active operation or functioning; direct or internal cause; indirect cause or condition; direct effect; indirect result—what is one and indivisible. As the text above says, it makes "*a variety of distinctions*" for pedagogical purposes. The tenth aspect, "*the absolute identity of their beginning and end*" (*honmatsu kukyōtō*, the ultimate identity of the first and the last) is interpreted by Tendai Zhiyi to mean that since the first nine aspects are mutually interrelated or interpenetrating in any and all phenomena, they are ultimately the same. In other words, phenomena are constituted as a dynamic totality of several aspects that can be grasped and expressed categorically (see Nitta Masaaki, *Tendai jissōron no kenkyū* [Heirakuji Shoten, 1981], pp. 488–89; also p. 496n4). The tenth aspect is clearly the crucial one, since it is the inability of mundane thought and language to encompass all aspects in one "suchness" at every moment that presumably necessitates the somewhat mystical language used to point to it, viz., "only a Buddha and a Buddha can exhaust their reality."

6. A reference to one of the verse passages in the *Lotus Sutra* III, "Parable":

> "If there are beings / who know not the root of suffering / and are deeply bound to the causes of suffering, / unable to cast them off even for a while, / for their sakes / I devise the means to preach the Way. / *The causes of a multitude of sufferings / are rooted in insatiable desire* [*shoku no yoru tokoro wa / ton'yoku o moto to nasu*]; if insatiable desire is extinguished, / they would have no place to anchor." (*Hokkekyō* 1: 204, my translation; see also *Scripture of the Lotus Blossom*, trans. Hurvitz, p. 75)

Appendix: Biographical Notes

List of Entries

Biographical Notes

BONTŌ, or Bontōan-ju (secular name Asayama Morotsuna) (1349–ca. 1417). Member of a warrior clan that had been Ashikaga retainers since Takauji's day. Bontō himself served the Shōgun Yoshimitsu and was sent to Satsuma in Kyūshū as the Shogun's representative in 1391 and 1398. He spent the next twenty years in the provinces, traveling from Kumano (in Wakayama) westward to Shikoku and then north to the Tōhoku region. While in Tōhoku, he built himself a hut at Matsushima and assisted in laying the plans for the Kōmyōji, a Jishū-sect temple in what is now Yamagata Prefecture. He returned to the capital in 1408 and apparently took holy orders thereafter.

Like Imagawa Ryōshun, Bontō studied waka with Reizei Tamehide (d. 1372; Tamesuke's son) and renga with Nijō Yoshimoto. He transmitted Yoshimoto's teachings in the *Bontōan-ju hentōshō* (1417) and the *Chōtanshō* (1390). Other extant works are the *Bontōan sodejitashū* (1384), also a renga handbook, and the *Bontō renga-awase jūgoban* (1415), a collection of his best tsukeku, arranged in fifteen rounds and judged by the Rtd. Emperor Go-Komatsu (1377–1443; r. 1392–1412).

Shinkei called Bontō "the guiding light of the Way" in his generation because he transmitted Yoshimoto's teachings; however, he would also deplore the deleterious effects upon his art of his long exile from the capital. See the pertinent citation from *Oi no kurigoto* in *HF*, pp. 101–2.

[LAY MONK] DŌIN (ca. 1090–1182). Vice-director of the Horses Bureau, son of the Civil Affairs Ministry official Fujiwara Kiyotaka and a daughter of the Governor of Nagato province. Became known in waka circles in his later years, participating in the leading events and himself sponsoring large-scale waka contests at the Sumiyoshi and Hirota Shrines. Last known public appearance in 1179, at the contest sponsored by Minister of the Right Fujiwara Kanezane. Twenty poems included in the *Senzaishū*, the imperial anthology compiled by Shunzei in 1183–87. See also Chapter 51 above.

[RTD. EMPEROR] GO-TOBA (1180–1239; r. 1183–98). Arguably the best known of Japan's monarchs in literary history, due to his active promotion and practice of poetry, including renga in its early stages, and his sponsorship of the greatest of the imperial waka anthologies, *Shinkokinshū*, and of major poets like Shunzei, Saigyō, and Teika. Succeeding to the throne while barely out of infancy during the Gempei civil wars (1180–85), he abdicated before twenty in order to rule as retired emperor, pursuing a policy aimed at restoring the power of the court in defiance of the newly triumphant military class. In 1221, he issued an imperial decree chastising the Hōjō leader Yoshitoki and mustered an army against Kamakura in what is now known as the Jōkyū Disturbance. Unfortunately, Yoshitoki heard of the plan and took the offensive by sending the Eastern warriors to take the capital. The imperial forces met defeat, and Go-Toba was deposed and sent into exile in Oki Island, off Shimane on the Japan Sea coast, there to spend the nineteen years until his death in 1239. On Go-Toba's acumen as a statesman and details of the court-bakufu conflict, see George Sansom, *A History of Japan to 1334* (Stanford: Stanford University Press, 1958), pp. 376–85.

A man of many talents, Go-Toba practiced the arts of music as well as poetry, but also more vigorous activities like horsemanship and kickball (*kemari*). His greatest enthusiasm, however, was reserved for the *Shinkokinshū*, whose compilation he decreed in 1201, the year after he reestablished the then defunct Wakadokoro and sponsored the first of the two 100-poem sequences that would provide material for the anthology. Other events of lasting literary historical consequence that he sponsored and participated in himself are *Rōnyaku gojisshu uta awase* (Fifty-poem Match by Old and Young [1201]), *Minase-dono koi jūgoshu uta awase* (The Minase Palace Fifteen Love Poems Match [1202]), *Sengohyakuban uta awase* (Poem Contest in 1,500 Rounds [1201–2]), *Kasuga no yashiro no uta awase* (Poem Contest for the Kasuga Shrine [1204]), *Genkyū shiika uta awase* (Chinese-Japanese Poetry Match in the Genkyū Era [1205]), *Saishōshitennōin shōji waka* (Waka for the Saishōshitennō Temple Painting Screens [1207]), and *Entō on'uta awase* (Poetry Match in the Distant Island [1236]), commissioned by correspondence from Oki Island. Involving scores of contemporary poets and generating thousands of poems, these events may be viewed as an assertion of the court's cultural supremacy in the face of the new political dominance by the warrior class. However, they also undoubtedly stimulated what is now considered the highest development of the ancient art of waka poetry; certainly, by the Muromachi period, the efflorescence sponsored by Go-Toba would be viewed with nostalgia and admiration by Shōtetsu, Shinkei, and subsequent artists of the word. It is interesting to note that even after the *Shinkokinshū*'s completion in 1205, Go-Toba kept reediting the collection; indeed, he continued work on it in his exile, as evidenced in the existence of a variant version called the Oki Text *Shinkokinshū*. Aside from his commentaries during the poetry contests above, the treatise *Go-Toba-in onkuden* (post-1221?; trans. Robert Brower as "Ex-Emperor Go-Toba's Secret Teachings: *Go-Toba no In Gokuden*," *HJAS* 32 (1972): 5–70) is an important critical work presenting his concept of the ideal waka style and his evaluation of the leading poets of his day. He identified Shunzei's style of "gentleness and grace, profound heart-mind, and moving quality" (*yasashiku en ni, kokoro mo fukaku, awarenaru tokoro*) as ideal, and was critical of Teika's more involved, obscure syntax. Go-Toba's own poetry is said to conform generally to the *Shinkokin* mode, chiefly manifesting itself in a refined, fluid syntax, loftiness of tone, or at times a vivid and fresh visual impression. This style underwent no major change in his exile, except for a perhaps predictable increase in deeply moving poems around the thematics of longing for the capital and for times past.

GUSAI, or Kyūsei (ca. 1282–1376). The most famous renga master of the Nambokuchō period, and renga's first major poet. A disciple of Zen'a from an early age; first became known when already around 38 years old, when he began participating in the annual 1,000-verse sessions at the Kitano Shrine around 1319. He seems to have studied waka under Reizei Tamesuke (b. 1263) after this, but there is no information about him for the next twenty years, probably because of the civil disorders that preceded the division into the Northern and Southern Courts. He composed verses in 1339 for the *Toki Yoritō-ke renga* and again in 1341 for the *Kiyomizudera renga* and a session at his home called the *Gusaitaku renga*. For the next eighteen years, until the compilation of the *Tsukubashū* (1356–57), in which he assisted his student Nijō Yoshimoto, he became increasingly prominent. His friends included such members of the nobility as the Cloistered Prince Son'in (1306–59), and such powerful warrior officials as Ashikaga Tadayoshi (1307–52; brother of the Shōgun Takauji), and Takauji's lieutenant Sasaki Dōyo. By the end of the Nambokuchō era, he was recognized as the greatest contemporary authority and poet of linked verse. Gusai's tutorship of Yoshimoto had a fateful influence on the history of renga. It was his teachings that were reflected in Yoshimoto's critical works—notably the *Renrihishō* (1349), a treatise that, among other things, reiterated the principle that linking should be an internal process designed to produce the qualities of *yūgen* (ineffable depth) and *yojō* (suggestiveness, overtones)—and it was also he who helped Yoshimoto to compile the *Renga shinshiki* (also called *Ōan shinshiki*, 1372), the handbook that consolidated existing practices into a coherent body of rules governing renga composition.

Gusai's renga style is the most representative example of the intermingling of commoner and court renga circles that characterized the Nambokuchō period and was especially promoted by Nijō Yoshimoto. However, while evincing the new aesthetic of profundity and overtones, its essential characteristics are firmly rooted in the commoner tradition, as well as the character and talent of the man himself. As summarized by the renga historian Kidō Saizō, his verse style is marked by a firm integral unity and starkness of tone or rhythm. In linking, he does not eschew the verbal correspondences and antithetical structure developed within the commoner tradition, but at their best, his tsukeku generate a wide separation between themselves and the maeku, signifying a purely inward and profound connection, while simultaneously effecting a startling transformation of the maeku. His central position in the contemporary renga milieu is amply confirmed in the *Tsukubashū*, which includes 126 of his verses, by far the highest number among all the poets anthologized there. *RS* 1.20–21, 238–52. It is clear from Shinkei's writings that he had a high regard for Gusai's profundity and distinctive manner of linking; the same goes for Sōgi, who begins his critical handbook of model renga verses, *Oi no susami*, with examples from this poet.

[FUJIWARA] HIDEYOSHI, or Hidetō (1184–1240). Son of Hidemune, Governor of Kawachi (Osaka) and Yamato (Nara), junior fifth rank; his mother was the daughter of Minamoto Mitsumoto, the Governor of Iga (Mie). At fifteen, Hideyoshi became one of the "north-facing warriors" (*hokumen bushi*), a guards group in the special service of the retired sovereign. Subsequently, he was an officer of the Gate Guards, and later Governor of Dewa Province (Akita and Yamagata), as well as Kawachi, with junior fifth rank. As a loyal warrior who enjoyed the friendship and patronage of Go-Toba, he fought as a general of the imperial troops against the bakufu forces during the Jōkyū Disturbance (1219–21). After Go-Toba's defeat and banishment, and with his own children and brothers dead in battle, he took the tonsure and went into reclusion in the mountains of Kumano under the priestly name Nyogan. He traveled to Iwami in 1236 to see Go-Toba, though it is not known whether he made it across to Oki Island. He was, however, one of the participants in Go-Toba's 1236 *Entō on'uta awase*. Only seventeen when he began appearing in poetry meetings in 1201; appointed to the Wakadokoro, he remained an active participant in all the major contests and poetry sessions of his day. He has 17 poems in the *Shinkokinshū* and 939 in the individual anthology *Nyogan- hōshi shū*. Go-Toba writes that Hideyoshi's poetry has a loftiness (*take*) unexpected in someone of his class, and that even his ordinary poems are remarkably attractive (*Go-Toba-in onkuden*, ed. Hisamatsu Sen'ichi, *NKBT* 65: 147). Unlike the major *Shinkokinshū* poets, Hideyoshi seldom employs *kakekotoba* and allusive variation in his work, which hews instead to direct expression of feeling and simple but strong descriptions of nature.

[FUJIWARA] IETAKA, or Karyū (1158–1237). Born to the daughter of an official of the Empress Dowager's household and Mitsutaka, at the time Minister of Civil Affairs and Governor of Etchū (Toyama), later Acting Middle Counselor with senior second rank. Ietaka himself was successively Governor of Etchū and Kazusa (Chiba), then Minister of the Imperial Household from 1206. He first became eminent in poetic circles in the 1190s, and thereafter his name figures in practically all the meetings and contests of his day; his several children were also talented poets. Go-Toba, who appointed him one of the *Shinkokinshū* editors, deemed him a strong, effective poet who produced so many superior pieces that he outstripped everyone else (*Go-Toba-in onkuden*, ed. Hisamatsu, p. 147). In 1216, he attained to the junior third rank, thus joining the senior nobility at age fifty-eight; he reached the pinnacle of his official career in 1235 at age seventy-seven, when he was awarded the junior second rank. The following year, 1236, Go-Toba, then in his fifteenth year of exile on Oki Island, commanded him to gather ten poems each on ten given topics from fifteen poets (including himself), which the sovereign then arranged into a poetry contest, significantly matching his own poems against Ietaka's (this is the *Entō on'uta awase*). Taken ill late in the same year, 1236, Ietaka took the tonsure with the priestly name Busshō ("buddha nature"), subsequently retiring to Tennōji. where he died in 1237, leaving seven poems composed just the day before. He was indeed a prolific poet. His individual anthology, *Minishū* (also *Mibu-nihon shū* or *Gyokuginshū*), compiled by the former Palace Minister Kujō Motoie in 1245, includes 2,857 (plus some 340 more in variant texts) poems. Forty-three appear in the *Shinkokinshū*, putting him in seventh place, after Teika's forty-six. In the imperial anthology compiled by Teika himself in 1235, the *Shinchokusenshū*, Ietaka has the highest number of all at forty-three. See also Chapter 50 above.

IMAGAWA RYŌSHUN. See under "Ryōshun."

[LADY] ISE (ca. 877–940). One of the three best-known woman poets of the Heian period, the others being Ono no Komachi and Izumi Shikibu. Her name derives from her father's title as Governor of Ise Province. She came to court as lady-in-waiting to Empress Onshi during the reign of Emperor Uda (r. 887–97), and bore him a son who died young. Later, she was loved too by Uda's son Prince Atsuyoshi; Lady Nakatsukasa, whose poems appear in the *Shūishū*, was the result of that union. The recognition given Ise's skill may be seen from her participation in the *Teijin no uta awase* (913), where she competed on an equal footing with such illustrious figures as Ki no Tsurayuki and Oshikōchi Mitsune. Her individual anthology, the *Ise shū*, includes 483 poems; 15 are in the *Shinkokinshū*. (*WBD*, pp. 52–53)

JAKUREN (1139?–1202). Adopted by Shunzei when his father Shunkai, Shunzei's younger brother, entered the priesthood at Daigoji; thus from an early age received the direct influence of Shunzei's teachings. He was Junior Assistant Minister at the Ministry for Central Affairs, with Junior Fifth Rank, when he took the tonsure, presumably around 1172, when Shunzei's own son, Teika, was ten years old. He would then have been in his early thirties. As a monk, Jakuren traveled and undertook religious austerities in various provinces, including Kawachi and Yamato, in 1173–80, and in Izumo and the Azuma region in 1190–91. He was already participating in poetry matches in the capital in 1167 and kept up his poetic endeavors even after entering the priesthood, composing numerous *hyakushu* with the new innovative poets Yoshitsune, Teika, and Ietaka. His running debate with the rival Rokujō-school poet Kenjō during the *Roppyakuban uta awase* of 1193–94 is well known, and he proved himself an important member of the Mikohidari school in other ways as well. When Go-Toba became the center of the poetic milieu from 1200, Jakuren was one of its leading members and was appointed to the Wakadokoro as one of the compilers of the *Shinkokinshū*. Unfortunately, he passed away in the early autumn of 1202, before the completion of that anthology, which includes thirty-five of his poems, eighth place in number. Go-Toba, who awarded him property in Akashi, apparently had great admiration for his work and he lauds his skill in composing on *musubidai*, linked or compound topics, and gives the following evaluation:

> Jakuren was someone who did not compose poems in a cavalier manner. He labored over them so minutely, they fell just short of the truly sublime. Yet when he did set out to compose in the lofty mode, as in the poem "Masses of white clouds trailing / beyond the peak of Tatsuta" [*Tatsuta no oku ni / kakaru shirakumo*], for the Three Styles meeting, the result was awesome. On occasion, he would compose rapidly, producing renga and even "mad poems" [*kyōka*] in an instant and still managing to make sense, so that he seemed to me a genuine adept. (*Go-Toba-in onkuden*, ed. Hisamatsu, pp. 146–47)

Kamo no Chōmei recounts Jakuren's dissatisfaction with the cavalier attitude of Minamoto Tomochika to poetry, comparing him unfavorably to his sister Kunaikyō, one of the major poetesses in the *Shinkokinshū*, who is said to have perished from her poetic exertions (*Mumyōshō*, p. 77). Jakuren's individual anthology, the *Jakuren-hōshi shū*, exists in five variant editions, possibly an indication of the popular esteem in which his work was held. See also Chapters 50 and 56; the poem "Masses of white clouds trailing . . . ," cited above by Go-Toba, appears in Chapter 7.

JIEN. See under "Jichin."

JICHIN (posthumous name of Jien) (1155–1225). Priest with exceedingly high connections in the sociopolitical world. Son of the Regent Fujiwara Tadamichi; younger brother of two other Fujiwara regents, Motofusa and Kanezane; and the uncle of still another, the poet Yoshitsune. At eleven, Jichin began his studies at Hieizan; at fourteen, he took the tonsure. By 1178, when he was twenty-four, he had risen to the rank of Abbot of the Hōshōji. Six years later, his close friendship with Rtd. Emperor Go-Toba earned him the position of *gojisō* (Imperial Exorcist). In 1192, as Acting Archbishop, he became Abbot of the Tendai sect, a position to which he was reappointed four times. An influential personage who bridged the clerical and political spheres, Jichin is the author of the famous *Gukanshō* (ca. 1220), a historical chronicle covering the early times until the Jōkyū era (1219–21) and considered the first attempt to interpret, rather than merely record, events. He is represented in the *Shinkokinshū* by ninety-two poems, a number second only to the ninety-four by Saigyō, the other prominent poet-priest of the period.

JŪBUTSU (dates unknown). One of Zen'a's followers in the popular renga milieu, he was a priest from Yamato who was known for his many talents, including waka, Chinese, and medicine. He was invited by the first Ashikaga shōgun, Takauji, to lecture on the *Man'yōshū* and is the author of the travel record *Daijingū sankeiki* (Record of a Pilgrimage to the Great [Ise] Shrine [1342]). He is reported to have written also a thirty-volume reference work on renga called *Shūjinshō*, which has unfortunately not survived.

JUNKAKU (1268–ca. 1355). Priest of the Shōmyōji Temple and learned renga in Kamakura. He came to Kyoto around 1309 and enrolled as Zen'a's disciple, participating like Shinshō in the Hōrinji 1,000-Verse Sequence of 1312. After staying for several years in Kyoto, he went back to live in Kamakura, remaining in the Shōmyōji until the defeat of the Hōjō in 1333. The *Junkaku-bon Ise monogatari* is a copy of that classic that Junkaku wrote, according to its colophon, in 1341, when he was seventy-three. That he was still alive around 1355 may be surmised from the fact that he was the first renga teacher of Imagawa Ryōshun (1325–1420), and Ryōshun first came to renga in his early thirties. Junkaku's diction and rhythm is as plain and stark as Shinshō's, but he occasionally exhibits in addition the qualities of depth and loftiness. He has nineteen verses in the *Tsukubashū*. *RS* 1.211–14.

KENZAI (1452–1510). Renga poet from Aizu District in Iwashiro Province (Fukushima Province); first taught by Shinkei as a young priest of eighteen, when he came to Edo and subsequently invited the master to Aizu in 1470; it was also probably around this time that he met Sōgi. After Shinkei's death in 1475, he moved to Kyōto, where he quickly attained success as a renga poet, succeeding Sōgi as Kitano *bugyō*, Master of the Kitano Renga Meeting Hall, in 1489. In 1490, he visited Yamaguchi (Suo Province) at the invitation of Ōuchi Masahiro, to whom he presented the renga handbook *Renga entokushō*. He was back in Yamaguchi in the Ninth Month of 1495 in order to show the dying Masahiro the manuscripts for the *Shinsen Tsukubashū*. The diary *Ashita no kumo* is a moving account of Masahiro's death on the eighteenth day of the Ninth Month (1495) and of the subsequent funeral ceremonies. It includes an elegiac poem jointly composed by Sanjō Kin'atsu and the priest Shōnin, as well as memorial renga *hyakuin* held daily for the rest of the Ninth Month.

Back in the capital, Kenzai participated in renga sessions sponsored by Emperor Go-Tsuchimikado (1442–1500; r. 1465–1500) and later by Emperor Go-Kashiwabara (1464–1526; r. 1500–1526), at the same time studying waka with Gyōe (1430–ca. 1498). Later, he went back to live in Iwashiro, where he was well known among the feudal lords of the eastern and northern regions. One of his last works was the *Ashina-ke kitō hyakuin* of 1505, a 100-verse sequence composed as a prayer for the reconciliation of the warring father and son of the Ashina clan in Aizu.

Kenzai's verses from 1469 to 1508 are gathered together in the extensive four-part anthology, *Sono no chiri*. They are written in a poetic style whose sharply delineated, realistic quality is often contrasted to Shinkei's spirituality and Sōgi's lyrical descriptions of scenery. Apart from *Sono no chiri*, there are extant some thirty volumes of his *hyakuin*, and his most famous composition, the *Seibyō hōraku senku*, a votive offering 1,000-verse sequence, read from the tenth day of the Second Month, 1494, as part of the Kitano Shrine sessions.

Among Kenzai's renga handbooks are the *Shinkei sōzu teikin* (1488), which records Shinkei's teachings on the proper training for a beginner in renga, and the *Renga honshiki* and *Yōshinshō*, both dealing with renga rules or *shikimoku.* For an account of Kenzai's early training and association with Shinkei, see *HF*, pp. 132–33, 141–47, and 173–74.

[MINAMOTO] KINTADA (889–948). Grandson of Emperor Kōkō (r. 884–87). Served variously as Chamberlain and Governor of Yamashiro and Ōmi provinces during the reigns of Daigo (r. 889–931) and Suzaku (r. 931–47), reaching the junior fourth rank and position of Controller of the Right. Counted among the Thirty-Six Poet Immortals [*Sanjūrokkasen*], he was a close friend of Ki no Tsurayuki, enjoyed the trust of his cousin, the Emperor Daigo, and was a frequent participant at poetry matches and picture screen poem compositions at the palace. Also a practitioner of hawking and incense-making, he is mentioned in the *Genji monogatari* as a famous expert at incense competitions. The *Kintada shū*, his individual anthology, includes seventeen, thirty-nine, or fifty-two poems, the number varying according to the textual lineage. He also figures in anecdotes told in *setsuwa* collections like *Yamato monogatari* and *Uji shūi monogatari*. See also Chapter 46 above.

KODAI NO KIMI, or Koōgimi (dates unknown). Woman poet of the mid-Heian period; one of the so-called Thirty-Six Poet Immortals, but very little is known about her life, except that she was a Lady Chamberlain when Rtd. Emperor Sanjō (976–1017; r. 1011–16) was still Crown Prince. Still, the fact that her poem opens the *Goshūishū* imperial anthology (ca. 1086–87) and that she figures in poetry matches with leading poets indicate a high place in the cultural milieu of her day. The *Goshūishū*, it must be noted, is distinguished by the exceptionally high percentage, 31.5 percent, of poems by women; that is, 384 poems by ninety-nine female poets, indicating their active role in poetry as well during the height of Heian women's prose writing, a period that coincided with the reign of Emperor Ichijō (980–1011; r. 986–1011) and the regency of the Fujiwara. The individual anthology, *Kodai no Kimi shū*, exists in four variant texts, the first of which includes 161 poems.

[LADY] KUNAIKYŌ (fl. 1200–1205). Lady-in-waiting to Rtd. Emperor Go-Toba; regarded as one of the most accomplished woman poets of her age, a reputation that she shared with the poet known as Shunzei's Daughter. Her father Minamoto Moromitsu was also an active participant in poetic meetings, but reached only the position of Acting Master of the Capital, Right Division (*ukyo daibu*), with senior fifth rank. Her mother, the daughter of the painter Kose Munemochi, was a lady in-waiting to Rtd. Emperor Go-Shirakawa called Aki. Kunaikyō's ability in painting, perhaps an influence from her maternal grandfather, manifested itself in an impressionistic poetic style that revealed a high sensitivity to the colors of nature. It was her undoubted poetic talent that led Go-Toba to invite her to his court; unfortunately, her career was all too brief; she is said to have been less than twenty when she died, in contrast to Shunzei's Daughter, who was still writing in her eighties. "Kunaikyō's poetic labors were so exhausting she spat blood," we are told in *Sasamegoto*. (See Chapter 21 and n. 4 there for a revealing anecdote about her from *Mumyōshō*.) Fifteen of her poems appear in the *Shinkokinshū*.

KYŌUN, or Keiun (ca. 1293–1369). Along with his father Jōben (ca. 1265–1344), Ton'a (1289–1372), and the author of *Essays in Idleness*, Kenkō (ca. 1283–1352), one of the so-called "four deva kings of waka" (*waka shitennō*) in the late Kamakura period who were leading disciples of the Nijō-school master Tameyo (1250–1338). Kyōun was particularly close to the Cloistered Prince Sondō of the Shōren'in, the Tendai *monzeki* temple in Higashiyama, and was appointed acting superintendent of the Gion Shrine. He received the *Kokin denju* from Nijō Tamesada (1293–1360), compiler of the eighteenth imperial anthology, *Shinsenzaishū* (1359), but in his late years associated with Reizei Tamehide (d. 1372), to whom he is said to have transmitted the said *Kokinshū* received traditions. In the *Kinrai fūteishō* (The Styles of Recent Times [1387]), Nijō Yoshimoto evaluates his poetry thus: "It favors the sublime and is imbued with the loneliness of things; tending slightly to the old styles, its form and feeling are affecting, in a way that makes the ears prick up" (quoted in *WBJ*, p. 173). The *Keiunshū*, his individual anthology, includes some 300 poems. See also Chapter 56 above.

[FUJIWARA OR ASUKAI] MASATSUNE (1170–1221). Son of a daughter of Acting Middle Counselor Minamoto Akimasa, senior second rank, and Fujiwara Yoritsune, Minister of Punishments and Governor of Bugo (Ōita), junior fourth rank. When his father was banished to Izu in 1189, Masatsune too went east and lived in Kamakura, where he married the daughter of a senior retainer of the bakufu and learned the art of kickball (*kemari*), eventually becoming so expert as to found the Asukai school of that genteel sport. Summoned back to the capital in 1197 by Go-Toba, he became one the sovereign's close personal attendants, serving as Captain of the Palace Guards and later Commander of the Military Guards, Right Division. His debut in the poetry milieu was in 1198; thereafter, recognizing his talent, Go-Toba included him in subsequent matches, finally appointing him to the Waka Bureau and the editorial board of the *Shinkokinshū* in 1201. Masatsune retained his ties to Kamakura and conveniently served as the link between Teika and his waka student, the young Shōgun Minamoto Sanetomo (1192–1219; r. 1203–19). He attained to junior third rank in 1218 and was appointed Consultant in 1220, but died the following year at age fifty-one. The *Asukai wakashū* includes 1,672 poems; 22 appear in the *Shinkokinshū*. Masatsune was a dexterous poet who gave careful thought to his compositions, *Go-Toba-in onkuden* notes (ed. Hisamatsu, p. 147).

[FUJIWARA] NAGAYOSHI, or Nagatō (b. 949?). Mid-Heian poet, son of the Governor of Ise, Fujiwara Tomoyasu (senior fourth rank, upper grade), and younger brother of Michitsuna's mother, the author of *Kagerō nikki* (Gossamer Diary). In 1005, he achieved his highest rank, junior fifth, upper grade, and was appointed Governor of Ise, but he disappears thereafter from public records. Numbered among the Thirty-Six Poet Immortals, Nagayoshi also has the distinction of being the teacher of the famous poet-priest Nōin (b. 988) and of founding the practice of formal poetic transmission. The *Nagatō shū*, his individual anthology, has 147 poems, including pieces on daily life in the provinces and poetic exchanges with women, while a variant text features more public pieces from poetry contests and inscriptions on painting screens.

NIJŌ YOSHIMOTO (1320–88). The greatest patron of renga in the Nambokuchō period (1336–92). A son of the Minister of the Left Fujiwara Michihira, Yoshimoto was at first attached to Emperor Go-Daigo's court, but elected to remain in Kyoto with the northern faction during the split into the two courts. He gradually rose in the official hierarchy until he became Prime Minister (*Daijōdaijin*). He was appointed Regent (*Sesshō*) four times, and thus enjoyed great influence both at court and among the military throughout the incumbency of the first three Ashikaga shōguns. Yoshimoto was well versed in waka and waka poetics, both of which he had studied with the Nijō school poet Ton'a (1289–1372). Nevertheless, he made renga his main avocation, having begun studying it from his early twenties with the renga master Gusai, with whom he would collaborate in the task of establishing the basis of an orthodox renga tradition.

Yoshimoto's most important achievement was undoubtedly his compilation of the first *renga* anthology, the *Tsukubashū*, between 1356 and 1357. He seems to have gone to enormous effort to secure for the *Tsukubashū*, over the objections of those who wished to preserve the primacy of waka, the status of a quasi-imperial anthology comparable to the imperial waka collections. In this, he received valuable assistance from some of the powerful warrior officials, especially Ashikaga Takauji's trusted ally Sasaki Dōyo (1306–73).

Besides compiling the *Tsukubashū*, Yoshimoto produced a body of critical writings which established a theoretical foundation for the renga as a poetic form. His *Renga shinshiki* (1372) took the various poetic practices employed in actual sessions on the one hand, and existing handbooks of rules such as the *Kenji shinshiki* established by Zen'a on the other, and synthesized them into a new, relatively complete set of rules governing renga composition. Although partially revised in later periods, the book remained the definitive renga authority until the nineteenth century. After the *Renga shinshiki*, Yoshimoto's most important works are the *Renrihishō*, the *Tsukuba mondō* (1357–72), and the *Kyūshū mondō* (1376). The last two are couched in the form of dialogues—the first illuminating the history and origins of linked verse, its connection with Buddhism, and elements of practice and technique; and the second (written for Imagawa Ryōshun, who was then Commissioner of Kyūshū) explaining Yoshimoto's ideal of excellence in verse-making.

Yoshimoto's most decisive influence on the subsequent development of renga was his introduction of the aesthetic ideals of the waka tradition into the literary foundations of this new poetic form. What might be called the new style of the Nambokuchō period was a combination of the formal structural strengths developed in the commoner renga tradition and the *yūgen* aesthetic advocated by

Yoshimoto. In turn, the renga revival represented by Sōzei, Shinkei, and the other "seven sages" of the Muromachi period had its basis in the Nambokuchō style on the one hand and moved even further in the direction of the classical tradition on the other through these poets' simultaneous training in waka with Shōtetsu, for whom Teika and the *Shinkokinshū* represented the apogee of waka development.

NŌIN (988–ca. 1051). Numbered among the "thirty-six poet immortals of mid-antiquity" (*chūko sanjūrokkasen*); the wandering poet who became a model for Saigyō in the early medieval period. A son of the provincial Governor of Higo (Kumamoto), Nōin attended the university in the capital and received the usual degree in Chinese letters (*monjōshō*), but at twenty-six in 1013, he embarked on the path of reclusion and wandering that would characterize his life. His hermitage was in Kosobe (modern Osaka) and from there he went on travels to nearby provinces, across the sea to Shikoku, and twice on foot pilgrimage all the way up to the deep North. He also studied waka poetry with Fujiwara Nagayoshi (or Nagatō, see entry above), a relationship that reportedly established the practice of master-disciple transmission in the field of poetry. He was a participant in the prominent poetry matches at court, including those sponsored by the Regent and Minister of the Left Yorimichi in 1035, by the Palace in 1049, and by the household of Imperial Princess Yūshi in 1050. At the same time, he was an active member of the informal middle-class poetry milieu composed of retainers of noble households and families of provincial governors. The *Nōin hōshi shū* is his self-selected anthology, dating from sometime after 1045 and containing some 256 poems. The *Nōin utamakura* (Nōin Poem Pillow), a lexicon of poetic words, monthly poem topics, and famous sites in various provinces is considered the very first of its genre, valued by poetry students through the ages, as witness its wider dissemination in a woodblock print edition from the Genroku period (1688–1704). He was reportedly also the author of a travel journal, the *Yasojima no ki* (Record of the Eighty Islands), and another work on poem topics, *Daishō* (Notes on Poem Topics), but these manuscripts have been lost. That he was one of the earliest readers and owners of Sei Shōnagon's *Pillowbook* may be gathered from the existence of the *Nōin-bon Makura sōshi* (the *Nōin-Text Pillowbook*), a textual lineage stemming from his copy, and one of the valuable source texts for this work. Nōin is probably best known today among readers of Japanese literature for the poem he composed upon reaching Shirakawa Barrier, the gateway to the far North; subsequent poets, including Saigyō, Shinkei, Sōgi, Kenzai, and Bashō would allude to it on their own journeys there. It is *GSIS* 518: Travel.

miyako o ba	When I left,
kasumi to tomo ni	the haze was just rising
tachishikado	over the capital—
akikaze zo fuku	Across Shirakawa Barrier now
shirakawa no seki	the autumn wind is blowing.

REIZEI TAMEHIDE (d. 1372). Second son of Tamesuke, attained to the second rank with the office of Middle Counselor. Losing his father and elder brother in his twenties, he made the Kantō his base of activities during the period of rivalry between the Kyōgoku and Nijō schools, but gradually came into his own, establishing connections with the Shōgun Ashikaga Takauji (1305–58; r. 1338–58), as well as with the court poetic milieu, until he was appointed one of the officials in charge of compiling the seventeenth imperial anthology, *Fūgashū* (comp. 1345–48). Patronized by the Regent, Nijō Yoshimoto, he also became the poetry master of the Shōgun Yoshiakira (1330–67; r. 1358–67) in the 1360s and acted as judge in the poetry contest sponsored by him at the dedication of the Shintamatsushima Shrine in 1367. Tamehide was at one period a member of the monthly poetry meetings led by the Nijō leader, Tamesada, but a falling-out occurred between them, and he was subsequently excluded from the *Shinsenzaishū* (1359) anthology compiled by Tamesada that would mark the beginning of the Nijō dominance. In general, he maintained the liberal principles of his father, composed in a Kyōgoku-influenced style, and counted among his disciples Imagawa Ryōshun who in turn transmitted the Reizei principles to his disciple Shōtetsu. It was, of course, through Shōtetsu's mentorship of Shinkei and other Muromachi renga poets that the Reizei school influenced the course of renga.

[IMAGAWA] RYŌSHUN, or Sadayo (1326–1420). Military general and waka scholar; belonged to the prominent eastern daimyō clan, Imagawa, based in Tōtōmi and Suruga (modern Shizuoka) provinces, and related to the Ashikaga shogunal clan. He entered the Shōgun Yoshiakira's service as a young man and in 1370 was appointed by the Shōgun Yoshimitsu as Commissioner [*tandai*] of Kyūshū, with the task of subduing the loyalist (Southern court) forces entrenched in the island. He held the position for twenty-five years, during which he successfully broke the back of the loyalist resistance by means of his brilliant military strategies. In 1395, he was recalled to the capital on false charges of disloyalty to the bakufu brought against him by the daimyō Ōuchi Yoshihiro (1355–1400). A few years later, his loyalty once more came into question, and he was subsequently stripped of his offices as Constable of Suruga and Tōtōmi provinces. Thereafter, he retired to the country and devoted his time to composing waka and renga, his main preoccupation before being called upon to serve in Kyūshū.

Ryōshun was a major figure in the poetic milieu of the fourteenth century, having studied waka with Reizei Tamehide for a period of around twenty-five years, and renga with Nijō Yoshimoto principally, and at other times with Gusai, Junkaku, and Shūa. He vigorously defended the ideals of the innovating Reizei school of waka poetry against the conservative Nijō school in such works as *Wakadokoro e fushin no jōjō* (Questions to the Waka Bureau on Dubious Points [1430]), *Ryōshun isshiden* (Ryōshun's Legacy to His Son [1409]; or *Benyōshō*), and *Rakusho roken* (Admitting Authorship of the Lampoons [1412?]). The last two also record Yoshimoto's teachings and Ryōshun's explanations of them. *HD*, p. 799; see also George Sansom, *A History of Japan, 1334–1615* (Stanford: Stanford University Press, 1961), pp. 109–15.

SAIGYŌ (1118–90), lay name Norikiyo. His father was Satō Yasukiyo, a lieutenant of the Left Gate Guards, and his mother a daughter of Minamoto Kiyotsune, an

Inspector (*Kenmotsu*) in the Central Affairs Ministry. The Satō was a warrior clan descended from Fujiwara Hidesato, the eastern Constable who put down the Taira Masakado revolt in 940. The Satō had served for generations in the guards units in the capital, and Saigyō himself was named to the post of Lieutenant of the Left Military Guards at eighteen. He also served as Junior North-Facing Warrior (Shimo Hokumen Bushi), Sixth Rank, to Rtd. Emperor Toba (1103–56, r. 1107–23) through the Satō connection to Toba's empress, Taikenmon'in Shōshi. Shōshi belonged to the Tokudaiji regental family, who held in fief the Satō estate in Kii Province, and so Saigyō at this time was in effect a retainer of the Tokudaiji, or of its head, the Minister of the Left Tokudaiji Saneyoshi. The reason for Saigyō's sudden turn to reclusion in 1140 at the unusually young age of twenty-three remains speculative; the numerous popular legends about this venerated poet-priest ascribe it to either political causes or a hopeless love for a woman far above his station. The woman is said to be the aforementioned Shōshi, Toba's empress and mother of the emperors Sutoku and Go-Shirakawa. At any rate the experience was tremendous enough to move him to abjure mundane society, despite his outwardly happy situation in it. In 1142, we find Saigyō visiting the Palace Minister Fujiwara Yorinaga to request him, as he had the two retired sovereigns and others, to copy out a chapter of a sutra on the occasion of Shōshi's taking the tonsure following her son Sutoku's forced abdication in 1141. The anecdote is recounted in Yorinaga's diary, *Taiki* (entry for 3.15.1142), which continues with this observation about Saigyō: "He rendered service to the Cloistered Emperor with the courage of several generations of stalwart warriors. Having set his heart on the Buddha Way even as a layman, though affluent of family and young in age, and with a heart unclouded by sorrow, in the end he fled the world. People were moved to admiration."

Saigyō spent the next few years at various temples in Higashiyama and Saga, near the capital, but around 1144, he embarked on a journey north to the Mutsu region, following the traces of the early Heian poet-priest Nōin (see separate entry for Nōin) and visiting sites famous for their poetic associations. (Bashō would later follow the same course north in his travel memoir, *Narrow Road to the Deep North*). On his return, he settled in Mount Kōya, the great Shingon monastery in Kii (Wakayama) that would be his base for the next thirty years. From here he would occasionally embark on journeys of religious pilgrimage and self-discipline, as well as to solicit contributions for the temple. He also wrote poetry wherever he was and visited or corresponded with other lay monks in and around the capital, such as the three well-known sibling recluses known as the Ōhara Sanjaku (Jakunen, Jakuchō, and Jakuzen) and his old warrior friend Saijū. He was in the capital to attend the funeral of his former sovereign, Rtd. Emperor Toba, in 1156, right before the outbreak of the Hōgen Disturbance that ended with the banishment of Rtd. Emperor Sutoku (1119–64; r. 1123–41) to Sanuki in Shikoku. Saigyō traveled from the Chūgoku region to Shikoku in 1168 in order to visit places associated with Kōbō Daishi, Mount Kōya's founder, but also to pray at the grave of the ill-fated Sutoku. In 1180, at sixty-three, he left Mount Kōya and moved to a hermitage in the mountains of Futami no Ura in Ise Province, perhaps to avoid the disorders of the Gempei Wars. From here in the autumn of 1186, he undertook another long journey to the deep North in order to raise the gold for the rebuilding of the Tōdaiji and its Great Buddha Hall, which had been razed by Taira Shigehira in the course of the war. He stopped in Kamakura for a famous visit with the Shōgun Yoritomo, doubtless to obtain his cooperation in his venture.

Saigyō passed away at the Hirokawa Temple in Minami-Katsuragi, Kawachi Province (Osaka), on 2.16.1190, aged seventy-three. In his last years at Ise, he made a selection of his poems and arranged them in two solo poem contests (*jika awase*), intended as offerings to the Great Shrine. For the first, the *Mimosusogawa uta awase* (1187), he requested and obtained Shunzei's judgment, while for the second, *Miyakawa uta awase* (1189), he asked the young Teika. Teika took so long over his evaluation that Saigyō had to write Shunzei to urge him on, and it was not until the winter of 1189, when Saigyō was already ailing in Hirokawa, that the manuscript reached him. The letter expressing his joy at finally receiving Teika's response is still extant. The widespread admiration for Saigyō's work among the court poets is clearly manifest in the fact that all of fifteen years after his death, they gave him the highest number of poems—ninety-four—in the *Shinkokinshū*. Go-Toba confirms this high esteem, writing: "Saigyō is interesting, and what is more, his mind is remarkably profound; it is marvelous that both qualities are present in even his difficult poems. I believe him to be a born poet. His poetry is not such as can be learned by those of lesser talent. His ability is beyond explanation" (*Go-Toba-in onkuden*, ed. Hisamatsu, p. 145). Because he did not participate in the various meetings and contests in the capital but evolved his own style outside their studio-like contexts, mostly in solitude in natural settings, Saigyō was able to write freely according to the promptings of personal experience. His unaffected love of nature, as manifest in his numerous poems to the moon and flowers, his attitude of self-examination, and the devotion to the deepest truths of Buddhism in his poetry all bear witness to a deep sense of humanity and have endeared him to readers to the present day. There are numerous stories about Saigyō in the anecdotal literature, apocryphal or otherwise, showing that his life and poems struck a chord in the popular imagination. The influence of his spirit and words on subsequent poetry, including renga and haikai, was incalculable; Shinkei and Bashō clearly saw him as an inspiring precursor. There exist several versions of Saigyō's individual anthology, the most representative being the *Sankashū* (Mountain Recluse Collection), with 1,552 poems in the Yōmei Bunkō edition.

[IMPERIAL PRINCESS] SHIKISHI, or Shokushi (1152?–1201). Daughter of Emperor Go-Shirakawa (1127–92; r. 1155–58). For eleven years (1159–69) until her father took the tonsure, she held the position of High Priestess of the Kamo Shrine. Unlike other leading *Shinkokinshū* poets, her attendance at contemporary poetry meetings was infrequent; she apparently developed her skills through study of the anthologies and close association with Shunzei, her waka mentor, and his son Teika. It was at her request that Shunzei wrote one of the most important treatises in the history of Japanese poetry, *Korai fūteishō* (Poetic Styles from Ancient to Modern Times [1197]). Her later life was marked by lonely isolation, particularly after her father

Go-Shirakawa's demise in 1192. She became a nun around 1194, and was apparently implicated in a political conspiracy in 1197. Nineteen of her poems are included in the *Senzaishū* (1188), the imperial anthology compiled by Shunzei, and forty-nine in the *Shinkokinshū*, the fifth highest number by any poet there. The individual anthology *Shikishi-naishinnō shū*, which includes three *hyakushu*, has around 373 poems. Go-Toba ranks her with Yoshitsune and Jien as one of the best poets of her time and characterizes her style as particularly intricate and involved (*momimomi to aru yō ni*) (*Go-Toba-in onkuden*, ed. Hisamatsu, p. 146). There is indeed, in her most distinctive poems, a deep interiority, a subtle intellectuality that suggests a thoroughgoing absorption in a symbolic mental realm and is somewhat similar to Teika's manner.

SHINSHŌ (fl. ca. 1312–45). First attracted notice when he participated in the Hōrinji 1,000-Verse Sequence of 1312 in the company of his teacher Zen'a. He became a regular member of the annual spring flower sessions thereafter and was apparently popular also among the nobility. He is known to have been summoned once by the Retired Emperor for a renga session on Mount Takao held after the regular waka and Chinese-poetry meetings were over. However, unlike Zen'a's most famous disciple, Gusai, he remained firmly in the *jige*, or commoner, tradition, exhibiting a haikai-like humor in some of his verses, and surpassing his teacher Zen'a in his skill in verbal figures. There are twenty verses by him in the *Tsukubashū*. *RS* 1.208–11.

SHŌTETSU (1381–1459). The major Reizei-school poet of his time; born to a samurai family in the Oda village of Bitchū Province (Okayama), and went to the capital at around age ten. He was thirteen when he met Imagawa Ryōshun and Reizei Tametada (1361–1417) at a monthly poetry meeting and subsequently enrolled as Ryōshun's disciple. At seventeen, he was sent to be in attendance at the Kōfukuji Temple in Nara, foreshadowing his later interest in Zen. By the time he was thirty-four, his reputation as a poet was established.

In 1417, he became a scribe at the Tōfukuji, the Rinzai Zen temple in Kyōto. Sometime later, he seems to have spent some years in the village of Kiyosu in Owari Province (Aichi), where he expounded on the design and composition of the *Genji monogatari* to local enthusiasts and composed two 100-poem sequences. He returned to the capital in 1420 and was privileged to have an audience with the Shōgun Yoshimochi (1386–1428; r. 1394–1423, 1425–28). In the same year, he went on a retreat to Ishiyamadera Temple to mourn his teacher Ryōshun's death. Thereafter, he was active in the anti-Nijō movement in poetry. Unfortunately, he seems to have earned the displeasure of the Shōgun Yoshinori (1394–1441; r. 1428–41), with the result that his property in Oda was confiscated; similarly, despite his work and reputation, he was excluded from the very last imperial anthology, *Shinzoku Kokinshū* (1439). The ten years from 1449 until his death are recorded in detail in the poetic diary *Sōkonshū* (Grass-roots Collection), which includes some 11,238 poems, a number unrivaled by any other individual waka anthology.

Shōtetsu had a large following among the ruling warrior class and the priestly intelligentsia and was, in short, acknowledged to be the greatest *jige* (commoner) waka poet of his time. His last years were spent on pilgrimages to various temples and mountain retreats, where he composed 100-poem sequences and participated in poetry sessions held as prayer-offerings. Among his other works are the poetic diary *Nagusamegusa* (Grasses of Solace [1418]), and the treatise *Shōtetsu monogatari* (Conversations with Shōtetsu [1448 or 1450]). The most significant aspect of Shōtetsu's poetics, and the one in which he influenced his disciple Shinkei, is his advocacy of the aesthetic ideals of Teika, especially his insistence on the supremacy of *yugentei* above all other styles. *WBD*, pp. 511–12; *WBJ*, pp. 325–26. On his relations with Shinkei and the other leading renga poets of the Muromachi period, see *HF*, chaps. 2 and 3; for his treatise, see *Conversations with Shōtetsu*, trans. Robert Brower (Ann Arbor: Center for Japanese Studies, University of Michigan, 1992). And see also Chapter 43 above.

SHŪA (d. ca. 1377). Gusai's most gifted disciple; his quick wit and verbal facility early attracted the notice of Nijō Yoshimoto, and in the early years, he was a regular participant in the monthly sessions held at Yoshimoto's residence, as well as Sasaki Dōyo's. He emerged as the most likely successor to Gusai in the period after the compilation of the *Tsukubashū*. Whereas in a *senku* (1,000-verse sequence) held at Yoshimoto's residence in 1355, Shūa composed only 56 verses as compared to Gusai's 104, In the *Murasakino senku* held a few years later, he produced all of 168 verses, a number quite close to Gusai's 179. Along with Gusai, he was engaged in Yoshimoto's project of selecting *yoriai* (verbal correspondences) from both Chinese and Japanese classical works, including the *Wen hsüan, Mao shih, Man'yōshū*, and *Genji monogatari*, in preparation for consolidating the renga rules of composition. For a while at least, Yoshimoto was quite impressed with Shū'a verse style; he ranked it as high as Gusai's and envisioned a new style that would be an amalgam of the two. However, in his later years, Yoshimoto apparently became disenchanted with Shūa's preoccupation with verbal technique and figures. This was not the case in popular renga circles, where Shūa's dexterity, imagistic conceits, and ornate diction won him a large following and became the model for the renga of the middle period, immediately before the age of the seven sages.

SHUNZEI, or Toshinari (1114–1204). With his son, Teika, one of the two greatest poet-critics of the mid-classical period. The son of a Consultant of the third rank, he was awarded the junior fifth rank in 1127 and appointed Governor of Mimasaka (Okayama); subsequently, he also held the governorships of Kaga (Ishikawa), Tōtomi (Shizuoka), Mikawa (Aichi), and Tango (Kyoto). After a stint as Master of the Capital, Left Division, he was advanced to senior third rank in 1167, thus arriving at the highest rungs of the aristocracy. His final office was Head Chamberlain of the Empress Dowager's (Kinshi, Go-Shirakawa's empress) Household from 1172; four years later, he retired due to a grave illness. Shunzei completed the compilation of the *Senzaishū* imperial anthology in 1188, just two years after the end of the Gempei Wars (it will be recalled that he figures in a famous anecdote in the *Heike monogatari*). Rtd. Emperor Go-Toba, who held him in the highest esteem, sponsored his ninetieth birthday celebration in 1203, the year before his death. Shunzei was the most respected poet-critic of his day and into the Muromachi period of Shinkei and Shōtetsu. As the grand old man of poetry, his judgment was eagerly sought for private compositions, as well as for public poetry matches. His most enduring contribution was to establish *yūgen* as an all-encompassing aesthetic ideal, especially as manifested in the aura [*kehai*] of ambiguity that hovers about a poem without being overtly expressed in its words. Like Shinkei, he was less concerned, in his criticism, with diction and form than with the "deep mind" (*fukaki kokoro*) concealed in the poem's plain verbal surface. See Chapter 45 above.

SHUNZEI'S DAUGHTER (ca. 1171–1252?). Actually Shunzei's granddaughter, brought up by him. Her father was the Governor of Owari Province (Aichi) and her mother, Shunzei's daughter. She was married to the poet Minamoto Michitomo (1171–1227) around the early 1190s and bore him two children, but they shortly afterward became estranged, and around 1202, she started to serve as lady-in-waiting in Rtd. Emperor Go-Toba's court. It was from this time that she first became known in the poetic milieu, eventually becoming the main female member during the matches sponsored by Go-Toba; 29 of her poems were selected for the *Shinkokinshū*. In 1213, in her forties, she took the tonsure, though remaining active in the poetry circle around Go-Toba's son, Emperor Juntoku (1197–1242; r. 1210–21). With the support of her uncle Teika, her poetic production continued even after she went into seclusion in Saga, west of Kyoto, in her sixties, as is evident from her participation in the poem matches and meetings at the residence of the Regent Michiie and of the Saionji family. After Teika's death in 1241, she retired farther out in the family's estate in Koshibe, Harima Province (Hyōgo), where she died in her eighties. The individual anthology *Shunzei-kyō no musume no shū* developed from a core of 83 poems chosen by herself as material for *Shinchokusenshū*, the imperial anthology compiled by Teika around 1234; it exists in three other variant texts with additions by other editors, the longest including 246 poems. An extant letter known as *Koshibe no Zenni shōsoku* (Letter from the Koshibe Zen Nun [1252]) was sent to her cousin Tameie, Teika's son, then fifty-four years old. It has lavish praise for the balance and harmony of Tameie's choice of poems for the just completed imperial anthology *Shokugosenshū* (1251), compiled by him at the order of Rtd. Emperor Go-Saga (1220–72; r. 1242–45). It expresses her joy at having lived to see three royal anthologies compiled by three generations of her family and reveals her enduring loyalty to Go-Toba in praising the present Rtd. Emperor Go-Saga as his grandson (pp. 342–44). The following passage is particularly arresting in its veiled reference to Go-Toba's defeat and exile:

> Now I have no more lingering resentment, for I have lived to see the reign of my lord [Go-Saga].

sora kiyoku	Suns and moons I once
aogishi tsukihi	gazed upon in a clear sky,
sono mama ni	just as they were

kumorazarikeru	have emerged from the clouds,
kage no ureshisa	a shining splendor to bring joy.

(*Koshibe no Zenni shōsoku*)

As the letter also contains poetic references to impending death, it is presumed that the poetess died in Koshibe not long afterward.

SONE YOSHITADA (fl. ca. 986). One of the Thirty-Six Poet Immortals whose poems were selected by Fujiwara Norikane (1107–65) in the mid-classical anthology *Nochi no rokurokusen* (Later Selections from Thirty-six Poets). A low-ranking official in the Tango provincial office, he was known for eccentric behavior, such as appearing at a party uninvited. Although the unconventional diction and imagery of his poems were not always acceptable in the literary milieu of his time, a century later, he was belatedly recognized as an innovative poet. His individual anthology, the *Sōtanshū* (586 poems), includes such interesting features as a series of 30 poems for each month of the year and a *hyakushu* (100-poem sequence) for which the poet Minamoto Shitagō (911–83) composed another hyakushu in response. (For more on Yoshitada, see *JCP*, pp. 179–85.)

SŌZEI (secular name Minamoto Tokishige) (d. 1455). A retainer of the powerful daimyō Yamana Sōzen (1403–73), with the official title of Junior Assistant Minister in the Ministry of Popular Affairs (Mimbu shōyū), but by 1427, for reasons unknown, he had taken the tonsure and was living in priestly seclusion on Mt. Kōya, south of the capital in Kii Province (Wakayama). He studied waka and the *Genji monogatari* with Shōtetsu, and renga with Bontō, whose teachings he recorded in the treatise *Shoshin kyūeishū* in 1428, a year after Bontō's death. He participated in the famous Kitano *manku* (a 10,000-verse sequence) sponsored by the Shogun Yoshinori in 1433, around which time he apparently returned to live in the capital, for we find him sponsoring a "poetry meeting on the occasion of building a new hut" in the Tenth Month.

In the years that followed, Sōzei gradually became the central figure in the world of the renga, participating in the annual *manku* of the Kitano Shrine and composing verses with warrior-officials of Ise Province (Mie), among others. Between 1444 and 1448, he wrote the *Kokon rendanshū*, a poetic treatise in three sections. The first and third sections trace the evolution of two styles of renga from Zen'a and other early masters of the Kamakura period, and the second section explains the manner of composition of some verses taken from the Kitano Shrine *senku* of 1439. This work is an important source for the development of *jige renga* during the Kamakura period, and especially for the transmission of tradition from one teacher to another. The peak of Sōzei's career came in 1448, when he was appointed *bugyō* (official Renga Master) of the Kitano Renga Kaisho. As *bugyō*, he undertook the revision of the renga code of rules with the statesman and poet Ichijō Kanera (or Kaneyoshi, 1402–81), Nijō Yoshimoto's grandson. In 1450, he collected his verses in the *Sōzei kushū*, which was intended for inclusion in Kanera's projected renga anthology of twenty volumes, the *Shingyokushū*. Two years later, in 1452, came the *Hana no magaki*, in which he put together forty-five tsukeku by Gusai, Ryōa, Shūa, and Bontō, plus two by himself, and classified them according to ten styles.

In 1454, Sōzei followed his feudal lord, Yamana Sōzen, who had incurred the displeasure of the Shōgun Yoshimasa, in his retreat to Tajima Province (Hyōgo Prefecture). He died there the following year, in 1455. For Sōzei's role in the contemporary renga milieu, see *HF*, pp. 52–62 passim; 80–83.

[FUJIWARA] SUKEMUNE (eleventh century). Very little is known of the poet Sukemune. He belonged to the northern branch of the Fujiwara; his father was the Consultant and Provisional Master of the Crown Prince's Household, Fujiwara Sukefusa of the senior third rank; his mother was the daughter of a Minamoto provincial governor. He was variously Director of the Imperial Stables of the Right, Governor of Settsu, and Minor Captain, and had reached the fourth rank upon retiring in 1087. The poem cited in Chapter 46 above is the only one by him in the *Shinkokinshū.*

[FUJIWARA] TAKANOBU (1142–1205). Son of Tametsune or Jakuchō, one of the three sibling poet-recluses known as "the three recluses of Ōhara" (*Ōhara sanjaku*). His mother, a daughter of the Wakasa Provincial Governor Chikatada, was also known as Bifukumon'in Kaga, and later became Shunzei's wife. Thus Takanobu and Teika were half brothers. Takanobu was successively appointed Provincial Governor of Kazusa, Echizen, and Wakasa, and ended his official career as Provisional Master of the Right Capital, with the Senior Fourth Rank, before taking the tonsure in 1202 at age sixty. He was an active participant in the poetry meetings and contests of his time and was, like his contemporary Kamo no Chōmei, an official of the Waka Poetry Bureau during the compilation of the *Shinkokinshū.* He apparently had a reputation as a ladies' man, but was equally prominent for his skill as a painter. He is indeed said to have founded portrait painting in Japan; the famous portraits of Minamoto Yoritomo, Taira Shigemori, and Fujiwara Mitsuyoshi (designated a National Treasure) in the Jingōji are all ascribed to him. A man of many talents, he is also mentioned as the author of the fictional tales *Ukinami* and *Iyayotsugi*, now unfortunately lost. His personal poetry collection, the *Takanobu-ason shū*, with 959 poems, is a useful source for the poetic milieu of the time, particularly his association with Saigyō, Shunzei, Teika, and the poetess Kojijū. (*WBJ*, p. 401)

[FUJIWARA] TAMEIE (1198–1275). Teika's eldest son and heir. His mother was the daughter of Palace Minister Fujiwara Sanemune. As a young man he was apparently more interested in kickball (*kemari*) than in acquiring solid poetic skills and so incurred his father's displeasure (see Chapter 22 above), but Teika's persistent admonitions and the loss of his protector, Emperor Juntoku, to exile in the Jōkyū Disturbance of 1221 finally turned him around after he reached twenty. His new seriousness as heir to the Mikohidari poetic house may be gauged by his feat of composing a thousand poems within five days in 1223 and otherwise polishing his skills. After Teika's death in 1241, he began to function as judge at poetry matches, solidifying his reputation until Rtd. Emperor Go-Saga appointed him sole compiler of the imperial anthology *Shokugosenshū* of 1251. In 1256, he retired following an illness, aged fifty-eight, and lived in Saga with his secondary wife, the nun called Abutsu, on whom he apparently lavished much affection, as for his son by her, Tamesuke (1263–1328), to whom he willed the Hosokawa estate in Harima (Hyōgo) and the family's literary manuscripts, including Teika's *Meigetsuki* diary. Thus started a rivalry between the Reizei school, of which Tamesuke was the founder, and the Nijō school of his first son and legitimate heir, Tameuji (1222–86), which would last for several generations.

Tameie is best known in literary history for his valorization of the qualities of simplicity and grace (as set forth in his instruction book, *Eiga no ittei* (One Mode of Poem Composition), most commonly associated with the Nijō school and the aesthetics of *heitanbi*, which ideally combines a surface plainness with deep feeling. In this, he diverged from the ideal of *yōen* (a composite of sensual allure and surreal mystery), associated with his father Teika during the *Shinkokinshū* period. The popularity, from the medieval period on, of Tameie's style probably owes as much to its broad, uncomplicated appeal as to his prestige as Teika's heir. His individual anthology exists in four variants, one of which includes 713 poems.

[FUJIWARA] TEIKA, or Sadaie (1162–1241). Son of the esteemed poet and critic Shunzei and the woman known as Bifukumon'in Kaga, daughter of the Provincial Governor of Wakasa (Fukui), Fujiwara Chikatada. He was successively Middle Captain (*Chūjō*) of the Inner Palace Guards, Consultant (1214), and Minister of Civil Affairs, among other offices, attaining junior third rank in 1211 at age forty-nine and an exalted senior second rank in 1227, when he was sixty-five. When he turned seventy at New Year's of 1232, he was appointed to the Council of State as Provisional Middle Counselor (*Gonchūnagon*), but he resigned at the end of the year. The following year, he left lay life and took the priestly name Myōjō ("clear tranquility") from the Tendai meditation treatise *Makashikan*. Teika was the object of Rtd. Emperor Go-Toba's royal favor from 1200 on, when the latter began to actively stimulate the poetic milieu by commissioning a series of 100-poem sequences and poem matches. Teika was appointed one of the *Shinkokinshū* compilers and labored to bring the anthology to completion. Nevertheless, disagreements arose between the two strong-willed men, and in 1220, Teika was subjected to an imperial reprimand over a poetic issue. By 1222, his waka production began to diminish, and he turned instead to impromptu renga composition, declaring it a solace in old age. However, in 1232, long after Go-Toba's exile to Oki, Teika was appointed by Emperor Go-Horikawa (1212–34; r. 1221–31) as sole editor of another imperial waka anthology, the *Shinchokusenshū*, a task that he completed in 1235. In the *Shinkokinshū*, his poems number forty-six, the sixth highest among the poets included there.

Apart from being recognized today as one of the two or three greatest waka poets of his time, Teika is the author of several poetic treatises that demonstrate his keenness as a critic. These include the *Kindai shūka* (Superior Poems of Our Time [1209]), *Eiga no taigai* (Essentials of Poetic Composition [before 1219 or after 1221]), and *Maigetsushō* (Monthly Notes [1219]); the instruction books *Hekianshō* (Partial Views [1226]), *Sandaishū no kan no koto* (On the Anthologies of Three Eras [1222]), and *Kenchū mikkan* (Secret Comments on Kenjō's Annotations [1221]); and the *Genji* annotations called *Genji monogatari oku'iri.* He also privately edited various anthologies and poem matches and even wrote a tale called *Matsura no miya monogatari* in his youth. His *kambun* diary, the *Meigetsuki* (Bright Moon Record), covers the years 1180–1235; he began it when he was only eighteen and continued until six years before his death at seventy-nine. He first put together his individual anthology, the *Shūi gusō,* in 1216, when he was fifty-four, adding and revising it until his later years; it includes a total of 3,661 poems.

Teika's most distinctive work is in the *ushintei* (mode of meditation) that is marked by a deep concentration in the poetic realm. It has an apparently simple structure and a finely modulated diction calculated to evoke a subtle, intricate, and richly ambiguous feeling. This style has been criticized as affected, obscure, or even abstract, in being trained upon a wholly constructed mental realm, but it represents one of the most ambitious developments in Japanese symbolist poetry and would have a major influence on later generations of poets.

[MINAMOTO] TOMOCHIKA (fl. ca. 1200–1262) was the elder brother of the poetess Kunaikyō (see separate entry on her). He reached the position of Minor Captain in the Palace Guards, junior fourth rank, by no means exalted, but one rank higher than that of his father, the Acting Master of the Capital, Right Division. He was a participant in Go-Toba's 100-verse sequences and other meetings, and was appointed to the Wakadokoro in 1201. He has only seven poems in the *Shinkokinshū,* whereas his sister has fifteen, and has suffered somewhat from Chōmei's unflattering observation about his lack of dedication compared to her, but his poetry indicates a positive enthusiasm for the new diction and conceptions of the *Shinkokin* mode. His last recorded participation in the contemporary milieu was at the *Sanjūrokunin ōuta-awase* (The Great Poetry Match of Thirty-six Poets) of 1262.

TON'A (1289–1372). Unquestionably the most famous of the four late Kamakura Nijō-school poets known as "the four deva kings of waka" (*waka shitennō*; see entry for Kyōun above). Son of a warrior family with Kamakura bakufu ties dating from the time of the first Shōgun, Minamoto Yoritomo, Ton'a took the tonsure and trained on Mt. Hiei from around age twenty. He left after three or four years to undertake pilgrimages in the eastern region, and in his later years, he settled in a hermitage at the Sōrinji in Higashiyama. In this, he was clearly inspired by the model of Saigyō, to whose poetry of reclusion he frequently alluded in his own work. Ton'a's poetic activities began soon after he left Hiei, as he became involved in the milieu around Nijō Tameyo, his son Tamefuji (1275–1324), nephew Tamesada, and grandson Tameakira (1295–1364). In 1318, for example, he participated with Jōben and Kyōun, among others, at the New Year's poetry meeting at the Waka Bureau, and is said to have received the *Kokin denju* from Tameyo in 1320. Subsequent to the Nambokuchō civil disorders, he was patronized by the Shōgun Ashikaga Takauji and his son Yoshiakira, becoming a pillar of Nijō-school interests and earning the trust of the family's poetic heirs. That even the Regent Nijō Yoshimoto (1320–88) valued his opinion is manifest in the treatise *Gumon kenchū* (Sage Comments on Foolish Questions [1363]), which records Ton'a's replies to Yoshimoto's queries on issues ranging from the nature of waka to its methods and traditions. Ton'a's other treatise, the *Seiashō* (late Kamakura to ca. 1360), is one of the most important critical sources for Nijō-school poetics, and was frequently reproduced until the Edo period. Similarly, his individual anthologies, the *Sōanshū* (Grass Hut Collection [1359?]), containing around 1,440 poems, and *Zoku Sōanshū* (Sequel to the Grass Hut Collection [1366 or 1368]), containing 560 poems, plus 100 renga verses, wielded a great influence in the poetic milieu, being considered the classic model of medieval poetic orthodoxy throughout the Muromachi and Edo periods.

[PRIEST] TŌREN (d. 1182?). A member of the Karin'en poetic milieu of courtiers, Shintō and Buddhist clerics, and court ladies active in the period around 1156–80, with its center at the Karin'en, the temple hermitage of Priest Shun'e, Kamo no Chōmei's mentor. The *Tōren-hōshi shū* includes 26 poems, and there is also extant a 100-poem sequence on love, the *Tōren-hōshi koi no hyakushu*.

[MINAMOTO] TSUNENOBU (1016–97). A member of the Uda Genji clan, sixth son of the Popular Affairs Minister Michikata and a daughter of the Harima Provincial Governor Minamoto Kunimori. He held various posts in the court bureaucracy from 1030 onward, being appointed to head the ministries of the Treasury and Popular Affairs, then Head Chamberlain of the Empress's Household, and reaching the exalted senior second rank in 1077. In 1091, he was appointed Major Counselor, and in 1094, Provisional Commissioner of Dazaifu in Kyushu, where he passed away in 1097. Tsunenobu excelled in Chinese and Japanese poetry, as well as in music, and was a frequent participant in the courtly poetic matches, becoming the leader of the poetic milieu during the reign of Go-Reizei (r. 1046–69). However, he apparently suffered some setbacks with the accession of Emperor Shirakawa (r. 1072–87), who in 1075 appointed a younger man, Fujiwara Michitoshi, as the compiler of the fourth imperial anthology, *Goshūishū* (ca. 1086). Tsunenobu expressed his disapproval in the critical polemical pieces *Goshūi mondō* (now lost) and *Nan Goshūi*. In the reign of Horikawa (r. 1087–1106), however, he was restored to an unchallenged position as the most senior authority in the waka field, acting as judge at poetry matches in the residence of the Shijō Princess Kanshi in 1089 and of the former Regent Morozane in 1094. His poetry, distinguished by a fresh handling of landscape description, was held in high esteem by Shunzei and Teika, who knew of it through Tsunenobu's son, Toshiyori (or Shunrai) (1065–1129), author of the treatise *Toshiyori zuinō* (Toshiyori's Essentials of Poetry [ca. 1111–13]). His poems are collected in the *Tsunenobu shū*, of which there are three variant texts, ranging in number of poems from 132 to 276. He also left a diary, *Sotsu-ki*. (*WBJ*, pp. 452–53)

[FUJIWARA] YOSHITSUNE (1169–1206). One of the great literary patrons of the mid-classical period; second son of the regent Kanezane, the leader of the hereditary regental branch of the Fujiwara during the Gempei Wars. As was expected, he swiftly ascended the career ladder, becoming Palace Minister in 1196, Minister of the Left in 1199, Regent in 1202, and finally Prime Minister, with junior first rank, in 1204. He began composing Chinese and Japanese poetry at age thirteen and became active in the contemporary poetic milieu under the guidance of his uncle, the Tendai Abbot Jien. He emerged as the early sponsor of the group that included Teika and Shunzei and would later form the core of Rtd. Emperor Go-Toba's poetic circle. He played an important role in the formation of the *Shinkokin* style, while continuing to cultivate Chinese poetry at meetings in his residence; some attribute the loftiness and strength of his characteristic style to his training in Chinese poetry. He was honored to write the Kana Preface to the *Shinkokinshū*, which includes seventy-nine of his poems, the third highest number, surpassed only by Saigyō and Jien. Yoshitsune died at age thirty-seven, just a year after the completion of the *Shinkokinshū*.

Go-Toba singles out loftiness of tone as characteristic of Yoshitsune's work. He thought there was something marvelous in his mastery of diction and remarked that Yoshitsune had composed so many superior poems that it might even be thought a flaw in a hyakushu, which requires some plainer pieces to set the others off (*Go-Toba-in onkuden*, ed. Hisamatsu, p. 146). To this day, Yoshitsune is praised for evocations of scenery that suggest deep feeling in apparently plain language. His individual anthology, the *Akishino gesseishū*, includes some 1,600 poems and carries an Epilogue by Teika from 1228. In addition, there are the manuscripts called *Go-Kyōgoku-dono onjika awase* (The Go-Kyōgoku Lord's Solo Poetry Contest [1198]), arranged in 100 rounds and judged by Shunzei; and the *Sanjūrokuban sumaidate shiika* (Chinese and Japanese Poem Match in Thirty-six Rounds), a good source for studying the mutual relationship between these two poetic languages in contemporary practice.

ZEN'A (fl. ca. 1275–1333). The central figure in the commoner renga milieu in the latter half of the Kamakura period. A priest in the Jishū branch of the Jōdo Shinshū sect, he frequently led the "renga under the flowers" in the temples, and was instrumental in establishing one of the early versions of the rules, called *Kenji shinshiki* (The New Code of the Kenji Era) in 1277. It was perhaps for this reason, and because he taught other well-known poets like Gusai, Junkaku and Shinshō, that he was hailed in the Muromachi period as "the father of true renga." His style of linking, which became the established one for his time, was characterized by the frequent use of verbal and conceptual parallelism, an antithetical structure that strengthened the syntactic independence of the single verse, and in turn the firm separation between successive verses. His diction, which is again typical of commoner renga in contrast to the waka-like language of the court poets, was economic and plain, and possessed a stark rhythm. Thirty-two of his verses are included in the *Tsukubashū*. (*RS* 1.202–7)

Bibliography

Primary texts, compendia, and reference works are listed under their titles. Abbreviations are as listed on pp. xiii–xiv. Unless otherwise noted, the place of publication for Japanese-language sources is Tokyo.

Akahane Manabu. *Yūgenbi no tankyū*. Shimizu Kōbundō, 1988.

———. "*Sasamegoto* ni okeru fumyōtei to yūgen." *Renga haikai kenkyū* 11 (March 1956): 28–39.

Asaji [Low Rushes], by Sōgi. In Kidō Saizō, ed., *Rengaronshū* 2. *Chūsei no bungaku*, 1st ser., 14: 315–75. Miyai Shoten, 1982.

Aston, W. G., trans. *Nihongi*. Charles E. Tuttle, 1972.

Brower, Robert, trans. *Conversations with Shōtetsu (Shōtetsu Monogatari)*. With introduction and notes by Steven D. Carter. Ann Arbor: Center for Japanese Studies, University of Michigan, 1992.

———, trans. "Ex-Emperor Go-Toba's Secret Teachings: *Go-Toba no In Gokuden*." *HJAS* 32 (1972): 5–70.

Brower, Robert, and Earl Miner. *Japanese Court Poetry*. Stanford: Stanford University Press, 1961.

———, trans. *Fujiwara Teika's Superior Poems of Our Time: A Thirteenth Century Poetic Treatise and Sequence*. Stanford: Stanford University Press, 1967.

Bukkyō jiten. Edited by Nakamura Hajime et al. Iwanami Shoten, 1989.

Bundy, Roselee. "*Santai Waka*: Six Poems in Three Modes." In *MN* 49, 2 and 3 (1994): 197–227 and 261–86.

Butten kaidai jiten. Edited by Mizuno Kōgen et al. Shunjūsha, 1966. 2nd ed., 1977.

Carter, Steven D. *The Road to Komatsubara: A Classical Reading of the Renga Hyakuin*. Cambridge, Mass.: Harvard University Press, 1987.

Chan, Wing-Tsit, trans. *A Sourcebook in Chinese Philosophy*. Princeton, N.J.: Princeton University Press, 1963.

Chikuenshō [Notes from the Bamboo Garden]. Attributed to Fujiwara Tameaki. In *NKT* 3: 410–28.

Chōtanshō, by Bontō. 1390. In Ijichi Tetsuo, ed., *Rengaronshū*, 1: 144–202. Iwanami Shoten, 1953.

Chūgoku shijin senshū. Edited by Yoshikawa Kōjirō and Ogawa Tamaki. 17 vols. Iwanami Shoten, 1958–59.

Cleary, Thomas, trans. *Shōbōgenzō: Zen Essays by Dōgen*. Honolulu: University of Hawaii Press, 1986.

———, trans. *Stopping and Seeing: A Comprehensive Course in Buddhist Meditation by Chih'i*. Boston: Shambhala, 1997.

Cleary, Thomas, and J. C. Cleary, trans. *The Blue Cliff Record*. Boston: Shambhala, 1992.

Confucius. Arthur Waley, trans. *The Analects of Confucius*. New York: Knopf, 1938. See also under *Rongo*.

Conze, Edward, trans. *Buddhist Scriptures*. Harmondsworth, England: Penguin Books, 1959.

Cranston, Edwin A. "'Mystery and Depth' in Japanese Court Poetry." In *The Distant Isle: Studies and Translations of Japanese Literature in Honor of Robert H. Brower*, ed. Thomas Hare, Robert Borgen, and Sharalyn Orbaugh, pp. 65–104. Ann Arbor, Mich.: Center for Japanese Studies, University of Michigan, 1996.

Daichidoron. *T* 25: 1–756.

Dainippon zokuzōkyō. Edited by Maeda Eun. 750 vols. Kyōto: Zōkyō Shoin, 1905–12.

Donner, Neal, and Daniel B. Stevenson, trans. *The Great Calming and Contemplation: A Study and Annotated Translation of the First Chapter of Chih'i's Mo-ho chih-kuan*. Honolulu: University of Hawaii Press, 1993.

Eiga ittei, by Fujiwara Tameie. Ca. 1275. Edited by Fukuda Hide'ichi and Satō Tsuneo. In Hisamatsu Sen'ichi, ed., *Karonshū I. Chūsei no bungaku*, 1st ser., vol. 1. Miyai Shoten, 1971.

Fude no susabi [Solace of the Brush], by Ichijō Kanera. In Ijichi Tetsuo, ed., *Rengaronshū*, 1: 281–303. Iwanami Shoten, 1953.

Fūgashū. In Tsugita Kasumi and Iwasa Miyoko, eds., *Fūga wakashū. Chūsei no bungaku*, 1st ser., 4. Miyai Shoten, 1974.

Fukui Kyūzō. *Renga no shiteki kenkyū*. Yūseidō, 1969.

———, ed. [*Kōhon*] *Tsukubashū shinshaku*. 2 vols. Waseda Daigaku Shuppanbu, 1936 and 1942.

Fūshikaden [Style and the Flower], by Zeami. Edited by Omote Akira. In *Rengaronshū, Nōgakuronshū, Haironshū*, *NKBZ* 51: 215–97. Shōgakkan, 1973.

Genji monogatari. In Abe Akio et al., eds., *Genji monogatari*. 6 vols. *NKBZ* 12–17. Shōgakkan, 1970–76.

Go-Toba-in onkuden [or *gokuden*]. Edited by Hisamatsu Sen'ichi. *NKBT* 65: 142–51.

Guhishō. Edited by Sasaki Nobutsuna. *NKT* 4 (1958): 291–312.

Gunsho ruijū. 18 vols. Keizai Zasshisha, 1903–4.

Gunsho ruijū. 24 vols. Tōkyō Naigai Shoseki, 1928–37.

Hachidaishūshō, ed. Yamagishi Tokuhei. 3 vols. Yūseidō, 1960.

Haga Kōshirō. *Chūsei Zenrin no gakumon oyobi bungaku ni kansuru kenkyū*. Vol. 3 of *Haga Kōshirō rekishi ronshū*. Kyoto: Shibunkaku Shuppan, 1981.

———, ed. *Geidō shisōshū. Nihon no shisō* 7. Chikuma Shobō, 1971.

Haikai daijiten. Edited by Ijichi Tetsuo et al. Meiji Shoin, 1972.

Haku Kyo-i [Ch. *Bai Juyi*]. Edited by Takagi Masakazu. 2 vols. *Chūgoku shijin senshū*, vols. 12–13. Iwanami Shoten, 1958–59.

Heike monogatari. Edited by Ichiko Teiji. 2 vols. *NKBZ* 29–30. Shōgakkan, 1973 and 1975.

Hekiganroku [Blue Cliff Record]. In *T* 48: 139–226.

Hightower, James Robert. *The Poetry of T'ao Ch'ien*. Oxford: Clarendon Press, 1970.

Higuchi Yoshimaro, ed. *Teika Hachidaishō to kenkyū*. 2 vols. Mikan Kokubun Shiryō Kankōkai, 1956, 1957.

Hirota, Dennis. "In Practice of the Way: *Sasamegoto*, an Introduction Book in Linked Verse." *Chanoyu Quarterly* 19 (1977): 23–46.

———, comp. and ed. *Wind in the Pines: Classic Writings of the Way of Tea as a Buddhist Path*. Fremont, Calif.: Asian Humanities Press, 1995.

Hitorigoto [Solitary Ramblings], by Shinkei. Edited by Shimazu Tadao. In *Kodai chūsei geijutsuron*, pp. 464–78.

Hōjōki, by Kamo no Chōmei. Edited by Kanda Hideo. In Kanda Hideo et al., eds., *Hōjōki, Tsurezuregusa, Shōbōgenzō zuimonki, Tannishō*. *NKBZ* 27: 27–49. Shōgakkan, 1971.

Hokkekyō [Lotus Sutra]. Bilingual Chinese-Japanese edition. Sakamoto Yukio and Iwamoto Yutaka, eds. and trans. 3 vols. Iwanami Shoten, 1976.

Hosshinshū. Edited by Kondō Keizō. In [*Kaitei*] *Shiseki sōran* 23: 1–188. Kondō Kappanjo, 1901.

Hurvitz, Leon, trans. *Scripture of the Lotus Blossom of the Fine Dharma*. Translated from the Chinese of Kumarajiva. New York: Columbia University Press, 1976.

Ijichi Tetsuo. *Renga no sekai*. Yoshikawa Kōbunkan, 1967.

Ikkai Tomoyoshi, ed. and trans. *Tō Emmei* [Ch. *Tao Yuan-ming*]. *Chūgoku shijin senshū* 4. Iwanami Shoten, 1958.

Ima kagami. Edited by Itabashi Tomoyuki. Vol. 53 of *Nihon koten zensho*. Asahi Shinbunsha, 1957.

Inada Toshinori. "Muromachi-ki no waka ni okeru rengateki hyōgen: Rengashi no waka o chūshin ni shite." In Kaneko Kinjirō-hakase Kokikinen Ronshū Henshū Iinkai, ed., *Renga to chūsei bungei*, pp. 149–65. Kadokawa Shoten, 1977.

———. *Shōtetsu no kenkyū*. Kazama Shoin, 1978.

Inada Toshinori et al., eds. *Chūsei bungaku no sekai*. Sekai Shisōsha, 1984.

Inoue Muneo and Katano Tatsurō, eds. *Shikawakashū*. Kazama Shoin, 1970.

Ise monogatari. Edited by Fukui Teisuke. In Katagiri Yōichi et al.

Ivanhoe, Philip J., trans. and commentary. *The Daodejing of Laozi*. New York: Seven Bridges Press, 2002.

Iwahashi no jo, batsu [Preface and epilogue to *Iwahashi*], by Shinkei. Edited by Ijichi Tetsuo. In *Rengaronshū*, 1: 331–39. Iwanami Shoten, 1953. The Epilogue also appears as *Iwahashi batsubun* in Kidō Saizō, ed., *Rengaronshū* 3: 321–29.

Jikkinshō. Edited by Nagazumi Yasuaki. Iwanami Shoten, 1942.

Jikkinshō shinshaku. Edited by Okada Minoru. Daidōkan Shoten, 1939.

Junshi [Ch. *Xunzi*]. 2 vols. *SKT* 5–6. Meiji Shoin, 1966.
Kaneko Kinjirō. *Tsukubashū no kenkyū*. Kazama Shobō, 1965.
———. *Shinsen Tsukubashū no kenkyū*. Kazama Shobō, 1969.
———. "Shinkei no renga jittei ni tsuite." *Shōnan bungaku*, no. 13 (March 1979): 1–16.
———. "Shinkei no fūga ishiki." *Bungaku, Gogaku* 90 (June 1981): 45–60.
———. "Shinkei no makoto no michi." *Shōnan bungaku* 11 (March 1977): 1–8.
———. "Shinkei no shochūgo-kan." *Kokugo to kokubungaku* (June 1956): 1–10.
———. "Yoshimoto rengaron no kotsu, koppō, koppū." *Gengo to bungei* (March 1959): 26–31.
———, ed. [*Renga kichōbunken shūsei kinen ronshū*] *Renga kenkyū no tenkai*. Benseisha, 1985.
Kaneko Kinjirō-hakase Kokikinen Ronshū Henshū Iinkai, ed. *Renga to chūsei bungei*. Kadokawa Shoten, 1977.
Kanke bunshō, Kanke kōshū, by Sugawara Michizane. Edited by Kawaguchi Hisao. *NKBT* 72. Iwanami Shoten, 1966.
Katō, Hilda, trans. *The Mumyōshō of Kamo no Chōmei and Its Significance in Japanese Literature*. University of British Columbia, Department of Asian Studies Reprint Series. Reprinted from *Monumenta nipponica* 23, 3–4 (October 1968), pp. 321–430.
Keene, Donald, trans. *Essays in Idleness: The Tsurezuregusa of Kenkō*. New York: Columbia University Press, 1967.
Keikandō, by Kenzai. In Ijichi Tetsuo, ed., *Rengaronshū*, 2: 128–46.
Kenzai zōdan [A Miscellany of Kenzai's Lectures]. In Sasaki Nobutsuna, ed., *NKT* 5: 390–425. Kazama Shobō,[1957] 1977.
Kidō Saizō. *Renga shironkō*. 2 vols. Meiji Shoin, 1973.
———. *Sasamegoto no kenkyū*. Rinsen Shoten, 1990. Originally published as *Kōchū Sasamegoto kenkyū to kaisetsu*. Rokusan Shoin, 1952.
———. "Yoriai, tsukeaigo gikō." *Nihon Joshi Daigaku kiyō: Bungakubu* 29 (March 1980): 1–8.
Kidō Saizō and Shigematsu Hiromi, eds. *Rengaronshū* 1. *Chūsei no bungaku*, 1st ser., vol. 2. Miyai Shoten, 1972.
———, eds. *Renga yoriaishū to kenkyū*. 2 vols. Toyohashi-shi: Mikan Kokubun Shiryō Kankōkai, 1978, 1979.
Kindai shūka [Superior Poems of Our Time] by Teika. Edited by Fujihira Haruo in *Karonshū*. *NKBZ* 50: 467–90. Shōgakkan, 1975.
Kirihioke [Paulownia-tub Brazier]. Attributed to Teika. Edited by Sasaki Nobutsuna. In *NKT* 4: 264–90. Kazama Shobō, 1956.
Knechtges, David R., trans. *Wen xuan, or, Selections of Refined Literature* [Comp. Xiao Tong]. 3 vols. Princeton, N.J.: Princeton University Press, 1982, 1987, 1996.
Kodai chūsei geijutsuron. Edited by Hayashiya Tatsusaburō. *Nihon shisō taikei* 23. Iwanami Shoten, 1973.
Kodai kayōshū, eds. Tsuchihashi Yutaka and Konishi Jin'ichi. *NKBT* 3. Iwanami Shoten, 1957.

Kokinshū. Edited by Ozawa Masao. *Kokinwakashū*. *NKBZ* 7. Shōgakkan, 1971.
Kokinshū. Edited by Saeki Umetomo. *Kokinwakashū*. *NKBT* 8. Iwanami Shoten, 1958.
[*Shimpen*] *Kokka taikan*. Edited by Shimpen Kokka Taikan Henshū Iinkai. 10 vols. with separate indexes. Kadokawa Shoten, 1983–92.
Kokon chomonjū. NKBT 84. Iwanami Shoten, 1966.
Konjaku monogatari. NKBT 22–26.
Koshibe no Zenni shōsoku [A Letter by Shunzei's Daughter]. Edited by Morimoto Motoko. In *Karonshū* 1: 339–45. Hisamatsu Sen'ichi, ed. *Chūsei no bungaku*, 1st ser., no. 1. Miyai Shoten, 1971.
Kubota Jun. *Saigyō, Chōmei, Kenkō*. Meiji Shoin, 1979.
———, ed. *Fujiwara Teika zenkashū*. 2 vols. Kawade Shobō, 1985, 1986.
Kubota Utsubo, ed. *Shinkokinwashū hyōshaku*. 3 vols. Tōkyōdō, 1964–65.
Kubota Utsubo et al., eds. *Waka bungaku daijiten*. Meiji Shoin, 1962.
Kunshishū [The Gentleman's Collection]. *ZGR* 32b: 946.9–12.
Kurokawa Yōichi, ed. *To Ho* [Ch. *Tu Fu*]. 2 vols. *Chūgoku shijin senshū* 9–10. Iwanami Shoten, 1957.
Kyoraishō. Edited by Kuriyama Ri'ichi. In *Rengaronshu Nōgakuronshū Haironshū*. *NKBZ* 51: 419–515. Shōgakkan, 1973.
[Laozi]. *Lao-Tzu: Tao Te Ching*. Translated by Stephen Addiss and Stanley Lombardo. Indianapolis: Hackett, 1993.
———. *Lao Tzu: Tao Te Ching*. Translated by D. C. Lau. Harmondsworth, England: Penguin Books, 1963.
Lamotte, Étienne. "The Assessment of Textual Interpretation in Buddhism." In Donald S. Lopez Jr., ed., *Buddhist Hermeneutics*, pp. 11–27. Honolulu: University of Hawaii Press, 1988.
Legge, James, ed. and trans. *The Chinese Classics*. 1861. Reprint. 5 vols. Taipei: SMC Publishing, 1994.
Lopez, Donald S., Jr. "On the Interpretation of the Mahayana Sutras." In id., ed., *Buddhist Hermeneutics*, pp. 47–70. Honolulu: University of Hawaii Press, 1988.
Lotus Sutra. *Scripture of the Lotus Blossom of the Fine Dharma*. Translated by Leon Hurvitz from the Chinese of Kumarajiva. New York: Columbia University Press, 1976.
Maigetsushō [Monthly Notes], by Teika. Edited by Fujihira Haruo in *Karonshū*. *NKBZ* 50: 511–30.
Makashikan [The Great Stillness and Insight], by Chih-i. Edited and translated by Sekiguchi Shindai. 2 vols. Iwanami Shoten, 1966.
Man'yōshu. In Kojima Noriyuki et al., eds. *Man'yōshū*. 4 vols. *NKBZ* 2–5. Shōgakkan, 1971–75.
Meigetsukishō [Selections from Teika's *Meigetsuki* Diary]. Edited by Imagawa Fumio. Kawade Shobō Shinsha, 1986.
Manyōshū. Edited by Kojima Noriyuki et al. 4 vols. *NKBZ* 2–5. Shōgakkan, 1971–75.

McCullough, Helen Craig, trans. *Tales of Ise*. Stanford: Stanford University Press, 1968.

———, trans. *Ōkagami, The Great Mirror: Fujiwara Michinaga (966–1027) and His Times*. Ann Arbor: Center for Japanese Studies, University of Michigan, 1991.

[*Kundoku*] *Meigetsuki* [Bright-Moon Record, the diary of Fujiwara Teika]. 6 vols. Edited by Imagawa Fumio. Kawade Shobō Shinsha, 1977–79.

Miraiki [Prophetic Record]. Attributed to Teika. In Sasaki Nobutsuna, ed., *NKT* 4: 380–83. Kazama Shobō, 1956.

Mizuno Kōgen et al., eds. *Butten kaidai jiten*. Shunjūsha, 1977.

Mōgyū [Ch. *Meng qiu*]. Edited by Hayakawa Mitsusaburō. 2 vols. *SKT* 58–59. Meiji Shoin, 1973.

Monzen [Ch. *Wen xuan*]. Edited by Kokumin Bunkō Kankōkai. 3 vols. Kokumin Bunkō Kankōkai, 1921–22.

Morrell, Robert E., trans. *Sand and Pebbles (Shasekishū): The Tales of Mujū Ichien, A Voice for Pluralism in Kamakura Buddhism*. Albany: State University of New York Press, 1985.

Mujū Ichien. *Shasekishū*. Edited by Tsukudo Reikan. 2 vols. Iwanami Shoten, 1943.

———. *Shasekishū*. Edited by Watanabe Tsunaya. *NKBT* 85. Iwanami Shoten, 1966.

Mumyōshō [Nameless Notes] by Kamo no Chōmei. Edited by Hisamatsu Sen'ichi. In Hisamatsu Sen'ichi and Minoru Yoshio, eds., *Karonshū, Nōgakuronshū*. *NKBT* 65: 35–98. Iwanami Shoten, 1961.

Murasaki Shikibu. *The Tale of Genji*. Translated by Edward Seidensticker. 2 vols. New York: Knopf, 1977.

Nakamura Hajime et al. [Iwanami] *Bukkyō jiten*. Iwanami Shoten, 1989.

Nihon kagaku taikei. Edited by Sasaki Nobutsuna. 10 vols. Kazama Shobō, 1956–63.

Nihon kagaku taikei. Edited by Sasaki Nobutsuna and Kyūsojin Hitaku. 15 vols. Kazama Shobō, 1977–81.

Nihon koten bungaku taikei. Edited by Takagi Ichinosuke et al. 102 vols. Iwanami Shoten, 1956–68.

Nihon koten bungaku zenshū. Edited by Akiyama Ken et al. 51 vols. Shōgakkan, 1970–76.

Nihon rekishi daijiten. Edited by Nihon Rekishi Daijiten Henshū Iinkai. 12 vols. Kawade Shōbō, 1968–70.

Nihon sandai jitsuroku. Edited by Kuroita Katsumi. *Kokushi taikei* 4. Kokushi Taikei Kankōkai, 1934.

Nihon shoki. Edited by Sakamoto Tarō et al. 2 vols. *NKBT* 67–68. Iwanami Shoten, 1965, 1967.

Nitta Masaaki. *Tendai jissōron no kenkyū*. Heirakuji Shoten, 1981.

Nomori no kagami [The Fieldkeeper's Mirror], attrib. to Rokujō Arifusa. 1295. In Sasaki Nobutsuna, ed., *NKT* 4: 65–96. Kazama Shobō, 1956.

Nose Asaji. *Renga kenkyū*. *Nose Asaji chōsakushū* 7. Shibunkaku Shuppan, 1982.

———. *Renku to renga*. Yōshōbō, 1950.

Oi no kurigoto [Old Man's Prattle], by Shinkei. Edited by Shimazu Tadao. In *Kodai chūsei geijutsuron*, pp. 410–22. Iwanami Shoten, 1973.

Oi no susami, by Sōgi. Edited by Kidō Saizō. In *Rengaronshū* 2. *Chūsei no bungaku*, 1st ser., vol. 14: 137–86. Miyai Shoten, 1982.

Okazaki Yoshie. *Bi no dentō*. Kōbundō Shobō, 1940.

Rakusho roken, by Imagawa Ryōshun. Edited by Sasaki Nobutsuna, in *NKT* 5: 190–212. Kazama Shobō, 1957.

Ramirez-Christensen, Esperanza. *Heart's Flower: The Life and Poetry of Shinkei*. Stanford: Stanford University Press, 1994.

———. "The Operation of the Lyrical Mode in the *Genji monogatari*." In *Ukifune: Love in the Tale of Genji*, ed. Andrew Pekarik, pp. 21–61. New York: Columbia University Press.

Renga entokushō, by Kenzai. In Ijichi Tetsuo, ed. *Rengaronshū* 2: 116–26. Iwanami Shoten, 1956.

Renga haikaishū. Edited by Kaneko Kinjirō et al. *NKBZ* 32. Shōgakkan, 1974.

Renga hidenshō [The Secret Traditions of Renga]. Edited by Ijichi Tetsuo. In *Rengaronshū* 2: 87–113.

Renga hikyōshū [A Collection of Analogies to Renga], by Sōchō. Edited by Ijichi Tetsuo. *Rengaronshū* 2: 161–85. Iwanami Shoten, 1956.

Renga jūyō [Ten Renga Lessons], by Yoshimoto. Edited by Ijichi Tetsuo in *Rengaronshū* 1: 101–5. Iwanami Shoten, 1953.

Rengaronshū. Edited by Ijichi Tetsuo. 2 vols. Iwanami Shoten, 1953, 1956.

Rengaronshū, Haironshū. Edited by Kidō Saizō and Imoto Nōichi. *NKBT* 66. Iwanami Shoten, 1961.

Renga shinshiki tsuika narabi ni Shinshiki kin'an-tō [The New Renga Code with Additions, Proposed Modern Revisions, etc.]. In Yamada Yoshio and Hoshika Sōichi, eds., *Renga hōshiki kōyō*. Iwanami Shoten, 1936.

Renju gappekishū, by Ichijō Kanera. In Kidō Saizō and Shigematsu Hiromi, eds., *Rengaronshū* 1, pp. 26–202. Miyai Shoten, 1972.

Renri hishō, by Nijō Yoshimoto. Edited by Kidō Saizō. In *Rengaronshū, Haironshū*. *NKBT* 66: 33–67. Iwanami Shoten, 1961.

Rimer, Thomas J., and Jonathan Chaves, eds. and trans. *Japanese and Chinese Poems to Sing: The Wakan Rōei Shū*. New York: Columbia University Press, 1997.

Rokkashō [Selections from Six Poets]. Edited by Katayama Jun and Kubota Jun. *Chūsei no bungaku*, 1st ser., 8. Miyai Shoten, 1980.

Rongo [Ch. *Lunyu, The Analects of Confucius*]. Edited by Yoshida Kengō. 1960. *SKT* 1. Meiji Shoin, 1980.

Roppyakuban uta awase [Poetry Contest in 600 Rounds]. Edited by Konishi Jin'ichi. Yūseidō, 1976.

Roppyakuban uta awase [Selections]. Edited by Taniyama Shigeru. In *Uta awase shū*. *NKBT* 74: 428–60. Iwanami Shoten, 1965.

Ryōshun isshiden [also known as *Ryōshun benyōshō*], by Imagawa Ryōshun. Edited by Sasaki Nobutsuna. *NKT* 5: 177–89. Kazama Shobō, 1977.

Sakaida Shirō and Wada Katsushi, eds. *Nihon setsuwa bungaku sakuin*. Rev. ed. Seibundō, 1976.

Sangoki [Full Moon Record], attributed to Fujiwara Teika. Edited by Sasaki Nobutsuna. In *NKT* 4: 313–53. Kazama Shobō, 1956.

Sansom, George. *A History of Japan to 1334*. Stanford: Stanford University Press, 1958.

———. *A History of Japan, 1334–1615*. Stanford: Stanford University Press, 1961.

Sanzōshi [The Three Books], by Hattori Dohō. 1776. Edited by Kuriyama Ri'ichi. In *Rengaronshū, Nōgakuronshū, Haironshū*. *NKBZ* 51: 519–624. Shōgakkan, 1973.

Sasamegoto [Murmured Conversations], by Shinkei. Rev. ed. Edited by Ijichi Tetsuo. *NKBZ* 51: 65–160. Shōgakkan, 1973.

Sasamegoto [Murmured Conversations], by Shinkei. Edited by Kido Saizō. *NKBT* 66: 119–204. Iwanami Shoten, 1961.

Sasamegoto [Murmured Conversations], by Shinkei. Edited by Suzuki Hisashi. In Haga Koshirō, ed., *Geidō shisō shū*: 89–227. *Nihon no shisō* 7. Chikuma Shobō, 1971.

Seiashō, by Ton'a. In Sasaki Nobutsuna, ed., *NKT* 5: 18–122. Kazama Shobō, 1957; 4th ed., 1977.

Sekida, Katsuki, trans. *Two Zen Classics: Mumonkan and Hekiganroku*. New York: Weatherhill, 1977.

Sengohyakuban uta awase, ed. Ariyoshi Tamotsu. 4 vols. *Koten Bunkō* 178, 181, 184, and 186. Koten Bunkō, 1962–63.

Senzaiwakashū [the seventh imperial waka anthology]. Edited by Kubota Jun and Matsuno Yō'ichi. Kasama Shoin, 1969.

Setsuwa bungaku hikkei. Edited by Hinotani Akihiko et al. Suppl. vol. to *Nihon no setsuwa*. Tokyo Bijutsu, 1976.

Shasekishū. See under Mujū Ichien.

Shichiken jidai renga kushū. Ed. Kaneko Kinjirō and Ōta Takeo. Kadokawa Shoten, 1975.

Shikashū. Edited by Kudō Shigenori. In *Kinyōwakashū, Shikawakashū*, eds. Kawamura Teruo et al. *SNKBT* 9. Iwanami Shoten, 1989.

Shimaji Daitō, ed. *Kanwa taishō Myōhōrengekyō*. Meiji Shoin, 1914.

Shimazu Tadao. *Rengashi no kenkyū*. Kadokawa Shoten, 1969.

Shinkei-sōzu jittei waka [Bishop Shinkei's Waka in Ten Styles]. In *ZGR* 15: 403.41–47; also in *Chūsei IV, ST* 6: 106–15.

Shinkei-sōzu teikin [Bishop Shinkei's Teachings], by Kenzai. In *ZGR* 17: 497.1120–26.

Shinkei sakuhinshū. Edited by Yokoyama Shigeru. *Kichō kotenseki sōkan* 5. Kadokawa Shoten, 1972.

Shinkeishū ronshū. Edited by Yokoyama Shigeru and Noguchi Ei'ichi. Kisshōsha, 1948.

Shinkokinshū. In Kubota Jun, ed., *Shinkokin wakashū zenhyōshaku*. 9 vols. Kōdansha, 1977.

Shinshaku kambun taikei. General eds. Uchida Sennosuke et al. 114 vols. plus 1 suppl. Meiji Shoin, 1960–.

Shioiri Ryōdō. "The Meaning of the Formation and Structure of the *Lotus Sutra*," in *The Lotus Sutra in Japanese Culture*, ed. George J. Tanabe Jr. and Willa Jane Tanabe, pp. 15–36. Honolulu: University of Hawaii Press, 1989.

Shokyō (Ch. *Shu jing*). Edited by Katō Jōken. 2 vols. *SKT* 25–26. Meiji Shoin, 1983.

Shōtetsu monogatari. Edited by Hisamatsu Sen'ichi. In Hisamatsu Sen'ichi and Nishio Minoru, eds. *Karonshū Nōgakuronshū*, 165–234. *NKBT* 65. Iwanami Shoten, 1961.

Sōkonshū, by Shōtetsu. In *Chūsei IV*, *ST* 5: 532–870. Meiji Shoin, 1976.

Shūi gusō, by Fujiwara Teika. In Kubota Jun, ed., *Fujiwara Teika zenkashū*. 2 vols. Kawade Shobō Shinsha, 1985–86.

Shūi ōjōden. In *DNBZ* 107.

Sōzei kushū. In [*Shichiken jidai*] *Renga kushū*, eds. Kaneko Kinjirō and Ōta Takeo. *Kichō kotenseki sōkan* 11. Kadokawa Shoten, 1975.

Suzuki Hisashi. "*Sasamegoto* mikkan." Published in seven parts, I to VII, in *Fukushima Daigaku Gakugeigakubu ronshū* in the following issues: I, no. 12 (March 1961): 31–44; II, no. 14 (March 1963): 23–37; III, no. 15 (March 1964): 13–32; IV, no. 16 (October 1964): 14–31; V, no. 17 (October 1965): 15–32; VI, no. 18 (October 1966): 56–69; VII, no. 19 (November 1967): 16–33.

Taishō shinshū daizōkyō. Edited by Takakusu Junjirō and Watanabe Kaigyoku. 85 vols. Taishō Issaikyō Kankōkai, 1924–32.

Takagi Masakazu, ed. *Haku Kyo-i* (Ch. *Bai Juyi*). 2 vols. *Chūgoku shijin senshū*, vols. 13–14. Iwanami Shoten, 1958–59.

Tamagami Takuya, ed. *Genji monogatari hyōshaku*. 14 vols. Kadokawa Shoten, 1967.

Taniyama Shigeru. *Yūgen no kenkyū*. Kyoto: Kyōiku Tosho Kabushiki Kaisha, 1943.

Teika jittei [Teika's Ten Styles of Poetry]. In *NKT* 4: 362–79.

Ten Grotenhuis, Elizabeth. *Japanese Mandalas: Representations of Sacred Geography*. Honolulu: University of Hawaii Press, 1999.

Thurman, Robert A. F. trans. *The Holy Teaching of Vimalakīrti: A Mahāyāna Scripture*. University Park: The Pennsylvania State University Press, 1976.

Tokoro-dokoro hentō [Replies Here and There], by Shinkei. In *SSRS*, pp. 195–227. Also in Ijichi Tetsuo, ed., *Rengaronshū*, 1: 305–30. Iwanami Shoten, 1953.

Toshiyori zuinō [Toshiyori's Essentials of Waka]. Edited by Hashimoto Fumio. In *Karonshū*. *NKBZ* 50: 39–270. Shōgakkan, 1975.

Tsukuba mondō [Tsukuba Dialogues], by Nijō Yoshimoto. *NKBT* 66: 71–106.

Tsukubashū. In Fukui Kyūzō, ed. *Kōhon Tsukubashū shinshaku*. 2 vols. Waseda Daigaku Shuppanbu, 1936, 1942. For an abridged edition, see Ijichi Tetsuo, ed., *Rengashū*. *NKBT* 39: 39–174. Iwanami Shoten, 1960.

Tsurezuregusa [Essays in Idleness], by Yoshida Kenkō. Edited by Nagazumi Yasuaki. In Kanda Hideo et al., eds., *Hōjōki, Tsurezuregusa, Shōbōgenzō zuimonki, Tannishō*. *NKBZ* 27: 85–285. Shōgakkan, 1971.

Uchūgin [Rainy Poems]. Attributed to Teika. In Sasaki Nobutsuna, ed., *NKT* 4: 384–85. Kazama Shobō, 1956.
Ui Hakuju, ed. *Bukkyō jiten.* Daitō Shuppansha, 1938. Reprint, 1965.
Waka bungaku daijiten. Edited by Kubota Utsubo. Meiji Shoin, 1962.
Waka bungaku jiten. Edited by Ariyoshi Tamotsu. Ōfūsha, 1991.
Wakan rōeishū. Edited by Kawaguchi Hisao. *NKBT* 73. Iwanami Shoten, 1965.
Watson, Burton, trans. *The Complete Works of Chuang Tzu.* New York: Columbia University Press, 1968.
———, trans. *Records of the Grand Historian.* 3 vols. Rev. ed. New York: Columbia University Press, 1993.
———, trans. *The Vimalakirti Sutra.* New York: Columbia University Press, 1997.
Wen xuan. See *Monzen.*
Yakumo mishō [The August Eightfold Cloud Treatise], by Rtd. Emperor Juntoku. In Sasaki Nobutsuna, ed., *NKT* 3: 9–94. Kazama Shobō, 1956.
Yoshida, Kenkō. *Essays in Idleness: The Tsurezuregusa of Kenkō.* Translated by Donald Keene. New York: Columbia University Press, 1967.
Yuasa Kiyoshi. *Shinkei no kenkyū.* Kazama Shobō, 1977.

Character List

Abe Kiyoyuki 安部清行
Abutsu 阿仏
Akahito 赤人
Akishino gesseishū 秋篠月清集
Amida 阿弥陀
Anrakushū 安楽集
anmarashiki / shinnyo engi 菴摩羅識・真如縁起
Andao (J. Andō) 安道
arayashiki engi 阿頼耶識縁起
Arima no miko 有間皇子
Ariwara Motokata 有原元方
  Narihira 業平
Asaji 浅茅
Ashikaga Tadayoshi 足利直義
  Takauji 尊氏
  Yoshiakira 義詮
  Yoshimitsu 義満
  Yoshimochi 義持
  Yoshinori 義教
Ashina-ke kitō hyakuin 蘆名家祈祷百韻
Ashita no kumo あしたの雲
Ashuku 阿閦
Asukadera 飛鳥寺
Asukai (Fujiwara) Masatsune 飛鳥井（藤原）雅経
Asukai wakashū 飛鳥井和歌集
Atsuyoshi, Prince 敦慶親王
Bai Juyi 白居易
Baopuzi (J. Hōbokushi) 抱朴子

Bashō 芭蕉
bekkyō 別教
Bifukumon'in Kaga 美福門院加賀
Bishamondō 毘沙門堂
Bo Ya (J. Hakuga) 伯牙
Bo Yi (J. Haku I) 伯夷
bodai 菩提
Bontō (Bontōan-ju, Asayama Morotsuna) 梵燈(梵燈庵主・浅山師綱)
Bontōan renga awase jūgoban 梵燈庵連歌合十五番
Bontōan-ju hentōshō 梵燈庵主返答書
bonzoku 凡俗
bosatsu 菩薩
bugyō 奉行
bumintei 撫民體
bunbu ryōdō 文武両道
Butsuzōgyō 佛蔵経
byōdōshō-chi 平等性智
Cangxie (J. Sōketsu) 蒼頡
chi 智
Ci En (Kui Ji) 慈恩（窺基）
chikuen 竹園
Chikuenshō 竹園抄
chinkasai 鎮花祭
chinshi 沈思
Chion'in 知恩院
Chirenshō 知連抄
Chishō Daishi 智証大師 (*see* Enchin)
Chisha Daishi 智者大師 (*see* Zhiyi)
Chiun 智蘊
Chōgonka (Ch. Chang-hen ke) 長恨歌
chōka 長歌
chōkōtei 長高體
Chōtanshō 長短抄
chū 中
Chuci (J. Soji) 楚辞
chūdō 中道
chūdō jissō no kokoro 中道実相の心
chūjō 中将

chūko sanjūrokkasen 中古三十六歌仙
Chunqiu (J. Shunjū) 春秋
Chuo Wenjun (J. Taku Bunkun) 卓文君
Chūron 中論
[Matsumuro] Chūzan［松室］仲算
Daibirushana jōbutsu shimpenkaji-kyō 大毘盧遮那成仏神変加持経
Daibirushana-kyō shiun 大毘盧遮那経指揮
Daibongyō 大梵経
Daibutchō shuryōgonkyō 大仏頂首楞厳経
daichi 大智
Daichidoron 大智度論
Daie Shūkō (Ch. Dahui Zonggao) 大慧宗杲
daiei 題詠
daienkyō-chi 大円鏡智
daigi 大偽
Daigo, Emperor 醍醐天皇
Daigoji 醍醐寺
Daigokuden 大極殿
Daihonhannyakyō 大品般若経
Daijikkyō 大集経
Daijingū sankeiki 大神宮参詣記
Daijōdaijin 太政大臣
Daijōkishin-ron 大乗起信論
Dai Kui (J. Taiki) 戴逵
daikū no jissō 大空の実相
Dainichi Nyorai 大日如来
Dainichi-kyō 大日経
Dainichikyō-sho 大日経疏
Daishō 題抄
danna haramitsu 檀那波羅蜜
Danrin 壇林・談林
Daode jing (J. *Dōtoku-kyō*) 道徳経
darani 陀羅尼
Dengyō Daishi 伝教大師
Di Huang 翼黄
Dōgen 道元
Dōin, Lay Monk 道因入道
dōjō 堂上

Dōjo 道助
Dōjo-hōshinnō-ke gojisshu waka 道助法親王家五十首和歌
Dōkaku, Cloistered Prince 道覚入道親王
Dong'a 東阿 (= Cao Zhi 曹植)
donyoku 貪欲
dōrui 同類
dōshin 道心
Dōsojin 道祖神
Du Fu (J. To Ho) 杜甫
Eiga no ittei 詠歌一体
Eiga no taigai 詠歌大概
en 縁
en 艶
Enchin 円珍
endon 円頓
engaku 縁覚
Engakukyō 円覚経
engi 縁起
engo 縁語
Engo (Ch. Yuanwu) 圜悟
engyō 円教
engyō ennyū 円教円融
enryū 艶流
Entō on'uta awase 遠島御歌合
Eshin 恵心 (*see* Genshin)
fu (Ch. fu) 賦
fū (Ch. feng) 風
Fu Yue 傅説
Fuboku wakashū 夫木和歌集
Fude no susabi 筆のすさび
Fūgashū 風雅集
Fugen, bodhisattva 普賢菩薩
Fujiwara Akisuke 藤原顕輔
  Ariie 有家
  Chikatada 親忠
  Hidesato 秀郷
  Hideyoshi (or Hidetō) 秀能
  Iemi 家躬

Ietaka (or Karyū) 家隆

Kanezane 兼実

Kinnori 公教

Masatsune 雅経

Michihira 道平

Michiie 道家

Motofusa 基房

Mitsuyoshi 光吉

Nagayoshi (or Nagatō) 長能

Nobuzane 信実

Norikane 教兼

Sadanaga 定長 (*see* Jakuren)

Shunzei (or Toshinari) 俊成

Suetsune 季経

Sukemasa 佐理

Sukemune 資宗

Tadamichi 忠通

Tadazane 忠実

Takanobu 隆信

Tameie 為家

Tametsune 為経 (*see* Jakuchō)

Tameuji 為氏

Tameyo 為世

Teika (or Sadaie) 定家

Tomoyasu 倫寧

Yorimichi 頼通

Yorinaga 頼長

Yoshitsune 良経

Yukinari 行成

Fujiwara Michitsuna's Mother 藤原道綱母

fukashigi no ze 不可思議の是

Fukūjōju 不空成就

fumyōtei 不明体

furyōgi 不了義

furyū 不立

furyū monji 不立文字

Fūshikaden 風姿花伝

fushimono renga 賦物連歌

Fuwa no seki 不破の関
futori atatakanaru ku 太り暖かなる句
ga (Ch. ya) 雅
Gan En (Ch. Yan Yuan) 顔淵
Gan Kai (Ch. Yan Hui; ≐ Gan En) 顔回
Gaotang fu 高唐賦
Gekimōshō 撃蒙抄
Gembin, Bishop 玄賓僧都
Genji monogatari oku'iri 源氏物語奥入
genke no chi 幻化の智
Genkyū shiika awase 元久詩歌合
genmō 幻妄
Genshin 源信 (*see* Eshin)
Giba 耆婆
giri 義理
gō 業
gochi 五智
godai shosei 五大所成
Go-Daigo, Emperor 後醍醐天皇
Go-Fukakusa, Emperor 後深草天皇
Go-Fushimi, Emperor 後伏見天皇
Go-Horikawa, Emperor 後堀河天皇
goin renjō 五韻連声
goin sōtsū 五韻相通
Go-Kashiwabara, Emperor 後柏原天皇
Gokōgon, Emperor 後光厳天皇
Go-Komatsu, Emperor 後小松天皇
Go-Kyōgoku-dono onjika awase 後京極殿御自歌合
Go-Kyōgoku Sesshō 後京極摂政 (*see* Fujiwara Yoshitsune)
gomi Zen 五味禅
gon 権
Gondaisōzu 権大僧都
gonzetsu 言説
Go-Reizei, Emperor 後冷泉天皇
gōrikitei 強力体
Go-Saga, Emperor 後嵯峨天皇
Go-Shirakawa, Emperor 後白河天皇
Goshūishū 後拾遺集

gotai 五体
Gotō egen (Ch. *Wudeng huiyuan*) 五燈会元
Go-Toba, Emperor 後鳥羽天皇
Go-Toba-in onkuden 後鳥羽院御口伝
Go-Tsuchimikado, Emperor 後土御門天皇
Go-Uda, Emperor 後宇多天皇
Guhishō 愚秘抄
gūji 窮子
Gukanshō 愚管抄
Gukenshō 愚見抄
Guku Shibakusa 愚句芝草
Gumei hosshinshū 愚迷発心集
Gumon kenchū 愚問賢注
Gusai (or Kyūsei) 救済
Gusaitaku renga 救済宅連歌
Gyōe 堯恵
Gyōjo 行助
Hachidaishū shō 八代集抄
Hachimangū 八幡宮
hagan mishō 破顔微咲
hai'e no mujō 敗壊の無常
haikai renga 俳諧連歌
hakai muchi no sōgyō 破戒無智の僧形
Hakushi monjū 白氏文集
hampi no ku 半臂の句
Hana no magaki 花能万賀喜
hana no moto renga 花の下連歌
hanka 反歌
hannya 般若
Hanshu 漢書
happiki no koma 八疋の駒
hasshiki 八識
heitanbi 平淡美
Hekianshō 僻案抄
Hekiganroku 碧巌録
Henjaku (Ch. Bian Que) 扁鵲
hen-jo-dai-kyoku-ryū 篇序題曲流
Heshang'gong 河上公

hi (Ch. bi) 比
Hideyoshi (*see under* Fujiwara)
hie yase 冷え痩せ
Hieizan 比叡山
hito no nasake 人の情
hitofushi no aru tei 有一節体
hitofushi no tei 一節体
Hitomaro 人麿
Hitorigoto 独言
hiyu 譬喩
Hō Koji (Hōun) 龐居士 (龐蘊)
hōben 方便
hōben anryūtai 方便安立諦
Hōgen Disturbance 保元の乱
Hōgen monogatari 保元物語
hōgo 法語
hōhen no uta awase 褒貶の歌合
hōjin 報身
Hōjō Yoshitoki 北条義時
Hōjōki 方丈記
hokkaitaishō-chi 法界体性智
Hokke gengi 法華玄義
Hokke mongu 法華文句
Hokkekyō 法華経
hokku 発句
Hokkugyō 法句経
hokumen bushi 北面武士
hongaku no myōshin 本覚の明心
hon'i 本意
Honchō hokke genki 本朝法華験記
Honchō kōsō den 本朝高僧伝
Honchō reisō 本朝麗藻
Honchō shinsenden 本朝神仙伝
honji suijaku 本地垂迹
honka 本歌
honkadori 本歌取り
honmatsu kukyōtō 本末究竟等
Honnōji 本能寺

honrai no chiken 本来の知見
hontai 本体
honzetsu 本説
hōraku 法楽
Horikawa, Emperor 堀河天皇
Horikawa-in ontoki hyakushu waka 堀河院御時百首和歌
Hōshōji 法勝寺
Hosokawa Katsumoto 細川勝元
hosshin 法身
hosshin no tei 法身の躰
Hosshinshū 発心集
Hossō (Ch. Faxiang) 法相
hotoke no sanjin 仏の三身
Houhan shu 後漢書
Huainanzi 淮南子
Huan (J. Kan), Duke of Qi 斉桓公
Hyakuban renga awase 百番連歌合
hyakuin 百韻
hyakushu 百首
i 意
ichidaiji no innen 一大事因縁
Ichigyō 一行
Ichijō Kanera (or Kaneyoshi) 一条兼良
ichinen soku goku 一念即極
ichinen sanzen no kan 一念三千の観
ichiryō musōkyō 一霊無相教
Ima kagami 今鏡
Imagawa Ryōshun (Sadayo) 今川了俊(貞世)
innen 因縁
Inryōken nichiroku 蔭涼軒日録
Inu Tsukubashū 犬筑波集
Ise 伊勢
Ise shū 伊勢集
ishin denshin 以心伝心
issai isshin 一切一心
isshin 一心
Iwahashi 岩橋
iwanu kokoro no nioi 言はぬ心の匂ひ

Izumi Shikibu 和泉式部
jahō 邪法
jakkō 寂光
Jakuchō 寂超
Jakunen (or Jakuzen) 寂然
Jakuren 寂蓮
Jakuren-hōshi shū 寂蓮法師集
jamyō seppō 邪命説法
ji amari 字余り
Jia Dao (J. Ka Tō) 價嶋
Jiandi song 澗底松
Jichin (= Jien) 慈鎮 (慈円)
jige 地下
jige renga 地下連歌
jika awase 自歌合
jikkai 十界
Jikkinshō 十訓抄
Jingōji 神護寺
Jinnōkyō 仁王経
Jion (Ch. Ci En) Daishi 慈恩大師
jisan no uta (jisanka) 自讃歌
Jisankachū 自讃歌註
Jishū 時宗
jissō 実相
jitsu 実
jittei 十体
jittoku 十徳
jo 序
jo no kotoba 序の詞
Jōben 浄弁
Jōdo Bosatsu Sutra 浄土菩薩経
Jōdo Shinshū 浄土真宗
jōe 定恵
Jōgen 浄眼
jo-ha-kyū 序破急
jōjū no myōkyō 常住の妙境
Jōkei 貞慶
jo-shō-ruzū 序正流通

jōshosa-chi 成所作智
Jōshū (Ch. Zhaozhou) 趙州
Jōzō 浄藏
jōzu 上手
Jubusen (= Ryōjusen) 鷲峯山
Jūbutsu 十佛
jūjō kanpō 十乗観法
Jūjūshin'in 十住心院
Junkaku 順覚
Junkaku-bon Ise monogatari 順覚本伊勢物語
Juntoku, Emperor 順徳天皇
jūnyoze 十如是
Jūringyō 十輪経
kabyō 歌病
kadō no shōji 歌道の生死
kadō wa zenjō shugyō no michi 歌道は禅定修行の道
Kagerō nikki 蜻蛉日記
kai 戒
Kai Shisui (Ch. Jie Zhitui) 介之推
Kaifūsō 懐風藻
kaishi 懐紙
kakekotoba 掛詞・懸詞
Kammu, Emperor 桓武天皇
Kamo no Chōmei 鴨長明
Kangyō jōzengi 観経定善義
kanjin 閑人
kanjin 観心
Kanjin ryakuyōshū 観心略要集
Kanke kōshū 菅家後集
Kanmuryōjukyō 観無量寿経
kan'ō (or kannō, Ch. ganying) 感応
kansei omokage yosei 感情・面影・余情
Kanzan 觀算
Karakuni 唐国
karakurenai 唐紅
Karin'en 歌林苑
kasen 歌仙
Kashō 迦葉

Kasuga no yashiro no uta awase 春日社歌合
katauta mondō 片歌問答
ke 仮
kechien 結縁
Kegonkyō 華厳経
kehai 気配
kehō shikyō 化法四教
keikandō 景感道
Keiso saijiki (Ch. Jingchu suishi ji) 荊楚歳時記
Keiunshū 慶運集
Kenchū mikkan 顕注密勘
kendai 兼題
Kenji shinshiki 建治新式
Kenkō 兼好
Kenzai 兼載
Kenshō 顕昭
Ki no Haseo 紀長谷雄
  Nagon 納言
  Tokibumi 時文
  Tsurayuki 貫之
  Yoshimochi 淑望
Kibi 吉備
Kidō Saizō 木藤才藏
kikon 機根・気根
Kin'yōshū 金葉集
Kindai shūka 近代秀歌
Kinrai fūteishō 近来風体抄
Kintada shū 公忠集
Kintō-kyō chū 公任卿注
kiratsutei 鬼拉体
Kirihioke 桐火桶
ki-shō-ten-gō 起承転合
Kitamura Kigin 北村季吟
Kitano tenjin renga jittoku 北野天神連歌十徳
Kiyohara Motosuke 清原元輔
Kōbō Daishi 弘法大師
Kodai no Kimi (or Koōgimi) 小大君
Kodai no Kimi shū 小大君集

Kōhon Tsukubashū shinshaku 校本菟玖波集新釈
Kojidan 古事談
Kojijū 小侍従
Kokin denju 古今伝授
Kokinshū 古今集
Kokinshūjo chū 古今集序註
Kokinwakashū ryōdo kikigaki 古今和歌集両度聞書
Kōkō, Emperor 光孝天皇
Kokon chomonjū 古今著聞集
Kokon rendanshū 古今連談集
kokoro 心
kokoro egatashi 心得難し
kokoro kotoba sukunaku 心言葉少なく
kokoro no en 心の艶
kokū 虚空
komayakanaru tei 濃體
Kombeiron 金錍論
Kōmyōji 光明寺
Kong Wenzi 孔文子
Kongō hannyaharamitsu kyō 金剛般若波羅蜜経
Kongōkai 金剛界
Kongzi (J. Kōshi, = Confucius) 孔子
Konkōmyō 金光明
kompon'in 根本因
Konrenji 金蓮寺
Korai fūteishō 古来風体抄
Koshibe no Zenni shōsoku 越部禅尼消息
Kōshikego (Ch. Kongzi jiayu) 孔子家語
koto shikarubeki tei 事可然體
kotoba 言葉・詞
kotobagaki 詞書
ku 句
ku wa kyō, i wa ri nari 句は教、意は理也
kū 空
kū ke chū no santai 空仮中の三諦
kufū 工夫
Kujō Motoie 九条基家
  Norizane 教実

Kūkai 空海
Kumano Sanzan 熊野三山
kūmon daigo 空門大悟
Kunaikyō 宮内卿
Kung Yu 孔圉
Kunshishū 君子集
kurenai 紅
kusari renga 鎖連歌
kyakku 隔句
kyō 教
kyō wa sunawachi gon nari 教は即ち権也
kyō (Ch. xing) 興
kyō 境
kyōchi 境智
Kyōdai, Priest 教待和尚
kyōgai betsuden 教外別伝
kyōgen kigyo 狂言綺語
kyōgon rijitsu 教權理実
kyoku 曲
kyōka 狂歌
Kyōun (or Keiun) 慶運
Kyoyū (Ch. Xu You) 許由
Kyūshū mondō 九州問答
Lady Ise (Ise no Go) 伊勢の御
Laozi 老子
Li Bai 李白
Li Yuan 李遠
lianju (J. renku) 聯句/連句
Lienü zhuan (J. Retsujoden) 列女伝
Liezi 列子
Liu Xiang 劉向
Liu Yiqing 劉義慶
Lü Buwei 呂不韋
Lunyu (J. Rongo) 論語
Lüshi chunqiu 呂子春秋
ma 間
maeku 前句
Maigetsushō 每月抄

Makashikan (Ch. Mohe zhiguan) 摩訶止観
makura kotoba 枕詞
Man'yōshū 万葉集
Manajo 真名序
manashiki 末那識
manku 万句
Maoshi 毛詩
Maoshi zhenyi 毛詩正義
Mashimo Mitsuhiro 真下満廣
Matsura no miya monogatari 松浦宮物語
Mazu 媽祖
Meigetsuki 明月記
meisei (or myōshō) 明聖
meishi 名師
Meng Haoran (J. Mō Kōzen) 孟浩然
Mengzi (J. Mōshi) 孟子
michi 道
Michiteru (*see under* Minamoto)
Mikkyō 密教
Mikohidari 御子左
Mimosusogawa uta awase 御裳濯河歌合
Minamoto Arihito 源有仁
  Kintada 公忠
  Michichika 通親
  Michiteru 道光
  Michitomo 通具
  Moromitsu 師光
  Saneakira信明
  Sanetomo 実朝
  Shitagō 順
  Tamenori 為憲
  Tokishige 時重
  Tomochika 具親
  Toshiyori (or Shunrai) 俊頼
  Tsunenobu 経信
  Yoritomo 頼朝
  Yoritsuna 頼綱
  Yorizane 頼実

Minase-dono koi jūgoshu uta awase 水無瀬殿恋十五首歌合
Minishū (Mibu-nihon shū, Gyokuginshū) 壬二集 (壬生二品集・玉吟集)
miraiki 未来記
miru tei 見体
Mitsudenshō 密伝抄
mitsuin 蜜印
Miyakawa uta awase 宮河歌合
Mōgyū (Ch. Meng Qiu) 蒙求
Mohe zhiguan (J. Makashikan) 摩訶止観
Mokuchin 木鎮
Mokuren (Mokkenren) (Skt. Maudgalyāyana) 目連 (目犍連)
monji 文字
monjōshō 文章生
Monju (Skt. Mañjuśrī) 文殊
mono no aware tai もののあはれ体
mono no na 物の名
Monshin 門真
monzeki 門跡
Motoyoshi, Prince 元良親王
motsuga ichinyo 物我一如
Mu Wang (J. Bokuō) of Zhou 周穆王
muen no chi o mote, musō no kyō o enzu 無縁の智をもて、無相の境を縁ず
muen no jihi 無縁の慈悲
mujishō 無自性
mujō jukkai 無常述懐
mujō no tai 無常體
Mujū 無住
Mumon Ekai (Ch. Wumen Huikai) 無門慧開
Mumonkan (Ch. Wumen guan) 無門関
mumyō no kokoro 無明の心
Mumyōshō 無名抄
Murakami, Emperor 村上天皇
Murasaki Shikibu 紫式部
Murasakino senku 紫野千句
musa 無作
musa sanjin 無作三身
mushi jigo 無師自悟
mushin 無心

mushin muen 無心無縁
mushin shojaku 無心所著
mushotoku 無所得
musō no kyō 無相の境
musubidai 結題
musubi-no-kami 結びの神
musubu fumi 結ぶ文
myōkanzatsu-chi 妙観察智
Myōshōgonnō 妙荘厳王
Nagatō shū 長能集
Nagusamegusa なぐさめ草
nakatsukoro 中つ比
Nakazane 仲實
Nangaku (Ch. Nanyue) 南岳
Nashitsubo (Shōyōsha) 梨壺 （昭陽舎）
Nehangyō 涅槃経
nehan myōshin 涅槃妙心
nembutsu 念仏
nenge mishō 拈華微咲
nenjū gyōji 年中行事
nennen no mujō 念々の無常
Nihon shoki (Nihongi) 日本書紀 （日本紀）
Nijō Tameakira 二条為明
  Tamefuji 為藤
  Tamesada 為定
  Tameyo 為世
  Yoshimoto 良基
Ning Yue (J. Neisetsu) 甯説
ninkyō funi 人境不二
Nintoku, Emperor 仁徳天皇
nitai wa tada kore kyōmon nari 二諦は唯是教門也
Nōa 能阿
nochi no rokurokusen 後六々撰
nōgei 能芸
Nōin 能因
Nōin-bon Makura sōshi 能因本枕草子
Nōin-hōshi shū 能因法師集
Nōin utamakura 能因歌枕

Nomori no kagami 野守の鏡
Nyogan 如願
Nyogan-hōshi shū 如願法師集
nyoraizō (Skt. tathāgata-garbha) 如来蔵
nyoze 如是
Ōe Chisato 大江千里
  Tokimune 時棟
  Tomotsuna 朝綱
Ōhara sanjaku 大原三寂
Oi no kurigoto 老のくりごと
Oi no susami 老のすさみ
ōjin 応身
Ōkagami 大鏡
Oku no hosomichi 奥の細道
ōmiyabito 大宮人
omokage 面影
omoshiroki tei 面白體
Omuro senka awase 御室千歌合
Ōnakatomi Yoshinobu 大中臣能宣
Ōnin War 応仁の乱
Ono no Komachi 小野小町
  Takamura 篁
  Tōfū 道風
Onshi 温子
Ōshikōchi 凡河内
Ōtomo no Yakamochi 大伴家持
Ōuchi Masahiro 大内政弘
  Yoshihiro 義弘
Owari 尾張
Pan Yue 潘岳
Pang, Layman (J. Hō Koji) 龐居士
Ping Yuan 平原
Pipa xing 琵琶行
Qin (dynasty) 秦
Qiu xing fu 秋興賦
Qu Yuan (J. Kutsugen) 屈原
rakudai 落題
Rakusho roken 落書露顕

reidan jichi 冷暖自知
Reizei Tamehide 冷泉為秀
Tamesuke 為相
Tametada 為尹
Ren Cha 仁差
renga 連歌
Renga entokushō 連歌延徳抄
Renga hidenshō 連歌秘伝抄
rengashi 連歌師
renga shichiken 連歌七賢
Renga shinshiki (Oan shinshiki) 連歌(応安)新式
Renrihishō 連理秘抄
ri 理
ri o nazukete jitsu to nasu 理を名づけて実と為す
ri wa kore shinnyo 理は是れ真如
rikugi 六義
rinne 輪廻
Rinzai Zen 臨済禅
riseitei 理政体
rōgo no suki 老後の数寄
Rokkashō 六家抄
rokudai muge 六大無碍
rokudō 六道
rokuharamitsu 六波羅蜜
Rokujō Arifusa 六条有房
Rongo (Ch. Lunyu) 論語
Rōnyaku gojisshu uta awase 老若五十首歌合
Roppyakuban uta awase 六百番歌合
Ryōa 良阿
Ryōgakyō 楞伽経
ryōgikyō, furyōgikyō 了義経・不了義経
Ryōgon 楞厳
Ryōshun isshiden (Benyōshō) 了俊一子伝 (弁要抄)
ryōsokuson 両足尊
sa no hō 作の法
sabi 寂
Sagoromo monogatari 狭衣物語
Saien 西円

Saigyō (Satō Norikiyo) 西行 （佐藤義清）
Saigyō monogatari e-kotoba 西行物語絵詞
saijōjō 最上乗
Saijū 西住
Saimei, Empress 斉明天皇
Saishōji 最勝寺
Saishōshitennōin shōji waka 最勝四天王院障子和歌
Sakanoue Mochiki 坂上望城
Sampo getsuroku 三輔決録
samuku yasetaru ku 寒く痩せたる句
Sandaishū no kan no koto 三代集間事
Sangoki 三五記
sanjō 三乗
Sanjō Kin'atsu 三条公敦
sanjūrokkasen 三十六歌仙
Sanjūrokuban sumaidate shiika 三十六番相撲立詩歌
Sanjūrokunin ōuta-awase 三十六人大歌合
Sankashū 山家集
sanmai 三昧
sanmaya 三昧耶
sanshin (or sanjin) 三身
santai (or sandai)三諦
santai ennyū 三諦円融
Santai waka 三体和歌
sanze 三世
sarikirai 去嫌
Sasaki Dōyo (Takauji) 佐々木道誉(高氏)
Sasamegoto さゝめごと
sataishō 左大将
satori 悟り
Seiashō 井蛙抄
seichoku no sugata 正直の姿
Seigan Shōtetsu 清巌正徹
Seison 性遵
sendatsu 先達
Seng Can 僧璨
Sengohyakuban uta awase 千五百番歌合
Senjun 専順

Senjūshō 撰集抄
Senzaishū 千載集
sesshō 摂政
setai, dai'ichigitai 世諦・第一義諦
Setchō (Ch. Xuedou) 雪竇
shakotei 寫古體
Shakumakaen-ron 釈摩訶衍論
Shakushi keikoryaku (Ch. Shishi jigulüe) 釈氏稽古略
Sharihotsu (Skt. Śāriputra) 舎利弗
Shasekishū 沙石集
Shibakusa kunai hokku 芝草句内発句
Shibakusa-nai renga awase 芝草内連歌合
shichi shōzai 七聖財
shichigon niku 七言二句
shichiho no sai 七歩の才
Shichinin tsukeku-han 七人付句判
shigaku no bodai 始覚の菩提
shigaku no mon 始覚の文
Shi ji 史記
Shi jing 詩経
shiika awase 詩歌合
Shiju hyakuinnenshū 私聚百因縁集
shikan 止観
shikashū 私家集
Shiki (Ch. Shi ji) 史記
shikimoku 式目
Shikishi (or Shokushi), Imperial Princess 式子内親王
Shikishi-naishinnō shū 式子内親王集
shimo hokumen bushi 下北面武士
shimpen 神変
shina 品
Shinchokusenshū 新勅撰集
Shingon 真言
Shingyokushū 新玉集
shinji 心地
Shinji Kakushin 心地覚心
Shinjikangyō 心地観経
Shinjinmei (Ch. Xinxin ming) 信心銘

Shinkei 心敬
Shinkei kushū kokemushiro 心敬句集苔筵
Shinkei-sōzu teikin 心敬僧都庭訓
Shinkokin nukigakishō 新古今抜書抄
Shinkokinshū 新古今集
Shinkokinwakashū kikigaki 新古今和歌集聞書
shinku 親句
shinnyo 真如
shinnyo jissō no ri 真如実相の理
Shinsenzaishū 新千載集
Shinshō 信照
shinzoku 真俗
Shinzoku (or Shinshoku) Kokinwakashū 新続古今和歌集
Shiseki shūran 史籍集覧
Shishuo xinyu 世説新語
Shitta (Skt. Siddhārta) 悉達
shō (Ch. song) 頌
shō to wa shōjitsu nari 聖とは正実也
Shōan Kanjō (Ch. Zhang'an Guanding) 章安灌頂
shōbō 正法
Shōbōgenzō 正法眼蔵
Shōhaku 消柏
shohō jissō 諸法実相
Shōin 松陰
Shōji ninen in'onhyakushu (or Go-Toba-in shodo hyakushu) 正治二年院御百首*(*後鳥羽院初度百首*)*
shōken 正見
shokū 諸苦
Shokugosenshū 続後撰集
Shokukokinshū 続古今集
Shokyō (Ch. Shu jing) 書経
shōmon 声聞
Shōren'in 青蓮院
Shōryōshū 性霊集
Shoshin kyūeishū 初心求詠集
Shōshō no Naishi 少将内侍
Shōtetsu 正徹
Shōtetsu monogatari 正徹物語

shōtoku 證得

Shōtoku-taishi 聖徳太子

Shōzaishū 聖財集

Shu jing (J. Shokyō) 書経

Shu Qi (J. Shuku Sei) 叔齊

Shūa 周阿

Shugo kokkaishō 守護国界章

Shugokyō 守護経

shugyō kufū 修行工夫

Shūgyokushū 拾玉集

Shūi gusō 拾遺愚草

Shūi ōjōden 拾遺往生伝

Shūishū 拾遺集

shūitsu 秀逸

Shūjinshō 袖珍鈔

Shukaku, Cloistered Prince 守覚法親王

shūku 秀句

Shun 舜

Shun'e 俊恵

Shunrai (or *Toshiyori*) *zuinō* 俊頼髄脳

Shunzei 俊成 (*see under* Fujiwara)

Shunzei's Daughter (Shunzei-kyō no musume) 俊成卿女

Shunzei-kyō no musume no shū 俊成卿女集

Shuryōgonkyō 首楞厳経

shuseki 手跡

Sima Xiangru (J. Shiba Shōjo) 司馬相如

Sōa 相阿

Sōanshū 草庵集

Sōchō 宗長

Soga Akae 蘇我赤兄

Sogen 素眼

sōji 総持

Sōkonshū 草根集

soku 疎句

sokushin jikiro 即身直路

Son'in, Cloistered Prince 尊胤法親王

Sondō, Cloistered Prince 尊道法親王

Sone Yoshitada 曾禰好忠

Sono no chiri 園塵
Sonshin (Ch. Sun Chen) 孫晨
Sōrinji 双林寺
Sosei 素性
Sōseki 宗碩
Sōseki renga awase hyakunijūban 宗碩連歌合百二十番
Sōtanshū 曾丹集
Sotsuki 帥記
Sōzei 宗砌
Sōzei kushū 宗砌句集
Su Dongpo 蘇東坂
Su Wu 蘇武
sugata 姿
sugata no yasabamitaru 姿の優ばみたる
Sugawara Fumitoki 菅原文時
  Michizane 道真
Suiko, Empress 推古天皇
suki 数寄
Taigong Wang (J. Taikōbō) 太公望
Taiheiki 太平記
Taikenmon'in Shōshi 待賢門院璋子
Taiki 台記
Taira Masakado 平将門
  Shigehira 重衡
  Shigemori 重盛
Taishi 泰子
Taiyuan 太源
Taizōkai 胎蔵界
Takanobu-ason shū 隆信朝臣集
take takaki tei 長高體
tama tebako 玉手箱
Tamatsushima Shrine 玉津嶋神社
Tanabata 七夕・棚機
tandai 探題
tanden 単伝
tanrenga 短連歌
Tao Qian 陶潛
Taohuayuan ji 桃花源記

tassha 達者
Teijiin no uta awase 亭子院歌合
Teika 定家 (*see under* Fujiwara)
Teika jittei 定家十体
teizen no hakujushi 庭前の柏樹子
Temmu, Emperor 天武天皇
ten 点
Tenchi (or Tenji), Emperor 天智天皇
Tendai 天台
Tendai sandaibu 天台三大部
tenja 点者
Tenmanjin 天満神
tenrin jōō 転輪聖王
Tō no Tsuneyori 東常縁
Tōdaiji 東大寺
Tōfukuji 東福寺
tōgenkyō 桃源郷
tōki 逗機
toku 徳
Tokudaiji Saneyoshi 徳大寺実能
tokunin 徳人
Tokushū 徳宗
Tomochika (*see under* Minamoto)
Ton'a (or Tonna) 頓阿
tongo jikiro 頓悟直路
Tongzi jiao 童子教
Tōren 登蓮
Tōren-hōshi koi no hyakushu 登蓮法師恋百首
Tōren-hōshi shū 登蓮法師集
tō-rinne 遠輪廻
torisute 取捨
toriyori 取寄
tōrushin 等流身
Toshiyori zuinō 俊頼髄脳
tōza 当座
tōza no ikkyō 当座の逸興
tsūgyō 通教
tsukeai 付合

tsukeku 付句
Tsukubashū 菟玖波集
Tsunenobu 経信
Tsurayuki (*see under* Ki)
Tsurezuregusa 徒然草
tsutome (gongyō) 勤め（勤行）
uchikoshi 打越
Uchūgin 雨中吟
Uda, Emperor 宇多天皇
ui hōbutsu muchū gonka, musa sanjin gakuzen jitsubutsu 有為報仏夢中權果、無作三身覚前実仏
Uji shūi monogatari 宇治拾遺物語
umon, kūmon 有門・空門
Unmon 雲門
Urabon-e 盂蘭盆会
uro 有漏
uruwashiki tei 麗體
ushin 有心
ushintei 有心體
usō 有相
uta no gotai 歌の五体
uta no michi 歌の道
utayomi 歌詠み
utazukuri 歌作り
utsuri うつり
uwagaki 上書き
waka 和歌
Wakadokoro 和歌所
Wakadokoro e fushin no jōjō 和歌所へ不審条々
Wakan rōeishū 和漢朗詠集
Wakanoura 和歌浦
waka shitennō 和歌四天王
wakō dōjin 和光同塵
wakō no hōben 和光の方便
Wang Su of Wei 魏王粛
Wang Wei 王維
Wani 王仁
Wen, Emperor of Wei 魏文帝 (= Cao Pi 曹丕)

Wenxuan (J. Monzen) 文選
Wu Ding 武丁
Wushan 巫山
Xie Lingyun 謝靈運
Xu Hun (J. Kyokon) 許渾
Xu Wugui 徐无鬼
Xuanzong 玄宗
Xunzi 荀子
Yahatayama 八幡山
Yakumo mishō 八雲御抄
Yamana Sōzen 山名宗全
Yamato monogatari 大和物語
Yamato Takeru no mikoto 日本武尊・倭建命
Yan Hui (J. Gan Kai; = Yan Yuan) 顔囘 or 顔回
Yan Yuan (J. Gan En; = Yan Hui) 顔淵
Yang Guifei (J. Yōkihi) 楊貴妃
Yao 堯
yasumetaru kotoba 休めたる詞
Yasuyori hōbutsushū 康頼宝物集
Yi Yin 伊尹
yingyan ji 応験記
Yixing 一行
yōen 妖艶
yojō (or yosei) 余情
yōon 幽遠
yoriai 寄合
Yoshimoto 良基 (*see under* Nijō)
yū 優
Yuan Zhen 元稹
Yuan Shaoyin ji 元少尹集
yūgen 幽玄
yūgentei 幽玄體
Yuima (Skt. Vimalakīrti) 維摩
Yuimagyō (Skt. *Vimalakīrti-nirdeśa sūtra*) 維摩経
yuishiki 唯識
Yuishikiron 唯識論
Yuishikiron jukki 唯識論述記
Yūsei 祐盛

Yūshi, Imperial Princess 祐子内親王
yūshin 幽深
Zeami 世阿弥
zehi 是非
Zen kōan 禅公案
Zenmui Sanzō 善無畏三蔵
Zen'a 善阿
zenna 禅那
Zhang Han (J. Chōkan) 張翰
Zhanran (J. Tannen) 湛然
Zheng Hong 鄭弘
Zheng Taiwei (J. Tei Tai'i) 鄭太尉
Zhiyi (J. Chigi) 智顗
Zhong Ziqi 鍾子期
Zhuangzi 荘子
Ziyou (Wang Xizhi) 子猷 (王羲之)
Zōbō ketsugikyō 像法決議経
zōbō mappō 雑法末法
Zōga, Priest 増賀上人
zōjōen 増上縁
Zoku honchō ōjōden 続本朝往生伝
Zoku zayū mei 続座右銘
zōkyō 蔵教
Zong Lin 從林
Zong Shi 宗史
Zōtanshū 雑談集
zuiki, tōki 随機・逗機
Zuo Zhuan (J. *Saden*) 左傳

Index of First Lines

For abbreviations of titles, see the List of Abbreviations; for numbering of the poems or renga verses, refer to the source text in the Bibliography. Where no poet's name is given, it is presumed unknown. This index includes the first lines of Japanese waka and renga (grouped under hokku and tsukeku) only. Chinese and Buddhist verses are not included; for these, refer to the annotations and the subject index.

Waka

mizuha sasu (Priest Zôga, *Hosshinshû*), 297n9
mononofu no (Hitomaro, *MYS* 264; *SKKS* 1648), 259n15
mubatama no (Anonynous, *KKS* 647), 281n66
mukashi hito (Shôtetsu, *SKS* 7455), 184
natsuyama no (Minamoto Yoritsuna, *GSIS* 271), 240n6
ninaimotsu (Jichin, *Shûgyokushû* 2396), 150
ofu no ura ni (Anonymous, *KKS* 1099), 228n28
omoiideyo (Fujiwara Ietaka, *SKKS* 1294), 168
omoiiru (Hideyoshi, *SKKS* 1317), 34
omoiiru (Ietaka, *SKKS* 1337), 33
omoiizuru (Rtd. Emperor Go-Toba, *SKKS* 801), 31
omoikane (Tsurayuki, *SIS* 224), 241n6
omou koto (Jichin, *SKKS* 1780), 32
oshikaranu (Anonymous, *Yakumo mishô*), 150
onozukara (*Shasekishû* V. A: 12), 304n7
sagi no iru (Teika, *FGS* 1784), 97
sakagame ni (Ôtomo Tabito, *MYS* 343), 168
sakurabana (Tsurayuki, *KKS* 59), 231n34
samidare ni (*Sangoki*), 305n2
saranu dani (Taikenmon'in no Horikawa, *Senzaishû* 310), 278n48
sasa no ha wa (Hitomaro, *MYS* 133; *SKKS* 900), 27
sato tôki (Teika, *Shûi gusô* 3314), 97
shii no ha no (Shôtetsu), 97
shikishima no (Tsurayuki, *KKS* 697), 104
shimeokite (Shunzei, *SKKS* 1558), 32
shinateru ya (Shôtoku Taishi, *Shasekishû*), 309n8
shirazariki (Teika, *Shûi gusô* 1401), 43
sorenagara (Princess Shikishi, *SKKS* 368), 31
sumu hito mo (Minamoto Tsunenobu, *SKKS* 1528), 305n2
tada tanome (Kiyomizu Kannon, *SKKS* 1917), 303n7
ta ga misogi (Anonymous, *KKS* 995), 105
tare zo kono (Jichin, *Shûgyokushû*), 28
te ni musubu (Fujiwara Yoshitsune [attrib. to Rtd. Emperor Go-Toba in *SSG*], *Sengohyakuban uta awase*), 45
teri mo sezu (Ôe no Chisato, *SKKS* 55), 289n2
tomoshisuru (Rtd. Emperor Juntoku, *Fuboku wakashû*), 45
tonomori no (Minamoto Kintada, *SIS* 1055), 156
toshi mo henu (Teika, *SKKS* 1142), 33
toshi no uchi ni (Ariwara Motokata, *KKS* 1), 215n1
toshi takete (Saigyô, *SKKS* 987), 35
tsukubane no ("A Song of Hitachi," *KKS* 1095), 210n2
ukaibune (Jichin, *SKKS* 251), 105
utsuriyuku ([Asukai] Masatsune, *SKKS* 561), 34
wabinureba (Prince Motoyoshi, *GSS* 961), 28
waga io wa (Anonymous, *KKS* 982), 232n35
waga yado wa (Bishop Henjô, *KKS* 770), 224n20
wasurenamu (Lady Ise, *SKKS* 858), 28
wasurenu ya (Teika, *Shûi gusô* 268), 28
yahatayama (Shôtetsu, *SKS* XI: 8342), 43
yamashiro no (Anonymous, *KKS* 759), 104
yamazato o (Sone Yoshitada, *SKKS* 495), 28
yo o umi ni (Akashi Lay Monk, *Genji monogatari*, "Akashi" chapter), 260n19
yo no naka o ([Fujiwara] Yoshitsune, *Rônyaku gojisshu uta awase*), 225n23
yoshinogawa (Tsurayuki, *KKS* 471), 105
yoshino naru (Prince Yuhara, *MYS* 375), 274n25
yoshinoyama (*Sengohyakuban uta awase*, Round 256) 289n2
yukusaki o (Akashi Lay Monk, *Genji monogatari*, "Matsukaze" [The Wind in the Pines] chapter), 272n20

Tsukeku

aki samuki (Ton'a), 127
aki wa tada (Gusai), 122
ashihiki no (Zen'a, *TKBS* 1320), 102
au made to (Gusai), 129
chirikakaru (Junkaku), 103
e ni kakeba (Ryôa), 130
fuji no ne wa (Junkaku, *TKBS* 1319), 130
fune ni tamareru (Junkaku), 129
furusato no (Gusai), 29
hana mishi yama no (Ryôa), 103
hana no ato / aoba (poet unknown), 269n4
hana no ato / konomoto (Ryôa), 128
harusame ni (Junkaku), 123
hayakawa no (Gusai), 25
hitogokoro (Shinshô), 129
hitoyo wa akenu (Teika, *TKBS*), 23
honobono to (poet unknown), 29
hototogisu (Shinshô), 131
idete iru made (Shinshô), 103
ikuyo to mo (Shinshô), 24
inazuma no (poet unknown), 96
irie no hotade (Gusai), 106, 130
itarikeri (Sôzei), 30
itazura ni (Ryôa), 29
itsu idete (Gusai), 29
iwashiro no (Junkaku, *TKBS* 825), 24
kaga nabete (hitomoshibito [the firelighter] in the *Kojiki*), 210n2
kakashi tatsu (Shûa), 131
kamome naku (Gusai), 126
karakuni no (Shûa, *TKBS* 1414), 25
kareno no tsuyu ni (Ryôa), 127
karigane kaeru (Ryôa), 123
karisome no (Ryôa), 25
karu wasaii wa (Yakamochi, *MYS* 1635), 211n4
kasugano no (Junkaku, *TKBS* 1030), 122
kasumedo imada (Ietaka, *TKBS* 11), 24
kataoka no (Ryôa), 98
kareno no tsuyu ni (Ryôa), 127

Hokku

Subject Index